Mastering™

Windows Server® 2008
Networking Foundations

Mark Minasi

Rhonda Layfield

John Mueller

WILEY

Wiley Publishing, Inc.

Acquisitions Editor: Tom Cirtin
Development Editor: Kim Wimpsett
Technical Editor: Jim Kelly
Production Editor: Christine O'Connor
Copy Editor: Kim Cofer
Production Manager: Tim Tate
Vice President and Executive Group Publisher: Richard Swadley
Vice President and Executive Publisher: Joseph B. Wikert
Vice President and Publisher: Neil Edde
Proofreader: Nancy Bell and Russ Mullen
Indexer: Ted Laux
Book designers: Maureen Forys, Happenstance Type-O-Rama and Judy Fung
Cover design: Ryan Sneed
Cover image: © Pete Gardner/Digital Vision/gettyimages

Library of Congress Cataloging-in-Publication Data.
Minasi, Mark.
  Mastering Windows Server 2008 networking foundations / Mark Minasi. -- 1st ed.
      p. cm.
  ISBN 978-0-470-24984-0 (paper)
  1. Computer networks. 2. Microsoft Windows server. I. Title.
  TK5105.5.M5666 2008
  005.4′476 — dc22

                                                       2008017696

Dear Reader,

Thank you for choosing *Mastering Windows Server 2008: Networking Foundations*. This book is part of a family of premium quality Sybex books, all written by outstanding authors who combine practical experience with a gift for teaching.

Sybex was founded in 1976. More than thirty years later, we're still committed to producing consistently exceptional books. With each of our titles we're working hard to set a new standard for the industry. From the paper we print on, to the authors we work with, our goal is to bring you the best books available.

I hope you see all that reflected in these pages. I'd be very interested to hear your comments and get your feedback on how we're doing. Feel free to let me know what you think about this or any other Sybex book by sending me an email at nedde@wiley.com, or if you think you've found a technical error in this book, please visit http://sybex.custhelp.com. Customer feedback is critical to our efforts at Sybex.

Best regards,

Neil Edde
Vice President and Publisher
Sybex, an Imprint of Wiley

To the newest members of the Minasi clan, my lovely young niece Aubrey and already-studly young nephew Joseph. I wish for you that by the time you need to use a computer then you won't need any of your uncle's books!

Acknowledgments

Most of us have heard of Elizabeth Kubler-Ross's five stages of grief (denial, anger, bargaining, depression, acceptance), a wise and concise overview of how people deal with loss. I find it strange, then, that no one has ever enumerated the five stages of book writing:

- Excitement ("This is gonna be soooo cool, I can't wait to find some folks to write about this neat stuff with me!")

- Writing ("How am I *ever* going to get this stuff done on time?")

- Editorial ("Aaugh, how am I supposed to finish this new chapter *and* review the editorial changes on time?")

- Cleanup ("I thought I was finished, and now I have to write the *introduction*?")

- Satisfaction ("Golly, doesn't that look nice on the bookshelf . . . that was easy, let's do another one!")

Author Peter DeVries explained this years ago with a wry summing-up: "I love being a writer — it's the paperwork I can't stand." Well, with this final bit of text, I get to move from Cleanup to Satisfaction . . . so let me tell you about the other stages.

I was very fortunate to find a few co-authors to help put this book together. The co-author who contributed the most chapters was John Paul Mueller. I've worked with John before and love the fact that he's a meticulous guy — the examples in his chapters are not just illustrative, they *work*! I also could not have gotten this book done without my partner Rhonda Layfield. Rhonda's been in the computer business for twenty-something years and in that time she's accumulated a wide variety of experience — experience that she's used to put together the chapters on Windows storage (an all-new chapter), the NetBIOS chapter, and the DHCP chapter. Derek Melber is one of the three smartest guys I know when it comes to group policies (Darren Mar-Elia and Jeremy Moskowitz are the other two, and I've been fortunate to work with them both on other books) and so I was delighted when he agreed to write the group policies chapter in this book.

Once the chapters get written, they need editing and technical review and as always, the Wiley folks provided us an all-star lineup. James Kelly did the tech review for the book, as he has for my last few books, and offered no end of useful advice. Kim Wimpsett kept us all on schedule, gave every chapter an editing pass, and patiently answered my questions about formatting my text so that it worked within the Wiley standards. Kim Cofer and Christine O'Connor completed the edits and assembled the chapters into the nicely-laid-out chapters that you hold in your hand right now. Our publisher Neil Edde, an old friend of many years, ran interference for us whenever the book ran into a snag, something for which I cannot thank him enough.

Finally, let me thank two other sources of help for this book. Without Microsoft to create Server 2008, we wouldn't have had anything to write — so thanks, Redmond, and thanks for letting us get a peek at Server 2008 before it was finished. More important than Microsoft's contribution, however, was the kind support of you folks — the readers. The only reason that I've been able to "love having been a writer" is because all of you keep buying my books — thank you very much!

Contents at a Glance

Introduction . . . . *xvii*

Chapter 1 • Why Network? 1

Chapter 2 • Building a Simple Network 15

Chapter 3 • Security Concepts in Windows 37

Chapter 4 • Installing Windows Server 2008: Basics 55

Chapter 5 • Controlling Windows Server: MMC 89

Chapter 6 • Controlling Windows Server: The Command Line 107

Chapter 7 • Controlling Windows III: The Registry 135

Chapter 8 • Controlling Windows Server: Group Policy 161

Chapter 9 • Windows Storage Concepts and Skills 183

Chapter 10 • TCP/IP and IPv4 Networking Basics 253

Chapter 11 • What's in a Name? Network Name Overview 313

Chapter 12 • Old Names: Understanding NetBIOS, WINS,
and NetBIOS over TCP/IP 319

Chapter 13 • New Names: How DNS Works 353

Chapter 14 • Automatic IP Setup: DHCP Essentials 435

Chapter 15 • Things to Come: A Peek at Active Directory 473

Index 477

Contents

Introduction . . . . *xvii*

Chapter 1 • Why Network? **1**
What's the Point of Networks and Networking? 1
   Choosing a Network Type 3
   Network Client and Server Software 3
   Networks Need Connection Hardware and Links 6
   Considering the Hardware 6
   Clients and Servers Must Speak the Same Protocols 10
A Brief History of Windows 12

Chapter 2 • Building a Simple Network **15**
Getting Your Free Copy of Windows Server 2008 16
   Downloading the Software 16
   Extending the 30-Day Version to 180 Days 17
   Performing the Installation 18
Performing the Basic Network Setup 22
   Changing the Machine Name 24
   Changing the Network Name 26
Creating User Accounts 27
Sharing Resources with Other Computers 30
Accessing Resources on Another Computer 33
   Accessing Resources Temporarily 34
   Making Resource Access Automatic 34

Chapter 3 • Security Concepts in Windows **37**
Understanding the Need to Secure Windows 37
Considering What You Need to Secure in Windows 38
Understanding Authentication versus Authorization 40
Understanding How Authentication Works 42
   Where Windows Stores Users and Passwords 43
   Securing the User Account Database 44
   Networkable, Centralized Accounts: Domains 44
   Secure Logons Across a Network 45
Understanding How Authorization Works 46
   Permissions and Access Control Lists (ACLs) 46
   Understanding What Tokens Do 48

Access to Earlier Security Systems 50
Defining File and Folder Security 50

Chapter 4 • Installing Windows Server 2008: Basics **55**
Choosing a Windows Server 2008 Edition 55
Performing a Windows Server 2008 Full Version Installation 57
Considering the Installation Choices 58
Using the DVD Installation Method 59
Using the Initial Tasks Page 65
Providing Computer Information 65
Update the Server 66
Customizing This Server 69
Understanding Roles and Features 70
Determining the Need for Specific Roles and Features 71
Installing Roles and Features 81
Adding Roles 82
Removing Roles 85
Adding and Removing Features 86

Chapter 5 • Controlling Windows Server: MMC **89**
Fixing the Server 2008 GUI 89
Restoring Your Desktop Icons and Start Menu 90
Setting Administrator-Friendly Folder Options 92
A Microsoft Management Console Primer 93
What Is This MMC Thing? 94
MMC Terms to Know 95
The Computer Management Console 97
Other MMC Tools 99
Building Your Own MMC Tools 101
Building a Simple Microsoft Saved Console 101
Creating the Removable Storage Manager Console 104

Chapter 6 • Controlling Windows Server: The Command Line **107**
Why You Give a Hoot about the Command Line Interface 108
Reasons to Use the Command Line 108
Situations Where the Command Line Is Less Useful 110
Elements of the Command Line 112
Command Line Rights 113
Command Prompt Window Configuration 114
Command Prompt Personalization 118
Internal Versus External Commands 121
Basic Command Examples 124
Getting Help at the Command Line 124
Checking the Status of the System 128
Viewing and Managing Tasks 129
Locating Specific Files Based on Content 130
Simple Batch Files 131

Chapter 7 · Controlling Windows III: The Registry **135**

Computer Configuration and the Registry 135
Why Should You Care About the Registry? 136
   The Registry Is the *Real* Control Panel 136
   Some Administrative Tasks Require Direct Registry Editing 137
Looking at the Registry 138
   The Keys 139
   Viewing the Registry from the Command Line 143
Changing Registry Entries 143
   Changing Registry Entries from the Command Line 145
   Registry Entry Types 145
Researching the Registry 146
   Discovering Registry Keys on Your Own 147
   Dealing with a "Hey, Where Is It?" Registry Value 148
Creating/Deleting a New Registry Entry 150
   Creating and Deleting Registry Entries from the CLI 151
Backing Up and Restoring a Registry Subkey 151
Securing the Registry 152
   Subkeys Have Permissions 152
   Registry Security: the Idea and the Effects 154
Where the Registry Lives: Hives 156
   A Look at the Hive Files 156
   Fault Tolerance in the Registry 157
Remote Registry Modification 158
Backing Up and Restoring a Registry 159

Chapter 8 · Controlling Windows Server: Group Policy **161**

The Power of Group Policy 161
Working with LGPOs 163
   Local Group Policy 165
   Administrators or Non-Administrators LGPO 166
   User Specific LGPO 167
Group Policy Breakdown: How LGPOs Are Organized and Structured 168
   Computer Node vs. User Node 168
   LGPO . . . Just a Glorified Registry Editor 169
   Introducing ADM Templates and ADMX Files 172
   Not All Group Policy Settings Are Registry-Based 174
   Introducing Client Side Extensions 176
   Essential Policy Settings 176
Using Scripts in Group Policy 180
Working with Active Directory–Based GPOs 181
   LGPOs and Active Directory GPOs 182

Chapter 9 · Windows Storage Concepts and Skills **183**

Disk Management versus DiskPart 183
   The Disk Management Gooey (GUI) 183
   Meet DiskPart, the Command-Line Interface 185

The Basics of Disk Management 186

    Physical/Logical Disks: How to Slice Them Up 186

    Basic Disks versus Dynamic Disks 189

    Server 2008 Setup and System Disk Meet Dynamic Disks 198

RAID in Server 2008 204

    Mirrored Volumes — RAID-1 205

    RAID-5 210

    Moving a Dynamic Disk 214

Performing Disk Maintenance 215

    Background: Disk Geometry and File Formats 216

    Formatting Disks 220

    Dealing Out Disk Space . . . Managing Disk Quotas 224

    Volume Shadow Copy Service 230

    Encrypting NTFS Files and Folders 235

    Tools of Disk Maintenance 244

    Defragmenting Disks 248

    Remote Storage 251

The Evolution of Storage 252

Chapter 10 • TCP/IP and IPv4 Networking Basics **253**

A Brief History of TCP/IP 254

    Origins of TCP/IP: From the ARPANET to the Internet 255

    Goals of TCP/IP's Design 257

Getting There: The Internet Protocol (IP) 259

    A Simple Internet 259

    Subnets and Routers: "Should I Shout, or Should I Route?" 259

    IP Addresses and Ethernet/Media Access Control (MAC) Addresses 260

    Where Your System Gets Its IP Address From 262

    IP Routers 265

    Routing in More Detail 265

Class A, B, and C Networks, CIDR Blocks,

  and Routable and Nonroutable Addresses 267

    A, B, and C Class Networks 268

    Routable and Nonroutable Addresses 269

    You Can't Use *All* of the Numbers 270

    Subnet Masks 272

    Exercise: Using IPConfig to View Network Information 273

    Classless Inter-Domain Routing (CIDR) 275

    What IP *Doesn't* Do: Error Checking 277

Transmission Control Protocol (TCP) 278

    Sequencing 279

    Flow Control 279

    Error Detection/Correction 279

Sockets, Ports, and the Winsock Interface 279

    How Ports and Sockets Work: An Example 281

    Routing the Nonroutable, Part II: PAT and NAT 282

    Winsock Sockets 285

Internet Host Names 285
   Simple Naming Systems (HOSTS) 286
   Domain Name System (DNS) 287
   E-Mail Names: A Note 288
Attaching to an Internet 289
   Dumb Terminal Connection 290
   PPP Serial Connection 290
   Cable Modem and DSL Connections 291
   LAN Connection 291
   Terminal Connections versus Other Connections 291
The Basics of Setting Up TCP/IP on Windows Server 2008
  with Static IP Addresses 292
   Configuring TCP/IP with a Static IP Address 293
   Setting Up MAIN 295
   Testing Your IP Configuration 295
   Configuration Continued: Setting Domain Suffixes 298
   Handling Old Names: Configuring Your Workstation for WINS 301
   Adding IP Addresses to a Single NIC 303
Lower-Cost LAN-to-WAN Routing with Internet Connection Sharing 305
   Step One: Connect the Internal Network — and Meet Automatic Private
     Internet Protocol Addressing (APIPA) 306
   Step Two: Get Connected to Your ISP 307
   Step Three: Turn ICS On 309
   Step Four: Configure the Intranet Machines 311
   What About the Firewall? 311

Chapter 11 • What's in a Name? Network Name Overview **313**
What Is Naming All About: What a Name Server Does for You 313
Name Resolution in Perspective: Introduction to WINS, NetBIOS,
  DNS, and Winsock 314
   The Old: WINS, NetBIOS, and LMHOSTS 314
   The New: Domain Naming System (DNS) 315
   Two Different Lineages, Two Different Names 316
   Application Program Interface = Modularity 316

Chapter 12 • Old Names: Understanding NetBIOS, WINS,
        and NetBIOS over TCP/IP **319**
NetBIOS and Winsock 319
   Handling Legacy and NetBIOS Names: The Windows Internet Name Service . . . 320
   NetBIOS atop TCP/IP (NBT) 320
   Name Resolution before WINS: LMHOSTS 326
   Introducing LMHOSTS 326
WINS: A NetBIOS Name Service for Windows 329
   WINS Needs NT or Later Server 329
   WINS Holds Name Registrations 329

WINS Client Failure Modes 330
It's My Name, but for How Long? 330
Installing WINS 331
Configuring a WINS Server 333
Designing a Multi-WINS Network 337
Adding the Second WINS Server 338
Keeping the Second Server Up-to-Date 339
Avoiding WINS Problems 343
Deleting, Tombstoning, and Purging WINS Records 344
WINS Proxy Agents 345
Name Resolution in More Detail 347
Review: Winsock versus NBT 347
DNS/Winsock Name Resolution 347
Controlling WINS versus DNS Order in Winsock 349
NetBIOS Name Resolution Sequence 350

Chapter 13 • New Names: How DNS Works **353**
What DNS Does 353
Anatomy of a DNS Name 354
DNS Labels 1: The Host Name 355
DNS Labels 2: DNS Domains or Zones 355
DNS Domains Versus Active Directory Names 355
DNS from the Client Side 356
Preferred and Alternate DNS Servers 356
Configuring Your DNS Client Software 356
Configuring Your DNS Domain Membership 359
Configuring the DNS Suffix Search List 360
Caching Query Results 361
Caching Negative Query Results 362
Setting Up a Simple DNS Server 363
Find Your IP Addresses 363
Installing the DNS Server Software 364
Point the DNS Client to the DNS Server 365
Try Your DNS Server Out 365
Meet a Better DNS Tool: NSLOOKUP 366
Troubleshooting the Simple DNS Server 367
We Just Built a "Caching-Only" DNS Server 367
DNS Concepts: "The Hierarchy" 368
Introducing the Hierarchy: Back to Left-to-Right 369
Why Build the DNS Hierarchy This Way? 370
The Root, Top-Level, Second-Level, and Child Domains 370
Building a More Complex DNS Server 376
Connect and Name the Systems 376
Set Up the IP Addresses and Preferred DNS Servers 377
Open the Firewalls to Allow Pings 377

Test Connectivity 378
Install DNS Suffixes 378
Make Winserver a DNS Server 379
Creating *bigfirm.com:* The Birth of a Domain 380
Configuring Your Zone with DNS Records 384
Adding Hosts to a Zone: "A" Records 384
Setting Up Reverse Lookups 386
Reading NS and SOA DNS Records 388
Working with A Records and Understanding Glue Records 390
Seeing All of the Records: The Zone Files Themselves 392
Giving a Host Multiple Names with CNAMEs 395
Identify Your E-mail Servers with MX Records 398
Modifying Your Zone's SOA Record 401
Spreading the Work: Secondary DNS Servers 401
Secondary DNS Servers Hold Read-Only Zone Copies 402
How Primaries Keep Secondaries Up-to-Date 402
Delegating: Child Domains/Subdomains 411
Revising Bigfirm 411
Time for a Subdomain: *test.bigfirm.com* 414
Easier Record Maintenance: Dynamic DNS (DDNS) 416
Seeing DDNS Work 416
What DDNS Does, Under the Hood 417
Why You Need a Dynamic Reverse Lookup Zone 418
Keeping Your Systems from Registering PTRs 418
What Triggers DDNS Registrations? 419
Stopping All DDNS Registrations 420
Troubleshooting Failed DDNS Registrations 421
Keeping Your Zones Clean with DNS Scavenging 421
DDNS and Security 426
Tweaking DNS Performance 426
Cheap "Clusters": Building Fault Tolerance with Multiple A Records
and Round-Robin DNS 427
dnscmd Cheat Sheet 430

Chapter 14 • Automatic IP Setup: DHCP Essentials **435**
DHCP: Automatic TCP/IP Configuration 435
Simplifying TCP/IP Administration: BOOTP 435
DHCP: BOOTP Plus 436
Installing and Configuring DHCP Servers 437
Monitoring DHCP 462
Rebuilding a Damaged DHCP Server 462
DHCP on the Client Side 463
DHCP in Detail: How DHCP Works 463
Designing Multi-DHCP Networks 471

Chapter 15 • Things to Come: A Peek at Active Directory **473**

Centralized User Accounts and Authorization 474

Group Policy Centralizes Management, Security, and Configuration 475

AD Provides a Central List of Resources 475

Your Data Follows You Around, and It's Easier to Secure 476

Index 477

Introduction

Hello and welcome to the *Mastering Windows Server 2008* series and in particular to this volume, *Mastering Windows Server 2008: Networking Foundations*! Now, I know that many people don't read introductions, but I *beg* of you: please stay with me for at least this page or two ... or you may waste your money. I say that because some of you reading this would be best served by skipping this book and going directly to the second book in the series, *Mastering Windows Server 2008: Essential Technologies*.

Don't Buy This Book If . . .

This is the 13th in a series of books about Windows Server that I've written since 1993, and as such, I'm lucky to have a group of loyal return readers for which I'm very grateful — and it's to *you* folks that I'm talking in this section. For a number of reasons I'll get to a bit later in this introduction, I've divided the *Mastering Windows Server 2008* book into *three* books. This is the first book, and it's mainly aimed at those just joining us in Microsoft networking. In this book, we ("we" meaning my coauthors and I, that is — my veins, I fear, completely lack royal blood) show you things like how to put together two very basic Windows Server 2008 systems so that we can get some initial experience with NET USE-ing, the basics of the four ways you can control Windows, how Windows security works (logons, file permissions, passwords), what an IP address is, how to set up a DHCP server to *provide* those IP addresses, the difference between a DNS and a NetBIOS name, the ins and outs of storage in a Windows server, and an explanation in plain English about what a *directory service* is and why you'd set one up.

> **NOTE**
>
> To those of you who *haven't* ever before read one of my Server books: if any of those phrases sounded confusing, or if you've never heard of DHCP, DNS, or the like, then don't worry — you've got the right book. We'll make all of that stuff nice and easy.

That's not to say that this book offers no value for all readers of a previous volume. As you'll see if you stay with me for the rest of the introduction, over half of this book is either completely new chapters or extensively rewritten ones, and in any case I'm sure that a goodly number of return readers will find the review that they offer useful. I suspect, though, that most return readers might benefit more by moving directly to the second volume, *Mastering Windows Server 2008: Essential Technologies*. (Again, if you're unsure, then keep reading — you'll see chapter-by-chapter synopses of the other books in this series later in this introduction.) In any case, I can't stress enough that I would absolutely *hate* having someone buy a book of mine that didn't teach anything, especially not one of my loyal readers, which is partially why this introduction is as long as it is.

With that caveat out of the way, we're ready to answer the more important question: for whom *did* we write this book?

Do Buy This Book If...

My coauthors and I wrote this first volume mainly for people who seek to move from "network user" to "network administrator." If . . .

◆ You are currently familiar with Windows networking in the sense that you've been on a network as a user, surfed the Web, or used e-mail and want to start *running* networks rather than using them, or if

◆ You are already smart on non-Microsoft networks and need the propaganda-free, no-sales-pitch scoop on Microsoft networking, or if

◆ You've been stuck working as an administrator in some very specific corner of Microsoft networking (Web administration, user support, SQL administration) and want a broader understanding of the Microsoft networking landscape, then . . .

. . . you're in the right place. Again, welcome!

In this book, you'll start from a quick look at why people want to build Microsoft networks in the first place and move from there to understanding how to make a network work. You'll learn how to make a computer into a Windows server, and then understand how to control it. Along the way, you'll see firsthand how Microsoft networks are secured and how to create an intranet infrastructure. At that point, you'll have a network foundation in place and ready for the next book, which tackles the business of building on that foundation to create a useful network.

Like any long-used and successful piece of software, Windows Server is multi-faceted, complex, and complicated, and for a number of reasons. First of all, there are a lot of goodies that come with Windows Server software, and it's not immediately obvious what they do or why you'd want them. And then there are the things that don't make any sense at all until someone explains that yes, that module isn't all that desirable, but that it's a necessary evil for some reason, and the explanation usually involves understanding some unfortunate design decision made back in the mid-'90s that we're stuck with for reasons of backward compatibility. Finally, there are the parts of Windows Server 2008 that seem to have been included for just one reason: to make a few very, very large and important companies happy. The problem is, how to know what's useful, what's necessary, and what can be safely ignored? All you need is a native guide, and these three books seek to act in that role for you. Think of it this way: it is entirely possible to find a great glass of beer in France, and a delightful glass of wine in Britain, and I have, in both cases, but experience tells me that it's going to be a lot easier the other way around. Let my associates and me show you the easy way from user to administrator!

What's in This Book

Somehow I suspect that me merely saying, "buy this book if you're new to the industry or want a broader perspective on Server," may not provide sufficient incentive for you to decide to part with thirty bucks. So here's what you'll find inside *Mastering Windows Server 2008: Network Foundations*.

First, I needed to ensure that people of all technical levels could make use of this book, and so Chapter 1, "Why Network?," starts us off from ground level by providing a quick background on Windows networking. It discusses the benefits of networks, their component hardware, software, and protocols, and some "baseline" concepts so you'll be ready for the rest of the book. In Chapter 2, "Building a Simple Network," we temporarily skip the concepts and go straight to the skills, as we show you how to build two Windows Server 2008 systems, create a file share, access that file share, and more. I don't know about you, but I can learn things much more quickly if I can get my hands around them by playing with them, so we provide a step-by-step "cookbook" about creating these two servers. I think you'll find that having two working servers will make following the rest of the book easier, as you can always put the book aside and try out what you've been reading.

Chapter 3 fixes a problem that I've been meaning to fix in the Server books for quite some time: a need for more security focus. Once upon a time, security in networking was something of an afterthought: first get the network working, and then go secure it. But unfortunately that's 20th century thinking; the modern network administrator must understand and be thinking about security from Day One. That's why this book has this all-new chapter, "Security Concepts in Windows," that explains how logons work; what a permission, right, and privilege are; and where they live in Windows. With a bit of hands-on and the "basic basics" out of the way, it's time to see how to install Windows Server 2008 in Chapter 4, "Installing Windows Server 2008: Basics." This is actually the first of three chapters in this series that talk about Windows setup and deployment, as the same topic reappears in the second and third books in this series. The chapter in this first book tells you about the several different flavors of Server available, some advice on acquiring Server-friendly hardware, a guide to running Setup and then the initial setup process, and ends with a cook's tour of the literally dozens of aspects of Server 2008 that you can enable or disable.

Once the system's set up, it's time to meet its dashboard or, rather, dashboards. In the next four chapters, you'll meet the four big tools that administrators use to reconfigure and control Windows Server: its GUI, its command-line interface (CLI) tools, its "Registry" (the place where Windows keeps the settings), and its group policy settings (a sort of all-in-one-place location for several thousand Windows settings, levers, dials, and switches). Chapter 5, "Controlling Windows Server: MMC," starts it off with coverage of the Microsoft Management Console, a graphical framework for small programs called "snap-ins" that can be mixed and matched to allow you to create your own administrative "cockpit," and also includes some advice for those moving from the Windows 2000 or Server 2003 user interface to Server 2008's new desktop — as usual, Microsoft's rearranged the furniture a bit. Chapter 6, "Controlling Windows Server: The Command Line," moves you from the GUI to the command line with an introduction to administration from the command line, a useful chapter that's a guaranteed cure for "C:\> "-sickness. (Get it, "seasickness?" You see, from the command line you sometimes just see "C:\> ," and ... okay, not my best joke, I admit it.) Chapter 7, "Controlling Windows Server: The Windows Server 2008 Registry," covers the Registry from tip to toe, starting from its structure and purpose and moving quickly to some straight-talk advice about its realities ("don't expect the meaning of different Registry settings to be consistent — there is no Registry Police!") and from there to procedures to modify the Registry when necessary, backing it up, securing it, and understanding how its structure can cause many of the software incompatibilities that we run into when moving from older versions of Windows to Vista and Server 2008, and what you can do about it. Chapter 8, "Controlling Windows Server: Group Policy," then offers a soup-to-nuts look at something called a "local group policy object," a very, very useful tool for local server administration — and one that's undergone some significant changes over the local group policy objects in Server 2003.

With all of that out of the way, it's time to see how to do just enough basic server management to get us past the "beginner" stage to the "intermediate" level that we need in order to tackle the second book in the series. Chapter 9, "Windows Storage Concepts and Skills," explores how to install, configure, and manage drives on Windows Server, as well as creating fault-tolerant stores, protecting them with volume shadows, and more. Chapter 10, "TCP/IP and IPv4 Networking Basics," introduces you to TCP/IP, the language of the Internet. You can't get your computer onto the Internet or, for that matter, even your home's network, without knowing what a "subnet mask" and a "default gateway" are, and you'll learn that in this chapter. You'll also see how to troubleshoot a failed Internet connection and how to get it back up and running there as well.

The next three chapters cover a topic that makes networks easier for users to use ... but often tougher for administrators to fix. I'm talking here about network names, the things that let you visit my Web site by typing www.minasi.com (the Web site's name) rather than **70.165.73.5** (its network IP address). In a perfect world, this would be a *really* simple topic, but it's not, because Microsoft networks use *two* completely different kinds of names — sort of like what life would be for me if half of the world knew me as Mr. Minasi and the other half knew me as Mark but if neither half could understand that I could have any name other than the one that they knew me by. Chapter 11, "What's in a Name? Network Name Overview" explains how we got into this mess in the first place. Chapter 12, "Old Names: Understanding NetBIOS, WINS, and NetBIOS over TCP/IP," explains how Microsoft networks *used* to do names — but can't quite seem to stop doing it — and how you can (and almost certainly *must*) make those names work on your network. Chapter 13, "New Names: How DNS Works," explains the Domain Name System (DNS), the naming system that the Internet uses and that Microsoft is using more and more.

You learned about TCP/IP from a "how to use it just on *my* computer" standpoint in Chapter 10, but as a network administrator you need to deliver an IP address to *everyone* in your network and believe me, you don't want to have to walk around to every system on your network and give them an address. Modern networks simplify this with a sort of service called the "Dynamic Host Configuration Protocol" or "DHCP server." If you've got an Internet router in your house, then it's currently serving in that role for your home network ... but Windows Server can act as an industrial-strength DHCP server that can do way more things than that little Internet router can do, and you'll learn about that in Chapter 14, "Automatic IP Setup: DHCP Essentials."

Everything that we'll have done up to that point is nice and useful, but here's the ugly truth: it's all just plumbing. I mean, don't get me wrong — plumbing is necessary and all, and when someone else's plumbing doesn't work, they'll usually be pretty willing to pay someone (like you, perhaps) decent money to fix the plumbing. But plumbing isn't all that interesting unless you've got something to attach to it — sinks, toilets, bathtubs, and the like. Get ready to meet our first big fixture, our first big "this is why we worked so hard to set up these servers" reason: Active Directory. AD is the main focus of the second book of the series, but I didn't want to end this first book without giving you a look at AD in Chapter 15, "Things to Come: A Peek at Active Directory": what it does, why you want it, and what you can do with it. And with that, we'll be done with our examination of networking foundations ... and ready to move to Windows' essential technologies in the second book of the series.

About the Series

If you've gotten this far, then I'm hoping that you've decided to stay and that you'll perhaps pick up another volume or two in this series. To that end, please permit me to introduce you to the basic ideas we kept in mind in creating the three books, and then I'll give you look ahead at the entire scope of the series.

Written from the Final Code, Not Betas

You may have noticed that these books didn't appear on the shelf on 27 February 2008, the date that Microsoft shipped Windows Server 2008. That's a break with tradition, as we normally try to get the book out at the same time as the product; what's different now?

There's always a problem with books delivered at the same time as a piece of software: to a certain extent, they're always wrong. Books like this take months and months to write and, after being written, publishers need another couple of months to edit, lay out, print, bind, and ship those books. If, therefore, we had created a "published at Server 2008 delivery date" book, then you wouldn't be reading a book about Server 2008; instead, you'd be reading a book about Server 2008, Beta 3 — an incomplete product. Does it really matter whether a book about a product matches that product exactly? I believe so, as it can be disturbing to try to follow an example in a book only to find that the example doesn't work because some button's in the wrong place or some command doesn't work as advertised by the book. It's also sort of disquieting to examine a screen shot of some dialog box where that screen shot doesn't match what you're actually seeing on the screen. As a result, I asked the publisher to let us wait until the final product was finished before releasing the book, and they agreed.

Accuracy Is the Watchword

I believe that this will also serve a very important goal — the best accuracy that we can provide. When books are rushed to print, then things fall through the cracks. That becomes apparent when you try to follow a step-by-step exercise in some chapter in a book, only to find that the chapter's author apparently wrote the exercise from his memory of how the software works, rather than actually trying out. Accuracy has of course always been important in books, but I believe that it's more important now than ever — after all, if you, the reader, were willing to put up with inaccurate advice and explanations, then why would you buy a book when you can always just search the Internet. (Sorry, I couldn't resist.) I'm not promising perfection, but we've tried to get it as right as possible. Furthermore, if there *is* an inaccuracy, I'll post information about it on my online forum at www.minasi.com/forum, which I'll get to later in this introduction.

The Command Line Is a Must!

A long time ago, I was asked to be on a panel of "industry experts" at some conference. We took Q&A from the audience, and someone asked me why I thought the Windows Server products were beating the pants off the Novell server products, which were excellent in their own right and were the unquestioned king of the server market as recently as the mid-'90s. My answer went something like, "The thing that NT Server [the name of Windows Server prior to the year 2000] has that Novell doesn't is the GUI. If you can figure out how to play Solitaire, then you're halfway to being an NT administrator." Okay, I was mostly looking for a laugh there, but in truth I think that Server's early GUI-centric nature made for an easier learning curve and contributed strongly to Windows Server's rapidly outpacing Novell, market share-wise.

I've always thought, however, that while GUIs are good for accomplishing things you only do occasionally, in the end analysis you can get a lot of tasks done more quickly with a command-line tool than a GUI tool, so I've always tried to learn both the GUI and CLI way to get things done, and I've always tried to teach my students and clients both ways, and since 1997 I've been writing a monthly column about command-line tools in *Windows IT Pro* magazine. Well, I guess I sort of got lucky, as Server 2008 includes a version of itself that runs basically without a GUI, a version called Server Core. It has a very, very minimal GUI, meaning that anyone running a Server Core system had better be pretty good with the CLI. To that end, my coauthors and I have attempted to offer both the GUI and CLI ways to get things done in these books, and I hope you find that useful.

Why Three Books? We, Um, Outgrew the Binding

So why *did* we break *Mastering Windows Server 2008* into three books? Two reasons: size and a better "fit" for those who've purchased an earlier *Mastering Windows Server* book.

I'm told that the machines that bind printed pages into a book have a semi-standard maximum size of about 3 and some inches. *Mastering Windows Server 2003* could apparently *just* fit that restriction, but adding a few more pages would have made it "unbindable." In addition, I've heard from many readers that while they liked the 2003 book, hauling around an eight-pound book was like having to carry a second laptop, and did I know that sitting the book in one's lap raised welts? Honest, I heard you folks, and besides, I *had* to add coverage of plenty of neat things that arrived after Server 2003's April 2003 debut. *Mastering Windows Server 2003*'s unwieldy nature and a need to cover a lot more of all that added up to one thing: the day of the single-volume *Mastering Windows Server* book was over.

Return Readers Will See More "New" Stuff . . . but No Deltas

As long as I had to divide *Mastering Windows Server 2008* into a few books, I decided to remedy a concern voiced by a small number of return buyers who felt that they shouldn't see any material repeated from previous books. For example, a couple of readers who first purchased my *Mastering Windows NT Server 4.0* book in 1997 and learned the fundamentals of TCP/IP in that book and later purchased my *Mastering Windows 2000 Server* book in 2001 objected to the fact that the basic "this is how IPv4 works" chapter hadn't changed very much and angrily wondered why I was "recycling" so much material. The answer is this: first-time readers of *any* Windows networking book need to know how TCP/IP works, but TCP/IP just doesn't change all that much from one version of Windows to another. It would, then, be crazy for me to waste time trying to write a whole new TCP/IP chapter that says pretty much the same things as the old one, just to word it differently from the previous book's coverage. TCP/IP is, of course, just one example — with the exception of the change from NT 4 to Windows 2000, we've never seen a new version of Windows Server that's more than about 20 percent different from its predecessor, and so of course every *Mastering* book on Windows Server will have large sections of text that have been revised from the previous version rather than completely rewritten.

Of course, an obvious answer would be to turn out *two* versions of every edition of *Mastering Windows Server*. One would be the "complete" version, and one the "delta" version, which covered only the changes in the operating system. I would truly love to produce both versions of each edition of the book, but the fact is that there's simply no money in it. I tried it in the update to *Mastering Windows Server 2003* in 2006's *Mastering Windows Server 2003 Upgrade Edition for SP1 and R2*. It covered only the very large variety of changes that 2003's SP1 brought, as well as the changes that the interim "R2" version of Server 2003 delivered. The result was a smaller 700 page book that offered just the new stuff, instead of a revised edition of *Mastering Windows Server 2003* . . . and it didn't sell worth a darn, unfortunately. Other book series that have tried delta books have run into similar troubles, so I wasn't all that surprised — but it was worth the experiment anyway.

I *can*, however, reduce the amount of "I've seen this before" for return readers by putting much of the basic stuff in a separate volume — this one. That's one benefit of separate volumes, and I hope the returning readers find if of value.

Meet the Second and Third Books in the Series

While this book will work just fine for someone just looking for a the basics of Microsoft networking, the three books together are designed to constitute a sort of soup-to-nuts course in planning, installing, maintaining, and troubleshooting networks based on Windows Server 2008. Here is, then, a quick overview on what you'll see in the second and third books, *Mastering Windows Server 2008: Essential Technologies* and *Mastering Windows Server 2008: Enterprise Technologies* or, as its friends know them, Books 2 and 3.

MASTERING WINDOWS SERVER 2008: ESSENTIAL TECHNOLOGIES

Book 2 aims to help people who already know earlier versions of Windows Server and those who've just finished *Mastering Windows Server 2008: Networking Foundations* to work with what I think are the everyone-needs-to-know technologies and concepts, the things that networks large and small need to know.

The book starts off with an overview of what's new in Server 2008 and then returns in Chapter 2 to the topic of 2008's Setup program. But this time, we show you how to set up a hands-off setup via an answer file, and what you'll need to add that first 2008 server to your existing Windows Server 2003–based network. Then it's time in Chapter 3 to meet the newest member of the Server family, a sleek, trimmed-down, lean-and-mean version called Server Core. You'll do most of your Server Core administration from the command line . . . so you'll save days by learning the particular command-line tools you'll need to run a Core system. (As a matter of fact, you'll find that all three books share the trait that wherever possible you'll learn not only the GUI method of getting something accomplished, you'll learn the command-line method as well.)

In Chapter 4, we move from the TCP/IP basics covered in *Mastering Windows Server 2008: Networking Foundations* to a look at what's new in 2008's networking code. Chapter 5 returns us to the topic of DNS for two reasons: to learn what new features 2008 brings to DNS and some step-by-step instructions to set up a DNS infrastructure that'll make your network Active Directory–ready.

With the last of AD's foundation laid, it's time in Chapter 6 to actually build an Active Directory, showing you how to implement the simplest — and most common by far — Active Directory implementation, called a "one domain, one site forest." Now that you've got an Active Directory, it needs users, so Chapter 7 explains the care and feeding of 2008-based user accounts, always with an eye to getting your work done in the least time. Then we return to the topic that we previously spent four chapters on in *Mastering Windows Server 2008: Networking Foundations* — control — as you'll learn how to expand and multiply the power of group policies with domain-based group policies in Chapter 8. Our examination of how to control AD continues in Chapter 9, where you'll learn how to divide up the work by creating administrative accounts with fine-grained control of those powers via something called "Active Directory delegation."

The earliest function of any local area network is file and printer sharing, and so Chapters 10 through 12 take you step-by-step through several aspects of those topics and in particular taking veteran Windows Server administrators through a potentially troublesome migration tool. Every Active Directory needs machines called "domain controllers" to run the AD, and every DC needs a special shared folder called SYSVOL. Server 2008 completely changes SYSVOL, requiring a migration that, well, can be a little tricky . . . unless you read Chapter 11.

That room where the company keeps the servers can get pretty hot and noisy, so most of us admin types like remote administration tools, the topic of the Chapter 13. After that, you'll see how to connect various kinds of Windows clients to your new Active Directory domain in Chapter 14. Then it's time in Chapter 15 to set up Microsoft's Web server, the completely rebuilt-from-the-ground-up Internet Information Server 7.0. Finally, you'll see how to monitor your system's health and performance in Chapter 16, and the last chapter shows 2008's new Active Directory maintenance and recovery tools.

MASTERING WINDOWS SERVER 2008: ENTERPRISE TECHNOLOGIES

Once you've worked your way through *Mastering Windows Server 2008: Essential Technologies*, you'll be well on the way to a good knowledge of the parts of Windows Server 2008 that virtually every Windows network will include (as far as I can see, anyway). Microsoft's made Windows Server into a fairly "big tent" in that it comes with a large number of other networking tools beyond what I think most networkers would consider the "essential" stuff. I think of those technologies as the "enterprise" tools and, again, you're not likely to come across *all* of them in any one organization, but I'm pretty sure you'll see differing combinations of *some* of them in virtually every organization.

You may have noticed a sort of narrative thread, a "story line" in the first two books: the first book lays the foundation, and the second raises your network's house, so to speak. They're each sort of like a novel in that reading their chapters out of order usually won't work well. In contrast, you'll see that *Mastering Windows Server 2008: Enterprise Technologies* is less of a "novel" and more a collection of "short stories," coverage of topics like (to continue the house metaphor) putting in an extra bathroom, extending the garage, finishing the basement, and the like.

As with the first two books, we again open on the topic of deployment, this time in Chapter 1 moving beyond the question of rolling out one server and continuing to coverage of Microsoft's more extensive technologies for rolling out systems by the truckload in a chapter that includes Microsoft's new imaging tools and their unifying software, Windows Deployment Services. In Chapter 2, you'll learn about a technology that's of limited interest by itself but that acts as a foundation for several of the topics covered later — certificate services and public key infrastructure (PKI). Chapter 3 returns to TCP/IP fundamentals, but this time to demystify IP version 6, the new networking software that Microsoft enables by default on all Vista and Server 2008 systems. If you've been shutting off IPv6 as a matter of course in your modern Windows systems, then this chapter may change your mind. Chapter 4 continues IP coverage with details about how to build an IP infrastructure, including using a Window Server system as an "Internet traffic cop" — an "IP router," and you'll learn how to divide your network into "subnets." You'll need to understand Windows-based IP routing and subnetting as a prerequisite for the next two chapters.

Chapter 5 shows you how to use a Windows Server computer to allow you to access your organization's intranet from home or on the road, with coverage of Windows-based virtual private networking (VPN) technologies. Knowing about IP routing and Windows-based VPNs prepares you for one of 2008's really big all-new technologies, Network Access Protection (NAP). One way that malware gets into your network is when someone with a laptop computer accidentally installs some malware on the laptop and then brings it into your organization. Modern networks, however, can stop the malware at the door through a "quarantining" system that refuses to give a computer an address on the network until that computer's been through a sort of "health check." Again, it is one of the few truly new-to-2008 pieces of Server 2008 and you can read all about it in Chapter 6.

In Chapters 7–11, we return to the topics of Active Directory and file shares. Chapter 7 expands on the basic AD structure that we discussed in *Essential Technologies* with a discussion of running ADs in organizations with multiple locations and branch offices. Chapter 8 introduces another one of Server 2008's all-new features, the notion of a Read-Only Domain Controller, or RODC. Microsoft originally created RODCs to address the problem of putting a DC — a server that contains user passwords and thus must be secured properly — into an insecure location like many branch offices. But now that RODCs are available, it's easy to see a number of other uses for them, as you'll see in Chapter 8. All of this talk of branch offices is then the jumping-off point for a new form of file server designed with branch offices in mind, "DFS Namespaces." They first appeared in a sort of incomplete form in Server 2003 R2, but they really take off in Server 2008, as you'll learn in Chapter 9. Chapter 10 discusses the whys and hows of creating a multi-domain forest, and Chapter 11 explains how to merge and migrate existing Active Directories, as you might do if your organization merges with another, or changes its name. It's one of the uglier tasks we can ever face as AD managers, but Chapter 11 shows you the most direct ways to get it done.

Chapter 12 discusses an aspect of Server that's been around for about ten years, but that gets a major overhaul and improvement — Windows Terminal Services. There's so much new about Terminal Services that this chapter is a must-read for anyone using this valuable tool! Chapters 13 and 14 help out enterprises with non-Windows clients, explaining how to attach Macintoshes and Linux systems to Windows networks as easily and effectively as possible.

Chapters 15 and 16 discuss setting up FTP and e-mail servers on Server 2008 (and here "e-mail servers" does *not* mean Exchange, Microsoft's premier e-mail server product, but rather simpler Internet e-mail systems). The File Transfer Protocol (FTP) is one of the oldest and still most-used ways to exchange files over the Internet, and Windows Server has always included an FTP server ... but nobody ever really liked it. It always sort of felt like an afterthought, something that Microsoft did because someone forced them to do. With Windows Server 2008, however, we get a brand-new and quite nice bit of FTP server software, as you'll see in Chapter 15. Chapter 16 looks at Microsoft's implementation of the workhorse e-mail standards that handle every byte of Internet e-mail, the Simple Mail Transfer Protocol (SMTP). (Server 2003 also included a module called the Post Office Protocol [POP3], which meant that Server 2003 had a complete [if bare-bones] e-mail server right in the box, but unfortunately that's no longer true in Server 2008.)

More and more Windows components need to store reasonably large and complex databases and the standard way to access databases has become the Structured Query Language or SQL. Several parts of Windows Server can't function without a database server present, and so Microsoft includes a basic version of their SQL Server engine in Server 2008. Called "Windows Internal Database," this server service, once added, requires a bit of care and feeding, as well as introduces new security requirements. Chapter 17 explains those issues, as well as offering a set of "cookbooks" on how to manage this SQL database engine.

The more software you have on your computer, the more potential bugs you've got on that computer, and so all the more patches you've got to apply. But keeping up with patching is becoming a part-time job ... which is why Microsoft includes an entire service to do that, the Windows Server Update Services (WSUS). Chapter 18 shows you what WSUS does, how to set it up, and how to manage it.

Microsoft tells us that file servers are a mere thing of the past, and that a Web application of theirs is an even better idea — an application called Windows SharePoint Services. SharePoint's been around for a while but it keeps getting better. It lets you share documents as file shares do, but with the added benefit of a Web interface, an easy way to not just share files but collaborate with others, share calendars, and tons of other things. SharePoint's more than just a Web app, it's an, um, way of life as far as I can see, and Chapter 19 covers it.

Enterprise Technologies continues with Chapter 20, where we return to the matter of user account management with some practical advice on how to use roaming profiles, group policies, and logon scripts to simplify things for users — which simplifies things for us administrators. Finally, it wraps up with a start-to-finish explanation of Server's new "Hyper-V" virtualization tool, something that Microsoft's put into Server with the intention of taking over the ever-growing "server virtualization" market. If you're not yet using virtualization to its fullest or if you'd like to see how to get the most out of 2008's server virtualization platform then you won't want to miss this chapter. And with that, the *Mastering Windows Server 2008* series is done ... until Windows Server 2008 R2 appears in a couple of years, that is!

Stay in Touch and Learn More

I surely hope that this book and its companions answer all of your questions ... but if you need more information, want to ask a question, have a suggestion for future editions or — oh, this is the painful part — you found an error in the book (eek!), then we're easy to get in touch with. You can find me at help@minasi.com, and I promise — I always answer my e-mail, even if it's just to say, "Um, I'm sorry, but I have no idea, but such-and-such guy might."

Also, I host an online community of several thousand members via my online technical help forum at http://www.minasi.com/forum. We've been running since 2002 and we're very fortunate to have some very smart members who are quite helpful on a wide variety of topics. Come on down, ask a question, join a discussion, or offer some of *your* expertise. Our prime directive at the forum is, "Be nice!" — no newbie flaming allowed.

Finally, I'm always learning new things and I just can't wait to tell you about them, so I put together a free technical newsletter every month or so. You can find out about them in any of three ways. First, I've got an RSS feed at http://www.minasi.com/rss.xml that'll tell you when I create a new newsletter, as well as seminars that I offer and the occasional news about my Web site. Second, you can sign up for e-mail alerts, short text e-mails that tell you when a newsletter is available; go to http://www.minasi.com/nwsreg.htm to sign up. If you're skittish about giving people your e-mail address, then I surely understand — but, as my privacy policy states, I've been collecting e-mail addresses for the newsletter since 1999, and I've never spammed anyone, I've never sold the list, and I never will. Third, you can read my newsletters at any time by visiting http://www.minasi.com/nwstoc.htm. And if you forget any of those URLs, then don't worry — just remember the home page at http://www.minasi.com, and you'll be able to navigate from there to any of those locations.

Again, welcome to *Mastering Windows Server 2008: Networking Foundations*. I hope you like it!

Chapter 1

Why Network?

If you're reading this book, then you have an interest in Microsoft networking. For some people, networking sounds like a scary topic, but it really isn't. Getting a network running doesn't need to be hard, and this chapter explains many of the reasons why you want to set up a network when you have multiple machines to use. Windows Server 2008 makes networking considerably easier than ever, in fact, so you'll find that you do less work than ever before to get a network up and running.

In this chapter, we'll give you a bit of history on Server 2008 and then take a very high-altitude look at why we're using Microsoft's networking software in the first place. This is not intended to prepare you for a test on networking essentials, nor is it a complete book on Windows past and present. What I'm trying to accomplish in this chapter is to answer these questions:

◆ Why should you care about all of this networking stuff, anyway?

◆ What do you need to create a simple network?

◆ Why does Microsoft's networking software approach networking the way that it does?

What's the Point of Networks and Networking?

In a way, this chapter is penance for my youthful misdeeds.

When I was in the seventh grade, I had a math teacher named Mr. Schtazle. Seventh-grade math was a kind of potpourri of mathematical topics — I recall one chapter that took pains to drill into our heads the difference between precision and accuracy — and I'd plague the poor man at the beginning of every chapter by asking him, "How will we use this?" — a slightly more-polite version of "Why do we care?" Well, nowadays I find that when I'm teaching a room full of people about Windows Server, *I've* got to be careful to answer the question "Why do you care?" even if it isn't asked. Because if I don't answer that, then many people in the room will leave the class with a pretty good notion of *how* to accomplish a bunch of tasks but not a really good feel for *why* they'd do the tasks in the first place. And you know what? Answering the "Why do I care?" question can be pretty rough some times.

So, Mr. Schtazle, if you're out there...my apologies.

Let's consider these two questions:

◆ Why network in the first place?

◆ If we agree that networking is a good thing, why do we do it this way?

The answer to the first question will turn out to be pretty straightforward: Networking solves a set of problems for us. The answer to the question, "Why do we do it this way?" is a bit longer.

First and foremost, you're doing this to try to solve some problem that networking can help you with. Your company might want, for example, a great Web site, or to be able to send and receive e-mail, or a simple file and print server for a small office, or to share data with others on the Internet, or to allow employees access to your server from remote locations. These are the goals; a network is the means or tool to reach them. In short, *the ultimate goal of any networking project is to provide some kind of service*. Everything else is just a necessary evil — but there are a *lot* of those necessary evils!

Second, networks can provide many kinds of services, and every kind of service needs different software to make it work. For example, suppose you wanted to set up a Web site on the Internet. Network services, including Web sites, need two main pieces: a *server* piece and a *client* piece. To put up that great Web site, you'll create the site itself with HTML and drop that HTML onto a Web server. One way to get a Web server is by taking one of your computers and putting a piece of software on that computer to make it function as a Web server. But that's only half the story — in order for your customers to enjoy that Web server's content, they will need a piece of client software called a *Web browser*. That's our first networking piece: *Every network service needs server software and client software*.

Third, you need to ensure that there's a way for your information to get from your server to your clients, a physical system that the service can travel over. If the clients and servers are in the same building, then you need only a local area network (LAN), and setting that up merely requires pulling wires through the building (plus a few pieces of additional hardware described in the "Networks Need Connection Hardware and Links" section of the chapter). If, however, you want to offer your service to the world, as in the case of a Web server, then you'll need some kind of wide area network (WAN) connection to the Internet. Most companies today rely on a virtual private network (VPN) to ferry data safely across the Internet. In other cases, you'll need a WAN connection, but not to the Internet: Many organizations with more than one location connect those locations via private communications links with names like *leased line, T1*, or *frame relay*. That's our next networking piece: *Networks need connection hardware (switches, hubs, routers, modems) and links (phone lines, network cables, frame relay, DSL, cable modem, ISDN, and so on), or the clients can't connect to the servers*.

Fourth, to provide a service over a network, your server and your clients must agree on how to transmit information over that network. That agreement is called a *network protocol*, and the one that you'll most probably use in the Windows 2008 world is called the Transmission Control Protocol/Internet Protocol (TCP/IP). You may have heard of it before, as it's the network protocol that the Internet uses, but you needn't be on the Internet to use it. In short, *clients and servers must agree to speak using the same network protocols*.

NOTE

Windows Server 2008 provides two different versions of IP: IP version 4 (IPv4) and IP version 6 (IPv6). IPv4 is the version of IP used by the Internet today. In most cases, it's the only version of IP you need to support today. IPv6 provides additional addresses, some extra security, and a few other features. This version of IP provides functionality you need tomorrow, but you don't need to worry about it today. Because Microsoft chose to install IPv6 by default in Windows Server 2008, you may want to disable this support in order to gain some additional system performance. Chapter 2 tells you how to create an optimal setup that uses IPv4 efficiently (the companion enterprise volume, *Mastering Windows Server 2008: Enterprise Technologies*, discusses IPv6 in detail).

Fifth, once you have the channels open and before information starts flowing in both directions, you'll almost certainly need to worry about security. When you use the tool that is networking, you want to be sure it doesn't increase your risk, and in fact you can shape the tool so it reduces hazards. Briefly: *Networks need security.* (Chapter 2 introduces you to the topic of security.)

Sixth, and finally, once you've set up that terrific network service, you need a way for people to *find* that great service. You do that with a "naming" system. Windows 2008 has two of them — one that appeared years ago before the first version of NT (NT was the earliest version of Windows Server that Microsoft initially offered in 1993) and a newer (than NT, anyway) method that the Internet has been using for years. The last network piece, then, is that *networks must provide a way for users to find their services.*

Let's examine these pieces in order, take a closer look at why they work the way that they do, and get some insight into how Windows 2008 in particular handles them. This chapter only begins the discussion of networks. Some topics are so important that we decided to discuss them in detail in Chapters 2 and 3. You won't actually install Windows Server 2008 until Chapter 4 — these initial chapters will help you understand and prepare for your network.

Choosing a Network Type

Windows networks fall into two categories: workgroup and domain. A *workgroup* network connects multiple computers in a peer-to-peer configuration, which means that every computer can serve as both a client and a server. Workgroups are very simple, and you normally use them for smaller groups of computers — usually less than 10, but I've seen much larger workgroups of up to 100 computers. A workgroup doesn't require a centralized server, but you can certainly use one. Workgroups typically require little time to set up and configure, but they can become a nightmare to manage when they exceed a certain size. The fact that you don't necessarily need to have a server also means that workgroups can be less expensive.

A *domain* provides fully centralized services. It always requires that you set up a server and the server must provide support for advanced management features such as Active Directory. Domains provide stronger security than workgroups do because everything is under the tight control of the server. In addition, domains provide centralized administration. Normally, you use domains for larger networks. They require a lot more time and effort to set up, configure, and administer for a small number of computers, but a domain also offers significant advantages over a workgroup. As the size of your network groups increases, administration costs go down and performance increases when compared to a workgroup.

Network Client and Server Software

The reason that we network computers in the first place is so that computers acting as clients can benefit from the services of computers acting as servers. For example, suppose you want to visit my Web site, www.minasi.com. Two of the ingredients that you'll need to make that possible are software applications:

◆ You'll need a computer running a program that knows how to request Web information and then how to receive it — in other words, a *client application*.

◆ I'll need a computer running a program that knows how to listen for requests for Web information and then how to deliver that information — in other words, a *server application*.

As sometimes occurs *too* often in the computer business, you've got choices about both the client and the server.

THE CLIENT PIECE: A WEB BROWSER

I've said that first you'll need a computer, of course, one that's running a Web browser program such as Firefox or Internet Explorer. But let me rephrase that in basic network client-server terms.

There is technically no such thing as "the World Wide Web." Instead, there is an agreement about how to transfer text, pictures, and the like, and that agreement is called the HyperText Transfer Protocol — which is normally shortened to HTTP. The phrase World Wide Web just refers collectively to all of the HTTP servers on the Internet. When you think you're surfing a Web page, what really happens is this:

1. Your client computer asks the Web server (oops, I meant *the HTTP server*) something like, "Do you have any documents?"

2. The Web server responds by saying, "Here's my default document," a simple text file that is the so-called home page for that Web server. The Web server sends that file to your client using the HTTP protocol.

3. Once your client receives the text file, it notices that the page is full of references to *other* files. For example, if the home page that you requested has pictures on it, your Web browser (HTTP client) didn't originally know to ask for them, so the Web server (HTTP server) didn't send them. Your client notices the lack of the images and requests that the server send them, which it does — again using HTTP.

Here, "HTTP client" just means a program that knows how to speak a language that transfers a particular kind of data — Web data. Your computer is deaf to the Web unless it knows how to request and receive data via HTTP.

Notice what *client* means here. It doesn't refer to you, or even to your computer. Instead, it just means a program that your computer runs.

THE SERVER PIECE: A WEB SERVER

Next, let's consider what's sitting on my side of the conversation.

I'll need a computer running a special piece of software that is designed to listen for your computer (or anyone else's, for that matter) requesting to see my Web pages via HTTP and that can respond to those requests by transferring those pages to the requesting client software. You *might* call such a piece of software an "HTTP server" program, although almost no one calls it by that name. You'd more *commonly* call it "Web server" software. There is a variety of Web server software that I might run on my Windows Server 2008 computer, but I'm most likely to run the one that comes free with Server 2008, a program called Internet Information Services (IIS) 7. Alternatively, I might find, download (probably using HTTP!), and install a popular piece of free Web server software called Apache.

Once again, notice carefully what "server" means here. It does not really refer to the particular computer hardware that I've got stashed in my network room connected to the Internet. Instead, *server* means "the program running on Mark's computer that listens for HTTP requests and knows how to fulfill them."

Now that I've gone through all of that, consider again the question that I asked at the beginning of the chapter — why are you bothering with a network? The answer is probably because you want to offer a Web site, either internally or on the public Internet, and you think that IIS is the best (highest-performance, cheapest, or some combination of the two) Web server software around — which means that you must use Server 2008, because it's the only operating system that supports IIS 7. (Or you could use an earlier version of Server and an earlier version of IIS, but why not go with the latest and greatest?)

OTHER TYPES OF SERVERS

I'll tend to use the Web client-server example for this discussion. But I don't want to lose sight of the fact that there are quite a few client-server systems, besides Web servers, that are in common use and that you may want to use 2008 to create. Returning to the theme of this chapter, then — "Why do I care or why do I need this stuff?" — networks offer several valuable services, and you may want to set up a computer to act as a server and offer some of those services. Here are a few besides the Web server example:

File Servers   File servers act as central places to store data files. Why put them on a server rather than just keep them on your local computer? Well, in some cases someone else created the file, and placing a file on a central server is a simple way to make the files available to others. The other good thing about storing files in a central location is that they're more easily backed up that way. Server 2008 comes with file server software built in.

Print Servers   Print servers let you share printers. Not everyone wants to put a printer on their desk, and besides, if you share the printers, you can afford more expensive (and presumably better) models. Server 2008 comes with print server software built in.

Application Servers   Application servers provide a method for sharing an application across the Internet. In addition, you can distribute pieces of the application so that you can use multiple servers to provide a complete solution. Windows Server 2008 provides the software required to create an application server and manage the applications it hosts from a central location. This is a new feature for Windows Server 2008.

E-mail Servers   Mail servers are essential if you're going to do e-mail. Some computer (or computers) must act as the post office, collecting e-mail from the local users and sending it to other mail servers across the Internet and acting as a receiving point for other mail servers to send mail destined for your organization. You *can* outsource this function by letting your ISP act as your mail server, but running your own mail server gives you more flexibility. (However, it *does* require a persistent connection to the Internet.) 2008's new features include a basic e-mail server. Yes, it's "basic" because Microsoft *really* wants to sell you Exchange as your mail server. But it's not a bad server for many people's needs.

Terminal Servers   A terminal server harks back to the days of mainframes (think about the huge computers you may have seen in older movies — a mainframe is a single large computer used to serve a number of people). Someone using a terminal would log into the mainframe from a remote location to access the features that the mainframe provides. Modern users rely on this feature to access the server from a remote location using less capable devices. Some companies use this service to save money. Administrators rely on this feature to manage the server. Using a terminal server application called Remote Desktop means you don't have to walk to the server to perform administration tasks.

Group Scheduling Servers   The centralized nature of servers means that they're a great place to keep track of scarce resources like meeting rooms or your time. Server 2008 does not come with a scheduling server, because Microsoft wants to sell you Exchange to do that sort of thing. But there are alternatives to Exchange; there are some terrific Web-based scheduling tools that work great on 2008 — for one example, take a look at www.mattkruse.com/scripts/calendar/ or other tools, such as Lotus Notes.

SharePoint Servers   A SharePoint server lets users collaborate with other users, even when they aren't physically located in the same place. Users from England, the United States, and Japan could work on documents together as if they were all located in the same place.

As with a local connection, users can also share information, such as contacts, with each other. An administrator can also use a SharePoint server to place (deploy) applications on remote systems without physically visiting those locations.

E-Commerce Online Stores   If you've got something great to sell, then the Web's one place to do it. There are thousands of online stores on the Web, and a good number of them run on 2008. While 2008 includes a Web server, it doesn't include the other software that you'd need to create a complete online store. But there are a lot of consulting and programming firms that would be happy to help you create an online store atop 2008!

Microsoft has adopted new terminology for Windows Server 2008 that makes it easier to understand the difference between a service that the server provides and a piece of software that makes the server perform better or provide improved capabilities. *Roles* are the pieces of software that define the services that a server provides. For example, if you want to make your server into a Web server, you install the Web Server (IIS) role. *Features* help your server perform certain tasks better. In some cases, you must install a feature to make a role work, but most features simply add functionality. For example, if you want to use your Web server to help remote users print documents, then you install the Internet Printing Client feature.

Networks Need Connection Hardware and Links

If I want to offer a server service and ensure that you can enjoy that service, then we'll both need to be physically attached to the same network — the same series of cables, satellite links, or whatever — or your computer's requests will never get to my computer in the first place. That probably means that we're both on that huge network-of-networks called the Internet, but we could just be working for the same company in a single wired building, or a multilocation firm connected by a private intranet.

Now, notice that if I'm going to run a Web server, I'll need to be connected to our common network (Internet or otherwise) persistently: I couldn't decide to run a Web server out of my house and just dial in to the Internet now and then. Of course, if I'm only serving some private network that we share, then an Internet connection is unnecessary, because we already have a connection to a common network.

People who worry about the physical connection part of networking concern themselves with getting cables run through walls, calling the phone company to arrange for persistently connected data links of various kinds (links with names like *digital subscriber line, cable modem, frame relay, leased lines, T1* or *T3 lines*) and then working with a family of hardware that helps get the bits going off in the right direction (devices with names like *switches, hubs,* and *routers*).

Does 2008 help you with this part of the job? In some parts, it can. Switches and hubs are very basic, simple devices, and 2008 has nothing to do with them — although clearly 2008 depends on their presence in order to network! Routers are, however, more complex devices. You probably know that the market leader in the router world is a firm named Cisco Systems, but you might not know that a router is really just a small, single-purpose computer. If you wanted, you could use a computer running Server 2008 to replace a Cisco router. Additionally, if you wanted to allow people outside your network to dial in to your network, you could use a Windows Server 2008 to make that possible.

Considering the Hardware

This chapter has already discussed a lot of hardware. Although the hardware part of the picture isn't hard to understand, you do need to understand it in order to create your network. Networks have some basic hardware that you must have in order to ensure that everyone can communicate.

In some cases, you install optional hardware to make the network perform certain tasks or to add to the functionality that the network provides.

When PC networks first came into existence, you could find a wide range of distinctly incompatible components. Network hardware could use all kinds of odd-sounding technologies such as Token Ring and ArcNet. (Don't worry if these technology names are unfamiliar to you, we'll discuss them in more detail as the book progresses. For now, all you need to know is that they provide a kind of physical connection between computers.) Today, most networks rely on Ethernet connections and use standard components. You might have heard that networks are hard to put together, partly because they really were in the past, but luckily standardization has made creating a network significantly easier. Here are the common pieces of hardware you find on a network:

Connector For many people, the lowly connector isn't even worth mentioning, but you suddenly discover the importance of this element when your network is no longer connected and nothing is apparently wrong. The typical Ethernet connector looks just like a larger version of the connector for your telephone, as shown in Figure 1.1. In fact, that's one of the first things you need to avoid — mistaking the two types of connector. Notice that the RJ45 connector is larger and that it has 8 pins in it, rather than the 4 or 6 pins of an RJ10, RJ11, or RJ12 connector used for a telephone. When you plug a connector into a NIC, hub, switch, or router, the receptacle normally lights up to show you have a good connection. You should look for these lights when you need to find a loose connection. It's a bad idea to plug and unplug connectors too often because the connection can become loose and cause you a lot of trouble.

FIGURE 1.1
Typical Ethernet connectors. The male connector appears on each end of the cable, while the female connector appears with the computer, hub, switch, router, or other device connection.

8   1

Male RJ45 Connector

1

Female RJ45 Connector

Typical Ethernet connectors, the male connector appears on each end of the cable, while the female connector appears with the computer, hup, switch, router, or other device connection.

Network Interface Card (NIC) A network interface card (NIC) connects the computer to the network. It provides all of the hardware features required to make an electrical connection and perform low-level networking tasks. A NIC won't provide the connection by itself. Windows provides software required to make the NIC functional. Most machines today have one or two NICs supplied with them. You must have one NIC for each connection you want to create. A machine with two NICs can use one of them to connect to a local network and the other to connect to the Internet. NICs have specific characteristics — some of which are important for everyone to know and some of which are only helpful to technicians. The most important NIC characteristic is its connection speed because the connection speed determines how fast the NIC can communicate with other machines connected to the network.

Cable A cable provides a physical connection between the NIC contained within the machine you want to connect to the network and the hub, switch, or router used to distribute signals to the rest of the network. Cables come in a confusing array of sizes and types. The most important characteristic of the cable is the connection speed it supports. You must match the connection speed of the cable to the NIC. Otherwise, the NIC won't be able to connect at full speed. In some special cases, you need cables with other characteristics. For example, if you want to run the cable through a false ceiling or through air ducts, you may need special cable designed for that purpose (often called *plenum cable*). Plenum cable resists burning and doesn't produce as many noxious chemicals if it does burn, but it costs a lot more than standard cable. Check the local electrical code to ensure you use the right kind of cable for a specific purpose.

Hub   A hub is the least expensive connectivity solution for a network. You connect one end of the cable into the NIC and the other end into the hub. *Voilà*, you are now part of the network. Every computer or other device (such as a printer) that wants to be part of the network has the same connection setup. Hubs can usually have 2, 4, 8, 16, or 32 computers or other devices connected to them, with 8 being the most common. Each connection to a hub is a port. You should buy a hub with enough ports to support all the devices on your network, with a few to spare. When you run out of ports, you can purchase another hub, connect the two hubs together using a special port, and then plug additional computers into the new hub. Connecting multiple hubs together is *daisy chaining*. Because hubs are very simple devices, they are also extremely reliable. However, the reliability and cost savings comes at the price of performance and ease of maintenance. If you need a high-speed connection or you have many devices to connect, then a switch is a better option than using a hub. The most important characteristic of a hub is the connection speed it supports. The connection speed must match the speed of the NICs on a network.

Switch   Switches work precisely the same as hubs from the outside. You connect one end of the cable into the NIC and the other end into the switch to create a connection to the network. However, switches include additional internal circuitry and provide performance benefits. A switch can make smart connections between two devices on the network to speed communication between them. When working with a hub, all of the computers on the network hear the message that another computer sends, but switches direct the message specifically to the computer that needs to hear it. In addition, switches normally contain diagnostic hardware to make it easier to find problems on your network. Of course, you don't get this extra circuitry free — switches cost more than hubs do. As with hubs, the switch connection speed must match the connection speed of NICs on the network.

Router   A router is similar to a switch or hub, but it includes something extra — the ability to connect to the outside world. A router is similar to a computer with two NICs in it. One set of connections is for the local network, while the second set of connections is for the outside world. The vendor labels the connections so you can't make a mistake in creating the required connections. Routers also include some of the features of a server, including a firewall for security purposes. The features you obtain with the router depends on the kind of router you buy. For example, some routers include special support for standard TCP/IP features, and some even include a wireless access point (WAP) to connect with wireless devices. Make sure you get a router that includes all the features you need. For example, if you have wireless devices, then getting a router with a built-in WAP is a better buy than purchasing the WAP separately.

Network-Ready Device   In days gone by, most devices such as printers, camcorders, and cameras were dependent on a connection with a computer to gain network connectivity. You plugged the device into the computer and shared the device with others on the network, and then other people would access the device through this shared connection. This approach to networking wastes resources because you now need a computer to create the required connection. Network-ready devices have a NIC built into them and provide the software required to create the network connection. You access a network-ready device the same way you do any computer on the network. The network-ready devices do cost more than standard devices, so you need to weigh the added cost of the device against the cost of using the computer to provide a connection. In some cases, such as a small network that has a server and only a few devices, using standard devices may actually prove less expensive in the long run. Most routers support only two networks. However, it's possible to find routers that support more — all the way up to 128 networks — but you'll pay a hefty price for them.

Wireless Access Point A wireless access point (WAP) is a type of router. It creates a connection between a wired network and wireless devices. The wireless devices use radio waves to communicate with the WAP. As with most network devices, you plug the WAP into a hub, switch, or router to create the connection to the wired network. The critical consideration for a WAP is the standards to which the WAP adheres. For example, if your laptop provides an 802.11g connection, then your WAP must support the 802.11g specification or the two devices won't communicate with each other. The 802.11b and 802.11g specifications are the most common in use today, but you must check your wireless devices to determine which standard they follow. In some cases, the WAP will support multiple standards. You'll want all your wireless devices to use the same standard because some wireless connection standards don't work well with others because of radio wave interference. Another consideration is the antenna range for the WAP. This range determines the maximum distance that can separate the wireless device and the WAP. Always remember that the distance between the wireless device and the WAP affects transmission speed. You may think that you'll get 54 Mbps transmission speed, but you won't when you're at the maximum distance. In fact, most WAPs provide multiple fallback speeds so you need to know the slowest speed you can expect before losing the connection completely.

It often helps to view network diagrams put together by other people before you create your own network. For example, you can see a basic home network with a WAP at http://www.homenethelp.com/web/diagram/wireless-bridge-xp.asp. The diagrams at http://msdn2.microsoft.com/en-us/library/aa934598.aspx show you how you might attach a network-ready device. The diagram at http://www.weresc.com/home.php is significantly more complex than the other two, but it shows you that networks can be any size. If you want to create your own network diagram using the hardware discussed in this chapter, check out the free program at http://www.supershareware.com/info/edraw-network-diagrammer.html.

After you look at a number of designs put together by other people, you'll want to spend some time creating your own diagram. The diagram need not be very complicated. However, you need to provide enough information to ensure you can create a good network setup. Figure 1.2 shows a network diagram that includes many of the elements that you'll probably have on your network. This diagram doesn't represent your network any more than the diagrams I referenced earlier through Web sites — it's just another example that you can use to create your own diagram.

This diagram shows a number of important features. Every computer and network-ready device can have a NIC that is separate from that device. Yes, the NIC appears inside the unit, but it may not come with the unit — you may have to purchase this item separately and ask the vendor to install it for you. The connector (shown in Figure 1.1) will appear somewhere on the case. You connect a cable from the device to the hub or switch as shown. In some cases, you might actually connect the computers and network-ready devices directly to the router, instead of using a separate connection as shown. Notice that the router provides a connection to the Internet — the hub or switch won't provide this connection.

Do you see that lightning bolt next to the WAP? That lightning bolt represents a connection made using radio waves — a wireless connection. Any device, such as a laptop, designed to use the wireless standard supported by the WAP can connect to the network through the WAP as shown. You shouldn't add a WAP to your network unless you actually need it because a WAP can cause security breaches that you wouldn't experience when using wired connections. As shown in Figure 1.2, the WAP provides a bridge between the wired and wireless connections on your network.

FIGURE 1.2
Creating a diagram of your network is important if you want to get good results.

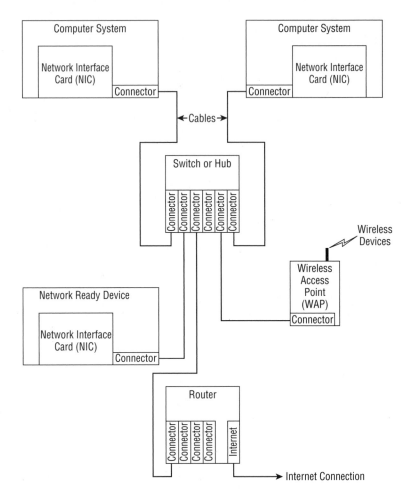

Clients and Servers Must Speak the Same Protocols

But simply being connected to the same wire isn't enough — we need a common communications language. If I were to pick up a phone and dial some number in Beijing, I'd have a physical connection with whatever poor soul picked the phone on the other end — but that would be the extent of our interaction. In the same way, computer networks need to agree on things like, "What's the biggest block of data that I can ever send you?" and "How shall I acknowledge that I actually *got* that block of data?" or "Should I bother acknowledging receipt of data at all?" and hundreds of other questions.

The answers to all those questions are contained in the "network language," or, in network techie terms, the *network transport protocol*. It probably won't surprise you that more than one network transport protocol exists, and over the years NT and other versions of Windows Server have generally supported three of them:

◆ NetBEUI (Network Basic Input/Output System Extended User Interface), an old Microsoft/IBM/Sytek protocol designed to support small networks

◆ IPX/SPX (Internet Packet Exchange/Sequenced Packet Exchange), the protocol that Novell NetWare predominantly used for years

◆ TCP/IPv4 (Transmission Control Protocol/Internet Protocol), the protocol of the Internet and intranets

Windows Server 2008 changes this equation somewhat. You won't find support for IPX/SPX in Windows Server 2008, which means it won't communicate with that old NetWare server on your network. In addition, you won't find NetBEUI support in Windows Server 2008 because Microsoft has replaced this protocol with TCP/IP. However, Windows Server does add support for TCP/IPv6, which provides additional address space (which means it supports additional devices) and better security. The article at `http://technet.microsoft.com/en-us/library/bb878121.aspx` provides great information on the new features provided by TCP/IPv6.

Your only choices for transport protocols in Windows Server 2008 are TCP/IPv4 and TCP/IPv6. It's a good bet that you're using TCP/IPv4 right now. Why TCP/IPv4? Well, there have been some really great protocols over the years, but because the Internet uses TCP/IP and the Internet is so popular, TCP/IP has sort of trumped the other protocols. In fact, it's impossible to do a fair number of things that 2008 and its predecessors Windows 2000 and, to a lesser extent, Windows NT 4 are capable of doing *without* TCP/IP. Because TCP/IPv6 is so new, few Internet service providers (ISPs) require it and it's doubtful you need this protocol for your company. So, I'm going to assume for our discussion and indeed for most of this book that your network will use TCP/IPv4.

Oh, and one more thing — once you've decided that TCP/IP is your network protocol of choice, then you'll need to install several *more* servers to support TCP/IP's infrastructure. And here again, when I say "more servers," I'm not suggesting that you have to buy more PCs, although you might. What I mean is that you'll have to install software on some computer or group of computers to perform three basic pieces of plumbing or infrastructure jobs:

◆ A Domain Naming System (DNS) server keeps track of the names of the computers in your network (an important task, believe it or not). When working with a workgroup, you can obtain DNS support automatically (without any configuration) by using the Internet Connection Sharing (ICS) feature of Windows Server 2008. You must install DNS support separately for a domain.

◆ A Dynamic Host Configuration Protocol (DHCP) server configures the specifics of TCP/IP on each computer in your network, both great and small. Many routers provide DHCP support, so make sure you check your router before you configure this feature on your Windows Server 2008 installation because it may be a redundant service/role that your Windows Server can do without.

◆ A Windows Internet Name Server (WINS) does something like what DNS does — keeps track of names — but isn't really necessary on a "pure" Windows 2008 network — its main job is to support older Microsoft operating systems like Windows 9x, Me, and NT 3.x and 4.

You'll learn more about the specifics of DNS, DHCP, and WINS in Chapter 11. I should point out that if you're a one-person shop, then you might not need all of that, as your ISP might be handling it for you — but I'm assuming throughout this book that you are probably a network administrator/manager for a network of at *least* a few computers, and possibly for a tremendous number of computers.

A Brief History of Windows

Let's finish this chapter with a look at how NT has grown into Windows Server 2008 today.

Even in the early 1980s, Bill Gates knew that networking was a key to owning the computer business. So, on April 15, 1985, Microsoft released its first networking product, a tool called MS-NET, and its companion operating system, DOS 3.10. Most people knew about the new DOS and were puzzled at its apparent lack of new features. What it contained, however, were architectural changes to DOS that made it a bit friendlier to the idea of networks.

Now, Microsoft wasn't big enough at that time to create much hoopla about a new network operating system, so it let others sell it — no matter how high or low you looked, you couldn't buy a product called MS-NET. Instead, it sold mainly as an IBM product under the name of the IBM PC Network Support Program; IBM viewed it as little more than some software to go along with IBM's PC Network LAN boards and, later, its Token Ring cards. The server software was DOS-based, offered minimal security, and, to be honest, performed terribly. (Believe me, I *know*; I used to install them for people.) But the software had two main effects on the market.

First, the fact that IBM sold a LAN product legitimized the whole industry. IBM made it possible for others to make a living selling network products. And that led to the second effect: the growth of Novell. Once IBM legitimized the idea of a LAN, most companies responded by going out and getting the LAN operating system that offered the best bang for the buck. That was an easy decision: NetWare. In the early days of networking, Novell established itself as the performance leader. You could effectively serve about twice as many workstations with Novell NetWare as you could with any of the MS-NET products. So Novell prospered.

As time went on, however, Microsoft got better at building network products. 3Com, wanting to offer a product that was compatible with the IBM PC Network software, licensed MS-NET and resold it as their 3+ software. 3Com knew quite a bit about networking, however, and recognized the limitations of MS-NET. So, 3Com reworked MS-NET to improve its performance, a fact that didn't escape Microsoft's attention.

From 1985 to 1988, Microsoft worked on its second generation of networking software. The software was based on its OS/2 version 1 operating system. (Remember, Microsoft was the main driving force behind OS/2 from 1985 through early 1990. Steve Ballmer, Microsoft's number-two guy, promised publicly in 1988 that Microsoft would "go the distance with OS/2." Hey, the world changes, and you've got to change with it, right?) Seeing the good work that 3Com did with MS-NET, Microsoft worked as a partner with 3Com to build the next generation of LAN software. Called Microsoft LAN Manager, this network server software was built atop the more powerful OS/2 operating system. As with the earlier MS-NET, Microsoft's intention was never to directly market LAN Manager. Instead, Microsoft envisioned IBM, 3Com, Compaq, and others selling it.

IBM did indeed sell LAN Manager (it still does in the guise of OS/2 LAN Server). 3Com sold LAN Manager for years as 3+Open but found little profit in it and got out of the software business. In late 1990, Compaq announced that it would not sell LAN Manager because it was too complex a product for dealers to explain, sell, and support. Microsoft decided then that if LAN Manager were to be sold, it would have to do the selling, so on the very same day as the Compaq withdrawal, Microsoft announced it would begin selling LAN Manager directly.

> **NOTE**
>
> Here's an interesting side note: Ten years after Compaq (now HP) decided that its sales force couldn't sell network software, it reversed direction and said it would sell a special version of Windows 2000 called Datacenter Server. It's special because you cannot buy it from Microsoft — you must buy it preinstalled on specially certified vendor hardware. In other words, the hardware vendors (HP is not the only one selling Datacenter) now believe that they can sell complex network operating systems. I wish them the best of luck, but stay tuned to see the outcome of this particular marketing maneuver!

LAN Manager in its first incarnation still wasn't half the product that Novell NetWare was, but it was getting there. LAN Manager 2 greatly closed the gap, and in fact, on some benchmarks LAN Manager outpaced Novell NetWare. Additionally, LAN Manager included administrative and security features that brought it even closer to Novell NetWare in the minds of many network managers. Slowly, LAN Manager gained about a 20 percent share of the network market.

When Microsoft designed LAN Manager, however, it designed it for the 286 chip (more accurately, I should say again that LAN Manager was built atop OS/2 1.*x*, and OS/2 1.*x* was built for the 286 chip). LAN Manager's 286 foundation hampered its performance and sales. In contrast, Novell designed their premier products (NetWare 3 and 4) to use the full capabilities of the 386 and later processors. Microsoft's breakup with IBM delayed the release of a 386-based product, and in a sense, Microsoft never released the 386-based product.

Instead of continuing to climb the ladder of Intel processor capabilities, Microsoft decided to build a processor-independent operating system that would sit in roughly the same market position as Unix. It could then be implemented for the 386 and later chips, and it also could run well on other processors, such as the PowerPC, Alpha, and MIPS chips. Microsoft called this new operating system NT, for "new technology." Not only would NT serve as a workstation operating system, but it would also arrive in a network server version to be called LAN Manager NT. No products ever shipped with that name, but the wallpaper that NT Server displays when no one is logged in is called LANMANNT.BMP to this day.

In August 1993, Microsoft released LAN Manager NT with the name NT Advanced Server. In a shameless marketing move, it was labeled version 3.1 in order to match the version numbers of the Windows desktop products. This first version of NT Advanced Server performed quite well. However, it was memory-hungry, lacked Novell connectivity, and had only the most basic TCP/IP connectivity.

September 1994 brought a new version and a new name: Microsoft Windows NT Server version 3.5. Version 3.5 was mainly a "polish" of 3.1; it was less memory-hungry, it included Novell and TCP/IP connectivity right in the box, and it included Windows for Workgroups versions of the administrative tools so network administrators could work from a Workgroup machine rather than an NT machine. Where many vendors would spend 13 months adding silly bells and whistles, NT 3.5 showed that the Microsoft folks had spent most of their time fine-tuning the operating system, trimming its memory requirements, and speeding it up.

In October 1995 came NT version 3.51, which mainly brought support for PCMCIA cards (a real boon for us traveling instructor types), file compression, and a raft of bug fixes.

NT version 4, 1996's edition of NT, got a newer Windows 95–like face and a bunch of new features, but no really radical networking changes. Under the hood, NT 4 wasn't much different from NT 3.51.

From mid 1996 to early 2000, no new versions of NT appeared, an "upgrade drought" such as we'd not seen in quite some time from Microsoft. Then, in February 2000, Windows 2000 ("NT 5.0") shipped. Windows 2000 included a whole lot of new stuff, but perhaps the most significant was a new way of storing and organizing user accounts and related information: Active Directory (AD) domains. Closely following AD in importance was the then-new notion of Group Policy, something you'll see has become quite important to anyone wanting to run a network based on XP and Server 2003.

The next version of NT shipped in pieces for the first time since 1993. First NT Workstation 5.1 or, as it's better known, XP Professional and its lesser sibling, XP Home. Microsoft intended to follow up with the server version of NT 5.1, but events conspired to compel them to wait a bit longer and produce NT Server 5.2 — that is, Windows Server 2003. Windows Server 2003 is a "1.1" version of Windows 2000, a welcome improvement to 2000's fit and finish.

And now we reach Windows Server 2008, which builds a wealth of functionality onto the previous offerings. Of course, it now supports TCP/IPv6, which is an addition for the future. The best news is that Windows Server 2008 provides significant new security features. For example, even the administrator doesn't have access to the root directory, \Windows folder, or \Windows\ System32 folder, so trying to corrupt executables within these folders is significantly more difficult. The new Windows firewall provides both incoming and outgoing firewall support, so outsiders will find it much more difficult to gain entry to your server, especially if you have other firewalls in place. The administrator also runs as an average user now and must give permission to perform certain tasks. This feature makes it much harder for an outsider to do something without the administrator's knowledge. In short, Windows Server 2008 is a welcome improvement to the one issue that people complain about most — Windows security.

For those of you who fought through Windows network configuration tasks in the past, you'll find that Windows Server 2008 greatly automates the task. Microsoft has added functionality that automatically detects your network card and begins the setup process for you as part of the installation. In some cases, you might not need to do anything with the NIC or associated connections at all except verify that your configuration is correct. You don't need to worry about these details now. The next chapter shows how to put your network together, Chapter 3 reviews Windows security, and you'll see how to install Windows Server 2008 in Chapter 4.

Well, I hope this chapter wasn't boring for those already expert in Windows while bringing the newbies up to speed. No matter what version of Windows you're running, however, you'll need to configure it. For example, Microsoft can't guess about which resources, such as hard drives, that you want to share, so the new automation can't do everything for you. And there are, as there always have been, two main ways to do it. The preferred way is through the GUI with windowed programs that offer help and a bit of error-checking, or its somewhat more complex relatives, the command-line tools. The less-preferred, but often necessary, way is to directly tweak some setting in its lair . . . a place called the Registry. The chapters that follow introduce these two configuration approaches.

Chapter 2

Building a Simple Network

In Chapter 1, you learned why you might want to network computers together. In this chapter, you'll begin to see how some of the pieces described in Chapter 1 fit together in a real-world scenario. You won't build anything complex in this chapter. However, these basics are important for the novice, so if this is your first time working with a network, you'll discover some amazing new things you can do with a computer system.

The goal of this chapter is to help you build a simple network, a network you can use to see how things work. This kind of network is an important first step to working with Windows Server 2008 because you can use it to build networking skills in a safe environment — one that isn't connected to the Internet or anything else for that matter. What we're trying to accomplish in this chapter is to answer these questions:

◆ Where do you obtain a free copy of Windows Server 2008 that you can use for testing?

◆ What do you need to do to make the two servers see each other?

◆ How do you set up user accounts for a basic setup?

◆ How can you share resources when working with a basic setup?

◆ Now that you have an account and shared resources on one server, how do you access them on another machine?

> **NOTE**
>
> This chapter assumes you have two machines that you can connect together to form a network. Because you're using the machines to perform only simple tasks, you don't need the latest product on the market — you only need a system that will provide the basic support required to run Windows Server 2008. You also need the cables required to connect the machine to a hub or switch, as well as the hub or switch. Each of the machines requires one network interface card (NIC) installed so it can connect to the network (in most cases, you'll find that the NIC comes installed with your machine).
>
> Theoretically, you can also accomplish all the tasks in this chapter using a virtual machine setup on a higher-end physical machine. Using this approach requires more setup time and experience on your part, but it does mean you can get by using just one machine. This chapter doesn't discuss the virtual machine approach because of the complexity of the setup. The focus of this chapter is to keep things simple, especially at the hardware level.

Getting Your Free Copy of Windows Server 2008

You may not realize it, but Microsoft does occasionally give things away. If you only want to set up a quick network and use it for testing purposes, then the 180-day free trial version of Windows Server 2008 may be all you need. This chapter assumes you're using the 180-day trial version, but you can also use it with a paid version of Windows Server 2008. The two versions are essentially the same, but the 180-day version quits working after 180 days. Also, these books focus on Windows Server 2008 *Standard* Edition (the version that runs roughly $1,000 to buy), and Microsoft offers its 180-day evaluation copy only in the form of Windows Server 2008 *Enterprise* Edition, the $4,000 version. Again, you won't see much in the way of differences, but some menus may look a little different.

Downloading the Software

To obtain your free copy of Windows Server 2008, you need to go to the main Windows Server 2008 Web site at `www.microsoft.com/windowsserver2008/default.mspx`. This Web site contains a number of links on the left side, one of which will take you to the download location for the free version of Windows Server 2008. The current URL for the download is `www.microsoft.com /windowsserver2008/audsel.mspx`. However, Microsoft likes to rearrange its Web site every week or so, so just in case the 180-day evaluation copy's not there, then go to Microsoft's Web site at `www.microsoft.com` and search for *Windows Server 2008 180 day evaluation*, and you'll probably find it.

After you get to the download location, you'll see links for a number of Windows Server 2008 editions. In fact, you'll see a link for each of the editions that you can get in a paid version, including the following:

♦ Standard

♦ Enterprise

♦ Datacenter

♦ Web Server

♦ Itanium

All of these editions, except Itanium, come in both 32-bit (x86) and 64-bit (x64) versions. Because most machines in use today have 64-bit processors, you can use either version of the product. This chapter assumes you're using the Windows Server 2008 Enterprise edition (again, because that's the free evaluation version), but any of the editions should work fine for the simple tasks that we'll perform. Check the "Choosing a Windows Server 2008 Edition" section of Chapter 4 if you want learn more about the various edition features. For simplicity, the chapter uses Windows Server 2008 for both machines. You need only one product key for both machines.

When you arrive at the actual download page, you must select the language you want to download. You'll also see several links. The links use names such as 6001.17051.071121-2029_ amd64fre_Server_en-us-KR1SXFRE_EN_DVD.iso that may look hard to read at first. The initial numbers tell you the version and build number of the file. The amd64 part tells you that this is a 64-bit version of Windows Server 2008 for an AMD processor. When you see x86 in place of the amd64, you know that you're downloading the 32-bit version. The word Server means that this is a server version of the product (the only version available). The letters en-us tell you that you're downloading a U.S. English language version. The .iso file extension tells you that this file is in International Standards Organization (ISO) format and you use a product such as Nero (http://download-psp.net/Nero/), a product you can download free, to create a DVD from the file.

TIP

Even though your processor can support either the 32- or 64-bit version of Windows Server 2008, you may experience problems using the 64-bit version on some machines. The hardware drivers, the special pieces of software used to communicate with the hardware, must match the operating system. When you install a 64-bit operating system, you must also use 64-bit hardware drivers. The only problem is that some hardware vendors don't provide 64-bit drivers for their products. Although most enterprise-level server hardware will have 64-bit drivers, you might find those drivers lacking in some inexpensive systems, so you need to exercise care when buying your system. Before you install a 64-bit version of Windows Server 2008, make sure you have 64-bit hardware drivers for every piece of hardware on the server. It's also important to remember that the 64-bit version of the operating system will require some extra hard drive space. Even though the 64-bit version consumes only a few extra megabytes of hard drive space, you should plan on the extra hard drive space when considering the size drive to get.

Extending the 30-Day Version to 180 Days

The Windows Server 2008 download you get is good for only 30 days, so where does the 180-day version come into play? Notice that there is a link for registering for a product key and a guided tour. The following steps take you through the registration process:

1. Click the Register for Product Key and Guided Evaluation link. You'll see a new Web page where you can obtain a product key.

2. Choose your language in the Select Your Language (Country) field and click the right arrow next to the field. You'll likely see a prompt asking for your Windows Live ID. If you're already signed into Windows Live or have your machine set up to provide this information automatically, go to step 4.

3. Sign into Windows Live by typing your email address and password. If you don't have a Windows Live ID, click Sign Up Now and follow the prompts to create a Windows Live ID. After you enter the required Windows Live information, click Sign In.

4. At this point, you should see a list of Windows Server 2008 product identifiers. Click the link that matches your product. You'll see a product key for that edition of Windows Server 2008. This product key won't work with any other edition of Windows Server 2008. Microsoft lets you download up to five product keys.

5. Save the Web page containing your product key to disk so you can refer to it later. You can also print the Web page to make it easier to reference.

The registration process provides Microsoft with your contact information and you receive a 180-day trial version in exchange. You can count on receiving some email from Microsoft touting the new features of Windows Server 2008. These emails include some helpful information, so I encourage you obtain a product key and benefit from both the emails and the added product evaluation time.

NOTE

The installation procedure in this chapter assumes you have obtained a product key for your copy of Windows. Make sure you obtain a product key before you begin the procedure found in the "Performing the Installation" section of the chapter.

Performing the Installation

Now that you have everything you need, it's time to perform an installation. This section provides a very brief overview of the process. We'll simply tell you about the steps you need to perform to install Windows Server 2008. Don't worry about the details of each step for right now. The "Performing a Windows Server 2008 Full Version Installation" section of Chapter 4 provides you with detailed information for a basic installation. You must perform this installation on both of your test machines. Don't advance to the "Performing the Basic Network Setup" section of the chapter until you complete the installation of Windows on both machines.

WARNING

Make sure the machines you use don't have any data you want to keep on them. This procedure will remove any existing data on the hard drives. In fact, the installation is completely new — you'll need to add user accounts, set up any shared resources, and reinstall any applications. In short, if you can't afford to lose everything on the hard drive, don't start this procedure.

1. Start the system and place the DVD into the boot DVD drive as soon as possible before the system begins looking for a boot drive. The system will display a message asking whether you want to boot from the DVD. If you miss this sequence, you can always place the DVD into the drive and press the Reset button on the front of the computer system to restart it. You'll see the required message during the next boot sequence.

2. Press Enter to boot from the DVD. You'll see a message that Windows is loading files. This message will appear for several minutes, so be patient. After the initial file load completes, you'll see an Install Windows dialog box that contains entries for language, time and currency format, and keyboard or other input method as shown in Figure 2.1.

FIGURE 2.1
Choose the installation language, time and currency format, and keyboard options.

3. Choose an installation language, time and currency format, and a keyboard or other input method. Click Next. You'll see a dialog box with three options as shown in Figure 2.2.

FIGURE 2.2
Begin the installation by clicking Install Now.

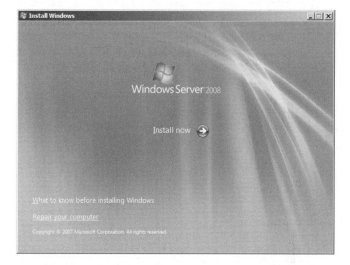

4. Click Install Now. The installation program performs some additional tasks and eventually displays a dialog box that asks for your product key as shown in Figure 2.3.

FIGURE 2.3
Type your product key to gain access to the Windows edition you purchased.

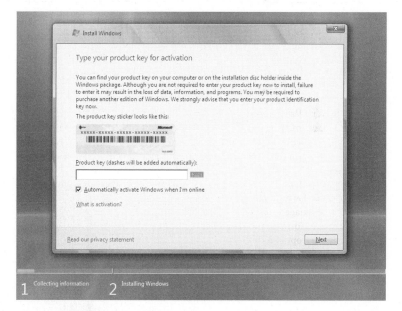

5. Type your product key. If you don't have a product key, see the "Extending the 30-Day Version to 180 Days" section of the chapter for information on obtaining one. Click Next. You'll see a list of options for the editions of Windows Server 2008 you downloaded as shown in Figure 2.4.

6. Select the Full Installation option (not the Server Core Installation) and click Next. You'll see the licensing dialog box.

FIGURE 2.4
Choose the version of the product that you want to install.

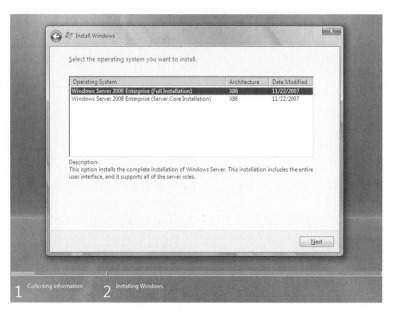

7. Check I Accept the License Terms and click Next. You'll see an installation type dialog box as shown in Figure 2.5. The Upgrade option is always disabled when you perform a DVD installation.

FIGURE 2.5
The setup program provides two options for installing Windows.

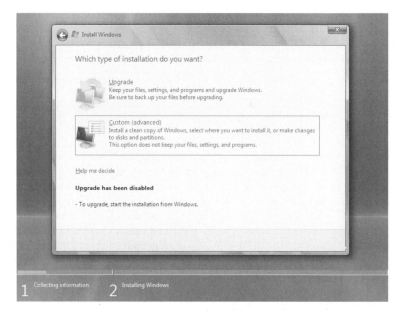

8. Click Custom (advanced). The installation program asks where you want to install Windows as shown in Figure 2.6. If you already have a copy of Windows installed on your hard drive, select the existing partition.

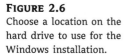

FIGURE 2.6
Choose a location on the hard drive to use for the Windows installation.

9. Choose the hard drive you want to use for Windows and click Next. The installation program now has enough information to proceed. The installation is automatic at this point. You'll see Windows accomplish these tasks for you. The installation process requires about 20 minutes to complete. Eventually, you'll see a logon screen telling you that you must change the user's password before logging in the first time. There may also be a reboot or two during the install process; don't let that worry you.

10. Click OK. You'll see an Administrator screen where you must type in a new password, and then confirm the new password.

TIP

Windows Server 2008 will require you to use a complex password. This requirement is another safety feature that helps guard the security of your system. A password like Secret won't work well because it's easy to guess. Use a password like H3 l1o_Th3r3. This second password is easier for you to remember but harder to guess because it contains a combination of uppercase and lowercase letters, numbers, and special characters (the minimum that Windows will accept — the password must also be a minimum of 6 characters long). You can also use a passphrase such as "My dog's birthday is on 12-02-98." Because it also includes a combination of uppercase and lowercase letters, numbers, and special characters, the longer passphrase is significantly harder to guess.

---

11. Type a new password and click the Right Pointing Arrow icon. Windows will tell you that it has changed the password.

12. Click OK. You'll see a flurry of activity as Windows Server configures itself. Eventually, you'll see an Initial Configuration Tasks page where you can perform initial configuration. You now have Windows Server 2008 installed.

Performing the Basic Network Setup

When working with previous versions of Windows, you had to know all kinds of arcane facts to obtain a working network. Windows Server 2008 makes it considerably easier to setup a basic network. If you're willing to accept the default settings and have all of the physical connections in place before you install Windows, you might not have to do anything at all. That's right! Microsoft does enough work now that the setup program automatically detects the networking hardware, configures drivers and other software, and even creates the connections for you.

In fact, you may have already noticed that you can see the other machine in your setup in the Network window. To see the Network window, choose Start ➢ Network to see the Network window shown in Figure 2.7.

FIGURE 2.7
Use the Network window to see the machines and other resources on your network.

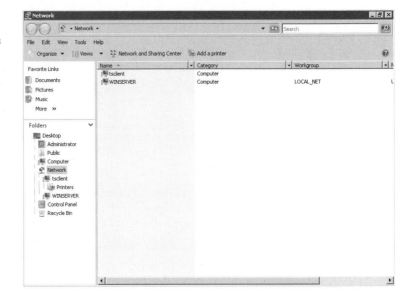

If you can't see the other computer, you may have to turn Network Discovery on. Use these steps to perform that task:

1. Open the Start menu.

2. Right-click Network and choose Properties. You'll see a Network and Sharing Center window similar to the one shown in Figure 2.8.

3. Click the down arrow next to the Network Discovery feature in the Sharing and Discovery section of the window. You'll see some information about this feature, along with some options for working with the Network Discovery feature.

4. Choose the Turn On Network Discovery option and click Apply. Windows will make the Network Discovery feature active.

FIGURE 2.8

The Network and Sharing Center window provides access to the Network Discovery feature.

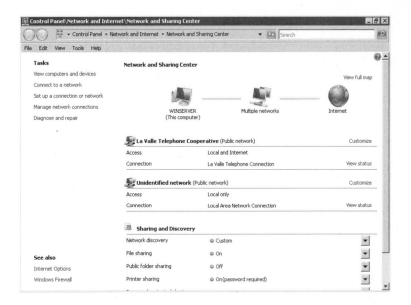

The network configuration for this example is simple. It looks like the one shown in Figure 2.9. Of course, just because you can see the other computer, doesn't mean you can do anything with it. Any computer that acts as a server must tell Windows what to share. The default Windows Server 2008 configuration is to share nothing at all. If you want, you can try to access the other computer right now by choosing Start ➢ Network to display the Network window and you'll find that it won't allow you any access at all. You'll discover how to provide access to your server in the "Creating User Accounts" and "Sharing Resources with Other Computers" sections of the chapter.

The following sections tell you how to perform basic tasks that you'll normally do to make your network easier to understand and access. Giving a machine a name that matches its purpose helps people find it more quickly. Providing a unique name for your network also makes it easier for people to find, but makes guessing the name more difficult for outsiders.

FIGURE 2.9
This chapter uses a simple network setup you can use to see how networks work.

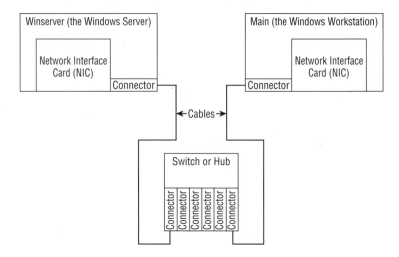

Changing the Machine Name

The weird machine names can be a problem because searching for them can prove difficult when Microsoft has used gobbledygook character combinations. If you feel as I do that the names Microsoft chooses for your machine are too difficult (or too vague) to work with, then use the following steps to change the machine names:

1. Open the Start menu and right-click Computer. Choose Properties from the context menu. (A context menu is a special window that appears when you right-click an object in Windows — it contains a list of tasks you can perform using the object.) You'll see the System window shown in Figure 2.10.

2. Click the "Advanced system settings" link to display the System Properties dialog box. Choose the Computer Name tab to display the computer name information as shown in Figure 2.11.

FIGURE 2.10
Open the System window to gain access to system settings.

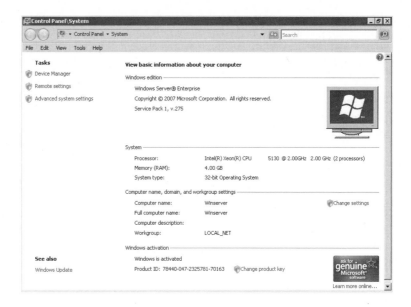

FIGURE 2.11
The Computer Name tab displays the current computer name.

3. Click Change. You'll see the Computer Name/Domain Changes dialog box shown in Figure 2.12.

4. Type a new name for your computer in the Computer Name field. The example systems use Main (for main workstation) and Winserver (for Windows server) for the two machines. The machine that provides shared resources will use the Winserver name. You could literally use any names you desire for the two machines as long as they meet the Microsoft naming criteria.

5. Click OK. Windows will tell you that you must restart your system before any changes will occur.

FIGURE 2.12
Use this dialog box to change your computer name, workgroup, or domain.

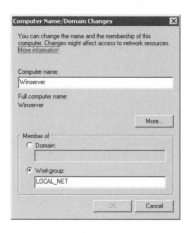

6. Click OK. Windows will ask whether you want to restart your system now.

7. Click Restart Now. The system will restart and will use the new name you choose when it reboots.

Changing the Network Name

The network name can pose a security problem. Although the name Workgroup is easy to read and understand, Workgroup is also a name that everyone with a penchant for snooping on your network knows. If you plan to use your basic setup to access the Internet, you'll definitely want to change your network name. The following steps show you how to change the network name:

1. Open the Start menu and right-click Computer. Choose Properties from the context menu. You'll see the System window shown earlier in Figure 2.10.

2. Click the "Advanced system settings" link to display the System Properties dialog box. Choose the Computer Name tab to display the computer name information as shown earlier in Figure 2.11.

3. Click Change. You'll see the Computer Name/Domain Changes dialog box shown earlier in Figure 2.12.

4. Type a new name for the workgroup in the Workgroup field. The example systems use a name of LOCAL_NET (for local network), but you can use any name that meets the Microsoft naming criteria.

5. Click OK. Windows will tell you that you must restart your system before any changes will occur.

6. Click OK. Windows will ask whether you want to restart your system now.

7. Click Restart Now. The system will restart and will use the new name you choose when it reboots.

The important issue to remember when working with networks is that all of the computers that want to share resources must appear as part of the same workgroup. You can't use two different workgroup names and expect to access resources on the other computer easily. When you change the workgroup or domain name, Windows will search for that workgroup or domain and then display a welcome dialog box telling you that you have become part of the domain or workgroup you requested. As with a computer name change, you must reboot the computer before any name change will take effect.

Creating User Accounts

Microsoft provides many ways to create user accounts, and you'll probably use each of them at some point. For example, you can create user accounts using the User Accounts applet in the Control Panel, a command-line utility (a text-based program), a .NET application (described in Chapter 6), or a Microsoft Management Console (MMC) console (Chapter 5 describes how to work with MMC).

All of these methods work fine, but some methods are easier to work with than others are — the command-line utility approach is definitely viewed as the hardest by people who are used to working with the Graphical User Interface (GUI), but can prove to be easier once you know the required commands. You also use some methods in special situations. For example, you'd proba-bly use a command-line utility when working with a batch file (a kind of automation).

This chapter shows you the easiest method you can use to create a user account when working with the GUI — the special Control Panel applet. You won't use this method in every case because ease-of-use translates into lack of flexibility in this case. However, using the applet is fast and simple and you should think about using it when you can. The following steps show how to create a user account using the User Accounts applet. You perform this task on Winserver (the machine you're using as a server in this case).

1. Choose Start ➤ Control Panel. You'll see the Control Panel window shown in Figure 2.13. The Control Panel contains a list of special applications called *applets* that help you config-ure your machine in various ways. You don't need to worry about all of the applets right now — the rest of the book tells you how to use the most important applets in the Control Panel.

FIGURE 2.13
The Control Panel pro-vides access to a wealth of system configura-tion applets.

2. Click "Add or remove user accounts." You'll see the Manage Accounts window shown in Figure 2.14. This window shows any existing accounts on the system. It also provides links you can use to create a basic account or removing any existing account.

FIGURE 2.14
Add or remove accounts using the Manage Accounts window.

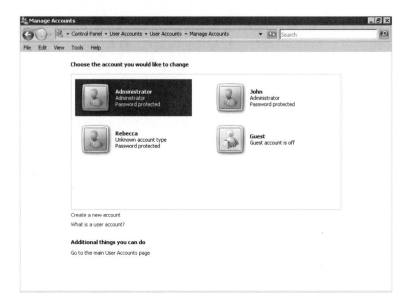

3. Click "Create a new account." You'll see the Create New Account window shown in Figure 2.15. As you can see, this window provides only the basics, but it provides enough functionality for our purposes.

FIGURE 2.15
Use the Create New Account window to create basic accounts that don't require special settings.

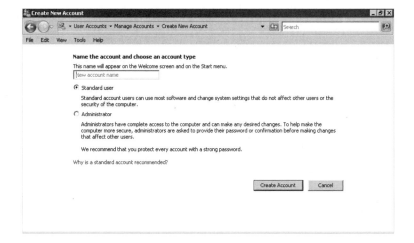

4. Type your name in the "New account name" field. The example system uses an administrator named George, but you should use your own name.

5. Choose the Administrator option. Because you want to perform administrative tasks, you must create an administrator account for yourself. Users who don't perform administrative tasks should use the Standard User option instead.

6. Click Create Account. Windows creates the new account for you and displays it in the Manage Accounts window shown in Figure 2.14. The account currently doesn't have a password associated with it and lacks other configuration features.

7. Click the new account and you'll see it displayed in the Change an Account window. Figure 2.16 shows a typical example. The window you see will have a different name as a minimum (unless your name is George).

FIGURE 2.16
The Change an Account window contains options to perform basic configuration tasks.

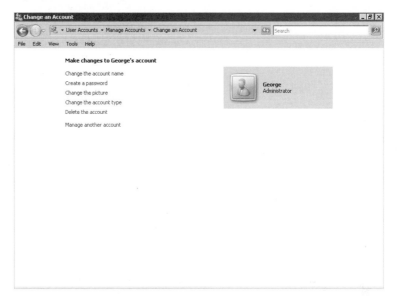

8. Click "Create a password." You'll see the Create Password window shown in Figure 2.17. It's important to password protect accounts immediately after you create them, even if you only plan to use the machine on a local network without Internet access. Passwords are a basic security feature that every account should have.

9. Type a password in the "New password" field and repeat typing it in the "Confirm new password" field. It's important to use passwords that no one else can easily guess. However, you also have to choose a password that is easy to remember. The example system uses He1!0_Wor!d as the password. It's actually a little too short, but it does include numbers, uppercase and lowercase letters, and special characters, making it harder to guess.

10. Type a hint that doesn't include the password in the "Type a password hint" field.

11. Click "Create password." You'll see the Change an Account window shown in Figure 2.16 again. Notice that the Create a Password link is gone now and Windows has replaced it with two new options: "Change the password" and "Remove the password." The process for changing a password is similar to the process you just used to create a password — the major difference is that a few of the prompts have changed to show that you're changing, rather than creating, a password.

FIGURE 2.17
Modify the password to keep the network free from prying eyes.

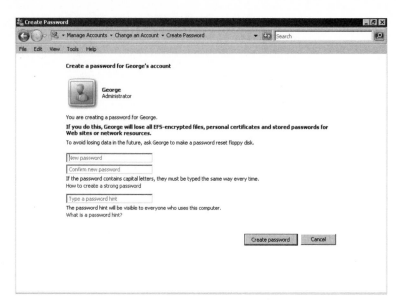

12. Close the Change an Account window.

Sharing Resources with Other Computers

One of the main reasons to give someone else an account on your machine is to share resources with them. A resource is any device, data, or piece of software on your server. Often, you'll share a device such as a printer because it's expensive and you can't afford to provide one for each user on the network. Other situations require that you share data between people collaborating on a project by sharing a hard drive or folder. In fact, you'll find many reasons to share server resources and that's really the main reason that you have a server in the first place.

In this chapter, you see how to share the most common resource, the hard drive. Microsoft provides a number of methods to share resources with others (many similar to the techniques used to create user accounts). The best policy is to know all of these techniques so that you can use the technique that works best in a particular situation. Of course, you don't want to learn all of those techniques on the first try. The following steps show the easiest method for sharing hard drive resources. You'll find other methods in the chapters that follow.

1. Choose Start ➢ All Programs ➢ Accessories ➢ Windows Explorer. You'll see a copy of Windows Explorer, similar to the one shown in Figure 2.18, open. The copy of Windows Explorer you see will likely have a few differences from the one on my system. Don't worry about these differences; they're normal. As part of this example, you'll create a folder to hold shared data and provide a share to it.

2. Right-click in the right pane (on any white/open space) and choose New ➢ Folder from the context menu. Type **My Shared Folder** as the folder name and press Enter. At this point, you have a folder that no one can access outside of the current machine.

FIGURE 2.18
Use Windows Explorer to share hard drive resources.

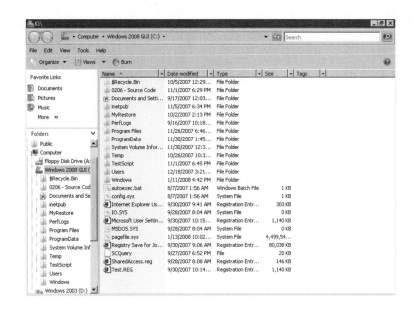

3. Right-click the folder you just created and choose Share from the context menu. You'll see the Sharing tab of the My Shared Folder Properties dialog box shown in Figure 2.19. This tab lets you share the folder outside of the current server. It makes the folder visible to anyone who wants to use it.

FIGURE 2.19
Create a share for the folder so other people can access it.

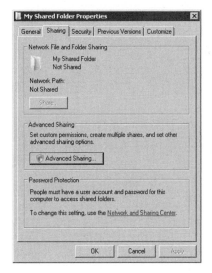

4. Click Advanced Sharing. You'll see the Advanced Sharing dialog box shown in Figure 2.20 (I've already made some changes to this dialog box so you can see the fields clearly in the book).

FIGURE 2.20
Define the share requirements using this dialog box.

5. Check "Share this folder." Windows will automatically supply an appropriate name for the share.

6. Click Permissions. You'll see the Permissions for My Shared Folder dialog box shown in Figure 2.21. These permissions affect the share — they don't actually provide access to the resource. You must set both share security and Windows security to access a resource from a remote location. Share security only determines what someone can do from a remote location, while Windows security determines both local and remote access.

FIGURE 2.21
Set permissions for the share to control what others can do from a remote location.

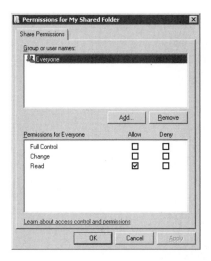

7. Highlight the Everyone group and click Remove. This action prevents anyone other than the selected groups from accessing the share.

8. Click Add. You'll see a Select Users or Groups dialog box like the one shown in Figure 2.22. For this example, you'll simply type the name of the user or group that can access the share. (Groups are a collection of users who have the same rights and access — we'll talk about them more in Chapter 3.) However, you can also click Advanced to search for users or groups when needed.

FIGURE 2.22
Choose the users or groups that can access the share.

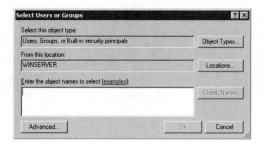

9. Type **Administrators** and click OK. Windows adds the Administrators group to the Group or User Names list shown in the Permissions for My Shared Folder dialog box (Figure 2.21).

10. Check Full Control. This option gives the Administrators group full control over the shared resource.

11. Click OK twice. The Sharing tab of the My Shared Folder Properties dialog box now shows that this folder has a share associated with it.

12. Choose Security. This tab shows you the Windows security for the folder. Because the Administrators group no longer has access to the root directory of the hard drive, they also don't have access to the folder.

13. Click Edit. You'll see a Permissions for My Shared Folder dialog box similar to the one shown in Figure 2.21. Remember that you're setting Windows security this time, not share security.

14. Highlight the Administrators group in the list. Check Full Control in the Permissions for Administrators list. Click OK. The Administrators group now has full control over this shared folder, both locally and from any remote location.

15. Click Close. You have now successfully created a share for My Shared Folder.

Accessing Resources on Another Computer

Throughout this chapter, you have worked with Winserver performing various configurations. It may seem as if setting up Main (the workstation) was a waste of time and effort. Now, however, you'll see how Main comes into play — you'll use it to access the resources that you made available on Winserver.

As with other activities you've performed so far, you have many different options for accessing resources on another computer. In many cases, you'll want to set up those access options so that they happen automatically every time you boot your machine. For example, when you work on the same set of files on a particular server every day, looking for those resources is a waste of time. You need to set the access up so that the data is at your fingertips.

Of course, you can also obtain temporary access to a resource. For example, if you only use a printer once a month, setting aside resources to access it locally every day is a waste of resources. Configuring automatic access always uses system resources. Your machine will spend time looking for the resource and making a connection to it every time you start Windows, so you should only set automatic access when you need to use the resource regularly. The following sections describe how to set up both temporary and automatic access of resources on another system.

Accessing Resources Temporarily

The easiest and fastest method for accessing resources on a server is to know the server name. Open a copy of Windows Explorer by choosing Start ➤ All Programs ➤ Accessories ➤ Windows Explorer. In the address field, type **\Winserver** and press Enter. Because you have access to Winserver from Main, you'll see a list of the resources on Winserver as shown in Figure 2.23. In this case, I've shared a number of resources so you can see what a typical server display will look like. What you should see is the My Shared Folder entry.

FIGURE 2.23
Use Windows Explorer to access any resources on your server temporarily.

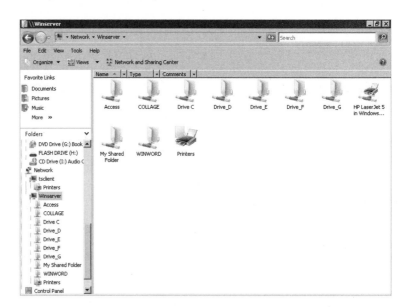

To see how this access works, double-click My Shared Folder. The folder is empty right now, so let's add a file to it. Right-click the right pane and choose New ➤ Text File. Press Enter to accept the default name. Now, go to the Winserver console and choose the same folder using Windows Explorer. See, the file is actually stored on the server, even though you're seeing it on the Main workstation!

Making Resource Access Automatic

Most people don't want to hunt around the network every time they want to access a server resource — it's time consuming. You can configure your system to access common resources automatically. To see how this works, right-click the My Shared Folder entry and choose Map Network Drive from the context menu. You'll see the Map Network Drive dialog box shown in Figure 2.24.

FIGURE 2.24
Create drive mappings
so that you can access
remote resources as a
local resource.

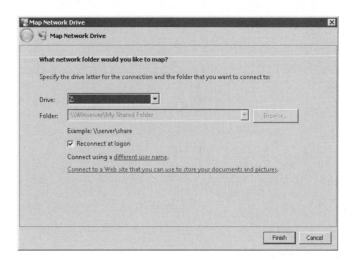

The Drive field contains the drive letter you want to use to access the remote resource. Windows automatically chooses the last available drive letter for remote resources and the first available drive letter for local resources. You work toward the middle of the drive letters as you access more resources. In this case, you'll accept the default drive letter.

The "Reconnect at logon" option lets you choose whether Windows always attempts to map the drive letter to the resource. You must check this option for resources you want to access permanently. Click Finish and Windows will create the drive mapping for you. Windows Explorer will now display the shared resource as drive Z.

TIP

You don't have to use the method shown in this section to create a share — you can easily use a command prompt instead. To open a command prompt, choose Start. Right-click the Command Prompt entry and choose Run as Administrator from the context menu. Using this technique opens a command prompt where you can execute administrator level commands. Type **Net View \\Winserver** and press Enter to see the list of resources that Winserver has available. To use the My Shared Folder resource on Winserver, type **Net Use Y: "\\Winserver\My Shared Folder"** and press Enter. You'll find that the Y and Z drives both provide the same access to My Shared Folder now. If you want to restore the connection automatically the next time you boot the system, then you add the /Persistent:Yes command line switch by typing **Net Use Y: "\\Winserver\My Shared Folder" /Persistent: Yes** and pressing Enter.

You may later decide that you really don't want to continue accessing a resource. In this case, right-click the drive in Windows Explorer and choose Disconnect from the context menu. Windows will remove the drive mapping. Using drive mappings carefully lets you access remote resources as if they exist on your local system. There are many other ways to make remote resources look like local resources. You'll discover these other techniques in Chapter 10 of the companion enterprise volume, *Mastering Windows Server 2008: Enterprise Technologies*, of this series.

Chapter 3

Security Concepts in Windows

Wait! Before you skip this chapter on security because you think it's boring or beyond you, think about what your data means to you. Many users view security as some kind of mystical undertaking that only seasoned administrators can understand and appreciate. The reverse is actually true. Security, at least the basic concepts of it, is actually quite understandable.

Think about security this way — when you go home at night, you stick your key in the lock, turn it, open the door, and then lock the door behind you. Would it surprise you to know that security in Windows amounts to the same thing? Really! Just as you lock your house to make sure that no one steals your television, you lock Windows to ensure no one steals your data.

If you've ever *heard* computer security folks talk, then you may have come away with the impression that you've got to really *live* security in order to know how to secure your system. But in fact it's not all that hard, certainly not much harder than knowing where your door's lock is and to remember to lock it. So don't skip this chapter — it's an essential part of administering a Windows Server 2008 setup and isn't as hard as you might think. What I'm trying to accomplish in this chapter is to answer these questions:

◆ Why do you need to secure your Windows server?

◆ What do you need to secure on your Windows server?

◆ What is the difference between authentication and authorization?

◆ How does authentication work?

◆ How does authorization work?

◆ How does Windows use authentication and authorization to secure your system?

Understanding the Need to Secure Windows

You secure Windows for many of the same reasons that you secure your home. Of course, you do it to protect your property. Like your home, a computer has resources that you want to protect — your "personal data property." For example, any files you create contain priceless data. Most organizations have more money invested in their data than they'll ever have invested in their hardware. Interestingly enough, someone who accesses your system without your permission can steal your data and then turn your system into a worthless chunk of metal should they decide to do so.

Most outsiders won't make their presence known, though. They'll steal your data so that they can get credit cards in your name or ruin your finances in other ways. However, they won't modify the data files in any way because they don't want to alert you to the stolen data. If you don't secure your system, you could end up losing your personal data or, worse yet, the personal data of thousands of clients. You could end up as part of the headlines for the next trade press article. (Just look to the company that owns T.J. Maxx, Marshalls, and a number of other retail store chains. Hackers got into their customer database in January 2007, and the company basically had to contact everyone who'd ever used a credit card in one of their stores to warn them of possible false credit card charges. The lawsuits ensued, and, well, don't be surprised if someone else is running the T.J. Maxx near you sometime soon.)

An outsider need not express any interest in your data at all. They might simply need a place to park files containing viruses that they plan to serve to someone else. Because the access to your system is traceable, you may find the FBI knocking at your door. Sure, this is the extreme view of things, but the fact remains that someone is using your server to send viruses to other people, so your reputation is at stake. At the very least, your ISP could express its displeasure by shutting off your account until you get your server cleaned up.

Speaking of viruses, every virus, adware, or other unauthorized third-party application that appears on your server consumes resources that you could use for other purposes. Sometimes people complain about how their system used to work quickly, but now it takes forever to complete the same task. In many situations, the problem isn't with the computer — it's with the viruses and adware executing on the computer. Those outside parties don't care about your computing needs. They'll hog every resource possible to ensure their crud runs as fast as possible on your machine.

NOTE

Some administrators are under the mistaken notion that viruses and adware attack only client machines and only then because users are so stupid (according to the administrator). Viruses and adware can appear on any machine that can run them. The only way to avoid them completely is to disallow the server access to any outside source ever. Given the connected nature of networks today, you can be sure that your server is a target for virus and adware attacks and that the probabilities of getting an infection are nearly as high unless you're proactive in your protection of these vital resources.

Other interesting and other unwanted things happen when your server becomes the target of outside interest. For example, you can spread all of those lovely viruses to every other machine on the network. Someone could also use the primary server access to gain access to every other machine on the network. You may suddenly find that several machines have unauthorized data access and not know where the access is coming from and may not even be able to trace it with any ease.

I didn't write this section to scare you to death, and I know that scare tactics seldom work. This section provides you with good reasons to secure your system. It also provides ammunition you can use to convince management to allot more time and resources to security needs. Many organizations, including home users, fail to secure their systems properly today and the result is lost time and money for everyone. You wouldn't leave your front door open when you go to work, so why leave your server open so just anyone can walk through the front door?

Considering What You Need to Secure in Windows

The most secure server in the world is the one that no one can access for any reason whatsoever. Of course, building a server like this one would mean that you wouldn't get any return on your investment. A server that doesn't provide access to something is worthless. Because access necessarily incurs security risks, you'll always have security issues to consider for your server. Balancing the risk of access against the need for access is the cornerstone of any good security plan. You must begin any security plan you create with the idea that access by someone that is supposed to have access automatically implies access by someone who doesn't have your permission. Monitoring is part of any good security plan because monitoring lets you see what others are doing with your server.

Now that I've dispelled the notion that you can create a perfect security plan, it's time to discuss the risk element of security in Windows. Previous versions of Windows assumed that everyone was good and allowed unrestricted access to the server unless you secured it. Windows Server 2008 takes nearly the opposite approach — with this operating system, Microsoft assumes everyone plans to do evil things to your computer. You have to tell Windows Server 2008 to provide access.

When you first install Windows Server 2008, it doesn't provide any access at all — you actually have to open access to the server by configuring the firewall, adding roles and features, setting up shares, and granting or denying permissions. Microsoft forces you to install roles and features that provide services to the caller and then open security holes in your configuration to provide access to those services. This is an important change in Windows because you now have full control over everything anyone does. You also can't claim ignorance when you open the wrong security hole.

The services you provide and the security holes you open determine your security risk. You can reduce that risk by opening the security holes carefully. For example, when the Administrators group requires access to a file but no one else requires that access, you can give access to only the Administrators group. The "Understanding How Authorization Works" section of the chapter tells you more about how this process takes place in Windows. For now, all you need to know is that you can reduce your risk by using the right management techniques.

NOTE

You'll see the terms *rights* and *permissions* used throughout this chapter. From a security perspective, both terms mean the same thing. A right or permission is the access you have to a resource such as files, folders, printers, other user accounts, services, and other Windows objects. In early versions of Windows, Microsoft used the term *rights*. Possibly because it's more descriptive, Microsoft began using the term *permissions* instead of rights in recent versions of Windows. A right or permission is an act you can perform with the resource. For example, you can read and write files. These two acts are actually separate permissions in Windows Server 2008. You even have to have permission to see the file, so permissions cover every act you can perform with the resource.

Now that you understand how Windows Server 2008 differs from its predecessors, you can finally consider what to unsecure on your system. As mentioned, your server begins with full security in place. When you create a new folder on the server and place data files in it that you want to share with other people, the other people can't access it until you open a security hole that allows them access. Even if there is a share for the folder, the user will still see a message stating that they can't access the folder. To provide remote access to those files, you must perform these three steps:

1. Add the File Server role to the server.

2. Create a share for the folder you want to share.

3. Provide access to that folder by telling Windows who can access it.

> **NOTE**
>
> The three steps in this section are the minimum you would do. In most cases, though, you must install additional protection. For example, if the server has any kind of outside access, you must install a firewall, virus, and adware protection. However, given the way that Windows Server 2008 protects your system, you must also consider keeping unnecessary roles and features uninstalled to protect the server — install only those roles and features you actually need to accomplish a given task.

It's interesting to note that not even the administrator can access the server from a remote location after a server has been installed. Unlike previous versions of Windows, the administrator doesn't have access to the root directory of the server. The administrator can access only personal files and folders located in the My Documents folder. Consequently, you must give yourself access locally before you can access the server properly from a remote location. Some people claim that Windows Server 2008 has become so secure that it's worthless, but really, it's only worthless until you perform the configuration that Windows should have forced you to perform all along.

Administrators will perform a lot more configuration for Windows Server 2008 because Microsoft has focused on security features that create a secure server environment from the outset. It's important to remember that Windows Server 2008 doesn't authorize access to anything unless you tell it to provide the access. This change can lead to all kinds of authorization problems (authorization is explained in the next section). No longer can you assume that the user has default access to a particular folder — you must check the folder to ensure that you have authorized access to it. The only exception to this rule is the user's personal folder (`Documents and Settings \User Name\`).

In fact, some administrators are going to be surprised to learn that Windows Server 2008 disallows access to folders that users could access in previous versions of Windows Server. The Windows folder is locked down (you don't have access to it, just as Joe didn't have access to the `Second.TXT` file in the examples that appear later in the chapter), as is the System32 folder. Windows locks these folders down separately. Giving access to the Windows folder doesn't provide access to the System32 folder — you must give separate access to each. More problematic is access to the Program Files folder. No one has access to this folder by default either. All of these security changes make it harder for someone to access these sensitive areas without alerting you to a potential problem. In the past, adware and virus writers would often access these sensitive areas without permission and no one knew about it.

Understanding Authentication versus Authorization

Although there's a lot to security, it basically boils down to two things: *authentication* and *authorization*. Some people get the two confused, but it's easy to keep them separate once you understand that authentication and authorization occur in a specific order. The way we're going to start this section is to try out an example that demonstrates the difference between authentication and authorization. Follow these steps and you'll see how the two work (don't worry too much about the details of these commands for now; you'll examine them more closely in Chapter 6):

1. Log onto your test server using the Administrator account.

2. Open the Start menu. Right-click Command Prompt, and choose Run as Administrator from the context menu. This action will open a command prompt that you can use for the steps that follow. Using the command prompt can prove faster and easier for some tasks

than working with the Graphical User Interface (GUI). This book shows you techniques for administering your computer using both approaches (GUI in Chapter 5 and command prompt in Chapter 6).

3. Type **Net User Joe HiJoe! /Add**, and press Enter to add a new user named Joe with a password of HiJoe!. Now that you have a new user, you can provide a place for the new user to go.

NOTE

Remember that Windows requires that you provide a complex password that includes uppercase letters, lowercase letters, special symbols, and numbers. The password also has to meet a minimum password length requirement. The password in this example meets all the requirements — it would be very hard to guess. You can also use passphrases to make the password even harder to guess, but significantly easier to remember, such as "My dog Sam's birthday is 10/10/2008." This passphrase includes uppercase letters, lowercase letters, numbers, and special symbols, yet it's incredibly easy to remember.

---

4. Type **MD C:\Test**, and press Enter to create a new directory on the C drive named Test.

5. Type **CD C:\Test**, and press Enter to go to the new directory you just created.

6. Type **Echo This is the first file. > First .TXT**, and press Enter to create a file named First.TXT that has the content of "This is the first file." The Echo command displays any text that you type on the screen. The > (greater than sign) is called a redirection symbol. It sends the text displayed by the Echo command to the file, instead of to the display.

7. Type **Echo This is the second file. > Second.TXT**, and press Enter to create a file named Second.TXT that has the content of "This is the second file." Now it's time to set security on the two files you just created. The next two steps tell what Joe can do with the file.

8. Type **ICACLS First.TXT /Grant Joe:F**, and press Enter to grant Joe full access to the First.TXT file. Joe can do anything with this file because he has full access to it (he has permission to manage, read, write, execute, and delete the file, among other things).

9. Type **ICACLS Second.TXT /Deny Joe:F**, and press Enter to deny Joe any access to the Second.TXT file. Joe won't be able to do anything with this file because Windows will prevent any access to it.

10. Log off the Administrator account.

11. Log into the Joe account. Remember that your password is HiJoe!.

12. Choose Start ➢ Command Prompt to display a command prompt.

13. Type **CD C:\Test**, and press Enter to go to the Test folder you created earlier.

14. Type **Type First.TXT**, and press Enter. You see "This is the first file." displayed on screen. The Type command displays the content of any text file, so it can prove handy for seeing information in files when you're working at the command prompt.

15. Type **Type Second.TXT**, and press Enter. Windows will display an "Access is denied." error message because Joe doesn't have access to this file. The First.TXT and Second.TXT

files demonstrate authorization. Joe is authorized to work with the `First.TXT` file, but he isn't authorized to work with the `Second.TXT` file.

16. Log out of the Joe account.

17. Log back into the Joe account. However, this time use the wrong password — any incorrect password will do. Windows displays an error message saying, "The user name or password is incorrect." This error message demonstrates authentication. Joe isn't authenticated to use Windows, so he can't gain any access to it until he supplies the correct password.

Now that you've seen authentication and authorization in action, it's time to consider what the two actions really mean. Here are how the two steps occur:

1. First, you want to be able to identify who's entering your network. That's authentication. When you enter your name and password to access the local system, it generates *credentials* for you that Windows uses on your behalf to gain access to all kinds of local and remote resources. The system actually authenticates you many times during a particular session, once for every resource that requires it, but you generally need to log in only once. It's important to remember that authentication occurs every time the system needs to identify you in some way. Authentication addresses identification only.

2. Second, once you know for sure who you're talking to — once you've authenticated — then you must be able to look up somewhere what that person is allowed to do, his *permissions*. For example, a network logon could figuratively go something like, "Okay, now I know you're Jack . . . but I've been told to deny Jack access to everything." Merely being authenticated doesn't mean that you get access! After the server knows what permissions the caller (Jack in this case) has, it authorizes the caller to use the resources affected by those permissions. The permissions also determine what activities you can perform with those resources, so authorization is akin to a parent telling a child that they can go to the party, but only until 11 p.m. and that they can't drink anything stronger than soda.

Authentication and authorization are two separate processes in Windows Server 2008 or, indeed, any secure modern operating system. Whenever someone attempts to access a server, the server tries to authenticate them. Only when the server successfully authenticates the person do they gain access to the system. Consequently, if you give Joe permission to use the MyStuff folder on the C drive but don't give Joe permission to log into the system, Joe still can't access the MyStuff folder.

> **NOTE**
>
> Windows also automatically disables access to an account when certain events occur, such as Joe typing his password incorrectly several times. When someone says that they can't access their data folder and you know that you provided the required access, the place you should look for problems is in their account.

Understanding How Authentication Works

The first part of security is *authentication*, and you usually accomplish it either by supplying Windows with a user name and password or through a special credit card–type storage device called a *smart card* that you slide through a card reader.

On some systems, you can use somewhat more science-fiction-ish means of authentication. One day, the computer may recognize you by your fingerprint, face, voice, retina blood vessel pattern, or some other item that's distinctly you. The geek term for those authentication approaches is *biometrics*. Many "business-level" laptops such as the IBM Thinkpad "T" series, or the Hewlett-Packard "HP Business" series laptops can be equipped with fingerprint readers. You can find fingerprint readers on some desktops as well.

You recognize your friends and business associates by looking at their faces, but computers aren't so good at recognizing people, no matter *what* the Homeland Security folks tell us. We therefore need some way for Windows to recognize — authenticate — a user sitting at a workstation computer. I'm sure you're already familiar with this recognition process: we call it logging on. I realize that nearly everyone who's reading this book has undergone an authentication at some point — you've logged into a network or perhaps a membership Web site at some time. Logons surely *seem* simple, don't they — just type in your name and password, click "OK," and you're in, right? As with many *seemingly* simple things, you'll soon see that what goes on under the hood isn't so simple.

Where Windows Stores Users and Passwords

In order to support authentication in an operating system, you'll need some kind of program that lets administrators create user accounts and store them in a file secured in some manner. You met such a program in the previous chapter when you created a user account. (As you'll see over the course of the three books in the *Mastering Windows Server 2008* series, it's not the only one. Lots of tools let you create and manage user accounts.) Secure systems then store user accounts in a file of some sort, what is essentially a database of user names and passwords. Windows systems store the simplest kind of account, a "local" account in a file named SAM. The name is short for Security Account Manager, and it's in the \windows\system32\config folder of every modern Windows system. If you have a local account (I keep saying "local" because there's another kind called a "domain" account that you'll meet soon) on a Windows workstation or server, your account information lives in the SAM on that system.

"Wow," you might be thinking. "You mean I can just go to your computer, open SAM in Notepad, and look at your passwords?" Nope, it's not that easy. For one thing, SAM doesn't really contain passwords. Instead, it contains encrypted versions of your passwords called *hashes*.

NOTE

In actuality, the passwords aren't encrypted. Instead, they are "hashed," which means that Windows takes your password and runs it through a mathematical function that's easy to *do*, but very hard to *undo*. The math is major-league ugly, but here's an easy example of "mathematical doing" that's easier than "mathematical undoing." If I asked you to multiply 26 × 13 by hand, you could probably fairly quickly compute the answer, 338; multiplication is pretty easy. But what about "undoing" multiplication — long division? Not as easy, is it? I could ask you to "undo" the multiplication problem by asking, "What's 338 divided by 13," and, I'd bet, the average person would take about three times as long to do that division problem as it would that same person to do the original multiplication problem. Now imagine a mathematical function where *undoing* that function took not three times longer, but *trillions* of times longer than doing it, and you'll understand how hashing works. It's a mathematical function where you stuff a password in one side, and a 128-bit number comes out the other side. Computers can compute hashes in fractions of seconds. But undoing it? About a septillion years. (That assumes that you didn't pick a really simple password — they're *way* easy to crack.)

Securing the User Account Database

Despite the fact that passwords are hashed and hashes of well-chosen passwords are tough to crack, it's a fact that most folks pick easy-to-crack passwords. So, Windows and other secure operating systems encrypt their user account databases.

So SAM is secure, between the hashing and the encrypting? Sort of. Microsoft keeps coming up with better ways to secure SAM, but the bad guys keep figuring out how Microsoft did it. That means that you can't really be sure that someone won't copy your SAM onto a USB stick, take it home, and use some hacker tool to crack the passwords at their leisure. This is a Windows security vulnerability, but you're basically vulnerable only *if you leave the bad guys alone with your computer*. Don't let 'em into the same room as the server, and they're not going to walk out with that SAM on the USB stick.

That's an important security concept called *physical security*. Put simply, if you let me spend a little "alone time" with your computer, then you will have no idea afterward what I did, what files I replaced, what files I copied, and so on. (You'll find that there's a class — a minority, but a large one — of security people who have a propensity to swagger when they talk, so their version of the advice would be a pronouncement something like, "if you let me touch your computer, I *own* your computer." Promise me and promise yourself — no matter how much you learn about security, don't *ever* talk to people like that.) Anyway, the moral of the story is that servers really ought to be physically secured, meaning that they should be in a locked room, one of those security cages, or the like.

> **NOTE**
>
> OK, there's one exception to that: what about when business realities (that is, the reality that your boss can fire you and he insists that there's no need to secure some server) *force* you to leave a server in an insecure position? Server 2008 actually offers a solution. As you'll read in one of the companion books in this series, *Mastering Windows 2008: Enterprise Technologies*, you can encrypt the entire hard disk on a Server 2008 machine. Thus, if the bad guys steal the computer, then they'll have to figure out how to decrypt that hard disk before they can even *start* attacking your SAM . . . and it'd probably take a few billion years to crack the drive encryption.

Networkable, Centralized Accounts: Domains

Let's look more closely into this notion of "local accounts," how we'd use them, where they limit us, and how to go beyond them with a concept called "domains." Suppose you have a user account on a given system and so you sit down at that system, press Ctrl-Alt-Del, and then punch in your user name and password. You have now done what's called a *local logon* or, sometimes, an *interactive logon*. Your password only traveled from your computer's keyboard to its CPU and RAM — the network's not involved yet.

You mostly do local logons to workstations, not servers: almost no one wanting to print an image at a print server would put the image on a USB drive, walk over to the server, sit down, log in locally, and print from the server. Instead, the more common server logon scenario entails you sitting at your workstation, logging onto that workstation, and then trying to access something on a remote machine — a server — across a network. That's no longer a *local* logon, but instead a *network* logon.

Let's review something here: when the workstation logged you on, it did it using your user account information on the SAM on that workstation. How, in contrast, would the server, a completely separate computer, get the information to authenticate you? Simple: because the server must have an account in your name as well, meaning that there's a user account with your name and password on that server's SAM. That may seem sort of obvious, but let me be clear about what that means.

◆ **Before you can access a server, that server's administrator must create an account for you on that server**. So if you interact with 15 servers, then each one of their SAMs needs a user account and password for you.

◆ **Nothing automatically synchronizes the different servers' SAMs**. There's no guarantee that the passwords are the same on all 15 servers, and when you change your password every few months (you really should change passwords regularly for security's sake), then you've got to remember to change them on all 16 machines — the 15 servers and your workstation. Ugh.

◆ **There's no easy way to keep track of how many accounts you have**. So an employee leaves the company and we want to clean out the inactive accounts. Which servers have an account for her? Sounds like a security nightmare in the making.

The answer? Well, instead of having every SAM in every workstation and server in your organization contain an account for every user in your organization, Windows lets you store a central database of user accounts and passwords on a small number of servers, sort of like a "shared SAM." The idea is that it's possible with Windows servers and workstations to tell them, "if someone tries to log on and tells you that his account isn't in your SAM but instead on some server's user database, then ask that server to authenticate the user for you." Such a notion is called a *Windows Active Directory domain*. More specifically:

◆ The servers that maintain centralized user databases are called *domain controllers* (DCs).

◆ The workstations and servers that rely upon the domain controllers to perform authentication services are said to *trust* the DCs. ("Trust" because when I sit down at a workstation and say, "log me on with my *domain* account," then that workstation must trust a DC to say "yes, judging by the password, that is indeed Mark." These trusting systems are said to be *members* of the domain.

◆ When a member is first configured to trust authentications from the DCs, that system is said to have *joined the domain*.

DCs don't store the central user database in SAMs; instead, they store the Active Directory (AD) user database in a file called `NTDS.DIT`. (The name means "NT Directory Services," which was the original name for Active Directory, which first appeared in Windows 2000, and "Directory Information Table," which is apparently a fancy way of saying "database file.") Domains are, as you'll see, extremely useful in Windows networks. They aren't required, though — if you wanted to, you really could set up a network like the 15 servers that I imagined a page or two back. A network like that one is called not a domain but a *workgroup*. Thus, a domain is a group of systems that all trust a set of domain controllers to do authentication for them; a workgroup, then, is a group of systems that *aren't* a domain.

Secure Logons Across a Network

Suppose I'm sitting at my Vista workstation and I want to get to some files on a file server named `files-r-us.bigfirm.com`. Before files-r-us will give me access, I have to log on. One of the many programs that comes with every version of NT since version 3.1 is called `winlogon.exe`, and it's the program that pops up when you first turn your workstation on, asking you to punch in your user name and password.

So imagine that I'm trying to access some data on files-r-us. Files-r-us responds by asking my workstation, "What's his name and password?" *Now* I've got a problem.

You see, what I'd *like* to do is to just say over the network line, "This is Mark and his password is 'swordfish.'" Then files-r-us can just look in its directory file of user names and passwords and see if it has a user named Mark with a password of "swordfish." If so, then I've been properly authenticated, and it lets me in. If not, it doesn't. Simple, eh?

Well, there's one flaw here — the part where my workstation passes "swordfish" over the network. A class of programs called "sniffers" can record and display any data that passes over a network wire (it's even easier when using a wireless connection). So passing passwords around on an unencrypted Ethernet cable isn't a great idea. That means you've got another challenge: how to prove to a server across the network from you that you've got Mark's password without actually showing that password to the server.

Over time, networks have come up with different answers, but Windows versions 2000 through 2008 that are members of an Active Directory domain use an old authentication method called Kerberos, which some folks at MIT first invented in the mid '80s. It replaces an older method employed by NT 3.*x* and 4 called NTLM, which was short for NT LAN Manager, a reference to one of NT's predecessors. What follows is an extremely simplified version of how Kerberos works. (It's actually a wildly simplified description, but it'll help you understand the more complete explanation that you'll see in the next section.)

Let's return to files-r-us. I try to access its data, so files-r-us needs to first log me in. It does that by saying, "I'll tell you how to access my data," and sends me some instructions on how to get to its data. But the data is *encrypted* — with my password! In other words, *anyone* could claim to be me, and files-r-us would happily send these vital instructions-for-connection. But only I can decrypt those instructions, so only I can benefit from them. So files-r-us ensured that only someone with my password could gain access, without sending my password over the wire.

Understanding How Authorization Works

After you gain access to the server, you need *authorization* to use resources on it. It was relatively easy to gain access to general resources such as files, folders, and printers in past versions of Windows, but Windows 2008 tightens things considerably. For example, you must now have specific rights to access the Programs, Windows, and System32 folders. That said, the actual process for authorizing a user to access resources once the system knows who they are hasn't changed from previous versions of Windows.

Permissions and Access Control Lists (ACLs)

Once a server has determined that I am indeed me, does that mean that I'll get access to the server's information? Not necessarily. Authentication just identifies me. The next step in security is access control, also known as (depending on what network operating system you are using) *rights*, *permissions*, or *privileges*.

Ever since its earliest versions, NT (which includes Windows Server 2008) has had a very flexible system of object permissions. An object can be a file, folder, printer, or just about any other resource that Windows manages. As you'll see later in this chapter, you can exert very fine-grained control, such as specifying that Mary can read or write to a given file, that Bill can only read it, and that June cannot access the file at all. Don't get the idea, however, that permissions refer only to files. There are permissions to do things like create, modify, and destroy user accounts, and even permissions to create domains in the first place. The flexibility of these permissions is one of Microsoft networking's great strengths.

Just about everything in the Microsoft networking world has security on it. Want to read a file? You need the permissions to read it. Want to shut down the program that provides the Web server? You need the permissions to shut it down. Want to create a new user account on your network? You need the permissions to create a new user.

These permissions are stored as a list. In the case of the file, the operating system sets aside a little space for every file that it creates, and keeps the permissions in that space. A set of permissions for a file, then, might look like

◆ A user named June can do anything that she wants to the file.

◆ Another user, Joe, can only read it.

◆ Any user in a group named Cube-dwellers can read or modify the file, but not delete it. (A *group* is a group of security resource requestors that can include the operating system, software running on the system, users, and even other groups.)

◆ The operating system can do anything that it wants to the file.

In Microsoft networking-speak, that list is called an access control list or, inevitably, *ACL*. (You say it as an acronym, "ackel," rather than "A-C-L." It's technically called a *discretionary* ACL — discretionary because when you create a file, you have the discretion to put whatever permissions in it that you like, so you'll also see it called a DACL, pronounced to rhyme with "spackle."

The DACL could get lost if Microsoft didn't package it in some way. Microsoft places the DACL, along with some other information, within a bit of data that they call a "security descriptor," as shown in Figure 3.1. A security descriptor is a kind of lock. It describes what an authenticated caller must provide in order to access an object in Windows.

FIGURE 3.1
Windows relies on a security descriptor to hold the ACLs.

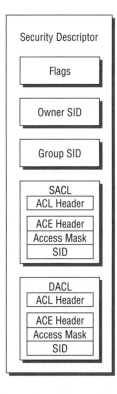

The security descriptor begins with a group of *flags* (a kind of on/off switch) that define the kind of object and some information about the security descriptor itself. In most cases, you'll never worry about these flags, but it's useful to know that they exist.

The next two entries are Security Identifiers (SIDs), a special number that identifies security information within Windows. Everything in Windows has a SID, including you. SIDs are either unique (as in your SID) or well-known (as in the SID for the Everyone group). You can find a list of well-known SIDs at http://support.microsoft.com/kb/243330. The two SIDs shown in Figure 3.1 identify the owner of the resource, such as a file, and the resource group. The owner SID is important because the owner of the resource can do anything with it. The group SID isn't important for now and you don't need to worry about it.

Let's get back to the ACLs now. An ACL includes a header that provides information about it. Normally, you won't ever have to work with this header, but it contains the information you might expect, such as the kind of ACL. The ACL header also contains a number that tells Windows how many users and groups can access the resource.

Within the ACL, you see a number of Access Control Entries (ACEs) that define access to the resource. Each ACE contains information about the user or group that can access the object. The ACE contains a header that tells Windows about the ACE, a list of rights for this particular ACE, and a SID, the unique identifier for the user or group. The combination of the rights mask (the list of rights) and the SID, define security for that particular user or group for this specific object.

Technically, then, if I create an ACE that gives Mary complete control of a file and John only the ability to read the file, then the file's DACL contains two ACEs. In reality, nearly everyone in the Windows world would say, "I gave Mary a full control *permission* and John read permission" — "permission" is the colloquial phrase for "access control entry." You'll also hear people say, "I gave Mary a full control ACL on that file," which is totally wrong — there's almost certainly other ACEs on the file — but, again, it's a common bit of phrasing among Windows admins.

Understanding What Tokens Do

The whole process of authenticating you every time you need a resource could become quite monotonous and time consuming. Microsoft came up with a method to overcome this problem called a *token*. When you authenticate on a system, you receive a token. Remember our first security metaphor, the notion that you secure your house by putting locks on the door and by carrying a key in your pocket that fits those locks? In our locking-the-house metaphor, the lock is a permission ("ACE"), and the key is the token.

But there's more to the token than just proof that "I am Mary Smith." In some senses, you can think of the token as you would a driving license. The token identifies who you are, provides a list of resources you can access, and determines how you can access them. Figure 3.2 shows what an access token looks like.

An access token begins with your SID. You may recall that SID is short for "Security ID," and the SID uniquely identifies you for security purposes. After your SID, you see a number of group SIDs. (Yes, groups have SIDs, too.) Each of these SIDs identifies a group to which you belong. You automatically receive any privileges assigned to the groups, so Windows looks these rights up to determine the full set of rights that you have to resources on the system.

The main portion of the access token contains a list of resources that you can access as an individual, rather than as part of a group. Windows stores a count of your rights at the beginning of the list. It then provides one entry for each right that you have. A resource has an identification number, but it's not the same as a SID. In this case, the system uses a Locally Unique Identifier (LUID). Every file, printer, disk drive, or other resource has a LUID. Your access token contains a list of the LUIDs that you can access as a user and the rights (or privileges) for that LUID in the form of attributes (or flags). Setting one flag to "on" might mean you can read the file, while a separate flag means that you can write to it. Don't worry about these flags for right now. However, if you're truly curious, you can see examples of these attributes at `http://msdn2.microsoft.com/en-us/library/aa375728(VS.85).aspx`.

FIGURE 3.2
You receive an access token when you log onto Windows.

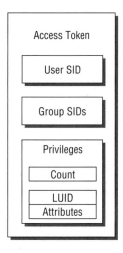

The access token you receive stays with you throughout the session. If you change a right, the access token won't reflect it because the access token is Windows' way of making things more efficient — Windows never updates the access token after it creates the access token for you. To update the access token, you must log out, and then log back into the system. Thus, if you ever join a new group or get a new user right/privilege, you will not see the benefits of that new group membership or right until you log off and log back on. To illustrate how this feature works, try these steps (don't worry about the specifics of the commands for the moment, simply focus on the results of each step).

1. Log onto the server as Joe. Remember that Joe's password is HiJoe!. Now, Joe isn't an administrator, so he can't normally perform any special acts, such as setting folder security. So, the first thing you need to do is give Joe access to an Administrator command prompt.

2. Choose Start. Right-click Command Prompt, and choose Run as Administrator from the context menu. You'll see a User Account Control dialog box telling you that Windows must have your permission to continue.

3. Type the Administrator password in the field provided, and click OK. You'll see an Administrator: Command Prompt appear. Notice that it actually has the name Administrator as part of the title bar to differentiate it from a normal command prompt.

4. Type **ICACLS C:\Test /Deny Administrators:F**, and press Enter. This command will deny the Administrators group access to the `C:\Test` folder. Joe still has access to this folder, but the Administrator account doesn't.

5. Log out of the Joe account and into the Administrator account.

6. Choose Start. Right-click Command Prompt, and choose Run as Administrator from the context menu. Notice that because you're already authorized to use the administrator command prompt, you don't have to do anything special, as you did when you opened the command prompt as Joe.

7. Type **CD C:\Test**, and press Enter. Hey, wait a minute! You're the administrator, and you don't have access to this folder. The system displays the "Access is denied." error message.

8. Type **ICACLS C:\Test /Grant Administrators:F**, and press Enter. Notice that you get a success message, so you know that the change is in place.

9. Type **CD C:\Test**, and press Enter. Wait a second, you still can't access the folder!

10. Log out and log back into the Administrator account.

11. Choose Start. Right-click Command Prompt, and choose Run as Administrator from the context menu.

12. Type **CD: C:\Test**, and press Enter. You now have access. This example illustrates how a token works. In order to update the token, you log out and back into the system.

Access to Earlier Security Systems

The last challenge that Windows 2000 and 2003's security designers faced was the so-called legacy support — ensuring that they could interact with the security systems built into Windows for Workgroups, Windows 9x, NT 3.x, and 4. I've described in very broad strokes how Kerberos works, but Windows and NT didn't use anything like that and in fact *couldn't* do Kerberos logons; Kerberos first appeared in the Microsoft networking world in February 2000, with the introduction of Windows 2000. Microsoft knew that you wouldn't be very happy if it required you to throw away all of your old Windows 9x and NT systems before you could implement Active Directory, so newer versions of Windows know a variety of logon methods — NTLM 1.2 for Windows 9x and NTLM 2.0 for NT 3.x and 4 — in addition to Kerberos.

Defining File and Folder Security

Now that you know the theory of security, it's time to see security in action. This example shows how the various pieces of Windows security work together to create a secure environment. This is actually a very simple example, but it does demonstrate the principles in a way that you'll find very useful. In fact, you'll use this procedure to grant users access to the file and folder resources on your server, which is a primary use of a server in many cases.

1. Choose Start ➤ All Programs ➤ Accessories ➤ Windows Explorer. You'll see a copy of Windows Explorer open. You can use Windows Explorer to manage many of the resources on your server from a security perspective.

2. Right-click anywhere in the right pane, and choose New ➤ Folder from the context menu. Type **SecureFolder** as the folder name, and press Enter.

3. Right-click SecureFolder, and choose Properties from the context menu. Select the Security tab. You'll see the SecureFolder Properties dialog box shown in Figure 3.3. This dialog box shows you the DACL for the SecureFolder object. It helps to look at Figure 3.1 when you view this dialog box. Each entry in the Group or User Names list is an ACE. Windows automatically translates the SID into a human readable name for you. The Permissions list shows you the individual flags found in the access mask. A check next to an entry shows that the flag is on and that the group or user has the specified right.

FIGURE 3.3

The Security tab shows the DACL for the Secure-Folder folder.

4. Click Advanced. You'll see the Advanced Security Settings for SecureFolder dialog box shown in Figure 3.4. Now you're seeing the entire security descriptor described in Figure 3.1. The Permissions tab shows the DACL, while the Auditing tab (Figure 3.5) shows the SACL. Your Auditing tab is going to be blank — I filled this one out for explanation purposes. The SACL works just like the DACL from a storage perspective, but you can see a bit more of its inner workings. For example, Figure 3.5 shows the effect of the ACE header. In this case, you see a success or a failure audit based on the contents of one of the flags in the ACE header. Like a DACL, however, there is a SID (the Everyone group in this case) and an access mask (what to audit). The Owner tab shows the owner SID entry of Figure 3.1. Because Windows doesn't actually use the group SID entry, you don't see it in this dialog box. The Effective Permissions tab is a special tool for checking the access that a user actually has and we'll look at it next.

FIGURE 3.4

This dialog box shows you the entire security descriptor.

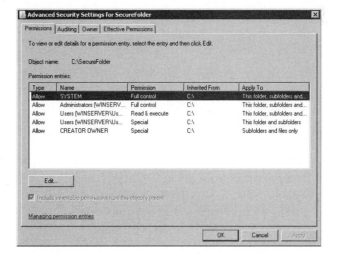

FIGURE 3.5
The SACL contains a list of auditing entries for a particular group or user.

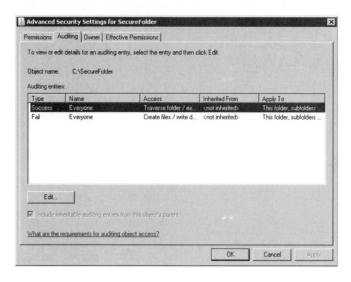

5. Select the Effective Permissions tab. You'll see the tool shown in Figure 3.6 (this dialog box shows the results of a test). An *effective permission* is the combination of:

◆ The rights you assign to the user or group individually

◆ The rights the user or group has (inherits) from higher levels in the folder hierarchy (rights always flow down to the lower levels from upper levels unless you specifically take them away)

◆ The rights of any groups to which the user or group belongs

FIGURE 3.6
Check the effective permissions of users or groups to determine what they can actually do.

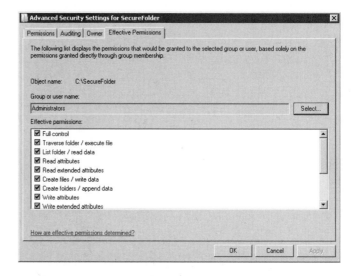

6. Click Select. You'll see the Select User or Group dialog box shown in Figure 3.7.

FIGURE 3.7
Provide the name of
the user or group that
you want to check.

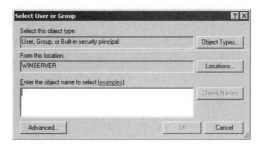

7. Type **Administrators** (the group) in the Enter the Object Name to Select field. Click OK. You'll see the output shown in Figure 3.6. This tool lets you check the effective permissions of any user or group for the selected object.

8. Click Cancel to close the Advanced Security Settings for SecureFolder dialog box. Of course, the question at this point is how to change the rights of a user or group. You can use the Advanced Security Settings for SecureFolder dialog box if you want, but Windows provides an easier method that you can use in most cases.

9. Click Edit in the Security tab of the SecureFolder Properties dialog box (shown earlier in Figure 3.3). You'll see the Permissions for SecureFolder dialog box shown in Figure 3.8. This dialog box lets you change the basic security settings for any user or group that has access to the file or folder you selected. You can use this dialog box to perform the following tasks.

FIGURE 3.8
Modify the basic secu-
rity for any file or folder
using this dialog box.

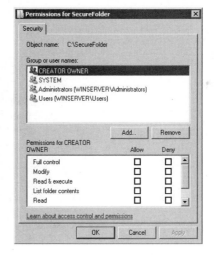

a. To add a new user or group, click Add. You'll see a Select Users or Groups dialog box where you can type the name of the user or group that you want to add to the security descriptor.
b. To remove a user or group, highlight its entry in the list and click Remove.
c. To modify the existing permissions of a user or group, highlight its entry in the list and check or clear the appropriate permission in the Permissions list.

10. Click OK when you want to save changes you've made to security or Cancel when you don't want to save them. Windows doesn't make any security changes until you signal that the changes are complete.

11. Click Cancel to close the SecureFolder Properties dialog box.

12. Remind any users with added Allow/Deny permissions to log off and then log back on to have these changes implemented.

This section has provided you with an overview of how to work with security for files and folders. The amazing thing is that you've also learned how to set security for a considerable number of other objects in Windows. For example, when you open a printer's Properties dialog box, you'll see a security tab that looks nearly the same as the one for a file or folder (see Figure 3.9 as an example). When you compare the permissions for each object, you'll notice that they're different (naturally, since you use each object in a different way). However, the concepts you use for modifying security remain the same.

FIGURE 3.9
The techniques you use for modifying file and folder security also apply to other objects.

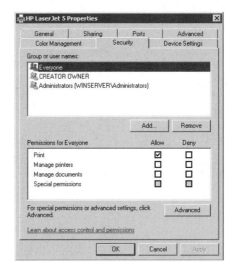

Whether you use the GUI or the command prompt to work with security in Windows, you'll find that you can change access to any Windows resource when you have the required permissions. When working with the Joe account, you had to ask Windows for permission to perform this task, but the administrator account has this permission by default. Some administrators like the GUI, as shown in this section of the chapter, and others like the command prompt, as shown in the "Understanding Authentication Versus Authorization" and "Understanding What Tokens Do" sections of the chapter.

Chapter 4

Installing Windows Server 2008: Basics

A great house begins with a great foundation; likewise, a great Windows Server begins with a great installation. Chapters 1 through 3 helped you understand how to create a basic network setup. This chapter takes you though the process of installing Windows Server 2008.

The element that differentiates a good installation from a great installation is planning. After all, you wouldn't just start pouring concrete before you planned where you were going to put your new house, would you? The first time you go through this chapter is actually a planning phase — you should read the chapter with the idea of thinking about all of the tasks you need to perform, before you actually do them. You should determine which edition of Windows Server 2008 best meets your needs, determine the installation technique that works best in your situation, define the roles your server needs to accomplish a given task, and then specify the features needed to extend the server to meet certain requirements.

This chapter focuses on a basic installation. The installation will meet the needs of anyone with general requirements. What I'm trying to accomplish in this chapter is to answer these questions:

- ◆ Which edition should you choose?

- ◆ How do you perform an initial setup?

- ◆ What is the difference between a role and a feature?

- ◆ When should you install roles or features?

- ◆ How do you install roles and features?

Choosing a Windows Server 2008 Edition

Microsoft seems to provide a mind-numbing array of editions for its products, and Windows is no exception to the rule. Of course, there is a good reason for variety — not everyone needs the same level of functionality. A small business certainly doesn't need the same number of features that a large corporation requires. Likewise, a workgroup has a different set of priorities from the corporation as a whole and probably uses a different edition of Windows than the corporation does to meet its needs. The most important preinstallation step for Windows Server 2008 is choosing the correct edition. Windows Server 2008 comes in a number of editions.

An *edition* defines the feature set of a particular operating system package (the unit that Microsoft uses to sell Windows Server 2008). You choose an edition based on your needs. Of course, editions that include more features come with a higher price tag. The following list describes the Windows Server 2008 editions:

Standard The Standard edition provides functionality that the average work center, small business, or even medium-sized business will require. You receive all of the virtualization, a full-featured Web server, and new security features described in this book as part of the Standard edition. (We focus mainly on Standard edition in the three books in the *Mastering Windows Server 2008* series.) In addition, you'll see the tools described in this book for managing your server. The main limitations for the Standard edition are the number of processors (up to 4 processors in a single server) and the amount of memory you can use (4 GB for the 32-bit version and 32 GB for the 64-bit version). Standard Server costs about $1,000 list and additionally requires you to purchase a client access license (CAL) for each user. They cost around $40 apiece, although that varies depending on whether you're upgrading or building a new system from scratch.

NOTE

When Microsoft talks about processors, it means processors that Windows can recognize. If your system uses dual-core processors, each core counts as a processor. Consequently, when working with Standard edition, you can install up to four single-core processors or two dual-core processors. If you're lucky enough to have a quad-core Xeon processor, you can install only one processor when working with Standard edition.

Enterprise The Enterprise edition provides functionality that a medium-sized business will normally require for a centralized server. You also find this edition in larger businesses as part of a large workgroup. In addition to all the functionality that the Standard edition provides, the Enterprise edition also provides greater memory support (64 GB for the 32-bit version and 2 TB for the 64-bit version) and the ability to use more processors (up to 8 processors in a single server). Additional features include clustering and hot-add memory support, as well as Microsoft's permission to create up to four "virtual" servers from one license. Enterprise costs around $4,000 and also requires the same sort of CALs as Standard Server.

Datacenter The Datacenter edition provides support for large businesses as part of the centralized server setup. It provides the maximum processor (up to 64 processors in a single server) and memory support (64 GB for the 32-bit version and 2 TB for the 64-bit version) allowed by Windows Server 2008. In addition to the features found in the Enterprise edition, you'll receive improved clustering support and the ability to dynamically partition hardware. Additional features include hot-replace memory and hot-add/replace processor support, as well as the ability to create as many virtual servers from one license as you like. Datacenter Server costs about $3,000 *per processor* and requires CALs.

Web The Web edition is a special Windows Server 2008 setup for the sole purpose of supporting Web sites. Consequently, you won't find many of the features found in other editions in the Web edition. This edition focuses on .NET Framework, IIS 7, and ASP.NET support. The reason you want to get this edition for Web sites is that it uses resources more efficiently and helps you support Web sites with fewer resources. In addition, having fewer features actually translates into a more reliable and secure server because there are fewer ways in which the server can fail. The processor limits for the Web edition are the same as for the Standard edition. The memory limits are 2 GB for the 32-bit version and 32 GB for the 64-bit version. You also can't use the Web edition to create virtualized images, nor can a copy of Web edition ever be a domain controller in an Active Directory domain. (It *can* be a member of an AD, though.) Web edition costs around $470 and requires CALs.

Itanium   Microsoft specifically designed the Itanium Processor edition to run on the Itanium processor. Except for not supporting a 32-bit version (since this processor doesn't come in a 32-bit format), the features of the Itanium Processor version are pretty much like those found in the Enterprise edition. Consequently, this chapter discusses the Itanium Processor version as part of the Enterprise edition.

The various editions also have role and feature differences that define the tasks each product can perform. You can see a list of these differences at www.microsoft.com/windowsserver2008 /editions/features.mspx. The "Understanding Roles and Features" section of the chapter highlights the differences between roles and features. You'll find a role and feature summary in the "Determining the Need for Specific Roles and Features" section of the chapter. The important issue is to ensure that the edition you purchase includes the roles and features you need to perform any needed tasks with the server.

Performing a Windows Server 2008 Full Version Installation

This section of the chapter considers the installation process for Windows Server 2008. Before you can do anything, you must make sure that your system fulfills the basic Windows Server 2008 hardware requirements and provides enough capacity to run any applications that you need to run. The Windows Server 2008 hardware requirements appear at www.microsoft.com /windowsserver2008/sysreqs.mspx. Remember that these specifications only tell you what Windows Server 2008 requires — you must have additional memory, hard drive space, and other hardware resources to run applications on the server. I recommend a minimum of 4 GB of RAM and a large (500 GB or above) single partition Small Computer System Interface (SCSI) hard drive. If at all possible, make sure you get hardware with the device drivers required to support 64-bit operation.

The edition of Windows Server 2008 that you purchase normally comes in more than one version. A *version* defines specifics about the product such as whether it operates in 32-bit or 64-bit mode and which interface it uses. One of the preinstallation choices you must make is which version to install to maximize the potential of your system.

NOTE

Windows Server 2008 breaks with tradition in that it also offers a Server Core version. This new lightweight version is Windows without the windows (the graphical interface). All you see when you install the Server Core version is a command prompt. Consequently, you must know how to work at the command prompt to use this version. The Server Core version comes in Standard, Enterprise, and Datacenter editions. You can't get Server Core in the Web or Storage Server editions because these editions require use of a graphical interface and Server Core doesn't provide the required support.

This chapter doesn't present you with all the installation choices that Microsoft provides for Windows Server 2008. Instead, you'll learn about the most common and reliable method of installing Windows Server 2008 using the DVD. Upgrade and slipstream installations present challenges that most novice users won't want to face. In fact, upgrade installations can be downright unreliable and cause you significant pain in getting Windows configured for use.

You'll find more advanced installation options in the other books of the *Mastering Windows Server 2008* series.

Considering the Installation Choices

At this point, you've decided on which Windows Server 2008 edition to install. Before you install Windows Server 2008, however, you must make some additional choices. Windows Server 2008 comes in a number of versions. Harkening back to the house foundation example, choosing a version is akin to deciding on the depth of the footings, choosing the type of tiling used to divert water, and determining whether you want to use a French drainage system. A version affects functionality in some way. For example, if your server requires a 32-bit operating system, then you'd use the 32-bit version of the product. Likewise, anyone with an Itanium processor will require the Itanium version of the product. The 32-bit version lacks the memory access and a few other features of the 64-bit version but provides better access to drivers in most cases.

In addition to choosing a processing model, you must choose an interface type. Windows Server 2008 also comes in a Full and a Server Core version. The Full version provides the complete Graphical User Interface (GUI), the same GUI that you've always used with Windows. The Server Core version comes only with a command prompt and some very basic graphical capabilities. This book doesn't consider the Server Core version because this version requires advanced configuration techniques and is for special needs, but you'll notice that almost all places where you see how to accomplish something with a GUI, we include the corresponding command-line commands so you'll be ready for Server Core when you get around to it. (Chapter 3 of the second volume in the series, *Mastering Windows Server 2008: Essential Technologies*, covers Server Core.)

Before you begin the installation, you must consider both the processing and interface model. Consequently, you may find yourself installing the 32-bit version of the Windows Server 2008 Full edition on one machine and the 64-bit version of the Windows Server 2008 Server Core edition on other machine. Even though the basic functionality of Windows is the same in both cases, the results of the two installations are quite different.

Once you determine the edition and version choices you want to install, you have to decide on an installation technique. The DVD installation provides the easiest method of getting Windows Server 2008 onto a system that doesn't include an operating system. You can also use this technique when you don't want to save the settings on a system (you want to perform a clean install) or you want to perform diagnostics before performing the installation. For example, you may want to test system memory. As previously mentioned, this book discusses only the DVD installation method because this method is the easiest to perform and provides a more reliable installation.

WHAT ABOUT THE WINDOWS INSTALLATION METHOD?

Microsoft does provide other installation methods, with the Windows installation method being the next most common. The Windows installation method begins the process within Windows instead of during the boot cycle. You use the existing copy of Windows as a starting point. Taking that approach normally lets you preserve your existing setup by performing an update installation, unless the installation program encounters a problem. (When the setup program does run into a problem, you can still perform a custom or clean installation, as described in this chapter.) In many respects, the update approach isn't much different from installing an application because you begin by inserting the media in the drive and waiting for the automatic installation process to start (you can also start the setup by locating `Setup.exe` on the installation media and double-clicking it in Windows Explorer).

The main problem with this type of installation is that the environment and the Registry aren't clean. Consequently, you can experience problems even if the installation should proceed flawlessly. Scrupulous attention to detail helps prevent problems. For example, you'll want to remove any applications that Windows Server 2008 doesn't support. You'll also want to downgrade your display adapter to use a generic driver to ensure you can see the display once Windows restarts. You'll find complete instructions for performing an update installation in the second volume, *Mastering Windows Server 2008: Essential Technologies*.

Using the DVD Installation Method

When working with the DVD installation method, you create an entirely new Windows installation. This installation doesn't preserve any of your old settings, and you'll need to install your applications from scratch. Of course, you also won't carry any of the old baggage around that could cause you problems later. Not only does your existing Windows installation contain potentially harmful applications, but it also includes Registry settings that aren't attached to anything (or worse yet, misconfigure your applications), and device drivers that may not work with Windows Server 2008. This installation provides you with a reliable and stable setup in most cases. The following steps describe how to perform a DVD installation:

1. Start the system and place the DVD into the boot DVD drive as soon as possible before the system begins looking for a boot drive. The system will display a message asking whether you want to boot from the DVD. If you miss this sequence, you can always place the DVD into the drive and press the Reset button on the front of the computer system to restart it. You'll see the required message during the next boot sequence.

2. Press Enter to boot from the DVD. You'll see a message that Windows is loading files. This message will appear for several minutes, so be patient. After the initial file load completes, you'll see an Install Windows dialog box that contains entries for language, time and currency format, keyboard, or other input method as shown in Figure 4.1.

FIGURE 4.1
Choose the installation language, time and currency format, and keyboard options.

3. Choose an installation language, time and currency format, and a keyboard or other input method. Click Next. You'll see a dialog box with three options as shown in Figure 4.2.

FIGURE 4.2
Begin the installation by clicking Install now.

Here's a description of the three options:

◆ *Install now*: Lets you install the operating system immediately.

◆ *What to know before installing Windows*: Displays a Help and Support dialog box where you can discover information about the Windows release and preinstallation requirements. The help screen includes information on the minimum processor, RAM, and disk space requirements. Make sure you pay close attention to requirements such as disconnecting your UPS serial cable before you begin the installation or the installation may fail. All these special requirements appear in the Before Your Start Setup section of the help file (scroll about halfway down).

◆ *Repair your computer*: Displays the system recovery options, which include: Windows Complete PC Restore (to restore your system from a backup), Windows Memory Diagnostic Tool, and access to a command prompt. The command prompt is especially flexible because it gives you access to any command that's available on the installation media or on the disk drives. For example, I used the command prompt to start my screen capture program so I could capture screenshots for this section of the chapter. Before you see the recovery options, however, you'll see a System Recovery Options dialog box where you choose which partition to work with on your hard drive. You can also load any drivers required to perform system recovery tasks on your system.

4. Click Install now. The installation program performs some additional tasks and eventually displays a dialog box that asks for your product key, as shown in Figure 4.3. If you want to install a particular version of Windows Server 2008, you must provide your product key now to ensure the best installation. However, you can also provide a product key later, after you complete the installation. The Windows Server 2008 installation media contains all available editions and versions of Windows Server 2008. Use the following steps to see all the editions contained on the DVD.

FIGURE 4.3
Type your product
key to gain access to
the Windows edition
you purchased.

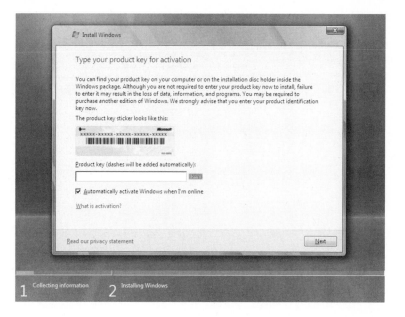

a. Click Next at the product key dialog box. Windows will display a warning dialog box.

b. Click No to bypass the warning dialog box. Windows displays a list of Windows editions that you can install. You must eventually provide a product key for your installation, but this option lets you try a Windows operation system edition for a predefined timeframe (120 days as of this writing).

c. Choose the edition you want to install, and check the I have selected the edition of Windows that I purchased option.

d. Click Next and proceed to step 7.

5. Type your product key. Check the Automatically activate Windows when I'm online option. Click Next. You'll see a list of options for the editions of Windows Server 2008 you purchased as shown in Figure 4.4.

NOTE

Usually, the options shown in Figure 4.4 include a GUI version (Full Installation option) and a Server Core version. The GUI version has all the features that you normally associate with Windows. This is the version of Windows Server 2008 described throughout this book. The Server Core version contains only a command prompt. You won't see most of the GUI features usually associated with Windows when working with this version, but this version does provide certain reliability, performance, and security features that offset the lack of a GUI.

---

6. Select the GUI version (Full Installation option) of the operating system, and click Next. You'll see the licensing dialog box.

FIGURE 4.4
Choose the version of
the product that you
want to install.

7. Check I accept the license terms, and click Next. You'll see an installation dialog box, as shown in Figure 4.5. The Upgrade option is always disabled when you perform a DVD installation. You must start the setup program from within Windows to perform an upgrade installation.

FIGURE 4.5
The setup program pro-
vides two options for
installing Windows.

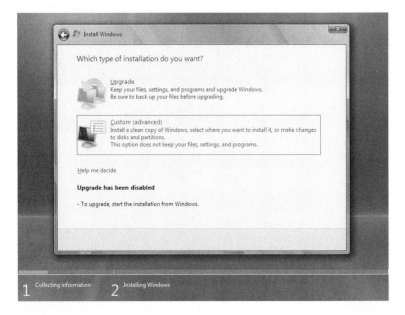

Here's a description of the two installation options:

◆ *Upgrade*: An upgrade installation lets you keep your files, settings, and programs intact on the host system. The upgrade installation performs most tasks automatically. When you select Upgrade you can simply sit back and watch the installation program perform most of the work for you (all you'll need to do is perform any custom configuration after the operating system installation completes; the topic of the rest of this book).

◆ *Custom (advanced)*: A custom installation lets you perform a clean install of the operating system. The new version of the operating system can appear on a separate partition from an existing operating system installation or you can completely replace an existing copy of the operating system. This procedure continues with the custom installation.

WARNING

A clean installation over an existing copy of Windows always removes the old copy of Windows, any settings, applications, data, and everything else in the partition. Consequently, you should perform a backup before you install Windows Server 2008 over an existing partition if you want to keep any of this information from the previous installation. Otherwise, you'll lose absolutely everything in that partition.

---

8. Click Custom (Advanced). The installation program asks where you want to install Windows, as shown in Figure 4.6. If you already have a copy of Windows installed on your hard drive, you can choose to install Windows in the existing partition or in an unallocated area of the hard drive. In some cases, you may have to load a driver or perform other special tasks to work with the drive. When this situation occurs, click Drive Options, and the display will change, as shown in Figure 4.7 to provide access to specialized drive features.

FIGURE 4.6
Choose a location on the hard drive to use for the Windows installation.

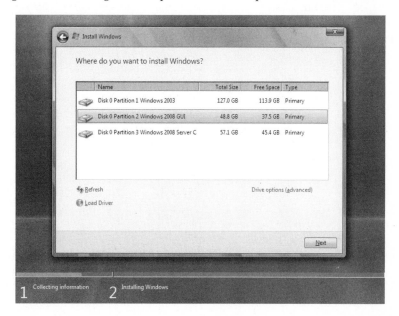

FIGURE 4.7
The setup program provides access to special drive features when needed.

9. Choose the hard drive you want to use for Windows, and click Next. If you choose a partition with an existing copy of Windows on it, you'll see an Install Windows dialog box that warns you about the potential problems of using the partition (namely that the installation will overwrite any existing data). Click OK to get past the Install Windows dialog box or Cancel to choose a different partition. The installation program now has enough information to proceed. The installation is automatic at this point. You'll see Windows accomplishes these tasks for you:

   a. Windows begins copying and expanding the files needed for the operating system. Since this process can require quite a bit of time (depending on the capabilities of your server; my server required about 10 minutes to complete the task), now might be a good time to get that cup of coffee you've been wanting.

   b. At some point, the server will reboot to continue the installation process. This is perfectly normal.

   c. After the server reboots, it will perform a number of additional tasks and may reboot again (this sequence can occur multiple times depending on the complexity of your setup; again, it's normal behavior during an install).

   d. Eventually, you'll see a message telling you that you must change the user's password before logging in the first time. This is a new safety feature that ensures you have an opportunity to change the administrator password before you perform any other task with Windows server.

10. Click OK. You'll see an Administrator screen where you must type in a new password, and then confirm the new password.

11. Type a new password and click the Right Pointing Arrow icon. Windows will tell you that it has changed the password.

12. Click OK. You'll see a flurry of activity as Windows Server configures itself. Eventually, you'll see an Initial Configuration Tasks window where you can perform initial configuration. You now have Windows Server 2008 installed.

Using the Initial Tasks Page

After you complete the installation on your system, you'll see the Initial Configuration Tasks window shown in Figure 4.8. This window is essentially a checklist. You start at item 1, move down the list of icons in item 1, and then go to item 2. Microsoft provides this checklist so that you can configure your server quickly, without missing any essential configuration tasks. The following sections provide a brief overview of each of these configuration items. You'll find more detailed information on these configuration tasks as the book progresses.

FIGURE 4.8
The Initial Configuration Tasks window provides a sort of checklist of things you should do.

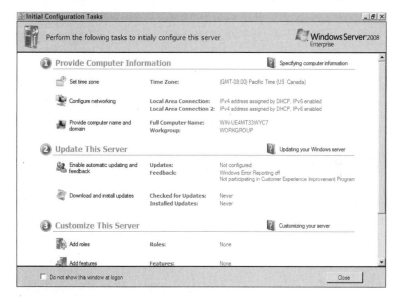

Providing Computer Information

The first step in configuring your computer is to provide some information about it. Click Set time zone and you'll see the Date and Time dialog box where you can set the system time if necessary. As a minimum, you should click Change Time Zone to change the time zone for your area (unless you happen to live in the US Pacific time zone).

Click Configure networking and you'll see the Network Connections window. For now, you'll probably leave the network settings alone unless you know that you need specific settings to make your network operational. For example, you may have used this machine on a network in the past and wish to use the same setting with Windows Server 2008. Chapters 9 through 13 of this book tell you how to work with the network settings.

When you click Provide computer name and domain, you see the Computer Name tab of the System Properties dialog box. This is the dialog box where you change the odd Microsoft generated computer names (such as WIN-UE4 MT33WYC7), to something more readable. You may recall that you've previously performed this task in the "Changing the Machine Name" section of Chapter 2. After you change the machine name and choose a workgroup or domain, you'll need to reboot the system. Don't worry, the Initial Configuration Tasks window will reappear.

Update the Server

The second step in configuring your server is to determine how updates occur. Most companies don't want to set the server to update automatically because automatic updates can result in data loss and other nasty problems when the server reboots unexpectedly after an update. What you want to do is have the server check for updates and then let you decide when to make them in most cases. You may even want to make the process manual.

When you click Enable automatic updating and feedback, you'll see the Enable Windows Automatic Updating and Feedback dialog box. Click Manually Configure Settings and you'll see a list of choices like the one shown in Figure 4.9. The settings for Windows Automatic Updating and Windows Error Reporting won't work unless you interact with the console directly — Windows won't perform these tasks unless you're logged into the server. The Customer Experience Improvement Program setting will work because it's set not to do anything at all.

FIGURE 4.9
Define server update settings that make sense for your server environment.

Click Change Setting in the Windows Automatic Updating section and you'll see the "Change settings" window shown in Figure 4.10 where you can select an update strategy that will work with your server environment. In most cases, you aren't going to want to choose the "Install updates automatically (recommended)" setting because the server can reboot unexpectedly and you don't know how the update will affect your server unless you test it on another test system first. The option that I find works best for smaller networks is the "Check for updates but let me choose whether to download and install them" option. If your network has a central update server, use the "Never check for updates (not recommended)" option instead. After you choose an automatic update option, click OK to close the "Change settings" window.

FIGURE 4.10
Choose an automatic update option that matches your network setup.

After you choose an automatic update option, click Change Setting in the Windows Error Reporting section of the dialog box. You'll see the Windows Error Reporting Configuration dialog box shown in Figure 4.11. The option shown won't work particularly well if you aren't monitoring the computer console. You should choose an automatic setting or the option not to participate at all. Given that most companies today are very concerned about giving out too much information, the non-participation option is probably the best choice. Choose a setting and click OK to close the Windows Error Reporting Configuration dialog box. Click Close to close the Manually Configure Settings dialog box.

Your server probably has outdated software on it the second you install Windows Server 2008. That's because the media you get from Microsoft doesn't have any of the updates that Microsoft provides. Before you begin any customization or product installation, it's a good idea to get the server updated. Click Download and install updates in the Initial Configuration Tasks window. You'll see the Windows Update window shown in Figure 4.12.

FIGURE 4.11
Decide whether you want to submit error reports to Microsoft.

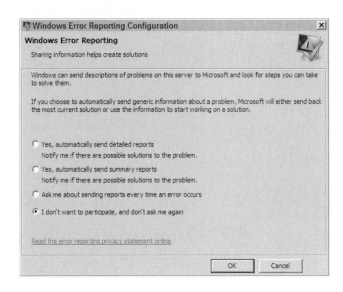

Click Check for Updates. Windows will check online for any updates to your server. Follow the prompts that Windows provides if it finds any updates to install. If there aren't any new updates, you'll see a "Windows is up to date" indicator, as shown in Figure 4.12.

FIGURE 4.12
Perform an update of your system before you customize it.

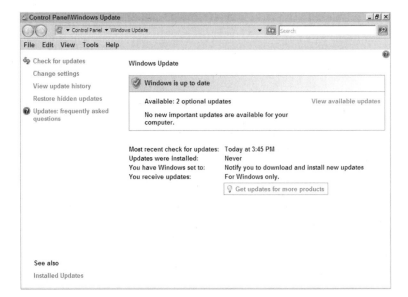

Customizing This Server

The third step in configuring your server is to customize it. The "Understanding Roles and Features," "Determining the Need for Specific Roles and Features," and "Installing Roles and Features" sections of the chapter describe the first two entries in this section. You'll find that working with roles and features is something you do as you work with the server and not just a task you perform once as part of working with the Initial Configuration Tasks window.

Most administrators don't work with their servers by going to the server console. The server is very likely locked up in its own air-conditioned room somewhere and accessing it directly is inconvenient to say the least. Consequently, one of the features that you'll want to enable immediately is Remote Desktop. Simply click Enable Remote Desktop, and you'll see the Remote tab of the System Properties dialog box shown in Figure 4.13.

FIGURE 4.13
Remote Desktop connectivity is a must-have for most administrators.

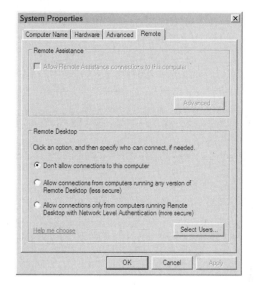

You have three choices when enabling Remote Desktop. The first choice is not to allow any connections at all, which is the default configuration. The second choice is to allow a less secure connection for computers running any version of Remote Desktop. Unless all your administrator workstations use Vista, this is the option that you'll need to choose. If you work for one of the few companies that currently use Vista everywhere, you can choose to use the third option, which requires that the caller uses Network Layer Authentication (NLA) for greater security.

After you make a choice to enable Remote Desktop, you'll see a dialog box warning you that the selection enables Remote Desktop for all connections. Click OK to dismiss the dialog box. Click OK in the System Properties dialog box to enable Remote Desktop. You may wonder why you didn't need to click Select Users. Windows automatically allows any member of the Administrators group to connect using the Remote Desktop Connection utility on a workstation. The only time you have to select users is when you want people outside of the Administrators group to have access as well.

If you test the Remote Desktop connection at this point, you'll see that it's already active. Of course, this begs the question of how you're gaining access through Windows Firewall. Windows automatically makes exceptions in Windows Firewall for you when you perform certain activities such as enabling Remote Desktop. When you first install Windows, the firewall doesn't have any exceptions, but you already have several of them in place simply by configuring the server to perform certain tasks. To see these changes, click Configure Windows Firewall. When you see the Windows Firewall window, click Change Settings. Choose the Exceptions tab in the Windows Firewall Settings dialog box and you'll see that a number of exceptions already appear in the list. Figure 4.14 shows a typical example.

FIGURE 4.14
Windows automatically performs certain firewall configurations for you.

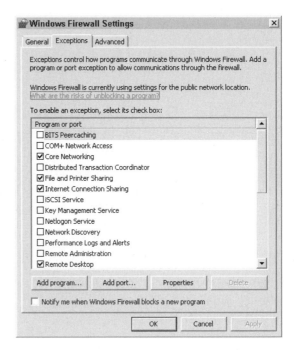

Understanding Roles and Features

In previous versions of Windows, you selected Windows functionality using the Add or Remove Programs applet. You simply selected Add/Remove Windows Components to see which features you could install. Apparently, using this approach was too easy to understand, so Microsoft made things a little more complicated in Windows Server 2008. You now need to know whether the functionality you want to add is a role or a feature, and the distinction between the two seems arbitrary at best, which is certain to frustrate many administrators — especially those who have worked with Windows for a while.

In general, a *role* is a major task that the server must perform, such as providing file and print services. Of course, one of the biggest roles is Active Directory, and you'll find that Windows Server 2008 actually provides several subroles in this area. If you find that you can't locate a particular function that you know Windows Server 2008 supports, then check out the "Determining the Need for Specific Roles and Features" section of the chapter for details on the roles and features that you'll find in this product.

A *feature* is something that augments the server in some way, at least in most cases. For example, you can probably argue that the .NET Framework 3.0 and Windows PowerShell are ancillary features. However, it's not always the case that you can say something is a feature or a role just by looking at it logically. DHCP Server and DNS Server are roles, while Peer Name Resolution Protocol and WINS Server are features. It's hard to tell why Microsoft made this distinction. Perhaps features somehow fall into the less necessary category of functions that Windows Server performs. It's really hard to tell.

The one thing that you can count on is that roles and features both add to the functionality of your server. Windows Server 2008 provides a significant list of functions that it can perform. The main reason that Microsoft probably decided on splitting the list into two is that a single list is becoming unwieldy.

You don't always need to know which role or feature to install because sometimes Windows installs it for you. For example, when you share a hard drive resource on your server, Windows automatically installs the File Services role for you. If you later remove the File Services role because you don't know what task it performs, you'll also disable the shares you created. The shares will still exist; they simply won't do anything useful. Consequently, always verify that you don't need a particular role or feature before you remove it. In addition, sometimes a role or feature requires another role or feature to work. Windows will make you aware of these dependencies when you work with the roles or features.

NOTE

After you complete the initial configuration, you can check the "Do not show this window at logon" option at the bottom of the Initial Configuration Tasks window. This window will go away and you'll see the Server Manager start up automatically instead. Server Manager provides significantly more functionality than the Initial Configuration Tasks window and I recommend moving to Server Manager as soon as you can after you finish the initial system setup.

Determining the Need for Specific Roles and Features

Windows Server 2008 provides support for a vast range of functionality — more than any previous Windows product. As mentioned in the "Understanding Roles and Features" section of the chapter, a role is something that provides major server functionality. Table 4.1 provides a complete list of the roles found in the Windows Server 2008 Enterprise Edition. Other editions may not support all these roles, so the table also tells you whether you'll find a particular feature in the most commonly purchased edition, Standard.

TABLE 4.1: Windows Server 2008 Roles

ROLE NAME	DESCRIPTION	FOUND IN STANDARD EDITION?
Active Directory Certificate Service	You install this role to create a new certificate authority (CA). A CA is a special server used to issue certificates, such as those used to sign applications or enhance the security of your e-mail. The certificate tells someone else who you are and helps them determine whether they can trust you. These are the same certificates you see when you go to a secure Web site. In fact, you can use this role to help you create a certificate for your Web server, making secure communications possible.	Yes, but limited to creating certificate authorities
Active Directory Domain Services	You can't install this role by itself. This is the role that Windows Server 2008 installs when you promote the server to a domain controller. Active Directory is a special kind of database that holds all the settings for everything on your network. You'll find user, application, and system settings in this database. In addition to storing settings, Active Directory provides support for major applications such as Microsoft Exchange Server. The Domain Services portion of an Active Directory setup is essentially the Database Management System (DBMS) that provides access to the Active Directory database.	Yes
Active Directory Federation Services	One of the problems with modern networks is that the user has to remember so many logons. Every time the user wants to access another resource, it requires a logon of some sort. When you install Active Directory Domain Services (AD DS), you obtain federated logon capability for the local network. A federated logon is one in which a Single Sign On (SSO) acts as a key to access all areas of the network for which the user has the appropriate credentials. Using SSO makes working with the network considerably easier.	No
Active Directory Lightweight Directory Services	Most of the applications on your network won't use Active Directory at all for data storage. Only the large applications, such as Exchange Server, require extensive data storage in Active Directory. However, some applications fall between these two extremes of not needing any Active Directory support at all and requiring the complete package. In this case, the application may need Active Directory Lightweight Directory Services (AD LDS). You may actually know AD LDS by a different name, Lightweight Directory Access Protocol (LDAP). LDAP is actually a standardized technology that you'll find on many platforms, not just Windows (see the LDAP standards at www.ietf.org/rfc/rfc1777.txt and www.faqs.org/rfcs/rfc1823.html for further information).	Yes

TABLE 4.1: Windows Server 2008 Roles *(CONTINUED)*

Role Name	Description	Found in Standard Edition?
Active Directory Rights Management Services	Using this role implies that you want to protect access to your data when that access occurs outside your network. The whole purpose of Active Directory Rights Management Services (AD RMS) is Digital Rights Management (DRM). The features this role provides help you protect your data by checking the credentials of each user requesting data access. It doesn't matter where the access occurs, the user must have proper rights to work with it.	Yes
Application Server	An application server is a special way of providing services to a client machine. The application executes partially on the server and partially on the client. Precisely how the application works depends on where the developer determines the particular piece of code works best. The Application Server role provides this functionality to Windows Server 2008 users. Microsoft has designed it to work with Microsoft's Enterprise Services (www.microsoft.com/biztalk/solutions/soa/esb.mspx and www.microsoft.com/downloads/details.aspx?FamilyId = B4FF0934-2CF1-423B-B273-D482E60442BA) and .NET Framework 3.0 (www.microsoft.com/events/series/msdnnetframework3.aspx and http://msdn2.microsoft.com/en-us/library/ms687307.aspx) applications.	Yes
DHCP Server	The Dynamic Host Configuration Protocol (DHCP) is a standard means for client computers to request an Internet Protocol (IP) address from a server. You normally need just one such server for a small to medium network. You must have a DHCP server installed before you can promote your server to a domain controller.	Yes
DNS Server	The Domain Name System (DNS) is a standard means of converting IP addresses into a human readable form. For example, when you want to access Microsoft's main page, you type www.microsoft.com, not the IP address of the Microsoft Web site. The DNS server converts this human readable name into the actual IP address. You must have a DNS server installed before you can promote your server to a domain controller.	Yes
FAX Server	Installing the FAX Server role lets you use your server to send and receive faxes, provided you have the required hardware and software installed. This role also requires that you install the Print Server role.	Yes

TABLE 4.1:   Windows Server 2008 Roles *(CONTINUED)*

ROLE NAME	DESCRIPTION	FOUND IN STANDARD EDITION?
File Services	Installing the File Services role lets you share files on the network. This is the one role that you'll always install on the server since a server isn't much good if you can't share files. Adding the File Services role only provides basic file sharing.	Yes but limited to one standard Distributed File System (DFS) root (see the information at `http://technet` `.microsoft.com` `/en-us/library` `/bb727150.aspx` or Chapter 11 of *Mastering Windows Server 2008 Server Volume Two: Essential Foundations* for additional details)
Network Policy and Access Services	The name of this particular role is a bit misleading because it provides a lot more functionality than the name implies. In fact, installing this particular role provides these services: Network Policy Server (NPS), Network Access Protection (NAP) Health Policy Server, Secure Wireless Access (IEEE 802.11), Secure Wired Access (IEEE 802.3), Central Network Policy Management, Remote Access Dial-In User Server (RADIUS) Server and Proxy, Remote Access Service (RAS), Routing, Health Registration Authority (HRA), Host Credential Authorization Protocol (HCAP), and Tools Required to Manage All Access Services. The scope of this particular role is incredible. It provides many of the features that modern servers must provide for outside communication.	Yes but limited to 250 Routing and Remote Access Service (RRAS) connections, 50 Internet Authentication Service (IAS) connections and 2 IAS Server Groups (see `http://technet2` `.microsoft.com` `/windowsserver/en` `/library/7f26a61e-` `8dfa-455f-b596-` `53aa6349f0511033` `.mspx` for details)
Print Services	Providing print services is another common role for servers. At one time, printers were extremely expensive (and good printers still are) so issuing one to each user wasn't cost effective. This role helps you manage all the printers connected to the server and offers their use to any users with the required access.	Yes
Terminal Services	Terminal Services offers remote connectivity to anyone who needs to work with the server directly. In many cases, this activity means using a light client or involves an administrator performing configuration tasks. The two most common ways to use Terminal Services is through Remote Desktop or through RemoteApp applications.	Yes but limited to 250 Terminal Services Gateway connections

TABLE 4.1:   Windows Server 2008 Roles *(CONTINUED)*

ROLE NAME	DESCRIPTION	FOUND IN STANDARD EDITION?
UDDI Services	The Universal Description, Discovery, and Integration (UDDI) service is the Microsoft method of making Web services and their associated applications easily accessible from the server. For the most part, you'll never install this role unless you have a custom application that relies on it.	Yes
Web Server (IIS)	Web servers traditionally serve content over the Internet or through an intranet. Users view the content using a browser or through a special application. Modern Web servers provide fully distributed application support in addition to dynamic and static content. IIS 7.0 is a completely new version of IIS with many changes that will surprise you if you haven't worked with it before.	Yes
Windows Deployment Services	If you normally install Windows through your server, then you'll need to install this role. The Windows Deployment Services lets a client log into the server and install a complete copy of Windows without any interaction on the part of the user or administrator. Of course, you have to perform a number of configuration tasks to make this feature work. You can learn more about Windows Deployment Services at `http://msdn2.microsoft.com /en-us/library/aa967394.aspx`.	Yes
Windows SharePoint Services	SharePoint Services is a technology that lets application users share data through the server. The application must provide the functionality required to work with SharePoint Services. For example, advanced versions of Office 2007 provide the functionality required to use SharePoint Services. Of course, before you can use SharePoint Services, you must have a server with the SharePoint Services role installed to provide the required connectivity, which is the only reason that you'd install this role. You can learn more about SharePoint Services at `www.microsoft.com /technet/windowsserver/sharepoint/default.mspx`.	Yes

Features are something that augment the server functionality in some way. Table 4.2 shows a complete list of all the features found in the Windows Server 2008 Enterprise Edition. Other editions of the product may not provide all these features.

TABLE 4.2: Windows Server 2008 Features

FEATURE	DESCRIPTION
.NET Framework 3.0 Features	The .NET Framework provides all the managed functionality that you need to run managed applications. Microsoft is promoting managed applications, those that rely on the .NET Framework, as safer, more reliable, and more secure. Theoretically, managed applications do offer all these features, but many of these features are only available when the developer provides the proper support within the application code.
BitLocker Drive Encryption	BitLocker is a full drive encryption technology that relies on one of several key technologies to unlock the drive during the boot process. The theory behind BitLocker is that the drive is secure unless you provide someone with the key. Even removing the drive from the system and placing it in another system won't provide access to the required key. No one can boot the drive and gain access to your data, at least in theory. Many servers will have a Trusted Platform Module (TPM) chip installed (see the Web site at `https://www.trustedcomputinggroup.org/groups/tpm/` for details on this technology). This chip holds the key to unlocking the drive. You must provide a Personal Identification Number (PIN) to activate the key. As an alternative, you can place the key on a flash drive (those little key fob devices that contain several GB of storage). Placing the flash drive (see `www.usbflashdrive.org/` for details on this technology) in a Universal Serial Bus (USB) port provides the key to access the encrypted hard drive during the boot process.
BITS Server Extensions	If you've ever used Windows Update, then you've used the Background Intelligent Transfer Service (BITS). BITS provides the means to continue an upload or download despite poor line conditions, disconnections, and even reboots. The BITS Server Extensions feature lets clients upload files to your server using the BITS technology. The server can also send files to the client using BITS technology. If your server provides files to client systems or requires the client to perform uploads, this is a great feature to install because you already have access to it on the client.
Connection Manager Administration Kit (CMAK)	The CMAK functionality helps you define connection scenarios for clients accessing your server. The connection scenarios can include everything from a dial-up connection used on the weekend to upload or download files to a full Virtual Private Network (VPN) connection used to conduct business from a remote location.
Desktop Experience	You'd install this feature to make your server look a lot more like Vista, rather than an improved version of Windows 2003. The problem is that all the Vista eye candy consumes a lot of resources, yet doesn't really provide any improvement in operating system functionality, reliability, security, or performance. Given that you probably won't use your server as a workstation, installing this feature is probably the worst thing you can do. Installing this feature will give you lots of Vista eye candy, but it'll also reduce server performance and response time as a minimum.

TABLE 4.2:   Windows Server 2008 Features *(CONTINUED)*

FEATURE	DESCRIPTION
Failover Clustering	If your organization has multiple Windows Server 2008 installations, you can use failover clustering to improve overall system reliability. When a server fails, the load that server was carrying is transferred to another server. The user will likely notice a drop in performance, but will still continue using the network, oblivious to the failure. The servers must communicate with each other to implement this feature, so you'll see the effects of the additional overhead. Generally, the servers will become a little less responsive. Depending on your setup, no one may even notice that change. In essence, you trade some performance to obtain additional reliability. Failover clustering can't overcome certain kinds of failures. For example, if your entire network goes down, then failover clustering isn't going to help.
Group Policy Management	Group policy management is an important part of the enterprise. You can use it to control everything from the local machine, to network connections, to the server. Everything on your entire network probably has a setting you can use to control policy for it. Of course, this feature only works with Active Directory since you need the Active Directory database to store the settings.
Internet Printing Client	Sometimes clients will need to print from the Internet using the local server. The Internet Printing Protocol (IPP) helps the client perform this task with relative ease. Using this feature lets the client send a report to a collaborator or perform other printing related tasks.
Internet Storage Name Server	The Internet Storage Name Server (iSNS) feature lets you make your local system hard drive available to Internet clients as an Internet Small Computer System Interface (iSCSI) drive. A correctly configured iSCSI drive looks like a local drive to the client system.
LPR Port Monitor	You'd only need this feature when working with UNIX systems. The Line Printer Remote (LPR) port monitor tracks printers that are running the Line Printer Daemon (LPD) on a remote system. When this service is available, the local machine can use the remote printer as if it were a locally attached device.
Message Queuing	Message Queuing is akin to using the post office. Someone sends a letter, the post office delivers it, and the recipient picks the letter up. No one has to see anyone else in this entire scheme. The sender need not see anyone at the post office, the people at the post office need not see the recipient, and the recipient doesn't have to retrieve the letter at any particular time. Even so, this system of delivering mail is consistent and relatively reliable. Working with Message Queuing in Windows Server 2008 is even more reliable than the post office — in fact, the post office guarantees delivery. You configure a server to use Message Queuing when you have one or more applications installed that use this feature.

TABLE 4.2: Windows Server 2008 Features *(CONTINUED)*

FEATURE	DESCRIPTION
Multipath I/O	This feature, along with the Microsoft Device Specific Module (DSM) provides the means to support multipath Input/Output (I/O) on the server. A multipath solution is similar to clustering, in that it provides a high reliability solution. However, it differs from clustering by focusing on the storage device, rather than an entire system. Consequently, Microsoft Multipath I/O (MPIO) has some significant advantages from a cost perspective.
Network Load Balancing	Network Load Balancing (NLB) distributes an application load across several servers. A main server accepts requests from the caller and then sends that request to the server in a server farm that has the smallest load. Using NLB helps your server farm scale better by distributing the load evenly. It also provides many of the same reliability benefits of clustering, but you use this solution (along with MPIO) in different circumstances.
Peer Name Resolution Protocol	Finding resources on a network relies on someone providing an identifier and someone else providing a name for that identifier. Sometimes the identifier is simply part of a search and, in other cases, the caller is looking for something specific. Most networks rely on DNS to resolve names, such as www.mycomputer.com, into an IP address, which is essentially an identifier. Sometimes DNS doesn't work as well as it should, so Microsoft came up with Peer Name Resolution Protocol (PNRP) to overcome DNS problems and to augment the DNS functionality.
Quality Windows Audio Video Experience	The Quality Windows Audio Video Experience (Qwave) provides a number of Audio Visual (AV) performance enhancement and management features. For example, using the Quality of Service (QoS) feature guarantees a specific level of performance, assuming your network can support the performance level in the first place. This isn't a run-of-the-mill corporate feature — Microsoft designed it with the home enthusiast in mind. However, it can work in the corporate setting for delivering training materials and engaging in conference calls, among other tasks.
Remote Assistance	The Remote Assistance feature works the same on the client system as it does on Windows Server 2008. You use this feature to provide remote assistance to the person using the computer. Generally, this feature makes sense on a workstation, especially workstations used by less experienced users, but it's probably not a feature that you'll need on Windows Server 2008 very often. Don't confuse this feature with Remote Desktop, which lets you control the server from a remote location.
Remote Differential Compression	In times past, whenever an application sent data across the network, it sent the entire dataset. Because the dataset was small, the cost of sending the entire dataset was also small. However, as the size of the dataset for any given transfer has increased, so has the cost of sending it. The Remote Differential Compression (RDC) feature makes it possible to send just the information that has changed, rather than the entire dataset across the network, which saves considerable time and resources. You can find more information about RDC at http://msdn2.microsoft.com/en-us/library/aa372948.aspx. The Web site at http://technet2.microsoft.com/windowsserver/en/library /8c4cf2e7-0b92-4643-acbd-abfa9f189d031033.mspx tells you how the Distributed File System (DFS) feature relies on RDC to perform its work.

TABLE 4.2:   Windows Server 2008 Features *(CONTINUED)*

FEATURE	DESCRIPTION
Remote Server Administration Tools	Installing this feature installs a number of Microsoft Management Console (MMC) snap-ins you can use to perform remote server administration of roles and features. Microsoft lets you install all the snap-ins, just the snap-ins for roles or features, or individual snap-ins for roles or features.
Removable Storage Manager	The Removable Storage Manager (RSM) catalogs any removable media you use on your server. It's also possible to use this feature to manage the catalogs that RSM creates.
RPC over HTTP Proxy	The Remote Procedure Call (RPC) technology has been around for many years. It's a technique for distributing an application across multiple systems. An application on one system calls a procedure found in a component on another system. Although the application is distributed and the client doesn't even necessarily know where it's calling for assistance, the entire system appears as a local application to the user. This technology is so old and stable you can find a 1988 specification for it at www.faqs.org/rfcs /rfc1050.html. Unfortunately, RPC doesn't work well across the Internet. Firewalls and other obstacles tend to break connections and cause other problems. An application that works perfectly on a LAN might break due to the new methods in which computers communicate over the Internet. The RPC over HTTP Proxy feature helps correct these problems by making it possible to use HTTP to perform the actual data transfer, rather than rely on older technologies to perform the task. RPC over HTTP Proxy is a technology that you install to meet specific application needs. In fact, the application may install it for you automatically. Never uninstall this feature unless you know you don't have any applications installed that require it. You can learn more about RPC over HTTP Proxy at http://technet.microsoft.com/en-us/library/bb124035.aspx. The Web site at www.computerperformance.co.uk/exchange2003/exchange2003_rpc_http.htm tells how Microsoft Exchange Server can use RPC over HTTP.
Simple TCP/IP Services	The Simple Transmission Control Protocol/Internet Protocol (TCP/IP) Services feature is a compatibility support item. You won't normally need to install this feature because it's unlikely that you'll need the services it provides. This feature provides support for the following TCP/IP requests: Character generator, Daytime, Discard, Echo, and Quote of the day. You can find additional information about these requests at www.tcpipguide.com /free/t_MiscellaneousTCPIPTroubleshootingProtocolsEchoDisc.htm.
SMTP Server	The Simple Mail Transfer Protocol (SMTP) is the basis for e-mail systems. You can actually combine various pieces of Windows Server 2008 to create a rudimentary e-mail system. However, most people will use this feature with a full-featured e-mail program. Generally, you'll install this feature to support a role such as the Web Server (IIS) role or you'll install it as part of your setup for a third-party e-mail product.
SNMP Services	The Simple Network Management Protocol (SNMP) is one of a number of methods you can use to manage your server. Windows Server 2008 actually provides a number of management technologies and the one you choose depends on your server and network setup. The advantage of SNMP is that it's standardized across many platforms. In fact, you can read the SNMP standard at www.cse.ohio-state.edu/cgi-bin/rfc /rfc1157.html.

TABLE 4.2:   Windows Server 2008 Features *(CONTINUED)*

FEATURE	DESCRIPTION
Storage Manager for SANs	A Storage Area Network (SAN) provides a means for maintaining hard drive storage external to a server. The SAN provides hard drives to a server and you can configure specific servers to rely on certain hard drives. By placing the hard drive external to the server, you can move storage around as needed to meet specific requirements. In addition, when a server becomes unavailable, you can quickly move its storage to another server.
Subsystem for UNIX-based Applications	The Subsystem for UNIX-based Applications (SUA) feature provides a level of cross-platform compatibility support. This support is relatively limited and you'll find that most modern UNIX applications can't use it. You can read more about SUA at `http://technet2.microsoft.com/WindowsServer/en/library/695ac415-d314-45df-b464-4c80ddc2b3bc1033.mspx`.
Telnet Client	Telnet is an ancient (in computer terms) technology for creating a connection between computers. It provides a basic connectivity option that works across most platforms today. In fact, you'll find Telnet used with devices such as routers too. Although Telnet doesn't provide much in the way of functionality, it does provide a rudimentary connectivity option that you should consider when other options are either inaccessible or not working. Generally, you can run most command line applications on the remote system using Telnet. Of course, this means knowing the command line utilities you want to use.
Telnet Server	A Telnet client requires a Telnet server in order to gain access to any system. The Telnet server doesn't provide access to everyone. In fact, Windows Server 2008 allows only members of the Administrators group access when using the default setup. However, you can configure Telnet for other scenarios as needed.
TFTP Client	The Trivial File Transfer Protocol (TFTP) client feature helps you perform file transfers from remote systems. This technology is standardized across platforms — you can read the specification for it at `www.faqs.org/rfcs/rfc1350.html`. In most cases, you'll use TFTP to work with embedded devices or other specialty devices using TCP/IP as the communication medium. You can read more about this technology at `www.tcpipguide.com/free/t_TrivialFileTransferProtocolTFTP.htm`.
Windows Internal Database	You'll never need to install the Windows Internal Database feature. That's because this feature provides a relational database for other Windows Server 2008 roles and features. Consequently, leave this particular feature alone because if it's installed, you actually do need it to meet a particular need.
Windows PowerShell	Windows PowerShell is the new command line. Unlike the command line that you've probably used in the past to manage Windows, this command line includes additional security features and provides access to managed applications (those supported by the .NET Framework). As with the command line you've used since the days of DOS with only a few changes, Windows PowerShell supports scripting. However, you'll find that the scripts you create using Windows PowerShell are significantly more powerful than those created for the command line and more reliable as well.

TABLE 4.2:   Windows Server 2008 Features *(CONTINUED)*

FEATURE	DESCRIPTION
Windows Process Activation Service	Microsoft has rebuilt IIS from the ground up. In fact, the IIS in Windows Server 2008 bears little resemblance to the IIS that you've worked with in the past. IIS has a completely new interface and the inner workings are equally different. One of the changes that Microsoft made was to implement a new process activation strategy — one that doesn't necessarily rely on an HTTP request. The Windows Process Activation Service feature is the new way to make your applications run with IIS and you'll find that it has a lot of offer. Like everything else Microsoft is doing these days, the Windows Process Activation Service also relies on managed code, so it relies on the Windows Communication Foundation (WCF) to accomplish tasks.
Windows Recovery Disc	At some point, a catastrophe will occur on your system and you'll find that it has reduced capability or may not boot at all. You may not receive any warning about the problem or even have a feeling of impending doom, but it will happen. A Windows Recovery Disc can help you overcome massive system failures. Although you can't rely on this strategy to recover your data, you can use it to recover your system quickly. Consequently, you'll also want to have a good system backup to help restore your data.
Windows Server Backups	It's impossible to have a good maintenance strategy without including a good backup. Any maintenance you perform must include a backup because a backup is the only good form of data protection at your disposal. Although Windows backup no longer provides the flexibility you obtained with previous versions of Windows, it's better than nothing at all.
Windows System Resource Manager	Your server has a number of valuable resources. It's possible for one application to attempt to grab all those resources and for other applications to become resource starved. Users may notice that the server's slow on some days, but not on others, and for apparently no reason at all. The Windows System Resource Manager (WSRM) feature helps you manage the CPU and memory resources on your server to improve performance and ensure applications work reliably.
WINS Server	The Windows Internet Naming Service (WINS) is another in a long line of methods of mapping a human readable name for an object into something the computer can understand. In this case, WINS maps a Network Basic Input/Output Service (NetBIOS) name into an IP address. Depending on your organization, you may not even use WINS any longer because other mapping services have replaced it. However, you may still need WINS, in some cases, especially when working with multiple platforms on the same network.
Wireless LAN Service	Most organizations have some number of wireless devices today. The Wireless Local Area Network (WLAN) service helps you configure your server to automatically poll for and configure wireless devices.

Installing Roles and Features

You'll install and uninstall roles and features as the needs of your organization change. In fact, you may install only the required roles and features first and then install others as you install applications. In short, this isn't a task that you'll perform just once. Whether you add roles or features using the Initial Configuration Tasks or Server Manager windows, the process is the same. You can only remove roles or features using Server Manager. The following sections focus on Server Manager because you'll use this utility the most. If you don't see Server Manager when you start your system, you can always open it using the Start ➢ Server Manager command.

Adding Roles

In Windows Server 2008, you still have access to the Add or Remove Programs applet as you did in the past. However, Microsoft has changed the name of this feature to Programs and Features. It's still possible to add or remove roles using this approach. Server Manager provides another option that you might want to try. Adding and removing roles can now rely on a wizard that helps you create a complete role, rather than installing a particular piece of software and finding that you didn't install enough.

This section describes the process of adding roles using the wizard. When accessing this wizard from the Initial Configuration Tasks window, start with step 2 on the wizard screen. You'll find the removing process described in the "Removing Roles" section of the chapter. The following steps describe how to add a role:

1. Open Server Manager, and choose Roles in the left pane. You'll see a Role summary view, as shown in Figure 4.15.

FIGURE 4.15
Server Manager
provides a list of the
roles installed on
your system.

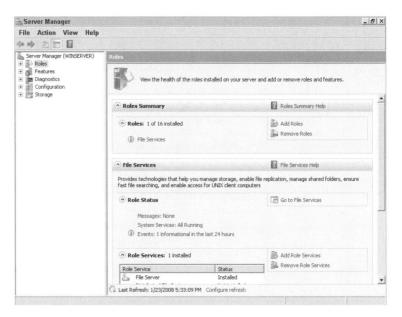

2. Click Add Roles. The Add Roles Wizard displays the Before You Begin page of the Add Roles Wizard dialog box. Make sure you read the instructions on this page before you proceed. You can avoid displaying this page every time you start the wizard by checking Skip this page by default.

3. Click Next. The Add Roles Wizard displays a list of available roles, as shown in Figure 4.16. The wizard automatically grays out any installed roles so you don't install them a second time.

FIGURE 4.16
Choose the roles you want to install on the server.

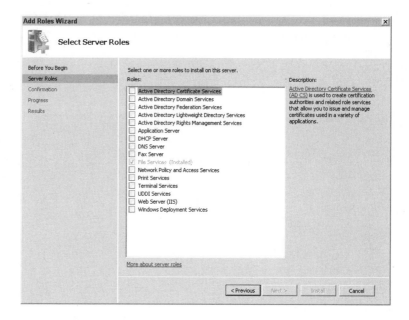

4. Check each of the roles you want to install. Notice that the wizard automatically grays out any roles you have already installed. When you select some roles, you'll see an Add Roles Wizard dialog box, such as the one shown in Figure 4.17 that tells you that you must install another role to obtain the desired functionality.

FIGURE 4.17
Some roles rely on other roles to work properly.

5. Click the Add Required Features button as needed to install dependent roles. As you add roles, the Add Roles Wizard also adds configuration steps as shown in Figure 4.18. These additional steps vary by role, so you may see many steps, in some cases, and only one or

two in others. An overview page at the beginning of each configuration step (such as the one shown in Figure 4.18) tells you what to expect and details the purpose of each step. Individual steps perform specific configuration tasks for that role. Be absolutely certain to read this information because it frequently contains configuration settings and recommendations that are extremely important to the proper functioning of the roles and features you will be adding.

FIGURE 4.18
Adding roles adds steps to the wizard to provide role configuration.

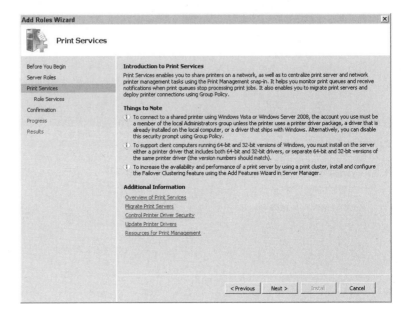

6. Perform any required configuration. Click Next for each additional configuration step. Sometimes a configuration step will add other roles to the server. For example, if you choose Internet Printing in the Role Services step for the Print Services role, you'll see an Add Roles Wizard dialog box like the one shown in Figure 4.17 to add the Web Server (IIS) role and Windows Process Activation Service feature when you don't have these elements installed.

7. Perform step 6 as often as necessary to configure each role. Eventually, you reach the Configuration Installation Selections page. This page tells you what the wizard will install.

8. Verify the installation information, and then click Install. You'll see the Installation Progress page. An indicator at the bottom of the page provides information on how much of the installation is complete. When the installation is complete, the Add Roles Wizard displays the Installation Results page where you can see the results of the installation. At this point, the installation is complete.

9. Click Close.

Removing Roles

At some point, you may decide to remove a role that you no longer need. Removing a role in the past was error prone because you couldn't be sure you had removed all the component parts. Windows Server 2008 improves on this process through the Remove Roles Wizard. The following steps describe how to remove a role you have installed on the server:

1. Open Server Manager, and choose Roles in the left pane. You'll see a Role summary view, as shown in Figure 4.15.

2. Click Remove Roles. The Remove Roles Wizard displays the Before You Begin page of the Remove Roles Wizard dialog box. Make sure you read the instructions on this page before you proceed. You can avoid displaying this page each time you start the wizard by checking "Skip this page by default."

3. Click Next. The Remove Roles Wizard displays a list of roles, as shown in Figure 4.19. The wizard automatically grays out any roles that you haven't installed.

FIGURE 4.19
Choose the roles you want to remove from the server.

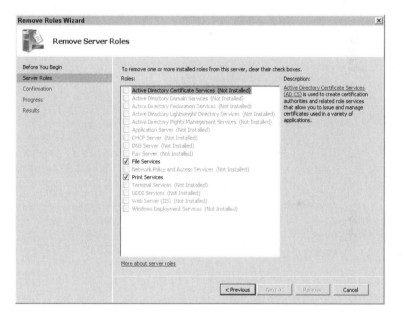

4. Click the check mark next to the role you want to remove. The Remove Roles Wizard adds steps to the process as necessary to remove the role completely. Not every role requires that you perform additional steps, so you may not see any additional roles.

5. Perform any required configuration. Click Next for each additional configuration step.

6. Perform step 5 as often as necessary to configure the removal process for each role. Eventually, you'll reach the Configuration Installation Selections page. This page tells you what the wizard will remove.

7. Verify the removal information, and then click Remove. You'll see the Removal Progress page. An indicator at the bottom of the page provides information on how much of the removal process is complete. When the removal process is complete, the Remove Roles Wizard displays the Removal Results page where you can see the results of the removal process. In most cases, this page will also tell you that you must reboot the server to complete the removal process.

8. Click Close. The Remove Roles Wizard will ask whether you want to restart the server now. To prevent damage to your server, you'll normally want to reboot immediately.

9. Click Yes. The server reboots. After the server reboots, you see a Resuming Configuration dialog box. Eventually, the Removal Results dialog box returns, and you'll see the results of the configuration process.

10. Click Close.

Adding and Removing Features

Windows Server 2008 comes without having any features installed. However, you'll find that it supports a host of features (some of which are required to support roles) as described in the "Determining the Need for Specific Roles and Features" section of the chapter. When you select Features in the left pane of Server Manager, you'll see a summary of the features currently installed on the server as shown in Figure 4.20.

FIGURE 4.20
Features help extend the functionality of your server.

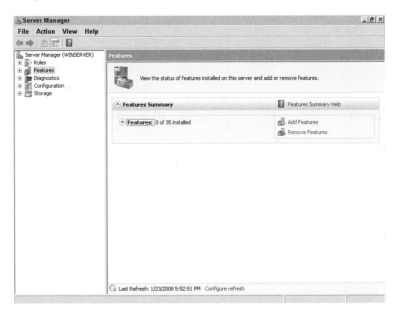

Adding and removing features is almost the same as adding and removing roles (see the "Adding Roles" and "Removing Roles" sections of the chapter for details). The main difference is that you'll see the Add Features Wizard shown in Figure 4.21 or the Remove Features Wizard in place of the Add Roles Wizard or Remove Roles Wizard. The basic concepts are the same, however.

FIGURE 4.21
Add new features using
the Add Features
Wizard.

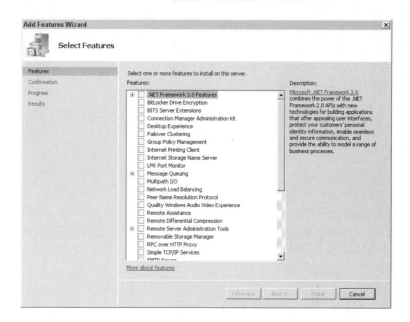

As with roles, some features will require you to add or remove other roles or features. For example, when you install the full .NET Framework 3.0 feature, you also need to install the Web Server (IIS) role and the Windows Process Activation Service feature. You'll even see the same dialog box shown in Figure 4.17 (except that the title bar says Add Features Wizard). In short, if you know how to add or remove a role, you also know how to add or remove a feature.

Chapter 5

Controlling Windows Server: MMC

How do you get Windows to work the way you want it to work? The answer is to perform configuration tasks — to manage Windows so that it acts the way you expect it to work. Think of management as a kind of training for Windows. Microsoft provides a number of tool types for managing Windows.

The tool that most administrators discover first is the Microsoft Management Console (MMC). MMC is a special kind of application that holds tools, rather than acting as a tool itself. This chapter describes how MMC works and shows you a few examples of working with it to perform useful tasks. You'll find a number of examples of working with MMC throughout the book. In fact, you've already worked with MMC to an extent without even realizing it when you added new users to Windows using the GUI, added or removed roles and features in the previous chapter, and performed other configuration tasks.

Before you start working with MMC, though, you'll want to spend some time configuring your Desktop. The default Desktop is better suited to a user who is using Windows to work with a word processor or to perform other data-specific tasks. Since you're an administrator, you'll want an administrator's Desktop, and this chapter shows you how to create one. An administrator's Desktop is exceptionally efficient, and it shows more information than a Desktop that a user needs. What I'm trying to accomplish in this chapter is to answer these questions:

- How do I make Windows Server 2008 look more like the Windows 2000/2003 environment?

- What is the MMC, and why do I need it?

- Which tools does Microsoft make available as part of MMC?

- How do I create a custom console should I need to do so?

Fixing the Server 2008 GUI

An administrator's Desktop normally focuses on Windows and the applications it supports. You want quick access to Windows features that make it possible to perform configuration tasks such as changing network settings or setting up new system features. The Desktop found in Windows Server 2008 is pretty barren — Microsoft designed it to look clean and simple for someone who works with data all day. At a minimum, an administrator's Desktop requires quick access to the Computer icon for system configuration, the Network icon for network configuration, and Internet Explorer to obtain updates and additional information about Windows functionality.

Along with the Desktop, Microsoft has redesigned the Start menu, which isn't a bad thing, except for a couple of nuisances. For one, the Run link has been moved from its former home right above the Shut Down and Log Off options to the adjacent column. If, like me, you are accustomed to rapidly launching programs from Start ➢ Run by entering the program filename (for example, Start ➢ Run ➢ CMD or Start ➢ Run ➢ COMPMGMT.MSC), this change can be a little disorienting. Another little nerve plucker is the new Start menu's way of putting links to your most recently used programs right above the place where the Run link used to be. Even worse, the list keeps changing as you work. All of these features are great for a user who works with data all day, but an administrator wants a stable Start menu to make it easier to find applications quickly.

TIP

You can use the Start Search field shown on the Start menu as a partial replacement for the Run dialog box. Simply type the name of the application you want to run and press Enter. Although this technique may seem a little odd given that you're theoretically performing a search, it does work.

The following sections describe how to configure your Desktop and Start menu to make them more efficient from an administrator perspective. Not everyone uses this setup, but many administrators do because it makes them more productive. Of course, if you also use your system for data-specific tasks, you may choose not to make all of these changes. The choice is ultimately yours to make. That's one of the reasons that the flexibility Windows provides is so great. My advice is to at least read through the following sections and decide whether you'd like to try the administrator's Desktop on your own machine.

NOTE

If you've already worked with Windows Server in previous versions, the following sections also provide some information about how things have changed in this version. For example, you'll discover that the Network icon is the replacement for the My Network Places icon found in previous versions of Windows. Anyone who hasn't worked much with Windows can safely ignore these little extras.

Restoring Your Desktop Icons and Start Menu

To restore the Computer and Network icons to your Desktop, right-click the Desktop, and choose Personalize. You'll see the Personalization window shown in Figure 5.1. Those of you who have worked with the Desktop Properties dialog box in the past won't see anything remotely familiar here. Microsoft still provides some, but not all of the elements of the Desktop Properties dialog box, but they're hidden several layers deep now. The main reason that Microsoft has made this change is to reduce the complexity of the interface.

To show Computer (formerly the My Computer icon) and Network (formerly My Network Places) on your Desktop, click Change Desktop Icons. You'll see the Desktop Icon Settings dialog box shown in Figure 5.2. Notice that Microsoft has provided access to additional icons in this version of Windows. Check the boxes next to those items in the Desktop Icons Settings dialog box that you want to display and click OK. You can also choose to display User's Files (used to be My Documents, but now it has the user's name under the icon), Control Panel, and Recycle Bin on your Desktop. Missing from previous versions of Windows is the ability to add or remove the Internet Explorer icon.

FIGURE 5.1

The Personalization window is Microsoft's attempt to make things easier.

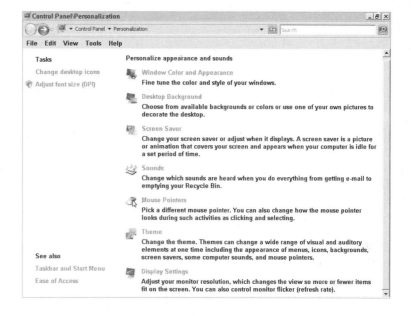

FIGURE 5.2

Customize your Desktop items.

To change the Start menu back to the Windows 2000 style, right-click the Start menu and choose Properties. Alternately, you can right-click the taskbar, choose Properties, then go to the Start Menu tab. Choose the radio button for the Classic Start menu (see Figure 5.3), and click OK.

FIGURE 5.3
The Start Menu Properties tab

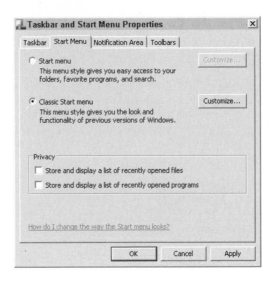

> **NOTE**
>
> If you configure your Display applet to show Computer on the Desktop, you can still right-click it and choose Manage, which launches the Server Manager (the alternative for the Computer Management console), or choose Properties to access the System window (the replacement destination for the System Properties dialog box). Likewise, after putting it back on the Desktop, right-click Network and choose Properties to launch the Network and Sharing Center applet (the replacement destination for the Network Connections window). The System Properties dialog box and Network Connections window both exist, but at a lower access level in Windows Server 2008.

Finally, if you like the new Start menu in general, but don't like every little thing about it, you may be able to fix it to suit you. Just click the corresponding Customize button in the taskbar and Start Menu Properties applet to see your options. For instance, many items on the new Start menu can be configured to act either as menus (they expand when you hover your mouse over them) or links (they open in a new window when you click them) or to not display at all.

From this same window, notice that Microsoft has added a new feature to Windows Server 2008 in the Privacy section. You can choose to clear both the recently opened files and recently opened programs lists. Although clearing these lists means that you have to do a little extra work to open files and start applications, these options do reduce the amount of information available to others who gain access to the system. It's a small change, but it's worthwhile clearing those lists to reduce the information left behind for other people to grab.

Setting Administrator-Friendly Folder Options

For administrators, the default folder options for Explorer can also be annoying. The context-sensitive task links that appear on the left side of every window may be helpful to some people, but they are just a waste of space to me. I need to see the hidden and system files, and in general,

Details view is best for maintenance operations. Unfortunately, Microsoft makes it impossible to remove the address bar in Windows Server 2008 and forget about removing the space-wasting buttons as well. However, there is still a lot you can do to make your environment "administrator friendly."

The first thing that I must do, then, when faced with a new system is to get Explorer into "administrator-friendly" mode. To save you time, here are the steps:

1. Open Computer.

2. From its menu bar, choose Tools ➤ Folder Options.

3. In the General tab, under Tasks, choose Use Windows Classic Folders.

4. Click the View tab.

5. Check the box labeled Display the Full Path in the Title Bar.

6. Click the radio button labeled Show Hidden Files and Folders.

7. Uncheck the box labeled Hide File Extensions for Known File Types.

8. Uncheck the box labeled Hide Protected Operating System Files (Recommended) and click Yes when it asks you to confirm your choice.

9. Click OK.

10. Back in the main Computer folder, click View ➤ Details.

11. Click the close icon on the Computer window — the icon in the upper-right corner that looks like an *X*.

Now reopen Computer, and apply those settings to all folders:

1. Click Tools ➤ Folder Options.

2. Click the View tab.

3. Click the button toward the top of the page labeled Apply to All Folders.

4. Click Yes to confirm the message.

5. Click OK to close Folder Options.

6. Close Computer.

Without all those empty calories, Explorer is now a lean, mean administrator's machine. To make it even leaner, you can navigate to individual folders and select Choose Details from the View menu to add or remove the details you want to see for that folder. For example, you might want to see the file system types for each logical drive in Computer, or you might not want to see the lengthy service descriptions in the Control Panel.

A Microsoft Management Console Primer

To master Windows Server administration, you must master the MMC. In the following sections, I'll discuss the key MMC terms you should know and briefly show the Computer Management console to illustrate these terms.

What Is This MMC Thing?

Before Windows 2000 came onto the scene, NT administrators had to master multiple administration tools plus independent third-party tools. With all the different menus, buttons, toolbars, wizards, tabs, HTML, Java (you get the picture), mastering a new tool's concepts took second place to learning how to navigate the software. NT Administrative software also lacked granularity. There was no simplified version of User Manager for Domains for Account Operators to use, and no way to hide sensitive menu items for those without full administrator rights. Administrative folks would typically install the full set of NT administrator tools on their workstations, whether they needed them all or not; if administrators failed to guard access to their desktops, or if regular users were permitted to log onto these administrative workstations, then anyone with the ability and knowledge could gain access to the entire range of management tools — not smart.

MMC was designed to overcome these limitations and accommodate the requirements of today's increasingly complex networks.

MMC is a framework for management applications, offering a unified administrative interface for Microsoft and third-party management tools. MMC doesn't replace management applications; it integrates them into one single interface. There are no inherent management functions in MMC at all. It uses component tools called *snap-ins*, which do all the work. MMC provides a user interface; it doesn't change how the snap-ins function.

MMC KEY BENEFITS

MMC offers the following benefits:

◆ You only have to learn one interface to drive a whole mess of tools.

◆ Third-party (ISV) tools are now using MMC snap-ins. IBM, HP, Seagate, and Symantec are all using the MMC framework to build admin tools for their products.

◆ You can build your own consoles, which is practical and fun. Admins can even create shortcuts on the console to non-MMC tools like executables, URLs, wizards, and scripts.

◆ By customizing MMC consoles, admins can delegate tasks to underlings without giving them access to all functions and without confusing them with a big scary tool.

◆ Help in MMC is context sensitive; it displays help subjects for only the appropriate components.

WHAT'S NEW WITH MMC?

Windows Server 2003 relies on the 5.*x* version of MMC 2, which provides a few enhancements over the original version of MMC. Microsoft makes a few changes to each version of MMC to improve it. MMC hasn't changed much since Windows Server 2003. When you move to Windows Server 2008, you'll notice a few minor changes in the new version (MMC 3 version 6.0).

◆ The Actions pane now appears to the right of the snap-in console. As you select items in the snap-in, the options in the Actions pane change. If you find the Actions pane unnecessarily uses a lot of screen real estate (as I do), then click the Show/Hide Actions Pane toggle button on the toolbar.

◆ The Add or Remove Snap-ins dialog box has a number of improvements that makes it easier to work with snap-ins. You can also easily control the extensions that you make available to snap-ins and control whether MMC can automatically enable snap-ins that become available later. Most importantly, you can rearrange snap-ins in a number of ways to make them easier to find. You can even nest snap-ins that rely on each other so you can see dependencies.

♦ Improved error handling is possibly one of the changes that you'll notice most. MMC is more proactive about catching errors now so it doesn't crash as often. You also have more options as to how the system responds to errors.

WHAT *CAN'T* YOU DO WITH MMC (NON-MMC TOOLS)?

When I said that MMC offers a unified interface for administration, I didn't mean that all administrative tools in Server 2008 are MMC-based. Many system-level functions are accessed using wizards or plain old executables. In general, you will use a wizard to add or remove new software and services or to set system-level options locally. Then, once a new service (DNS, Remote Access, DHCP, Active Directory) is installed, you can use an MMC tool to remotely configure it and monitor its activity. Let's also not forget all the new command-line tools that Microsoft has written for Server 2008. On the other hand, because MMC tools can be created and customized, you can integrate non-MMC apps into the MMC interface by creating links to them in your custom tools.

MMC Terms to Know

This section defines important terms you'll need to know when working with MMC.

A *console*, in MMC-speak, is made up of one or more administrative tools in an MMC framework. The admin tools that are included with Server 2008, like Active Directory Users and Computers, are console files. You can configure your own console files without any programming tools — you needn't be a C or Visual Basic programmer, as I'll discuss a bit later. The saved console file is a *Microsoft saved console (MSC)* file and it carries the .MSC extension.

It's important to distinguish between the Microsoft Management Console and console tools. The terms *console* and *tool* are sometimes used interchangeably when discussing MMC. Strictly speaking though, a console is not a tool, and as I pointed out in the previous section, not all tools are consoles. MMC.EXE is a program that presents administrators (and others creating console tools) with a blank console to work with. When you create a Microsoft Word document, you first load the program (WINWORD.EXE), then create or modify documents within that context. Similarly, you create MMC tools by first loading a blank console (MMC.EXE) and then creating a customized "document" based on the available options and add-ins. In this way, MMC provides a framework for your tool, and the new console you create is the finished product.

Snap-ins (also called *plug-ins*) are the administrative tools that can be added to the console. For example, the DHCP admin tool is a snap-in, and so is the Disk Defragmenter. Snap-ins can be created by Microsoft or by other software vendors. (You *do* need programming skills to make these, in other words.) A snap-in can contain subcomponents called *nodes*, or *containers*, or even *leaves*, in some cases. Although you can load multiple snap-ins in a single console, most of the prepackaged administrative tools contain only a single snap-in (including the Computer Management tool, COMPMGMT.MSC).

An *extension* is basically a snap-in that can't live by itself on the console but depends on a stand-alone snap-in. It adds some type of functionality to a snap-in. Sometimes the same code is implemented as both a snap-in and an extension. For example, the Event Viewer is a stand-alone snap-in, but it's also implemented as an extension to the Computer Management snap-in. The key point is that extensions are optional. You can choose not to load them. For example, Local Users and Groups is an extension to the Computer Management snap-in. If you remove the extension from the COMPMGMT.MSC file used by your support folk, or simply don't include it in a custom console that uses the snap-in, those who use the tool won't have the option to create or manage users and groups with the tool. They won't even see it. (Please note that this will not prevent them from creating users and groups by other means, if they have the correct administrative privileges.)

To create a new MSC file, customize an existing MSC file or create one from a blank console. The MMC.EXE plus the defined snap-ins, views, and custom tasks create the tool interface. Although it's possible to open multiple tools simultaneously, each one runs in a single instance of the MMC.EXE process. To see what I mean, open an MSC file and check out the Task Manager while it's running — you only see the MMC.EXE process running, not the MSC file, just as you see WINWORD.EXE running in Task Manager, but not the Word document's name. However, you can open separate *nodes* in separate windows within the tool. You could have separate windows open to the Event Viewer and the Device Manager within the same tool, for instance.

By default, prepackaged console tools open in *User mode*. Changes (both in look/layout and in tools used) cannot be made to the console design. You can't add or remove snap-ins, for example. To create or customize a console, use *Author mode*. When a user is running a tool and not configuring it, it should be running in one of the User modes. When a tool is running in Author mode, additional items will appear on the File and Action menus. Also, the Favorites menu doesn't appear in User mode consoles. Favorites can only be configured in Author mode.

Figure 5.4 shows a sample console tool, with the parts of the interface labeled. This console is running in Author mode to show all the parts of the MMC interface. This is a custom console, but to open any existing tool in Author mode, invoke it from the Start/Run dialog box with the /a switch. Alternately, right-click the tool's icon and choose Author to open it in Author mode. This does work with the links to tools in the Administrative Tools group, but remember not to overwrite the original file!

FIGURE 5.4

Anatomy of a console tool

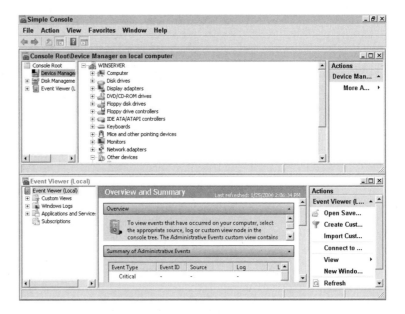

In addition to its traditional functions (New, Open, Save, Save As) the File menu in the Main window is used to add and remove snap-ins and set console options. The Action menu and the Toolbar are context sensitive and will reflect the options of the selected snap-in tool or component.

The Favorites menu functions like the Favorites menu in Explorer; however it stores only links to locations in the console tree.

The hierarchical list of items shown by default in the left pane is called the *console tree*, and at the top is the *console root*. The center pane is called the *details pane*. Snap-ins appear as nodes on the console tree. The contents of the details pane change with the item selected on the console tree.

The Computer Management Console

Now it's time to practice the new MMC terms you've learned as we take a look at the Computer Management console. COMPMGMT.MSC is *the* main tool for administering a single server, local or remote. If you only have one or two Server 2008 servers on your network (and are not implementing Active Directory), the Computer Management console contains most of the tools you'll need. You'll find Computer Management in the Administrative Tools program group, or right-click Computer on the Start menu and choose Manage.

USING COMPUTER MANAGEMENT REMOTELY

There are several ways to use COMPMGMT.MSC to manage remote servers on your network:

◆ Run COMPMGMT.MSC with the switch /COMPUTER = *COMPUTERNAME*.

◆ If you are working in an Active Directory context, within Active Directory Users and Computers, right-click the machine's icon and choose Manage.

◆ Open Computer Manager and highlight Computer Management (local) at the root of the console, then right-click and choose Connect to Another Computer.

◆ If you are creating a custom console that includes the Computer Management snap-in, specify the remote server the tool will point to when you add the snap-in, or check the box that allows you to specify the remote computer at the command line, as described in the first option.

There are three nodes in the Computer Management console tree: System Tools, Storage, and Services and Applications (see Figure 5.5). Notice that the tool manages the Local machine by default; to connect to other computers on the network, highlight the Computer Management icon at the root of the tree, right-click, and choose Connect to Another Computer. You can also choose Connect to Another Computer from the Action menu, but right-clicking an object in the console tree reveals both the Action and View menu options, so it's more efficient.

FIGURE 5.5

The Computer Management console tree

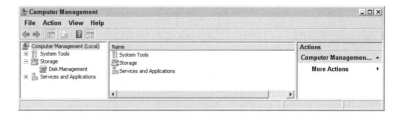

Expand the nodes in the Computer Management console tree to reveal the configuration tools and objects, as shown in Figure 5.6. Most of the core functions are under System Tools.

FIGURE 5.6
The expanded Computer Management console tree

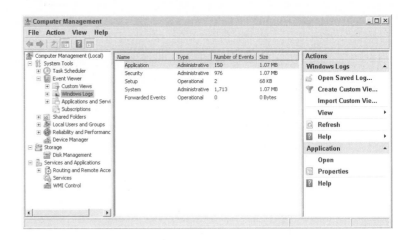

In the System Tools node, you can perform the following tasks:

◆ Schedule tasks that you want to perform automatically. The Task Scheduler can save you time by letting the machine remember to perform redundant tasks. In addition, it can make maintenance more reliable on your system by ensuring these tasks occur on time and at regular intervals.

◆ View events and manage the event logs. The Event Viewer is available as a snap-in, an extension to the Computer Management tool (as shown in this section), or as a stand-alone prepackaged tool (EVENTVWR.MSC). Some services, such as DNS and Active Directory, have their own logs and these will appear in the details pane if the service is installed on the system.

◆ Manage shared folders. View, create, and manage shares; view sessions and open files; and disconnect sessions.

◆ Create and manage local users and groups. If the system is a domain controller running Active Directory, however, the local users and groups extension will not load.

◆ Set up performance logs and alerts.

◆ Manage devices. This version of Device Manager functions in read-only mode when it's looking at remote systems, but it's still a good resource if you want an overview of the remote system's hardware or are troubleshooting a resource conflict.

TIP

For a better (but still read-only) look at a remote system's hardware and software configuration information, run MSINFO32.EXE. This little tool is powerful and includes options to run a search, view a history of changes, print system information, or export the data to a file.

The Storage node includes options for managing localized storage. Gone are features such as the Disk Defragmenter and Removable Storage snap-ins. Fortunately, the Removable Storage

Manager snap-in still exists — all you need to do is create a console to use it. The "Creating the Removable Storage Manager Console" section of the chapter describes how to perform this task.

The Services and Applications node includes, at a minimum, remote access settings, services configuration, and an indexing extension. As new services are installed on the system, the components available in the Services and Applications node will change. For instance, if the server is a DHCP server or is running DNS, the appropriate management tools will appear under Services and Applications — otherwise, you won't see them. I'm quite fond of this feature; when I'm checking out a server for the first time, I can determine what key services are installed on the system and look at the configuration for those services using the same tool.

Other MMC Tools

If you're like me, you don't want to get carpal tunnel syndrome just trying to open something from the Administrative Tools group. If you want to have quick and easy access to your tools, and you prefer to use Start/Run as much as possible to open programs, it's nice to know their filenames. To save your hands and your sanity, Table 5.1 lists most of the core MSC filenames. Keep in mind that some tools, like DNS and DHCP, may not be available on the system until the corresponding service is installed. Also, remember to include the program extension in the Start/Run box. For example, entering just DSA to open Active Directory Users & Computers doesn't work. You'll need to enter DSA.MSC.

TABLE 5.1:   Core MSC Files

MSC FILENAME	COMMON NAME
AzMan.MSC	Authorization Manager
CertMgr.MSC	CertMgr (Certificates – Current User)
COMExp.MSC	Component Services
CompMgmt.MSC	Computer Management
CompMgmtLauncher.EXE	Server Manager
DevMgmt.MSC	Device Manager
DiskMgmt.MSC	Disk Management
EventVwr.MSC	Event Viewer
FSMgmt.MSC	Shared Folders
GPEdit.MSC	Group Policy Editor
iSCSICPL.EXE	iSCSI Initiator
LUsrMgr.MSC	LUsrMgr (Local Users and Groups)
MdSched.EXE	Memory Diagnostics Tool

TABLE 5.1: Core MSC Files *(CONTINUED)*

MSC FILENAME	COMMON NAME
MSConfig.EXE	System Configuration
NAPC1Cfg.MSC	NAPClCfg (NAP Client Configuration)
ODBCAd32.EXE	Data Sources (ODBC)
PerfMon.MSC	Reliability and Performance Monitor
RSOP.MSC	Resultant Set of Policy
SCW.EXE	Security Configuration Wizard
SecPol.MSC	Local Security Policy
ServerManager.MSC	Server Manager
Services.MSC	Services
StorageMgmt.MSC	Share and Storage Management
StorExpl.MSC	Storage Explorer
TAPIMgmt.MSC	Telephony
TaskSchd.MSC	Task Scheduler
TPM.MSC	Trusted Platform Module
tsadmin.MSC	Terminal Services Manager
TSConfig.MSC	Terminal Services Configuration
TSMMC.MSC	Remote Desktops
WBAdmin.MSC	Windows Server Backup
WF.MSC	Windows Firewall with Advanced Security
WMIMgmt.MSC	WMIMgmt (Console Root \WMI Control)

Most of the tools listed in Table 5.1 are in the \Windows\system32 directory and are therefore in the default search path; you'll have no problem running them from a command line or using Start/Run. A couple, however, are in other directories that are not included in the default search path. If you need to run any of these tools on a regular basis, and they aren't in your search path and you still don't want to use the Start menu (boy, we admins sure can be stubborn), you have several options to make these tools more readily accessible. You can copy the tool(s) to the \Windows\system32 directory; or if you don't mind a cluttered Desktop, just create Desktop shortcuts to the tools. Another approach is to change the search path to include the directories that contain your tools. This is a bit more of a pain; you'll need to open the System applet and go to the

Advanced tab, then choose the Environmental Variables button to edit the system variable called Path. Oh, yes, and then reboot. Is it worth it? Many don't think so. In the past, I used this strategy: I copied all the tools I needed to a separate directory, and then added *that* directory to the search path. That way I didn't have to edit the path variable multiple times.

You may think this is a lot of trouble just to use a couple of tools, but after you install a bunch of third-party tools on your server you may change your mind. They'll probably all use their own installation directories.

Building Your Own MMC Tools

If the existing MMC tools don't fit your needs exactly, you can create a customized tool with your most frequently used components. Creating your own admin tool is easy using the MMC framework and snap-ins provided by Microsoft and third-party software vendors.

Although it's quite simple to create a customized MMC tool, there are so many options for customizing that I can't tell the full story here. Nevertheless, no discussion of MMC would be complete without an example or two of authoring administration tools.

Building a Simple Microsoft Saved Console

To configure your own custom admin tool, open a blank MMC in Author mode by opening Start/Run and typing `mmc.exe`. This will open an untitled console (Console1) and display a generic console root, shown in Figure 5.7. You can now open existing MSC files (just as you open DOC files in Word or XLS files in Excel) by choosing Open from the File menu. These files will automatically open in Author mode if you open them in a blank console. If you wish to open and fiddle with existing MSC files, most (but not all) of them are in the `\Windows\system32` directory. Just be sure to leave the original MSC files intact; you might need them again. In the example that follows, you'll be creating a tool from scratch, starting with a blank console and loading snap-ins.

FIGURE 5.7

A generic console root

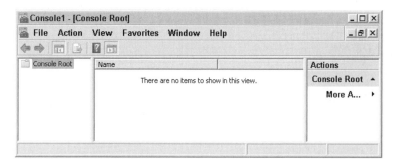

Suppose you need a tool for hardware management and troubleshooting. To create it, follow these steps:

1. Start by renaming the console root Hardware Tools; right-click the console root and choose Rename (you can perform this step later if you prefer).

2. Now you're ready to add snap-ins. Choose Add/Remove Snap-in from the File menu in the Main window. As you can see in Figure 5.8, you must choose where to add the snap-in. All you need to do is highlight one of the entries in the Selected snap-ins list. Right now, it's only possible to add snap-ins to the console root (now called `Hardware Tools`), but you can group related tools by first adding folders to the console root. Folders are implemented as snap-ins, permitting you to organize tools into groups on the console tree.

FIGURE 5.8
Choosing where to
add snap-ins

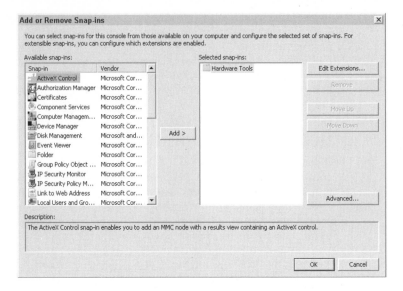

FIGURE 5.8
Choosing where to
add snap-ins

3. To add folders to the console root, highlight the Folder entry in the Available Snap-ins list and click Add. MMC will add a new folder to the list as shown in Figure 5.9. You can rename the folder later (after you leave the Add or Remove Snap-ins dialog box) by right-clicking its entry and choosing Rename from the context menu. For the purposes of this example, add three folders to the hierarchy. Click OK to close the Add or Remove Snap-ins dialog box.

FIGURE 5.9
Add a folder to the
hierarchy to group
snap-ins together.

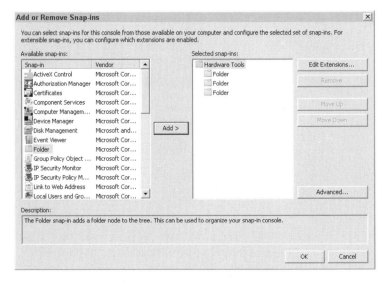

4. Back at the console in progress, right-click the folders to rename them. Figure 5.10 shows a Hardware Tools console with three folders, renamed to Disk Tools, Other Tools, and Web Sites.

FIGURE 5.10
Console1 with three
new folders

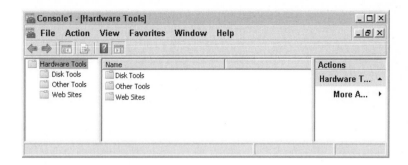

5. The Web Sites folder will contain snap-ins that are hyperlinks to hardware vendor and support sites. To add links to the Web Sites container, open the Add or Remove Snap-ins dialog box again (choose Add/Remove Snap-in from the File menu). In order to add an entry to the Web Sites folder, you must make it accessible. Click Advanced. Check the Allow changing the parent snap-in option in the Advanced dialog box, and click OK. The Add or Remove Snap-ins dialog box changes as shown in Figure 5.11. You can now add content to each of the folders you created earlier.

FIGURE 5.11
Customizing the console

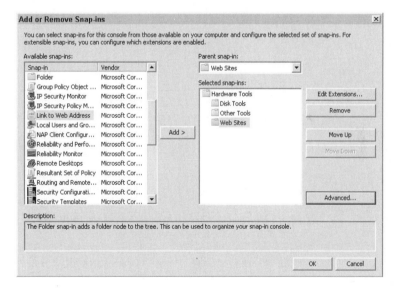

6. Select the Web Sites folder as the container in the Parent Snap-in list. Locate the Link to Web Address snap-in. Click the Add button, and follow the wizard prompts to create a new Internet shortcut; simply fill in the URL and give the shortcut a friendly name. Click OK to close the Add or Remove Snap-ins dialog box and return to the console. Now when you select the link in the console tree, the Web page will appear within the details pane (be patient, it can take a few seconds for the Web site to appear). You can surf the Web from within the console, although technically you'll need links to leave that particular site.

To add tools to the other folders, follow the same process and choose the appropriate tools from the list of snap-ins available. Some third-party software vendors are now implementing their tools as snap-ins, so this list will expand and vary with the system configuration and software installed. Some tools will prompt you to select a computer to manage. Others, such as the Event Viewer snap-in, also present the option to choose the machine when you start the tool from the command line, as shown in Figure 5.12. To specify a remote system to manage when you open the tool, enter **FILENAME.MSC /computer = computername** in the Start/Run box or at a command prompt.

FIGURE 5.12
Selecting a computer for the snap-in to manage

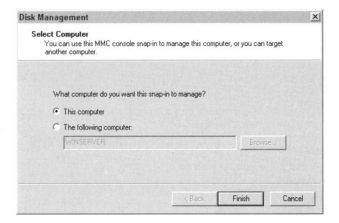

While adding the stand-alone snap-ins, be sure to check out the available extensions for them. To change the extensions, highlight the snap-in entry and click Edit Extensions. Choose the Enable Only Selected Extensions option and clear the checks next to any extensions you don't want to use. It's interesting to note that the Computer Management snap-in components are all implemented as extensions (see Figure 5.13), although most of these also exist as stand-alone snap-ins. When loading the Computer Management snap-in, you have the option to deselect the extensions that aren't needed for your custom tool. All available extensions are added by default.

In Figure 5.14, you can see what your final tool could look like: a customized Hardware Tools console. This one consists of a Disk Tools folder (with Disk Management), a folder called Other Tools that includes the Device Manager and the Event Viewer, and a Web Sites folder that can be filled with helpful hardware support links.

To save the custom console, choose Save from the File menu, name the file and click Save. Now the MSC file is ready to use.

Creating the Removable Storage Manager Console

The Removable Storage Manager (RSM) helps you work with storage that isn't a permanent part of the server. You use the RSM to monitor removable storage on your server (or any other machine, for that matter) such as DVDs, CDs, and flash disks. These devices work, even if you don't install RSM. All the RSM does is provide a monitoring capability.

FIGURE 5.13
Select or deselect
extensions.

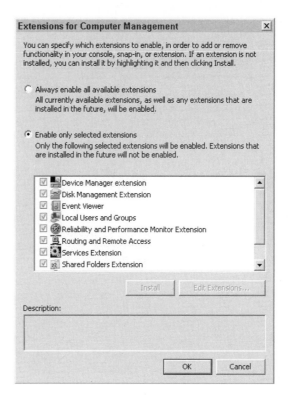

FIGURE 5.14
A custom Hardware
Tools console

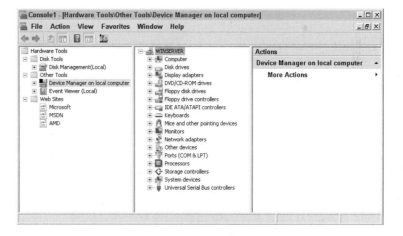

One oddity of the RSM installation is that Microsoft doesn't create a console for you in the Administrative Tools folder of the Control Panel. This feature used to appear as part of the Computer Management console, but Microsoft has removed it. A monitoring feature isn't much good without some means of performing the monitoring, so you need to create a console on your own. The following steps tell you how to perform this task:

1. Open a blank MMC console using the technique described in the "Building a Simple Microsoft Saved Console" section of the chapter.

2. Choose File ➤ Add/Remove Snap-in. The Microsoft Management Console (MMC) displays the Add or Remove Snap-ins dialog box.

3. Locate the Removable Storage Management entry and then click Add. MMC displays the Select Computer dialog box.

4. Choose the computer you want to monitor using this dialog box. In fact, a single console can contain multiple copies of the same snap-in, all of which are monitoring a different computer.

5. Select the Local Computer option.

6. Check the Allow the selected computer to be changed when launching from the command line option.

7. Click Finish. MMC adds the snap-in to the Selected Snap-ins list.

8. Click OK. The blank console now contains the Removable Storage Management snap-in you configured.

9. Choose File ➤ Save. Windows displays the Save As dialog box. Notice that this dialog box automatically chooses the Administrative Tools folder as the storage place for the console you just created. Unless you have a good reason for not sharing the console with other administrators, maintain this storage location.

10. Type **Removable Storage Manager.MSC**, and click Save. MMC changes the title of the console to match the name of the Microsoft Console (MSC) file, as shown in Figure 5.15. In addition, you now see the Removable Storage Manager in the Administrative Tools folder of the Control Panel, where you can access it as needed.

FIGURE 5.15
The new console provides complete information about RSM.

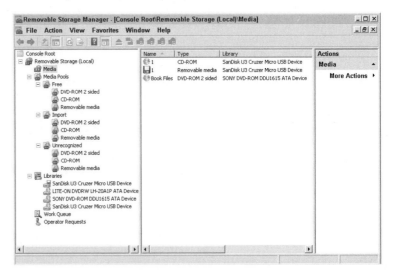

Chapter 6

Controlling Windows Server: The Command Line

When you get to this chapter, you might ask the question, "What is a command line — I thought Windows was about graphics?" Many years ago there was DOS — the Disk Operating System. DOS was very basic. You could only run one task at a time and it didn't have many of the features that people expect today. To run a task, you simply typed its name at the command line (or the command prompt as some people say — Microsoft uses both terms). Everything on the computer was in text back then. The task ran and then the computer waited for you to type another command. The command line in Windows is a legacy of DOS. Just like DOS, you type in the name of a command, press Enter, wait for the results, and type the next command.

Of course, this sounds easy, so why do we need graphics? People said DOS was hard to use because you had to remember tons of commands and type them at the command line without error, so vendors created Graphical User Interfaces (GUIs) to make issuing the commands easier. Unfortunately, GUIs have grown to the point that now *graphical* things have become hard to find! Now, the GUIs are gooey and many administrators are returning to the command line to gain some level of productivity. In fact, some experienced administrators never left. The command line isn't this scary place that only geniuses use — it's the root of computer use that people have forgotten over the years.

The command line is actually pretty neat. You can type commands quickly without traversing endless menus. The commands can easily appear within batch files (an automated way of executing commands), so you don't have to type them at all. Of course, you still have to type the batch filename, but after that, everything is automated. The reason that smart administrators never left the command line is because it's incredibly flexible, simple to understand, and works precisely the same way every time. The only problem is remembering all of those commands, but there is even a somewhat easy method for overcoming that problem.

You've already used the command line several times in this book to perform some basic tasks. For example, you used it in Chapter 2 to create a share. Chapter 3 relied on the command line to work with a guy named Joe. The command line helped you configure part of Joe's account. Chapter 5 showed you how to start a console from the command line. In sum, you already know something about the command line and it probably turned out to be quite useful for you. This chapter fills in some of the details for you. What I'm trying to accomplish in this chapter is to answer these questions:

- ◆ Why do you want to use the command line?
- ◆ How do I work at the command line?

◆ What are some of the ways in which I can use the command line to perform useful work?

◆ How do I automate the command line so I don't have to remember quite so many of the commands on my own?

Why You Give a Hoot about the Command Line Interface

Many people think of the command line as an antiquated leftover from the past. It's true that you can perform most of the tasks that you perform at the command line using a GUI equivalent. However, the command line excels at meeting some needs, such as accomplishing a task quickly or automating specific kinds of tasks. In some cases, the command line really isn't the best tool and you need to know about those situations as well. For example, the command line doesn't provide graphic output (such as a colored pie chart showing disk usage or fragmentation), so you need to use a GUI for that task.

Before you go any further, you'll want to open a command prompt on your server machine (make sure you log on as Administrator). Choose Start ➢ Programs ➢ Accessories. Right-click the Command Prompt entry and choose Run as Administrator from the context menu (make sure you log in at the UAC prompt as required). Use this command prompt to try out the commands listed in the following sections so you can see how they work. It's important to try the commands out so you can better see what the command prompt can do for you.

The following sections tell you about the wonders of the command line. You'll also discover when you might consider replacing it with a GUI equivalent so you can get the best of both worlds.

Reasons to Use the Command Line

There are many good reasons to rely on the command line as one of the tools in your administrator toolbox. For example, when you want to create a share, you can use Windows Explorer to do it or you can go the command line route. Let's just look at the share issue. When you want to create a share in Windows Explorer, you'll spend several minutes clicking through dialog boxes to do it. Check out the "Sharing Resources with Other Computers" section of Chapter 2 again and you'll see that it requires no less than 15 steps to create a share with Windows Explorer. To create the same share at the command line, you use a single command, Net Share. For example, if you want to share the D drive on your machine as Drive_D, you'd type **Net Share Drive_D=D:** and press Enter. That's it! The command line displays a success message saying, "Drive_D was shared successfully." Of course, you have to know the Net Share command, but you have to admit that using it is fast. Therefore, the first reason to use the command line is speed — it lets you work incredibly fast.

TIP

If you find that your command line display is getting messy, type **CLS**, for clear screen, and press Enter. The window will clear and all you'll see is the standard command prompt.

Now, let's extend this conversation about shares a little. Let's say you want to see everything you're sharing quickly. Well, if you're using the GUI, you have to rely on several tools to get this information. For example, you can open the Computer Management console we discussed in Chapter 5 and view System Tools\Shared Folders\Shares to see which drives you're sharing.

Unfortunately, this view doesn't tell you anything about printers. When you type **Net Share** and press Enter, you see a complete list of every share on your system, printers included, from one location as shown in Figure 6.1 (your display will contain different shares from the ones shown in Figure 6.1). Using the command line is convenient. You can often get more information with less effort at the command line. Of course, you trade this convenience for formatting — no one will ever accuse of the command line of outputting pretty data.

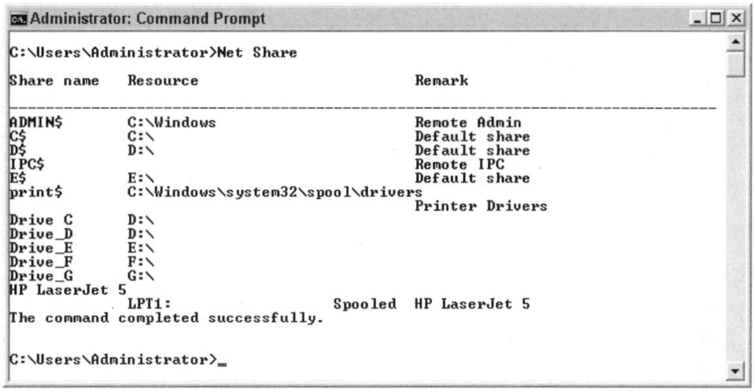

FIGURE 6.1

Use the Net Share command to obtain a complete list of shares on your system.

Talking about getting more information, the command line often provides you with information that you can't find in the GUI at all. For example, if you want to obtain a full list of the service packs and patches installed on a system, type **WMIC QFE List Full** and press Enter. Figure 6.2 shows typical results (in this case, you're actually looking at a Windows XP system, but the results are the same on Windows Server 2008). What you'll see is a list of all of the service packs and patches on the local system. The information includes the service pack or patch name, description, installation date, and who installed it, along with a wealth of other useful information, such as the hotfix identifier. The hotfix identifier is specially important because you can use this number to look up complete information about the service pack or patch on Microsoft's Knowledge Base (http://support.microsoft.com/). Just type the hotfix identifier into the Search field and press Enter. You'll find it difficult to obtain this information in the GUI because the GUI doesn't even display all of the services packs and patches in most cases.

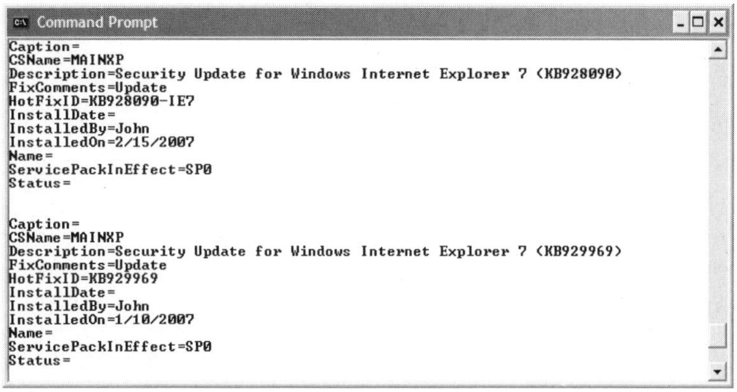

FIGURE 6.2

Obtain a complete list of the service packs and patches on your system.

The command line can also provide access to special features of your GUI applications. You may not realize it, but the Notepad application has command-line switches associated with it. For example, to print a document named Hello.TXT, you'd type **Notepad /p Hello.TXT** at the command line and press Enter. In this case, you're typing the name of the application, which is the Notepad application, the /p command-line switch (print), and the name of the file. Notepad will start, load Hello.TXT, send the file to the printer, and close, all without you clicking anything. Of course, this command line sends the file to the default printer. If you want to send the file to another printer, you'd type **Notepad /pt Hello.TXT MyPrinter** and press Enter. The difference is that you're using the /pt command-line switch (print to) and adding the name of a printer to use. Many other programs offer the same functionality. You can exercise program features without ever opening the program yourself. This example also points out that GUI applications and command line applications aren't necessarily different — you simply work with the application in a different way. The "Basic Command Examples" section of the chapter tells you about a number of other useful commands you should know about when working at the command line.

Sometimes you'll encounter a situation where there isn't any other way of performing a task than to use the command line. For example, you may find that you can't configure your router without using a command line application. Many older routers use a special application named Telnet to perform the task. Likewise, your motherboard may use a command line application to perform certain kinds of updates, and you'll find other hardware that relies on the command line as well. Although the situations where you must use the command line are rare, knowing how to use the command line when you need it is an important part of being an administrator.

Working at the command line can help you automate tasks. By placing the commands you want to execute on individual lines in a text file, you can create a *batch* file. A batch file has a BAT file extension and it contains a list of things you want the operating system to do for you. To execute the batch file, you simply type its name at the command line and press Enter. Consequently, the efficiency gains you see by using the command line can greatly increase with a little extra work. The "Simple Batch Files" section of the chapter tells you more about creating your own batch files.

TIP

Microsoft has introduced a new version of Windows called Server Core. The Server Core version is stripped of GUI tools for the most part — no Start menu, no Toolbar, no Desktop to speak of, and no Administrative Tools folder. In fact, Server Core is missing most of the tools that you have used in the past, so the Server Core environment requires that you know the command line. Why would you use such an environment? It provides a significant improvement in performance, reliability, and security. You can actually use Windows Server 2008 Full version to discover the command line and then move to Server Core to obtain all of the benefits it provides.

Situations Where the Command Line Is Less Useful

When you think about working at the command line, think fast and efficient — don't think beautiful or user friendly. In fact, I normally suggest that new administrators spend time working with the command line on a test machine because seemingly small spelling errors can cause all kinds of problems. The issue isn't one of being afraid to use the command line — you truly can't escape it — it is one of learning to type the commands correctly. The only way you can learn to type the commands correctly is to practice them as you work. It usually doesn't take long for you to memorize your favorite commands and discover how to use them for the tasks you commonly perform.

The "Getting Help at the Command Line" section of the chapter describes how you can overcome some of the difficulties of using the command line, but the fact remains that it isn't user friendly. When you need to perform a task with close to 100 percent reliability, the GUI is often the best choice.

The ease of use issue can also come into play when you need to perform complex tasks. The example in this section shows that you can use a friendly GUI utility to share resources without error and without learning arcane command line syntax, or you can use the error prone command line interface. The Share utility example in the previous section is quite fast and easy. However, it gives access to the share to the Everyone group, which may not be what you expect. Yes, you can still use the ICACLs utility as you did in the "Understanding Authentication Versus Authorization" section of Chapter 3 to secure the folder, but setting proper security for the share is also a requirement. Unfortunately, the Share utility doesn't provide this functionality. In order to set the share to use a particular security setup from the command line, you must download a separate utility called SubInACL (`http://www.microsoft.com/downloads/details.aspx?FamilyId=E8BA3E56-D8FE-4A91-93CF-ED6985E3927B`). So, the first problem with the command line is that it may not provide all of the functionality you need to perform every task.

Go ahead and download this tool now — it's incredibly useful. Install the tool by double-clicking the `SubInACL.MSI` file and following the prompts. Now, let's deny access to the Everyone group and give full access to the Administrators group. You'll need to change directories to the SubInACL tool. Type **CD `"C:\Program Files\Windows Resource Kits\Tools\"`** (many command line utilities require that you add double quotes when an argument has spaces in it — the CD command is one of the few that will work with or without the spaces, try it both ways to see for yourself) and press Enter.

TIP

You may have noticed that the CD command used in this section requires a lot of typing. One of the command line shortcuts you should try is the Tab key. Try typing **CD `C:\Pr`** and pressing Tab. The command prompt automatically converts this input to CD `"C:\Program Files\"`. Notice that the command prompt automatically adds the quotes for you, even though you didn't type them. Press the left arrow, type **`\Win`** and press Tab again. The command prompt will probably display CD `"C:\Program Files\Windows Mail"` at this point. Don't worry, press Tab again and you'll notice that the directory changes. Keep pressing Tab until the command prompt chooses the correct subdirectory (Windows Resource Kits) for you. This technique helps you type long directory entries quickly and without error.

Now that you're in the correct directory, you can perform the required tasks. To remove access to the Everyone group, type **SubInACL /Share Drive_D /Revoke=Everyone** and press Enter. Wow, that's a lot of odd typing, but this example doesn't even begin to illustrate how long some command line sequences can become! Of course, you can reduce the complexity by breaking the command into its components. The `SubInACL` utility requires that you provide an object type, which is `/Share` in this case. You must follow the object type with an object name, which is Drive_D in this case. After the object information comes an action. You want to remove the Everyone group, so you use the `/Revoke` action. Finally, you must specify any arguments for the action, which is the Everyone group in this case.

Your display will look like the one shown in Figure 6.3 after you execute the `SubInACL` command. The output tells you that the system permanently removed the Access Control Entry (ACE), numbered 0, for the Everyone group. Removing this ACE required one change to the security for this share. The time to perform this task was unbelievably fast. The SubInACL utility performed one task, it was a modification task, and the utility didn't experience any failures or syntax errors. Failures can occur for a number of reasons, such as a lack of rights on your part. A syntax error occurs when you type the information at the command line incorrectly. The SubInACL utility will usually provide help to fix the typing mistake.

FIGURE 6.3
Remove users and groups as needed from the share to prevent them from using it.

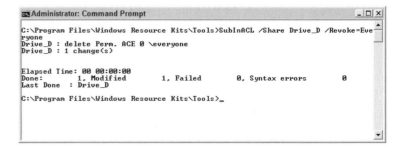

To give the Administrators group full access to the share, you type **SubInACL /Share Drive_D /Grant=Administrators=F** and press Enter (see Figure 6.4 for the results). This command follows the same pattern — you provide an object type, object name, action, and arguments. The letter F tells the application to give the Administrators group full access. This little demonstration also points out that working with the command line isn't always straightforward. Sometimes you have to combine several commands to achieve a desired result. This example also shows that you may not always have all of the tools you require to get the job done.

FIGURE 6.4
Add users and groups as needed to the share to allow them to use it.

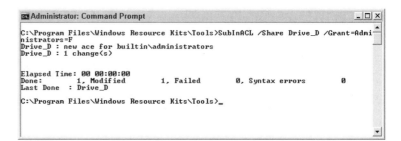

Some command line limitations are almost instantly obvious. For example, you won't get heavily formatted output from the command line. Even the text you do get is quite plain. You normally need to perform additional work to create the reports you need that are based on command line utility output. Forget about getting graphics from command line applications. If you need graphics, then you need to use the GUI. Even with these limitations, however, using the command line can be exceptionally productive.

Elements of the Command Line

The command line is a different environment from the GUI provided by Windows. For example, you can open two kinds of command line — one has fewer rights than the other. The Command Prompt also provides a number of configuration options, such as the color of the text and background. You can control the size of the text, the window, and features such as the amount of information the Command Prompt stores for later use. It's also possible to personalize the appearance of the prompt and control how the command line works from a functional perspective. Finally, you also have access to special command lines. The sections that follow describe these and other environmental topics.

Command Line Rights

Windows Server 2008 provides additional security for the user, including administrative users, over previous versions of Windows. The User Account Control (UAC) feature affects the administrator as much as it does any other user. When you perform certain tasks, Windows Server 2008 asks your permission to escalate (increase) your rights. This protection may seem annoying at first, but it can save you many headaches later.

Unlike the GUI environment, the command line doesn't ask your permission to escalate your rights when you need to perform a task that requires administrator privileges. Instead, the command will simply tell you that it failed — no explanations offered. When you open a command line by simply choosing Start ➤ Programs ➤ Accessories ➤ Command Prompt, you have the rights of a standard user (the Administrator account always works in the Admin Approval mode in Windows Server 2008, unless you change the security settings to work otherwise). These rights work for most of the command line tasks you perform and you should use the restricted command line whenever possible. Try the following steps to see how this works for yourself.

1. Log into the Joe account you created in Chapter 3.

2. Choose Start ➤ Programs ➤ Accessories ➤ Command Prompt to open a standard command prompt.

3. Type **CD C:\Program Files\Windows Resource Kits\Tools** and press Enter.

4. Type **SubInACL /Share Drive_D /Grant=Joe=F** and press Enter. Instead of seeing the success message shown in Figure 6.4, you now see the failure message shown in Figure 6.5. At least the SubInACL utility provides you a clue as to the source of the problem by providing the "Access is denied." error message. The problem is that you don't have the rights required to use the command line. Notice that the title bar in Figure 6.5 simply says Command Prompt and not Administrator: Command Prompt. This difference is your clue that you need more security. Now let's see how to fix this problem.

FIGURE 6.5
A lack of rights can cause problems when using some utilities.

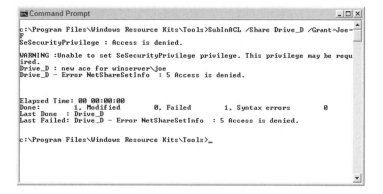

5. Choose Start ➤ Programs ➤ Accessories. Right-click Command Prompt and choose Run as Administrator from the context menu. You'll see a User Account Control dialog box.

6. Select the Administrator account and type the administrator password in the field provided. Click OK. Notice that the new window displays Administrator: Command Prompt on the title bar.

7. Type **CD C:\Program Files\Windows Resource Kits\Tools** and press Enter.

8. Type **SubInACL /Share Drive_D /Grant=Joe=F** and press Enter. This time, you are able to grant Joe full access to the Drive_D share. The only difference is that you used an administrator command line to perform the task.

Command Prompt Window Configuration

Most Windows elements provide some level of configuration and the command prompt is no exception. You can configure the command prompt to use different colors (the default is a black background with light gray text), fonts, font sizes, and even a different window size so you can see more of what's going on. You can also set special options, such as creating a larger cursor or modify the way that you edit command line text.

You can change the command prompt configuration at two levels. The first level is a custom setting for a particular command prompt based on the title bar text. For example, you can configure the Command Prompt window to use different colors from the Administrator: Command Prompt so that you don't confuse the two. To access this level of configuration, click the icon in the upper-left corner and choose Properties from the menu.

The second level is the default setting for any command prompt that doesn't have a custom setting. If you don't define custom settings for the command prompt that displays Hello Joe in the title bar, then you'll see the default configuration for it. To access this level of configuration, click the icon in the upper-left corner and choose Defaults from the menu. In both cases, you'll see a Properties dialog box like the one shown in Figure 6.6.

FIGURE 6.6
Modify the command prompt settings to meet your specific needs.

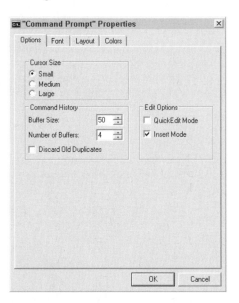

Now that you can see the settings, let's talk about them in detail. The following sections describe each of the tabs found in the Properties window.

Setting the Window Options

The Options tab shown in Figure 6.6 defines how the command window reacts when you open it. The Cursor Size option controls the size of the cursor, with small being the default. The Large option provides a block cursor that is very easy to see on a laptop.

TIP

Those of you who have worked with other versions of Windows may notice that the Display Options group is missing from Figure 6.6. The Display Options determine whether you see the command window full screen or as a window. Full screen mode uses the entire display area for the command prompt. Using the full screen mode when you have a number of tasks to perform is easier on the eyes. However, Microsoft has removed this option for some reason. If you want to change to full screen mode as the default setting, open the Registry Editor (explained in full detail in Chapter 7) by choosing Start ➤ Run, typing **RegEdit** in the Open field, and clicking OK. Highlight the HKEY_CURRENT_USER\Console key. Double-click the Full Screen value and type **1** as the value. Click OK. The command prompt will now open in full screen mode. As an alternative to using the Registry Editor, you can also use the Reg command to make the change. Type **Reg Add "HKCU\Console" /v "FullScreen" /t REG_DWORD /d 1 /f** and press Enter to accomplish this task. The Reg command begins with the location of the key you want to change. The /v command-line switch provides the value you want to change. The /t command-line switch tells the data type of the value you want to change. The /d command-line switch contains the new value you want to use. The /f command-line switch forces the Reg command to complete the change without asking about overwriting existing values.

The Command History group is especially important because it determines how the command prompt stores previous commands that you issue. Here is the meaning of each of these entries.

◆ The Buffer Size option determines the number of commands the buffer will store. Every command requires memory, so increasing this number increases the amount of memory the command prompt requires. Increase this number when you plan to perform a number of complex commands. A smaller number will save memory for larger command line applications.

◆ The Number of Buffers option controls the number of individual histories. You need one history for each process (application environment) you create. Generally, the four shown work fine.

◆ The Discard Old Duplicates option tells the command prompt to remove any old commands from the history that duplicate current commands. Using this feature can save space for a larger number of unique commands.

The Edit Options determine how you interact with the command window. Here is the meaning of each of these entries.

◆ Check the QuickEdit Mode when you want to use the mouse to work with the entries directly. The only problem with using this feature is that it can interfere with some commands such as Edit that have a mouse interface of their own.

◆ The Insert Mode option lets you paste text into the command window without replacing the text currently there. For example, you might copy some information from a Windows application and paste it as an argument for a command.

CHANGING THE FONT

The Font tab shown in Figure 6.7 controls the font used to display text. The font size automatically changes when you resize the window, but you can also control the font size directly using this tab. The Font list selection controls the kind of font the command prompt uses as described in this list.

FIGURE 6.7
Use the Font tab to control the size of the text in the command window.

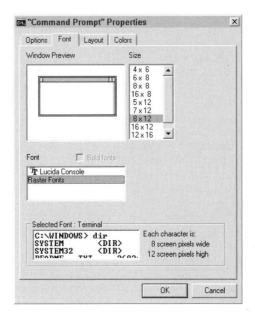

◆ The Raster Fonts give the typical command line font appearance that works well for most quick tasks. This is also the best font to use in full screen mode.

◆ The Lucida Console font works better in a windowed environment. It's easier on the eyes because it's smoother, but you might find that some applications won't work well with it if they create "text graphics" using some of the extended ASCII characters. The extended ASCII characters include corners and lines that a developer can use to draw boxes and add visual detail.

The Size list displays a list of font sizes you can use with the current Font selection. A larger size is easier on the eyes, while a smaller size lets you display more information. You can see the results of the Font and Size field selections you make in the Selected Font: Terminal window.

CHOOSING A WINDOW LAYOUT

The Layout tab shown in Figure 6.8 has the potential to affect your use of the command window greatly when working in windowed mode. You use the settings to control the window's physical size and position, as well as the virtual window used to store information that scrolls off of the physical display area. The following list describes the three configuration groups.

FIGURE 6.8
Change the size and positioning of the command window using the Layout tab.

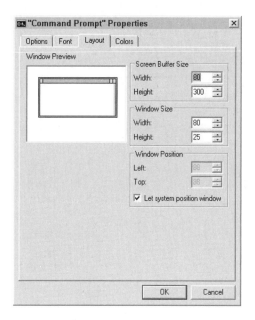

- ◆ The Screen Buffer Size controls the width and height of the screen buffer, the total area used to display information. This is the virtual display area — the whole area that you have to store command information. You can make this area larger than the physical display area of your screen.

- ◆ The Window Size controls the physical screen area used to display command prompt information. This setting must fit within the physical limits of your screen. When the Window Size setting is smaller than the Screen Buffer Size, Windows provides scroll bars so you can move the window around within the buffer area and view all it contains. Some commands require a great deal of space for display purposes. Adjusting the Screen Buffer Size and Window Size can help you view all of the information these commands provide.

- ◆ The Window Position determines where Windows places the command window when you first open it. Some people prefer a specific position on the screen so they always know where a new command window will appear. However, it's generally safe to check "Let system position window" to allow Windows to place the command window on screen. Each command window will appear at a different, randomly chosen, position on screen.

DEFINING THE TEXT COLORS

Text colors can affect how easy the screen is to see as well as cue you into specific command prompt windows. Microsoft assumes that you want a black background with light gray letters for the command window. Although DOS used this setting all those years ago, many people today want a choice. The Color tab lets you choose different foreground, background, and pop-up colors for the command window (even though Figure 6.9 doesn't show the colors, it does present the dialog box layout). You can modify the window to use any of the 16 standard color combinations for any of the text options. Use the Selected Color Values options to create custom colors.

FIGURE 6.9
Modify the text colors
for an optimal display
using the Colors tab.

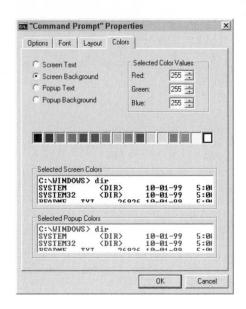

Command Prompt Personalization

The default command prompt provides the drive, current location on the drive (directory), and a greater than sign as shown in most of the screenshots in this chapter. For example, when you first open a command prompt, you'll probably see C:\Users\Administrator> as the prompt.

You don't have to maintain the default prompt if you don't want to. In fact, many people create a custom prompt to display specific information. For example, if you work at the command prompt in full screen mode all day, you may want the prompt to display the current date and time. Fortunately, you don't have to stick with Microsoft's choice of prompt. Table 6.1 displays a list of special items you can display at the prompt.

TABLE 6.1:   Command Prompt Personalization Values

VALUE	DESCRIPTION
$N	Current drive
$P	Current drive and path
$T	Current time in HH:MM:SS.mm format
$D	Current date in DayOfWeek MM/DD/YY format
$V	Windows version number
$H	Deletes the previous character
$G	Displays a greater than (>) sign
$L	Displays a less than (<) sign

TABLE 6.1:   Command Prompt Personalization Values *(CONTINUED)*

VALUE	DESCRIPTION
$C	Displays an opening parenthesis: (
$F	Displays a closing parenthesis:)
$S	Displays a space
$_	Creates a new line
%computername%	Displays the computer name
%EnvironmentVariable%	Displays the value of the specified environment variable
Other Text	Displayed as text

You use the Prompt environment variable to store the custom prompt. To see the current value of the Prompt type **Echo %Prompt%** and press Enter. When you type the name of an environment variable between percent signs, you tell the command prompt to expand it so that you can see the value it contains. Figure 6.10 shows the default Prompt value.

FIGURE 6.10
Set a Prompt value that helps you use the command line with greater ease.

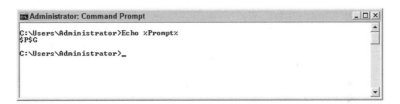

The default value is PG, which displays the current drive and path, along with a greater than sign. If you want to temporarily change the command prompt to try out new values, simply type **Prompt=** followed by the values shown in Table 6.1. Let's try it now. Type **Prompt=Hello$SJoe$_ PG** and press Enter. The command prompt will change as shown in Figure 6.11 to display Hello Joe on one line and the usual information on the next line. Try out a few other combinations as shown in Table 6.1 to see what you can come up with.

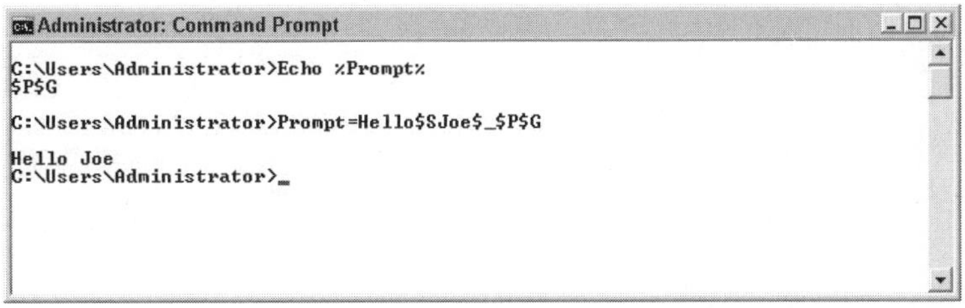

FIGURE 6.11
The command prompt can change to display any information you like.

Unfortunately, changing the Prompt environment variable at the command line won't make the change permanent. The next time you open a command prompt, you'll see the standard Microsoft value. Use these steps to create a permanent command prompt change.

1. Right-click Computer and choose Properties. You'll see the System window shown in Figure 6.12.

FIGURE 6.12
Gain access to the advanced system settings through the System window.

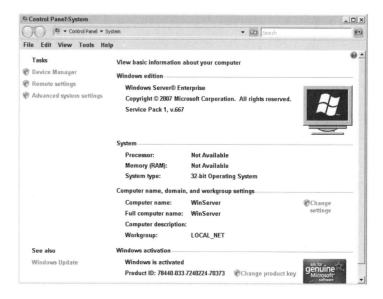

2. Click "Advanced system settings." You'll see the Advanced tab of the System Properties dialog box shown in Figure 6.13.

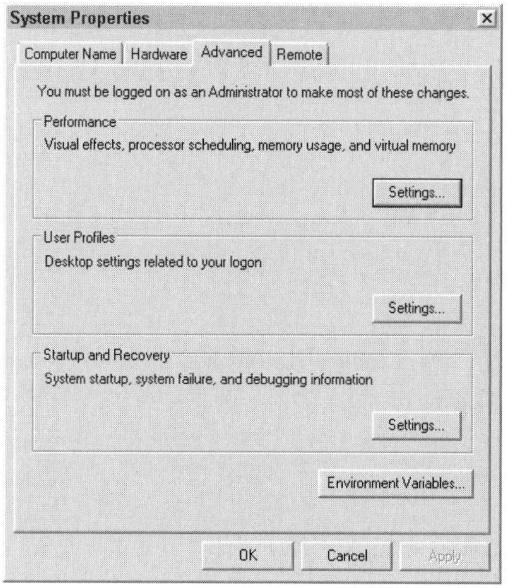

FIGURE 6.13
The Advanced tab of the System Properties dialog box

3. Click Environment Variables. You'll see the Environment Variables dialog box shown in Figure 6.14. This is where you'll create a Prompt environment variable to hold your specialized command prompt settings.

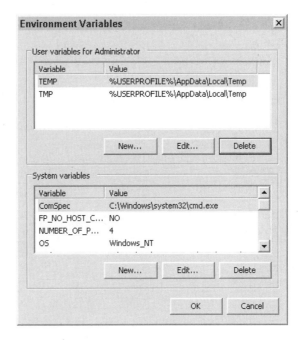

4. Click New in the "User variables for Administrator" section. You'll see a New User Variable dialog box containing two fields.

5. Type **Prompt** in the Variable name field.

6. Type the command prompt you want to use, such as PG, in the Variable value field.

7. Click OK three times to close all of the dialog boxes. The command prompt will now display the custom prompt you want to use.

If you later decide to change the prompt, follow steps 1 through 3 to open the Environment Variables dialog box. Highlight the Prompt entry in the "User variables for Administrator" section and click Edit. Change your prompt and click OK three times to change the setting.

Internal Versus External Commands

This chapter has used the term *command* for everything you execute at the command line. In reality, you need to view the command line as having multiple command types. The first command type you need to know about is the CMD program (CMD.EXE). The CMD program is different from other utilities. It doesn't end after it opens the command prompt; it remains in the background to receive and react to your keystrokes. In fact, you'll often hear this program called the command interpreter. That's because this program receives the commands that you type, interprets them, and tells the system how to handle them.

The second command type is internal commands. CMD begins looking for commands that you type within itself. When CMD finds that it has access to a particular command, it immediately executes it for you. For example, the `Dir` (directory) command is an internal `CMD.EXE` command. You won't find `Dir` listed as an executable anywhere on your hard drive. To test this out for yourself, type **`CD C:\`** and press Enter to get to the topmost directory on your hard drive. Type **`Dir Dir.* /S`** and press Enter. This command tells the `Dir` command to look for any file that uses Dir as its name anywhere on the hard drive. The `/S` command-line switch tells `Dir` to check every subdirectory on the hard drive. Depending on the size of your hard drive, this command could require a while to execute. Eventually, you'll see the "File Not Found" result message. Now, you just type `Dir` to locate the file, so you know the command exists, but it doesn't exist outside of the `CMD.EXE` program.

If you want to see the full list of commands that `CMD.EXE` supports, type **`Help`** and press Enter. You'll see the list as shown in Figure 6.15 (the list in the screenshot isn't complete — it continues past the bottom of the command window).

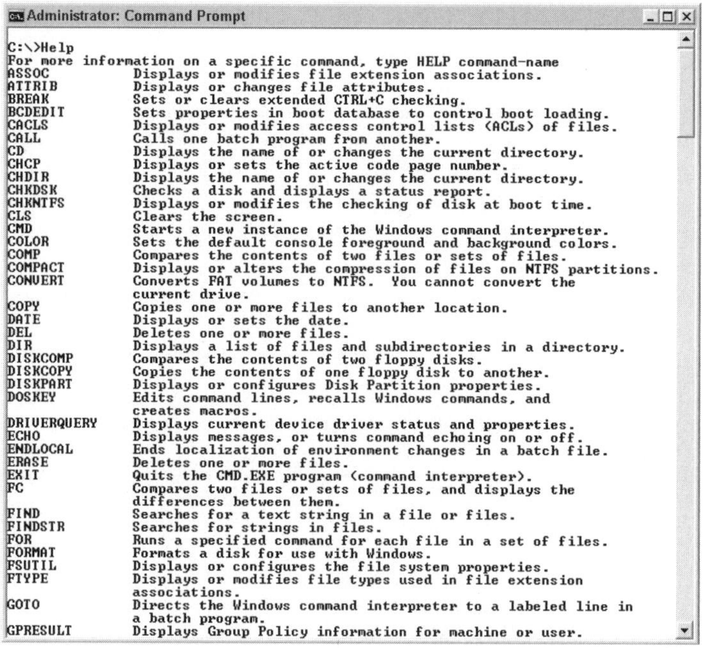


```
C:\>Help
For more information on a specific command, type HELP command-name
ASSOC          Displays or modifies file extension associations.
ATTRIB         Displays or changes file attributes.
BREAK          Sets or clears extended CTRL+C checking.
BCDEDIT        Sets properties in boot database to control boot loading.
CACLS          Displays or modifies access control lists (ACLs) of files.
CALL           Calls one batch program from another.
CD             Displays the name of or changes the current directory.
CHCP           Displays or sets the active code page number.
CHDIR          Displays the name of or changes the current directory.
CHKDSK         Checks a disk and displays a status report.
CHKNTFS        Displays or modifies the checking of disk at boot time.
CLS            Clears the screen.
CMD            Starts a new instance of the Windows command interpreter.
COLOR          Sets the default console foreground and background colors.
COMP           Compares the contents of two files or sets of files.
COMPACT        Displays or alters the compression of files on NTFS partitions.
CONVERT        Converts FAT volumes to NTFS.  You cannot convert the
               current drive.
COPY           Copies one or more files to another location.
DATE           Displays or sets the date.
DEL            Deletes one or more files.
DIR            Displays a list of files and subdirectories in a directory.
DISKCOMP       Compares the contents of two floppy disks.
DISKCOPY       Copies the contents of one floppy disk to another.
DISKPART       Displays or configures Disk Partition properties.
DOSKEY         Edits command lines, recalls Windows commands, and
               creates macros.
DRIVERQUERY    Displays current device driver status and properties.
ECHO           Displays messages, or turns command echoing on or off.
ENDLOCAL       Ends localization of environment changes in a batch file.
ERASE          Deletes one or more files.
EXIT           Quits the CMD.EXE program (command interpreter).
FC             Compares two files or sets of files, and displays the
               differences between them.
FIND           Searches for a text string in a file or files.
FINDSTR        Searches for strings in files.
FOR            Runs a specified command for each file in a set of files.
FORMAT         Formats a disk for use with Windows.
FSUTIL         Displays or configures the file system properties.
FTYPE          Displays or modifies file types used in file extension
               associations.
GOTO           Directs the Windows command interpreter to a labeled line in
               a batch program.
GPRESULT       Displays Group Policy information for machine or user.
```

FIGURE 6.15
`CMD.EXE` supports a number of additional commands in Server Core.

The third command type is external commands. These commands, such as `TaskList.EXE`, appear as separate files. To demonstrate this fact for yourself, type **`Dir TaskList.EXE /S`** and press Enter. If your system is anything like mine, the first location you'll see is `C:\Windows\System32`. However, `TaskList.EXE` actually appears in a number of locations on your hard drive as shown in Figure 6.16.

CMD can execute any internal command anywhere on your hard drive, so these commands are always available to you. However, to execute an external command, CMD must know where to find the file on disk. After CMD checks itself to see it if has the command, it looks at the local directory for the command. That's why you needed to change directories to the `C:\Program Files\Windows Resource Kits\Tools\` folder when working with the `SubInACL` utility earlier in the chapter — to ensure that CMD could find the file.

FIGURE 6.16

External commands appear as separate files on the hard drive.

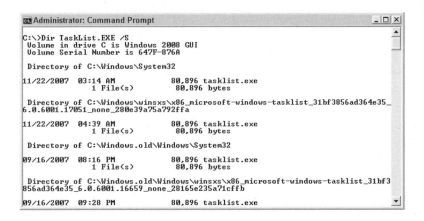

If CMD doesn't have the command and it doesn't find it in the local directory, it searches all of the locations defined in a special environment variable called Path for the command file. To see these locations, type **Echo %Path%** and press Enter. The default path includes: C:\Windows \system32, C:\Windows, and C:\Windows\System32\Wbem. Notice that the Path environment variable separates each of the locations using a semicolon. You should always place the paths that you plan to use most often first in the list because CMD searches the paths in the order that they appear in the Path environment variable. When CMD finishes searching all of these locations and still doesn't find the command you specify, it displays the " '<ProgramName>' is not recognized as an internal or external command, operable program or batch file." error message.

Some programs automatically modify the Path environment variable for you when you install them. The modification ensures that CMD can always find the application commands when you type them at the command line. Sometimes you need to add a new path to the Path statement manually. In this case, use these steps to complete the task.

1. Right-click Computer and choose Properties. You'll see the System window shown in Figure 6.12.

2. Click "Advanced system settings." You'll see the Advanced tab of the System Properties dialog box shown in Figure 6.13.

3. Click Environment Variables. You'll see the Environment Variables dialog box shown in Figure 6.14. This is where you'll modify the Path environment variable to hold the required path information.

4. Highlight the Path entry in the System variables group and click Edit. You'll see an Edit System Variable dialog box. Notice that Windows automatically highlights the Variable value field for you. Be very careful not to change the contents of the Variable name field. Otherwise, CMD won't be able to find the Path environment variable at all.

5. Press End. This action takes the cursor to the end of the current Path value.

6. Type ; (semicolon) if you don't see one at the end of the list.

7. Type the path you want to add, such as C:\Program Files\Windows Resource Kits \Tools\.

8. Click OK three times to complete the process.

Any changes you make to the Path environment variable won't take effect until you close and reopen the command prompt. You can also change the Path environment variable at the command prompt by typing **Path=%Path%;<New Path>** and pressing Enter. Using this command retains the current path information, adds a semicolon to it, and then adds the new path to the end. Changing the Path environment variable at the command line is temporary. The change will go away the moment you close the Command Prompt window.

Basic Command Examples

Windows provides access to literally hundreds of commands. You can download still more commands from online sources (such as the SubInACL utility used in this chapter). Third-party applications install still more commands. Some people will spend an entire lifetime at the command prompt and still won't execute every command. In addition, some of these commands become quite complex, making it unlikely that you'll use every feature even if you use the command regularly.

What I'm trying to say is that I can't hope to cover even a small portion of the available commands in a single chapter and it's not even necessary that you know them all. The following sections provide you with basic command examples that demonstrate how to perform common tasks. You can use this information to build your command line vocabulary as you spend more time with the command line.

Getting Help at the Command Line

One of the most important things to know about the command line is how to get help. If you know how to get help, you can figure out most of the commands that you'll find. Commands have a number of executable file extensions that include BAT, EXE, CMD, and COM (among others). When you see a command that you want to learn about, type its name followed by the /? command switch. The /? command-line switch is one of the only common switches that you'll find. Try it now with TaskList.EXE. Type **TaskList /?** and press Enter. You'll see the help information shown in Figure 6.17.

NOTE

If you type the name of a command, followed by a /?, and press Enter you should always see some type of help information. When you don't see help information, it's usually an indicator that you aren't supposed to use the command at the command line. There are a very few cases where you won't see help information and can still use the command, such as when working with Notepad. As a rule, if you don't know what the command does and you don't obtain any help information using the /? switch, then it probably isn't safe to use the command.

COMMAND LINE SYNTAX

One of the things that makes the command line difficult to use is that the programs you access aren't the work of one person. Thousands of programmers have all contributed to the command line and they all seem to have somewhat different ideas of how the command line should work. However, there are some common elements that you should know about when working with the command line.

FIGURE 6.17
Command line help is usually terse, but helpful when you know how to use it.

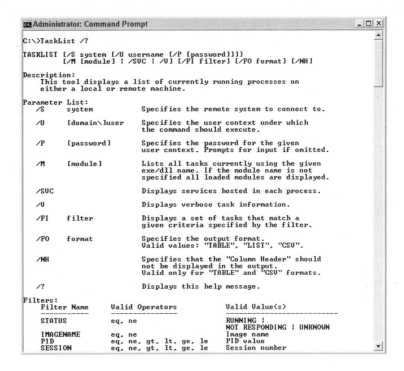

Typing the command by itself won't do much for you in most cases. In fact, you may very well see a message telling you that the command is wrong and that you should type **<CommandName>** **/?** to obtain help on using the command.

A command normally accepts a combination of command-line switches and arguments. The command-line switches change the behavior of the command. For example, a command-line switch may change the output mode from a table to a list. Command-line switches are preceded by either a slash (/) or a hyphen (-). Some commands accept either a slash or a hyphen, but other commands require the slash or hyphen specifically. You need to pay attention to the command-line help to see which form of command-line switch the command prefers.

Arguments provide some kind of data input that the command processes. For example, when you type **Dir Hello.TXT**, the Hello.TXT portion of the command is the argument. This argument tells the Dir command which file to look for. You'll often see arguments with command-line switches. A command-line switch-related argument provides data that the command-line switch requires to work properly. For example, when you see the /S (system) command-line switch, it requires the name of a remote system to work properly.

Some arguments can use wildcard characters. A wildcard character is a special character that represents one or more other characters. The most common wildcard characters are * (asterisk) and ? (question mark). The * can represent any number of characters. For example, when you type **Dir T*.***, you're telling the Dir command to find any file that begins with the letter T. Consequently, Dir will find Time.EXE and Telephone.TXT. The ? replaces a single character. Consequently, when you type **Dir T???.***, the Dir command will find Time.EXE, but not Telephone.TXT. The Telephone.TXT file has too many characters in it — Dir is only looking for four character filenames that begin with T.

Some commands are also case sensitive. A -a may not be the same as a -A (as an example, just type **nbtstat /?** at the command line and look at some of the options). The help screen provided with the command shows you the case you should use for each command-line switch. In a few cases, arguments are also case sensitive, so you need to be aware of this particular problem and type the argument in the case the command expects. Now that you have some preliminaries, let's look at a specific example. The TaskList help shows the common elements you'll find in command line help. The Help listing begins with the command syntax — the special words and values you use to work with the command. Notice the square brackets around each of the special words. This means that the term is optional. Consequently, you can type TaskList by itself and it'll work fine. Type **TaskList** and press Enter to see a list of tasks currently running on your system like the one shown in Figure 6.18.

FIGURE 6.18
Some commands work fine by themselves.

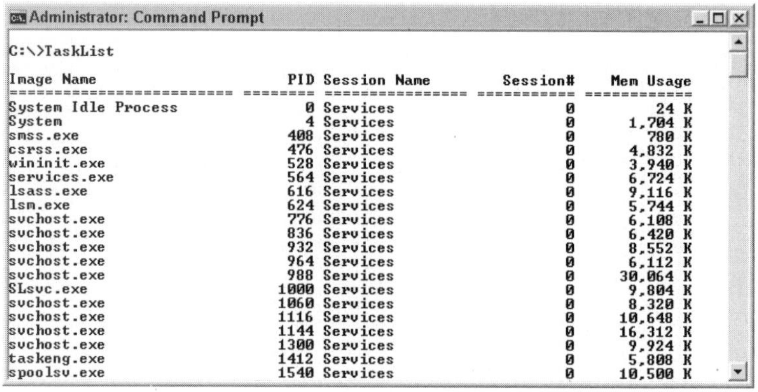

The entries inside the square brackets tell you about special things you can do with TaskList. For example, if you type **TaskList /SVC** you'll see a list of services associated with each SvcHost .EXE application as shown in Figure 6.19.

FIGURE 6.19
Use the /SVC command-line switch to obtain more information from TaskList.

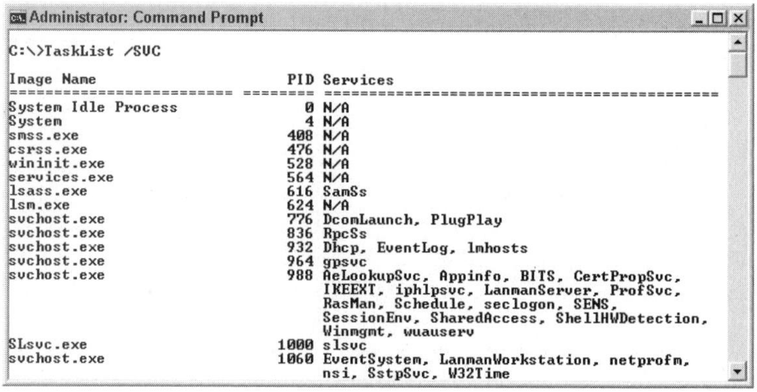

Notice that the command-line syntax shows the /SVC switch with two other switches within the same square brackets as:

```
[/M [module] | /SVC | /V]
```

When you see an entry like this, you know that you can use only one of the command-line switches. You can't use the /SVC command-line switch with the /V or the /M command-line switches. The pipe symbol (|) always tells you that you must make a choice between several potential options. You can, however, use the /SVC command-line switch with the /NH command-line switch because the /NH command-line switch appears in a different set of square brackets.

In some cases, one command-line switch will depend upon another command-line switch. For example, look at this portion of the command line syntax:

```
[/S system [/U username [/P [password]]]]
```

If you want to connect to a remote machine, you must first supply the /S command-line switch, along with the system name. This command-line switch is optionally followed by the /U command-line switch and you must supply a user name with it. Finally, you can optionally supply the /P command-line switch. Notice that the [password] argument appears in square brackets. This use of the square brackets means that you don't have to supply a value with the /P command-line switch. If you don't supply a value, then Windows will ask you to supply the value later. These command-line switches are also positional. You must provide the /S, then the /U, and finally the /P command-line switches to ensure the command works as anticipated.

TIP

Sometimes it pays to leave a variable out when you don't want other people to see it. For example, if you leave out a password, Windows will display a password dialog box. When you type the password, you'll see asterisks in place of the actual letters you type. Someone looking at your screen won't be able to decipher your password simply by looking at the screen, which adds a modicum of safety.

DESCRIPTION

The description you see in help is a short synopsis of what the command can do. In most cases, the description is too short to provide much useful information, but it does give you a general sense of whether you want to learn more about the command or not.

PARAMETER LIST

The parameter list provides extended information about each of the command-line switches in the syntax. When a command-line switch also requires an input argument, the parameter list tells you about it. In some cases, the information isn't quite enough to figure out how to use the command-line switch. When this problem occurs, you'll want to review any special usage information and examples that the help screen provides.

In some cases, the command-line switch requires specific input values to work. Look at the /FO command-line switch in Figure 6.17. The format argument can only accept TABLE, LIST, or CSV as input values. If you supply any other value, the command will fail. Consequently, you want to be sure to review the parameter list information for specific values that the command requires to work.

SPECIAL USAGE INFORMATION

Special usage information areas of a help screen provide additional help that you need to use the command. When working with TaskList, you need this information to create filters using the /FI command-line switch shown in Figure 6.17. You replace the filter argument with information you create using the help found in the Filters section. For example, if you want to filter the output by tasks that are running, you would type **/FI "Status eq Running"**. Notice the double quotes. Most complex values, such as a filter, require that you enclose them in double quotes or they won't work properly.

USAGE EXAMPLES

The basic information that a help screen contains may not provide enough information to use the command. Scroll down a little and you'll usually see some additional information provided as part of the help screen. Most help screens end by showing you some usage examples as shown in Figure 6.20. Usage examples take what you have learned in the upper portion of the help screen and show you how to use it to create commands.

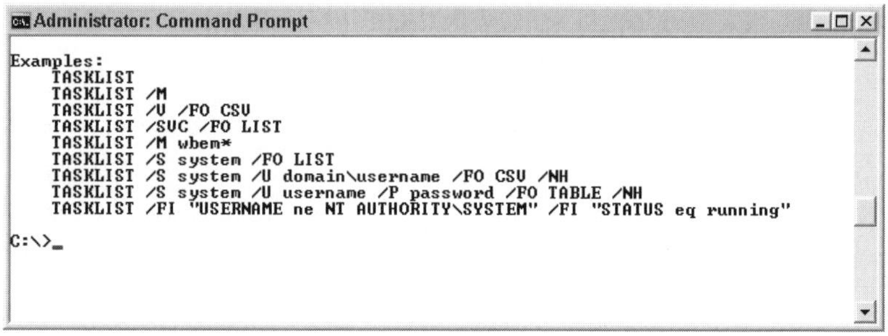

FIGURE 6.20
Examples can help to make the help screen easier to understand.

```
Administrator: Command Prompt                                            _ □ ×
Examples:
    TASKLIST
    TASKLIST /M
    TASKLIST /U /FO CSU
    TASKLIST /SVC /FO LIST
    TASKLIST /M wbem*
    TASKLIST /S system /FO LIST
    TASKLIST /S system /U domain\username /FO CSU /NH
    TASKLIST /S system /U username /P password /FO TABLE /NH
    TASKLIST /FI "USERNAME ne NT AUTHORITY\SYSTEM" /FI "STATUS eq running"

C:\>_
```

These examples provide helpful tips on working with the command. In addition, they clue you in on command-line switch position and capitalization, the requirements for using arguments, and any other special information you need to know to use the command. For example, by looking at the examples, you can determine that you can use TaskList by itself. The examples also show several cases of logging into another system. Notice that the last example tells you that you can use more than one /FI command-line switch to provide multiple filter criteria. This particular tidbit of information isn't readily available by looking at the other areas of the help information provided.

Checking the Status of the System

Most administrators need quick information about the systems they manage. You may need to know how much memory a system has or what kind of processor it's running. The SystemInfo utility can supply quick information about any machine on your network. To use SystemInfo locally, type **SystemInfo** and press Enter. The utility will output information similar to that shown in Figure 6.21.

Of course, obtaining local information isn't very hard anyway. Even though SystemInfo does provide a nice package of information, you'll probably want to use it most often on other machines. To obtain a remote connection, you need to use the /S command-line switch. For example, to locate information about a machine named Main with Joe's account, you'd type **SystemInfo /S Main /U Joe /P** and press Enter. SystemInfo will ask you to provide a password for the remote system and then display information similar to that shown in Figure 6.21.

FIGURE 6.21

SystemInfo outputs a lot of helpful information for the administrator.

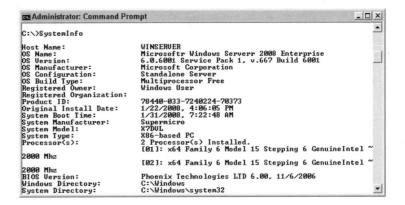

```
C:\>SystemInfo

Host Name:                     WINSERVER
OS Name:                       Microsoftr Windows Serverr 2008 Enterprise
OS Version:                    6.0.6001 Service Pack 1, v.667 Build 6001
OS Manufacturer:               Microsoft Corporation
OS Configuration:              Standalone Server
OS Build Type:                 Multiprocessor Free
Registered Owner:              Windows User
Registered Organization:
Product ID:                    78440-033-7240224-70373
Original Install Date:         1/22/2008, 4:06:05 PM
System Boot Time:              1/31/2008, 7:22:48 AM
System Manufacturer:           Supermicro
System Model:                  X7DUL
System Type:                   X86-based PC
Processor(s):                  2 Processor(s) Installed.
                               [01]: x64 Family 6 Model 15 Stepping 6 GenuineIntel ~
2000 Mhz
                               [02]: x64 Family 6 Model 15 Stepping 6 GenuineIntel ~
2000 Mhz
BIOS Version:                  Phoenix Technologies LTD 6.00, 11/6/2006
Windows Directory:             C:\Windows
System Directory:              C:\Windows\system32
```

TIP

When you need to collect information from a lot of systems, it's helpful to have that information in a form that you can easily import into a database or a spreadsheet. Use the /FO CSV /NH command-line switches to output the information in Comma Separated Value (CSV) format and without a header. Using this approach, you get just the information you need and in a format that you can easily format. Redirect the output to a CSV file by typing **SystemInfo /FO CSV /NH > LocalInfo.CSV** and pressing Enter.

Viewing and Managing Tasks

Administrators often need to check the status of tasks and sometimes they need to stop them from executing when the application encounters an error. The "Getting Help at the Command Line" section of the chapter described the TaskList utility. One of the ways in which you can use the TaskList utility is to detect applications that aren't running. Simply set a filter to detect this condition. For example, to check for frozen applications on the local machine, you'd type **TaskList /FI "Status eq Not Responding"** and press Enter.

One of the pieces of output information from the TaskList utility is a Program Identifier (PID). Every program running on your system has a unique PID. Consequently, if you have two copies of Notepad running, each copy will have a different PID associated with it. Use these steps to try this out now.

1. Open two copies of Notepad.

2. Type **TaskList /FI "ImageName eq Notepad.EXE"** at the command line and press Enter. Notice that you must include the file extension as part of the command. You'll see two copies of Notepad running as shown in Figure 6.22. Notice that each copy has a different PID.

The TaskKill utility lets you end an application you no longer need without using the normal methods to end it. Because using TaskKill can cause data loss, you'll want to use this utility as a last ditch effort to keep the system from becoming unstable. As with TaskList, you can use TaskKill from a remote system. You can also kill a range of tasks using a number of filters.

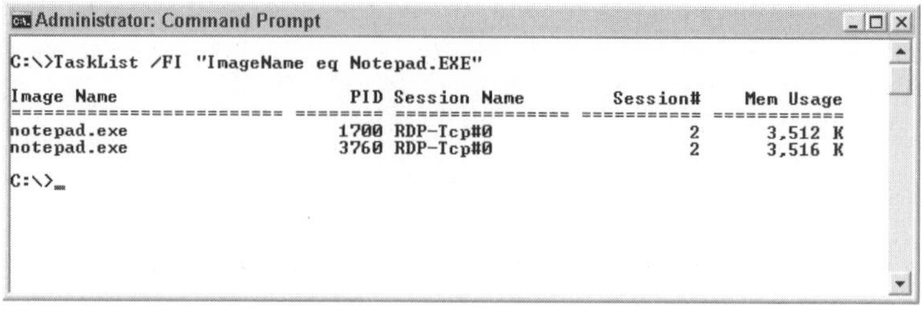

FIGURE 6.22
Every program has a unique PID.

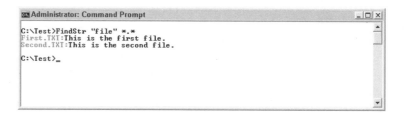

The safest way to use TaskKill is to supply a PID. Using a PID ensures that you kill only one task, specifically the task that isn't responding. For example, to kill the second copy of Notepad shown in Figure 6.22, you'd type **TaskKill /PID 3760** and press Enter. Try this with the second copy of Notepad you opened earlier. Make sure you supply the PID that corresponds to Notepad on your machine (not 3760, as it was on my machine). When you press Enter, you'll see a "SUCCESS: Sent termination signal to the process with PID <PID>." message. You'll also notice that the second copy of Notepad is gone.

Locating Specific Files Based on Content

There is a very cool utility hiding on your machine. The FindStr utility can find any file based on its content in an extremely short time and with 100 percent accuracy. Does it sound too good to be true? I haven't used GUI tools for years. Between the Dir command for locating files based on name and FindStr for locating files based on content, it's really hard to find a reason to use those other products. They do have their place, of course, but GUI search tools are often slow, cumbersome, and inaccurate.

The amazing thing about FindStr is that it can search any file anywhere on your hard drive. FindStr does have a considerable number of command-line switches that provide great flexibility, but many people are looking for specific kinds of information, which is what I discuss in this section. To make things easy, go to the C:\Test folder you created in Chapter 3.

FindStr works by looking for a single word or phrase. To look for files that contain the word file, type **FindStr "file" *.*** and press Enter. You'll see results like those shown in Figure 6.23 for the C:\Test folder. The minimum FindStr command line includes the word you want to locate (file in this case) and a file specification. As shown in this example, you can use the * or ? wildcard characters (the * replaces any number of characters, while the ? replaces a single character).

FIGURE 6.23
FindStr searches the content of files on your system.

Sometimes the text excerpt from the file can get rather lengthy and many administrators only want to know the filename anyway. The /m command-line switch tells FindStr to display just the filename. Try typing **FindStr /m "file" *.*** and pressing Enter this time. Notice that FindStr only displays the filenames this time.

You can't type a phrase on the command line without using the /c command-line switch. That because FindStr will look for any of the words in your list, rather than the phrase. For example, if you type **FindStr /m "second file" *.*** and press Enter, you'll still see both filenames displayed. Try typing **FindStr /m /c:"second file" *.*** and pressing Enter. This time, FindStr correctly reports that only Second.TXT contains the phrase you wanted to find.

Text searches are either case sensitive or case insensitive. For example, a case-sensitive search would treat Hello and HELLO as different strings, while a case-insensitive string would view them as the same. FindStr normally performs a case-sensitive search to find only the text that you specifically want. Consequently, if you type **FindStr /m /c:"Second file" *.*** and press Enter, FindStr will report that it didn't find any files matching the requested phrase. This is where the /i command-line switch comes into play. This command-line switch tells FindStr to perform a case-insensitive search. Try typing **FindStr /m /i /c:"Second file" *.*** and pressing Enter. Now FindStr will report that Second.TXT contains the phrase you wanted to find.

FindStr provides incredible power for a command line utility. I've only touched on a few of the more common command-line switches in this chapter and yet you have everything you need to perform some very specialized searches. Before you grab that GUI tool next time, try using some of the features of FindStr to locate the file you need.

Simple Batch Files

You may have heard of batch files in the past and think that they're for programmers. Batch files aren't necessarily hard to understand or difficult to write. Yes, you can make them do a lot of very interesting tasks by adding some programming elements to them, but even the most complex batch file is really just a list of commands. You've already typed many commands at the command line; all you need to do now is combine them into a text file. Table 6.2 shows a list of my favorite commands and an example of how you use them (the commands are capitalized in a certain way in the table to make them easier to remember — you can type them using any case at the command line — PING, Ping, ping, and PinG are all the same).

The basic reason to use batch files is to automate tasks that you'll perform more than once. If you don't plan to perform the task several times, then you really don't want to create a batch file for it. Writing a batch file will always require more time than performing the task manually once. You save time when you create a batch file to perform tasks multiple times.

A batch file is simply a text file. You can open a copy of Notepad to create one. In fact, open a copy of Notepad now and type the following text (make sure you press Enter at the end of each line).

```
Echo Hello
@Echo Hello
Pause Press Any Key...
Dir
@Pause Press Any Key...
```

You have to do something a bit different to save this file. Choose File ➢ Save As to display the Save As dialog box shown in Figure 6.24. Type **C:\Test** in the Address field. Notepad will change the directory to the test folder you created earlier. Choose All Files in the "Save as type" field. Type **TestMe.BAT** in the "File name" field. Your dialog box should look like the one shown in Figure 6.24 now. Press OK. The batch file is ready to go.

FIGURE 6.24

Make sure you save your batch files correctly.

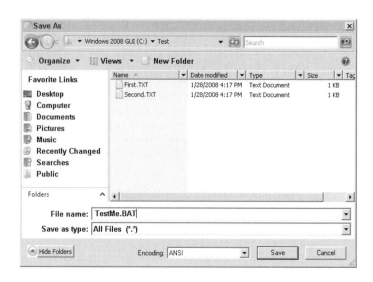

TABLE 6.2:   Common Commands and Usage

COMMAND	DESCRIPTION	USAGE EXAMPLE
CD	Changes directory to the location specified.	CD C:\ changes directories to the root directory. Executing commands in the directory where they appear can make it easier to use the command. You can also change directories to specific data to make the data more accessible.
ChkNTFS	Checks the hard drive for potential errors. You use this command to determine the state of the hard drive. A check of the boot drive will require a reboot.	ChkNTFS C: checks the boot drive for potential file and directory damage.
Dir	Locates files using a wealth of command-line switches and wildcard character descriptions. I like using Dir because it often finds files faster than any other method and it's always accurate.	Dir *.EXE /S /AH /ON locates all of the hidden executables on a hard drive and sorts them in name order. Viruses often hide their executables, making this command particularly useful.
FindStr	Locates files based on their content versus other factors.	FindStr /M /C:"Microsoft" /S *.EXE locates all of the executable files that contains the name Microsoft. It's often helpful to locate executables put out by a specific vendor on your hard drive.

TABLE 6.2:   Common Commands and Usage *(CONTINUED)*

COMMAND	DESCRIPTION	USAGE EXAMPLE
GetMAC	Obtains the Media Access Control (MAC) information for each of the Network Interface Cards (NICs) installed on the system. The MAC address is a unique identifier for the NIC.	GetMAC /v displays the connection name, network adapter name, address, and associated transport for each NIC.
IPConfig	Displays information about the current IP configuration. You can also use the command to renew connections.	IPConfig /All displays detailed information about each of the IP connections on a system.
Net	Manages a complex array of network information, including accounts, groups, computers, services, and files, among other network elements. You can even use it to decrypt some of those odd message numbers that Windows displays using the HelpMsg argument.	Net Session displays a list of the current sessions for the local computer. Net LocalGroup displays a list of all of the local groups.
NetStat	Displays statistics about the network connections for a computer. You can use this utility to determine which IP addresses and ports are open. The output also includes status information so you know whether the IP address and port are actually in use. This particular utility is very helpful in locating potential adware and viruses on a computer because you can detect them through the ports they use.	NetStat -a shows a complete list of the open IP addresses and ports. If you want to determine which executable opened the connection, use NetStat -a -b instead.
PING	Determines the status of a network connection. You can specify the name or IP address of the remote machine. The -4 command-line switch forces a check using IPv4, while the -6 command-line switch forces a check using IPv6.	PING MyServer checks the status of the MyServer connection.
PowerCfg	Manages power configuration information. You can simply list the power configuration, change the battery setup, create new power configuration, or anything else you need to do with the power configuration.	PowerCfg /Export BalancedPwrCfg.POW 381b4222-f694-41f0-9685-ff5bb260df2e exports the Balanced power scheme on my machine. That long number is a Globally Unique Identifier (GUID) that you obtain using the PowerCfg /List command. To restore the configuration you saved, you use the PowerCfg /Import BalancedPwrCfg.POW command.

TABLE 6.2: Common Commands and Usage *(CONTINUED)*

COMMAND	DESCRIPTION	USAGE EXAMPLE
WhoAmI	Displays user identification information. As a minimum, you obtain the user name and domain. However, by using various command-line switches, you can discover a great deal more about the current user.	WhoAmI /User displays the user name, domain, and Security Identifier (SID). The SID is especially helpful when working with security setups. If you want to know everything about a user, use WhoAmI /All instead.

Let's go ahead and run the batch file so you can see how it works. Type **TestMe** and press Enter. Notice that you see the two Echo commands at work. In the first case, you actually see Echo Hello, and then the word Hello. Adding an @ symbol in front of a command prevents you from seeing that command. At this point, you see a message, "Press any key to continue…" Press Enter. You see a directory of the current folder and then another "Press any key to continue…" message. Your display should look like the one shown in Figure 6.25. Press Enter one last time to complete the batch file.

FIGURE 6.25
Batch files need not be complicated to perform useful work.

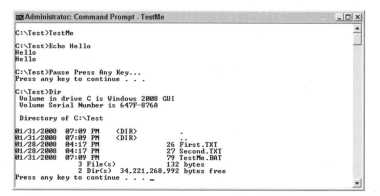

The code for this batch file displays two messages, performs a directory command, and pauses execution twice. You also see the effect of adding the @ sign in front of the command. Congratulations, you just create a batch file, albeit, not a very useful batch file.

The point is that you didn't have to do anything weird to create this batch file. All you did was type a few commands — one on each line. Since you already know the commands you want to use, you really don't need to know anything special to create a basic batch file. Just type the commands in the batch file in the same order and with the same switches you would normally use at the command line.

As you can see from the examples in this chapter, working at the command line can be very fast and efficient. You have to remember a few rules, however, the first of which is to experiment on a test machine before you assume anything about the command. It's also helpful to check out the help screens so that you know what the command expects from you. Remember that some command-line switches are positional or require special capitalization. Arguments can also require special capitalization to work properly and are either associated with the command or a particular command-line switch. Try creating a few batch files of your own and you'll quickly find out how valuable they are to the administrator.

Chapter 7

Controlling Windows III: The Registry

Any explanation of how to solve problems and get things done in Server 2008 or, indeed, *any* of the NT family of Windows will soon turn to a bit of software fiddling called "modifying the Registry" or "hacking the Registry." This chapter explains exactly what the Registry is, why you should care about it, and how to work with it. If you've already met the Registry in previous versions of Windows, then you may already know at least some of this information, but even if that's so, then I suggest that you read this chapter — I promise you'll see a few new things that will make running your Windows server a bit easier!

Every user and every administrator of every copy of any operating system in the world end up having to adjust that OS to meet their needs. Some adjustments are minor, such as changing a background color or swapping how Windows uses the right and left mouse buttons, and some are more important ones, such as giving your system a name or changing its network address. Furthermore, it isn't just Windows that needs adjusting; applications do also, directing them where to save files, how the application should start up, whether to use English or Metric units, and the like. Once we've made those changes, of course, then we expect the operating system and/or applications to remember the changes. That means that Windows needs someplace to store those changes somewhere between reboots and, not surprisingly, that someplace is the hard disk. But *where* on the hard disk, and how is it stored? Well, the answer to that has changed over time.

Computer Configuration and the Registry

Years ago, Windows stored information like "what is my network address?" or "what color should I use for the desktop background?" in simple ASCII text files whose names ended in .ini, like SYSTEM.INI. Storing configuration information in text files was pretty effective, as text files are easy to examine and fix with simple programs like Notepad. In fact, many modern PC applications use text files formatted with something called XML (short for "the eXtensible Markup Language," something we'll meet many times in each of the three books in this series) to store moderately complex databases of information, including their own configuration information. Windows, however, is an extremely complex piece of software — although no more so than every other modern OS — and so its configuration files got so big that Microsoft ran up against a weakness in text files: they're relatively slow to read and write, in comparison with other data file structures. By the early '90s, Microsoft saw that Windows had outgrown text files for configuration.

So they opted to start storing configuration information in a set of files formatted in a faster, non-text format. That set of files is collectively called, as you've probably guessed, the *Registry*. (Microsoft always capitalizes it — "the Registry" — so I will, too, but that seems a bit overdone, don't you think?) The Registry is terrific in that it's one big database that contains almost — I'll explain the "almost" later in this chapter — all of Server 2008's configuration information. From color settings to local user accounts' passwords to network addresses to whether you want Notepad to format lines in "Word Wrap" mode, it's in there. (In case you're wondering, you can't simply view those account passwords in the Registry — they're encrypted.) Even better, the Registry uses a fault-tolerant approach to writing data to ensure that the Registry remains intact even if there's a power failure in the middle of a Registry update.

Why Should You Care About the Registry?

By now, this discussion might make it sound like the Registry is just another obscure part of Windows living way down below the surface, something only of interest to the small group of people who like understanding operating system internals just for their own sake . . . you know, geeks like me. But in fact just about everybody who runs a Windows box will have to spend at least *some* time in the Registry, so here's a few reasons why you'll benefit from knowing how to twiddle the Registry.

The Registry Is the *Real* Control Panel

Even if you've never run a Windows server, I suspect that you've run *some* kind of Windows — an XP or Vista desktop, perhaps. And so I'll guess that you've had to spend at least some time in Control Panel, Computer Management (rebuilt as "Server Manager" in Server 2008, but unchanged in previous versions of Server), and similar programs, much of that time when you first got your computer up and running in the first place and then tweaking it to your liking afterwards. Well, in fact, most of that clicking and typing that you did in those programs ended up as changes to the Registry. That means that you could probably do three-quarters of your administrative tasks on a computer by directly modifying the Registry (in theory, anyway), although it wouldn't be much fun — as you'll see, the tools that let you work in the Registry aren't the most user-friendly ones on the computer. Control Panel and its ilk are more inviting, *but* — and here's the interesting part — there are times that hey, a bit of Registry spelunking is the *only* way to get a job done.

For example, you may have noticed by now that Server 2008 enables a screen saver by default, and to get access to the desktop again you've got to press Ctrl-Alt-Del and punch in a password. Security-minded techies at Microsoft made 2008 do that by default to protect unthinking administrators from themselves, as walking away from a server while still logged in allows anyone to sit down and do anything that an administrator can do. In theory, then, this is a good thing . . . usually.

In my case, you see, I often work with servers whose sole purpose in life is to let me experiment with Windows. Those servers don't contain any data that anyone cares about, including passwords, and in truth nothing much bad would happen if I handed one of those test servers to a random hacker . . . there's nothing to steal. Thus, I find Server 2008's default behavior of "don't touch the mouse for ten minutes and aha, I'm going to force you to log in again" irritating sometimes. So, one of the first things that I do upon building a *test* server (never on a production server!) is to right-click the Desktop, choose Personalize, and then, in the resulting Control Panel page, click Screen Saver and un-check the box that says "On resume, display logon screen." That's a fair amount of clicking, but under the hood, all Control Panel did was to find a particular location in the Registry and modify a setting at that location named ScreenSaverIsSecure from 1 to 0.

As it turns out, however, I can't always use Control Panel to turn off that blasted screen saver. Why? Well, you may recall that every copy of Server 2008 lets you choose to install it in one of two ways: the full GUI version and a GUI-less version called Server Core. Server Core's attraction is that it requires less RAM and CPU power to run than does the full version, and it's more secure to boot. But the price we pay for Server Core is that it's almost completely lacking in a GUI. So upon building my first Server Core test system, I soon wanted to turn off the screen saver ... but lacked Control Panel. The answer? I figured out the Registry entry that disabled the screen saver, and directly modified ScreenSaverIsSecure in the Registry, and my problem was solved. In fact, we will often see in our discussion of Server Core that the answer to "how do I ..." is often "modify such-and-such entry in the Registry."

Server Core is only one example of Registry worth. In another example of the value of Registry-fiddling over the GUI, I've seen cases in earlier versions of Windows Server where a server was sick and couldn't manage to boot up enough to get to the Control Panel. It *could*, however, start up enough to let me get to the Registry, and I could then cure the sick server (and save the day!) by modifying things in the Registry.

Still not convinced? Then consider that another much-used tool for controlling Windows is called "group policy settings" and you'll meet them in the next chapter. Group policy settings are a nice, easy-to-understand way to control your computer ... but under the hood, most group policy settings are actually nothing more than pretty front-ends to settings in the Registry. Again, sometimes a group policy setting gets corrupted, and that corrupts the Registry. Should that happen, a bit of knowledge of how the Registry fits together can save you from having to watch Setup run, if you know what I mean. As I've already suggested, the end result of much of your administrative tasks is ultimately nothing more than a sequence of Registry modifications ... so why not truly understand where all that work goes?

Some Administrative Tasks Require Direct Registry Editing

Still not convinced? Then consider this: there are things in Windows that you can only activate or repair with direct Registry editing. Yes, Control Panel, Server Manager, group policy settings, command line tools, and the like manipulate your computer's Registry settings ... but not *all* of them. Things get interesting when you discover that a small percentage of the Registry's settings are both largely undocumented (save in some obscure Knowledge Base article) *and* quite power-ful. The occult nature of these Registry settings has predictably become the source of countless "tips and tricks" about how to tune up Windows performance or how to solve some knotty prob-lem. Perhaps the most remarkable of these appeared over a decade ago when Windows internals expert Mark Russinovich discovered that the only real difference between the 1996-vintage NT Workstation 3.51 and NT Server 3.51 was *a few Registry settings*! Twiddling the Registry directly, then, is often of value to Windows troubleshooters.

The tough part about working with the Registry is in grasping the programs and terminology used in editing the Registry. You're just supposed to *understand* sentences like these:

> *You can adjust the display data prioritization settings of your Terminal Services session by mak-ing changes to the registry of the terminal server. You can increase or decrease the priority of the bandwidth given your display data (over the bandwidth given to your printing data) by changing the value of the FlowControlDisplayBandwidth entry. FlowControlDisplayBandwidth is of type REG_DWORD and is located in the HKEY_LOCAL_MACHINE\SYSTEM\CurrentControl Set\Services\TermDD subkey.*

Sentences like these are a major reason for this chapter. (That snippet refers to a new feature in a part of Windows Server 2008 called "Terminal Services" and it's quite a welcome new feature that we'll explain — in English, no less — in the companion book *Mastering Windows Server 2008: Enterprise Technologies*.) You will come across phrases like the previous quote in Microsoft litera-ture, magazine articles, and even parts of these books. Much of that information contains useful advice that will make you a better network administrator if you understand how to carry it out.

With hope I've convinced you by now that the Registry is well worth understanding, let's dive in and start working with it.

Looking at the Registry

The Registry is a hierarchical (that is, multi-level, tree-structured) database of settings that describe how your computer's operating system is set up, the contents of all local user accounts, your preferences about how the computer should start up and run your services, how the computer should interact with you, how the computer should interact with its hardware, and how you've configured the applications on the computer. Those things are a bit easier to understand when we can see them, so fire up a Server 2008 system, log in as the Administrator account, and then start up the most common Registry editing tool, Regedit, like this:

1. Click Start.

2. Just above the Start button, there's a text field containing the words "Start Search." In that field, type **regedit** and press Enter.

You'll see Regedit open up as in Figure 7.1.

FIGURE 7.1
Regedit opening screen

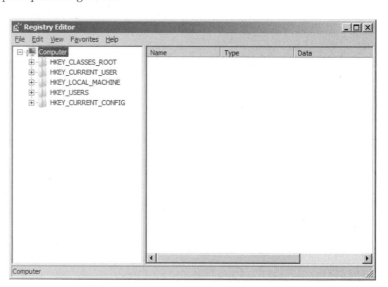

Remember, I warned you that Regedit ain't pretty! What you're seeing in Regedit are the five major parts of the Registry, but before I explain them, I want to include an important note.

WARNING

Now that we've got Regedit open, you may feel the irresistible urge to do a little typing. *Don't!* Never make changes to the Registry unless you truly want them. It's reasonable to expect that because Regedit is an "editor" that it's like Notepad or Word in that none of your changes actually take effect until you choose to Save them — but that is not the case at all. Make a change in Regedit and Regedit changes the Registry *immediately*. And, worse yet, there is no "undo" key for Regedit changes, and it's fairly easy when randomly changing the Registry to make your system unusable. So please until you know what you're doing, look — but don't touch! (Unless you like re-installing from scratch, that is — as you might have to do if you mess around with the Registry randomly.)

The Keys

Microsoft calls each of those five major parts a "key," although, as you can see, each key's icon in fact depicts a folder. The keys all have names that start with "HKEY" because "HKEY" is Microsoft's internal shorthand for "handle to a key," which is just programmer-ese for "this connects you to the actual key," the idea being that Regedit isn't showing you the key itself, it's actually made a connection — "handle" in programmer-ese — to that key. In actual fact you needn't worry about any of that — just understand that there are five keys and their names all start with "HKEY."

Of the five trees, you will probably never look at HKEY_CLASSES_ROOT, HKEY_USERS, or HKEY_CURRENT_CONFIG; since I've started working with the NT branch of Windows in 1993, I doubt I've spent more than an hour in the three of them collectively. So you'll mostly be interested in HKEY_LOCAL_MACHINE and HKEY_CURRENT_USER. To understand that, however, let's first look at the notion of *profiles*.

PROFILES: MACHINE SETTINGS AND USER SETTINGS

As you've already read, Windows contains thousands of switches, dials, and levers that collectively configure Windows so it'll run the way that you want it to, on the hardware that you've installed it on. But the configuration settings aren't all stored in one big lump. Instead, Windows recognizes that there are two distinct entities when it comes to configuration: the basic operating system itself and the person — or people — who sit down to work on it. That first part is called the "machine profile" and it encompasses all of the things that the operating system must control whether or not anyone's actually logged onto the system. That's important because server software runs whether someone's logged in at the server or not, or indeed has *ever* logged in or not.

For example, a server needs to be connected to your local network via the TCP/IP network protocol, and so it needs something called an "IP address." Again, that server needs an IP address in order to be useful to the network, even if someone isn't sitting at the server logged into it. In fact, the first time that you boot the server up, it has *never* had anyone log onto it yet — so where would it store that IP address? Clearly not in a user profile, as — again — there essentially *are* no user profiles yet. (That's not exactly right, but it's close enough.) Therefore the server's IP address must be stored in the Registry in the machine profile part. That's what Regedit calls "HKEY_LOCAL_MACHINE."

Windows systems all have just one machine profile, but they can have many, many user profiles, because any number of users may log into a given Windows system *interactively*. "Interactively?" Yes. There are two ways for users to log onto a Windows system, whether a desktop or server OS: network logins and interactive logins.

When you access a computer across a network, such as when you sit at your workstation and connect to a file server, then you're not sitting at the file server, but you must still log onto the file server, so that it knows who you are and what permissions you're allowed. That's a network logon.

In contrast, we can alternatively log onto our workstations (or servers, if we've got the permission) locally, meaning that we can sit down at the computer, press Ctrl-Alt-Del, punch in our user names and passwords, and be authenticated on that computer. That's known technically as an "interactive login." Window computers want to remember whatever preferences you've configured so that they can show you those preferences the next time you log onto them, and so every time you log onto a system *interactively* then that system creates a folder \Users*yourlogonname* wherein it keeps those preferences. That folder is your *user profile* and, among other things, it contains what the Registry knows about your preferences. (As you'll see later, it's a file called NTUSER.DAT, but let's just stay with the Registry settings for now.) Unless you enable a feature called "roaming profiles" (we'll take them up in the companion books then each computer that you log onto maintains a separate user profile for you. Thus, if you were to log onto PC21 one day and specify that you wanted a green background for your desktop and log onto SERVER7 the next day and specify that you wanted a blue desktop background, then SERVER7 would always show you a blue background upon subsequent logons, and PC21 would show green desktops upon subsequent logons.

When you log onto a system, Regedit shows you your user profile settings, but not as "c:\ users\susan\ntuser.dat"; instead, those settings show up under your HKEY_CURRENT_USER key. Remember that whole "handle" notion? Here's where it comes in. Open up HKEY_ CURRENT_USER, and it's like you're opening your NTUSER.DAT . . . but not exactly. Instead, you're reading/writing this key that contains "subkeys" and "sub-subkeys" and so on, and what you're doing gets translated into actually reading and writing ntuser.dat. Every person who's ever logged interactively into a given system, then, causes that system to create a folder for himself in the system's Users file, and to create a separate Registry key for him.

I said before that all Windows systems can have more than one user profile in their Registries. Windows Server systems have at least six user profiles on them because one of them stores the user profile of the built-in Administrator account and the rest support a bunch of accounts we won't really need to worry about for now called *service accounts*. You can see those profiles in the HKEY_USERS key, as each user profile gets its own subkey with a name like S-1-5-18. (You may recall from the previous chapter that "S-1-5-18" is a security ID, the "internal name" that Windows gives users.) If you create a new local user account on a server, then that user will get its own profile — and subkey under HKEY_USERS — but not until that user logs on interactively the first time. Again, network logins don't lead to user profiles; interactive logins do.

FIGURE 7.2

Regedit with machine and profile keys expanded

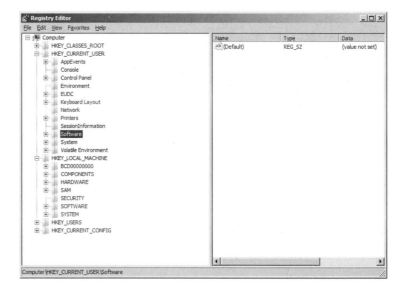

Let's return to the two big keys and examine what's in them. To see that, find "HKEY_LOCAL_MACHINE" and "HKEY_CURRENT_USER" in Regedit and click the plus signs next to them to expand the keys. You'll see something like Figure 7.2.

You'll only care about some of the subkeys in the two "big keys"; here's a quick tour.

HKEY_LOCAL_MACHINE

HKEY_LOCAL_MACHINE, which we'll see abbreviated HKLM by many parts of Windows, has two subkeys that you'll visit now and then — HKEY_LOCAL_MACHINE\SYSTEM and HKEY_LOCAL_MACHINE\SOFTWARE. (Just for the curious, SAM and SECURITY contain user accounts and security rules. BCD00000000 contains the commands to control how your server boots. Earlier versions of Windows had a text file called BOOT.INI that contained this data. You'll access boot parameters not through the Registry, though, but instead with a command called bcdedit that we'll meet later. HARDWARE contains plug-and-play information about, not surprisingly, your system's hardware. I honestly have no idea what COMPONENTS does, nor have I ever had a reason to mess with it.)

SYSTEM contains a subkey named CurrentControlSet that then contains a subkey for every service and driver in Windows. Services are the pieces of software that, not surprisingly, provide some sort of service to Windows. For example, the information in HKLM\SYSTEM\Current ControlSet\Services\Tcpip contains the configuration settings for the TCP/IP software system, HKLM\SYSTEM\CurrentControlSet\Services\BITS does the same for a service called the Background Intelligent Transfer Service, which automatically downloads bug fixes for various Microsoft programs, and HKLM\SYSTEM\CurrentControlSet\Services\W32Time contains configuration information for the service that enables all systems in a Windows network to maintain synchronized time. "Services" in Windows-ese also includes device drivers, the essential programs that enable Windows to use the computer's hardware. There's also a key HKLM\SYSTEM\CurrentControlSet\Control that contains information on boot information, print drivers, and other Windows components, so don't be surprised if you see technical articles or other parts of this book point you there to solve problems.

SOFTWARE, as its name suggests, contains configuration information on various pieces of software on your system. Manufacturers are supposed to create their own subkeys under HKLM\ SOFTWARE wherein they can store configuration information about their software. Thus, if we purchased an imaginary technical drawing program called EDraw sold by an imaginary firm named "Bigfirm Software," then we'd probably find many of the configuration settings for EDraw in HKEY_LOCAL_MACHINE\SOFTWARE\Bigfirm\Edraw. Why would we only find "many" of the settings? Because some of them would probably show up in *another* key, HKEY_CURRENT_USER\Software\Bigfirm\EDraw. Which provides a convenient segue to a discussion of the *other* big key, HKEY_CURRENT_USER.

HKEY_CURRENT_USER

As we just saw, HKEY_LOCAL_MACHINE holds settings that aren't user-specific, like configuration information for device drivers. HKEY_CURRENT_USER, often abbreviated "HKCU" by some software and "HCU" by others, holds configuration information for the currently-logged-on user. (That would be you.) Within HKEY_CURRENT_USER there are 12 subkeys, but the only ones that I ever mess with are "Control Panel," where Windows stores many of the settings that you choose in Control Panel, and "Software," which is where most of the rest of your personal preferences go. Did you notice the difference in spelling there? It's not an error: for some reason HKLM spells its subkey "SOFTWARE" and HKCU uses the more genteel "Software."

What's the difference? Well, extending my EDraw example of a fictitious technical drawing program, suppose after installing EDraw I start it up and soon notice that it seems to be using the metric measurement system. As I live in one of the three countries in the world that don't use that system (Liberia and Myanmar are the other two, I'm told), I look around EDraw's menus and eventually find where I can instruct it to use the English measurement system. EDraw wouldn't save that in HKEY_LOCAL_MACHINE\SOFTWARE\Bigfirm\EDraw, but instead would create a new subkey HKEY_CURRENT_USER\Software\EDraw and then make a note to itself to use the English measurement system.

But of course my EDraw example is just an imaginary one, so let's poke around HKCU a bit to see a real one. Remember a few pages back when I said that the Registry contained something called ScreenSaverIsSecure? You can see where that lives by opening up HKEY_CURRENT_USER, then its Control Panel subkey, and inside that you'll see a subkey named "Desktop." Click that and you'll see a lot of settings in the right-hand pane of Regedit. Scroll down a bit and you'll see something like Figure 7.3.

FIGURE 7.3

Desktop settings, including screen saver settings

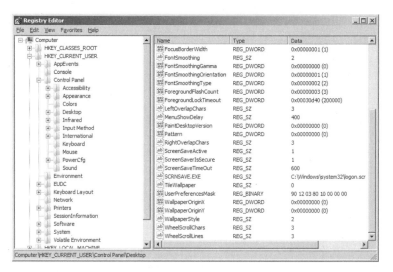

What you're seeing in that right-hand pane are called *entries*. They each act like a "switch" in the Registry to control something. For example, take ScreenSaveActive, which has a value of 1. As you may have already guessed, the ScreenSaveActive controls whether or not you're running a screen saver at all, and that "1" means you're using a screen saver and "0" means that you're not.

NOTE

It's true in this case, but beware: there are no hard-and-fast rules in Registry settings! Some Registry on/off items aren't represented by the numbers 1 and 0, but instead by the words "yes" and "no," "true" or "false," or some other combination. In general it's a really bad idea to change a Registry value unless you've found documentation on what the value does, or what values it understands. You see, there is no "central Registry emperor" at Microsoft; instead, every programmer gets to create any Registry entries that she likes, give them whatever names she likes, and whatever values she likes, and some programmers like "yes" and "no," others like "true" and "false," and still more like "1" and "0." Worse yet, as I've already noted, many Registry entries are either undocumented or documented in obscure places.

Viewing the Registry from the Command Line

Regedit is a convenient GUI tool, but we need to know how to manipulate the Registry from the command line as well. (After all, I promised that in the Introduction.) We can do that with the "reg.exe" command. Its subcommand "reg query" lets us view Registry entries and subkeys from the command line. For example, to view the current state of ScreenSaverIsSecure, we'd type

```
reg query "hkcu\control panel\desktop" /v ScreenSaverIsSecure
```

and we'd get a response like

```
HKEY_CURRENT_USER\control panel\desktop
    ScreenSaverIsSecure    REG_SZ    1
```

In that command, you specify `reg query`, followed by the subkey that your desired entry is in, followed by `/v` and the name of the entry. Without `/v ScreenSaverIsSecure`, reg would dump all of the contents of the subkey. Notice also that key names and entry names aren't case sensitive; I could just as effectively typed that line

```
reg query "hkcu\ContRol panel\desKtop" /v xcrEEnSaverisSeCure
```

Changing Registry Entries

Until now, we've just been tourists in the Registry, so let's try a bit of Registry "hacking." As this is our first tinkering trip, however, let's avoid the flashy (and, um, sometimes dangerous) Registry hacks and just go for something simple (and low-risk). We'll go into the Registry settings for Notepad to change its appearance, and then start Notepad to see the effects.

1. First, open Notepad (Start / All Programs / Accessories / Notepad), and close it. If you don't do this, then you won't find any Registry subkey for Notepad at all — for some reason, Windows doesn't set up an area for Registry settings for Notepad until you've run Notepad and closed it once.

2. Open it again so that you'll be able to see the differences that we'll make. Type "Notepad before" in Notepad and then minimize it.

3. Open Regedit, if you don't already have it open.

4. Navigate to HKEY_CURRENT_USER\Software\Microsoft\Notepad. You may be surprised when you see the number of Registry settings in Notepad — I certainly was. Who knew it could *re-format drives*? (Kidding.)

5. Next, we'll tell Notepad to format lines by wrapping the lines. You can normally control this by clicking Format / Word Wrap, but, again, all that clicking actually does is modify an item in the Registry, so we're going to cut out the middleman and zap the Registry directly. (When people mean to say "modify the Registry," you'll hear a number of variations, like "hack the Registry" or "do a Registry zap.") Locate the entry named "fWrap." Double-click it and you'll see a dialog box allowing you to change fWrap's value. Change it to 1. Click OK to close the dialog box.

6. Notice that Regedit identifies fWrap as having a "type," and that is "REG_DWORD." That means that fWrap can only hold numeric values. Note that a few other entries are of type "REG_SZ." That means that they can hold any string value. (The phrase "string" just means "a sequence of any sort of character — numbers, letters, punctuation" in computer-ese. "Mark Minasi" is a string, as is "171-66-93621.") Nearly all Registry entries are either REG_DWORD or REG_SZ; there are three other kinds, and we'll meet them a bit later in this chapter.

7. Just as you changed fWrap, locate and change fFaceName, which is a REG_SZ. Change it from "Lucida Console" to "Segoe UI" and note that there's a space between "Segoe" and "UI." This will change the typeface that Notepad displays.

8. Locate and change "StatusBar" from 0 to 1. This will cause Notepad to display a status bar at the bottom of its window.

9. At this point, we've made three configuration changes to Notepad; what must we do to see them take effect? Well, take a look at the copy of Notepad that you minimized before starting work with Notepad's Registry, the one that says "Notepad before" in it. Notice that the font hasn't changed, the Status bar hasn't appeared, and clicking "Format" will show that "Word Wrap" isn't checked.

10. *Now* open a second copy of Notepad and type "Notepad After" in the second copy of Notepad. Notice the new font, notice the Status Bar (which is, admittedly, not terribly impressive as status bars go), and click "Format" to see that Word Wrap is now checked.

11. Finally, close the *first* copy of Notepad, the "Notepad before" copy. Looking at the right-hand pane of Regedit again, press F5 to refresh the view. What did you see? Strange, eh — all of our work was undone!

So what did we just see? First, we saw that changing the Registry didn't change an already-running copy of Notepad. That's because Notepad only reads the Registry when Notepad starts up. That means that as expected it was no surprise that running Notepad a second time reflected the changes we'd made in the Registry. Third, you should have seen that fWrap, fFaceName, and Status Bar reverted to their original values. That's because the first copy of Notepad still retained those settings, and when we closed the first copy of Notepad, then apparently Notepad always re-writes its Registry settings when closed.

NOTE

When do Registry changes take effect? It depends on when an application's programmer decides. In the case of Notepad, its designer decided to read Notepad's Registry only when you start up a copy of Notepad; it also saves changes based on the latest copy of Notepad that you've closed, as we just saw. That's a perfectly valid approach, although some applications check the Registry on a regular basis looking for changes, which they then cause to take effect. In my experience, however, the majority of applications and Windows components only read their Registry entries when started, like Notepad. That's why you've got to reboot Windows to cause some Registry entries to take effect — the programs that they affect may be a bedrock piece of Windows that only reads its Registry entries upon startup, and those programs only start up when Windows starts up.

Changing Registry Entries from the Command Line

Sometimes you want to tell Windows to modify a Registry entry from the command line, perhaps to put it in a batch file. As with examining Registry information, you can change the Registry with the Reg command. When used to modify an existing value in the Registry, it looks like

```
reg add "subkey" /v entryname /d newvalue /f
```
So, for example, to change fWrap to 1, we'd type (from an elevated command prompt)

```
reg add "HKCU\Software\Microsoft\Notepad" /v fWrap /d 1 /f
```

Notice that reg.exe allows you to use the "HKCU" abbreviation for "HKEY_CURRENT_USER." The /f tells reg.exe not to stop and ask, "are you sure you want to overwrite this Registry entry?"

Registry Entry Types

While poking around Notepad's Registry above, we met REG_DWORD and REG_SZ types of Registry entries, but as I said, they're not the only types you'll run into. Occasionally you'll run into one of the Registry's three other types. I summarize all five types in Table 7.1.

TABLE 7.1:   Data Types as Defined by the Registry Editor

DATA TYPE	DESCRIPTION
REG_BINARY	Raw binary data. Data of this type usually doesn't make sense when you look at it with the Registry Editor. Binary data shows up in hardware setup information. If there is an alternative way to enter this data other than via the Registry Editor — perhaps if there's some well-suited Control Panel applet or MMC snap in relevant to the binary entry — then do it that way. Editing binary data can get you in trouble if you don't know what you're doing. The data is usually represented in hex for simplicity's sake.
REG_DWORD	Another binary data type, but it is 4 bytes long. We usually enter it in decimal, but Regedit lets you choose to enter the data as hex if you prefer.
REG_EXPAND_SZ	A character string of variable size, it's often information understandable by humans, like path statements or messages. It is "expandable" in that it may contain information that will change at runtime, like *%username%* — a system batch variable that Windows automatically changes from "%username%" to your user name. As user names can vary tremendously in length, the resulting value in the Registry entry is unpredictable beforehand, hence the need for an "expandable" string.
REG_MULTI_SZ	Another string type, but it allows you to enter a number of parameters in this one value entry. The parameters are separated by binary zeroes (nulls).
REG_SZ	A simple string.

And if you're wondering how on earth you'll figure out what data type to assign to a new Registry value, don't worry about it; if you read somewhere to use a particular new value entry, you'll be told what data type to use. Failing that, I usually just guess REG_SZ if it's textual in nature, REG_DWORD if it's numeric.

Researching the Registry

Now you've seen the Registry, poked around a bit, and changed a few safe things. But you may be thinking by now, "how did he know where the Notepad Registry settings were or, more important, how do *I* find out what exactly is in the Registry, and how can I make it work for me?" That's the part of Registry fiddling that incorporates the most guessing, so let's take a few moments and let me save you some time by offering some pointers about searching for Registry information.

◆ **There's no central overall Registry list.** When first exposed to the Registry, many Windows newcomers ask where every Registry setting is documented. While that *sounds* like it'd be a great idea, the fact is that there is no one single document that covers every single Registry setting, nor will there ever be. Compiling such a text would actually be fairly difficult, as any programmer can write an application that reads and writes entries that he created in the first place, and somehow whoever maintained this Registry reference compilation would have to know about every single application from every vendor and all of those applications' Registry entries.

But what about a central listing of just the Registry entries in Windows? That, too, would be difficult and, once you think about it, sort of pointless. Recall that Registry entries are just the switches, dials, and levers that let us configure different pieces of software. Thus, the documentation on Registry settings should be in the *software's* documentation. For example, merely picking up some incredibly thick book that said that the entry MakeAZLookupOptimal was a REG_DWORD that allowed you to optimize something called connectoid lookups in something called Authorization Manager if you set it to 1, but disabled optimization if set to 0, then what real good is that? (That's not a real Registry entry, it was mostly just technical bafflegab for the example's purposes, so don't go looking for the setting or worry about what "Authorization Manager" or "connectoids" might be, much less how they'd interact.) As far as I can see, information on my fictitious MakeAZLookupOptimal belongs in the documentation for Authorization Manager, just as you'd expect an explanation for the "Popcorn" button in your microwave's documentation, not your "kitchen documentation."

◆ **You often can find documentation on a Registry entry, *once* you know that it exists.** This wasn't always true, but you can find out about almost any Windows Registry entry by searching on Microsoft's online msdn.microsoft.com site. Or, failing that, simply Googling a Registry entry sometimes nets useful information, although in truth I've found more misinformation when searching the Web for Windows internals information than actual useful information, so keep a few grains of salt around when Googling that sort of stuff.

I hope that doesn't discourage you from doing your own Registry exploration. I've been poking around the Registry since 1993, and I still get a little pleased grin when I discover some new bit of "Registry gold." (Then again, my friends *do* tell me that I need to get out more often. Or maybe they're just jealous of my Registry mastery. Yeah; that's it.)

Discovering Registry Keys on Your Own

Surfing the Web's not the only way to find Registry gold. Another avenue involves searching the Registry. For example, here's a problem that I ran into years ago and how I searched the Registry for the answer.

If you ever click Help/About for most Windows applications, you get a dialog box identifying the application and then reporting the person to whom the application is registered, as well as the organization that person belongs to. Years ago, I changed my company name and wondered how to change that in Windows without re-installing. It had to be in the Registry, I figured, but where? So I searched the Registry with Regedit.

Between "name" and "organization," I guessed that the word "Name" would appear a lot in the Registry, so looking for a field called "Name" didn't sound promising. But "Organization" isn't as common, so I figured I'd try it. Here's how you can, too:

1. Start Regedit, if you haven't already got it running.

2. Click the My Computer icon in Regedit.

3. Click Edit/Find and a Find dialog box will appear. It looks like Figure 7.4.

FIGURE 7.4
Regedit's "Find"
dialog box

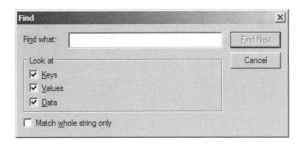

4. In the Find What text field, type in **organization**. Note that Regedit will search key names, value entry names, and the actual data in value entries. There is a lot more data in the Registry than there are key and value entry names, so skip searching data whenever possible; uncheck the Data check box and click Find Next.

On my system the first hit I got was for a key called MSExtOrganization, which was clearly not what I wanted, so I pressed F3 to tell Regedit to find the next match.

Several false hits later, I found a value named RegisteredOrganization. It's in HKEY_LOCAL_MACHINE\SOFTWARE\Microsoft\Windows NT\CurrentVersion and of course it's a REG_SZ. Or I could do it from the command line with reg query. The query looks like

```
reg query HKLM /f "Organization" /t REG_SZ /s
```

That tells Reg to search the HKEY_LOCAL_MACHINE key (a guess, but given that my name and organization are system-wide values, it seems unlikely it'd be sitting in HKCU) for anything with the phrase "Organization" in it. Just put whatever you're searching for after the "/f," and add "/s" to tell Reg to search subkeys — otherwise it only looks in the top level of HKCU and then stops. The "/t REG_SZ" is optional if you want to tell Reg what sort of data it's looking for — a character string or a number. (On my system, RegisteredOrganization appeared as the 36th — and last — result.)

Dealing with a "Hey, Where Is It?" Registry Value

While I'm on the subject of "unexpected and confusing things about Registry entries," permit me to explain something that can be confusing when first encountered: Registry values that aren't there yet. Remember Notepad's Status Bar Registry entry? It was a REG_DWORD entry that controlled whether or not Notepad displayed its simple "your cursor is at this row/column location" status bar at the bottom of its window. A value of zero meant "don't show the status bar," and a value of one showed the status bar. Recall also that the first time you looked in HKEY_CURRENT_USER\Software\Microsoft\Notepad that the Status Bar entry was already there, and had a value of zero in it. As a matter of fact, looking at all of the possible entries in HKEY_CURRENT_USER\Software\Microsoft\Notepad showed me a few Registry entries that I didn't know about, making Registry spelunking sort of useful — in this case.

THE CASE OF THE "HIDE" THAT HID

Unfortunately, I must report that most developers don't work as hard to reveal Registry entries as did Notepad's developer(s). For example, if you look in HKEY_LOCAL_MACHINE\SYSTEM\CurrentControlSet\Services\LanManServer\Parameters on a newly installed copy of Server 2008, then you'll see something like Figure 7.5.

FIGURE 7.5
Initial state of file server service parameters in the Registry

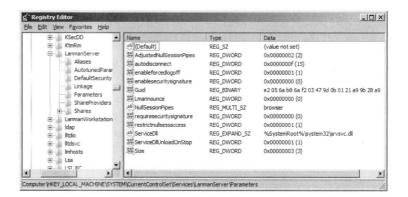

This Registry subkey holds the configuration parameters — the switches, dials, and knobs — of the file server service in Server 2008. Don't worry about what any of those switches do. Instead, get online and read Microsoft's Knowledge Base article number 265284. (Google "KB 265284" and it'll probably be the first entry you get.) Or heck, you needn't even bother (I just remembered — you could be reading this in bed, in the bathroom, or on a plane flight; sorry). Basically it says that you can hide your server's existence from your network by going to the Registry subkey that you're already looking at (HKLM\SYSTEM\CurrentControlSet\Services\LanManServer\Parameters, which I'm going to abbreviate to "...\LanManServer\Parameters" for the rest of this chapter) and setting a REG_DWORD value named "hidden" to 1, and then rebooting the computer.

NOTE

In actual fact, it doesn't *really* hide your server and it's in general more trouble than it's worth, so trust me, don't bother. We're just using this for example's sake.

Ah, but a look in the . . .\LanManServer\Parameters subkey shows that there *isn't* any entry named "hidden." That's because the majority of Registry hacks that you'll come across require you to create entirely new Registry values. In other words, *just because Windows understands and will respond to a Registry entry doesn't mean that the Registry entry is visible in Regedit by default.* We sort of saw that before in the Notepad example when I said to start the exercise by opening Notepad and closing it. You see, if you'd take a brand-spanking-new copy of Server 2008, installed it on some hardware, logged on that new server, opened up Regedit, and looked for HKEY_CURRENT_USER\Microsoft\Notepad, then you'd have found that entire subkey wasn't there at all. Only when you first exit Notepad does Notepad create its subkey and populate it with its default values.

REGISTRY SWITCH SETTINGS ARE "ON," "OFF," OR "DEFAULT"

But wait — and this was the confusing part, at least to me — what should the file server software do if there *isn't* a "hidden" REG_DWORD value in . . .\LanManServer\Parameters when the file server software starts up? I mean, you're either hiding or you're not, right, so in the absence of any instructions from the Registry about whether to turn on the Microsoftian Cloaking Device, what does the file server software do?

In the case of the file server software, the programmer who devised that code included instructions that said "if the Registry doesn't explicitly contain a Registry entry named "hide" with value 1, then don't hide." Notice that while I've been calling settings like "hide" a "switch," then I've not really used a perfect metaphor, as switches generally have an "on" and an "off" setting. The "switch" metaphor worked well for Notepad's fWrap setting, as it appears from the beginning. But the file server service's "hide" switch is sort of like having one of those "punch-out" locations on your car's dashboard, a place where there could be a switch, if you installed it. Before you install the switch, the car behaves in some manner, but installing the switch (perhaps to disable, say, an air bag) gives you the option to turn something on or off that you didn't have before.

Thus, whenever you learn of an on/off Registry entry, understand that if you must create that new entry in order to use it then Windows already has some default setting, and it can be useful to figure out what the setting is. Microsoft has gotten a lot better in recent years about explaining the "if there's no entry there in the first place, then the software behaves in such-and-such way," so if you can find any documentation about the entry, then you'll probably find information about the default behavior as well. (Probably.)

NOT EVERYTHING USES THE REGISTRY, OR USES IT PARTIALLY

While I'm on the subject of Registry quirks, let's talk about a related topic: *application* quirks when it comes to the Registry. In theory, it'd be great if every application stored all of its configuration data in the Registry, as the Registry's a fast and efficient place for storing that sort of data. But you'll see a wide variation in how much any given application relies upon the Registry, even *if* the application is, say, part of Windows Server. In general, I see three levels of Registry-reliance in Windows and Windows applications:

◆ **Total reliance.** From a central control point of view, I think it's great when an application stores all of its configuration information in the Registry. Most services do, and most of the built-in Windows "applets" like Notepad and WordPad do. Very nice for backing up and standardizing configurations.

◆ **Partial reliance.** Some applications store simple on/off settings in the Registry and then use extra files to store other information. One example I've run across in this category is Adobe Photoshop, which stores a bare minimum of settings in the Registry, and the rest in a mélange of files scattered across the computer. Not so good, but then perhaps that's because Photoshop was originally a Macintosh application, and the Mac doesn't use a Registry. In a Microsoft-related example, Internet Information Server, Windows Server's Web server software, has stored configuration information outside of the Registry since IIS 4.0.

◆ **Complete ignorance.** I use a freeware image viewer called Irfanview and I like it quite a lot, as it doesn't take up much disk space and is quite quick. But for some reason it doesn't use the Registry at all, storing all of its settings in an old-style file called i_view32.ini. Actually this isn't bad from a control and consistency point of view, as it's a snap to back up a file like this and put it where the application expects it, making backup and restore of application configuration fairly easy. But Irfanview's a simple program — apps of any complexity, as I've noted, soon grow out of their ASCII configuration files. Why didn't the author use the Registry? I can only guess, but figuring out how to use the Registry takes a bit of work, and perhaps he was a novice programmer when he started building his useful (and free!) image viewer.

So, just clarify once again: there's no Registry police. Any developer can choose to use the Registry or not, and to use the Registry in any way that she sees fit.

Creating/Deleting a New Registry Entry

Now that I've teased you with the promise of perhaps creating a new Registry entry, let's actually do it — let's put the "hide" entry into ...\LanManServer\Parameters and set it to 0. (No, it won't have any effect, but when it comes to the Registry, I'd much rather not cause you to accidentally make your server stop working. Or, worse, a *client's* server!) Accomplish that like so:

1. In Regedit, right-click on the HKEY_LOCAL_MACHINE\SYSTEM \CurrentControlSet \Services \LanmanServer \Parameters subkey.

2. In the context menu that appears, choose New /DWORD (32-bit) Value.

3. In the right-hand pane, you'll see a new entry with a highlighted name "New Value #1." You should be able to just overtype "New Value #1" with "Hide" (case doesn't matter) and press Enter.

4. Now give Hide a value. Right-click the new Hide entry and choose "Modify ..."

5. That raises an "Edit DWORD (32-bit) Value" dialog box like the one we saw back when were modifying the Notepad's Registry values. Note that its current value data is 0, which is what we wanted anyway. Click OK.

Perfectly simple. But let's review — what if we wanted to tell the server to hide and so set the "hide" value to 1. When would we see that change take effect? The answer is when you next start the file server software. As it's a separate service, you could stop and start the service (there's an interface in Server Manager that makes it easy), or you could just reboot the server. (Restarting the service is a better idea, as it reduces downtime to that server's users.)

Deleting Registry entries and/or keys works just as you'd expect it to — click the key or entry and press the Delete key. But don't do it very often — Registry deletion often leads to unhappiness if you're not sure of what you're doing.

Creating and Deleting Registry Entries from the CLI

To accomplish the previous task — create the Hide REG_DWORD entry and set it to 0 — then you use the REG ADD command that we've already met, except you've got to add an extra parameter to tell Windows what sort of entry it is — REG_DWORD, REG_SZ, and so on. It looks like this:

```
reg add "subkey" /v entryname /t entrytype /d newvalue /f
```

The only difference is in the /t option, which you should follow with "REG_sz," "REG_dword" or whatever entry type you're creating. In this case, the full REG command would look like

```
reg add "HKLM\SYSTEM\CurrentControlSet\Services\LanManServer\Parameters" /v
    hide /d 0 /t REG_DWORD
```

Note that if I hadn't included the "/t REG_DWORD" parameter, then REG would have assumed that I wanted a REG_SZ ... which wouldn't have worked very well at all. Notice also that REG recognizes the "HKLM" abbreviation.

Backing Up and Restoring a Registry Subkey

Given the Registry's importance, it's probably a good idea to perform a backup and restore parts of it. You can do that with Regedit and with Reg. Suppose we were going to experiment with the items in the HKCU\Software\Microsoft\Notepad subkey but wanted to easily restore them to their original state once we were done. From Reg, you could back up the key to a file called notepadback.reg (".REG" is the default extension for Registry backup files) like so:

1. Open an elevated command prompt.

2. Type **reg export "HKCU\Software\Microsoft\Notepad" notepadback.reg**.

3. Press Enter. You should see the result "The operation completed successfully."

4. Type **type notepadback.reg** and press Enter. You'll see the data from Notepad's Registry entries, formatted as ASCII text.

Now let's modify Notepad's settings a bit and then import the backed-up settings to see that an import really does restore the Registry's previous values.

1. Open Regedit, if you don't already have it open.

2. Navigate to the Notepad settings: HKCU\Software\Microsoft\Notepad.

3. Open Notepad.

4. Click Format /Font ... and choose any font that you like.

5. Close Notepad.

6. Return to Regedit. Press F5 to refresh the screen. You should see your new font reflected in the "fFaceName" entry.

7.   From the command prompt where you exported the Notepad settings, type **reg import notepadbak.reg** and press Enter. Again you should see the result "The operation completed successfully."

8.   Returning to Regedit, again press F5. You'll see that fFontName has been restored to whatever it was before, probably "Lucida Console" (the default).

You can also export and import from the Registry with Regedit. To export a subkey or import an existing .REG file to that subkey, click on the subkey in Regedit and choose File /Export and tell Regedit where to save the file in the resulting dialog box to export, or File /Import and, again, respond to the dialog box asking what file to import from. There is yet another way to import — use Regedit from the command line. In the previous exercise, we could have typed not this:

```
reg import notepadbak.reg
```

but instead this:

```
regedit /s notepadbak.reg
```

Securing the Registry

Inasmuch as the Registry is sort of the master control room for your server software, it stands to reason that the control room ought to have a door with a lock on it. It does, which is why we're next going to examine Registry permissions.

Subkeys Have Permissions

While it's not been obvious so far, each Registry subkey has a set of Windows permissions for restricting who can modify or even *view* that subkey's contents. (You can't set permissions on an entry, just a subkey.) By default, Windows blocks any "standard" users ("standard user" is Microsoft's phrase for user accounts that are not members of the Administrators group) from writing anything to HKEY_LOCAL_MACHINE, and in fact those accounts can only write to their own HKEY_CURRENT_USER key. To demonstrate that, we need a non-administrative account, so let's create a user named "nopower," log on with that account, and view our Registry permissions. (Note: if you're skipping around the book and want to do this exercise but you've skipped ahead and already created something called an "Active Directory domain controller," then you will not be able to do this exercise, as standard users may not log onto an AD DC. It *will*, however, run fine on any member server or domain member, such as an XP or Vista workstation. If you *didn't* skip ahead, then don't worry, this will work fine.)

1.   Open an elevated command prompt.

2.   Type the following:

```
net user nopower Panda12 /add
shutdown -l
```

(That's two separate lines, and the option on "shutdown" is a lowercase "L," not a "1.") That creates the "nopower" user and logs you off. Log on as "nopower" with password

"Panda12." (Be sure to capitalize it or the system will reject the password as not being suffi-ciently "complex.")

3. Open Regedit.

4. Right-click the HKEY_CURRENT_User key.

5. In the resulting context menu, choose "Permissions . . ."

6. Find the "nopower" name in the upper pane so that you can see what permissions "nopower" gets in the bottom pane.

You'll see a screen like Figure 7.6.

FIGURE 7.6

Permissions on
HKEY_CURRENT_USER
for a standard user

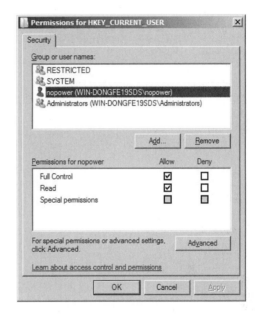

Notice that "Full Control" is checked, meaning that nopower can do anything it wants to anything in its HKEY_CURRENT_USER key. That makes sense, as nopower's HKEY_CURRENT_USER key exists for pretty much one reason: to store nopower's preferences. Click Cancel to clear that dialog box and then examine the permissions on HKEY_LOCAL_MACHINE, as you see in Figure 7.7.

Hmmm . . . there are only four groups here, but none explicitly names nopower. It's not a member of the RESTRICTED group (the multi-head icons refer to *groups* of users rather than par-ticular users), it's not the SYSTEM account (and no, I have no idea why SYSTEM gets a two-head ("group") icon when it should get a one-head ("user account") icon), nor is nopower a member of the Administrators group. nopower *is*, however, a member of the Everyone group, which, as you can see, only gets "read" access to HKEY_LOCAL_MACHINE. There's an example of how Windows tries to keep non-administrative users' fingers out of the gears.

But even administrators don't have *carte blanche* in the Registry. Ready for a surprise? Log off nopower and log back on as the Administrator account. Then look at permissions for HKLM\ SAM\SAM, the key in the Registry that stores local accounts, groups, and passwords. You'll notice that there's a part of the Registry that even administrators can't read, much less write! (Actually, that's not entirely true. The Administrators group may lack read and write permissions, but it has the ability to write *new permissions* for the key. Thus, if you really wanted to, you could give yourself read and write access to HKLM\SAM\SAM . . . but believe me, there's no real reason to do it.)

FIGURE 7.7
Permissions on
HKEY_LOCAL_MACHINE

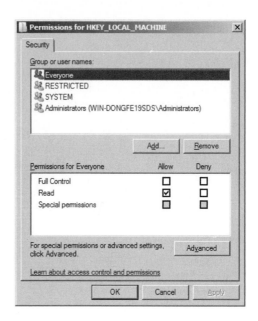

Registry Security: the Idea and the Effects

Why exactly did Microsoft lock down HKEY_LOCAL_MACHINE? Because the idea was that machines are shared, either in the sense that they are workstations on desktops used by different people at different times, or in the sense that the machines act as servers, offering their services to perhaps thousands of people. Just as a large company wouldn't leave the door to their headquarters' electrical control room unlocked, so also don't *you* want some random user walking up to a server, sitting down, logging in, and making a mess. Basically, the idea is that anything in HKEY_LOCAL_MACHINE affects everyone who uses the computer, and so only trusted administrators can modify HKLM.

Perhaps this makes the most sense if I zero in on a particular set of subkeys — call it "A Tale of Two 'Softwares.'" In the process, we'll also solve a mystery from a bit earlier in the chapter.

Recall that the Registry contains two different keys named "Software": HKLM\SOFTWARE and HKCU\Software. There are two keys named Software because of Windows' support for multiple users on a single system. Because more than one person might share a computer *and* share a piece of software, then those multiple people might want to configure that piece of shared software differently. So the familiar installation programs that we run to put new software on our systems copy all of the files necessary to run that new software to some folder on our systems, usually C:\Program Files. Then they create a new subkey *inside* the HKEY_LOCAL_MACHINE\SOFTWARE subkey, and put most of the configuration information for that software in the machine's profile. Then whenever a new user logs in (interactively) and runs the software, then Windows stores that user's preferences in his HKEY_CURRENT_USER\Software.

For example, suppose Jane and Tom share a computer; perhaps Jane works the day shift and Tom works the night shift. Let's say that their job is to draw engineering diagrams and they use the imaginary program that I wrote of earlier, a program called EDraw from a company called Bigfirm. Let's examine how HKLM\SOFTWARE\Bigfirm\EDraw and HKCU\Software\Bigfirm\EDraw get created.

First, someone's got to install EDraw. Notice that installing EDraw requires creating HKLM\SOFTWARE\Bigfirm\EDraw, which means writing to HKLM ... and standard users can't do that. (I find Microsoft's relatively new term "standard users" sort of amusing and I am *dying* to make a joke about non-standard users ... but I'm going to show manly restraint. For now.) That's moderately handy because the standard way to install an application on a Windows box involves copying the application's files to the Program Files directory (which standard users cannot write to), and the application's initial configuration settings to HKLM\SOFTWARE. In this way, Microsoft hopes to reduce the number of applications that a standard user could install, making "software installation" the province of administrators. It's not foolproof, of course, but it does help to reduce the amount of extra junk that users tend to put on their workstations, junk that makes the workstations less reliable and harder to troubleshoot.

Second, when does HKCU\SOFTWARE\Bigfirm\EDraw get created? That's a trick question, actually. Remember that I said that Tom and Jane share a machine, which means that there are two active users on the machine, and each user gets his or her own profile. Thus, when Jane's logged in, the HKCU that she sees is hers, and when Tom's logged in, then the HKCU that he sees is his. That'd mean that there are three Bigfirm\EDraw subkeys on this system — the central one in HKLM, the one in Jane's profile, and the one in Tom's profile. (Note that any other user accounts, like Administrator, would *not* have an HKCU\SOFTWARE\Bigfirm\EDraw subkey, as they've never started EDraw up.)

Why's this useful? Because now, when Tom's logged in and decides that he really likes drawing with English units against a black background, then that preference gets stuck in Tom's Bigfirm\EDraw subkey, not Jane's. That way, Jane always gets the background color and measurement units that she likes, and Tom keeps the one that he likes.

I should explain that what I just talked about is more of a *workstation* Registry concern than a Server Registry concern, but I threw it in (1) to help explain why Microsoft structured the Registry as they did and (2) to explain some issues that you'll end up having to deal with when helping users with application compatibility problems (which you'll get to do whether you like it or not). In general, it's worth mentioning that desktop systems like XP and Vista are very concerned about the people who *sit down* at those systems and log into them. Servers, in contrast, aren't (or shouldn't be), as they don't really have people sitting down at them and logging in very often — nearly never, in fact. As we'll see in the second book, good administrators in actual production environments should do their server administration from other systems (XP or Vista boxes, most likely) and then use remote administration tools. Why? Well, in the course of the day we admins, like everyone else, tend to surf the Web for documents, patches, etc., and look at e-mail — two very good ways for an inattentive user/admin to accidentally infect a system with some sort of malware. In the past year, for example, I probably haven't spent more than a few hours total actually sitting at the server (also known as an "interactive login"); most of the time I'm administering it over the network with various remote administration tools. In those cases, I'm still logged on, but it's called a "network login" to distinguish it from an interactive login. So in actual fact most users' connections to servers are network logins rather than interactive logins. (You'll make use of that information as you work with systems, trust me.)

Before I leave my tale of two Softwares, however, let me tell you about a fairly common problem in software compatibility. Recall that only administrators can write the HKLM\SOFTWARE, but any user can write to his personal HKCU\Software, and Registry permissions block any attempt to violate that. That's the theory, but some software vendors have taken quite a while to understand it. For example, prior to the 2007 version of AutoCAD, the most-used engineering drawing program in the world, the application would store user preferences in HKLM, not HKCU. Result: you had to be an administrator to draw a blueprint on your computer! Why'd Autodesk, the creators of AutoCAD, do something so dumb? Well, the first popular 32-bit version of Windows was Windows 95, which didn't have any security at all, and that's the version that Autodesk used when first implementing AutoCAD on 32-bit Windows. Their developers clearly didn't understand the distinction between HKLM\SOFTWARE and HKCU\Software, and never *had* to understand the distinction, because Windows 95's lack of security meant that the HKLM-centric AutoCAD worked fine. Years went by and people started moving to the versions of Windows that included security (Windows 2000, Windows XP) and all of a sudden AutoCAD began failing unless the user was an administrator. "XP is buggy, it's incompatible!," people cried, when in fact the problem lay with the application vendor. Nor is this an unusual story; as I write this sentence in 2008, there are hundreds of applications whose designers still haven't figured out the difference between HKLM and HKCU, even if Autodesk finally has!

Where the Registry Lives: Hives

I don't know about you, but I can't help wondering where things like the Registry actually *live*. I mean, they're on the hard disk, right, so *where* on the hard disk? We'll see in this section.

The Registry is mostly contained in a set of files called *hives*. ("Mostly" because some of it is built automatically every time you boot up your system. For example, Server doesn't know what devices are on a SCSI chain until you boot.) Hives are binary files, so there's no way to look at them without a special editor of some kind, like Regedit. Knowing where hives are sometimes helps troubleshoot system problems.

Most, although not all, of the Registry is stored in hive files. Most of the hive files themselves are kept out of view by being stored with Hidden and, in some cases, System file attributes. They're always open, so you're kind of limited in what you can do with them directly — any real hive manipulation should happen via Regedit or Reg.

A Look at the Hive Files

The machine-specific hive files are in the \WINDOWS\system32\config directory. The user-specific hive files are in the \Users*username* directories. (Note that location is new to 2008 — Windows 2000, XP, and 2003 stored user profiles in a folder called \Documents and Settings*username*.) You can see the hive files that correspond to parts of the subtree listed in Table 7.2.

Table 7.2 needs a few notes to clarify it. First, about the HKEY_CLASSES_ROOT subtree: It is copied from HKEY_KEY_LOCAL_MACHINE\SOFTWARE\Classes at boot time. The file exists for use by 16-bit Windows applications (which is odd, given that I'm running a 64-bit copy of Server and 64-bit Windows is incapable of running any kind of 16-bit apps). While you're logged onto Server 2008, however, the two keys are linked; if you make a change to one, the change is reflected in the other.

The local user profiles live in \Users*username*, where each user gets a directory named *username*. For example, I've got a user account named mark, so there's a directory named \users\mark on my computer. If I look in it, I find the files ntuser.dat and ntuser.dat.log, provided I tell Explorer to show me hidden and system files.

TABLE 7.2: Hive Files

SUBTREE/KEY	FILENAME
HKEY_LOCAL_MACHINE\SAM	SAM (primary) and SAM.LOG (backup)
HKEY_LOCAL_MACHINE\SECURITY	SECURITY (primary) and SECURITY.LOG (backup)
HKEY_LOCAL_MACHINE\SOFTWARE	SOFTWARE (primary) and SOFTWARE.LOG (backup)
HKEY_LOCAL_MACHINE\SYSTEM	SYSTEM (primary) and SYSTEM.ALT (backup)
HKEY_USERS\DEFAULT	DEFAULT (primary) and DEFAULT.LOG (backup)
HKEY_USERS\Security ID	NTUSER.DAT (in the Users*username* folder of the particular user)
HKEY_CURRENT_USER	NTUSER.DAT (in the Users\username folder of whatever user is currently logged in)
HKEY_CLASSES_ROOT	(Created from current control set at boot time)

To summarize, then, the core of the Registry is the four *S*s and DEFAULT:

◆ SAM

◆ SECURITY

◆ SYSTEM

◆ SOFTWARE

SAM contains the user database; SECURITY complements SAM by containing information such as whether a server is a member server or a domain controller, what the name of its domain is, and the like. Domain controllers don't make much use of SAM files (although they do have them), but workstations (XP, Vista, etc.) and member servers all have SAMs. SYSTEM contains configuration information like what drivers and system programs the computer uses, which should be loaded on boot-up, and how their parameters are set. SOFTWARE tends to contain more overall configuration information about the larger software modules in the system, configuration information that does *not* vary from user to user. And then every user has an NTUSER.DAT with their specific application preferences in it.

One question remains about the hive files, however. Why do all the files have paired files with extensions .LOG1 and .LOG2? Read on.

Fault Tolerance in the Registry

Notice that every hive file has at least one file with the same name but an extension like .LOG1, .LOG2 or the like. (I'll generically call them "LOG" files.) That's really useful because Server 2008 (and in fact every version of NT) uses it to protect the Registry during updates.

Whenever a hive file is to be changed, the change is first written into its LOG file. The LOG file isn't actually a backup file; it's more a journal of changes to the primary file. Once the description of the change to the hive file is complete, the journal file is written to disk. When I say "written to disk," I *mean* written to disk. Often, a disk write ends up hanging around in the disk cache for a while, but this write is "flushed" to disk. Then the system makes the changes to the hive file based on the information in the journal file. If the system crashes during the hive write operation, there is enough information in the journal file to "roll back" the hive to its previous position.

The exception to this procedure comes with the SYSTEM hive. The SYSTEM hive is really important because it contains the CurrentControlSet. For that reason, the backup file for SYSTEM, SYSTEM.ALT, is a complete backup of SYSTEM. If one file is damaged, the system can use the other to boot.

Notice that HKEY_LOCAL_MACHINE\HARDWARE does not have a hive. That's because the key is rebuilt each time you boot so Server 2003 can adapt itself to changes in computer hardware. The Plug and Play Manager, which runs at boot time, gathers the information that Server needs to create HKEY_LOCAL_MACHINE\HARDWARE.

Confused about where all the keys come from? You'll find a recap in Table 7.3. It's similar to Table 7.2, but it's more specific about how the keys are built at boot time.

TABLE 7.3: Construction of Keys at Boot Time

KEY	HOW IT'S CONSTRUCTED AT BOOT TIME
HKEY_LOCAL_MACHINE:	
HARDWARE	Plug and Play Manager
SAM	SAM hive file
SECURITY	SECURITY hive file
SOFTWARE	SOFTWARE hive file
SYSTEM	SYSTEM hive file
HKEY_CLASSES_ROOT	SYSTEM hive file, Classes subkey
HKEY_USERS_DEFAULT	DEFAULT hive file
HKEY_USERS\Sxxx	Particular user's NTUSER.DAT file
HKEY_CURRENT_USER	Particular user's NTUSER.DAT file

Remote Registry Modification

You can modify another computer's Registry, perhaps to repair it or to do some simple kind of remote maintenance, by loading that computer's Registry. Regedit lets you do that simply; just click File/Connect Network Registry, and Regedit then asks for the name of the remote computer. You fill in the name, click OK and, if necessary, Regedit will ask for a user name and password with permissions to access the remote computer's Registry. Once Regedit is satisfied that you're Da Man permission-wise, you get a new icon under your My Computer icon and the HKEY_LOCAL_MACHINE and HKEY_USERS subtrees of that remote computer. (The others don't show up, as they're all either dynamic or are simply mappings to subsets of the other subtrees.)

NOTE

As with all remote operations, this won't work if the remote server's firewall blocks whatever ports Regedit needs to do remote Registry control.

You can then edit the remote computer's Registry as if you were there. When done, just click File/Disconnect Network Registry and Regedit breaks the connection.

You can also load a particular hive with the Load Hive or Unload Hive commands. More specifically, you can load or unload the hives only for HKEY_USERS and HKEY_LOCAL_MACHINE. Here's how:

1. Start Regedit.

2. Under My Computer, click either the HKEY_LOCAL_MACHINE folder or the HKEY_USERS folder.

3. Click File/Load Hive.

4. In the resulting dialog box, point to the exact hive file itself — a particular NTUSER.DAT on a share somewhere.

The hive shows up as another key. You can then edit it and use File/Unload Hive to disconnect from it.

WARNING

And I know you're getting tired of me reminding you, but I have to point out that Unload is not the same as Save. Those changes you made happened immediately.

Again, the Load Hive option appears only if you've selected one of those two subtrees. Unload Hive is available only if you've selected a subkey of one of those two subtrees.

Why, specifically, would you load a hive or a remote Registry? In my experience, you typically load a hive in order to get to a user's profile. Suppose a user has set up all of the colors as black on black and made understanding the screen impossible. You could load the hive that corresponds to that user, modify it, and then unload it.

You could load and save hive files to a USB stick, walk the floppy over to a malfunctioning machine, and load the hive onto the machine's hard disk, potentially repairing a system problem. To do that, you'd need to be able to access the system's hard disk *while the system wasn't running*, as you can't swap out a hive file while the OS is running — the OS locks it open. You can get around that, however, by popping your Server 2008 installation DVD into your DVD drive and booting from the DVD. Don't choose to reinstall the operating system; instead, at the page that says "Install Now," choose the "Repair your computer" option (it's in smaller print) and from there choose "Command prompt." Now you can swap hives to your heart's content.

There is yet another way to control Registries remotely, through something called domain-based group policies, which are covered in the second book in the chapter by that name.

Backing Up and Restoring a Registry

By now, it should be pretty clear that the Registry is an important piece of information and that it should be protected. It protects itself pretty well with its LOG files, but how can you back it up?

Unfortunately, the fact that Registry hive files are always open makes it tough to back up the Registry since most backup utilities are stymied by open files. Server 2008 will back up your entire Registry, but unfortunately you can't tell 2008's backup program to only back up the Registry. You see, Windows Server 2008 completely changed the way backup works, and as of Windows Server 2008 two new things happen. First, no server can back itself up without adding a "backup role" — not the end of the world, but I'm not certain why anyone would create an actual production server without being able to back it up. Second, the new-to-2008 Server backup program only backs up entire drives, so there's not really a way to back up just the Registry in Windows, starting with Windows Vista and Windows Server 2008. That's probably not terrible given the low cost of extra hard disks, but, again, it is a bit odd and you can learn more about it in the last chapter of the second book. Furthermore, it's sort of a shame that 2008 makes it so hard to back up and restore some or all of the Registry — years ago, NT 4.0 had a neat little program called RDISK that would do it. Sadly, RDISK is gone with no replacement.

What if you want to back up and restore only a portion of the Registry? Actually, you already know — remember REG EXPORT? That'll do the trick, but only for small portions of the Registry. Trying to import entire keys like HKLM or HKCU is almost useless because you can't *export* either key — as you'll see if you try, it always fails because the operating system wants to control *any* writes of some keys. But exporting an entire subkey for a particular application can be useful, as you can always import the subkey back, so long as the application's not running at the time. When would that be useful? Well, suppose you've painstakingly set up an application for a user, spending an hour or two noodling around with all of its settings and configuration parameters. You don't want to have to do all that ever again, so you *might* be able to save your work by just exporting that application's Registry subkey. (Why did I say "might"? Remember — not every application stores its configuration in the Registry, and some apps only store *some* configuration in the Registry. You'll need to experiment a bit and find out what'll work for any given application.)

No one *wants* to play around in the Registry, but in real life, most network administrators will find a bit of Registry spelunking to be the only answer to many problems. Knowing how the Registry is organized and what tools are available to modify it will prove valuable to all Server repair folks.

Chapter 8

Controlling Windows Server: Group Policy

Group Policy is a technology that has been around since Windows 2000 was introduced. Since its introduction, it has proven to be the most powerful and efficient technology available to centrally manage Windows computers. To top it off as a viable technology, it is free within every Windows computer that is released.

Group Policy provides a centralized solution for managing all aspects of the computer and user environment. Within a single Group Policy Object (GPO), there are thousands (more than 5,000 on last count!) of potential settings that you can configure. The options in a single GPO can configure settings both for the computer and for the user. Settings can be configured that control security, desktop settings, printer installation, mapped drives, local group membership, and Registry settings. Of course, with 5,000 settings, these are just a few of the potential settings.

Group Policy is a technology that you can leverage on a single computer or using Active Directory. The power of Group Policy within Active Directory is substantial and impressive. We will discuss Group Policy for Active Directory in the companion book in the series, *Mastering Windows Server 2008: Essential Technologies*; here, we will discuss working with Group Policy on an individual computer, which are referred to as Local Group Policy Objects (LGPOs).

Every Windows Vista and Windows Server 2008 computer comes with the ability to configure the LGPOs. These LGPOs provide the power to manage every user who logs into the computer in a like manner or, if desired, by exception with a unique set of policy settings. This granular approach to policy management gives any administrator ultimate control over desktops and servers as well as the users who might log into them.

The Power of Group Policy

Group Policy provides a monolithic approach to desktop and server management. Ever since the introduction of Group Policy with Windows 2000, Microsoft has constantly improved and expanded the capabilities of Group Policy. With the current release of Windows Vista and Windows Server 2008, Microsoft has made a distinct decision to make Group Policy the preferred method for managing desktops and users within a Microsoft environment.

Whether you are in a domain or working with just a single computer, Microsoft has provided LGPOs for managing the computer where the LGPO resides and any user who logs onto that computer. The capabilities within a single LGPO are quite impressive (if used), providing control over nearly every aspect of the Windows computing environment. Remember, LGPOs can be leveraged or not; consider them an advanced control that can be used, abused, or completely ignored.

LGPOs manage both the computer and the users who log onto the computer. There are, however, different areas that can be configured on each. Figure 8.1 provides a snapshot of an LGPO and the settings that can be configured for the computer.

FIGURE 8.1
The LGPO provides numerous settings to control the computer environment.

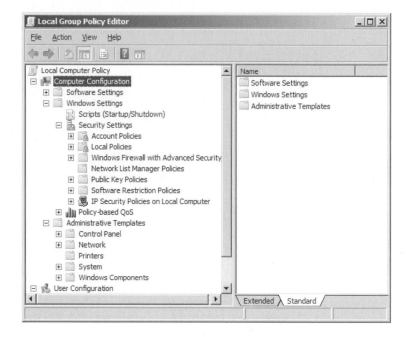

Here are some ideas of how you can use the settings to control the computer environment:

◆ Run a script that maps drive letters, maps printers, updates Registry values, and much more.

◆ Map a connection to a printer that every user who logs on will have access to.

◆ Establish a password policy for any local user account.

◆ Modify the User Rights for the server to allow a subset of server administrators the ability to back up files and folders.

◆ Establish an IPSec policy to restrict the communication of the server in order to protect the data residing on it.

LGPOs also provide settings that can manage the users who log onto the computer, as shown in Figure 8.2.

Here are some ideas of how you can use the settings to control the user environment:

◆ You can configure logon scripts to create individual drive mappings, printer mappings, Registry settings, and virtually anything else that can be placed in a script.

◆ You can configure individual printer mappings that only the user being targeted will receive after logon.

◆ You can configure Internet Explorer including every toolbar, drop-down list, check box, and setting.

FIGURE 8.2
The LGPO provides numerous settings to control the user environment.

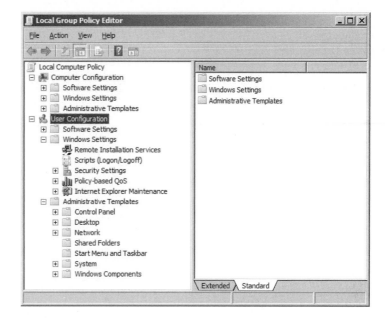

- You can tweak the Start menu to meet the need of the user.

- You can remove Control Panel to limit what the user can see and thus manage.

- You can modify the desktop icons and settings to add functionality (such as Active Desktop) or eliminate distractions for the user.

The true power of all the settings is that they reside on the computer after configuration and apply every time the computer is started or a user logs on. This type of management is extremely useful and provides a way to consistently manage all desktops and servers in the environment.

Working with LGPOs

You control LGPOs using a few tools on your Windows computer. Depending on which LGPO you want to manage and configure, you will need to select the appropriate tool. There is not a default LGPO management tool, and you cannot access any of the LGPOs from the Start menu or Administrative Tools.

To better understand how to access the LGPOs, it is first important to understand the different levels of LGPOs that can be configured. Before Windows Vista, there used to be a single LGPO that controlled the computer and every user who logged onto the computer. This was not very flexible or efficient, because every user, administrator and nonadministrator, were controlled the same way. Now there are three levels:

- Local Group Policy

- Administrators or Non-Administrators LGPO

- User Specific LGPO

These three levels of LGPOs provide a very granular control mechanism, allowing ultimate control over the computer no matter who logs onto it.

We'll define the three levels in more depth in the following sections, but for now, to show you how the LGPOs function, we'll take a look at an example. Specifically, we'll show how to control access to the Control Panel for a Windows Server 2008 computer as an example.

Imagine there are two admins for the server, both of whom have membership in the local Administrators group. There are also two help-desk employees who also need to log onto this server, but they should not have the ability to modify anything in the Control Panel. They don't have membership in the local Administrators group. Finally, there is the IT Director. Her name is Vanessa. She does not have membership in the local Administrators group, but she should be able to access the Control Panel to perform some of her duties.

To accomplish this, you will need to set up three LGPOs, as shown in Table 8.1. Figure 8.3 illustrates what the final LGPO structure will look like.

TABLE 8.1: LGPOs to Configure Control Panel Example

LGPO	GPO POLICY CONFIGURED	POLICY SETTING
Administrators	User Configuration\Administrative Templates\Control Panel\Prohibit access to the Control Panel	Disabled
Non-Administrators	User Configuration\Administrative Templates\Control Panel\Prohibit access to the Control Panel	Enabled
Vanessa	User Configuration\Administrative Templates\Control Panel\Prohibit access to the Control Panel	Disabled

FIGURE 8.3
LGPOs configured in the Control Panel scenario

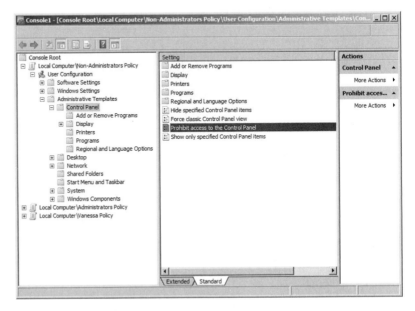

You could also accomplish this with the Local Group Policy being set to disable the policy. The result would be the same.

These LGPOs have a hierarchy that is adhered to. The most generic of the LGPOs is applied first and has the weakest precedence, which is the Local Group Policy. The most granular and targeted LGPO is applied last and has the highest precedence, which is the User Specific LGPO. The other LGPO is applied in the middle and has the appropriate precedence between the other two LGPOs.

Local Group Policy

The Local Group Policy is the generic LGPO that you have always had on a desktop or server. The Local Group Policy is the easiest to access and provides the widest scope of configuration. Every user who logs onto the computer will be affected by this LGPO.

This is also the only LGPO that can control computer settings, because the other two LGPOs can only modify user-based settings. You should use this LGPO to configure the generic or baseline settings for a computer. Then, you can use the other LGPOs to modify these settings or append to these settings, depending on the user or type of user who is logging on.

You can access the Local Group Policy in two ways. The first way is the most common way, since it has been around for the longest and is the most efficient. This method is to just run `gpedit.msc` in the Run dialog box from the Start menu.

The alternate method is to load the Local Group Policy into the Microsoft Management Console. This method requires that you run `mmc.msc` in the Run dialog box from the Start menu. From there, add the snap-in for the Group Policy Object editor for the Local Computer, as shown in Figure 8.4.

FIGURE 8.4
To load in the Local Group Policy, select Local Computer from the Group Policy Object text box.

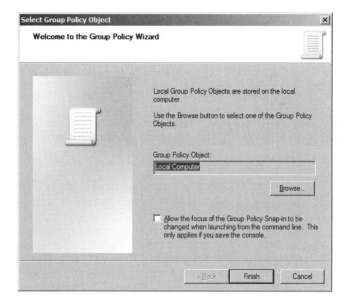

To access this GPO, you will use the local Group Policy Object editor. To access the local Group Policy editor, simply follow these steps:

1. Click the Start button.

2. Select the Run menu option.

3. Type **gpedit.msc** in the Open text field.

4. Press Enter.

NOTE

This is an administrative task; therefore, if you have UAC enabled, you will have to agree to the permissions or provide the credentials to open the Group Policy editor in the MMC.

Administrators or Non-Administrators LGPO

As the name represents, the settings in these LGPOs will target either the users in the Administrators group or users in all other groups. The idea is that when a user has membership in the local Administrators group, that user could/should have more privileges than a user who is not in this group.

Note that the LGPOs that control these settings only modify user-based settings. There are no settings under these LGPOs that control computer-based settings, which are located under the Computer Configuration node.

Since there are two "types" of groups, there are two LGPOs that control them. For you to control both of these "types" of users, you will need to configure both LGPOs. To access these LGPOs, you must use the MMC. The steps are similar to those in the previous section, with a slight alteration in the scoping of the Group Policy Object that is loaded in the MMC. Instead of choosing the Local Computer from the Group Policy Object text box, click the Browse button to look for the Administrators or Non-Administrators group listed under the Users tab, as shown in Figure 8.5.

FIGURE 8.5
You can find the Administrators and Non-Administrators LGPOs by using the MMC.

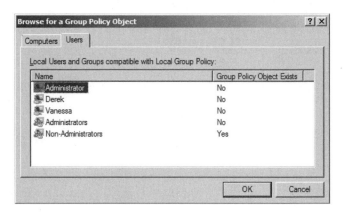

To access both of these local GPOs for editing, follow these steps:

1. Click the Start button.

2. Select the Run menu option.

3. Type **MMC** in the Open text field.

4. From within the MMC console, select the File menu from the toolbar.

5. Select Add/Remove Snap-in from the drop-down menu.

6. Select Group Policy Object editor from the list of snap-ins.

> **NOTE**
>
> This is an administrative task; therefore, if you have UAC enabled, you will have to agree to the permissions or provide the credentials to open the Group Policy editor in the MMC.

7. Leave Local Computer as the entry under Group Policy Object.

8. Select the Browse button.

9. Select the Users tab from the Browse for a Group Policy Object dialog box.

10. Select Administrators from the list, and then select the OK button.

11. Select Finish from the Select Group Policy Object dialog box.

12. Select OK from the Add or Remove Snap-ins dialog box.

13. Expand the Local Computer\Administrators Policy node from the console window.

14. Repeat steps 5–13 for the Non-Administrators local GPO, replacing Non-Administrators for Administrators in the appropriate steps.

User Specific LGPO

Finally, there is a very granular LGPO that can be configured on every Windows Server 2008 and Windows Vista computer. This policy is geared to target individual user accounts. There are only user-based policy settings in the LGPO, and the settings target only a single user.

The caveat to using this LGPO is that the user must have an account in the local Security Accounts Manager (SAM) of the computer that you are configuring. (In today's networked world, this is usually not found anymore because user accounts are stored in a centralized location such as with a domain configuration and Active Directory, but there are exceptions.)

To view and configure this LGPO, you will also use the MMC and follow the same steps as you did for the Administrators and Non-Administrators LGPO, except you will select the user account listed on the Users tab for which you want to create a LGPO when adding the Group Policy Object editor snap-in to the MMC. If you have selected the Administrator account, it will show up in the MMC similar to Figure 8.6.

Here are the steps that you would follow to access the local User Specific GPOs:

1. Click the Start button.

2. Select the Run menu option.

3. Type **MMC** in the Open text field.

> **NOTE**
>
> This is an administrative task; therefore, if you have UAC enabled, you will have to agree to the permissions or provide the credentials to open the Group Policy editor in the MMC.

4. From within the MMC console, select the File menu from the toolbar.

5. Select Add/Remove Snap-in from the drop-down menu.

6. Select Group Policy Object editor from the list of snap-ins.

FIGURE 8.6
Once a user is selected for management of the LGPO, it will show up in the MMC with all the User Configuration settings exposed.

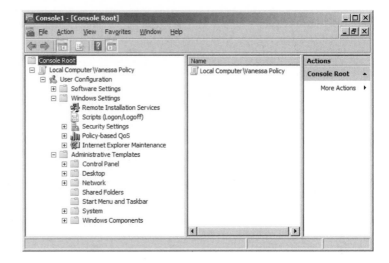

7. Leave Local Computer as the entry under Group Policy Object.

8. Click the Browse button.

9. Select the Users tab from the Browse for a Group Policy Object dialog box.

10. Select the desired user account from the list, and then select the OK button.

11. Select Finish from the Select Group Policy Object dialog box.

12. Select OK from the Add or Remove Snap-ins dialog box.

13. Expand the Local Computer\<username> Policy node from the console window.

Group Policy Breakdown: How LGPOs Are Organized and Structured

LGPOs are very logical and have the same structure on each computer where they exist. Understanding the structure, as well as the files that create that structure, will help with administration, configuration, and troubleshooting of each LGPO. It is also important to understand what is changed on a computer when an LGPO setting is made, as well as how that change is processed.

Computer Node vs. User Node

When you are looking at an LGPO within an LGPO editor, you will see a distinct separation of the settings. The settings are broken down into two different sections. The first section is related to the computer itself and labeled Computer Configuration. The second section is related to the user who logs onto the computer and is labeled User Configuration. Figure 8.7 shows these two sections.

It's important to understand the application of each of these sections. All the settings under the Computer Configuration node apply to the computer when it starts up. These settings will not apply to individual users when they log on; they are targeting the computer at startup.

In a similar manner, the settings under the User Configuration node target users who log onto the computer. These settings will not configure the computer at startup. These settings don't apply until the user logs on.

FIGURE 8.7
Each LGPO is broken down into two different sections: Computer Configuration and User Configuration.

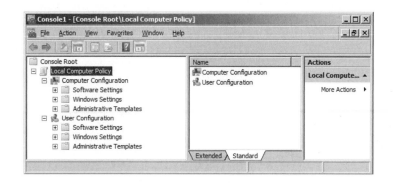

LGPO . . . Just a Glorified Registry Editor

If you break down the settings that are available in an LGPO, you will find that many of them simply modify a Registry value. Group Policy has been compared to a centralized management tool for the Registry, and in some ways that is exactly what it is. Thousands of policies in an LGPO do nothing but expose areas of the Registry in a friendly format, allowing the centralized management of the settings in the Registry without needing to open any Registry-editing tools.

To understand how the LGPO matches up with the Registry, first a summary of the Registry structure is in order. Although many HKEYs show up when you edit the Registry, two primary keys construct the Registry. The two primary HKEYs for the Registry are HKEY_Local_Machine and HKEY_Users.

HKEY_Local_Machine is the computer part of the Registry. These settings are directly controlling only the areas of the Registry that pertain to the computer itself, not the user. This is the area of the Registry that deals with security of the computer, network communications, installed applications, user rights, and the Security Accounts Manager (SAM).

HKEY_Users is all about user accounts that have logged into the computer, as well as there is a default portion of this HKEY that controls the initial user profile for all users that log onto the computer. The settings that are stored in this section of the Registry control what the user sees on their desktop, Internet Explorer settings and configurations, default folders, Start menu, Control Panel, and much more.

If you look under the hood of a GPO setting that updates the Registry, you will find that most of the settings are located in one of four different locations in the Registry. The four locations are as follows:

HKLM\SOFTWARE\Policies

HKLM\SOFTWARE\Microsoft\Windows\CurrentVersion\Policies

HKCU\SOFTWARE\Policies

HKCU\SOFTWARE\Microsoft\Windows\CurrentVersion\Policies

These locations are easy so spot, because they are the four locations that end in the Policies subkey. These four locations were created in Windows 2000 to accommodate the issue with "tattooing" that was prevalent with System Policies back in the Windows NT/95 days.

GROUP POLICY TATTOOING

The concept of tattooing has been around for a long time. The concept is rather simple to understand, but not that easy to eliminate. For the most part, settings that are configured in a GPO (LGPO or one in

Active Directory) are Registry modifications. If the GPO modifies the Registry value, and then the GPO is deleted, the Registry value will remain altered. The only way to change the Registry value back or alter it again is either to create another GPO with the setting altered or to manually alter the Registry setting.

The policies for an LGPO can be found under one of two nodes when editing the GPO in the GPME. Both nodes have the same name, Administrative Templates, but they are located under each of the top-level nodes within the GPME: Computer Configuration and User Configuration. Figure 8.8 illustrates where you will find the two nodes in the GPME.

FIGURE 8.8
Administrative Templates nodes contain the policies that come with a GPO by default.

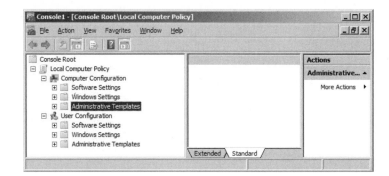

Preferences are not readily available in a default LGPO. If you add in a custom `.adm` template or ADMX file, you will see additional settings available in the GPME, as shown in Figure 8.9.

FIGURE 8.9
Custom Registry entries show up in the GPME and are considered Preferences.

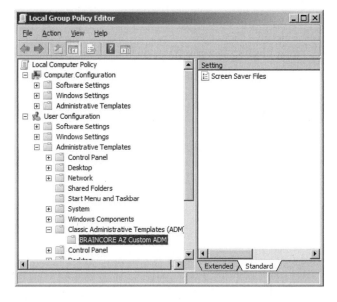

POLICIES VS. PREFERENCES

There is a distinct difference between policies and preferences within a GPO. These settings are clearer when you look at a GPO stored in Windows Server 2008 Active Directory; however, the concepts and definitions are still valid for any GPO, going back to Windows 2000.

A *policy* is an enforced setting. Policies are written to one of the four locations in the Registry that Group Policy uses, which are protected from standard users making routine modification to them. The Policies subkeys in the Registry have additional access control list (ACL) entries that prohibit them from being modified by anyone who is not in the local Administrators group. In conjunction with locking down the Registry entry, most of the applications that use these Registry entries disable the user interface, prohibiting the setting from being modified by the user.

A *preference* is a setting that is not enforced on the computer. These settings are designed to function outside of the Policies subkeys located in the Registry. Since these settings reside outside of these subkeys, they do allow for the modification of applications and operating system functions that are not Group Policy–aware. The new preference settings that are available with Windows Server 2008 domains are not valid in a local GPO. However, "preferences" can be created by customizing .adm templates or ADMX files. Any setting configured in one of these two file types will behave almost identically to that of a Group Policy Preference setting.

Table 8.2 summarizes the main differences between policies and preferences with regard to the LGPO.

TABLE 8.2:   Policies vs. Preferences for an LGPO

GROUP POLICY POLICIES	GROUP POLICY PREFERENCES
Settings are enforced	Settings are not enforced
User interface is disabled (in most cases)	User interface is not disabled
Not flexible or useful for custom Registry entries, or file/folder management	Custom entries for Registry entries, and file/folder management is easy
Supports Group Policy–aware applications	Does not support Group Policy–aware applications
Removing the policy setting restores the original setting	Removing the preference setting does not restore the original setting
Settings in Registry are secured to only allow administrators access	Settings in the Registry are not secured, allowing standard users access
Stored in one of the four Policies subkeys in the Registry	Stored outside of the four Policies subkeys in the Registry

Introducing ADM Templates and ADMX Files

When you edit an LGPO in the GPME, you will see a common structure. The structure is created by default files that reside on the local computer. The Registry-based settings that were just discussed, Policies and Preferences, show up under the Administrative Templates nodes when editing the GPO in the GPME.

These templates are essential for managing Registry-based settings. If these files are deleted or not available during the editing of an LGPO, the nodes and policies within the GPME will not be available. The reason for this is that the .adm templates and ADMX files not only dictate which Registry value should be updated, but they also create the interface in the GPME for configuring the entries.

ADM TEMPLATES

ADM templates are legacy files that were used with Windows 2000, Windows XP, and Windows Server 2003 to create the Administrative Templates nodes within the Group Policy Object editor (now called the Group Policy Management editor). The files also defined the Registry path, value, and data for each setting available for configuration in the editor.

There were five default ADM templates with Windows XP and Windows Server 2003, which were automatically loaded in the GPO when it was edited. These files are located in the C:\Windows\System32 folder. These files could be customized too, which allowed for virtually any Registry setting to be configured and modified using Group Policy.

If you have an ADM template that needs to be added to the GPO, follow these steps, which add in the Visio11.adm template:

1. Right-click the Administrative Templates node under the Computer Configuration section of the GPO and choose Add/Remove Templates.

2. In the Add/Remove Templates dialog box, click Add.

3. In the Policy Templates dialog box, select Desktop in the left pane.

4. Select the Visio11.adm template in the list. Click Open. You will see the Add/Remove Templates dialog box with the Visio11.adm template listed, as shown in Figure 8.10.

5. Click Close.

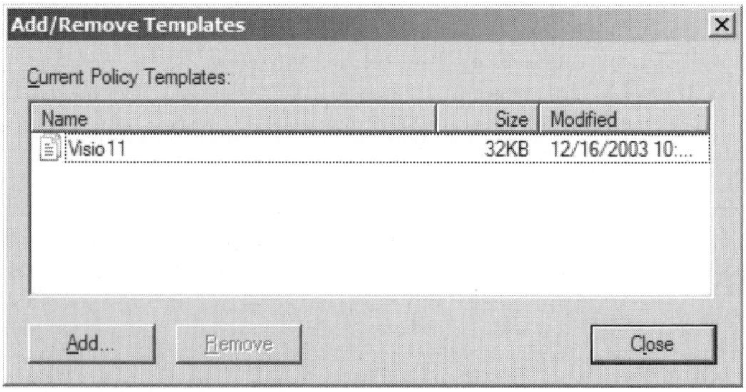

FIGURE 8.10
The Visio11.adm template added to a GPO

6. After the ADM template has been imported to the GPO, you can see the Visio 2003 node and policy settings in the GPO, as shown in Figure 8.11.

FIGURE 8.11
Policy settings for Visio 2003 are available after the `Visio11.adm` template is added to the GPO.

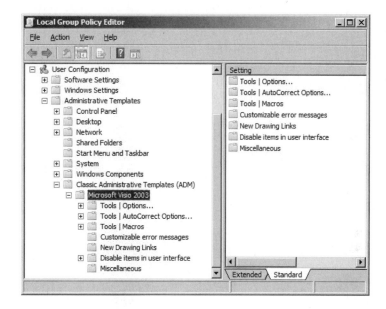

USING AND CREATING ADM TEMPLATES

ADM templates are still supported and valid in a Windows Vista and Windows Server 2008 environment. If you have custom ADM templates, you can convert them to ADMX files or keep them in the `.adm` template format.

If you want to convert the ADM templates to ADMX files, you can use a tool that is designed to perform this function. The tool is called the ADMX Migrator and can be downloaded at `http://www.microsoft.com/downloads/details.aspx?FamilyID = 0f1eec3d-10c4-4b5f-9625-97c2f731090c&DisplayLang = en`.

You can create additional custom ADM templates or use current templates. If you need to create a custom ADM template or need to modify an existing one, you can find additional information for these tasks at `http://www.microsoft.com/downloads/details.aspx?FamilyID = e7d72fa1-62fe-4358-8360-8774ea8db847&displaylang = en`.

The main reasons that ADM templates were replaced with the new ADMX files were many. The main reason was for language flexibility, since ADM templates were not flexible for multiple languages. The other reasons that ADM templates were replaced include the following:

◆ ADMX files create a multiple language environment for custom Registry entries in a GPO.

◆ ADMX files eliminate SYSVOL bloat, which means the inclusion and duplication of the ADM templates in the SYSVOL of every domain controller within the domain. This causes the domain controller to store duplicate files, which takes up storage space and can cause replication performance issues.

◆ ADMX files ease version updates of Registry entries through custom files.

◆ ADMX files remove decentralized administration of custom .adm templates.

ADMX FILES

ADMX files were first introduced with Windows Vista and are the new file format used to create default Administrative Template settings in a GPO, as well as the preferred method for creating custom Registry-based entries available for management in a GPO.

The ADMX structure is more granular than the ADM template structure, which is quickly obvious when you compare the default 133 ADMX files to that of only five ADM templates. The ADMX files reside in the C:\Windows\PolicyDefinitions folder on Windows Server 2003 and Windows Vista computers.

ADMX files are now based on XML, which is more flexible and feature capable compared to the legacy ADM templates. ADMX files are language-neutral files, which define the policy settings within the GPME. The text that is displayed in the GPME is not defined in the ADMX file. Instead, each ADMX file comes with an ADML file, which has the same filename as the ADMX file, just a different file extension. It is the ADML file that contains the language-specific text that shows up in the GPME. The ADML files are also in the C:\Windows\PolicyDefinitions folder, but they are tucked into language-specific folders under this location. To take a look at the full list of the English version of the ADML files, follow these steps:

1. Click the Start button.

2. Click Computer from the Start menu.

3. Double-click the C: drive from the list of Hard Disk Drives.

4. Double-click the Windows folder.

5. Double-click the PolicyDefinitions folder.

6. Double-click the en-US folder to see the list of ADML files.

The benefits of the ADMX files are substantial, especially when moving to a domain environment. However, the overall benefits are still there when using ADMX files in the LGPO:

◆ Language neutral ADMX files work with language specific ADML files

◆ ADMX files are granular, allowing for more control over newer versions of ADMX and ADML files

◆ ADMX files are not stored in the SYSVOL on domain controllers (domain specific benefit)

◆ A central store can be used for centralized management and consumption of ADMX and ADML files (domain specific benefit)

Not All Group Policy Settings Are Registry-Based

It is true that most settings in an LGPO modify the Registry. As mentioned, the two key areas of the Registry that are configured are the HKLM and HKCU nodes and settings. There are, however, other areas of the computer that can be configured and controlled. Each of the areas is dealt with in a unique way, because each specific area must be controlled using variables, files, or some other mechanism to control the settings.

To get an idea of how some settings don't affect the Registry but still configure the computer, let's look at one specific setting. One setting that does not configure the Registry but still affects the computer is the security setting that can Enable/Disable the Administrator account. The setting is located under the Computer Configuration\Windows Settings\Local Policies\Security Options and is the first policy listed, "Accounts: Administrator account status," as shown in Figure 8.12.

FIGURE 8.12
Policy that can enable or disable the local Administrator account

Unlike the Administrative Templates settings that are stored in the `Registry.pol` file, this setting and all other security settings are stored in the `security.sdb` file located at %windir%\ Security\database. This file is used in lieu of the `GptTmpl.inf` file that is stored in the GPT for domain based GPOs. The contents of this file includes the setting that toggles the variable for whether the account is enabled or disabled. There is no Registry path associated with this entry; it is simply a variable, named EnableAdminAccount.

There are numerous other common settings that are also not Registry-based. A small list of these settings include the following:

- Password Policies
- Audit Policies
- User Rights
- IPSec Policies
- Software Restriction Policies
- Scripts (logon, logoff, startup, shutdown)

As you can see, there are plenty of LGPO settings that are not Registry-based. This means that the LGPO is not exactly a fancy Registry editor tool, as it is perceived in the industry many times. An LGPO is a complex and powerful tool that can configure many areas of the computer and user environment.

Introducing Client Side Extensions

At the core of Group Policy processing and application are the files that perform most of the work within Group Policy. These files, referred to as Client Side Extensions (CSEs), are located on every target computer and must be present for a computer to consume Group Policy settings.

CSEs are the core of Group Policy due to the way that Group Policy processes and applies the settings that are configured through the GPME. We just saw that Group Policy settings are stored in a variety of different files, such as `registry.pol`, `secedit.sdb`, etc. If you crack open these files and look inside, you will find nothing more than text entries that describe a raw setting. The settings will typically include Registry paths, values, and their data, or they will include system variable names with the value the variable should be set to.

When Group Policy refreshes or processes on a computer, these raw settings contained within these files must be processed by the computer in some way. The process of Group Policy is detailed in Figure 8.13.

FIGURE 8.13
Group Policy Processing relies on the Group Policy Engine and Client Side Extensions to perform most of the work.

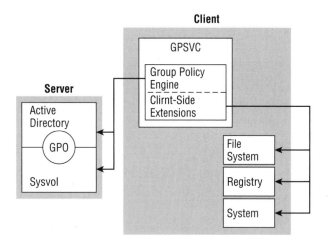

The CSEs are stored as `.dll` files, as well as they are referenced in the Registry. With every new operating system there are newly added CSEs. Windows Server 2008 is no exception, with the number of CSEs tallying a grand total of 37.

The `.dll` files are located in the C:\Windows\System32 folder. Within the Registry, the CSEs are defined and referenced under HKLM\SOFTWARE\Microsoft\Windows NT\CurrentVersion\Winlogon\GPExtensions.

Table 8.3 lists the CSEs, the DLL file that controls the CSE, and the Registry information that is associated with the CSE.

Essential Policy Settings

With more than 2,400 settings and 38 CSEs, you can choose from numerous settings. For most administrators to be productive with Group Policy, it is important to have a place to start with Group Policy. Most administrators that dive into a new GPO without having a plan of attack can get overwhelmed very quickly.

Here are some guides and helpful hints for you to get started with LGPOs. With so many options and variations of the settings within the LGPO, there is nothing that will provide you with the secret settings that will work specifically for your environment. Use these tools and guides as a way to start making settings within the LGPO only.

TABLE 8.3:   CSEs for a Windows Server 2008 Computer

CLIENT SIDE EXTENSION	CSE DLL	GUID
Wireless Group Policy	Wlgpclnt.dll	{0ACDD40C-75AC-47ab-BAA0-BF6DE7E7FE63}
Group Policy Environment	Gpprefcl.dll	{0E28E245-9368-4853-AD84-6DA3BA35BB75}
Group Policy Local Users and Groups	Gpprefcl.dll	{17D89FEC-5C44-4972-B12D-241CAEF74509}
Group Policy Device Settings	Gpprefcl.dll	{1A6364EB-776B-4120-ADE1-B63A406A76B5}
Folder Restriction	Fdeploy.dll	{25537BA6-77A8-11D2-9B6C-0000F8080861}
Microsoft Disk Quota	Diskquota.dll	{3610eda5-77ef-11d2-8dc5-00c04fa31a66}
Group Policy Network Options	Gpprefcl.dll	{3A0DBA37-F8B2-4356-83DE-3E90BD5C261F}
QoS Packet Scheduler	Gptext.dll	{426031c0-0b47-4852-b0ca-ac3d37bfcb39}
Scripts	Gpscript.dll	{42B5FAAE-6536-11d2-AE5A-0000F87571E3}
Internet Explorer Zonemapping	Iedkcs32.dll	{4CFB60C1-FAA6-47f1-89AA-0B18730C9FD3}
Group Policy Drive Maps	Gpprefcl.dll	{5794DAFD-BE60-433f-88A2-1A31939AC01F}
Group Policy Folders	Gpprefcl.dll	{6232C319-91AC-4931-9385-E70C2B099F0E}
Group Policy Network Shares	Gpprefcl.dll	{6A4C88C6-C502-4f74-8F60-2CB23EDC24E2}
Group Policy Files	Gpprefcl.dll	{7150F9BF-48AD-4da4-A49C-29EF4A8369BA}
Group Policy Data Sources	Gpprefcl.dll	{728EE579-943C-4519-9EF7-AB56765798ED}
Group Policy Ini Files	Gpprefcl.dll	{74EE6C03-5363-4554-B161-627540339CAB}
Windows Search Group Policy Extension	Srchadmin.dll	{7933F41E-56F8-41d6-A31C-4148A711EE93}
Security	Scecli.dll	{827D319E-6EAC-11D2-A4EA-00C04F79F83A}
Deployed Printer Connections	Gpprnext.dll	{8A28E2C5-8D06-49A4-A08C-632DAA493E17}
Group Policy Services	Gpprefcl.dll	{91FBB303-0CD5-4055-BF42-E512A681B325}
Internet Explorer Branding	Iedkcs32.dll	{A2E30F80-D7DE-11d2-BBDE-00C04F86AE3B}
Group Policy Folder Options	Gpprefcl.dll	{A3F3E39B-5D83-4940-B954-28315B82F0A8}
Group Policy Scheduled Tasks	Gpprefcl,dll	{AADCED64-746C-4633-A97C-D61349046527}

TABLE 8.3: CSEs for a Windows Server 2008 Computer *(CONTINUED)*

CLIENT SIDE EXTENSION	CSE DLL	GUID
Group Policy Registry	Gpprefcl.dll	{B087BE9D-ED37-454f-AF9C-04291E351182}
EFS Recovery	Scecli.dll	{B1BE8D72-6EAC-11D2-A4EA-00C04F79F83A}
802.3 Group Policy	Dot3gpclnt.dll	{B587E2B1-4D59-4e7e-AED9-22B9DF11D053}
Group Policy Printers	Gpprefcl.dll	{BC75B1ED-5833-4858-9BB8-CBF0B166DF9D}
Group Policy Shortcuts	Gpprefcl.dll	{C418DD9D-0D14-4efb-8FBF-CFE535C8FAC7}
Microsoft Offline Files	Cscobj.dll	{C631DF4C-088F-4156-B058-4375F0853CD8}
Software Installation	Appmgmts.dll	{c6dc5466-785a-11d2-84d0-00c04fb169f7}
IP Security	Polstore.dll	{e437bc1c-aa7d-11d2-a382-00c04f991e27}
Group Policy Internet Settings	Gpprefcl.dll	{E47248BA-94CC-49c4-BBB5-9EB7F05183D0}
Group Policy Start Menu Settings	Gpprefcl.dll	{E4F48E54-F38D-4884-BFB9-D4D2E5729C18}
Group Policy Regional Options	Gpprefcl.dll	{E5094040-C46C-4115-B030-04FB2E545B00}
Group Policy Power Options	Gpprefcl.dll	{E62688F0-25FD-4c90-BFF5-F508B9D2E31F}
Group Policy Applications	Gpprefcl.dll	{F9C77450-3A41-477E-9310-9ACD617BD9E3}
Enterprise QoS	Gptext.dll	{FB2CA36D-0B40-4307-821B-A13B252DE56C}

BEFORE YOU DEPLOY AN LGPO SETTING

You have heard it over and over again, and once again you will hear it: Before you roll out any setting that is related to security, settings, applications, or production of your company environment, you should test the setting.

Group Policy settings are no different. There are many settings that can be configured in a GPO that can cripple a computer or destroy the Registry. Without fully knowing what the setting will do or can do, and without fully testing the setting within your environment, you never know what the result will be.

Therefore, it is suggested that you fully read up on each setting before you deploy a setting, and test it on a non-production computer before you push any setting through an LGPO into production.

For more information on the settings that are available in a GPO on a Windows Server 2008 computer, refer to the following link and downloadable document: http://www.microsoft.com/downloads /details.aspx?FamilyID = 2043b94e-66cd-4b91-9e0f-68363245c495&DisplayLang = en.

To get you started with some common settings in an LGPO, Table 8.4 lists some settings that will configure different areas of the computer in a typical environment.

TABLE 8.4:   Common Settings in a LGPO

NODE WITHIN GPME	SETTING OR NODE OF SETTINGS
Computer Configuration\Windows Settings\Scripts (Startup/Shutdown)	Startup
	Shutdown
Computer Configuration\Windows Settings\Security Settings\Account Policies	Password Policies
	Account Lockout Policies
Computer Configuration\Windows Settings\Security Settings\Local Policies	Audit Policy
	User Rights Assignment
	Security Options
Computer Configuration\Administrative Templates\Windows Components	Internet Explorer
	Terminal Services
	Scripts
	Logon
	Group Policy
	Printers
User Configuration\Windows Settings	Internet Explorer Maintenance
User Configuration\Windows Settings\Scripts (Logon/Logoff)	Logon
	Logoff
User Configuration\Administrative Templates	Start menu and Taskbar
	Desktop
	Control Panel
User Configuration\Administrative Templates\Windows Components	Internet Explorer
	Windows Explorer
	Microsoft Management Console
	Terminal Services

Additionally, Microsoft has developed an entire suite of best practice and security setting documents that can help any company get started with Group Policy. The documents are part of the hardening guides and can be downloaded at `http://www.microsoft.com/downloads/details`
`.aspx?familyid = 8A2643C1-0685-4D89-B655-521EA6C7B4DB&displaylang = en`.

Using Scripts in Group Policy

One of the benefits of using Group Policy is the ability to utilize the scripting options for the different entry and exit processes that computers and users perform. For computers, these would be startup and shutdown. For users, these are the logon and logoff processes.

There can be a script associated with each of these activities. The script needs to be created outside of the GPO, but it can then be associated with the GPO. Figure 8.14 shows both nodes that can accept scripts, under Computer Configuration and User Configuration.

FIGURE 8.14
There are scripts for both computers (startup and shutdown) and users (logon and logoff).

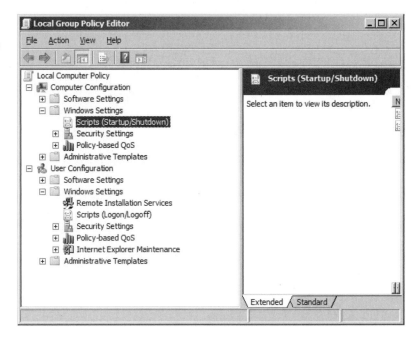

In most cases, the information that is stored in the script is related to the type of script that it is associated with. Table 8.5 describes some of the most common tasks that are configured in scripts, which are deployed using Group Policy.

Scripts can be created in many formats and file types. The supported list of scripts through a GPO include the following:

- BAT files
- VBS files
- EXE files
- JS files

TABLE 8.5:   Common Script Contents

SCRIPT CATEGORY	SCRIPT CONTENT
Startup Script	Initialize services
	Create and delete folders
	Create and delete files
	Modify Registry values
Shutdown Script	Back up files and folders
	Copy files and folders
	Stop services
Logon Scripts	Map folders and printers
	Configure Registry values
	Create, delete, copy files
	Create, delete, copy folders
	Install applications
Logoff Scripts	Back up files and folders
	Copy files and folders

Working with Active Directory–Based GPOs

This chapter focuses on the LGPO. The LGPO is a great way to configure isolated computers, kiosks, branch office computers, or those computers that are not joined to a domain. However, once a computer has joined an Active Directory domain, an entirely new environment of Group Policy management becomes available.

Once a computer has joined a domain, using LGPOs is not efficient or suggested. There is a new setting that will disable the functionality of the LGPO altogether, of which the policy is named "Turn off Local Group Policy objects processing." Some of the benefits that you can obtain when you move to using Group Policy in a domain environment include the following:

◆ Centralized management of GPOs using the Group Policy Management Console

◆ Efficient use of Group Policy inheritance, with GPOs linked to organizational units within Active Directory

◆ Additional security settings available in domain-based GPOs, not available in LGPOs

◆ Use of Group Policy Preferences, which are not available in LGPOs

◆ Leverage ADMX Central Store for centralized management of ADMX and ADML files

---

NOTE

For more information about using Group Policy in Active Directory, please refer to the companion essentials volume, *Mastering Windows Server 2008: Essential Technologies* (Wiley, 2008). For more information about managing Group Policy, refer to the Advanced Group Policy Management, which is part of the Microsoft Desktop Optimization Pack at `http://www.microsoft.com/windows/products/windowsvista/enterprise/features/tools.mspx#agpm`.

LGPOs and Active Directory GPOs

Group Policy is by far one of the most powerful and useful technologies in a Windows environment. Using Group Policy for a local computer is not only a best practice, but a practice that should never be passed up. Microsoft has spent a tremendous amount of time, effort, and money on building more into Group Policy for Windows Server 2008 and Vista, which should be taken advantage of immediately.

LGPOs provide a hierarchical structure for controlling settings depending on the type of user that is logging in. With the three different tiers of LGPOs, any situation can now be handled for your computers that are not joined to an Active Directory domain, such as kiosks, stand alone servers, servers in the DMZ, and special purpose servers.

With the power of Group Policy coming in the ability to control any Registry-based setting, you can control just about every aspect of a computer. If the default ADMX files don't provide enough control, there is still the ability to customize Registry settings using custom `.adm` templates or ADMX files.

Of course, the settings in the LGPO are not only Registry-based. There are settings that control environment variables, services, security settings, and much more. With this wide variety of potential settings, there is not much you can't do with an LGPO.

If you are missing any feature or function through the use of LGPOs, most likely moving the computer to an Active Directory domain and leveraging GPOs from the domain level can provide immediate benefits and provide more efficient control over all computers in the environment.

Chapter 9

Windows Storage Concepts and Skills

Computer storage refers to many things. In this chapter I will cover everything you need to know about Windows Server 2008's hard drives, partition styles and types, volumes, file systems, encryption, disk quotas, Remote Storage, and Volume Shadow Copies. I will show you how to perform disk management tasks in both the Disk Management GUI and from the command-line interface tool DiskPart.

Disk Management versus DiskPart

The Disk Management tool made its debut in Windows 2000 and allows you to perform disk management tasks. Some of those tasks are to create and delete partitions and logical drives, as well as gather status information concerning partition sizes, available free space, volume labels, drive-letter assignment, file system type, and the health of your disks. The Disk Management tool is the GUI way of managing your storage and is a very effective tool for seeing the logical layout of your disks, complete with a color-coded legend to help identify the kind of disk and the various flavors of partitions or volumes contained on those disks.

The command-line utility that allows you to manage your disks is `Diskpart.exe` and is installed by default with Server 2008. Why should I bore you with the command-line interface (CLI)? Well, there are a few reasons. Microsoft's new Server 2008 OS called Server Core contains no GUIs at all, so DiskPart is the only way to configure your disks. DiskPart is also easily scriptable. When we get into some of the more complex DiskPart commands, I will show you how to script them. Scripted DiskPart commands are great for setting up a large number of servers with the same disk configuration. Or, what about disaster recovery? Wouldn't it be nice to have a script that contains your entire disk configuration for a server just in case your server dies and you need to quickly build a new server with the same disk configuration? Lastly, DiskPart is more flexible and powerful than the Disk Management GUI utility. In other words, DiskPart can do things that the Disk Management utility cannot. Let's start with the Disk Management utility and then take a look at DiskPart.

The Disk Management Gooey (GUI)

There are many ways to open the Disk Management utility. The quickest is to select Server Manager from the Quick Launch bar at the bottom of the screen to the right of the Start button, as shown in Figure 9.1. Within Server Manager, expand Storage in the console pane, and highlight Disk Management, as shown in Figure 9.2. Or you could click the Start button and type **Diskmgmt.msc** in the Start Search box.

FIGURE 9.1
Opening Disk Management utility

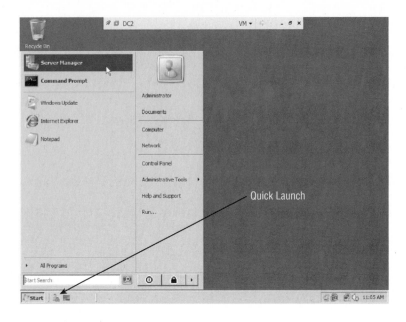

FIGURE 9.2
Disk Management utility

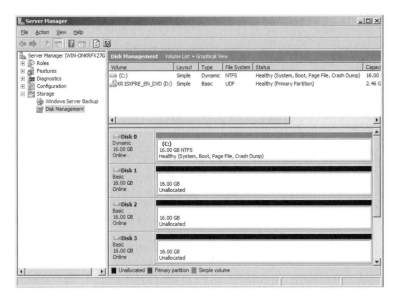

When Disk Management first opens, there will be an Actions menu to the far right of the screen. The Actions pane displays the same menu options as if you had right-clicked an object. I usually close the Actions pane so I have room for more important information like my disks and their configuration. To hide the Actions pane, click the Show/Hide Action Pane button on the toolbar. The Disk Management utility shows the Console pane to the left of the screen, and the volume list in the top portion lists all your existing volumes in a text list. The graphic view at the bottom of the window shows your disks and how they are currently configured. You can change the look and feel of your Disk Management utility by clicking the View menu item and choosing how you want the top portion of the window displayed: Disk List, Volume List, or Graphical View. And, you have the same options for the bottom of the screen with one addition: Hidden. Hidden is a nice option if you want to set your top view to Graphical (which is currently the view at the bottom of the screen) and the bottom to Hidden. It would be a bit confusing to see the graphical view on both top and bottom because it would appear that you have twice as many disks as you do because all disks would be displayed twice.

Disk Management uses a color-coded legend to help identify the different types of partitions or volumes. If the default colors in the legend are not to your liking, you can change them by clicking the View menu and choosing Settings. In the Settings dialog box, there are two tabs: Appearance and Scaling. The Appearance tab (shown in Figure 9.3) lets you select the type of partition or volume in the "Disk region" box and customize your color and patterns. I could, for example, choose that all unallocated space be displayed in purple. The Scaling tab allows you to change how the size of your partitions and volumes are displayed. For example, you could choose to have them all displayed as the same size but I have found that to be a bit confusing. Me? I like the defaults on this.

FIGURE 9.3
Choosing colors for the legend

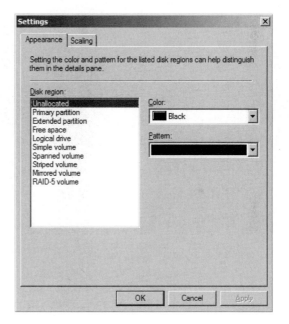

Meet DiskPart, the Command-Line Interface

Before we get into the meat of the material, I'd like to introduce you to some DiskPart terminology. DiskPart allows you to perform disk management tasks from the command-line interface (CLI) manually or by scripting. In the past, we used the fdisk utility for our command-line configuration of disks. Now that fdisk has been deprecated, we'll use the new and improved DiskPart utility. Okay, it's been around for a while, but most of us continued to use fdisk because it was what we knew (I did too). DiskPart is more powerful than fdisk ever dreamed of being and offers a higher degree of manageability than the Disk Management utility. At the end of each main topic, look for the "How to Do X Using DiskPart" section with numbered steps for specific tasks.

But, before I start throwing DiskPart syntax at you, let's look at some of the basics. Please don't be put off if you don't understand some of the language now. I promise you will shortly. To use DiskPart, launch a command prompt by clicking the Start button and typing **cmd** in the Start Search box. Then press Enter. At the CLI, type **diskpart**, and press Enter. You are now at the DISKPART> prompt.

A lot of DiskPart commands use the number of a disk to work with a specific disk. To find out how your disks are numbered from the DISKPART> prompt, type **list disk**, and press Enter. It will look like:

```
DISKPART>list disk
```

Figure 9.4 shows that I have four disks numbered 0, 1, 2, and 3. There is some additional information the list disk command shows (these will all make sense shortly): the status of the disk (online or offline); size of disk; amount of free space; whether the disk is basic or dynamic (if Dyn = *, then the disk is dynamic; otherwise it is a basic disk); and the type of partition style, which is either MBR or GPT (if GPT = *, then the disk is configured to use a GPT partition style instead of MBR).

FIGURE 9.4
DiskPart list disk results

The Basics of Disk Management

To begin with, you'll need to know the difference between physical and logical disks and how the OS views them. Then I'll cover how to introduce new disks to Server 2008, which is called *initializing a disk*. The two types of partition styles — master boot record (MBR) and GUID partition table (GPT) — have been around since Server 2003, but unless you had an Itanium server, you probably are not familiar with GPTs. I'll cover the difference between MBR and GPT and when to use one versus the other. Lastly in this section I'll explain what basic and dynamic disks are and how to create partitions or volumes and how to convert from basic to dynamic and from dynamic to basic.

Physical/Logical Disks: How to Slice Them Up

Let's begin by understanding the difference between physical disks and logical drives. A *physical disk* is that contraption of plastic and metal that you inserted in your server's case or have stacked up next to it. Physical drives are identified by numbers (Disk 0, 1, 2) that you cannot change.

NOTE

If you have multiple disks in your computer, they're numbered by their status on the drive controller. For example, in a SCSI chain, the disk with SCSI ID 0 will be Disk 0, the drive with the next SCSI ID will be Disk 1, and so on. The SCSI ID and the disk number are not directly related and will not necessarily match — the only correspondence lies in the disk's priority in the system.

You cannot change the size of a physical disk. What you purchased from the manufacturer of the hard drive is the fixed size of the physical disk. Once you have physically installed a new disk, you can use the built-in Disk Management tool within Server Manager to introduce the new disk to the operating system. There are three steps to this introduction: Initialize the new disk, select your partition style and size, and choose which file system format you want to use.

A logical disk is how you carve out space from the physical disk or disks into multiple storage areas each containing their own drive letters or a mounted folder name (mount folders are in the advanced section). For now, let's stick with drive letters. Each drive letter represents an area on the physical disk, and these areas are referred to as either *partitions* or *volumes*. Here is how it works: Once you have installed a physical drive, Server 2008 should recognize that a new drive has been added, but you won't be able to read it until the drive has been initiated or introduced to Server 2008's OS. If for some reason your new disk is not being displayed in Disk Management, from the Action menu choose Rescan. Rescanning using DiskPart is done by opening a command prompt and typing **diskpart**. Wait until you get the DISKPART> prompt and then type **rescan**; it will look like this:

```
DISKPART> rescan
```

In a perfect world when you open Disk Management, the OS knows that drives exist that it can't read, so the Initialize Disk Wizard launches automatically, as shown in Figure 9.5. The disk or disks that you have installed will appear here with check marks already in the "Select disks" box. You can choose to deselect a disk and initialize it later, but you won't be able to use the disk at all until it has been initialized and formatted. Think of initializing a disk as an introduction from the disk to the operating system: "Disk, meet the OS. OS, meet the disk." If you cancel out of the Initialize Disk Wizard, you can launch it again by right-clicking the gray area to the left of the drive in the graphical view portion where drives are listed with their drive number. For example, if I wanted to initialize drive 1, I would right-click the Drive l label and click Initialize Disk. Before you click OK in the Initialize Disk dialog box, you will need to choose your partition style. Your choices are either (MBR) Master Boot Record or (GPT) GUID Partition Table.

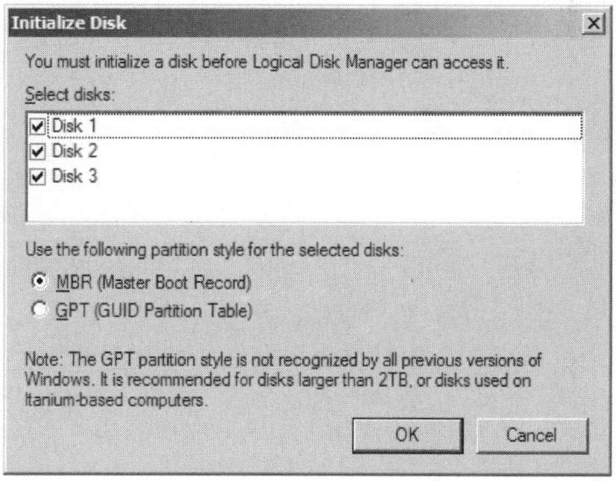

FIGURE 9.5
The Initialize Disk dialog box

PARTITION STYLES

The partition style is one of those settings that isn't easy to change once you have chosen either MBR or GPT. Let's look at the differences between the two so you can make an informed decision. I mentioned that it isn't easy to change your partition style but it is doable.

The MBR and GPT partition styles perform the same function, but GPT offers some advantages. Each disk needs to store information about that disk, such as the number of sectors on the disk and the beginning and ending addresses of those sectors along with the type and size of partitions or volumes that exist on the disk. The partition style information is read when the system boots looking for the initial boot program files that begin the process of loading the OS. So, what's the difference then, right? Well, the MBR uses a standard BIOS partition table that has some limitations. The MBR's partition table is only 64 bytes in size and resides in the first sector of the disk. Each time you create a partition a description of that partition is placed in the MBR's partition table. Each description is 16 bytes in size, so if you look at the size of the MBR partition table that is 64 bytes and divide that by 16 for each description, you get 4. That's why you can have only four partitions in an MBR partition style. We'll get to types of partitions a little later.

The GPT partition style uses extensible firmware interface (EFI). And instead of the BIOS partition table, a 1 MB database file is created to store the partition information of each disk. This database is stored on every hard disk for redundancy. Another big advantage of GPT disks is that they support up to 18 exabytes in size and up to 128 volumes per disk. GPT is also a requirement if you have disks larger than 2 terabytes (MBR supports only up to 2 TB).

Changing Your Partition Style

After initializing a disk with either GPT or MBR, you can change it as long as the disk does not contain any partitions or volumes. To change from GPT to MBR, right-click the drive number (I right-clicked Drive 2 as shown in Figure 9.6) and select Convert to MBR Disk. If you had previously initialized the disk with the MBR partition style, then you would see the option to Convert to GPT Disk. If, however, you right-click a drive and the option to convert is grayed out, then that drive already has partitions defined, and you can't change the partition style after you have defined partitions. If you really wanted to change the partition style, you would need to back up all of the data and delete the existing partitions by right-clicking each and choosing Delete Volume. Then, you'll have the option to convert the disk's partition style.

FIGURE 9.6
Converting your partition style

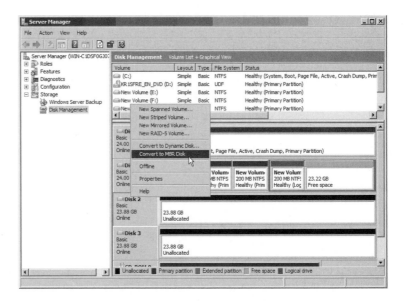

HOW TO CHANGE YOUR PARTITION STYLE USING DISKPART

1. At a command prompt, type **diskpart**. You will now be at the DISKPART> prompt. Type list disk as shown in step 2 to get the numbers of the existing disks.

2. DISKPART> **list disk**
   Note the number of the disk whose partition style you want to convert.

3. To select a specific disk you will use the select disk option. For example to select disk 1 type:

   DISKPART> **select disk 1**

   You should see "Disk 1 is now the selected disk." To convert the partition style, from the DISKPART> prompt type: convert mbr or gpt as shown in step 4.

4. DISKPART> **convert mbr**
   or
   DISKPART> **convert gpt**
   Typing **exit** allows you to exit from the DISKPART prompt.

Basic Disks versus Dynamic Disks

Server 2008 supports two types of disks: basic and dynamic. All disks start out as basic disks. Figure 9.6 shows that once a disk is initialized, it is listed as basic by default; all my disks — Disk 1, Disk 2, and Disk 3 — are set to Basic. All Microsoft operating systems can recognize basic disks, but only Windows 2000 and later OSes can detect dynamic disks. Basic disks can be converted to dynamic disks if you choose. Why would you want to convert a basic to a dynamic? Well, dynamic disks allow you to implement fault tolerance for your data. Fault tolerance will keep your data safe even in the event of a physical disk failure and was originally called Redundant "Array" of Inexpensive Disks (RAID), but is now known as Redundant "Array" of Independent Drives (still RAID).

Both basic and dynamic disks can contain multiple areas of storage. These areas of storage are defined for basic disks as partitions and dynamic disks as volumes. If you were familiar with partitions in the past, you can think of them as the same thing as a volume. If partitions and volumes are new to you, imagine that you have a 2 terabyte (TB) physical disk you have installed in your server and you want to dedicate 1 TB of space for users to store their data and 1 TB on which you want to install applications. For backup purposes and security reasons, it's a good idea to logically separate these by creating two distinct volumes. Then, when you looked at Windows Explorer on this server, you would have a C drive where you installed the OS and then (depending on your CD/DVD drive letter, most are D), there would also be E and F partitions.

In the following sections, I'll discuss basic disks, dynamic disks, and converting from one to the other and back again. I'll cover RAID when we have some partitions or volumes to work with.

BASIC DISKS

When you install Server 2008, the Setup program will automatically create a primary partition to put the OS on. Once Server 2008 is installed, you can create more partitions to store data that's separate from the partition that contains your operating system. As stated earlier each disk that you initialize will be basic by default. Basic disks can contain two different types of partitions: primary and extended. A *primary partition* is a portion of a physical hard disk and cannot be further divided into smaller partitions. An *extended partition* can be subdivided into smaller partitions called logical drives; where each logical drive has its own drive letter. In fact, you can't put any data into an extended partition or assign it a drive letter until you create one or more logical drives within that extended partition. Until then, it's just free space.

In the past basic disks were rather limited and could only contain three primary partitions and one extended partition that could be broken up into logical drives. But now you need to take into account the partition style, MBR or GPT. There are two major differences between a basic disk with an MBR partition style versus a basic disk with a GPT partition style. A basic disk with the partition style set to MBR is still restricted to three primary partitions and one extended partition (there can never be more than one extended partition) due to the limitation of the partition table. The partition table is stored in a hidden sector on the disk — sector 0, and the disk configuration information for that one disk only is stored there. This creates a single point of failure because none of the other disks in your server knows anything about the other disks. A basic disk with the partition style set to GPT allows for up to 128 individual storage locations referred to as volumes, and the configuration information is stored on each and every hard drive to alleviate the single point of failure concern.

There are two special partitions you should be very familiar with: System and Boot. The System partition contains hardware-specific files needed to start Windows, such as `BootMGR` and `WinLoad.exe`. The system partition must be a primary partition marked as active. This can be any drive that the system BIOS searches when the operating system starts. The Boot partition contains the Windows operating system files and supporting files. By default, Windows operating system files are in the WINDOWS folder, and the supporting files are in the WINDOWS\System32 folder. The System and Boot partitions can be the same but they don't have to be. While there can only be one System partition, you can have more than one boot partition if you have more than one operating system to boot such as Linux.

Creating a Primary Partition

To create a primary partition on a basic disk with the partition style set to MBR within Disk Management, right-click the unallocated space (this is the space that is available to create primary or extended partitions from) and choose New Simple Volume, as shown in Figure 9.7. The name for this wizard is a little strange because I am creating a partition, not a volume, and, yes, there is a difference — more on that later.

FIGURE 9.7
Launching New Simple
Volume Wizard

When the New Simple Volume Wizard launches, click Next on the Welcome page. A spin box labeled "Simple volume size in MB" will display the largest size that a new partition can be (Figure 9.8). Either accept the entire amount of unallocated space or type in exactly what you want the size to be in megabytes and click Next.

FIGURE 9.8
Specify Volume Size
page

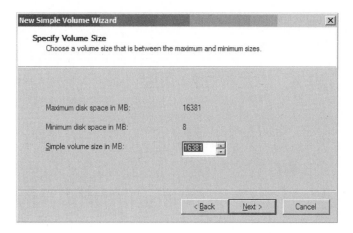

Then, you'll need to choose the drive letter for this partition. The next available drive letter will be displayed, or you can choose another drive letter that is not currently in use. Select the file system you want to format with. The available file systems will depend on the size of the partition you're formatting. A 4 GB (4096 MB) partition or smaller can be formatted with FAT, FAT32, or NTFS. For volumes larger than 4 GB, only FAT32 or NTFS will be available (more on file systems later). Choose the allocation unit size and volume label if you want one. The allocation unit size is the block size of data that will be stored on the physical disk. I always choose to do a Quick Format, which wipes the volume clean but doesn't check for bad clusters; it's much quicker. The last option allows you to enable file and folder compression or not. Click Next and Finish.

I created three 250 MB primary partitions. When I right-clicked the resulting 23.27 GB of unallocated space and chose New Simple Volume to create another 250 MB partition, I got a 23.27 GB Extended partition (notice extended partitions receive no drive letter) with a 250 MB logical partition and 23.02 GB of Free space. The logical partition will receive the next available drive letter; you can always change the drive letter later if you wish. Free space is different from unallocated space in that free space is the space within an extended partition, which can be further subdivided into logical drives, each containing its own drive letter. Unallocated space is the space that has not been assigned to any partition at all — primary or extended. There can only be one extended partition on a disk so the OS knows to take the remaining unallocated space and include that space in the extended partition. To create another logical partition within the extended partition, right-click the free space and choose New Simple Volume. This will launch the same New Simple Volume Wizard that you saw before. At this point I have only created one 250 MB logical drive within that extended partition. Figure 9.9 shows Disk 1 has been subdivided into three 250 MB primary partitions, one 250 MB logical drive, and 23.02 GB of free space. If you're not sure which partition is primary, extended, or logical, there is a color bar at the top of each volume and a corresponding legend at the bottom of the screen, as shown in Figure 9.9. Dark blue indicates a primary partition, light blue is a logical drive, and green is free space within the extended partition that can be divided to create additional volumes.

FIGURE 9.9
The color legend

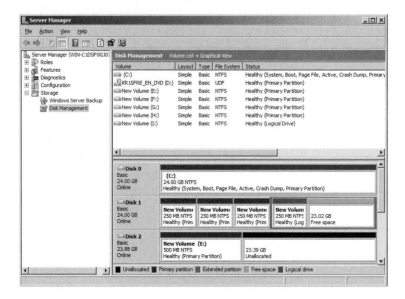

HOW TO CREATE A PRIMARY PARTITION USING DISKPART

1. At a command prompt, type **diskpart**. You will now be at the DISKPART> prompt. Type list disk as shown in step 2 to get the numbers of the existing disks.

2. DISKPART> **list disk**
   Note the number of the disk you want to create a simple volume on.

3. To select a specific disk you will use the select disk option. For example to select disk 1 type:

   DISKPART>select disk 1

4. To create a simple volume that is 250 MB in size on disk 1 type:
   DISKPART> *create volume simple size=250 disk=1*

5. Assign a drive letter (H in this example) by typing:
   DISKPART> *assign letter=H*

Marking a Partition as Active

Under Server 2008 and older Microsoft OSes you can have multiple partitions on a drive, but only one partition at a time can be marked as active. Marking a partition Active means you can boot from it. When you install Server 2008, the partition that you choose to install the OS on is automatically marked active. How can you tell which partition is currently active? The Disk Management utility will display the word Active in the status area of the partition. If you want to change the active partition or mark a partition active on another drive, (maybe one you installed a non-Microsoft OS) keep in mind that there are a few rules. Only one active partition per disk allowed, the partition style must be MBR, and logical partitions cannot be marked as Active.

To mark a partition as Active, right-click the partition you want to make active and choose Mark Partition as Active. If you are changing which partition is active you will receive a warning message that states "Changing the active partition on a disk might make the disk not startable if the partition does not have valid system files. Do you want to continue?" Choosing Yes changes which partition is active.

HOW TO MARK A PARTITION AS ACTIVE USING DISKPART

1. At a command prompt, type **diskpart**. You will now be at the DISKPART> prompt. Type list partition as shown in step 2 to get the numbers of the existing partitions.

2. DISKPART> **list partition**
   Note the partition number you want to mark as active.

3. Select the partition number from the list in step 2. For this example I am setting partition 2 as active. DISKPART> **select partition 2**

4. To set the selected partition to active type: DISKPART> **active**

When changing which partition is active, Disk Management and DiskPart only verify that the partition is capable of containing operating system startup files, not that the files exist on the partition. So, if you mistakenly change from the default "active" partition to one that does not contain the OS's startup files, your computer may not boot.

Extending Partitions

You can't do a lot with basic disks, there is no way to protect your data from a hard drive failure, but you can extend and shrink them. If you find that you need more storage space than an existing volume has to offer you can extend an existing basic volume using unallocated space from the same disk. In the past extending a partition could only be accomplished by using DiskPart but now you can do it in the GUI as well. A volume residing on a basic disk cannot be extended to another disk. Only dynamic disks can be extended to another disk. Also, the volume you wish to extend must be formatted with the NTFS file system to be able to extend it. For this example, I have a 500 MB volume on disk 2 that I want to extend to be 1 GB. To extend a volume using the GUI, right-click the volume you want to extend and choose Extend Volume. The Extend Volume Wizard launches. I right-clicked Disk 2 so Figure 9.10 shows that disk 2 is already selected. Enter the amount of space you want to extend it by in the "Select the amount of space in MB" box (I entered 524). The "Total volume size in megabytes (MB)" displays what the total volume size will be once the additional space has been added. Click Next and Finish to complete the Extend Volume Wizard. One thing you should note is that you cannot extend the System or Boot partitions.

HOW TO EXTEND A PARTITION USING DISKPART

1. At a command prompt, type **diskpart**. You will now be at the DISKPART> prompt. Type list volume as shown in step 2 to get the numbers of the existing volumes.

2. DISKPART> **list volume**
   Note the number of the volume you want to extend.

3. To select volume 1 type:
   DISKPART> **select volume 1**

4. To extend volume 1 that is currently 524 MB in size and residing on disk1 type:
   DISKPART> **extend size=524 disk=1**

FIGURE 9.10
Extending a volume

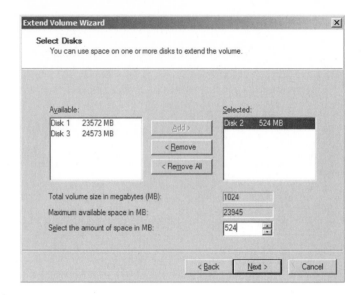

Shrinking Partitions

Shrinking partitions can come in handy when you have a simple or spanned volume that was previously set up as one large partition and you now want to create multiple partitions from it. You needn't worry about data when you shrink a disk; all files are automatically relocated on the disk to create the new unallocated space. And you'll like this: No formatting required to simply shrink a partition.

To shrink an existing partition from the Disk Management GUI, right-click the partition and choose Shrink Volume. The Shrink Volume Wizard queries the volume for available shrink space and presents you with a dialog box (Figure 9.11) that shows you how much you can shrink the volume by. You can choose to shrink it less but not more. And, be very careful if you attempt to shrink the volume that contains the operating system; if you shrink it too much the computer will no longer boot.

FIGURE 9.11
Shrinking a volume

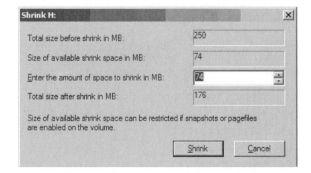

HOW TO SHRINK A VOLUME USING DISKPART

1. At a command prompt, type **diskpart**. You will now be at the DISKPART> prompt. Type list volume as shown in step 2 to get the numbers of the existing volumes.

2. DISKPART> **list volume**
   Note the number of the partition you want to shrink.

3. To shrink volume 3 type:
   DISKPART>**select volume 3**

4. To determine the amount of disk space that can be reclaimed or shrunk by type:
   DISKPART> **querymax**
   When I ran the querymax I received:
   The maximum number of reclaimable bytes is: 300 MB

5. For example, to shrink a 1 GB volume by 500 MB, type:
   DISKPART> **shrink desired=500**

Deleting a Partition

When you delete a partition all data on that partition is lost and there is no way to recover it, so please back up your data before you delete a partition. To delete a partition with Disk Management, right-click the partition and choose Delete Volume. A warning dialog box will pop up informing you that "Deleting this volume will erase all data on it. Back up any data you want to keep before deleting. Do you want to continue — Yes or No." When you delete a primary partition it will revert to unallocated space on the drive. Deleting a logical drive within an extended partition will revert to free space in the extended partition.

HOW TO DELETE A PARTITION USING DISKPART

1. At a command prompt, type **diskpart**. You will now be at the DISKPART> prompt. Type list disk as shown in step 2 to get the numbers of the existing disks.

2. DISKPART> **list disk**
   Note the number of the disk your partition resides on.

3. To select a specific disk you will use the select disk option. For example to select disk 1 type:
   DISKPART> **select disk 1**

4. To list the partitions that reside on disk 1 type: DISKPART> **list partition**
   Note the number of the partition you want to delete.

5. Select a partition, for this example I will choose partition 3 from disk 1 by typing:
   DISKPART> **select partition 3**

6. Delete the partition by typing: DISKPART> **delete partition**

DYNAMIC DISKS

Dynamic disks were first introduced in Windows 2000 and are not supported by any Windows OSes prior to W2K. Dynamic disks can be divided into volumes, whereas basic disks can be divided into partitions. Volumes work a little differently than partitions in that volumes may reside on a *single large expensive drive* (SLED), or across multiple physical disks. SLED is a way of arranging your data on one very large and hopefully reliable drive. But, the problem with SLED is, if that one very large drive fails, then your data goes with it. When you have more than one physical disk you can protect your data even in the event of a physical hard drive failure by implementing Redundant Arrays of Independent Drives or RAID. RAID keeps track of your data so that if one disk fails completely your data will still be safe and accessible. The way RAID keeps track of your data depends on the type of RAID you implement. In this section I'll cover converting a basic disk to dynamic, five different types of volumes, and explain which *types of volumes* are considered to be RAID and which are not. Lastly, I'll explain how to implement, troubleshoot, and relocate RAID volumes.

Converting Basic Disks to Dynamic

In the past you had to convert a basic disk to dynamic before you could create volumes, but not anymore. Now, when you attempt to create a volume that requires a dynamic disk the disk will be converted automatically. If, however, you want to convert a basic disk that already contains partitions to a dynamic disk you must have at least 1 MB of free space on that disk. Why? Well, dynamic disks store their configuration information in a 1 MB database. This database contains volume information such as the number of volumes on the disk and the type and size of volumes for each dynamic disk in the server. The 1 MB database is replicated to all the other dynamic disks in the system. The contents of the database on each disk is identical. Changes to the database are time-stamped, so that if a disk happens to be missing for a while (maybe it got mis-seated), the newer changes will be automatically replicated to the disk when it returns, without any intervention on your part. If you were to add another disk and convert it to dynamic, the new disk's information would be added to the existing database on the other disks and the database would be copied to the new disk itself so they all contain the same database information.

When you convert a basic disk that already has partitions defined to a dynamic disk, you'll have the original partition table to deal with. Each of the preexisting partitions retains a legacy-style partition table entry (type 42 for primary and type 05 for extended), even after upgrading the disk to dynamic. During the conversion to dynamic all partition information is moved into a 1 MB database at the end of the disk. Only one partition table entry of type 0x42 is entered in the master boot record (MBR) at sector 0, which indicates that the disk is dynamic and the disk configuration information is now stored in the 1 MB database at the end of the disk.

When you boot a computer with dynamic disks, the BIOS reads the partition table, looks for the active partition, and reports the boot partition to work from.

Not all disks are upgradeable. Only fixed-disk drives may be converted to dynamic disks. Removable disk drives such as Jaz drives can only be basic disks. Why? Remember I mentioned that dynamic disk volumes may extend over more than one physical disk. The problem with removable disks is that they might not always be present.

If the disk has a sector size larger than 512 bytes, then you won't be able to convert it. Notice that I said *sector* size, not *cluster* size. I'll get into the difference more in the later section on Disk Geometry, but for the moment know that (a) this is a problem you're unlikely to encounter with today's hard disks, and (b) you can't change the sector size of your disks with Server 2008. Cluster size, yes; sector size, no.

For those using Windows Server 2008, Enterprise Edition or Windows Server 2008, Datacenter Edition, you can't make the shared storage system in a cluster dynamic.

Dual-boot computers can be problematic. So, if you have more than one operating system installed on a server remember that only Windows Server 2000 and later can recognize dynamic disks. If you have a second OS installed that cannot read dynamic disks (something other than Microsoft or older than W2K) you could render the other OS unbootable.

Dynamic disks cannot be used on clustered storage devices natively, although there are third-party products that allow for dynamic disks to be clustered.

To convert a basic disk to dynamic, right-click the gray area at the far left of the disk you wish to convert and choose Convert to Dynamic Disk as shown in Figure 9.12. The OS first performs a system check to ensure the existing partitions (if there are any) are readable and that the disk is not currently experiencing I/O errors. If a problem is encountered at this stage the conversion process will abort.

FIGURE 9.12

Converting a basic disk to dynamic

The Convert to Dynamic Disk dialog box lists all your basic disks as seen in Figure 9.13. The disk you right-clicked on will already be selected (I right-clicked Disk 1). You can select as many as you like by putting a check mark in the box to the left of the Disk number. Click OK after you have made your selection and wait a few seconds; this is usually pretty quick.

FIGURE 9.13

Selecting basic disks to convert to dynamic

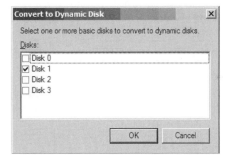

HOW TO CONVERT FROM BASIC TO DYNAMIC DISKS USING DISKPART

1. At a command prompt, type **diskpart** and press Enter. You will now be at the DISKPART> prompt. Type list disk as shown in step 2 to get the numbers of the existing disks.

2. DISKPART> **list disk**
   Note the number of the disk you want to convert to dynamic.

3. To select Disk 1 type:
   DISKPART> **select disk 1**

4. Convert disk 1 to dynamic by typing: DISKPART> **convert dynamic**

Converting Back to a Basic Disk

Once you convert a basic disk to dynamic it's not easy to convert back to a basic disk again. Dynamic disks can only be converted to basic if they do not contain any volumes. Huh? If your dynamic disks contain volumes with data on it, you'll need to delete all volumes before you can convert the dynamic disk back to basic. Until all volumes are deleted the option to Convert to Basic Disk will be grayed out. What happens to data that resides on a volume when you delete the volume? The data is also deleted. To save your data be sure to back it up first, then delete the volume.

If the disk you want to convert from dynamic to basic doesn't contain any volumes the process is simple. Right-click the gray area of the physical disk (where you see the disk name, Disk 1, Disk 2, etc. . . .) and choose Convert to Basic Disk. That's it. No muss, no fuss, no reboot required.

Server 2008 Setup and System Disk Meet Dynamic Disks

Microsoft Windows Server 2008 can only be installed to a basic disk. For troubleshooting purposes there may be a need to install a parallel installation of the OS. If for some reason you cannot boot your existing Server 2008 computer, installing another instance of Server 2008 would allow you to access the files from the original installation. You can install Server 2008 to free space on an existing disk or to another disk. But, keep in mind you can only install Server 2008 to basic disks. So, let's say you have converted all your disks to dynamic, created volumes, and stored data on them, and your server will not boot. Performing a parallel installation in order to access files from the original OS will be a bit more difficult and could result in data loss, because you would have to convert a dynamic disk to basic. And, the only way to do that would be to delete all volumes on a disk, convert that disk back to basic, and then complete the installation.

CREATING THE DIFFERENT TYPES OF DYNAMIC VOLUMES

Microsoft Server 2008 supports five different types of dynamic volumes: Simple, Spanned, Striped, Mirrored, and RAID-5. Not all of these *types of volumes* offer protection for your data. In fact, only two of the five can protect your data: Mirrored Volumes and RAID-5. Simple, Spanned, and Striped volumes provide no fault tolerance for your data at all. Not all types of volumes will always be available to create. You must have at least the minimum number of disks required to create certain types of volumes. If you have a single dynamic disk with unallocated space, the only option will be to create a simple volume. Two dynamic disks with unallocated space allow you to create a striped volume, spanned volume, or mirrored volume. To create a RAID-5 volume you will need at least three dynamic disks with unallocated space. Let's start with the non-RAID volume types first and then get into the more complex Mirrored and RAID-5 volume types.

Simple Volumes

A simple volume is a dynamic volume that consists of disk space from *one* dynamic disk. A simple volume can be created from a single region on a disk or multiple regions of the same disk that are linked together. If you convert a basic disk to dynamic with existing primary partitions and logical drives within extended partitions, they will become simple volumes.

To create a simple volume right-click the unallocated space and choose New Simple Volume. The New Simple Volume Wizard prompts you for the size, drive letter, and file system to format as and you have a new simple volume.

HOW TO CREATE A SIMPLE VOLUME USING DISKPART

1. At a command prompt, type **diskpart** and press Enter. You will now be at the DISKPART> prompt. Type list disk as shown in step 2 to get the numbers of the existing disks.

2. DISKPART> **list disk**
   Note the number of the disk you want to create a simple volume on.

3. To create a 250 MB simple volume on disk 1 type:
   DISKPART> **create volume simple size=250 disk=1**

4. Next, you will need to assign the new drive a drive letter.
   To assign the new drive the drive letter E:
   DISKPART> **assign letter=E**

Spanned Volume

Spanned volumes are volumes that span across multiple physical disks. You can expand an existing simple volume formatted with NTFS by extending it across additional disks to create a spanned volume. Or, you can create a spanned volume in unallocated space on two basic or dynamic disks. Spanned volumes require at least two disks and can consist of space on as many as 32 physical disks. Neither the system nor boot volumes can be included in a spanned volume because there is no fault tolerance provided and it would introduce a higher level of risk to the OS.

Create a spanned volume using the Disk Management UI by right-clicking *unallocated* space on a disk and choosing New Spanned Volume. The New Spanned Volume Wizard launches; click Next. Select the disks from the Available box in Figure 9.14. Once you have added the disks, select the amount of space you want from each disk by highlighting the disk number in the Selected box and typing in the size in the "Select the amount of space in MB" box.

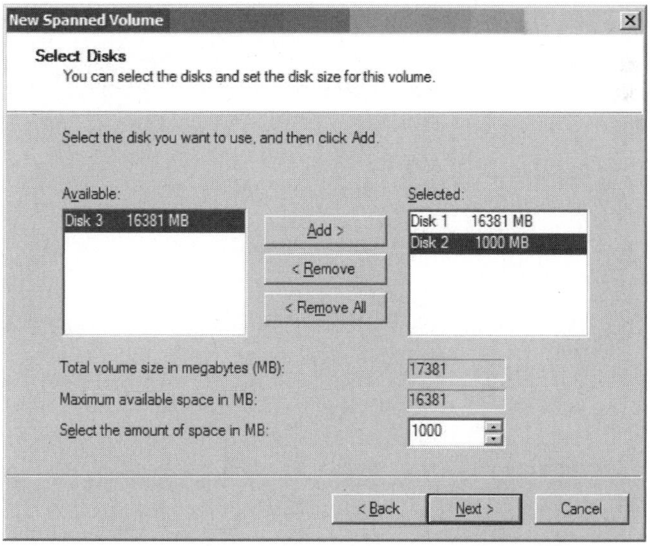

FIGURE 9.14
Select Disks and Size
dialog box

I have chosen to use all of the disk space on disk 1 and only 1000 MB from disk 2 for my spanned volume. Click Next, and assign a drive letter by accepting the next available drive letter (mine was E) or choose any available one. Choose the file system (NTFS is recommended), allocation unit size, and if you like, a volume label. Click Next and Finish; you should receive an informational message stating "The operation you selected will convert the selected basic disk(s) to dynamic disk(s). If you convert the disk(s) to dynamic, you will not be able to start installed operating systems from any volume on the disk(s) (except the current boot volume). Are you sure you want to continue?" Answering Yes to this message will convert the basic disk to dynamic and create the spanned volume.

Figure 9.15 shows how a spanned volume appears in the Disk Management UI. My E: drive resides on both Disk 1 and a portion of Disk 2. It is important to understand how files will be placed on the E: drive. Files being stored on the E: drive will fill the space on disk 1 completely before storing files on disk 2. You may have heard this called the "fill and spill" method, because disk 1 must be completely filled before anything spills over onto disk 2. Spanned volumes provide no fault tolerance; if either disk 1 or disk 2 fails all data stored on the E: volume would be lost. This is why neither the system nor boot volumes can be included in a spanned volume. Also to help protect your data — backups are imperative when implementing spanned volumes.

FIGURE 9.15
Spanned volume

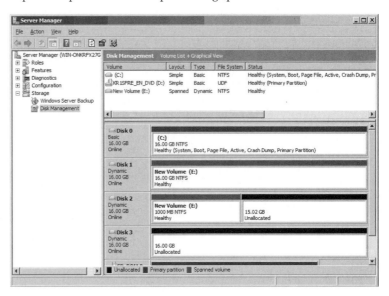

To extend an existing partition (primary or logical drives) that resides on a basic disk, the partition must be formatted with NTFS. If the partition you want to extend is currently formatted with FAT or FAT32, then the option to Extend Volume will be grayed out. You will need to convert the partition to NTFS before it can be extended. Converting a partitions file system to NTFS is done at a command prompt. Click the Start button and type **cmd** in the Start Search box or select Command Prompt from the shortcut menu. To convert the E: volume from FAT or FAT32 to NTFS, type the following:

```
convert E: /FS:NTFS
```

Then, right-click the partition and choose Extend Volume. The Extend Volume Wizard launches; click Next. From the list of available disks choose the disk(s) you want to extend to by double-clicking the disk number or highlighting it and clicking the Add button. Once you have added the disks you want to include in your spanned volume, choose how much space from each disk you want to use. Spanned volumes do not require the same amount of space on each disk. For example, you could right-click an existing partition from disk 1 and add 1000 MB from disk 2 and 2000 MB of space from disk 3. Spanned volumes cannot be shrunk; the only way to make a spanned volume smaller is to delete the entire volume and then create a new one. Be sure to back up any data because when you delete a volume all data is deleted as well.

Striped Volumes

Striped volumes allow you to combine areas of unused disk space from multiple physical disks into a single volume. Striped volumes offer a performance boost by decreasing the amount of time it takes to read and write data to the physical disks (more on this in a second). But you need to keep in mind that striped volumes offer no protection for your data, which is why striped volumes are also known as RAID 0 (0 fault tolerance).

To create a striped volume you must have at least two physical disks and you can include unallocated disk space from up to 32 different physical disks. I have two physical disks (disk 1 and disk 2) that both have 16 GB of unallocated space. To create a striped volume I right-click either disk 1 or disk 2 and choose New Striped Volume. The New Striped Volume Wizard launches; click Next. On the Select Disks page, whichever disk you right-clicked to launch the New Striped Volume Wizard will be listed in the Selected box. The Available box lists the disks that can be included in your striped volume. To add disk 2, either double-click disk 2 in the Available box or highlight disk 2 and click the Add button. Once you have all the disks you wish to include in your striped volume in the Selected box, it's time to set the size of your new striped volume. The amount of unallocated space must be the same from each disk. In the "Select the amount of space in MB" box I have 16 GB displayed because that is how much unallocated space I have on each disk. The "Total size in MB" box reflects the size of the entire striped volume, which will be 32 GB. If you don't want to use all of the unallocated space you can change the amount of disk space in the "Select the amount of space in MB" box. But remember you must use the same amount of space from each disk so when you attempt to change disk 1 to use 5000 MB of space for the spanned volume, the amount of space from disk 2 changes to 5000 MB also as shown in Figure 9.16.

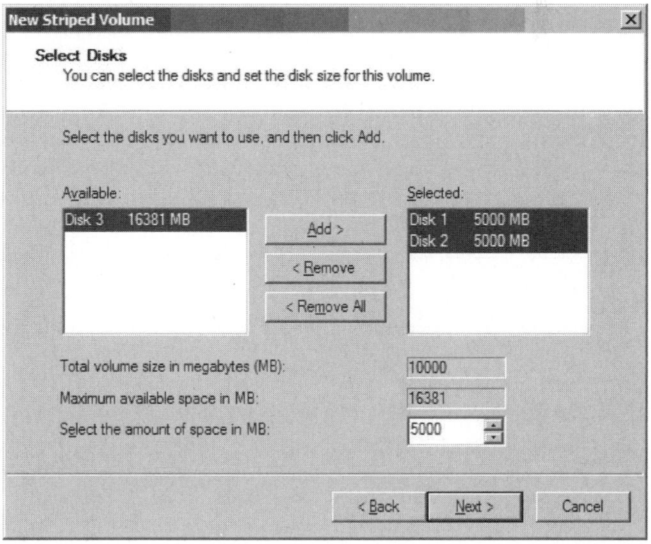

FIGURE 9.16
Selecting disks for a striped volume

After selecting the size of your striped volume, click Next. Choose either the next available drive letter (mine was F:), or select one from the drop-down box and click Next. Select the file system to format your striped volume as, click Next and Finish. I now have an E: drive that is a 10,000 MB striped volume that spans two physical disks, as shown in Figure 9.17.

FIGURE 9.17
Newly created striped volume

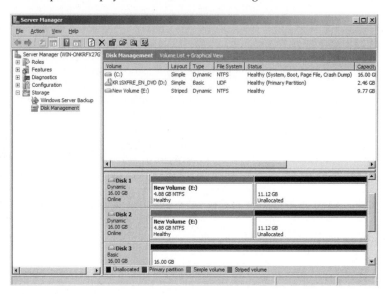

The data stored on a striped volume is different than the fill and spill method we saw with spanned volumes. With striped volumes the data is stored on the physical disks in a striped fashion (hence the name striped volumes). What does that mean exactly? I have a 1 MB file that I have stored on my E: drive. When the file was written to the E: drive the first 64 KB of data was stored on disk 1, the next 64 KB on disk 2, and then back to disk 1 again until the entire file is stored. Can you see how performance can be enhanced when every physical disk has a separate set of read/write heads? So think about a volume that has been striped over 20 physical disks — accessing data would be much faster. But, be sure to keep daily backups because if one physical drive fails then all data residing on the striped volume (in our scenario the E: drive) is gone as well. While striped volumes offer faster data access times there are some limitations. Striped volumes cannot be extended or mirrored. If you want to increase the size of your striped volume you will need to back up your data, delete the striped volume, create a new larger striped volume, and restore your data.

CREATING A STRIPED VOLUME VIA DISKPART

These steps create a 10,000 MB striped volume by using 5,000 MB of space from disk 1 and disk 2.

1. At a command prompt, type **diskpart** and press Enter. You will now be at the DISKPART> prompt. Type list disk as shown in step 2 to get the numbers of the existing disks.

2. DISKPART> list disk
   Note the numbers of the disks that you want to create the striped volume on. They need to be converted from basic to dynamic disks first (this is done automatically by Disk Management). Then assign a drive letter and format the volume.

3. To select disk 1 type: DISKPART> **select disk 1**

4. Convert disk 1 to dynamic by typing: DISKPART> *convert dynamic*

5. Select disk 2 by typing: DISKPART> **select disk 2**

6. Convert disk 2 to dynamic by typing: DISKPART> **convert dynamic**

7. DISKPART> **create volume stripe size=5000 disk=1,2**

8. Next, list the volumes by typing: DISKPART> **list volume**
   Notice that the new volume you have created (volume 0 in Figure 9.18) has no drive letter in the Ltr column. The next step is to assign a drive letter.

FIGURE 9.18
New Striped volume: No drive letter

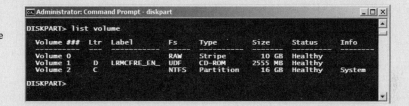

9. Select the new striped volume (in this example volume 0) by typing:
   DISKPART> **select volume 0**

10. Assign the next available drive letter by typing: DISKPART> **assign**
    assign by itself will assign the next available drive letter. If you want a specific drive letter, let's say J, then you would type:

    To specifiy a drive letter (such as J) type: DISKPART> **assign letter = J**
    The last step is to format volume 0. In step 9 I already selected volume 0 so the focus of DiskPart is still on volume 0.

11. The last step is to format the new striped volume by typing: DISKPART> **format**
    format by itself will use the NTFS file system to format.

To script these DiskPart commands for disaster recovery or Server Core 2008 you will need to know the disk numbers that you want included in the striped volume. Once again I am creating a 10,000 MB striped volume with disk 1 and disk 2 contributing 5000 MB to the total size of the striped volume. The striped volume will be assigned the drive letter J and formatted with NTFS. Open Notepad and type the following exactly as shown:

```
select disk 1
convert dynamic
select disk 2
convert dynamic
create volume stripe size=5000 disk=1,2
assign letter=J
format
exit
```

Next give the file a name and save it. I named mine NewStripe.scr and stored it in the root of C:. There are two methods for running your script. First, from a command prompt, type **diskpart /s C:\NewStripe.scr**. Second, create a batch (.bat) file that can execute the commands in the script NewStripe.scr. To create the batch file, open Notepad and type the following:

```
Diskpart /s <path to and name of file>
```
For my example:

```
Diskpart /s C:\NewStripe.scr
```

NOTE

The /s switch specifies that a script will be used.

DELETING DYNAMIC VOLUMES

Deleting dynamic volumes is a one-way process — there is no going back. So be sure you have backed up your data if you need to retain it. The steps for deleting dynamic volumes are the same whether the volume is simple, spanned, or striped. Right-click the volume (for a spanned or striped volume, right-click any portion of the volume) and choose Delete Volume. You'll receive a warning message stating "Deleting this volume will erase all data on it. Backup any data you want to keep before deleting, do you want to continue?" Choosing Yes deletes not only the volume but all data stored on it as well.

HOW TO DELETE DYNAMIC VOLUMES USING DISKPART

1. At a command prompt, type **diskPart** and press Enter. You will now be at the DISKPART> prompt. Type list volume as shown in step 2 to get the numbers of the existing volumes.

2. DISKPART> `list volume`
   Note the volume number you wish to delete.

3. To delete a volume (in this example volume 3) type: DISKPART> `select volume number`

4. To delete volume 3 type: DISKPART> `delete volume`

RAID in Server 2008

Server disks must be faster, more reliable, and larger than their workstation-based cousins. How do you achieve those goals of speed, reliability, and size? Well, you could always purchase faster, more reliable and larger drives but there is another solution. A group of drives can band together and, acting in concert, provide speed, capacity, and fault tolerance. This solution is called *Redundant Arrays of Independent Disks* or *RAID*.

Before we cover the last two *types of dynamic volumes* (Mirroring and RAID-5) let's talk about what RAID is and what it can do for you. RAID is a method of protecting your data by storing the same data on more than one physical disk or storing the instructions to rebuild the data on more than one disk. The function of RAID is to keep your data safe and accessible even in the event of a physical disk failure.

RAID is offered in both software and hardware solutions. Software-based RAID is easy to set up as long as your OS supports it. You can experiment with software RAID at no additional cost other than the additional drives needed to support your chosen level of RAID. But software RAID does have some limitations. Software RAID volumes are invisible to any OS other than Microsoft's Server 2000 or later. Recovery time of a failed physical drive could be an issue as well. Let's say you have four drives currently configured in a software RAID implementation and one of the four drives dies. While you can still access the data that used to live on the failed physical drive, you no longer have fault tolerance. Losing one physical drive is no big deal, but lose two and you've lost protection for your data. It is important to re-establish fault tolerance as quickly as possible. To do this you'll have to bring the server down, replace the bad drive with a new good one, and then regenerate the new disk into the RAID volume.

In contrast, *hardware* RAID systems usually come in a box containing several drives that are coordinated by a separate controller to act as one and they appear as one drive to Server 2008 systems. An external RAID box costs a bit more, but a hardware-based RAID system can rebuild itself faster than software RAID. And best of all, most hardware-based RAID systems allow you to hot-swap the bad drive — that is, you can replace the bad drive without bringing down the server. Hardware RAID is both more flexible and reliable than its software cousin. (And it's a heck of a lot easier on your computer — some software RAID can be ruinous to computer performance.) Software RAID offers a less expensive option for those who want this kind of data protection but can't afford hardware RAID solutions.

Most people who use Server 2008's built-in RAID use its mirroring capability, since the processing required to support RAID-5 seriously degrades server performance. However, if you're serious about data protection for Server 2008, you'll probably consider using hardware RAID, preferably one of the more advanced sorts, which offers its own processor and the ability to hot-swap failed disks.

Mirrored Volumes — RAID-1

Mirrored volumes are the simplest form of Server 2008 fault tolerance. They allow you to take an existing simple volume (including the System and Boot) and copy all the data to another physical disk, so you have an identical copy of the data. If one member of the mirrored volume fails you can still access the data on the working member. This is what makes mirrored volumes fault tolerant. You will need two physical disks with the same amount of space available.

When compared to other software implementations of RAID, this level has relatively good performance. Writing data to the mirrored volumes may be a little slower due to the fact that the data must be written to both disks. But, reading the data is faster because the I/O controller has two places to read information from.

Establishing a Mirrored Volume

You can mirror an existing simple volume or create a mirrored volume from unallocated space on two disks. When mirroring an existing volume the disk on which the volume resides must be dynamic. But, the disk you wish to mirror the existing volume to can be basic or dynamic (basic disks will automatically be converted to dynamic). To mirror an existing simple volume, right-click the volume and choose Add Mirror. A dialog box similar to the one in Figure 9.19 lists the disks available on which to mirror the data. Only disks that have at least as much unallocated space as the volume being mirrored will be listed. If no other drives contain enough unallocated space, then the option to Add Mirror will be grayed out. In Figure 9.20 I choose disk 1 to mirror my existing volume to. You must highlight the disk you want to add to your mirror (even if there is only one disk listed) and click the Add Mirror button. If you are mirroring the existing volume to a basic disk you will get a warning message stating the basic disk must be converted to dynamic, and if there are currently OSes installed on that disk they will become unbootable. If you are mirroring to a dynamic disk, the mirror will be created without any messages at all.

FIGURE 9.19
Adding disks to your mirror

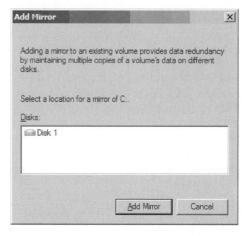

The new volume will be formatted with the same file system as the original volume. And, the data from the original volume will be copied to the new member of the mirrored volume. Depending on the size of the volume you're mirroring, this may take a while. It's not a fast process on large volumes. The new volume will have the same drive letter as the one you mirrored and will be available immediately — no reboot required. Figure 9.20 shows that I have mirrored my system volume (C:) so now both disk 0 and disk 1 contain the same files, which provides redundancy for my operating system. If either disk fails my server will continue to run from the working member of the mirrored volume.

FIGURE 9.20
Mirroring the system volume

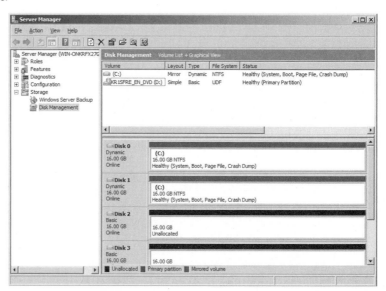

Create a mirrored volume from unallocated space by right-clicking an area of unallocated space and choosing New Mirrored Volume. The New Mirrored Volume Wizard launches; click Next. Select the disks you want to include in your mirrored volume and notice that the same amount of space is used on both disks. It wouldn't make a lot of sense to mirror 1 GB of data to a 2 GB volume — you would be wasting 1 GB of space. The rest of the wizard will look familiar; choose your drive letter and file system for formatting. Click Next and Finish. In a matter of minutes you'll have a new mirrored volume. From this point forward the data will be kept in sync on the two volumes.

DISK DUPLEXING

With the implementation of disk mirroring you can take it one step further in the world of fault tolerance by having each disk that is a member of the mirrored volume connected to its own disk controller. This is called *disk duplexing*. This ensures that the data is not vulnerable to controller failures and provides better disk-read performance and greater fault tolerance.

CONSIDERATIONS FOR MIRRORING VOLUMES

Partition styles can introduce some problems if you're not careful. The two types of partition styles (MBR and GPT) are explained in the earlier section "Partition Styles." You can create mirrored volumes using a combination of MBR and GPT disks, but the MBR cylinder-alignment restriction might cause difficulties when creating mirrored volumes. For this reason it is a good practice to always mirror MBR disks to GPT disks to avoid cylinder-alignment difficulties.

You cannot extend a mirrored volume. If you want your mirrored volume to be larger you will have to break the mirror (look for step by steps in the Breaking a Mirrored Volume section), extend the simple volume that you want to mirror, and then create a new mirror.

TROUBLESHOOTING AND DELETING MIRRORED VOLUMES

The status of the mirrored volume reflects whether the volume is successfully being mirrored or not. The status Healthy means that your data is being protected. If, however, the status is *Failed*, *Offline*, *Missing*, or *Failed Redundancy*, chances are your data is no longer protected. There are various reasons you may see a status other than Healthy: mis-seated disks, failed hard drives or disk controllers. In this section, I will explain how to recover from a failed mirrored volume and how to reclaim disk space by breaking, removing, and deleting mirrored volumes.

Recovering from a Failed Mirrored Volume

If the status of a disk is set to *Offline* or *Missing* it is possible that the disk has become mis-seated (common when moving servers). To repair your mirrored volume make sure that the disk is seated properly, and then within the Disk Management utility right-click the disk and choose Reactivate Volume. The status will switch to *Regenerating* and then hopefully back to *Healthy*.

HOW TO REACTIVATE A MIRRORED VOLUME USING DISKPART

1. At a command prompt, type **diskpart** and press Enter. You will now be at the DISKPART> prompt. Type list disk as shown in step 2 to get the numbers of the existing disks.

2. DISKPART> **list disk**
   Note the number of the disk reporting a status of Offline or Missing.

3. Select the number of the disk reporting a status of Offline or Missing. In this example that would be disk 3. DISKPART> **select disk 3**

4. To bring disk 3 back online type: DISKPART> **online**

If the status of the volume does not return to Healthy then you have either a failed physical disk or disk controller. Check the System log in Event Viewer to determine which is failing. Adding a new drive to a failed disk controller would be no help at all. If the failure is due to a bad disk you will need to break the existing mirror, replace the failed hard disk, and re-establish the mirrored volume again by right-clicking the dynamic volume you want to mirror and choosing Add Mirror. Select the new disk you added and you're done.

Breaking a Mirrored Volume

You can break the mirrored volume to reclaim disk space but the data will no longer be fault tolerant. Break the mirrored volume using Disk Management by right-clicking either member and choosing Break Mirrored Volume. You will receive a warning message letting you know that your data will no longer be fault tolerant and ask if you want to continue. Clicking Yes causes both members of the mirrored volume to become simple volumes. The original volume will retain the drive letter that had belonged to the mirrored volume, and the other volume will have the next available drive letter.

HOW TO BREAK A MIRRORED VOLUME USING DISKPART

1. At a command prompt, type **diskpart** and press Enter. You will now be at the DISKPART> prompt. Type list volume as shown in step 2 to get the numbers of the existing volumes.

2. DISKPART> **list volume**
   Note the number of the mirrored volume.

3. To select volume 1 type: DISKPART> **select volume**

4. The details of a mirrored volume list the drive numbers on which the mirrored volume resides. You will also see whether the volume has volume shadow copies or BitLocker enabled. Note the disk number of the half of the mirrored volume you want to remove.
   DISKPART> **detail volume**

5. To break the mirrored volume (in this example volume 2) into two simple volumes, both containing the data. The original member of the mirrored volume will retain the drive letter of the mirrored volume. The other simple volume will receive the next available drive letter by typing. DISKPART> **break disk 2**
   This command will break the mirrored volume into two simple volumes, both containing the data. The original member of the mirrored volume will retain the drive letter of the mirrored volume. The other simple volume will receive the next available drive letter.
   OR

6. Use the nokeep switch which breaks the mirrored volume and deletes the data from the disk you specified in this command. For example, I have a mirrored volume that spans disk 2 and disk 3. If I wanted to break my mirrored volume and retain only the data that lives on disk 2, I would type: DISKPART> **break disk=3 nokeep**
   Notice that the two commands are a little different; one requires the equal sign while the other does not. The volume would be deleted from disk 3 along with the data. Disk 3 would now contain unallocated space.

Removing a Mirrored Volume

Removing a mirrored volume works differently in Disk Management than from the command-line tool DiskPart. To remove a mirrored volume from Disk Management, right-click either member of the mirrored volume and choose Remove Mirror. Select the disk you want to remove the mirror from and click the Remove Mirror button as shown in Figure 9.21. When asked if you're sure, click Yes. The mirrored volume you selected will return to unallocated space. The disk that you *didn't* select will become a simple volume retaining the mirrored volume's drive letter and the data will still be in tact.

FIGURE 9.21
Removing a mirror

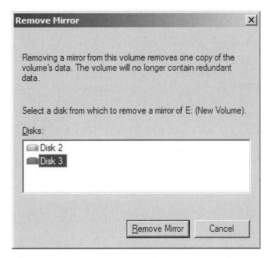

Did you want to retain the data on both disks, but no longer make them fault tolerant? This is where DiskPart is more flexible than the Disk Management snap-in. DiskPart gives you the option to remove the mirror and retain the data on one or both disks. In the "How to Break a Mirrored Volume Using DiskPart" sidebar, step 5 has been broken into two different scenarios. The first is to remove the mirror but leave the data intact on both volumes. The second is to delete the data and return one volume of the mirrored volume to unallocated space.

Deleting a Mirrored Volume

Deleting a mirrored volume also deletes the data in the mirrored volume. Delete a mirrored volume within the Disk Management by right-clicking either member of the mirrored volume and choosing Delete Volume. When asked if you're sure, click Yes. This deletes both halves of the mirrored volume — and destroys the volume. Be sure to back up your data prior to deleting a mirrored volume because there is no going back.

HOW TO DELETE A MIRRORED VOLUME USING DISKPART

1. At a command prompt, type **diskpart** and press Enter. You will now be at the DISKPART> prompt. Type list volume as shown in step 2 to get the numbers of the existing volumes.

2. DISKPART> **list volume**
   Note the number of the mirrored volume you want to delete.

3. To delete volume 3 from the mirrored volume type: DISKPART> **select volume 3**

4. Deleting the volume is done by typing: DISKPART> **delete volume**

RAID-5

RAID-5 volumes provide data protection and decrease the amount of time it takes to read data from the disks. RAID-5 volumes are the most cost-effective form of RAID that Server 2008 supports because they require less space for redundant data than mirroring does. Striping in RAID-5 is the same as striped volumes with one major difference. RAID-5 volumes store the instructions to rebuild data in case one of your hard drives fails. The instructions for rebuilding the data is called *parity*. In the event of hard drive failure the data can be regenerated from the parity information that is spread across the other drives. This is how it works: I have three disks in my RAID-5 volume (three is the minimum you can have, 32 is the max) and want to store a 1 MB file to my RAID-5 volume. The first 64 Kb of data is stored on the first physical disk, the second 64 Kb of data on the second disk, the third 64 Kb on the third disk, and the next 64 Kb of data would be stored on the first disk again until the entire file is stored. The data is not the only thing being stored. The parity must also be stored on the RAID-5 volumes, but parity and the data itself cannot reside on the same disk. Once the data is stored the parity is calculated, so the parity for data that resides on disk1 will be stored in equal parts to disk 2 and disk 3. The same thing happens for disk 2 - it's parity information is calculated and 1/2 the parity will be stored on disk 1 and the other 1/2 on disk 3. Data on disk three is no different: the parity is calculated and 1/2 of the parity is stored on disk 1 and the other 1/2 on disk 2. If disk 1 fails, the data that resides on disk 1 will still be accessible by rebuilding the data from the parity that is on disk 2 and disk 3. If in addition to losing disk 1, disk 2 dies, then half of the parity information for rebuilding the data on disks 1 and 3 would also be gone. This is why losing one disk is no big deal — maybe a little bit of a performance issue because when attempting to access data that resides on one of the failed disks, it has to be rebuilt using the parity information on the remaining working members of the RAID-5 volume.

But there are a couple of drawbacks. Most important, RAID-5 represents a serious drain on processor time. In high-end hardware RAID, the system is configured with a separate processor that handles all the calculations necessary. Software RAID, such as what we're discussing in this chapter, relies on the server's processor to do all that calculating. You almost certainly won't use software RAID-5 much on a production server because of the performance toll it extracts, especially on processor-intensive applications. Also, every time a document is saved to disk, its parity information must be updated to reflect its current status.

ESTABLISHING RAID-5 VOLUMES

Creating a RAID-5 volume can begin on either basic or dynamic disks. Right-click any area of unallocated space and choose New RAID-5 Volume (if you don't have three disks that you can dedicate to the New RAID-5 Volume, then the option New RAID-5 Volume will be grayed out). Click Next on the Welcome to the New RAID-5 Volume Wizard. The disk you right-clicked will be in the Selected box; choose at least two more disks from the Available box as shown in Figure 9.22. Notice that you can't click the Next button until you have at least 3 disks selected.

Next, you need to determine the size of your RAID-5 volume. In the "Select the amount of space in MB" box, the Disk Management utility will calculate the largest RAID-5 volume possible based on how much space is available on each of the drives. All drives must dedicate the same amount of space to the RAID-5 volume. If you have two drives with 10 GB of free space and one drive with only 500 MB, the largest your RAID-5 volume could be is 1500 MB (3 drives × 500 MB each). You can choose to make the volume smaller but not any larger. I typed in 1000 MB for the size and expected to get 1000 MB from each of the disks, 1, 2, and 3, for a total size of 3000 MB. But that's not what I got. My "Total volume size in megabytes (MB)" box shows only a 2000 MB drive, as shown in Figure 9.23, in which to store data. What happened to the other 1000 MB? The value in "Total volume size in megabytes (MB)" reflects the total amount of room available for *data*, not the total space in the RAID-5 volume. Since $1/n$ of the space in a RAID-5 volume (where n is the number of disks in the set) is used for parity information, the more disks you have, the larger percentage of room for data you'll get. For example, out of my 3000 MB RAID-5 volume, because there are three disks, one-third of the space is allocated to the storage of parity information. So, that 1000 MB is where our parity information for the RAID-5 volume lives.

FIGURE 9.22
Creating a New RAID-5
Volume

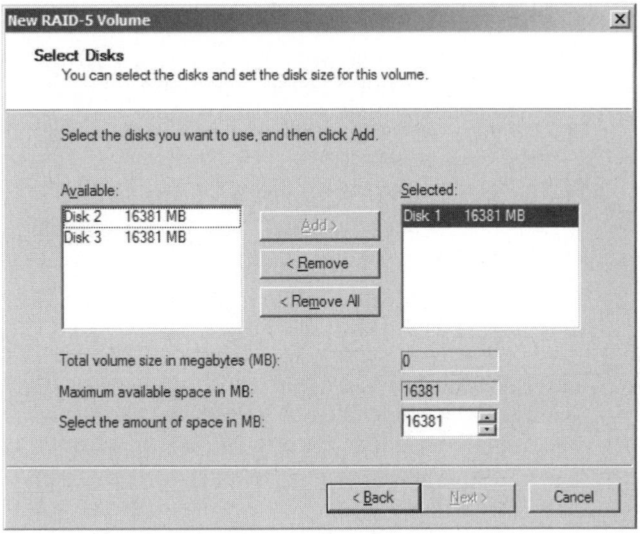

FIGURE 9.23
Selecting the disks for
the RAID-5 Volume

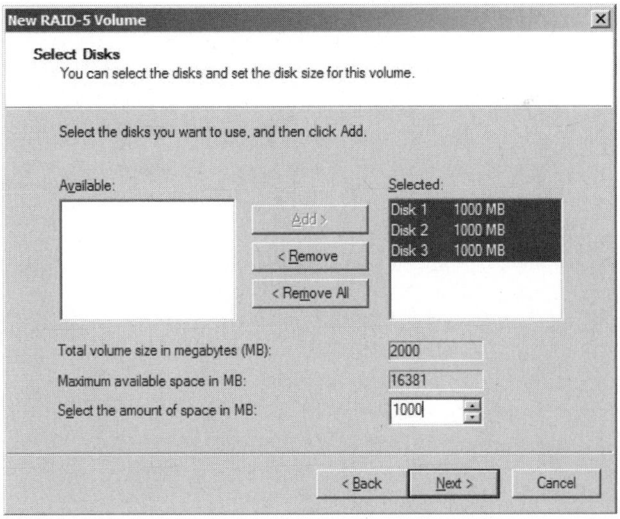

After you have chosen your disks and the size of your RAID-5 volume, click Next and assign the RAID-5 volume a drive letter. You don't have any choice as to the file system used for formatting; it will be NTFS. Server 2008 will grind away for a few minutes, setting up the new RAID-5 volume. When it's done, the RAID-5 volume will be immediately ready to use — no reboot necessary.

HOW TO CREATE A RAID-5 VOLUME USING DISKPART

When using DiskPart to create your RAID-5 volume, all disks must be dynamic. You cannot start with basic disks as you could in the Disk Management utility.

1. At a command prompt, type **diskpart** and press Enter. You will now be at the DISKPART> prompt. Type list disk as shown in step 2 to get the numbers of the existing disks.

2. DISKPART> **list disk**
   Note the disk numbers of the disks you want to include in your RAID-5 volume.

3. To create a 3000MB RAID-5 volume with 2000MB available to store data and 1000MB for storing parity type:
   DISKPART> create volume raid size=1000 disk=1,2,3

4. Assign a drive letter (F in this example) to the new RAID-5 volume by typing:
   DISKPART> assign letter = F

5. Format the new RAID-5 volume with NTFS by typing: DISKPART> **format**

RECOVERING FROM A FAILED RAID-5 VOLUME

If an unrecoverable error such as a disk failure occurs to one of the members of the RAID-5 volume, you'll still be able to read and write to the volume, but the volume will be marked *Failed* or *Missing* in Disk Management as shown in Figure 9.24. Losing one disk in a RAID-5 volume is not a problem; the data will still be accessible because the other two working members of the RAID-5 volume can build the data from parity. But, if you lose more than one disk the data will be inaccessible and unrecoverable. Notice in Figure 9.24 that each disk is flagged with Failed Redundancy.

FIGURE 9.24
RAID-5 failed redundancy

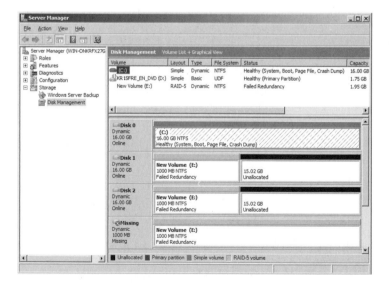

To re-establish the RAID-5 volume, replace the failed disk, initialize the disk, and if the disk does not appear in Disk Management from the Action menu, choose Rescan Disks. Once the disk appears in Disk Management, right-click the new disk and choose Reactivate Volume. If the status of the volume doesn't return to Healthy again, then right-click the RAID-5 volume and choose Repair Volume. A list of available disks will be listed (both basic and dynamic — the disk just needs enough unallocated space for its share of the data and parity). Choose the disk you want to include in the RAID-5 volume and click OK. You'll get the warning message about converting this disk to dynamic and how other OSes residing on this disk will no longer be bootable; click OK. The computer will chug away for a couple of minutes, rebuilding the missing data from the parity information on the remaining disks, and the RAID-5 volume will be back in one piece. No reboot required.

HOW TO BRING A FAILED RAID-5 DISK BACK ONLINE USING DISKPART

1. At a command prompt, type **diskpart** and press Enter. You will now be at the DISKPART> prompt. Type list disk as shown in step 2 to get the numbers of the existing disks.

2. DISKPART> **list disk**
   Note the number of the disk whose status is missing or offline and you want to bring it online again.

3. Select the disk with the Missing status. In my example that is disk 3. So type:
   DISKPART> **select disk 3**

4. To bring disk 3 back online type the following: DISKPART> **online**

DELETING A RAID-5 VOLUME

Deleting a RAID-5 volume is quite simple. Right-click any member of the RAID-5 volume and choose Delete Volume. You'll see the usual warning message telling you that you're about to delete the volume and lose data; click Next. The entire RAID-5 volume will return to unallocated space. Don't forget that deleting a RAID-5 volume destroys all the data and the parity information.

HOW TO DELETE A RAID-5 VOLUME USING DISKPART

1. At a command prompt, type **diskpart** and press Enter. You will now be at the DISKPART> prompt. Type list volume as shown in step 2 to get the numbers of the existing volumes.

2. DISKPART> **list volume**
   Note the number of the RAID-5 volume you want to delete.

3. To delete volume 3 type: DISKPART> **select volume 3**

4. To delete volume 3 type: DISKPART> **delete volume**

RAID-5 CONSIDERATIONS

RAID-5 volumes cannot be extended. They also place greater demand on your system due to the need to calculate parity information. Adding more memory and processor power to the server will help the performance of the RAID-5 volume.

Moving a Dynamic Disk

You might want to move a dynamic disk to a new computer, say, if you're moving half a mirrored volume to re-create duplicate data on a different computer. Server 2008 organizes dynamic disks into disk groups. When you move a dynamic disk from one computer to another, you're moving it to a new group. You'll need to introduce the disk you're moving to its new disk group — *without* deleting the data on the disk you're moving.

BEFORE YOU MOVE THE DISKS

Before you start moving disks from one computer to another ensure that all of your disks have a status of *Healthy* in the Disk Management tool. If any multidisk volumes don't have a status of *Healthy*, fix them before moving the disk. If you're planning to move both disks that comprise a mirrored volume or all disks contained in a RAID-5 volume, it is a *very* good idea to move all those disks at once. Spanned and striped volumes won't work unless all their disks are present — the data will be lost if you only move one of the disks supporting a striped or spanned volume. For example, say that you have a mirrored volume on Server1. If you *break* that mirrored volume and move half of it to Server2, then everything is fine. But if you move one member of the mirrored volume from Server1 to Server2 without breaking the existing mirror, things get a little strange. You can continue using the disks in both systems, meaning you can keep writing to a failed mirror volume in Server 2008; it'll just show up as Failed Redundancy in the Disk Management tool. If you later move the other half from Server1 to Server2, the data on the two mirror halves will be inconsistent. In such a case, Server 2008 will re-create the mirrored volume with the data from the physical disk moved first to Server2.

In this scenario, the computer you removed the disk from will be the *source* computer and the computer you moved it to will be the *destination* computer. When you remove a dynamic disk from a computer, information about it and its volumes is retained by the remaining online dynamic disks. The removed disk is displayed in the Disk Management tool on the source computer as a Dynamic/Offline disk with the name *Missing*.

Sometimes you can remove this Missing disk in the Disk Management UI by deleting all volumes on that disk, then right-click the disk and choose Remove Disk. Or, if Disk Management won't remove the Missing disk, DiskPart will. Follow these steps:

HOW TO REMOVE A MISSING DISK USING DISKPART

1. At a command prompt, type **diskpart** and press Enter. You will now be at the DISKPART> prompt. Type list volume as shown in step 2 to get the numbers of the existing volumes.

2. DISKPART> **list volume**
    Note the volume number of the Missing disk, status = Failed Rd, as shown in Figure 9.25. My failed volume is volume 0.

FIGURE 9.25
List disk - Failed Redundancy

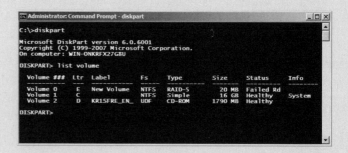

3. Select the failed volume o by typing: DISKPART> `select volume 0`

4. Then delete the volume o by typing: DISKPART> `delete volume`

INTRODUCING THE NEW DISK

After you physically connect the disks to the destination computer, if the disks do not appear in the Disk Management UI from the Action menu, choose Rescan Disks. The new disk will show up as Dynamic/Foreign. By default, a Dynamic/Foreign disk should be brought online automatically, but if it's not, then right-click the disk and choose Online.

To use Dynamic/Foreign disks, you'll need to import them. Right-click one of the moved disks and choose the Import Foreign Disks option. The importing procedure works slightly differently depending on whether there's already a disk group on the new computer. If there are no preexisting online dynamic disks, then the disk group is brought online exactly as it is. The disk group remains the same as it was; the database doesn't change. If a disk group was already present on the destination computer, then Server 2008 will merge the old disk group information with the new disk group information, so that all the dynamic disks contain the same information. The imported disks will become members of the local disk group on the destination computer.

CAN I USE THE DATA ON THE MOVED DISKS?

So what happens to the volumes on the dynamic disks you moved? Well, that depends on whether you moved enough data for the volume to work. Either the data itself or the parity information used to re-create the data must be on the destination computer.

Simple volumes, which are contained on a single disk, should be fine if they were fine before you moved the disk.

If you moved only part of a multidisk but non-fault-tolerant volume, such as a striped or spanned volume, that volume is disabled on both the source and destination computers until you move the disks containing the rest of it. So long as you don't delete the volume on either the source or destination computer, you should be able to move the rest of the volume to the destination computer and re-enable it, but you will need to move all the disks supporting that multidisk volume. If however, you deleted a volume after moving it to a new machine and noticing that the status was "Missing", you can't rebuild the volume.

If you move a disk containing part of a RAID-5 volume, then the data may be available even if you didn't move the entire volume to the destination computer; this depends on whether you moved enough parity data to regenerate what's missing. If the parity information is valid, one disk of the RAID-5 volume can be missing and the volume should still work, just as it would if one of the disks in the volume failed.

If you move a mirrored volume that's up to date, you can use the data on the new computer or even (if you broke the mirror set on the source computer) re-create the mirror volume using unallocated space from a disk on the destination computer.

Performing Disk Maintenance

The earlier sections in this chapter covered the basics, introducing the terminology of disk management in Server 2008 and showing you how to set up the various types of partitions and volumes. I'll now explain disk geometry, file formats, and how to change an existing drive letter.

Before getting into some of these routine maintenance chores, changing drive letters, formatting disks, defragmenting disks, and evaluating the health of your disks, let's take a quick look at the relationship between Server 2008 and hard disks.

Background: Disk Geometry and File Formats

A hard drive is not one but several disks called *platters*. Each platter is divided two ways: pie-shaped wedges and concentric circles. The pieces defined by the intersection of these divisions are called *sectors* and are the physical units of storage on a hard disk. Each sector on a disk is normally 512 bytes in size.

Server 2008 doesn't know a sector from a hole in the ground. To let its file storage component store and retrieve data on the disk, Server 2008 must impose some kind of logical structure over the physical structure of the disk. That logical structure is called a *disk format*. The disk format entails grouping sectors together in logical units called *clusters*. The number of sectors in a cluster varies, depending on the size of the disk partition. For this explanation, my disk is larger than 2 GB so the cluster size is 4 KB. How do clusters and sectors relate to each other? As most of you know, 1 KB is equal to 1024 bytes; therefore, the size of a 4 KB cluster would be $4 \times 1024 = 4096$ bytes. Now, if the sector size is 512 bytes, how many sectors does it take to make one cluster? The equation would look like this: $4096 / 512 = 8$, so the answer is there are 8 512-byte sectors to make up one 4096 KB cluster. When you format a volume, the clusters are numbered starting with 0. A cluster is the smallest organizational unit that a file system can recognize, which means you can store only one file per cluster. If a file is smaller than the cluster size, the entire file will be stored in one cluster, and any empty space in that cluster goes unused.

Sound irrelevant? Trust me: you'll need this background on clusters and sectors when it comes to performing the basic disk maintenance covered in the following sections. Let's get started.

CHANGING A DRIVE LETTER

If you find that you need to change an existing drive letter, it's a snap. Well, a snap for any drive that is not a System or Boot drive. The System and Boot drive letters cannot be changed. But, if you want to change other drive letters, right-click the volume whose drive letter you want to change and choose Change Drive Letter and Paths. Figure 9.26 shows the current drive letter. Click the Change button and you will see a screen similar to Figure 9.27.

FIGURE 9.26
Changing drive letters from within the Disk Management GUI

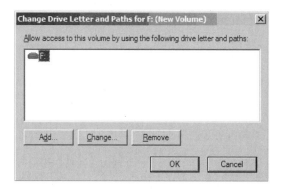

Select the new drive letter and click OK. You will then receive a warning message that says "Some programs that rely on drive letters might not run correctly. Do you want to continue Yes or No?" Click Yes, wait a few seconds, and voila — new drive letter. No more rebooting just to change a simple drive letter.

FIGURE 9.27
Change drive letter

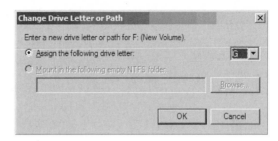

DISK FORMATS SUPPORTED IN SERVER 2008

Server 2008 supports three disk formats: the old FAT or FAT16 format that includes long-filename support, the FAT32 file format introduced with Windows 95 OSR 2, and an updated version of the NTFS format that's been around since NT 3.1.

FAT and FAT32

FAT is the oldest of Microsoft file systems, the one that all Microsoft operating systems support. It uses a simple catalog called the *file allocation table* to note which cluster or clusters a file is stored in. If a file's stored in more than one cluster, then the cluster includes a pointer to the next cluster used for that file until the final cluster includes an End of File marker.

FAT16 and FAT32 have a great deal in common: a simple set of attributes that note creation and access dates and the settings of the hidden, archive, system, and read-only bits. The main difference between FAT16 and FAT32 lies in their relative cluster sizes. FAT is actually FAT16, which means that it uses a 16-bit addressing scheme that allows it to address up to 216 (that is, 65,536) clusters.

FAT32, in contrast, has 32-bit addresses, which means that it can have up to 232 (that is, 4,294,967,296) clusters. Because of this, FAT32 can use much smaller clusters even on large volumes; on volumes up to 8 GB, it uses 4 KB clusters. Other than this difference, however, it's the same as FAT.

The main reasons FAT and FAT32 are included with Server 2008 is for backward compatibility with other OSes.

NTFS

Most often, the advanced features of NTFS will make it your first choice for a server file system.

◆ NTFS is designed for system security purposes and allows setting file and folder permissions. FAT and FAT32 do not allow setting file and folder permissions, but you can restrict access to *shared* directories when using FAT by setting permissions on the shared folder. To learn how file permissions work, see Chapter 11, "What's in a Name? Network Name Overview."

◆ Only NTFS volumes support Server 2008 file encryption, disk quotas, volume mounting, and data compression. Only volumes formatted with NTFS may be extended.

◆ NTFS keeps a log of activities in order to be able to restore the disk after a power failure or other interruption. The log is called the NTFS change journal and keeps track of any changes on that partition. Each partition contains its own NTFS change journal. The change journal doesn't replace *data* on the NTFS drives, but if it's interrupted in the middle of a write procedure, it will restore the volume structure. This prevents the disk's volume from becoming corrupted.

NAMING CONVENTIONS FOR LONG FILENAMES

All disk formats in Server 2008 support long filenames. Even FAT uses the extensions that make this possible. Filenames in Server 2008 can be up to 256 characters long with the extension, including spaces and separating periods. You can use any upper- or lowercase character in a long or short filename except the following, which have special significance to Server 2008:

? " / \ < > * | :

Even though NTFS supports long filenames, it maintains backward compatibility by automatically generating a conventional 8.3 FAT filename for every file. The 8.3 filename will consist of the first six characters of the long filename with a tilde (~) and a number attached to the end. When converting a long filename to the short format, Server 2008 does the following:

◆ Removes spaces.

◆ Removes periods, except the last one that is followed by a character — this period is assumed to herald the beginning of the file extension.

◆ Removes any characters not allowed in DOS names and converts them to underscores.

◆ Truncates the extension to three characters.

You may want to keep these points in mind when using long filenames so your filenames will make sense in both the 8.3 and long filename formats. For example, naming a file "Project for Migrating 2003 servers to 2008" DOC would generate an 8.3 filename of Projec ~ 1.DOC. If you then had another file named "Project for Migrating Office 2003 servers to office 2007" DOC the 8.3 filename would be Projec ~ 2.DOC. So now you have two files named so similarly it may be difficult to remember which one is which. If you will be depending on the 8.3 filenames (some applications can't read long file-names), it's a good idea to make the first six characters of the long filename more descriptive. For example, "2K3 Server migration project" and "2K3 Office migration project" would create 8.3 filenames of 2k3ser ~ 1.DOC and 2K3Off ~ 1.DOC. To see your 8.3 filenames, open a command prompt and navigate to the folder the files reside in and type **Dir /X** as shown in Figure 9.28.

FIGURE 9.28
Viewing 8.3 filenames

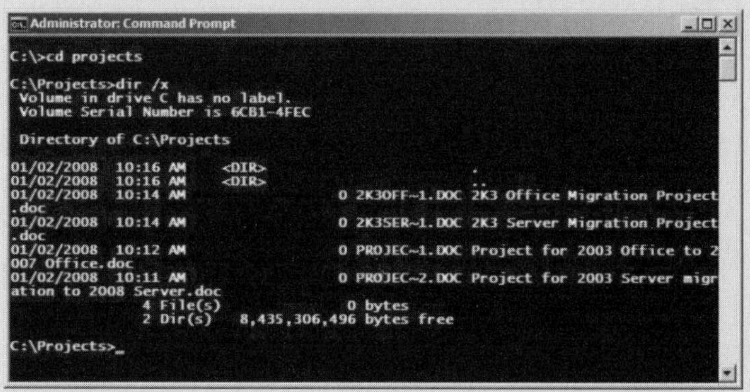

When it comes to floppies, you don't have much of a choice for file system formats. NTFS is not an option for floppies. There's a good reason for this: the NTFS file structure is complex, so finding data on large disks is fast and easy, but it takes up more room than a floppy disk can supply. You can, however, create files with long names on a floppy, since the Server 2008 version of FAT supports 256-character filenames.

Which File System?

Which file system should you use? Table 9.1 gives you an at-a-glance comparison of NTFS and the FAT file systems.

TABLE 9.1:   Comparing NTFS and FAT in Server 2008

FEATURE	NTFS	FAT32	FAT
Filename length	256 characters	256 characters	256 characters under Windows 9x, NT, Windows 2000; 8.3 under DOS
File attributes	Extended	Limited	Limited
Associated operating system	Server 2008, Windows 2000, and Windows NT	Server 2008, Windows 2000, Windows 9x, OSR2	DOS
Accessible when you boot the computer from a DOS floppy?	No	No	Yes
Maximum volume size supported	16 TB minus 4 KB	32GB	4GB
Cluster size on a 1GB volume	2 KB	4 KB	32 KB
Supports extending volumes?	Yes	No	No

NTFS is more efficient than FAT in the way it uses disk space, particularly on the large disks that are so common these days. There are specific scenarios that require NTFS such as mounted drives, encryption, and disk quotas. So, when *shouldn't* you use NTFS?

The only times NTFS won't work for you is when you need to support OSes prior to Windows Server 2000 that reside *on the same computer* as Server 2008. When it comes to accessing files from across the network the file system does not matter — a Windows 98 computer can read an NTFS volume across the network. FAT is widely supported by other OSes, so you should use it on any volume that you'll need to have accessible to other OSes on the same computer.

SHOULD I USE FAT ON THE SYSTEM PARTITION?

Mastering Windows NT Server 4 recommended that you format the system partition with FAT. If you did this, then you could copy the installation files from the CD to the system partition, and trouble-shooting a failed OS was much easier.

The only trouble with keeping all system files and said installation files on a FAT-formatted partition is that doing so is enormously wasteful of disk space. Like many of us, Server 2008/Windows 2000/NT has gotten fatter as it's gotten older. To be pretty sure I wouldn't run out of room, I'd need a system partition at least 2 GB in size. You can format a 2 GB partition with FAT — barely. That's the largest amount of disk space that FAT can "see" under Server 2008. But doing so is horribly wasteful. As dis-cussed earlier in this chapter, the FAT file system is wasteful of space on large partitions because it organizes the disk into very large clusters. 2 GB might not be enough to store all the system files.

Thankfully, a new tool first introduced in Windows 2000 called the Recovery Console makes format-ting the system drive with FAT no longer necessary. It's an NTFS-compatible command-line recovery tool that you can use to get at your system directory and make repairs. During the installation of Server 2008, if you accept the defaults, the OS will be placed on the C: partition and formatted with NTFS. If you want to format the system partition as FAT32 you will have to use the Shift F10 key com-bination to get to a command prompt and format from there.

Formatting Disks

Server 2008 lets you format volumes while creating them with the Disk Management tool. You can also format volumes from Explorer or the command prompt. And, yes, my fellow command-line junkies, you can use DiskPart as well.

If you chose not to format a volume that you created in the Disk Management tool, you can format it whenever you are ready to use it. Or you may also want to reformat an already formatted volume to quickly delete all data.

USING THE FORMATTING TOOLS

To format a volume on a disk that has been initialized (or you just want to delete all the data on the volume) within Explorer, right-click the volume and choose Format from the shortcut menu and you'll see a dialog box similar to the one in Figure 9.29.

If you choose to perform this task from the Disk Management tool, you'll see a slightly different dialog box, because it doesn't show you the Capacity of the volume, as it does from Explorer. Type in any name you like and then choose the disk format you want to use: NTFS, FAT32, or FAT. Click OK, and Server 2008 will format the selected volume. Of course, any data already on the disk will be deleted, so if you're reformatting, be sure that you've already saved any data on the volume that you want to keep.

Formatting from the Command Line

To format a partition or volume from the command prompt, open the command prompt from the Start menu and type: **format** *driveletter***: /fs:***file system*

For example, to format a newly created E: drive as NTFS, you would type

format e: /fs:ntfs.

Typing **format e:** will automatically format with NTFS. When formatting, keep in mind that if there is existing data on the partition it will be deleted so formatting the system or the boot volume

FIGURE 9.29
Formatting a volume in
Windows Explorer

would be a bad idea. But Server 2008 won't even allow it. If you choose to format the system or boot volume in Explorer or the Disk Management tool, the option to format will be grayed out. If you attempt to format the system or boot volume from the command prompt you will receive a message stating "System partition is not allowed to be formatted."

CONVERTING FAT OR FAT32 TO NTFS

If you have FAT or FAT32 volumes on your disk that you'd like to be NTFS, you don't have to worry about the data. You can simply use the CONVERT command-prompt utility. Here's the format: **convert *driveletter*: /fs:ntfs**

For example, to convert the P: drive to NTFS, you'd type the following:

convert p: /fs:ntfs.

You'd see output like the following:

```
The type of the file system is FAT32.
Volume Serial Number is B447-D3E5
Windows is verifying files and folders...
File and folder verification is complete.
Windows has checked the file system and found no
 problems.

  523,247,616 bytes total disk space.
        4,096 bytes in 1 files.
  523,239,424 bytes available on disk.
```

```
            4,096 bytes in each allocation unit.
        127,746 total allocation units on disk.
        127,744 allocation units available on disk.

Determining disk space required for file system
  conversion...
Total disk space:                512000 KB
Free space on volume:            510976 KB
Space required for conversion:     5329 KB
Converting file system
Conversion complete
```

In order to convert a partition/volume to NTFS you must have free space on the volume that you want to convert. The free space is where the data is stored while the clusters are being reorganized. If you don't have enough free space, then the option to convert will result in an error message or from Disk Management the option will be grayed out. For this reason it's a good idea to convert volumes before they get too full.

You can't convert to any file system other than NTFS, and there is no going back, or in other words, the conversion process is not reversible. In the past if you didn't have exclusive access (open files would prevent the conversion) to the partition you could not convert it without rebooting the computer. Not so in Server 2008 — once again no reboot necessary.

MOUNTED DRIVES

Normally we identify each logical volume with a drive letter. This method is simple and has the advantage of giving us a quick way to change from one volume to another: You just type the letter representing it. The disadvantage is that Server 2008 uses the Roman alphabet, so you're limited to 26 letters for all local drives and mapped network connections. To get around this limitation, Server 2008 supports mounting volumes and partitions to empty folders on NTFS volumes. Don't worry about basic and dynamic disks; both are supported.

The idea behind mounted volumes is they don't require drive letters, *only* an empty folder residing on an NTFS volume. I have an empty folder named Applications on my C: volume and a newly installed 16 GB drive, which is the fourth drive/disk in the computer, so the disk number would be 3. To mount the new 16 GB drive to the C:\Applications folder through the Disk Management GUI, right-click the 16 GB of unallocated space and choose to create a new simple volume (spanned volumes work also). On the Assign Drive Letter or Path page of the wizard, select "Mount in the following empty NTFS folder" and browse to the empty folder as shown in Figure 9.30.

When data is placed in the C:\Applications folder the I/O manager redirects all read/write calls to disk 3. What really happens under the hood is that a *junction point* is created for the C:\Applications folder that directs all data to the physical location of disk 3. Volume mappings are completely transparent to the user. The mounted volumes show up as drives in Windows Explorer as shown in Figure 9.31, but the users treat them as any other folder.

I mentioned simple and spanned volumes, but what about fault tolerance for those business-critical applications? You could have right-clicked unallocated space and chosen to create a mirrored or RAID-5 volume. Instead of giving the new volume a drive letter you can simply direct it to an empty folder. Once you have mounted a folder path, there is no way to modify it. So in order to make changes you'll need to remove the mount point and then re-create it.

FIGURE 9.30
Mounting a folder

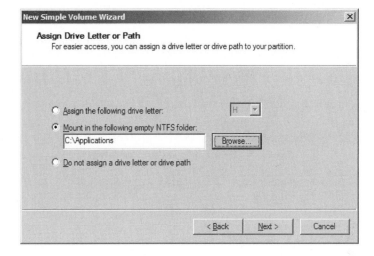

FIGURE 9.31
Mounted volumes in Windows Explorer

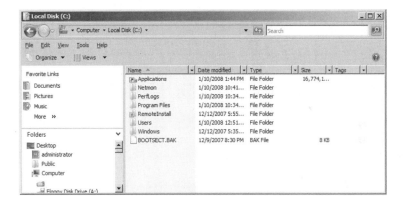

NOTE

After you have assigned a mount-point folder path to a drive, it's a good idea to check the System log in Event Viewer. Cluster service errors or warnings would indicate a failure in the mount-point folder path. These events would have ClusSvc in the Source column and Physical Disk Resource in the Category column of the event generated.

How to Mount a Volume Using DiskPart

You will need to create a volume first and then instead of assigning a drive letter, you will assign a mount point folder.

1. At a command prompt, type **diskpart**. You will now be at the DISKPART> prompt. Type list disk as shown in step 2 to get the numbers of the existing disks.

2. DISKPART> **list disk**
   Note the disk number of the disk on which you want to create the volume (3 in this example). If the disk is currently basic, you will need to convert it to dynamic first:
   DISKPART> **select disk 3**
   DISKPART> **convert dynamic**

3. To create a 500 MB simple volume on disk 3 (you could also create a spanned, mirrored, or RAID-5 volume) type:
   DISKPART> **create volume simple size=500 disk=3**
   In the following command, if you don't specify a file format, the volume will be formatted NTFS:
   DISKPART> **format**
   DISKPART> **list volume**
   Note the number of the newly created volume; in my example it is 5:
   DISKPART> **select volume 5**

4. The last step is to assign the mount point path. For example to assign the mount point path to C:\Applications, you would type:
   DISKPART> **assign mount=C:\Applications**

Dealing Out Disk Space . . . Managing Disk Quotas

We all have those users who attempt to store their entire MP3 collection in their Documents folder, which has been redirected to a server. Now, the reason their Documents folder was redirected to a server was to ensure that an administrator could back up the important work-related data. Windows 2000 introduced a simple quota management tool that is also included in Server 2008, and is better than ever. Disk quotas allow administrators to set limits on the amount of disk space a *user* (not a group of users) can use on a volume (not a folder). If you want to get more granular with your disk quotas you can use the File Server Resource Manager (FSRM), which made its debut in Server 2003 SP1. FSRM allows you to control the amount of disk space for each user within a volume *or* folder. And, with FSRM's file screening management you can even control the type of content based on the file's extension. There are some third-party products that provide a lot more functionality than the built-in quota management — but let's face it, why not use what you've already paid for?

Setting Up User Quotas

Keeping track of quotas in Server 2008 can be hard work. Quotas are tracked based on users' security identifiers (SIDs). That's why they are disabled by default in Server 2008 because keeping track of each user and the amount of disk space they have consumed can be CPU intensive. To enable quota management you'll need to get to the properties of a volume. You can access the properties of a volume in many ways: Windows Explorer, Start button / Computer, or the Disk

Management utility to name a few. The volume you are enabling quotas on must be an NTFS volume with a local drive or a drive letter mapped to another server running Windows 2000 or later. If you're defining quotas on a mapped drive you must have administrator rights on the computer the drive is connected to in order to set quota limits. Once you are on the properties page for the volume, go to the Quota tab shown in Figure 9.32 and place a check mark in the "Enable quota management" box. The settings you configure in this dialog box will apply to all users except Administrators. Administrators are exempt from all disk quotas.

FIGURE 9.32
Enabling quotas

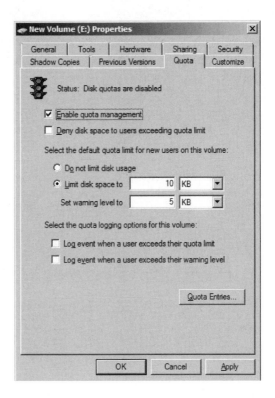

Next, choose whether you want to deny disk space to anyone who has exceeded their quota limit. Placing a check mark in the "Deny disk space to users exceeding quota limit" box creates a hard quota. Hard quotas prevent users from consuming more disk space than the administrator has allowed. If users attempt to store more data than they have allocated disk space they will receive a warning message as shown in Figure 9.33. If you don't check this box (it's not checked by default), then people violating their disk space quotas will be able to continue to store data well past what their quota allows. This is referred to as a soft quota. Soft quotas help administrators track which users are storing more data than allotted (via Event Viewer) while allowing users to continue working.

You set the quota limit by inputting a number in the "Limit disk space to" box in Figure 9.32. Notice that the default value is 10 KB, which means that unless you're in a particularly draconian mood, you're going to want to change the default to something a bit more reasonable. You might, for example, limit each user's quota on the volume containing home directories to 500 MB with a warning generated at 400 MB.

FIGURE 9.33
Hard quota disk space message

There are two logging options that can be set. Both options send an event to the System log in the Event Viewer tool. Choosing to log an event when users exceed their quota limit generates an event ID 37 whenever users attempt to store more data than their quota permits. But remember if you've set soft quotas, users will be able to continue to exceed their limit; only a hard quota would prevent them from storing any more data. You can also choose to log an event when users exceed their warning level. This creates event an ID 36. In both events (36 and 37), you will see the user's name in the User properties of the event as BIGFIRM\Rhonda as shown in Figure 9.34.

FIGURE 9.34
Event ID 37 details

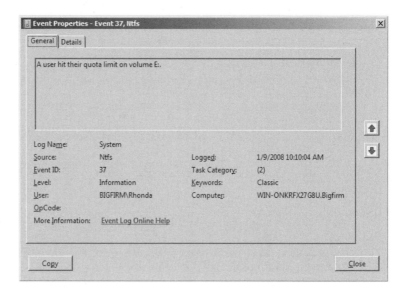

You've now set up basic quota management on the volume. So everyone (except administrators) will have the same quota limits. But, what about people who need a little more disk space, like the IT staff? To set more specific quotas for individual people you'll need to create quota entries. To do so, click the Quota Entries button in Figure 9.32. Your Quota Entries should look similar to Figure 9.35.

Figure 9.35 shows that the default BUILTIN\Administrators and local system accounts are excluded from the quota limits, but the amount of disk space used is still tracked (for the local group in Figure 9.35). Hey wait a minute, I thought it wasn't possible to set quotas based on group memberships? Well that's partially true. Administrators cannot apply quotas to groups of users. For those of you who have been waiting to implement quotas based on groups, I'm afraid you'll have to keep waiting; Server 2008 still doesn't allow it. Also listed will be users who have data stored on that volume along with their amount of disk space used, quota limit, and warning levels. For each user there are three possible statuses for quotas. A green up arrow indicates that the user is within their quota limit and beneath their warning level. A yellow yield sign means the user has exceeded their warning level and a red circle with a white exclamation point identifies that a user has exceeded their quota limit. You can sort the entries in the list by clicking the column heading, so if you need to find all the people who have exceeded the warning threshold for quotas, you'd click the Status column heading. Sadly, there's no mechanism from here to send people messages; you'll need to rely on e-mail or some other messaging technique. To add a new quota entry, from the Quota menu choose New Quota Entry; the Select Users window will pop up as seen in Figure 9.36.

FIGURE 9.35
Quota entries

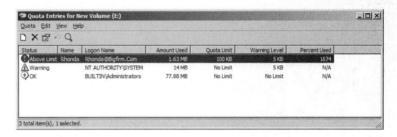

FIGURE 9.36
Select Users dialog box

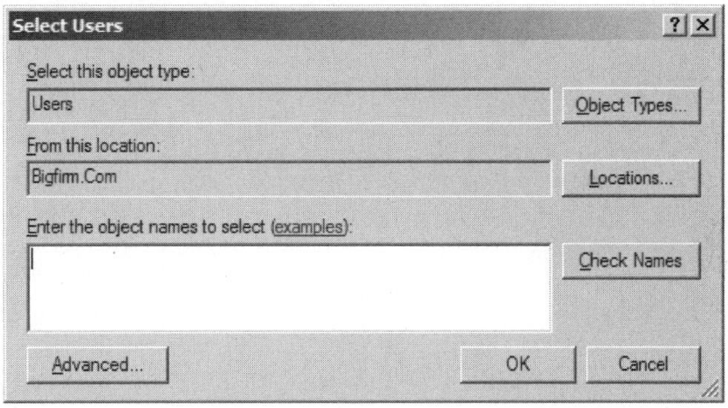

You can enter accounts from either the local user account database or the domain by clicking the Locations button and choosing either local machine or domain name. Select a user by either typing in each account name or click the Advanced button. The advanced Select Users dialog box is shown in Figure 9.37. You can search for accounts using queries or by clicking the Find Now button to enumerate a list of users from the location you specified in the first Select Users dialog box. You can also select a new location from which to search for user accounts by clicking the Locations button.

Because quotas are enforced on a per-user basis, you can create quota entries for multiple users by holding down the Ctrl key while selecting the users you want to add. All users will start with the same settings. When you have the users you want, click OK to return to the first Select Users dialog box and then click OK again. This will bring you to the Add New Quota Entry dialog box, as shown in Figure 9.38.

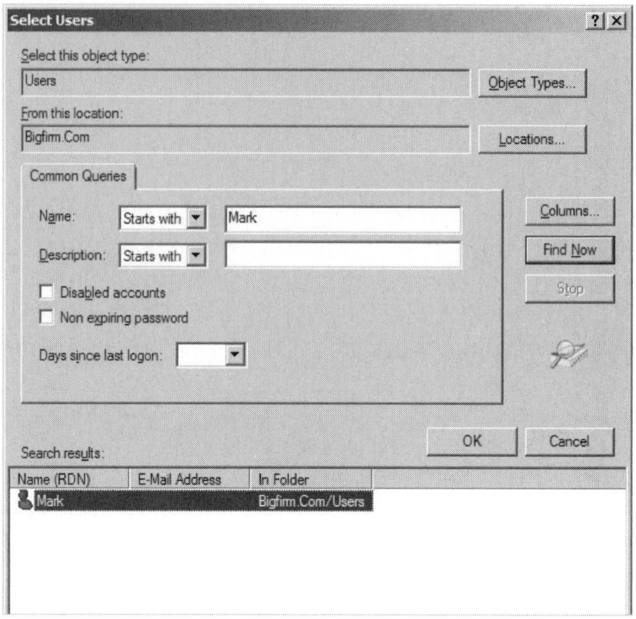

FIGURE 9.37

The Advanced Select Users dialog box.

FIGURE 9.38

Setting the quota limit

In this dialog box you can set the limit and warning levels for this specific user. Click OK to return to the list of quota entries. The new entries will be listed and take effect immediately. This is also the dialog box you will see if you double-click an existing quota entry (even quotas based on the basic quota limits) to modify the quota after it's been created.

MANAGING DISK QUOTAS

Once users have hit their quota limit they'll need to delete some of their files to get below quota. But, what about those users who have left the company? You as the administrator can take ownership of their files and then delete them from the quota entries list. Just right-click the user account and choose Delete. A list of their files will be displayed and you can highlight them all and take ownership, then delete them.

The files in the Recycle Bin are also considered part of a user's quota on the local volume. In addition, compressed files, although smaller than their original value, are calculated using the uncompressed value for the purpose of calculating quota limits.

NOTE

Some quota management software allows users a "grace write" when they're over quota, permitting them to save the file they're working on before locking them out. Server 2008's quota management does not.

If you want to use the same quota limits on more than one NTFS volume, you can export the quotas and import them on the new volume. To export a quota after creating it, highlight the quota in the Quota Entries list (Figure 9.35) and select Export or choose Export from the Quota menu. Choose a name for the file and save it (the extension for the export file is not displayed). To import the quota settings, go to the Quota Entries list for a volume, choose Import, and browse to the file.

SETTING DISK QUOTAS FROM THE COMMAND PROMPT

To enable, disable, or manage disk quotas from a command prompt you'll use the fsutil.exe (file system utility). To enable disk quotas on the E: volume, enter the following at the command line:

```
Fsutil quota enforce e:
```

To set a quota warning at about 750 MB with approximately a 1000 MB limit for everyone, type:

```
Fsutil quota modify e: 800000000 1000000000 everyone
```

Yes there are a lot of zeros; these numbers are input in bytes. Okay, you would end up with a 762.93 MB warning and a 953.67 limit, but I did use the words "about" and "approximately." If you wanted to modify the quota limits for a specific user you would need to replace *everyone* from the previous command with the user's name. For example, to set a different quota for Rhonda in the Bigfirm domain:

```
Fsutil quota modify e: 1000000000 2000000000 Bigfirm\Rhonda
```

To find out which users have violated their quota limits, type:

```
Fsutil quota violations
```

This command will search through the System event log and display all of the 36 and 37 event IDs. To get a listing of all users and their quota information on the e: volume, type:

```
Fsutil quota query e:
```

This will show you the same information that you would normally see listed in the Quota Entries screen, but at the command prompt.

Disabling quotas from the command prompt is done by typing:

```
Fsutil quota disable e:
```

Volume Shadow Copy Service

You are sitting at your desk, desperately trying to figure out how you will ever get enough done so you can spend just a little time at home tonight playing Death Match instead of working into the wee hours of the morning . . . again. Suddenly the phone rings. It's a (groan) user. "Um, I can't seem to find the spreadsheet that Mrs. Dickle needs to present at the World conference in Hawaii tomorrow. I think, somehow, it may have been deleted. Can you help me get it back?" This is an all-too-common scene in many a sysadmin's daily life and, usually, a huge waste of time. "Okay, what was the name of the file, and when did you last have a working copy of it? Where was it stored?"

Wouldn't it be great if you could, with just a little bit of user training, let your users help restore their own files simply by accessing the properties page of the file? "A pipe dream," you ask? No, my friends, it's true. This feature was new in Server 2003, but Server 2008 has made some great changes.

The Volume Shadow Copy Service (VSS for short) debuted in Server 2003 and offers two services I think you'll like. First, it allows users to access and/or restore previous versions of saved files using a client feature called Previous Versions. The server feature is known as Shadow Copy to us administrators. Secondly, VSS enables applications that take advantage of the volume shadow copy API to access locked files or files that are in use by other services or applications. We'll look at this first.

APPLICATIONS CAN USE THE API

"What does that mean," you ask? Well, let me give you an example. Since Server 2008's backup software has been built to take advantage of this API, it is now able to offer the new and improved functionality of backing up open or locked files. Here's what happens. There are four basic components of a VSS solution: the VSS Coordination Service, the VSS Requester, the VSS Writer, and the VSS Provider. To understand how they work together, let's look at each component's role.

- The VSS Coordination Service is part of the OS and was introduced in Server 2003. The coordinator role ensures that all VSS components can communicate with each other properly.

- The VSS Requester initiates the creation of shadow copies and other high-level operations such as importing shadow copies. The VSS Requester is built into Server 2008's backup utility and the System Center Data Protection Manager application. Third-party VSS requesters are quite common today; virtually all backup products that run on Server 2003 or later include a VSS requester.

- The VSS Writer guarantees a consistent data set is available to back up. The VSS writer is also integrated into software applications, like Exchange and SQL Servers. There is a basic VSS writer for the file system included with Server 2008. Third-party VSS writers are also included with many applications for Server 2008 that guarantee data consistency when a backup is performed.

- The VSS Provider takes care of keeping the shadow copies consistent with a specific date and time. Server 2008's VSS provider uses copy-on-write. If you use a SAN, you should install their VSS provider for more efficient storage of the shadow copies.

Now that you understand each component's role, let's look at a very simple explanation of how to back up a database using VSS technology. The VSS Requester in the backup software initiates a backup of a database. The VSS Writer in the database software enumerates all the volumes related to the database and then "freezes" the database, making sure that no changes can be made until further notice. This should only take a few seconds. During this time, all IO operations are queued and will only be written to the database after it's been "thawed." This is done so quickly that creating a shadow copy does not significantly impact the performance of the server. If the system is unable to queue the IO requests or if it takes longer than 10 seconds, the shadow copy creation process will fail and needs to be tried again later. The VSS Provider creates a snapshot of the data. The VSS Writer is notified that the shadow copy is finished and the database is thawed, allowing changes once again. The VSS Requester in the backup software notifies you that the shadow copy was created successfully.

VOLUME SHADOW COPY AND PREVIOUS VERSIONS

When an administrator enables volume shadow copies for a volume, it gives the users the ability to restore previous versions of the files and folders that reside on that volume. Shadow copies can only be enabled on a per-volume or per-partition basis. In the past to access the previous versions of a file you had to map a drive to a shared folder where your file was, but with the arrival of Vista comes a new and improved VSS that is included in Server 2008. You can access the previous versions of a file through a mapped drive or *locally*. Once enabled, VSS immediately takes a snapshot of the volume. You can also create a manual snapshot of the volume any time, or you can create a schedule for the VSS snapshots. The scheduler offers a very granular way to schedule this routinely.

When you initially enable VSS on a volume, you will find that a new hidden folder called System Volume Information appears in the root of the volume. This is where the snapshots are stored by default, along with the log files. This folder is created for each volume on which you enable VSS. The default storage space allocated for your shadow copies is 10 percent of the size of the volume and allows a maximum of 64 shadow copies to be stored. The minimum amount of disk space you'll need for a snapshot is 100 MB. You can configure a maximum allowable space for this folder, but you need to have a good idea of how much space you'll need for these snapshots, because going over the maximum means the deletion of the older Previous Versions files. You have to take into account both the number and size of your shadow copies. If they are relatively small you can store up to 64 shadow copies; when the 65th is created the very first one that was created will be overwritten. At the same time if you only allowed 500 MB of disk space for storing the shadow copies, and it takes 100 MB to store one shadow copy, you may run out of space when the sixth shadow copy is generated; once again, to store the sixth shadow copy the first shadow copy created will be overwritten. You'll need to experiment with your volumes to find out how much space is suitable for your environment. It is recommended that you store the shadow copy on a different volume from the one the files reside on. I'll show you where you can configure this, but first, let's look at how to enable VSS on a volume.

HOW TO ENABLE VSS

To enable shadow copies, right-click any volume and choose Configure Shadow Copies. The Shadow Copies property page will open, as shown in Figure 9.39.

Highlight the volume you wish to enable and click the Settings button to determine where you want to store the shadow copy data, configure the space allocated to the shadow copies, and set up a schedule for the service. Click OK to apply your settings and return to the Shadow Copies properties page. Accepting the default settings when you enable shadow copies creates shadow copies every day (Monday–Friday) at 7 a.m. and again at noon. As you can see in Figure 9.39, you can manually take a snapshot of your volume by clicking the Create Now button. Once you have snapshots you can also delete them here.

FIGURE 9.39

Shadow Copies properties page

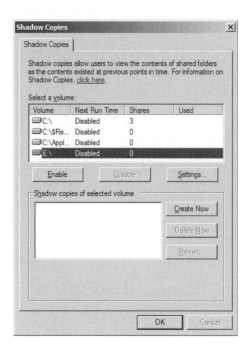

HOW IT WORKS

Here's how it works. When the administrator enables volume shadow copies on a volume, a snapshot is taken of the entire volume and all of its files. When I say snapshot, I don't mean a backup or a copy, just that the VSS records the "state" of the volume and all of the files that reside on it. VSS now has a "memory" of the volume and all the files on it at the moment that snapshot was taken. Let's say I, the user, have a Word document that resides on a volume where VSS is enabled and I am connected through a share. A snapshot was taken this morning at 7:00 a.m. before I arrived at work. When I arrive at 8 a.m., I edit a document and make some changes. As soon as I commit those changes to memory (i.e., save the file), the VSS goes to work.

VSS says, "Hey, I've got a file that has changed here. Do I have anything about this file in my snapshot?" The file existed on the volume when the snapshot was taken this morning, and it was in a different state than it is now that I am trying to commit changes to it. So, the VSS says, "Yup, that Word doc that is being saved is different from what I see in the snapshot." The VSS then creates and saves an exact copy of the Word doc as it existed at 7:00 a.m. this morning when the snapshot was taken, and it stores it in the System Volume Information folder. VSS then makes that file available to me, the user, by placing a link to that 7:00 a.m. version of the Word file in the Previous Versions tab of the property sheet of the Word document that I just saved. Now, if I access the file by double-clicking it or opening it from Word, I am editing the version that I saved at 8 a.m. But, if I access the properties of that doc and view the Previous Versions tab, I will have available to me the version of the file as it existed at 7:00 this morning because VSS saved that for me when I saved the file at 8:00 a.m.

Okay, stick with me here. Keep in mind that the VSS is scheduled to take a snapshot of the volume every morning at 7:00 a.m. Here's what that means to me, the user. Since the time that I edited that Word document at 8:00 a.m. this morning, I have made several more changes. It is now 10:00 a.m. and I decide to save the file again. When I last checked, I had one previous version available to me (the one from the 7:00 a.m. snapshot that was given to me because I changed the file at 8:00 a.m.). Since I am saving the file again, I should have two now, right? Actually, no.

Remember how I said that when I commit a change to a file, the VSS goes out and looks at the last snapshot it has of the volume to see if the file is different from the snapshot? And how, if the VSS finds that the snapshot is different, it creates and then saves an exact copy of that file, as it existed at 7:00 a.m. during the last snapshot? Well, I did this once already this morning at 8 a.m., and that file was copied and made available to me in the properties page of the file. Since the only information the VSS has to work from is the 7:00 a.m. snapshot, its job is done. The file, as it existed the last time the VSS recorded a snapshot, was made available to me at 8 a.m. and it can't be done again, not until two things happen. First, another snapshot has to be taken (at noon that day, according to the default schedule) and second, once that snapshot is taken, I have to make changes (and save those changes) to the file. Once those two things happen, I'll have another previous version available to me when I access the properties page of that file. I could make 10 more changes to that Word document today, and if I completely destroy the formatting and want to roll it back to a previous version, my only option is the copy of the file as it existed at either 7:00 a.m. or noon depending on the time I destroyed the document.

When users access the Previous Versions tab of a file's properties page, as shown in Figure 9.40, a list of the previous versions of that file will be displayed. There are three choices, in terms of what they can do with that file. They can view a read-only copy of the file by clicking Open; copy the file to another location (the permissions will be inherited from the new folder); or, a user could restore the file, which overwrites the current version of the file. Renaming a file will lose the previous versions that you have collected to date, so the previous versions process begins all over again. You won't have any previous versions of the newly renamed file available to you until: A, the next snapshot is taken for the volume and B, you commit changes to the newly named file.

FIGURE 9.40
The client's view of the Previous Versions property page

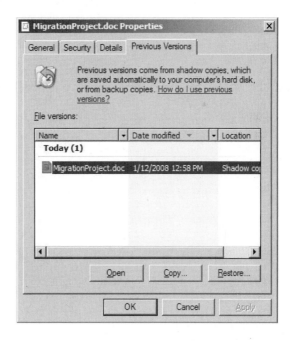

The Previous Version client is built into both Vista and Server 2008. For legacy clients (like XP) you can download `twcli32.msi` from Microsoft's download site or if you still have a 2003 Server, the Previous Version client for XP can be found in the Windows\system32\clients\twclient\x86 folder. Notice that it is an MSI file (`twcli32.msi`), which can be distributed through a network share, Group Policy, or SMS.

What happens if you accidentally delete a file and want to go to a previous version? You'll need to go to the previous version of the folder in which the file used to reside. Right-click the folder, and choose "Restore previous versions." Double-click the folder to open it, and you should see your deleted file. Right-click the filename, and choose Copy to place it on the clipboard. Then go to the folder where you want to put the file and paste it in or use the hotkey Ctrl-V. You could also choose to open the file and save it to the destination of your choice.

How to Work with Volume Shadow Copies from the Command Line

To enable and manage volume shadow copies from the command line, you will use the VSSadmin utility that is built into Server 2008:

```
vssadmin add shadowstorage/for=VolumeToEnableOn /on=VolumeToStore
/MaxSize=Max Size of the shadow storage area
```

For example, to enable volume shadow copies for the E: volume and store the shadow copies on E: you would type the following:

```
vssadmin add shadowstorage/for=E: /on=E:
```

If you want to set a maximum size of the volume shadow copy storage area you would add the /MaxSize=<InputSize>. Setting the max size to 1 GB looks like this: /MaxSize = 1GB (you could also specify size based on KB, MB, GB, TB, PB). If you do not supply a /MaxSize value then there will be no limit to the size of the volume shadow storage area. If you decide to make the storage area larger you can resize it by typing:

```
vssadmin resize shadowstorage/for=Volume/on=Volume
[/maxsize=MaximumSizeOfStorageArea]
```

To create a shadow copy for E: type:

```
vssadmin create shadow /for=E:.
```

To delete all existing shadow copies from E type:

```
Vssadmin delete shadows /for=E:.
```

There is a link created when you enable shadow copies and configure them to be stored on a volume. This link is called a storage association. As a cleanup item, when you are disabling volume shadow copies the last thing I would do is also delete the storage association, but how do you see them? Typing vssadmin list shadowstorage will show all shadow copy storage associations on the computer. To specify a specific volume's shadow copy, type:

```
vssadmin list shadowstorage /for=<InputVolume> /on=<VolumeShadowCopyIsStoredOn>
```

Once you have found the storage association to delete, then type:

```
vssadmin delete shadowstorage/for=<Volume> /on=<Volume> /quiet
```

To get a list of existing shadow copies type:

```
vssadmin list shadows /for = <Volume>
```

For a list of installed VSS providers or writers, type:

```
vssadmin list providers
```

Or

```
vssadmin list writers.
```

Encrypting NTFS Files and Folders

The ability to encrypt files and folders has been around since W2K, but in each new OS it has been improved upon. Server 2008's encryption allows you to secure your documents and folders so that only you — or the people you choose — can view the documents. It's a handy way of keeping even shared documents private or of protecting files on a machine that can be easily stolen, such as a laptop.

Encryption doesn't conceal the fact that the documents exist. Rather, when you attempt to open an encrypted file, Server 2008 checks to see whether you have a key to that file. If you don't, then you're forbidden access to the file, even if you have administrative permissions on that server (there is one exception that I'll cover later in the "Recovering Encrypted Files" section). This denial is not application dependent — for example, a Word document won't be accessible in Word *or* WordPad. The user without the key can't open the file at all.

TIP

The process of checking for an encryption key is processor intensive, so it's probably best not to encrypt files stored on a terminal server or other CPU-bound server.

Encryption is an NTFS attribute just like compression or the archive bit, so it's only supported on NTFS volumes in Windows 2000 and later.

HOW SERVER 2008 ENCRYPTION WORKS

When you encrypt data, you're generating a request for a new security certificate which identifies you to Server 2008. A *cryptographic service provider* (CSP) generates two 56-bit keys: a public key and a private key. This pair of keys is crucial to the encryption process, because it takes both keys for encryption to work properly. When encrypting data one key is used to encrypt and the other key is used to decrypt that same data. It doesn't matter which key encrypts the data — the other key is the one used to decrypt the data. The use of the keys is transparent to the user, but it becomes important when you want to make sure you have copies of the keys in case one became corrupt. If a key becomes corrupt encryption and even more importantly decryption would fail to work. I'll cover protecting your encryption keys a little later in this chapter but for now let's look at how to encrypt a file or folder.

Encrypting Files

To encrypt a file or folder from Explorer, right-click the file or folder (you cannot encrypt entire volumes) and open its property page. On the General tab, click the Advanced button to open the Advanced Attributes dialog box shown in Figure 9.41.

TIP

If there isn't an Advanced button visible, make sure that you're looking at an NTFS volume, not a FAT or FAT32 one.

To encrypt a file or folder simply put a check mark in the "Encrypt contents to secure data" box and click OK. While we're here it may be a good time to note that you can either enable encryption *or* compression on a file/folder, but not both. If you are encrypting a file within a folder that is not encrypted you will see a warning similar to Figure 9.42. Normally, it's a good idea to let Server

2008 encrypt the folder as well, which is the default if you just click OK on the Encryption Warning dialog box. Then all new files created within that encrypted folder will be encrypted as well.

FIGURE 9.41
Encryption is an Advanced NTFS Attribute

FIGURE 9.42
Encrypting a file in an unencrypted folder

TIP

If using encryption, encrypt the *Documents* folder for all users to ensure that their personal folder, where most Office documents are stored, will be encrypted by default.

The encryption attribute is now set. If anyone but you attempts to open the file or run an encrypted executable, they'll be denied access. That is, all users except the default Administrator account (more on this later). Encrypted folder and filenames will appear in green in Explorer if your folder options are set to the default. If they are not and you want for them to be displayed in an alternate color, from Windows Explorer's Tools menu choose Folder Options and go to the View tab. Scroll down and ensure a check mark is in the "Show encrypted or compressed NTFS files in color" box.

Users can encrypt data across the network, but the data is only encrypted when written to a disk, not while traveling across the network — you'll need network encryption for that. Server 2000 and later are the only OSes that can encrypt and decrypt data. Even though NT and Windows 9*x* users can read and open files on the newer NTFS volumes, they don't have the tools they'd need to encrypt or decrypt data.

COPYING, MOVING, AND BACKING UP ENCRYPTED FILES

New files in a folder inherit the encryption attributes of that folder: if the folder is encrypted, the file will be encrypted as well. If the folder is not encrypted, the file won't be encrypted. What about files *copied* to a directory? This is where it can get a little tricky:

◆ If you copy or move an unencrypted file to an encrypted NTFS directory, that file will become encrypted.

◆ If you copy or move an encrypted file to an unencrypted NTFS directory, the file will remain encrypted.

◆ If you copy or move an encrypted file to a FAT or FAT32 directory, you will receive a message stating that "Copying this encrypted file to a FAT or FAT32 volume does not support encrypting, do you want to continue?" Choosing yes un-encrypts the file. Choosing no will leave the file encrypted in its original location.

◆ Backups of encrypted documents are stored and restored in their encrypted state even if the backup media is a FAT-formatted drive.

ENCRYPTING FROM THE COMMAND LINE

You can also encrypt files from the command line with the CIPHER utility. To encrypt a single folder in the current directory named Project, type:

```
cipher /e Projects
```

To encrypt a file named migration.doc within the Projects folder you would change directories into the Projects folder (cd projects from the command line) and type:

```
cipher /e Migration.doc
```

To decrypt the Projects folder, replace the /e switch with /d, like this:

```
cipher /d Projects
```

To decrypt the Migration.doc file in the Projects folder, replace the /e switch with /d, like this:

```
cipher /d Migration.doc
```

The command will report back to you whether the operation succeeded or not.

Normally, CIPHER will only encrypt the files in the immediate folder you specify, not the subfolders. To encrypt all files within the specified folder and all subfolders within the folder, type:

```
cipher /e /s:foldername /a
```

Who Encrypted That Document?

The contents of an encrypted folder are displayed like any other shared or locally available data, except that they are displayed in green to identify them as encrypted (compressed files and folders are displayed in blue). The error message you get when attempting to access files that someone else has encrypted will look like Figure 9.43. Someone other than the person who encrypted the .txt file attempted to open it.

FIGURE 9.43

Users may not realize why they can't open an encrypted file.

Sometimes, you may just want to know who encrypted a file. Let's say that Mark created an unencrypted file so he is the owner of the file. He then allows Rhonda read and write permissions on the file. Then, Rhonda encrypts it. Mark will no longer be able to open the document because he is not the user that encrypted it. Still with me? Anyone with read and write permissions on an unencrypted file has the ability to encrypt it, rendering it unavailable to everyone else that also has rights to that file. To find out who encrypted the file, right-click the file and choose Properties, click the Advanced button, and then the Details button; you'll be presented with the window shown in Figure 9.44.

FIGURE 9.44

Details of an encrypted file

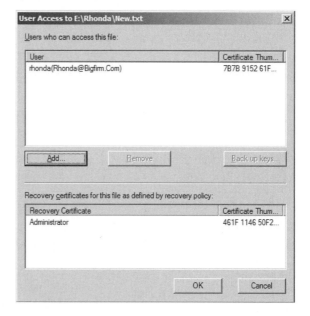

As you can see in the details of the encrypted file, Rhonda is the only user who can access the file so she must be the person who encrypted it. What if you wanted to allow other users to also access this document? You would click the Add button and select the users from the list then click

OK. If the user you are looking for doesn't appear in the list, click the Find User button shown in Figure 9.45. You will then see the Select Users dialog box, which is the same box you saw for setting disk quotas earlier.

FIGURE 9.45

Granting users access to encrypted files

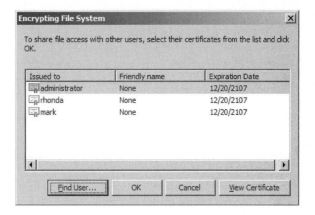

Recovery Agents are listed in the bottom box in Figure 9.43. As a recovery agent, you can fix things by decrypting files that were encrypted by other users. Recovery agents are covered in the section, "Recovering Encrypted Files."

Another way of finding out who can encrypt a file is by using a command-line Resource Kit utility named EFSINFO. You can run EFSINFO with the /u option (to show user information), the /r option (to show Recovery Agent information), and the /s option (to show directory and subdirectory information) like this:

```
efsinfo /u /r /s:c:\userdata
```

It'll tell you whether the folder and its files are encrypted, who encrypted the folder and files, and who can decrypt them. Here's the output from that command:

```
c:\userdata
.: Encrypted
  Users who can decrypt:
    BIGFIRM\Rhonda (Rhonda
  Layfield(Rhonda@Bigfirm.Com))
  Recovery Agents:
    DOTNETTEST\Administrator (Administrator)

Encrypted letter.doc: Encrypted
  Users who can decrypt:
    BIGFIRM\Rhonda (Rhonda
  Layfield(Rhonda@Bigfirm.Com))
  Recovery Agents:
    DOTNETTEST\Administrator (Administrator)

Recipes.doc: Not Encrypted

C:\>
```

Decrypting Files

Decrypting encrypted files is a cake walk if you're the person who encrypted the file in the first place. When the person who encrypted the file opens the file it is automatically decrypted. When the file is saved it is automatically encrypted again — the action is completely transparent to the user.

To permanently decrypt a file or folder from Explorer, open its property page and on the General tab click the Advanced button. Remove the check mark from the box next to "Encrypt contents to secure data." The file is now open to anyone who has the right to access it.

What's New in Server 2008?

In the past when a user encrypted a file or folder an EFS certificate was generated and stored on the local machine or in a domain environment in Active Directory. Now you can choose to store your certificates on Smart Cards. So, if someone were to steal your laptop, they would be unable to read any encrypted documents without the smart card containing your certificate. For this reason I strongly recommend storing your smart card somewhere other than your laptop bag. You can choose the behavior of the certificate stored on the smart card by using some new Group Policy options. You can choose to use smart cards in cached or non-cached modes.

Non-cached modes require that every time you attempt to encrypt or decrypt a document your private key would be read from the smart card, so no removing it. Cached mode creates a key that is derived from the user's private key stored on the smart card and stored on the local computer in a protected area of memory. Then whenever an encryption or decryption operation is performed the OS will use the key that is cached in memory. This way you can remove your smart card and still be able to encrypt and decrypt files.

Smart Card Single Sign-On (SSO)   Based on new Group Policy settings you can configure SSO settings to use the certificate stored on the smart card when one of two things happens. Either the user doesn't have a certificate stored locally on the machine and a GPO is configured to require smart card usage for EFS, or the user has a valid encryption key on their smart card.

Per-user Encryption of Offline Files   In the past there were some issues where multiple users on the same computer could access each others' encrypted files when using offline files. Not any more — when a user chooses to copy files via offline folders from a remote server, they can now be encrypted. If this option is enabled, each file stored in the offline files cache for that user will be encrypted using their public key. They could then supply their private key to decrypt the files.

New Encrypting File System Rekeying Wizard

This new wizard can migrate files that are currently encrypted with a certificate to use a newly created EFS certificate. The Rekeying Wizard also allows you to create new encryption certificates, back up existing certificates in case one is lost or becomes corrupt, and to set the local machine to look for EFS certificates on smart cards. This new wizard is a little advanced for this chapter so I am saving that for the second book in this series, *Mastering Windows 2008: Essential Technologies*.

Protecting Encryption Keys

One of the easiest methods of protecting encryption keys is storing users' certificates in Active Directory (AD), which is done automatically. In a domain environment (for more information on domains please see Chapter 15) all EFS certificates are stored in AD so they can be used throughout the domain. Microsoft developed these encryption services especially for laptop users who wanted to keep their data secure even if their laptop was stolen. However, there's one major hole in this security plan. If someone *does* steal a laptop and can log in with administrator rights, they can edit the certificate settings in a way that allows them to decrypt the data.

NOTE

Of course, if you don't password-protect your laptop, then decrypting your files is as easy as logging in as you.

To avoid this problem, Microsoft recommends exporting each user's certificate to a USB device or external disk, then deleting the certificate from the computer. To do so you'll have to go through Internet Explorer. In the past users who were not administrators could create a custom Microsoft Management Console (MMC) and add the Certificates snap-in. But not anymore. While I was doing a little research on Server 2008 I found countless documents that state "a user can create an MMC containing the Certificate snap-in." Every time I logged on as a standard user account, clicked the Start button, and typed MMC, I received the User Account Control (UAC) dialog box prompting me for administrator credentials. Now it appears as though you must be an administrator or turn off the built-in security features to be able to create a custom MMC. So open IE and tap the Alt button on your keyboard to bring in the menu. Then, from the Tools menu choose Internet Options and go to the Content tab as shown in Figure 9.46. In the Certificates box click the Certificates button. If you have a certificate it will be listed on the Personal tab.

FIGURE 9.46
Internet
Options/Content tab

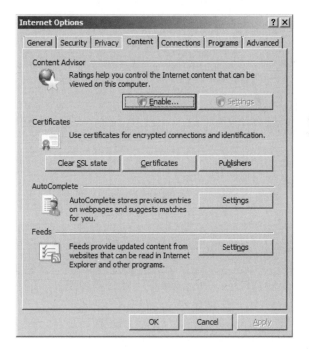

Highlight the certificate you want to export as a file and click the Export button as shown in Figure 9.47. This will start the Certificate Export Wizard, which asks whether you'd like to export the private key along with the certificate. You'll need the private key to decrypt data. On the next page, choose the file format of the certificate you want to export. If you are also exporting the private key you will need to choose "Personal Information Exchange - PKCS #12 (.PFX)". If you are not exporting the private key then you can choose Cryptographic Message Syntax Standard (PKCS #7) as your type of file format for the certificate. If you chose to export the private key, you'll need to supply a password that will need to be provided to import the key again. Choose a filename for the key by either typing a filename including the path to where you want to store it, or browse for the path and then input a filename. You can save the file on any volume, not just NTFS, but I recommend exporting to removable media such as a floppy drive, USB device, or a safe network location where it can get backed up, then delete it from the computer by clicking the Remove button (Figure 9.47).

FIGURE 9.47
Certificates dialog box

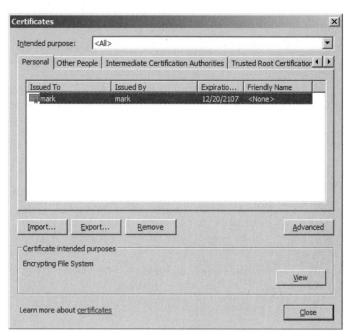

NOTE

The other two types of certificate file formats are DER (Distinguished Encoding Rules) Encoded Binary X and Base64 Encoded X.509, they provide interoperability with other than Microsoft Certificates .509 .

The final screen of the wizard summarizes your choices. Review them carefully and click Finish to export the keys. If the export operation worked, Server 2008 will pop up a quick message box to tell you it was successful.

To import the certificate to another computer or replace it on the same one, open the same IE / Content tab / Certificate button that you did to export the certificate. Click the Import button shown in Figure 9.47. This will start the Import Certificate Wizard. The wizard will prompt you to browse for the file you saved and click Next. Choose where you want to store the certificate or accept the "Automatically select the certificate store based on the certificate" option. The final page of the wizard summarizes your importing options. Click Finish to import the key. Server 2008 will tell you if the importing action succeeded.

NOTE

A shortcut for importing certificates is to simply right-click the certificate file that you exported earlier and choose to Install the certificate. If you exported the certificate as PKCS #12 file format you will see Install PFX. If you exported the certificate using the PKCS #7 file format you will see Install Certificate.

Recovering Encrypted Files

If Mark encrypts a file and then leaves the company, how can it be decrypted? This is where the recovery agent comes in. By default, workstations and member servers' recovery agents are the default Administrator account — not members of the Administrators group, but the Administrator *account*. The default recovery agent for a domain is the default administrator for the computer that was the first domain controller installed for that domain (or Forest, but that's jumping way ahead).

To recover a file for someone, you must log in as the recovery agent and decrypt the file, either through the GUI by removing its encryption attribute in the Advanced section of the file or folder properties, or with the CIPHER command that we discussed earlier.

In other words, EFS doesn't see any difference between the person who originally encrypted a file and the recovery agent. If you had an encrypted Word file and the recovery agent tried to open it, she'd see your file. If you've denied the recovery agent access to your Word file, then she won't be able to open it. Of course, if the recovery agent doesn't have access to your file, then she also can't decrypt it for you — but that's easily remedied by an administrator who can take ownership of the file and then grant read and write access for the file to the recovery agent. Again, if you haven't changed the defaults, then the recovery agent is the default Administrator account.

Let's look a bit further into the recovery agent account. First, do you really want to have to use the default Administrator account for anything? Probably not — that's a lot of power to give to the person in charge of making sure users can read their files — so how do you change which account can handle emergency decryptions? It's harder than you might expect. EFS encrypts and decrypts your files using a simple symmetrical algorithm; the same "password" (not a user password, but a special EFS "password") encrypts and decrypts your files. But it *stores* that password using an asymmetric, public key–type of encryption method. When you encrypt a file, EFS encrypts the password using your public key and stores the now-encrypted password in NTFS. When EFS needs to decrypt a file, it asks NTFS for that encrypted password. NTFS passes the request to an independent module of the EFS driver that handles all reads, writes, and opens on encrypted files and directories, as well as operations to encrypt, decrypt, and recover file data when it is written to or read from disk, and which passes the information back to NTFS. NTFS then gives the password to the EFS driver, which uses your private key to decrypt the password. Now that it has the password, it can decrypt the file. (You've probably guessed by now that encrypting files slows things down a bit.) How does EFS, then, allow more than one person to decrypt a file? By again exploiting NTFS: Not only can it store the file's password encrypted with your public key, EFS will also include that same password encrypted with the public key or keys of as many recovery agents as you like.

Where things get sticky is in the process of introducing EFS to a prospective recovery agent's public key/private key pair: in the past you needed a hierarchy of certificate authorities that were recognized by your computer. Without a certificate hierarchy, there were no certificates, and without certificates, you can't introduce new recovery agents to EFS. (With an exception — stay tuned.) But now you can run the new ReKeying Wizard by clicking the Start button, typing **rekeywiz**, and pressing Enter. One of the options of this wizard is to create a new certificate, either a self-signed certificate stored locally or on a smart card, *or* a certificate from a certificate authority.

But wait — at least one account requires a certificate without having to go through all of the certificate-authority stuff. Where did the first recovery agent, the default Administrator, get its certificate? Here's the exception. Apparently EFS generates a self-signing certificate for the default Administrator.

In Windows 2000, the absence of a recovery agent meant that you could not encrypt files, and EFS was basically disabled (a backward way of allowing you to turn encryption on or off). That was the only way that you could disable encryption on a system. With Server 2008, the EFS policy actually gives you the ability to turn EFS on or off, allowing you to decide which systems you enable EFS on. Because it is a computer policy, you can apply it wherever you want in the domain. This is a significant improvement; now you can turn it on, off, and back on again with just a flip of a Group Policy switch.

Tools of Disk Maintenance

Before we get into disk maintenance tools you need to understand the whole story. In the "Background: Disk Geometry and File Formats" section, I explained sectors and clusters and their relationship. Now it's time to learn about the $bitmap and $MFT (master file table) files.

When Server 2008 stores data on a disk two very important things happen: the first empty cluster must be found and a record of the first cluster a file is stored in is written to disk. Finding the first empty cluster is done by consulting a hidden system file called $bitmap. The $bitmap file contains one bit for each existing cluster. This bit indicates whether the cluster is empty or not (0=empty, 1=contains data). Then a record for each folder and file is created in the $MFT, which tells the OS which cluster the beginning of a file is stored in. If a file consumes more than one cluster there is a pointer at the end of the first cluster directing the OS to the next cluster that contains a portion of the file and so on until an *End Of File* marker is encountered.

Each NTFS volume also maintains a *transaction log* ($Logfile) of all proposed changes to the volume structure, checking off or *committing* each change as it's completed. When you restart the system, NTFS automatically inspects the transaction log and rolls the state of the disk back to the last committed change. But, transaction logging works only for *system* data, not for user data. FAT and FAT32 do not have transaction logging. If the disk fails — perhaps due to a power cord being unplugged unexpectedly (by the helpful janitorial staff) — before a write action is completed and you restart the computer, there's no way for the OS to know where it left off on writing data to the disk. So, you may need to run CHKDSK to ensure the pointers from one cluster to the next are still in tact. Does this mean that you only need to run CHKDSK on FAT and FAT32 and not NTFS volumes? No, it does not. There can be scenarios where running CHKDSK on an NTFS volume can fix cluster issues when the $bitmap and the $MFT get out of sync. Also, if the read/write head of the disk actually comes in contact with the disk, then it is possible that sectors (or clusters to the OS) of the disk have become unreadable. You can use the command-line version of the CHKDSK tool to check the disk for bad sectors and to edit the size of the transaction log. Read on to learn more about what CHKDSK is doing and how to use both the graphical and command-line versions.

What Is CHKDSK Doing?

Let's take a look at how CHKDSK works on an NTFS volume. When you run CHKDSK on a volume with no switches, it is running in report mode only; this is the mode we will begin with. CHKDSK makes three passes over the volume to examine the structure of the metadata on the disk. Metadata, what's that? Metadata is the data describing how user data is organized on the disk, or more specifically, the $MFT contains various files that make up the metadata such as $bitmap, $logfile, $badclus, and much more. Metadata helps the file system keep track of what data is stored in which clusters, how many clusters are free, where they are, and which clusters contain bad sectors.

During CHKDSK's first pass over the selected drive, it examines each file's record in the $MFT checking to see if the information stored in the $MFT is accurate according to what is physically stored in each cluster. After the $MFT is checked for consistency it then compares each record in the $MFT to the $bitmap. If the $MFT specifies that data is stored in a cluster but the $bitmap reports that the exact same cluster is empty, there is a discrepancy. Any discrepancies between the two are noted in CHKDSK's output.

During the second pass, CHKDSK checks the drive's directory structure. It makes sure that each index record in the $MFT corresponds to an actual directory on the drive and that each file's record in the $MFT corresponds to a file stored somewhere in the volume. CHKDSK also makes sure that all time and date stamps for all files and directories are up to date. Finally, it makes sure there aren't any files that have an $MFT record but don't actually exist in any directory.

The third pass CHKDSK ensures the integrity of the security descriptors for each file and directory object on the NTFS volume. During this pass, CHKDSK scans the security settings of files and directory objects in the volume to make sure they are not corrupt. It does not check the security settings to confirm that they're appropriate to a particular folder or even to check that the group or user account named exists.

How long does this process take? Depends on the size of the volume, the depth of the check, and what else the computer is doing during the check. CHKDSK is extremely CPU and disk intensive, and if other processes are competing for CPU time, the check will take longer. It is a good idea to close as many applications as possible when running CHKDSK. In any case, you can't run CHKDSK /f (fix problems found mode) on a volume that currently has files open. If you attempt to do so, CHKDSK will tell you that it can't get exclusive control of the volume and ask if you want to schedule the check for the next time the computer restarts.

There are three ways to run CHKDSK in Server 2008: the graphical tool (from Explorer), the command-line utility, and the Recovery Console. The graphical tool is simpler to use, but the command-line utility is more flexible.

> **NOTE**
>
> The version of CHKDSK changes as the file systems change. So be sure to use the version of CHKDSK that comes with the OS that you are working on.

Running CHKDSK from Explorer

The simplest way to run CHKDSK is from Explorer, as this tool doesn't demand that you know the command syntax and just uses the default options. To use the tool, select a drive in Explorer and open its property sheet. Click the Tools tab. In the Error-checking box click the Check Now button to open the dialog box in Figure 9.48.

FIGURE 9.48
The graphical disk
checker

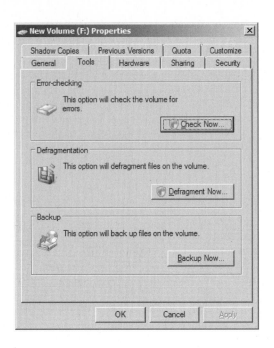

There will be two options to choose from: "Automatically fix file system errors" and "Scan for and attempt recovery of bad sectors." Choosing the first requires exclusive access to the drive and will prompt you with "Windows can't check this disk while it's in use. Do you want to check this disk the next time you start your computer?" You can choose to cancel or schedule disk check. If you choose to schedule disk check when the computer reboots CHKDSK will try to resolve any orphaned files — files that have entries in the file system catalog but don't appear in a directory on the volume. Choosing the second option instructs CHKDSK to check each sector on the disk instead of just those containing metadata and there is no reboot required. If you don't check either box and click the Start button, CHKDSK runs in report mode only. You will then see a dialog box stating "Your device or disk was successfully scanned." Clicking the down arrow to the left of the words "See details" shows you the report. To check another disk you will need to exit the current drive's property sheet and select another drive from Explorer.

RUNNING CHKDSK FROM THE COMMAND PROMPT

You have little control over how CHKDSK works when you run it from Explorer. If you'd like more control, you'll need to use the command prompt. The command-line options offer much more flexibility than the GUI.

Without any arguments, CHKDSK runs in read-only mode on the current drive. You'll see command-line output showing the progress of each pass over the volume, and then you'll get a report similar to the following:

```
[input chkdsk from the command line.png]
```

So — you've run CHKDSK in report mode. To instruct CHKDSK to actually do something if it finds a bad sector you'll need to use one or more of the switches explained in Table 9.2.

TABLE 9.2:   Command-Line Switches for CHKDSK

SWITCH	WHAT IT DOES
/f	Attempts to fix file system errors, such as orphaned files. The help file for this switch says that it fixes errors on the disk, but that's not really accurate. It fixes inconsistencies in the file system catalog.
/v	Has different results depending on whether you use the switch on FAT volumes or on NTFS. On FAT volumes, this switch lists the full path of every file on the volume. On NTFS volumes, it runs CHKDSK in verbose mode, reporting any cleanup messages relevant to fixing file system errors or missing security descriptors.
/r	Checks every sector on the disk to make sure it can be written to and read from. Any bad sectors are marked as bad in the $badclus file. On a fault tolerant volume if a detected bad sector was part of a cluster that contained data, CHKDSK regenerates and moves the data to a new cluster. If the volume is not fault tolerant the cluster with the bad sector will be marked as bad and no longer used. The data in the bad sector won't be recovered unless there's some redundant data to copy it from.
/x	Forces the volume to dismount first if dismounting is necessary to run CHKDSK (that is, if there are open handles to the chosen volume). Choosing this option will dismount the volume being checked.
/i	Tells CHKDSK to skip the second pass of the disk checking operation. Selecting this option saves time on volumes with a lot of directories. It's not a good idea to use this switch unless you must; using it causes any inconsistencies in the directory structure to go unnoticed.
/c	Tells CHKDSK not to check for cycles on the NTFS volume. Cycles are a rare kind of disk error where a subdirectory becomes a subdirectory of itself, creating an infinite loop. You can probably turn this switch on safely since cycles are rare, but it won't save you much time.
/l[:size]	On NTFS volumes, specifies a new size for the transaction log. The default size is 4096 KB, and for most purposes that's just fine.
volume	Specifies the mount point, volume name, or (if followed by a colon) the drive letter of the logical volume to be checked.
filename	On FAT volumes, tells CHKDSK to evaluate the specified filename to report on how fragmented it is. This option does not work on NTFS volumes.

The order of the switches is as follows:

```
chkdsk [volume[[path]filename]]] [/f] [/v] [/r] [/x]
  [/i][/c] [/l[:size]]
```

If you want to schedule CHKDSK to run at the next boot, from a command prompt you would type **chkntfs /c drive letter:** (nope that's not a typo — I meant chkntfs). For example, to schedule CHKDSK to run on the E: drive upon the next boot, type chkntfs /c e:.

When CHKDSK /f is run on FAT or FAT32 volumes, a repair would change the file allocation table and there may be data loss. If CHKDSK finds errors and attempts to fix them you will see a confirmation message stating that there are lost allocation units found. For example, if it found 10 lost allocation units you would see "10 lost allocations units found in 3 chains. Convert lost chains to files?" If you press Y for yes then each lost chain will be saved as a File*nnnn* (File0001–File0010) in the root directory of the volume being checked. You can then open these files and determine whether you need to save the data or not. If you do not need to save the data you can delete the files to save disk space.

Defragmenting Disks

When a disk is new, the available clusters are all next to each other. So, saving a file to disk is very efficient. Storing a file named Projects.DOC (which is a 16 KB file) to a brand new volume would require four clusters (assuming they are 4 KB in size). The first 4 KB of Projects.DOC would be stored in cluster 1, the next 4 KB in cluster 2, the next in cluster 3, and the rest of the file in cluster 4. Projects.DOC would then be stored in four contiguous clusters. As files are created and deleted clusters get freed up unevenly. If I deleted Projects.DOC then clusters 1–4 would now be available to place new data in them. When I then attempt to store a 32 KB file, the first 16 KB of the file would be stored in clusters 1–4 and then the next available cluster may not be until cluster 1000. So the next 4 KB would be stored in cluster 1000 and the next in 1500 and the last in 2004. When a file is spread among several noncontiguous clusters, it's said to be *fragmented*.

There is no utility that "automagically" realizes that after a file is deleted that was stored in clusters 5–8 that Projects.DOC could now be stored in contiguous clusters 1–8. Clusters 5–8 are simply available for the next time you store a file to disk. This normally wouldn't be cause for concern. You can still retrieve Projects.DOC; it is a pretty small file but think about a 10 MB file that is *very* fragmented. Opening the 10 MB file can take a lot longer to open due to being fragmented.

The process of defragging a disk is similar to the process you would use to clean out a closet. First you would take everything out of the closet, clean the closet, and put everything back in the closet in a more orderly fashion. Running the Disk Defragmenter does about the same thing for your files. You will need at least 15 percent of free space on a volume to run the defrag process. This space is used to store data that is being rearranged or placed in contiguous clusters. If the volume is too full, you'll need to remove files or (if possible) extend the volume before you can defragment it.

By default Server 2008 has a task that is scheduled to run every Wednesday at 1:00 a.m. named ScheduledDefrag. You can view this scheduled task by clicking Start ➢ Administrative Tools ➢ Task Scheduler, and then expand Task Scheduler Library ➢ Microsoft ➢ Windows and click Defrag. Any guess as to what this scheduled task runs? You got it — the Disk Defragmenter tool. Defragging users' data is nice but this tool also defrags system files including the $MFT.

For those times when you choose to run the Disk Defragmenter tool manually there are two ways to do it: through the GUI or the command line. But keep in mind that defragmenting the disk will *not* free up space on the disk. It will group all free space together to allow it to be used more efficiently, which can greatly improve the performance of your system.

Using the Disk Defragmenter

To use Disk Defragmenter to defragment a volume or see whether it needs to be defragmented, right-click the volume in Explorer or in the Disk Management tool and choose Properties, then go to the Tools tab. Click the Tools tab. Yes, this is the same place we ran CHKDSK from but this time in the middle box named Defragmentation. Click the Defragment Now button and you will see a dialog box similar to Figure 9.49.

FIGURE 9.49
Graphical Disk
Defragmenter

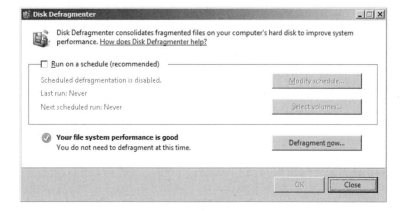

You can tell if the OS thinks your volumes need to be defragmented by looking in the bottom left corner. As you can see in Figure 9.49, the OS doesn't think that my volumes need to be defragged. If you wanted to defrag a volume anyway you would click the "Defragment now" button. A list of all the logical volumes on the server would be displayed as shown in Figure 9.50. If you have a large number of volumes in a server but only want to defrag one or two, the top selection "Select all disks" would come in handy because clicking that would deselect all volumes and you could choose only the ones you want.

FIGURE 9.50
Disk Defragmenter
shows all logical vol-
umes on the computer.

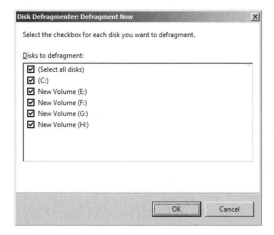

If you have some volumes that need to be defragged, select the volumes you wish to defrag and click OK. It can take some time to run; of course the amount of time it will take depends on how large the volume is and how fragmented it is.

DEFRAGGING FROM THE COMMAND LINE

Disk Defragmenter can also be run from the command line, which is really good news for those of you running Server Core 2008. The command-line version of the tool will both analyze and defragment your disks. To analyze a volume to determine whether it needs to be defragged or not from a command prompt, type **defrag volume -a**. For example, to run an analysis on the C: volume it would look like this:

```
Administrator: Command Prompt                                         _ □ ×

C:\>defrag c: -a
Windows Disk Defragmenter
Copyright (c) 2006 Microsoft Corp.

Analysis report for volume C:

    Volume size                        = 16.00 GB
    Free space                         = 8.23 GB
    Largest free space extent          = 7.58 GB
    Percent file fragmentation         = 0 %

    Note: On NTFS volumes, file fragments larger than 64MB are not included in t
he fragmentation statistics

    You do not need to defragment this volume.
```

The analysis report is fairly simple to understand. The Volume size reflects the size of the volume. Free space is the amount of space on the volume that is currently free to store data in. The Largest free space extent is the largest contiguous area that does not contain data. And, the Percent file fragmentation would tell you just how fragmented your volume is so you would know if you need to defrag that volume or not. To get more details on the analysis of a volume you would need to add the verbose switch. It would look like:

C: > Defrag C: -a -v

This command would give you a better breakdown on file, folder, and $MFT defragmentation.

There are some other switches you can use with the command-line defrag utility, as shown in Table 9.3.

TABLE 9.3:   Defrag Switches

SWITCH	WHAT IT DOES
-c	Defrags all local volumes on this computer.
-a	Performs an analysis only.
-r	Default setting. Only consolidates fragments smaller than 64 MB resulting in a partial defrag.
-w	Does a full defragmentation. Try to consolidate all file fragments, even 64 MB and larger.
-f	Automatically runs defrag of the volume when free space is low.
-v	Verbose mode. The defragmentation process and analysis output is much more detailed.
volume	Specifies the local volume name, or (if followed by a colon) the drive letter of the logical volume to be checked.

The following are some examples of using switches.

To perform an analysis on the C: drive, you should type the following:

```
defrag : -a
```

To both perform an analysis and see results of the analysis, type the following:

```
defrag : -a -v
```

To defragment the C: drive, type:

```
defrag :
```

If you want to both defragment a drive and see the defrag report for the C: drive, type the following:

```
defrag : /v
```

You can run only one instance of the defrag tool at a time. You must choose either the GUI or the command-line version, and you can run defrag on one volume at a time. If you try to run both the GUI and the CLI at the same time or you attempt to run defrag on two volumes, you will get an error that looks like this:

```
A defragmentation or volume shrink operation is already
 in progress. Only one of these operations can run at
 a time.
Wait until the current process finishes and then try
 again.
```

Remote Storage

One nice feature that was initiated in Windows 2000 and continues in Server 2008 is Remote Storage. What the Remote Storage feature does is allow you to mix tape-drive space and hard-drive space as if they were one unit.

The idea of Remote Storage is this. Suppose you have a 24 GB hard disk on your server; perhaps it's a nice amount of storage, but not quite enough for your users' needs. Suppose also that you've got a tape backup device, a carousel device that can automatically mount any one of 16 tapes into the tape drive without the need for human intervention. Perhaps it's a DLT loader and each tape can store 20 GB of data; that works out to about 320 GB of tape storage and, again, 24 GB of hard-disk storage. Here's what Remote Storage lets you do:

It lets you lie about the amount of hard disk space you have.

You essentially advertise that you've got a volume containing 320 plus 24, or 344 GB of online storage space. As people save data to that volume, Remote Storage first saves the data to the hard disk. But eventually, of course, all of that user data fills up the hard disk; at that point, Remote Storage shows off its value. Remote Storage searches the hard disk and finds which files have lain untouched for the longest time. A file could have, for example, been saved eight months ago by some user but not modified since. Remote Storage takes those infrequently accessed files and moves them from the hard disk onto the tape drives, freeing up hard-disk space.

Ah, but Remote Storage has been claiming the file that was untouched for eight months is ready and available at any time. What happens if someone decides to go looking for that file and it's on the tape? Remote Storage just finds the file on tape and puts it back on the hard disk, where the user can get to it. Yes, it's slow, but the fact is that many files are created and never reexamined, which means there is a good chance that putting the file on tape and off the hard disk will never inconvenience anyone.

I worked with mainframe systems that did things like this years ago, and it was quite convenient — files untouched for six months or so would be said to be "migrated" to tape. I could "unmigrate" the tapes, and that would take a while, but it wasn't that much of a nuisance and it helped keep the mainframe's disks free.

The Evolution of Storage

With the release of Server 2008, Microsoft has managed to add even more functionality to its storage management and has improved upon several of the features that debuted in Windows 2000. All told, Server 2008 is starting to look a lot more like an enterprise solution than NT 4 ever hoped to be. It's becoming a far more mature solution than many people ever expected and better than some Microsoft adversaries hoped it would ever become.

In this chapter, you saw how the Disk Management tool works to protect data and system disks and learned about the available options for choosing a disk format and the ways to logically divide those disks. You also learned about some of the advanced features of NTFS, such as disk quotas, encryption, Remote Storage, and the Volume Shadow Copy Service. I hope by now you feel pretty comfortable with the concepts of storage and how to better manage your systems. Using these tools, you should now be better able than ever to protect and manage your data files.

Chapter 10

TCP/IP and IPv4 Networking Basics

When you create a connection from one machine to another machine, the two machines don't just magically know how to talk with each other. They require a set of rules to perform the communication, rules called *protocols*. The Transmission Control Protocol/Internet Protocol (TCP/IP) combination defines the rules used to create a connection between two machines (TCP) and enables the two machines to exchange information in a particular way (IP). Don't worry if the idea of protocols seems confusing right now, the first section of the chapter provides you with a good definition and shows how they work. This chapter provides you with the details you need to understand how this communication occurs from an administrator perspective.

Windows hasn't always been TCP/IP-friendly, however. When Windows Server software first appeared, TCP/IP was a mildly scary, obscure, complex protocol used by just a few — those "oddballs" in research, education, and government who were attached to that large but then-still-private club called "the Internet." Some Windows Server users chose to use NetBEUI, Microsoft's proprietary networking protocol at the time. Others opted for IPX, the proprietary protocol offered by the then–market leader, Novell, for their NetWare software. Both NetBEUI and IPX are quite rare in networking now, because TCP/IP rules the roost.

Even if you don't know what TCP/IP is yet, you've been using it since Chapter 2. When we showed you how to build a network out of two Windows Server 2008 systems, the two machines were immediately able to network because that's the "in the box" protocol for modern versions of Windows. (That wasn't always true — you used to have scrounge around to find a version of TCP/IP that worked on Windows.) Even better, you didn't have to perform too much configuration to start the communication because Windows Server 2008's TCP/IP implementation does a lot of it for you in the background. But that automatic configuration is only really of value for small networks that don't talk to other networks or the Internet, so you have to know how to configure and troubleshoot Windows TCP/IP configurations, which is why this chapter is so important to you. What I'm trying to accomplish in this chapter is to answer these questions:

- What is TCP/IP all about?

- What does an IP address look like?

- How do subnets work?

- How do you use a default gateway?

- Where can I get an IP address when I need one?

- What is Automatic Private Internet Protocol Addressing (APIPA)?

- How do I use APIPA?

◆   What are sockets and ports?

◆   Is there a way to test connections to other machines?

◆   When do I need to enter a static IP address and how do I do it?

NOTE

This chapter doesn't discuss IPv6 because it still hasn't taken hold throughout much of the industry. To disable TCP/IPv6 support on your system so you don't have to worry about it, type **reg /add hklm\system\currentcontrolset\services\tcpip6\parameters /v DisabledComponents /t REG_DWORD /d 255** and press Enter at the command line. You can also clear the check next to the Internet Protocol Version 6 (TCP/IPv6) entry in the individual Properties dialog boxes for the connections, as described later in the chapter.

A Brief History of TCP/IP

Let's start off this chapter by answering, "What *is* TCP/IP?" TCP/IP is a collection of software created over the years, much of it with the help of large infusions of government research money. Originally, TCP/IP was intended for the Department of Defense (DoD). You see, the DoD tends to buy a *lot* of equipment, and much of that equipment is incompatible with other equipment. For example, back in the late '70s when the work that led to TCP/IP was first begun, it was nearly impossible to get an IBM mainframe to talk to a Burroughs (now Unisys) mainframe. That was because the two computers were designed with entirely different *protocols* — something like Figure 10.1.

FIGURE 10.1
Compatible hardware, incompatible protocols

To get some idea of what the DoD was facing, imagine picking up the phone in the United States and calling someone in Spain. You have a perfectly good hardware connection, because the Spanish phone system is compatible with the American phone system. But despite the *hardware* compatibility, you face a *software* incompatibility. The person on the other end of the phone is expecting a different protocol, which in this case is a different language. It's not that one language is better or worse than the other, but the English speaker cannot understand the Spanish speaker and vice versa. Rather than force the Spanish speaker to learn English or the English speaker to learn Spanish, we can teach them both a universal language such as Esperanto, the universal language designed in 1888. If Esperanto were used in my telephone example, neither speaker would use it at home, but they would use it to communicate with each other. With time, however, Esperanto might become so flexible and expressive that more and more people might find themselves using it both at home and in public, and English and Spanish might fall into disuse. That's what happened with TCP/IP.

TCP/IP began as a simple *alternative* communications language, an Esperanto for networks. But in time, however, TCP/IP evolved into a mature, well-understood, robust set of protocols, and more and more of the networking world has tossed aside their homegrown, "native" network language in favor of TCP/IP. In fact, today TCP/IP is the communication protocol of choice, and you'd probably have a hard time finding any of those alternatives. Let's first look at a little bit of the history of how that happened before we get into the specifics of TCP/IP on Server.

> **NOTE**
>
> This chapter describes the Internet Protocol version 4 (IPv4), which is the most common version of IP in use today. About 99.999 percent (or even more) of the world uses IPv4 today. The other version of IP is IPv6, and the main reason for this upgrade is to ensure the Internet doesn't run out of addresses. If you know how to work with IPv4, you already have a significant portion of the TCP/IP communications covered. In fact, IPv6 is so esoteric that we'll cover it in Chapter 3 of the third volume of the *Mastering Windows Server 2008* series as a separate topic. Because this chapter focuses entirely on IPv4, I'll use the term IP to describe it.

Origins of TCP/IP: From the ARPANET to the Internet

The original DoD network wouldn't just hook up military sites, although that was an important goal of the first defense internetwork, a network called the ARPANET. Much of the basic research in the United States was funded by an arm of the Defense Department called the Advanced Research Projects Agency, or ARPA. ARPA gave, and still gives, a lot of money to university researchers to study all kinds of things. ARPA thought it would be useful for these researchers to be able to communicate with one another, as well as with the Pentagon. Figure 10.2 and Figure 10.3 demonstrate networking both before and after ARPANET implementation.

FIGURE 10.2
Researchers before
ARPANET

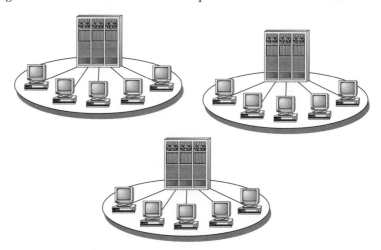

FIGURE 10.3
Researchers after
ARPANET

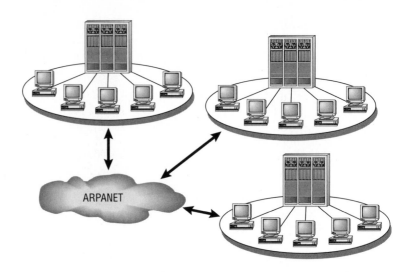

The new network, dubbed ARPANET, was designed and put in place by a private contractor called Bolt, Beranek, and Newman. (They're still around at www.bbn.com.) For the first time, it linked university professors both to each other and to their military and civilian project leaders around the country. Because ARPANET was a network that linked separate private university networks and the separate military networks, it was a "network of networks."

ARPANET ran atop a protocol called the Network Control Protocol (NCP). NCP was later refined into two components, the Internet Protocol (IP) and the Transmission Control Protocol (TCP). The change from NCP to TCP/IP is the technical difference between ARPANET and the Internet. On January 1, 1983, ARPANET packet-switching devices stopped accepting NCP packets and only passed TCP/IP packets, so in a sense, January 1, 1983 is the "official" birthday of the Internet.

ARPANET became the Internet after a few evolutions. (Well, that's a "few evolutions" unless you happen to believe that Al Gore invented it in his spare time while a senator.) Probably the first major development step occurred in 1974, when Vinton Cerf and Robert Kahn proposed the protocols that would become TCP and IP. (I say *probably* because the Internet didn't grow through a centralized effort, but rather through the largely disconnected efforts of several researchers, university professors, and graduate students, most of whom are still alive — and almost *all* of whom have a different perspective on what the "defining" aspects of Internet development were. And all of whom have a Web site on Internet history. . . .) Over its more than 20-year history, the Internet and its predecessors have gone through several stages of growth and adjustment. In 1987, the Internet could only claim a few thousand users. By 1993 it had grown to about 20 million. In 2002, there were nearly 600 million users, and in late 2007 1.3 billion users, according to http://www.internetworldstats.com/stats.htm. *All* of those numbers should be taken with a pound of salt, but no matter what numbers you believe, it's clear that the Internet's still growing pretty quickly.

Internet growth is fueled not by an esoteric interest in seeing how large a network the world can build, but rather by just a few applications that require the Internet to run. Perhaps most important is Internet e-mail, followed closely by the World Wide Web (WWW), and then the File Transfer Protocol (FTP). (And okay, let's tell the truth — if we took the pornography and the stolen MP3 and movie files off the Net, then the Internet's unused bandwidth would probably grow by a factor of 20.)

Originally, the Internet protocols were intended to support connections between mainframe-based networks, which were basically the only ones that existed through most of the 1970s. But the 1980s saw the growth of Unix workstations, microcomputers, and minicomputers. The Berkeley version of Unix (which, by the way, has a huge number of users, because it's the foundation of the Mac's OS/X operating system) was built largely with government money, and the government said, "Put the TCP/IP protocol in that thing." Adding IP as a built-in part of Berkeley Unix has helped both Unix and the Internet grow. The IP protocol was used on many of the Unix-based Ethernet networks that appeared in the '80s and still exist to this day — I know very few Linux boxes that run anything but TCP/IP, for example. In fact, you'll find that a majority of ISPs run Unix — however, Windows servers have been catching up over the last few years.

In the mid-1980s, the National Science Foundation created five supercomputing centers and put them on the Internet. This served two purposes: It made supercomputers available to NSF grantees around the country, and it provided a major "backbone" for the Internet. The National Science Foundation portion of the network, called NSFNet, was for a long time the largest part of the Internet. It is now being superseded by the National Research and Education Network (NREN). For many years, commercial users were pretty much kept off the Internet, because most of the funding was governmental; you had to be invited to join the Net. But those restrictions have vanished, and now the vast majority of Internet traffic is routed over commercial lines rather than government-run lines. In fact, commercial and private users dominate the Internet these days, so much so that the government and educational institutions are now working on a faster "Internet 2" that runs atop the newer version of IP, "IPv6."

It's customary to refer to the Internet as the information superhighway. I can understand why people say that; after all, it's a long-haul trucking service for data. But I think of it more as "Information Main Street." The Internet grew because businesses decided to use it to get things done and to sell their wares. All of this book was shipped back and forth on the Internet as it was being written. Heck, that sounds more like Main Street than I-95.

The network protocol wars are over, however. We're not running NetBEUI, or IPX, or X.25, or HDLC, or DDCMP (and if you've never heard of those, count yourself fortunate) — the TCP/IP-based Internet is *it*, and has been at least since 1995. It seems like there can't be more than one person left on the *planet* without an e-mail address . . . and I'm still working on my mother.

Let me not leave this section without defining a few terms: internet, Internet, and intranet:

◆ An *internet* is any network that uses TCP/IP.

◆ The *Internet* — capital *I* — is the informal term that I'll use to describe the public Internet, the one that connects networks the world over.

◆ An *intranet* is a term that popped up in the mid '90s because people found it confusing to have to say "THE Internet" when speaking of the worldwide public Internet rather than "AN internet" when referring to a private network that uses TCP/IP. *Intranet*, then, usually means basically the same thing as *internet* — little *i* — perhaps refined to mean "your internal network that not only uses TCP/IP but is also connected to the public Internet in some fashion, but usually protected by some sort of filtering software called a firewall."

Goals of TCP/IP's Design

Let's delve into some of the techie aspects of the Internet's main protocols. When the DoD started building this set of network protocols, it had a few design goals. Understanding those design goals helps in understanding why it was worth making the effort to use TCP/IP in the first place. Its intended characteristics include the following:

◆ Good failure recovery

◆ Ability to plug in new networks without disrupting services

◆ Ability to handle high error rates

◆ Independence from a particular vendor or type of network

I'm sure no one had any idea how central those design goals would be to the amazing success of TCP/IP both in private intranets and in *the* Internet. Let's take a look at those design goals in more detail.

GOOD FAILURE RECOVERY

Remember, this was to be a *defense* network, so it had to work even if portions of the network hardware suddenly and without warning went offline. That's kind of a nice way of saying the network had to work even if big pieces got nuked.

CAN PLUG IN NEW SUBNETWORKS "ON THE FLY"

This second goal is related to the first one. It says that it should be possible to bring entire new networks into an intranet — and here, again, *intranet* can mean your company's private intranet or *the* Internet — without interrupting existing network service.

This seems kind of basic nowadays, doesn't it? But a lot of the old network protocols were *really* fragile. Trust me, if we'd all stayed with some of the early PC networking protocols, then I'm only exaggerating a little bit when I say that we'd all have to reboot the Internet every time someone connected.

CAN HANDLE HIGH ERROR RATES

The next goal was that an intranet should be able to tolerate high or unpredictable error rates and yet still provide a 100 percent reliable end-to-end service. If you're transferring data from Washington, D.C., to Portland, Oregon, and the links that you're currently using through Oklahoma get destroyed by a tornado, then any data lost in the storm will be resent and rerouted via some other lines.

HOST INDEPENDENCE

As I mentioned before, the new network architecture should work with any kind of network and not be dedicated or tied to any one vendor.

This is essential in the twenty-first century. The days of "We're just an IBM shop" or "We only buy Novell stuff" are gone for many and going fast for others. (Let's hope that it doesn't give way to "We only buy Microsoft software.") Companies must be able to live in a multivendor world.

In fact, the Internet has achieved this wonderfully. When you connect to CNN, IBM, the White House, or my Web site, do you have any idea whether those Web servers are running some Microsoft Server OS, Unix, Linux, VMS, MVS, or something else? Of course not. My Web server runs atop a Microsoft OS and my e-mail server runs on Linux, and they get along just fine.

But enough about the Internet for now. Let's stop and define something that I've been talking about — namely, just what *are* TCP and IP? Originally, TCP/IP was just a set of protocols that could hook up dissimilar computers and transfer information between them. But it grew into a large number of protocols that have become collectively known as the *TCP/IP suite*.

Getting There: The Internet Protocol (IP)

The most basic part of the Internet is the Internet Protocol, or IP. (Although recall that we're talking here about IPv4, the most commonly used version. IPv6 is on the horizon, but, again, unless someone says differently, you can assume that "IP" means "IPv4.") If you want to send data over an intranet, then that data must be packaged in an IP packet. That packet is then *routed* from one part of the intranet to another.

A Simple Internet

IP is supposed to allow messages to travel from one part of a network to another. How does it do this?

An intranet is made of at least two *sub*nets. The notion of a subnet is built upon the fact that most popular Local Area Network (LAN) architectures (Ethernet and wireless networks) are based on something very much like a radio broadcast. Everyone on the same Ethernet segment hears all of the traffic on their segment, just as each device on a given wireless access point (WAP) on a wireless network must examine every message that goes through the network. The trick that makes an Ethernet or a wireless network work is that, while each station *hears* everything, each station knows how to ignore all messages except the ones intended for it.

You may have never realized it, but that means that in a single Ethernet segment or amongst all systems communicating wirelessly via the same WAP, there is *no routing*. If you've ever sat through one of those seemingly unending explanations of the ISO seven-layer network model, then you know that in network discussions, much is made of the *network layer*, which in ISO terms is merely the routing layer. And yet a simple Ethernet or WAP never has to route. There are no routing decisions to make; everything is heard by everybody. (Your network adapter filters out any traffic not destined for you, in case you're wondering.)

But now suppose you have *two* separate Ethernets connected to each other, as you see in Figure 10.4.

FIGURE 10.4
Multisegment internet

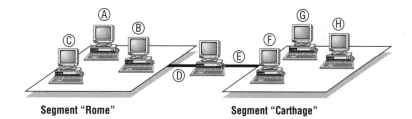

Segment "Rome"   Segment "Carthage"

In Figure 10.4, you see two Ethernet segments, named Rome and Carthage. (I was getting tired of the "shipping" and "finance" examples that everyone uses.) There are three computers that reside solely in Rome. Each one has an Ethernet card built into it, and I've labeled those Ethernet cards A, B, and C. Three more computers reside in Carthage; I've labeled their Ethernet cards F, G, and H. One PC has *two* Ethernet cards — one labeled D that's connected to Rome, and one labeled E that's connected to Carthage.

Subnets and Routers: "Should I Shout, or Should I Route?"

Much of intranet architecture is built around the observation that the PCs with Ethernet cards A, B, and C can communicate directly with each other, and the PCs with Ethernet cards F, G, and H can communicate directly with each other, but A, B, and C *cannot* communicate with F, G, and H without some help from the machine containing Ethernet cards D and E. That D/E machine will function as a *router*, a machine that allows communication between different network segments. A, B, C, and D could be described as being in each other's "broadcast range," as could E, F, G, and H. What I've just called a broadcast range is called more correctly in intranet terminology a *subnet*, which is a collection of machines that can communicate with each other without the need for routing.

For example, F and H can communicate directly without having to ask the router (E, in their case) to forward the message, and so they're on the same subnet. A and C can communicate directly without having to ask the router (D, in their case) to forward the message, and so they're on the same subnet. But if B wanted to talk to G, it would have to first send the message to D, asking, "D, please get this to G," so they're not on the same subnet.

Now, this whole trick of somehow knowing that F and H are on the same subnet and so do not need to enlist the aid of a router — F can just "shout" the message and H will hear it — or knowing that A and F are on different subnets — so A would need the help of D to get to F and F would require E's assistance to get to A — is IP's main job. Essentially, IP's job is to figure out "should I shout, or should I route?" and then, if routing's the way to go, IP has to figure out which router to use, assuming there's a choice of routers.

IP Addresses and Ethernet/Media Access Control (MAC) Addresses

Before continuing, let's briefly discuss the labels A, B, C, and so on, and how those labels actually are manifested in an intranet. Each computer on this net is attached to the net via an Ethernet board or, more likely, an Ethernet chip on the computer's motherboard, and each Ethernet board on an intranet has two addresses: an *Ethernet or Media Access Control (MAC) address* and an *IP address*. (There are, of course, other ways to get onto an intranet than via Ethernet, but let's stay with the Ethernet example as it's the most common one on TCP/IP intranets.)

ETHERNET/MAC ADDRESSES

Each Ethernet board's Ethernet address is a unique 48-bit identification code. If it sounds unlikely that every Ethernet board in the world has its own unique address, then consider that 48 bits offers 281,474,976,710,656 possibilities.

NOTE

A possible 281 trillion addresses sounds like a lot, doesn't it? Well, believe it or not, the networking industry reckons that we'll run out of unique 48-bit MAC addresses around 2100. (Don't roll your eyes — cut out the red meat, eat more fiber, hit the exercise bike three times a week, and hey, you might still be around then, right?) Anyway, they're trying to head that off by moving to a *64-bit* MAC address.

Ethernet itself uses only about one quarter of those 281 trillion possibilities (2 bits are set aside for administrative functions), but that's still a lot of possible addresses. In any case, the important thing to get here is that a board's Ethernet address is predetermined and hard-coded into the board. Ethernet addresses or, as they're more often called, MAC addresses (it's got nothing to do with Macintoshes), are expressed in 12 hexadecimal (16-bit) digits. For example, the Ethernet card on the computer I'm working at now has MAC (Ethernet) address 0020AFF8E771, or as it's usually written, 00-20-AF-F8-E7-71. The addresses are centrally administered, and Ethernet chip vendors must purchase blocks of addresses. In the example of my workstation, you know that it's got a 3Com Ethernet card because the Ethernet (MAC) address is 00-20-AF; that prefix is owned by 3Com.

NOTE

To see a Windows Server 2008 system's MAC address — or addresses, if it has more than one Network Interface Card (NIC) — just open a command line and type **getmac**, then press Enter. The string of numbers and letters under the column Physical Address is the MAC address of your NIC. If you want to find the vendor for your adapter, check out the Vendor/Ethernet MAC Address Lookup and Search utility at http://www.coffer.com/mac_find/.

IPv4 Addresses and Quad Format

In contrast to the 48 bits in a MAC address, an IPv4 address is a 32-bit value (an IPv6 address is a 128-bit value). IP addresses are numbers set at a workstation (or server) by a network administrator — they're not a hard-coded hardware kind of address like the Ethernet address. That means that there are four billion distinct Internet addresses.

It's nice that there's room for lots of machines, but having to remember — or having to tell someone else — a 32-bit address is no fun. Imagine having to say to a network support person, "Just set up the machines on the subnet to use a default router address of 10101110100-101010010101100010111." Hmmm, doesn't sound like much fun — we need a more human-friendly way to express 32-bit numbers. That's where *dotted quad* notation comes from.

For simplicity's sake, IP addresses are usually represented as *w.x.y.z*, where *w*, *x*, *y*, and *z* are all decimal values from 0 to 255. For example, the IP address of the machine that I'm currently writing this at is 199.34.57.53. Each of the four numbers is called a *quad*; as they're connected by dots, it's called *dotted quad* notation.

Each of the numbers in the dotted quad corresponds to 8 bits of an Internet address. (*IP address* and *Internet address* are synonymous.) As the value for 8 bits can range from 0 to 255, each value in a dotted quad can be from 0 to 255. For example, to convert an IP address of 11001010000011110101010000000001 into dotted quad format, it would first be broken up into 8-bit groups:

```
11001010   00001111   10101010   00000001
```

And each of those 8-bit numbers would be converted to its decimal equivalent. (If you're not comfortable with binary-to-decimal conversion, don't worry about it: Just load the Windows Server 2008 Calculator (Start ➤ Programs ➤ Accessories ➤ Calculator), click View, then Scientific, and then press the F8 key to put the Calculator in binary mode. Enter the binary number, press F6, and the number will be converted to decimal for you.) Our number converts as follows:

```
11001010   00001111   10101010   00000001
   202        15         170         1
```

which results in a dotted quad address of 202.15.170.1.

So, to recap: Each of these computers has at least one Ethernet card in it, and that Ethernet card has a predefined MAC address. Each of these computers are modern Windows systems, so they come with IP software right in the box. The operating system has assigned unique IP addresses to each of them. (Note, by the way, that the phrase "has assigned IP addresses to each of them" may not be true if you are using the Dynamic Host Configuration Protocol, or DHCP. For most of this chapter, however, I'm going to assume that you're not using DHCP and that someone must hand-assign an IP address to each Ethernet card.)

Let me redraw our intranet, adding totally arbitrary IP addresses and Ethernet addresses, as shown in Figure 10.5.

FIGURE 10.5

Two-subnet intranet with Ethernet and IP addresses

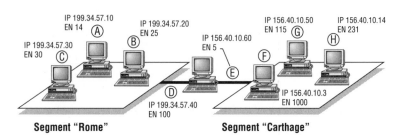

Segment "Rome"   Segment "Carthage"

NOTE

Remember, MAC addresses are burned into a network card; they come "out of the box," so to speak. IP addresses, in contrast, are assigned by a network administrator or software configured by a network administrator. There isn't any mathematical relationship between the two numbers; don't try to see if there's some connection between, say, the bottom 32 bits of a MAC address and the IP address — there won't be one.

Where Your System Gets Its IP Address From

At this point, I've introduced the notions of subnets, IP addresses, MAC addresses, and how we write IP addresses in dotted-quad format. I've also said that two systems in the same subnet can simply "shout" at each other, but that two systems in different subnets can communicate only if they "route" to one another. I'll explain more about IP routing in a minute, but before I do that, permit me to digress for just a moment and talk about just where a system gets an IP address in the first place.

Even if you've never seen dotted quad notation before, I assume that virtually everyone reading this book has spent at least some time on the Internet, if only to surf the Web and/or use e-mail. As you've just read, you can't get on an intranet, much less the Internet, without an IP address — and yet for the vast majority of us, getting on the Internet has been no more complicated than plugging our computer's Ethernet connection into a wall jack or turning on the wireless network connection in our laptop. Given that, you may be curious about how systems get their IP addresses in the first place — so here's a quick look. There are three ways:

- Servers running software that lets them perform as something called a "DHCP server" may provide a computer with an IP address, and that IP address may change over time.

- If a computer expects a DHCP server to provide it an address, but there either isn't a DHCP server or if the local DHCP server isn't working, then a system can provide itself a limited-value address called an "IPv4 link-local address" or an "automatic private IP address"

(APIPA). That'll probably turn out to be a different address every time that computer boots.

◆ In a fairly small number of cases, a system — usually a server — may need an unchanging address, leading an administrator to punch one right into the server; this is called a "static" IP address.

DHCP-PROVIDED ADDRESSES

As I'll cover briefly in this chapter and then in greater detail in Chapter 14, most networks provide IP configuration information (including IP addresses) automatically to their systems from a set of central servers that use something called the Dynamic Host Configuration Protocol (DHCP). The basic idea with DHCP is that a network administrator instructs a server running DHCP, "when someone asks for an IP address, then pick one from this pool of possible IP addresses (also known as a *scope*), making sure to never give two systems the same IP address." Having a way to hand out IP addresses automatically is convenient, and the vast majority of the systems on most intranets and on the Internet get their addresses from DHCP. A system basically gets an IP address from DHCP when it starts up by basically shouting, "hey, is there a DHCP server around here? I really need an IP address." The DHCP server then responds with an address and they're on the network.

DHCP servers are nearly everywhere — in fact, you might have one in your house. Ever plugged your laptop into your company's network and had it able to connect to that network, and probably the Internet? Then someone on that network set up a DHCP server, which might be running on a Windows Server box, perhaps a Unix server, or in some cases a dedicated appliance called a "Cisco Pix server." Ever fired up your computer's wireless network connection at an airport, coffee shop or like and gotten onto the Internet? Then someone there set up a DHCP server. For that matter, have you ever purchased an inexpensive wireless router, plugged into your cable modem or DSL connection, then turned on your computer's wireless network connection and gotten onto the Internet? Then that little Internet router of yours contains some software that acts as a DHCP server, and the manufacturer set that software up with some default settings that worked in your house.

When a DHCP server gives a machine an address, the server only gives it for a specific amount of time — the address is said to be "leased" to the target machine. Once the lease is up, the DHCP server may refuse to issue another (which is extremely unlikely) or the DHCP server may issue a different address (which is quite likely), and that new address is as good as the old one — you've probably worked on systems with changing IP addresses and not known it.

WHEN ALL ELSE FAILS: APIPA OR IPV4 LINK-LOCAL ADDRESSES

Sometimes, though, a system expects to get an IP address from a DHCP server, but either there is no DHCP server nearby, or the one that's supposed to be nearby isn't working. What happens then?

Well, for a number of years, what happened was that the computer didn't get an IP address, and so could not network. But when Windows 98 appeared over a decade ago, I noticed something odd. If I turned on a Windows 98 system on an isolated test network with no other systems on it and in particular no DHCP servers, the little Dickens ended up having an IP address! These "self serving" Windows 98 boxes all seemed to dish up IP addresses that looked like 169.254.x.y, where "x" and "y" were some random numbers between 0 and 255. To be honest, I largely ignored it — 98 was part of the old, lame Windows model, rather than the cooler, more robust NT family of Windows boxes.

So I was kinda surprised when Windows 2000 systems — members of that NT family, recall — started showing the same behavior. Stick 'em on a network segment without a DHCP server, and they'd just give themselves a 169.254.something.something address. I looked into it, and Microsoft called it an "APIPA" address. As there aren't many palindromic acronyms, I looked further. APIPA stands for Automatic Private IP Address. The idea is that if you've told a computer to look to DHCP for an IP address and none's to be had, then the next best thing would be to have the computer give itself an address that works, but only on its subnet, and thus, it can't talk to the outside world with that address — but it can talk to systems local to it.

Why is this useful? Well, consider the case of a few people who get together on a Saturday afternoon to hook up their laptops, fire up a multi-player game, and blast each other to virtual atoms. The game runs atop IP addresses, and so these systems need a set of IP addresses. Who wants to set up a DHCP server just for that? Or take the case of the two-system network that we had you set up in Chapter 2: we just wanted to hook up a couple of computers and demonstrate some networking. APIPA handled the networking.

APIPA, however, isn't just a Microsoft proprietary answer to building a "no planning necessary" network. It's a standard now. In 2005, the IETF, the folks who control standards in the Internet, accepted a new RFC, RFC 3927, which described a new way to give a limited-value, "if all else fails" sort of IP address. What was particularly interesting about the RFC is that it has three authors: an employee of Sun Microsystems, an employee of Apple Corporation, and an employee of Microsoft. You know if the three of those companies agree on something, it must be important! The name that the RFC gives to these kinds of addresses isn't APIPA, but instead "IPv4 link-local addresses." Here are few more details about how APIPA/IPv4 link-local addresses work:

◆ Again, a system can choose anything from 169.254.0.0 through 169.254.255.255, a range of 65,536 options.

◆ The system chooses an APIPA address randomly and then checks it by asking if any other system on the subnet currently has that address. If one does, the system just keeps spinning up random addresses in the 169.254 range until it finds one that doesn't conflict with another system. (The process is called Duplicate Address Detection, or DAD.)

◆ An IP packet sent from an APIPA address isn't allowed out of the subnet — no routing, just shouting.

In short, finding yourself with a 169.254 address usually means something's wrong . . . unless you intended to do it.

STATIC IP ADDRESSES

Back when I first started connecting to the Internet, my intranets were (like many people's in 1992) small, and I'm thankful for that because in those days Windows systems didn't know how to ask a DHCP server for an IP address, and APIPA was years in the future. How, then, did I get my early intranets working? By walking around to each networked computer and hand-entering IP configuration information onto that computer. It was a pain, because it took time and involved some recordkeeping on my part. That's called "static IP configuration."

Nowadays, I don't statically configure most of my systems, but I still must statically configure some of them. In particular, I must do static IP configuration on some of my servers because in general servers' IP addresses should be unchanging, and because Windows Server 2008 refuses to install some server modules on itself unless it's got a static IP address. We'll see how to do static IP configuration a bit later in this chapter.

Recapitulating, then, most systems get their IP addresses from DHCP servers, but there's got to be a DHCP server around to provide them. If a computer expects to get an address from DHCP but doesn't, it'll give itself an APIPA address, and, alternatively, you can tell your computer to skip talking to DHCP and just specify an unchanging — "static" — IP address for it.

IP Routers

Now let's return to the computer in the middle. It is part of *both* segments, both subnets. How do I get one computer to be part of two networks? By putting two Ethernet cards in the computer in the middle. (A computer with more than one network card in it is called a *multihomed* computer. Don't ask me why, the term has never made sense to me; I suppose it flows better than "multiNICced.") One of the Ethernet cards is on the Rome subnet, and the other is on the Carthage subnet. (By the way, each computer on an intranet is called a *host* in TCP-ese.)

Now, each Ethernet card must get a separate IP address, so as a result, the computer in the middle has *two* IP addresses, D and E. If a message is transmitted in Rome, adapter D hears it and E doesn't. Then, if a message is transmitted in Carthage, adapter E hears it but D doesn't.

How would we build an intranet from these two subnets? How could the computer with Ethernet card A, for example, send a message to the computer with Ethernet card G? Obviously, the only way that message will get from A to G is if the message is received on the Ethernet adapter with address D and then re-sent out over the Ethernet adapter with address E. Once E resends the message, G will hear it, because it is on the same network as E.

In order for this to work, the machine containing boards D and E must be smart enough to perform this function whereby it resends data between D and E when necessary. Such a machine is, by definition, an *IP router*. Any Windows Server 2008 computer (or even a Vista box, if you mess with its Registry a bit) can act as an IP router, as you'll learn later.

Under IP, the sending station (the one with Ethernet card A, in this case) examines the address of the destination (the PC with Ethernet card G, in this case) and realizes that it does not know how to get to G. (I'll explain exactly *how* it comes to that realization in a minute.) Now, if A has to send something to an address that it doesn't understand, then it uses a kind of "catchall" address called the *default router* or, for historical reasons, the *default gateway* address. A's network administrator has already configured A's default router as D, so A sends the message to D. Once D gets the message, it then sees that the message is not destined for itself, but rather for G, and so it resends the message from board E.

Routing in More Detail

Now let's look a little closer at how that message gets from A to G. Each computer, as you've already seen, has one *or more* IP addresses. It's important to recall that there is no relation whatsoever between an Ethernet card's address and the IP address associated with it: the Ethernet card's manufacturer hardwires the MAC address into the card, whereas in contrast network administrators assign IP addresses.

But now examine the IP addresses and you'll see a pattern to them. Rome's addresses all look like 199.34.57.z, where z is some number, and Carthage's addresses all look like 156.40.10.z, where, again, z can be any number in the range of 0 through 255. The Ethernet addresses, in contrast, follow no rhyme or reason and are grouped by the board's manufacturer. That similarity of IP addresses within Rome and Carthage will be important in understanding routing.

Now, let's reexamine how the message gets from A's computer to G's (for simplicity's sake, I'll say "A" instead of "the computer with the Ethernet card labeled A," and the same for G's computer and so on):

1. The IP software in A first says, "How do I get this message to G — can I just broadcast it, or must it be routed?" The way that it makes that decision is by finding out whether or not G is on the same *subnet* as A is. A subnet is simply a broadcast area. The host with Ethernet card A then, is asking, "Is G part of Rome, like me?"

2. A determines that it is on a different subnet from G by examining their addresses. A knows that it has address 199.34.57.10 and that it must send its message to 156.40.10.50. A's

computer has a simple rule for this: If the destination address looks like 199.34.57.z, where, again, z can be any value, then the destination is in the same subnet and so requires no routing. On the other hand, 156.40.10.50 is clearly *not* in the same subnet.

If, alternatively, G *had* been on the same subnet, then A would have "shouted" the IP packet straight to G, referring specifically to its IP and Ethernet address.

3. So A can't directly send its IP packets to G. A then looks for another way. When A's network administrator set up A's IP software, she told A the IP address of A's *default router*. The default router is basically the address that says, "If you don't know where to send something, send it to me and I'll try to get it there." A's default router is D. So now A has a sort of sub-goal of getting a message to nearby D, with IP address 199.34.57.40. We're almost ready to hand this over to the Ethernet card — *except* that Ethernet cards don't understand IP addresses; they understand MAC addresses.

TCP/IP has an answer for this: Address Resolution Protocol (ARP). A just sends a broadcast to the local segment, saying, "If there's a machine out there that goes by the IP address 199.34.57.40, please send me back your MAC address." D hears the request and responds that its MAC address is 100.

A then sends an Ethernet frame from itself to D. The Ethernet frame contains this information:

- Source Ethernet address: 14
- Destination Ethernet address: 100
- Source IP address: 199.34.57.10
- Destination IP address: 156.40.10.50

4. Ethernet card D receives the frame and hands it to the IP software running in its PC. The PC sees that the IP destination address is not *its* IP address, so the PC knows that it must route this IP packet. Examining the subnet, the PC sees that the destination lies on the subnet that Ethernet adapter E is on, so it ARPs to get G's MAC address; G responds, "My MAC address is 115," and then E sends out a frame, with this information:

- Source Ethernet address: 5
- Destination Ethernet address: 115
- Source IP address: 199.34.57.10 (note this is A's address, not E's)
- Destination IP address: 156.40.10.50

5. G then gets the packet. By looking at the Ethernet and IP addresses, G can see that it got this frame from E, but the original message really came from another machine, the 199.34.57.10 machine.

That's a simple example of how IP routes, but its algorithms are powerful enough to serve as the backbone for a network as large as the Internet.

TIP

There are different kinds of routing algorithms in TCP/IP. Windows Server 2008 now supports the Routing Information Protocol (RIP) version 2, Open Shortest Path First (OSPF), and Internet Group

Management Protocol (IGMP) version 2. For other routing approaches, or for very high-capacity routing needs, you need either third-party software or a dedicated hardware router to build large, complex intranets with Windows Server 2008. But Windows Server 2008 can handle a considerably larger set of routing tasks than did its predecessors.

Class A, B, and C Networks, CIDR Blocks, and Routable and Nonroutable Addresses

Before leaving IP routing, let's take a more specific look at networks, subnets, and IP addresses.

> **NOTE**
>
> We'll take up the matter of configuring a Windows Server to be an IP router in the third book of the *Mastering Windows Server 2008* series because in fact most people use dedicated appliances from Linksys, Cisco, Dlink, Netgear, and others to act as their IP routers.

The whole idea behind the 32-bit IP addresses is to make it relatively simple to segment the task of managing the Internet or, for that matter, *any* intranet.

To become part of the Internet, you'll need a block of IP addresses and a name (like `bigfirm.com`) or a set of names. Find a local Internet service provider (ISP) for the block of addresses. ISPs may also handle registering names for you, but it's just as easy to register a name yourself with Network Solutions or another name registrar; surf over to `http://www .networksolutions.com/` to find out how.

But how do the *ISPs* get their IP addresses? Originally, an organization named the Internet Assigned Numbers Authority (IANA) handed out addresses. In 1993, however, an Internet document RFC 1466 (see `http://www.faqs.org/rfcs/rfc1466.html`) explained that it made more sense to distribute the job as the Internet became bigger. (The rules describing how things work in the Internet are called Requests for Comment, or RFCs.) The IANA, which is now the Internet Corporation for Assigned Names and Numbers (ICANN) (`http://www.icann.org/`), divides its number-assigning authority among five Regional Internet Registries (RIRs):

◆ RIPE (Reseaux IP Europeens, or European IP Networks) handles Europe, the Middle East, and the better part of Asia

◆ APNIC (Asia Pacific Network Information Center) handles the rest of Asia and the South Pacific

◆ ARIN (American Registry for Internet Numbers) handles North America

◆ AFRINIC (African Network Information Center) handles all of Africa

◆ LACNIC (Latin American and Caribbean IP Address Regional Registry) handles South America

You can see a map of the five regions and get a list of the countries supported by each RIR at `http://www.arin.net/community/rirs.html`. Rather than say "The IANA/ICANN, RIPE, ARIN, APNIC, AFRINIC, LACNIC, or one of their sub-organizations," however, I hope you won't mind if I just say "ICANN" when referring to the IP-allocating groups.

A, B, and C Class Networks

The ICANN or an ISP assigns a company a block of IP addresses according to the company's size. That block of addresses is called a *network*. (As you'll soon see, a subnet is just a subdivision of that set of assigned addresses, hence *sub*net.) Big companies get class A networks (of course, there are none left; they've all been given out), medium-sized companies get class B networks (they're still around but pretty scarce), and others get class C networks (they're still available). Although there are three network classes, there are five kinds of IP addresses, as you'll see in Figure 10.6.

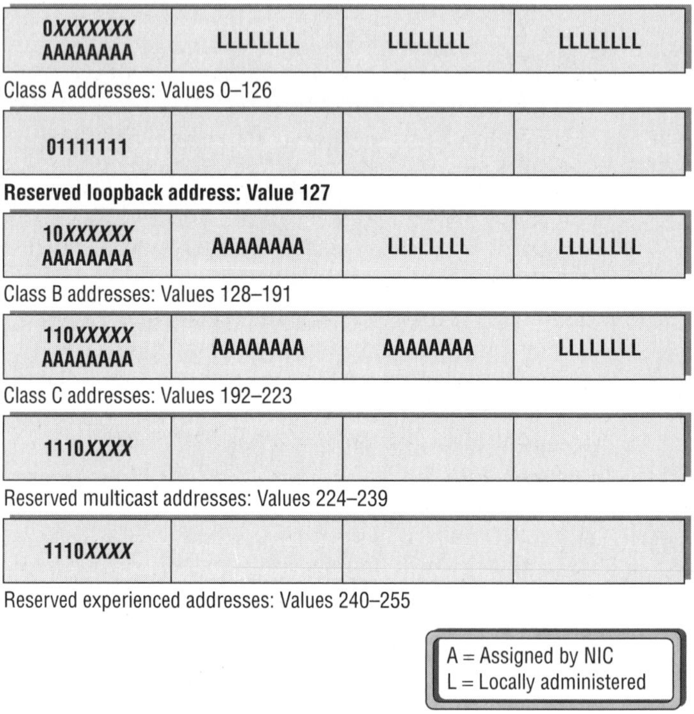

FIGURE 10.6

Internet network classes and reserved addresses

0*XXXXXXX* AAAAAAAA	LLLLLLLL	LLLLLLLL	LLLLLLLL

Class A addresses: Values 0–126

01111111			

Reserved loopback address: Value 127

10*XXXXXX* AAAAAAAA	AAAAAAAA	LLLLLLLL	LLLLLLLL

Class B addresses: Values 128–191

110*XXXXX* AAAAAAAA	AAAAAAAA	AAAAAAAA	LLLLLLLL

Class C addresses: Values 192–223

1110*XXXX*			

Reserved multicast addresses: Values 224–239

1110*XXXX*			

Reserved experienced addresses: Values 240–255

> A = Assigned by NIC
> L = Locally administered

Because it seemed, in the early days of the Internet, that four billion addresses left plenty of space for growth, the original designers were a bit sloppy. They defined three classes of networks of the Internet: Large networks, medium-sized networks, and small networks. The creators of the Internet used 8-bit sections of the 32-bit addresses to delineate the difference between different classes of networks:

Class A Networks A large network would have its first 8 bits set by the Internet Network Information Center (InterNIC; remember, now it's ICANN), and the network's internal administrators could set the remaining 24 bits. The leftmost 8 bits could have values from 0 to 126, allowing for 127 class A networks. Companies like IBM get these, and there are only 127 of these addresses. As only 8 bits have been taken, 24 remain; that means that class A networks can contain up to 2 to the 24th power, or about 16 million, hosts. Examples of class A nets include General Electric (3.*x.y.z*), Level 3 Communications (4), IBM (9), Xerox (13), Hewlett-Packard (15), Digital Equipment Corp, which is now part of HP (16) — *two* A networks for HP!, Apple (17), MIT (18), Ford (19), Eli Lilly (40), DuPont (52), Merck (54), the U.S. Postal Service (56), various defense groups — remember who built this — and some unexpected ones: Networld+Interop, which has the 45.*x.y.z* network set aside for its use (not bad, an A network for two week-long conferences a year!) and the U.K. Department of Social Security (51). You can see a complete list of Class A network assignments at `http://www.iana.org /assignments/ipv4-address-space`.

Class B Networks   Medium-sized networks have the leftmost 16 bits preassigned to them, leaving 16 bits for local use. Class B addresses always have the values 128 through 191 in their first quad, then a value from 0 to 255 in their second quad. There are then 16,384 possible class B networks. Each of them can have up to 65,536 hosts. Microsoft and Exxon are examples of companies with class B networks. (So Apple and IBM have class A networks and Microsoft only has a class B. What do you want to bet that this kind of thing keeps Bill up late nights?)

Class C Networks   Small networks have the leftmost 24 bits preassigned to them, leaving only 8 bits for local administration (which is bad, because it means that class C networks can't have more than 254 hosts), but because the InterNIC (now ICANN) has 24 bits to work with, it can easily give out class C network addresses (which is good). Class C addresses start off with a value from 192 to 223. As the second and third quads can be any value from 0 to 255, that means that there can potentially be 2,097,152 class C networks. The last C network, when it's assigned, will be 223.255.255.*z*; remember that the owner of that network will be able to control only *z*.

Reserved Addresses   Some addresses are reserved for multicast purposes and for experimental purposes, so they can't be assigned for networks. In particular, address 224.0.0.0 is set aside for *multicasts*, network transmissions to groups of computers.

Routable and Nonroutable Addresses

Once upon a time, getting hold of a bunch of IP addresses was easy. But nowadays, they're scarcer and scarcer. Four billion possible addresses sounds like a lot, but the A/B/C class approach tends to waste addresses on large companies and those who just got in line at the right time: With all due respect to the organizations involved, it's hard to believe that certain universities, Apple, and the Network+Interop conference each really need 16 million unique IP addresses. Don't misunderstand me, I'm not suggesting that we change their address allocation — first come, first served in the IP land rush is a reasonable first approach to allocation. But big and small firms alike need IP addresses, and they're not as plentiful as they once were.

RFC 1918's Nonroutable Addresses

We've heard for years that the Giant Brains of the IP world are working on promoting a replacement for IP called IPv6, a 128-bit–based addressing scheme that would allow more IP addresses than there are electrons in the universe (okay, I rechecked, it's only about the size of the *square root* of the number of electrons in the universe, but it's still a big number), but then I've been hearing about the "imminent" nature of IPv6 since about 1993. Although Windows Server 2008 does provide support for IPv6, it's unlikely that most outside connections do. Until it's more widely accepted, we need some way to stretch our IP addresses. And there *is* a way that's been widely adopted.

In RFC 1918 (`http://www.faqs.org/rfcs/rfc1918.html`), the Internet folks defined three nonroutable ranges of IPv4 addresses. They are

◆   10.0.0.0–10.255.255.255

◆   172.16.0.0–172.31.255.255

◆   192.168.0.0–192.168.255.255

The original idea with the ranges of nonroutable addresses was to set aside some addresses that people could use to build "test" intranets without having to go to the ICANN for a range of numbers — anyone can build an IP-based network using these addresses. Furthermore, even if networks based on the above addresses *were* attached to the Internet, then they couldn't cause any mischief, because Internet routers are programmed to *ignore* them! As messages sent from these ranges won't be routed on the public Internet, they are logically called the *nonroutable* ranges.

This means that literally millions of networks in the (for example) 192.168.1.0–192.168.1.255 range could exist, all at the same time, because they cannot communicate with the public Internet, and therefore can't cause any trouble. And that offers a kind of side benefit to companies choosing to use the nonroutable addresses: security. Clearly if my system has address 10.10.10.10, then I'm somewhat protected from certain sorts of network attack, because if the bad guys can't connect to me, then they can't cause trouble, right?

Because of this, most companies use at least two sets of IP addresses: Addresses used in their company's *internal* Internet (or "intranet," as we say nowadays) and a range of "official" Internet addresses obtained from an ISP or directly from a part of the ICANN.

THE OTHER NONROUTABLE ADDRESS: APIPA

Recall that there's *another* range of nonroutable addresses: the APIPA range. They're different from the RFC 1918 addresses, however, inasmuch as they are stuck in their subnets — none of the clever routing tricks that you're about to read about, like Network Address Translation, will route packets from a 169.254.x.y address.

ROUTING THE NONROUTABLE, PART 1: NETWORK ADDRESS TRANSLATION

Now, from what I've said so far, it sounds like the folks whose machines have nonroutable addresses are sort of left out in the cold; they can route *inside* their company's network, but they're shut out of access to the public, *routable* Internet. But not any more. In fact, a little technological trick has made it possible for companies to offer public Internet access to their nonroutable addresses. You see, there is a class of routers called network address translation (NAT) routers that can perform a small bit of magic and let you use private, non-ICANN–assigned IP addresses on your company's intranet and still be able to communicate with the Internet.

So, for example, suppose your firm had obtained a class C address range from the ICANN or an ISP: 256 addresses. Although you have thousands of computers, the fact that there are only 256 addresses is no problem as the NAT router can handle communications with the Internet. NAT is kind of interesting in that it lets machines with nonroutable addresses *initiate* conversations with machines on the routable public Internet, but doesn't allow machines out on the Internet to initiate conversations in the other direction. For example, if I were sitting at a machine with IP address 192.168.1.17 behind a NAT router and tried to surf www.microsoft.com, then I'd get in, no problem. But if someone in the public Internet tried to connect to my system at 192.168.1.17, they'd be rebuffed, because *their* local router would know better than to pass a request to a nonroutable address.

You'll see a bit more about NAT (and an important partner, PAT, *port* address translation) later in the chapter. And in case you wondered, NAT and PAT have a *down*side: under the wrong circumstances, NAT and PAT *can* let the bad guys in.

You Can't Use *All* of the Numbers

There are some special rules to IP addresses, however. There's a whole bunch of numbers that you can never give to any machine. They're the default route address, the loopback address, the network number, the broadcast address, and the default router address.

THE DEFAULT ROUTE ADDRESS

As you'll see later, the address 0.0.0.0 is another way of saying "the entire Internet." But as $0.x.y.z$ is in the class A range of addresses, all of $0.x.y.z$ must be set aside — all 16 million addresses.

THE LOOPBACK ADDRESS

The address 127.0.0.1 is reserved as a loopback. If you send a message to 127.0.0.1, then it should be returned to you unless there's something wrong on the IP software itself; messages to the loopback don't go out on the network, but instead stay within a particular machine's IP software. And so no network has an address 127.xxxxxxxx.xxxxxxxx.xxxxxxxx, an unfortunate waste of 16 million addresses.

THE NETWORK NUMBER

Sometimes you need to refer to an entire subnet with a single number. Thus far, I've said things like "My C network is $199.34.57.z$, and I can make z range from 0 to 255." I was being a bit lazy; I didn't want to write "199.34.57.0 through 199.34.57.255," so I said "$199.34.57.z$."

It's not proper IP-ese to refer to a range of network addresses that way. And it's necessary to have an official way to refer to a range of addresses.

For example, to tell a router, "To get this message to the subnet that ranges from 100.100 .100.0 through 100.100.100.255, first route to the router at 99.98.97.103," you've got to have some way to designate the range of addresses 100.100.100.0–100.100.100.255. We could have just used two addresses with a dash between them, but that's a bit cumbersome. Instead, the address that ends in all binary 0s is reserved as the *network number*, the TCP/IP name for the range of addresses in a subnet. In my $100.100.100.z$ example, the shorthand way to refer to 100.100.100.0 through 100.100.100.255 is 100.100.100.0.

Notice that this means you would never use the address 100.100.100.0 — you never give that IP address to a machine under TCP/IP.

For example, to tell that router, "To get this message to the subnet that ranges from 100.100 .100.0 through 100.100.100.255, first route to the router at 99.98.97.103," you would type something like **route add 100.100.100.0 99.98.97.103**. (Actually, you'd type a bit more information, and I'll get to that in the upcoming section on using your machine as a router, but this example gives you the idea.)

IP BROADCAST ADDRESS

There's another reserved address, as well — the TCP/IP broadcast address. It looks like the address of one machine, but it isn't; it's the address you'd use to broadcast to each machine on a subnet. That address is all binary 1s.

For example, on a simple class C subnet, the broadcast address would be $w.x.y.255$. When would you need to know this? Some IP software needs this when you configure it; most routers require the broadcast address (as well as the network number). So if I just use my class C network 199.34.57.0 (see how convenient that .0 thing is?) as a single subnet, then the broadcast address for my network would be 199.34.57.255.

DEFAULT ROUTER ADDRESS

Every subnet has at least one router; after all, if it didn't have a router, then the subnet couldn't talk to any other networks, and it wouldn't be an intranet.

By convention, the first address after the network number is the default gateway (router) address. For example, on a simple class C network, the address of the router should be $w.x.y.1$. This is not, by the way, a hard-and-fast rule like the network number and the IP broadcast address — it is, instead, a convention.

Suppose you have just been made the proud owner of a class C net, 222.210.34.0. You can put 253 computers on your network, because you must not use 222.210.34.0, which describes the entire network; 222.210.34.255, which will be your broadcast address; and 222.210.34.1, which will be used either by you or your Internet service provider for a router address between your network and the rest of the Internet.

Subnet Masks

If you had a trivially small intranet, one with just one segment where everyone can just "shout" to one another, then no routing is required. But that wouldn't be the case for most — routing is a great way to isolate parts of your network and is absolutely essential whenever connecting a wide area network to a local area network. Or you might simply have too large a number of IP addresses to fit on one segment even if you wanted to. Consider IBM's situation, with a class A network that can theoretically support 16 million hosts. Managing *that* network cries out for routers. For this reason, it may be necessary for your IP software on your PC to route data over a router even if it's staying within your company. Let's ask again, and in more detail this time, "How does a machine know whether to route or not?"

That's where subnets are important. Subnets make it possible, as you've seen, for a host (that is, a PC with an IP address) to determine whether it can just lob a message straight over to another host on the same Ethernet segment or a given WAP, or if it must go through routers. You can tell a host's IP software how to distinguish whether or not another host is in the same subnet through the *subnet mask*.

Recall that all of the IP addresses in Rome looked like 199.34.57.z, where z was a number between 1 and 255. You could then say that all co-members of the Rome subnet are defined as the hosts whose first three quads match. Now, on some subnets, it might be possible that the only requirement for membership in the same subnet would be that the first *two* quads be the same — a company that decided for some reason to make its entire class B network a single subnet would be one example of that. (Yes, they *do* exist: I've seen firms that make a single subnet out of a class B network, with the help of some bizarre smart bridges. Imagine it — 65,534 machines all able to broadcast to one another; yikes. And no, I don't recommend it because such large networks can experience performance problems due to increased collisions and are hard to troubleshoot due to the sheer number of computers to consider.)

When a computer is trying to figure out whether the IP address that it owns is on the same subnet as the place that it's trying to communicate with, then a subnet mask answers the question, "Which bits must match for us to be on the same subnet?"

IP does that with a *mask*, a combination of 1s and 0s like so:

```
11111111 11111111 11111111 00000000
```

Here's how a host would use this mask. The host with IP address 199.34.57.10 (station A in Figure 10.5) wants to know if it is on the same subnet as the host with IP address 199.34.57.20 (station B in Figure 10.5). 199.34.57.10, expressed in binary, is 11000111 00100010 00111001 00001010. The IP address for B is, in binary, 11000111 00100010 00111001 00010100. The IP software in A then compares its own IP address to B's IP address. Look at them right next to each other:

```
11000111 00100010 00111001 00001010 A's address
11000111 00100010 00111001 00010100 B's address
```

The leftmost 27 bits match, as does the rightmost bit. Does that mean they're in the same subnet? Again, for the two addresses to be in the same subnet, certain bits must match — the ones with 1s in the subnet mask. Let's stack up the subnet mask, A's address, and B's address to make this clearer:

```
11111111 11111111 11111111 00000000 the subnet mask
11000111 00100010 00111001 00001010 A's address
11000111 00100010 00111001 00010100 B's address
```

Look down from each of the 1s on the subnet mask, and you see that A and B match at each of those positions. Under the 0s in the subnet mask, A and B match up sometimes but not all the time. In fact, it doesn't matter whether or not A and B match in the positions under the 0s in the subnet mask — the fact that there are 0s there means that whether they match is irrelevant.

Another way to think of the subnet mask is this. The ICANN and friends give you a range of addresses, and you allocate them as you see fit. Of the 32 bits in your IP addresses, some are under your control and some are under the ICANN & Co.'s control. In general, however, the bits that the ICANN controls are to the left, and the ones that *you* control are to the right. For example, the ICANN controls the leftmost 8 bits for a class A network, the 16 leftmost bits for a class B network, and the leftmost 24 bits for a class C network.

How do you know what value to use for a subnet mask? Well, if you have a class C number and all of your workstations are on a single subnet, then you have a case like the one we just saw: A subnet mask of 11111111 11111111 11111111 00000000, which, in dotted-quad terminology, is 255.255.255.0. Remember that, by definition, the fact that I have a C network means that the ICANN has "nailed down" the leftmost or top three quads (24 bits), leaving me only the rightmost quad (8 bits). Since all of my addresses must match in the leftmost 24 bits and I can do anything I like with the bottom 8 bits, my subnet mask must be 111111111 1111111 11111111 00000000, or 255.255.255.0. Again, with subnet masks, the 1s are always on the left and the 0s on the right — you'll never see a subnet mask like "11111111 11110000 00001111 11111000" or "00000000 11111111 11111111 11111111."

Getting back to my C network, however, that 11111111 11111111 11111111 00000000 mask assumes that I'll use my entire C network as one big subnet. Instead, I might decide to break one class C network into two subnets. I could decide that all the numbers from 1 to 127 — 00000001 to 01111111 — are subnet 1 and the numbers from 128 to 255 — 10000000 to 11111111 — are subnet 2. In that case, the values inside my subnets will only vary in the last 7 bits rather than (as in the previous example) varying in the last *8* bits. The subnet mask would be, then, 11111111 11111111 11111111 10000000, or 255.255.255.128.

The first subnet is a range of addresses from *w.x.y*.0 through *w.x.y*.127, where *w.x.y* are the quads that the InterNIC assigned me. The second subnet is the range from *w.x.y*.128 through *w.x.y*.255.

Now let's find the network number, default router address, and broadcast address. The network number is the first number in each range, so the first subnet's network number is *w.x.y*.0 and the second's is *w.x.y*.128. The default router address is just the second address in the range, which is *w.x.y*.1 and *w.x.y*.129 for the two subnets. The broadcast address is then the *last* address in both cases, *w.x.y*.127 and *w.x.y*.255 respectively.

Exercise: Using IPConfig to View Network Information

We've been talking about networks for a while now, but you haven't actually seen any of this technology in action. You should perform the exercise in this section using the WinServer machine you set up in earlier chapters of the book. The following steps show how you can use a special command line utility called Internet Protocol Configuration (IPConfig).

1. Open an administrative command prompt.

2. Type **IPConfig /All** and press Enter. Depending on your system, you'll see a number of entries. Let's start with the Windows IP Configuration entry. These entries affect the machine as a whole. You only need to worry about three of the entries at this point.

   a. The Host Name entry tells you the name of the computer that you're working with.
   b. The Primary DNS Suffix tells you the DNS suffix, such as microsoft.com, used for a domain. Don't worry about this entry for right now, I discuss it later in the book.
   c. The Node Type entry tells you how the network is configured to send information to other nodes. The four possible values are: broadcast (no WINS support), peer (only WINS support), mixed (broadcast first, and then use WINS), or hybrid (use WINS first, and then broadcast). There is also a fifth value, unknown, that signifies an error condition. The Knowledge Base article at http://support.microsoft.com/kb/310570 tells how to fix this particular problem.

3. Now look at the Ethernet adapter Local Area Connection entry. Instead of looking at the machine as a whole, you're now looking at the settings for a particular adapter on your machine.

   a. The Connection-specific DNS Suffix entry is a domain, such as microsoft.com, for this particular adapter. As with the Primary DNS Suffix entry, I'll discuss this entry in detail later in the book. For now, all you need to know is that it's normally blank in a work-group scenario.
   b. The Description entry provides a human readable description of the adapter. This description information can be very helpful when working with technologies such as Internet Connection Sharing (ICS). For now, it simply confirms what you already know about the adapter.
   c. The Physical Address entry tells you the Media Access Control (MAC) address for the adapter. Remember that that MAC address is unique for each adapter. A special chip on the adapter provides the MAC address.
   d. The DHCP Enabled and Autoconfiguration Enabled entries determine ways that your adapter can get an IP address. The Dynamic Host Configuration Protocol (DHCP) requires that you install a DHCP server somewhere on your network to issue addresses to any adapter that requests one. Autoconfiguration provides an address for your adapter based on the Automatic Private Internet Protocol Addressing (APIPA), which is a form of automatic addressing discussed in the "Step One: Connect the Internal Network — and Meet Automatic Private Internet Protocol Addressing (APIPA)" section of the chapter.
   e. The IPv4 Address and Subnet Mask entries provide the information you've seen in the "Subnet Masks" section of the chapter. You can use this information to determine whether your adapter is on a class A, B, or C network, the subnet number of the network, and the computer's actual number on that subnet.
   f. The DNS Servers contains one or more IP addresses for the servers that provide name translation for this adapter. Remember that name translation takes a human readable computer name and turns it into an IP address, and vice versa.
   g. The NetBIOS over Tcpip entry tells you whether your adapter will route NetBIOS requests to other subnets using TCP/IP.

4. If your system contains another adapter, use the information you just learned to decipher the IPConfig output for that adapter. You'll see IPConfig used in a number of other situations in this book and in the other volumes of this series because it's extremely useful.

Classless Inter-Domain Routing (CIDR)

Now that we've gotten past some of the fine points of subnet masks, let me elaborate on what you see if you ever go to the ICANN or an ISP looking for a domain of your own.

The shortage of IP addresses has led the ICANN to curtail giving out class A, B, or C addresses. Many small companies need an Internet domain, but giving them a C network is overkill, because a C network contains 256 addresses and many small firms only have a dozen or so computers that they want on the Internet. Large companies may also want a similarly small presence on the Internet: For reasons of security, they may not want to put all of the PCs (or other computers) on the Internet but rather on an internal network not attached to the Internet. These companies *do* need a presence on the Internet, however — for their e-mail servers, FTP servers, Web servers, and the like — so they need a dozen or so addresses. But, again, giving them an entire 256-address C network is awfully wasteful. However, until 1994, it was the smallest block that an ISP could hand out.

Similarly, some companies need a few hundred addresses — more than 256, but not very many more. Such a firm is too big for a C network but a bit small for the 65,536 addresses of a B network. More flexibility here would be useful.

For that reason, the ICANN now gives out addresses without the old A, B, or C class restrictions. This newer method that the ICANN uses is called Classless Inter-Domain Routing, or CIDR, pronounced "cider." CIDR networks are described as "slash x" networks, where the x is a number representing the number of bits in the IP address range that ICANN controls.

If you had a class A network, then the ICANN controlled the top 8 bits and you controlled the bottom 24. If you decided somehow to take your class A network and make it one big subnet, then what would be your subnet mask? Since all of your A network would be one subnet, you'd only have to look at the top quad to see if the source and destination addresses were on the same subnet. For example, if you had network 4.0.0.0, then addresses 4.55.22.81 and 4.99.63.88 would be on the same subnet. (Please note that I can't actually imagine anyone doing this with a class A net; I'm just trying to make CIDR clearer.) Your subnet mask would be, then, 11111111 00000000 00000000 00000000, or 255.0.0.0. Reading from the left, you have eight 1s in the subnet mask before the 0s start. In CIDR terminology, you wouldn't have a class A network; rather, you would have a *slash 8* network. It would be written "4.0.0.0/8" instead of "4.0.0.0 subnet mask 255.0.0.0."

With a class B, the ICANN controlled the top 16 bits, and you controlled the bottom 16. If you decided to take that class B network and make it a one-subnet network, then your subnet mask would be 11111111 11111111 00000000 00000000, or 255.255.0.0. Reading from the left, the subnet mask would have 16 1s. In CIDR terms, a B network is a *slash 16* network. So if your firm had a B network like 164.109.0.0 subnet mask 255.255.0.0, in slash format that would be 164.109.0.0/16.

With a C class, the ICANN controlled the top 24 bits, and you controlled the bottom 8. By now, you've seen that the subnet mask for a C network if you treated it as one subnet is 11111111 11111111 11111111 00000000. Reading from the left, the subnet mask would have 24 1s. In CIDR terms, a C network is a *slash 24* network. Thus, one of my C networks (206.246.253.0, mask 255.255.255.0) can be written "206.246.253/24." Grasping this /24 nomenclature is important because you'll see it on some routers. My Ascend router never asks for subnet masks — just slashes.

Where the new flexibility of CIDR comes in is that the ICANN can in theory now not only define the A-, B-, and C-type networks, it can offer networks with subnet masks in between the A, B, and C networks. For example, suppose I wanted a network for 50 PCs. Before, ICANN would have to give me a C network, with 256 addresses. But now they can offer me a network with subnet mask 11111111 11111111 11111111 11000000 (255.255.255.192), giving me only 6 bits to play with. Two to the sixth power is 64, so I'd have 64 addresses to do with as I liked. This would be a *slash 26* (/26) network.

In summary, Table 10.1 shows how large each possible network type would be.

TABLE 10.1:   CIDR Network Types

ICANN NETWORK TYPE	"SUBNET MASK" FOR ENTIRE NETWORK	APPROXIMATE NUMBER OF IP ADDRESSES
slash 0	0.0.0.0	4 billion
slash 1	128.0.0.0	2 billion
slash 2	192.0.0.0	1 billion
slash 3	224.0.0.0	500 million
slash 4	240.0.0.0	250 million
slash 5	248.0.0.0	128 million
slash 6	252.0.0.0	64 million
slash 7	254.0.0.0	32 million
slash 8	255.0.0.0	16 million
slash 9	255.128.0.0	8 million
slash 10	255.192.0.0	4 million
slash 11	255.224.0.0	2 million
slash 12	255.240.0.0	1 million
slash 13	255.248.0.0	524,288
slash 14	255.252.0.0	262,144
slash 15	255.254.0.0	131,072
slash 16	255.255.0.0	65,536
slash 17	255.255.128.0	32,768
slash 18	255.255.192.0	16,384

TABLE 10.1:   CIDR Network Types *(CONTINUED)*

ICANN NETWORK TYPE	"SUBNET MASK" FOR ENTIRE NETWORK	APPROXIMATE NUMBER OF IP ADDRESSES
slash 19	255.255.224.0	8192
slash 20	255.255.240.0	4096
slash 21	255.255.248.0	2048
slash 22	255.255.252.0	1024
slash 23	255.255.254.0	512
slash 24	255.255.255.0	256
slash 25	255.255.255.128	128
slash 26	255.255.255.192	64
slash 27	255.255.255.224	32
slash 28	255.255.255.240	16
slash 29	255.255.255.248	8
slash 30	255.255.255.252	4
slash 31	255.255.255.254	2
slash 32	255.255.255.255	1

I hope it's obvious that I included all of those networks just for the sake of completeness, because some of them simply aren't available, like the slash 0, and some just don't make sense, like the slash 31 — it only gives you two addresses, which would be immediately required for network number and broadcast address, leaving none behind for you to actually use. The smallest network that the American subgroup of the ICANN, ARIN, will allocate to a network is a slash 20, a 4,094-address network.

CIDR is a fact of life if you're trying to get a network nowadays. With the information in this section, you'll more easily be able to understand what an ISP is talking about when it says it can get you a slash 26 network.

What IP *Doesn't* Do: Error Checking

Whether you're on *an* intranet or *the* Internet, it looks like your data gets bounced around quite a bit. How can you prevent it from becoming damaged? Let's look briefly at that, and that'll segue to a short talk on TCP.

An IP packet contains a bit of data called a *checksum header*, which checks whether the header information was damaged on the way from sender to receiver.

Many data communications protocols use checksums that operate like this: I send you some data. You use the checksum to make sure the data wasn't damaged in transit, perhaps by line noise. Once you're satisfied that the data was not damaged, you send me a message that says, "Okay — I got it." If the checksum indicates that it did *not* get to you undamaged, then you send me a message that says, "That data was damaged — please resend it," and I resend it. Such messages are called ACKs and NAKs — positive or negative acknowledgments of data. Protocols that use this check-and-acknowledge approach are said to provide *reliable* service.

But IP does not provide reliable service. If an IP receiver gets a damaged packet, it just discards the packet and says nothing to the receiver. Surprised? I won't keep you in suspense: It's TCP that provides the reliability. The IP header checksum is used to see if a header is valid; if it isn't, then the datagram is discarded.

This underscores IP's job. IP is not built to provide end-to-end guaranteed transmission of data. IP exists mainly for one reason: routing. We'll revisit routing a bit later, when I describe the specifics of how to accomplish IP routing on a Microsoft OS-based machine.

But whose job *is* end-to-end integrity, if not IP's? The answer: its buddy's, TCP.

Transmission Control Protocol (TCP)

I said earlier that IP handled routing and really didn't concern itself that much with whether the message got to its final destination or not. If there are seven IP hops (seven places where the message is retransmitted by a router) from one point to the next, then each hop is an independent action — there's no coordination, no notion of whether a particular hop is hop number three out of seven. Each IP hop is totally unaware of the others. How, then, could we use IP to provide reliable service?

IP packets are like messages in a bottle. Drop the bottle in the ocean, and you have no guarantee that the message got to whomever you want to receive it. But suppose you hired a "message-in-the-bottle end-to-end manager." Such a person (let's call her Gloria) would take your message, put it in a bottle, and toss it in the ocean. That person would also have a partner on the other side of the ocean (let's call him Gaston), and when Gaston received a message in a bottle from Gloria, Gaston would then pen a short message saying "Gloria, I got your message," put *that* message in a bottle, and drop that bottle into the ocean.

If Gloria didn't get an acknowledgment from Gaston within, say, three months, then she'd drop *another* bottle into the ocean with the original message in it. In data communications terms, we'd say that Gloria "timed out" on the transmission path and was *resending*.

Yeah, I know, this is a somewhat goofy analogy, but understand the main point: We hired Gloria and Gaston to ensure that our inherently unreliable message-in-a-bottle network became reliable. Gloria will keep sending and resending until she gets a response from Gaston. Notice that she doesn't create a whole new transmission medium, like radio or telephone; she merely adds a layer of her own watchfulness to the existing transmission protocol.

Now think of IP as the message in the bottle. TCP, the Transmission Control Protocol, is just the Gloria/Gaston team. TCP provides reliable end-to-end service.

By the way, TCP provides some other services, most noticeably something called *sockets*, which I will discuss in a moment. As TCP has value besides its reliability feature, TCP also has a "cousin" protocol that acts very much like it but does *not* guarantee end-to-end integrity. That protocol is called UDP (User Datagram Protocol).

That's basically the idea behind TCP. Its main job is the orderly transmission of data from one intranet host to another. Its main features include

◆ Handshake

◆ Packet sequencing

◆ Flow control

◆ Error handling

Where IP has no manners — it just shoves data at a computer whether that computer is ready for it or not — TCP makes sure that each side is properly introduced before attempting to transfer. TCP sets up the connection.

Sequencing

As IP does not use a virtual circuit, different data packets may end up arriving at different times and, in fact, in a different order. Imagine a simple intranet transferring four segments of data across a network with multiple possible pathways. The first segment takes the high road, so to speak, and is delayed. The second, third, and fourth do not and so get to the destination more quickly. TCP's job on the receiving side is to then reassemble things in order.

Flow Control

Along with sequencing is flow control. What if 50 segments of data had been sent and they all arrived out of order? The receiver would have to hold them all in memory before sorting them out and writing them to disk. Part of what TCP worries about is *pacing* the data — not sending it to the receiver until the receiver is ready for it.

Error Detection/Correction

And finally, TCP handles error detection and correction, as I've already said. Beyond that, TCP is very efficient in the way that it does error handling. Some protocols acknowledge each and every block, generating a large overhead of blocks. TCP, in contrast, does not do that. It tells the other side, "I am capable of accepting and buffering some number of blocks. Don't expect an acknowledgment until I've gotten that number of blocks. And if a block is received incorrectly, I will not acknowledge it, so if I don't acknowledge as quickly as you expect me to, then just go ahead and resend the block."

Sockets, Ports, and the Winsock Interface

Just about anything that you want to do with the Internet or your company's intranet involves two programs talking to each other. When you browse someone's Web site, you have a program (your Web browser, a *client* program) communicating with their Web server (obviously, a *server* program). Using the File Transfer Protocol (FTP), which I'll discuss later in this chapter, requires that one machine be running a program called an *FTP server* and that another computer be running an *FTP client*. Internet mail requires that a mail client program talk to a mail server program — and those are just a few examples.

Connecting a program in one machine to another program in another machine is kind of like placing a telephone call. The sender must know the phone number of the receiver, and the receiver must be around his or her phone, waiting to pick it up. In the TCP world, a phone number is called a *socket*. A socket is composed of three parts: the IP address of the receiver, which we've already discussed, the receiving program's *port number*, which we *haven't* yet discussed, and whether it's a TCP port or a UDP port — each protocol has its own set.

Suppose the PC on your desk running XP wants to get a file from the FTP site, which is really the PC on *my* desk running Windows Server 2008. Obviously, for this to happen, we have to know each other's IP addresses. But that's not all; after all, in my PC I have a whole bunch of programs running (my network connection, my word processor, my operating system, my personal organizer, the FTP server, and so on). So if TCP says, "Hey, Mark's machine, I want to talk to you," then my machine would reply, "Which *one* of us — the word processor, the e-mail program, or what?" So the TCP/IP world assigns a 16-bit number to each program that wants to send or receive TCP information, a number called the *port* of that program.

I said before that creating a socket connection is like placing a phone call, so let's extend this and perhaps make it clearer. Many buildings have just one incoming phone number, but many people in the building. Once you've gotten the operator for the building, how do you tell him who you want to speak of the many people? You give the operator that person's *extension*. Again, no server on the planet runs just one service; now think of each service that a server offers as being a separate office in a building. The server's "phone number" is its IP address; the "extension" for a particular "office" (service) is that office's TCP port number. Combining a machine's IP address with a service's port number results in a *socket address*.

The most popular Internet applications have had particular port numbers assigned to them, and those port numbers are known as *well-known ports*. You can see some well-known ports in Table 10.2.

TABLE 10.2:   Internet Protocols and Port Numbers

INTERNET PROTOCOL	PORT NUMBER
FTP	TCP 20/21
Telnet	TCP 23
Simple Mail Transport Protocol	TCP 25
DNS	UDP and TCP 53
Trivial FTP (TFTP)	UDP 69
Hypertext Transfer Protocol (Web)	TCP 80
Kerberos logons	UDP and TCP 88
Post Office Protocol v3 (POP3)	TCP 110
Network News Transfer Protocol (NNTP)	TCP 119
Simple Network Time Protocol (SNTP)	UDP 123

TABLE 10.2: Internet Protocols and Port Numbers *(CONTINUED)*

INTERNET PROTOCOL	PORT NUMBER
NetBIOS	UDP and TCP 137, UDP 138, TCP 139
IMAP4	TCP 143
SNMP	UDP 161/162
LDAP	TCP 389
Secure HTTP (SSL)	TCP and UDP 443
SMB over sockets (CIFS)	TCP/UDP 445
ISAKMP (key exchange for IPSec)	UDP 500
SQL Server	UDP/TCP 1433

Specific programs may use their own particular ports, as in the case of Active Directory's global catalog server, which uses port 3268. If you want to see a complete list of well-known ports, check out the list at http://www.iana.org/assignments/port-numbers. You can find an easier to read list at http://www.networksorcery.com/enp/protocol/ip/ports00000.htm.

How Ports and Sockets Work: An Example

So, for instance, suppose I've pointed my HTTP client (which you know as a Web browser, like Internet Explorer) to an HTTP server (which you know as a Web server, like a copy of Internet Information Server). Let's also assume that I'm going to visit www.bigfirm.com, that bigfirm.com's Web server is at 123.124.55.67, and that my computer has IP address 200.200.200.10.

My Web browser tries to contact the machine at 123.124.55.67. But just knowing a machine's IP address isn't sufficient; we need also to know the port address of the program that we want to talk to because, for example, this computer might also be a mail server, and I want to surf its Web pages, not send or receive e-mail. My Web browser knows that by convention the Web server lives at port 80. So my Web browser sets up a TCP/IP session with port 80 at address 123.124.55.67, commonly written 123.124.55.67:80, with a colon between the IP address and the port number. That combination of an IP address and a port is, again, called a *socket address*.

In order for the Web server computer to chat with my computer, the Web server computer must be *ready* to chat — there's got to be someone at the Web browser "listening" when I "call." That's a lot of what a Web browser program does — it just sits and waits, "listening" on port 80. When the Web browser first starts up, it says, "If anyone calls on port 80, wake me up — I'm willing to take calls on that port." That's called a *passive open* on TCP.

So my Web browser talks to the Web server at the Web server's port 80. But how does the Web server talk back — what port does it use on *my* computer, what port on my computer is now listening for the server's response? Well, port 80 might seem the logical answer, at first — but it can't be. Here's why: suppose I'm sitting at a computer that's *running* a Web server and I fire up Internet Explorer to surf a different Web site. Could that Web site talk back to my computer at port 80? No, because port 80 on my computer is *already* busy, because *my* Web server would be running there.

Instead, the Web server negotiates with my Web browser to pick a port that my system's not using. So the conversation might look like

1. *From my computer to the Web server*: "Hi there, anyone home at port 80 on 123.124.55.67?"

2. *From the Web server to my computer*: "Sure; how should we talk?"

3. *From my computer to the Web server*: "Ummm, how about port 40000?"

4. *From the Web server to my computer*: "Great, then, let's set up a connection to 40000."

So my questions to the Web server go to 123.124.55.67:80, and the answers come back on 200.200.200.10:40000. (And yes, I've left a few steps out, like "how did the Web server ask which port to use in the first place," but I'm trying not to turn this into a whole *book* on TCP/IP!) Here's the point that I want to make: Communications to a server employ a well-known port, like 80 on HTTP. In contrast, however, communications back to a client don't use any particular predefined port — the server and client just agree on one on-the-fly.

> **NOTE**
>
> And in case you're wondering, servers can carry on more than one conversation over a given port. If 500 people are all surfing a Web server, then the Web server can keep those conversations separate. To see the ports that your computer has passively open, open up a command prompt and type `netstat -an -p tcp`. All of the entries with the word "LISTENING" next to them are ports your system is listening on. Notice that your system listens on ports even if it's a workstation — every server sometimes acts as a client, and every workstation sometime acts as a server!

Routing the Nonroutable, Part II: PAT and NAT

Now that you know about ports, I can tell you how a bit of magic that you'll see a little later works. Windows Server 2008 includes a couple of tools called Internet Connection Sharing (ICS) and port address translation (PAT) that let you share a single routable IP address with any number of computers, even though those computers all bear *non*routable addresses. Let's look at how the simpler one, ICS, works.

WHAT'S INTERNET CONNECTION SHARING?

Suppose you have a bunch of computers in your home, all connected via an Ethernet network. Suppose also that you've got a high-speed Internet connection like a DSL or a cable modem connection. Those kinds of connections usually come with one — and one only — routable IP address, which you give to one of your computers.

But what about the other ones? How can you get all of your XP, Vista, Windows Server 2008 boxes, Macintoshes, and whatever else you've got in the house *all* on the Internet at the same time? After all, only one computer can use a given IP address, so trying to put that one routable IP address on every computer in the house not only won't help, it'll hurt — the Internet connection will work fine as long as only one computer's using the DSL or cable modem vendor-supplied address, but put it on a second system and *neither* system will be able to get to the Internet. Instead, here's how to put everyone in the house on the Internet. (This is a 10,000 foot view of how to do it — I don't intend in this explanation to show you how to set up ICS, but we will by the end of the chapter, I promise.)

First, connect all of the computers to your home Ethernet. Do not give those computers an IP address; instead, tell their TCP/IP software to obtain IP addresses via DHCP (I'll show you how soon — remember, 10,000 foot view right now.) Then, get a computer with *two* network interface cards on it and put Server 2008 on it. After that, connect the 2008 Server system to your DSL or cable modem connection. (Both provide their service ultimately as an Ethernet connection.) Fire up your Server 2008 system and check that you can, indeed, surf the Web. Nothing *else* on your home network can yet, and, remember, the 2008 system's only connected to the ISP, not your home network.

Now connect the unused NIC on your 2008 system so that now one of its NICs is connected directly to the Internet via your ISP, and the other NIC is connected to your home network — your "intranet." Start up the Internet Connection Sharing (ICS) service. Part of ICS's job is to act as a DHCP server, so reboot all of your computers on your home network except the 2008 box, and you'll find that all of those computers will be able to access the Internet ... and they'll each have one of those RFC 1918 nonroutable addresses.

Again, apologies for having to tease you with a sketchy plan on how to do this, but we'll actually go through the steps now — all I need you to do now is just get the overview.

How ICS Shares a Routable Address with Nonroutable Machines

What happened? Well, first of all, the routing computer — the one running ICS — distributes unique IP addresses to all of your other computers. But *what* IP addresses? Well, it's not kosher to start making up routable IP addresses and handing them out unless you actually *own* those addresses, so the routing computer hands out "safe" IP addresses from one of the nonroutable ranges specified in RFC 1918, the range from 192.168.0.2 through 192.168.0.254, and gives itself an extra IP address, 192.168.0.1. So far, so good — the computers in your home network can all "see" each other, even the routing computer.

Here's where the magic happens. Suppose one of your nonroutable computers (let's give it address 192.168.0.10) wants to surf my Web site at 206.246.253.200. That nonroutable computer says to the routing computer, the only one with a routable, acceptable-on-the-Internet address, "Please connect me to the Web server at 206.246.253.200." Now, clearly, the 192.168.0.10 system can't directly talk to my Web server, because 192.168.0.10 is a nonroutable address and no router will pass any 192.168.*y.z* traffic over the Internet. But the routable computer can employ its 200.200.200.10 address to establish that connection to the Web server at 206.246.253.200. The routable computer at 200.200.200.10 acts as a kind of "relay" to forward the nonroutable computer's request to my Web server, passing messages back and forth. My Web server hasn't a clue that the *real* client is sitting on a nonroutable address; as far as my Web server's concerned, it's talking to 200.200.200.10.

But the 200.200.200.10 computer running ICS can go further than that, because it can simultaneously relay requests for every single computer in your nonroutable network. So could you have 15 machines in your nonroutable network all talking to my Web site at the same time? Sure. But my Web site would think that the machine at 200.200.200.10 was holding 15 simultaneous conversations with it — peculiar, perhaps, but not unallowable. But what if each of the 15 people sitting at the 15 computers were surfing *different* pages on my Web site — how would the routing computer on your network keep it all straight? With ports. It could be that the session between the first nonroutable computer and my Web site took place on 200.200.200.10:40000, the second on 200.200.200.10:40001, and so on. The routing computer is then using the incoming port number to figure out which of its local, nonroutable computers made a particular request, so that it can *translate* that incoming port into a nonroutable address, so to speak. That's why the process is called *port address translation* or PAT. ICS is a piece of PAT routing software built into Windows Server 2008.

PAT IS ALMOST A FIREWALL, BUT ONLY *ALMOST*

PAT is, then, a pretty neat bit of routing magic. Say your ISP only gives you one routable IP address — here's a way to stretch it across dozens of machines. Even better, PAT offers a simple, basic kind of anti-hacker security. Consider that your nonroutable computers can access e-mail, Web, and other services on the public Internet, but still remain basically invisible in the sense that your internal computers can *initiate* a conversation with a server on the Internet, but no computer on the public Internet can initiate a conversation with one of your nonroutable computers. It's harder, then, for jerks — oops, I mean hackers — to attack your internal machines.

Harder, yes, but not impossible, I should point out. Once one of your internal, nonroutable systems establishes contact with a computer on the public Internet through your PAT routing computer, then there's obviously a channel now open from that computer on the public Internet and your nonroutable computer. While I'm not a security expert by any means, I'm told by people that I trust that this "open port," as they call it, can be a method for "e-bottom feeders" to potentially attack your system. And no matter what sort of security you use, remember that once you've downloaded a program to one of your internal computers and run that program, then the program can have malicious intent. Remember also that many kinds of files can contain programs nowadays: Web pages can contain VBScript macros, Word files can contain programs, and you might end up downloading and installing a kind of program called an ActiveX object simply by viewing a Web page. (That's why I keep my security settings fairly paranoid in Word, Outlook, and Internet Explorer, and I recommend that you do also — look in Tools/Macro/Security in Word and Outlook, or Tools/Internet Options/Security in Internet Explorer.)

And by the way, I've cast my PAT example as a home-based one, but don't think that only homes and small businesses can use it. Most large organizations only assign their routable addresses to a small number of systems, and put nonroutable addresses on the vast majority of their machines. Then they use PAT or PAT-like routers to let their employees access the Internet.

NAT VERSUS PAT

PAT's a nice piece of routing software built into Windows Server 2008 (and in fact every Microsoft OS shipped since 1998), but not the only one. ICS is nice, but it's pretty inflexible. It's supplemented by a more powerful bit of routing software called network address translation (NAT). In fact, it's far more likely that you've heard of NAT than PAT, because many PAT routers are mistakenly called NAT routers. (And understand that while a purist might quibble about whether a router is a PAT or NAT router, the fact is that the definitions have blurred so much in popular usage that in actual fact you'll probably *only* hear the phrase "NAT" rather than "PAT." As you'll see later in this chapter, Windows Server 2008 contains software that will do both NAT and PAT, but it calls the capability "NAT routing." So after this section, I'll surrender and just refer to NAT rather than PAT.)

A simple NAT router lets you connect a particular routable IP address with a particular nonroutable IP address. Thus, for example, if you had a Web server on a machine with the nonroutable address 10.10.10.50, then the outside world couldn't see or access that Web server. But suppose you had a few dozen routable addresses, including (for example) 100.50.40.10? You could put those addresses on a NAT router and tell the NAT router for example, "connect the routable 100.50.40.10 address with the nonroutable 10.10.10.50 address." When someone on the public Internet tried to surf the Web site at 100.50.40.7, then, the NAT router would transparently redirect all of that traffic to the system at the nonroutable address 10.10.10.50.

There's yet another permutation of port address translation that you'll see, built into Windows Server 2008's NAT routing software. In NAT, as you saw, the router completely assigned an entire routable IP address to a machine with a nonroutable IP address. But Windows Server 2008 also lets you assign a particular port on one system to a particular port on another system. So, for example, I could tell a Windows Server 2008 system acting as a router, "Whenever traffic comes in for 100.50.40.7 on port 80, send it to the nonroutable 10.10.10.50 system, on port 5000." (I'm not saying you would *want* to do it, I'm just explaining that it's possible.) So, in that case, you would set up the Web server on the 10.10.10.50 system and reconfigure the Web server so that it didn't use the standard port 80, but rather port 5000.

Winsock Sockets

Before moving on to the issue of Internet names (rather than all this IP address stuff that we've been working with), let me define a term that you'll hear in the Microsoft TCP/IP networking business: *winsock* or "windows sockets." The value of sockets is that they provide a uniform way to write programs that exploit the underlying Internet communications structure. If, for example, I want to write a networked version of the game Battleship, then I might want to be able to quickly turn out versions for Windows, Linux, the Mac, and Unix machines. But maybe I don't know much about communications, and don't *want* to know much. (I'm probably supposed to note here that Battleship is a registered trademark of Milton Bradley or someone like that; consider it done.) I could just sit down with my C compiler and bang out a Battleship that runs on Unix machines. Just a few code changes, and *presto!* I have my PC version.

But the PC market requires some customization, and so a particular version of the sockets interface, called Winsock, was born. It's essentially the sockets interface but modified a bit to work better in a PC environment.

The benefit of Winsock is that all vendors of TCP/IP software support an identical Winsock programming interface (well, identical in theory, anyway). TCP/IP-based programs should run as well atop FTP software's TCP/IP stack as they would atop the TCP/IP stack that ships with Windows XP, Vista, or even ancient versions of Windows such as Windows 98. That's why you can plop your Firefox Web browser on just about any PC with TCP/IP and it should work without any trouble.

NOTE

Windows Server 2008 provides less flexibility when it comes to binding protocols to a particular connection. In most cases, all you can bind or unbind is the File Printer and Sharing for Microsoft Networks service and Client for Microsoft Networks service. You can also choose to bind or unbind the Internet Protocol Version 4 (TCP/IPv4) and Internet Protocol Version 6 (TCP/IPv6) to each service. However, you can't bind or unbind protocols such as NetBIOS. To see the binding for your server, choose Advanced ➤ Advanced Settings in the Network Connections window. Select the Adapters and Bindings tab, and you'll see a list of bindings for each NIC in your system. Clearing a check mark in the list unbinds that service or protocol.

Internet Host Names

Thus far, I've referred to a lot of numbers; hooking up to my Web server, then, seems to require that you point your Web browser to IP address 70.165.73.5, TCP port number 80, which is written "70.165.73.5:80" in socket terminology.

Of course, you don't actually do that. When you send e-mail to your friends, you don't send it to 199.45.23.17; you send it to something like `robbie@somefirm.com`. What's IP got to do with it?

IP addresses are useful because they're precise and because they're easy to subnet. But they're tough to remember, and people generally prefer more English-sounding names. So TCP/IP allows us to group one or more TCP/IP networks into groups called *domains*, groups that will share a common name like microsoft.com, senate.gov, army.mil, or mit.edu.

> **NOTE**
>
> Internet naming, and in particular the Domain Name System (DNS), is a big topic — in fact, it'll fill the entirety of the upcoming Chapter 13; this section is just a brief summary. Stay tuned to Chapter 13 for the truly ugly (but necessary) details.

Machines within a domain will have names that include the domain name; for example, within my mmco.com domain I have machines named earth.mmco.com, narn.mmco.com, minbar.mmco.com, zhahadum.mmco.com, and vorlon.mmco.com. Those specific machine names are called *host names*.

How does TCP/IP connect the English names — the *host* names — to the IP addresses? And how can I sit at my PC in mmco.com and get the information I need to be able to find another host called archie.au when archie is all the way on the other side of the world in Australia?

Simple — with HOSTS, DNS, and (if you have a network that does not yet use Active Directory) Windows Internet Naming Service (WINS), which is covered in the Chapter 12. The process of converting a name to its corresponding IP address is called *name resolution*. Again, how does it work? Read on.

Simple Naming Systems (HOSTS)

When you set up your subnet, you don't want to explicitly use IP addresses every time you want to run some TCP/IP utility and hook up with another computer in your subnet — you'd much prefer to use more human-sounding names. So, instead, you update a file called HOSTS in the \Windows\System32\drivers\etc folder that looks like this:

```
199.34.57.50   keydata.mmco.com
199.34.57.129 serverted.mmco.com
```

This is just a simple ASCII text file and it already includes an entry for localhost. Each host goes on one line, and the line starts off with the host's IP address. Enter at least one space and the host's English name. Do this for each host. You can even give multiple names in the HOSTS file:

```
199.34.57.50   keydata.mmco.com markspc
199.34.57.129 serverted.mmco.com serverpc bigsv
```

You can even add comments, with the octothorp (#):

```
199.34.57.50   keydata.mmco.com markspc #The Big Dog's machine
199.34.57.129 serverted.mmco.com serverpc bigsv
```

Ah, but now comes the really rotten part.

You have to put one of these HOSTS files on *every single workstation*. That means that every single time you change anyone's HOSTS file, you have to go around and change *everybody's* HOSTS file. Every workstation must contain a copy of this file, which is basically a telephone directory of every machine in your subnet. It's a pain, yes, but it's simple. If you're thinking, "Why can't I just put a central HOSTS file on a server and do all my administration with *that* file?" — what you're really asking for is a *name server*, and I'll show you two of them, the Domain Name System (DNS) and the Windows Internet Name Service (WINS), in the upcoming Chapters 12 and 13.

HOSTS is reread every time your system does a name resolution; you needn't reboot to see a change in HOSTS take effect.

Domain Name System (DNS)

HOSTS is a pain, but it's a necessary pain if you want to communicate within your subnet. How does IP find a name outside of your subnet or outside of your domain?

Suppose someone at exxon.com wanted to send a file to a machine at minasi.com. Surely the exxon.com HOSTS files don't contain the IP address of my company, and vice versa?

Well, back when the Internet was small, HOSTS was sufficient — the exxon.com and minasi .com machines *would* have found each other in HOSTS back in 1980. The few dozen people on the early Internet just all used the same small HOSTS file. With the Internet's machine population in the billions, however, that's just not practical; we needed something better.

The Internet community came up with an answer in 1984: Distribute the responsibility for names. That's done by the Domain Name System (DNS). There is a central naming clearinghouse for *the* Internet, the Internet Corporation for Assigned Names and Numbers (ICANN), which you met earlier in this chapter. (Obviously, if you're only running a private intranet that's not connected to the public Internet, then *you* perform the function of name manager.) ICANN is the overall boss of DNS naming, but it delegates particular domains to particular *name registrars*, as for example when it delegates keeping track of all of the .com domains to VeriSign's Network Solutions subsidiary.

Instead of trying to keep track of the name and IP address of every single machine in the Internet, ICANN and its delegated registrars require that every Internet domain have at least two machines (although some now only require one) running that contain a database of that domain's machines. These machines are called *DNS servers*.

ICANN then needs only to know the IP address of the domain's DNS servers, and when a request for a name resolution comes to ICANN's servers, ICANN's servers just refer the questioner to the domain in question's local DNS machines. (We'll see how this works in greater detail in the next chapter.)

Thus, if you wanted to visit my Web site at `www.minasi.com`, you'd start up your Web browser and point it at `www.minasi.com`. Before your browser could show you anything, however, it would need to *find* the machine named `www.minasi.com`. So it would fire off a DNS query, "What's the IP address of `www.minasi.com`?" to its local DNS server. The local DNS server probably wouldn't know, and so it would ask ICANN's DNS servers. ICANN's servers would know that the `minasi.com` has two DNS servers, one at 70.165.73.5 and another at 70.165.73.6. So the ICANN DNS servers would tell your local DNS server that it could find `www.minasi.com`'s IP address by asking the question of the 70.165.73.5 or .6 machine. So your local DNS server would then re-ask the question, "what's the IP address of `www.minasi.com`?" this time of my local DNS server, and would then get the answer "70.165.73.5."

You've no doubt noticed that many Internet domains end with .com, but there are other endings as well. Initially, there were six naming domains: EDU was for educational institutions, NET was for network providers, COM for commercial users, MIL was for military users (remember who built this?), ORG was for organizations, and GOV was for civilian government. For example, there is a domain on the Internet called whitehouse.gov; you can send Internet e-mail to the President that way, at `president@whitehouse.gov`. There are more root domains these days, such as `.int`, `.museum`, `.name`, and a long list of two-letter codes for countries such as `.fi` for sites in Finland, `.uk` for sites in the United Kingdom, and so on.

What kind of computer do you need to run a DNS server? Just about any kind — there's DNS server software for IBM mainframes, DEC VAXes, Unix and Linux, and of course, Windows Server 2008 — in fact, a DNS server module not only ships with Windows Server 2008, you can't even run an Active Directory without a DNS server. You'll see how to set up a DNS server in Chapter 13.

E-Mail Names: A Note

If you've previously messed around with e-mail under TCP/IP, then you may be wondering something about these addresses. After all, you don't send mail to minasi.com, you'd send it to a name like `help@minasi.com`. `help@minasi.com` is an e-mail address. The way it works is this: A group of users in a TCP/IP domain decide to implement mail.

In order to receive mail, a machine must be up and running, ready to accept mail from the outside world (that is, some other subnet or domain). Now, mail can arrive at any time of day, so this machine must be up and running all of the time. That seems to indicate that it would be a dumb idea to get mail delivered straight to your desktop. So, instead, TCP mail dedicates a machine to the mail router task of receiving mail from the outside world, holding that mail until you want to read it, taking mail that you want to send somewhere else, and routing that mail to some other mail router. The name of the most common TCP/IP mail router program is *sendmail*. The name of the protocol used most commonly for routing e-mail on the Internet, by the way, is the Simple Mail Transfer Protocol (SMTP). Once e-mail is sitting on your local mail server, you then retrieve it via any of a number of protocols. One such is called the Post Office Protocol (POP3).

Windows Server 2008 can act as an SMTP server, but it doesn't have anything in-the-box like POP3 that would allow a client to retrieve her mail — Server 2008's sort of like a post office that *receives* mail, but doesn't send out letter carriers to deliver it. (In case you're wondering, you're right — it's a lame thing of Microsoft to do, because they included a POP3 module in Server 2003. I guess they want you to buy their feature-laden but relatively expensive and complex Exchange Server. Bah.) Or you could download any of a number of 2008-compatible e-mail servers, like the one you can find at `www.mailenable.com`. You can see how mail works in Figure 10.7.

FIGURE 10.7
The interrelation of host names, e-mail names, and the Internet

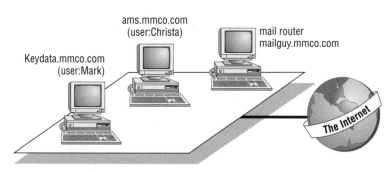

In this small domain, we've got two users: Mark and Christa. Mark works on keydata.mmco .com, and Christa works on ams.mmco.com. Now, suppose Christa wants to send some mail to her friend Corky, executive director for Surfers of America; Corky's address is `corky@surferdudes`

.org. She fires up a program on her workstation, which is called a *mail client*. The mail client allows her to create and send new messages as well as receive incoming messages. She sends the message and closes her mail client. Notice that her mail client software doesn't do routing — it just lets her create, send, and receive messages.

The mail client has been configured to send messages to an SMTP server, which is running in this subnet on mailguy.mmco.com. mailguy is kind of the post office (in Internet lingo, a *mail router*) for this group of users. The SMTP server on mailguy.mmco.com stores the message, and it then sends the message off to the machine with the DNS name surferdudes.org, trusting IP to route the message correctly to surferdudes. Hmmm ... there's no one machine named surferdudes.org; where should the mail go? As you'll learn in the next chapter, a DNS administrator can advertise that e-mail should go to a particular machine. Thus, surferdudes.org might have a machine named po.surferdudes.org; when mailguy.mmco.com tries to send the mail to corky, mailguy first asks DNS, "What machine is supposed to get mail for surferdudes?" and DNS replies, "po.surferdudes.org."

po.surferdudes.org is the server that is the interface to the outside world vis-à-vis mail, and its software knows that it is an e-mail server that handles e-mail for surferdudes.org. In fact, however, SMTP doesn't know *users*: for all it knows, surferdudes.org doesn't even have a user named "corky." DNS also no idea who Mark or Christa is; DNS is concerned with *host* names, not *e-mail* names. It's DNS that worries about how to find mailguy.mmco.com.

> **NOTE**
>
> The fact that neither SMTP nor DNS knows who corky is has a lot to do with why we get so much spam, unfortunately. Spammers find a domain like surferdudes.org and just start sending junk to tom@surferdudes.org, mary@surferdudes.org, administrator@surferdudes.org — they don't care, they just gunk up your server with names that might or might not create a "hit."

A bit later, Corky gets the message and sends a reply to Christa. The reply does *not* go to Christa's machine ams.mmco.com; instead, it goes to mailguy.mmco.com because Corky sent mail to christa@mmco.com. The mail system sends the messages to mmco.com, but what machine has the address mmco.com? Simple: DNS directs it to send mail for mmco.com to mailguy.mmco.com.

Eventually, Christa starts up the mail client program once again. The mail program uses POP3 to send a query to the local mail router mailguy.mmco.com, saying, "Any new mail for Christa?" There *is* mail, and Christa reads it.

Attaching to an Internet

So far, I've talked quite a bit about how an internet works and what kinds of things there are that you can do with an internet. But I haven't told you enough yet to actually get *on* an internet, whether it's your company's private intranet or *the* Internet.

◆ You can connect to a multiuser system and appear to the Internet as a dumb terminal. This doesn't happen much any more, so it's unlikely that you'll do this.

◆ You can connect to an Internet provider via a serial port and a protocol called Point-to-Point Protocol (PPP) and appear to the Internet as a host. This is what you're doing when you dial up with a modem to an Internet service provider (ISP) such as AOL.

◆ You can connect to an Internet provider via either a modified cable television network ("cable modem") or via modified phone lines ("digital subscriber line" or DSL).

◆ You can be part of a local area network that is an Internet subnet and then load TCP/IP software on your system and appear to the Internet as a host. This is probably how most people get on the Internet — either when the computer on your desk connects to the Internet via your company's network, or if you connect at home via a cable modem or DSL.

Each of these options has pros and cons, as you'll see. The general rule is that in order to access the Internet, all you basically have to do is to connect up to a computer that is already on the Internet.

The essence of any internet is in *packet switching*, a kind of network game of hot potato whereby computers act communally to transfer each other's data around. Packet switching is what makes it possible to add subnetworks on-the-fly.

Dumb Terminal Connection

This was once a common way to attach to the Internet. You'd dial up to a multiuser system of some kind — usually a Unix box of some stripe — and do simple terminal emulation. You'd then have a character-based session with typed commands only — no mouse, no graphics. Very macho, but not as much fun as surfing with a graphical Web browser. On the other hand, the distant multiuser machine did all the heavy lifting, computing-wise.

Unfortunately, this terminal access approach was kind of limited. Suppose, for example, that I live in Virginia (which is true) and I connect to the Internet via a host in Maine (which is not true). From the Internet's point of view, I'm not in an office in Virginia; instead, I'm wherever the host that I'm connected to is. I work in Virginia, but if I were dialing a host in Maine, then from the Internet's point of view I'd be in Maine. Any requests that I make for file transfers, for example, wouldn't go to Virginia — they'd go to my host in Maine.

Now, that can be a bit of a hassle. Say I'm at my Virginia location logged on to the Internet via the Maine host. I get onto Microsoft's FTP site — basically FTP is just a means to provide a library of files to the outside world — and I grab a few files, perhaps an updated video driver. The FTP program says, "I got the file," but the file is now on the host in Maine. That means that I'm only half done, because I now have to run some other kind of file transfer program to move the file from the host in Maine to my computer in Virginia.

PPP Serial Connection

If you've got one of those $10/month or $20/month dial-up Internet accounts, then you fit in this category. Instead of connecting to the Internet with an Ethernet card, you connect with a serial port connected to a modem, which in turn is connected to the ISP with phone lines.

To do this you will need software to support a protocol called the Point to Point Protocol or PPP. (Once upon a time PPP had a sibling protocol named the Serial Line Interface Protocol, or SLIP, but I've not seen anyone use it since 1997.) But you needn't look very far for PPP software — it's built into every version of Windows and NT since 1995. When setting up Windows Server 2008 systems to dial up to an ISP, you're using PPP by default.

Nor is PPP only for use in dialing up to ISPs. Windows Server 2008's Routing and Remote Access Server (RRAS) supports PPP, so if you dial into your company's servers, you do that with PPP.

Cable Modem and DSL Connections

Cable modem and DSL are a sort of halfway step between the previous connection type, simple dial-up, and the next type, direct network connection. Where dial-up is pure wide area network (WAN) connection and networks are pure LAN connection, cable modem and DSL are half and half in that they employ devices called "cable modems" and "DSL modems" that communicate on one side to a wide area network — the cable company's television signal network or the phone network in the case of DSL — and on the other side to your local area network.

Cable modems connect to cable networks using the same kind of "F" type connector that you'd use to connect your TV to a cable antenna. Then they connect to your computer or your local area network with an RJ-45 connector using Ethernet signals. To connect just one PC to a cable modem, then, you would put an Ethernet card in the computer and plug a standard Cat5-type patch cable between the cable modem and the Ethernet card. To connect an entire home or small office network, you'd hook the cable modem's RJ-45 port to an Internet sharing device like the roughly $50 devices you can find from DLink, Linksys, and others, or you could put a second NIC in your PC and then use the PC as an Internet sharing device. Many cable modems also offer Universal Serial Bus (USB) connections, although I strongly recommend against using them because of driver problems and speed issues. If you connect to your cable modem using an Ethernet card then the only drivers that your computer needs are the drivers for the Ethernet card, and those are usually pretty reliable. But connecting to the Internet via the USB connector on the cable modem requires a USB driver for the cable modem, and I've seen a number of cases where cable modem drivers were flaky.

DSL "modems" — I hate the term because they are by no means modems, but are instead something called a control service unit/data service unit (CSU/DSU) — typically have a standard familiar telephone-type RJ-13 connector that you use to connect them to a phone line in your house — one that's been specially tuned by the DSL provider — and then an RJ-45 jack that you use to make an Ethernet connection to a computer or a group of computers, in much the same way as you would with a cable modem. Some DSL modems have USB connections as well — my advice about cable modem USB connections also applies here.

LAN Connection

The most common way to connect to an internet is simply by being a LAN workstation on a TCP/IP-using network. Again, this needn't be *the* Internet — almost every LAN in existence today uses the TCP/IP protocol suite. This is the connection that Windows Server 2008 servers will use to provide TCP/IP services.

Terminal Connections versus Other Connections

Before moving on to the next topic, I'd like to return to the difference between a terminal connection and a PPP or LAN connection. In Figure 10.8, you see three PCs on an Ethernet attached to two minicomputers, which in turn serve four dumb terminals.

The minicomputer-to-minicomputer link might be SLIP or PPP, or then again they might be LANed together. Notice that only the *computers* in this scenario have Internet Protocol (IP) addresses. Whenever you send mail to one of the people on the PCs at the top of the picture, it goes to that person's PC. If you were to scrutinize the IP addresses — and most of the time, you will not — you'd see that everyone had the same IP address. In contrast, the people at the *bottom* of the picture get their mail sent to one of the minicomputers, and so in this example, each pair of terminals shares an IP address. If Shelly and George in your office access your company's intranet through terminals connected to the same computer, then a close look at mail from them would show that they have the same IP address. But, if you think about it, you already knew that; if you send mail to george@mailbox.bigfirm.com and to shelly@mailbox.bigfirm.com, then the machine name to which the mail goes is the same; it's just the user names that vary.

FIGURE 10.8
When Internet connections involve IP numbers and when they don't

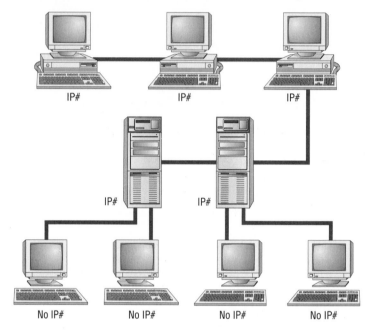

So, in summary: If you want to get onto *the* Internet from a remote location, then your best bet is to sign up with an ISP. To attach to a private intranet, you need to connect to that intranet's LAN either wirelessly or via an Ethernet cable. You then need to talk to your local network guru about getting their network hardware to allow your system to get an IP address so that it can be part of your intranet. You won't see too much SLIP or PPP much more, thank heavens, but it's not impossible!

NOTE

There is one case where Figure 10.8 isn't complete. If one of the terminals pictured is not simply a dumb ASCII terminal attached to a minicomputer but is instead a Windows Terminal — still a dumb terminal, but one built to work specifically with Windows Server 2008 Terminal Services or Citrix Metaframe — then that terminal will have its own IP address.

The Basics of Setting Up TCP/IP on Windows Server 2008 with Static IP Addresses

Enough talking about TCP/IP internetworking; let's do it, and do it with Windows Server 2008. For this first outing, let's return to the two systems WINSERVER and MAIN that we first built in

Chapter 2. If you don't have those running any more, however, it's no problem — you just need:

- Two systems running Windows Server 2008

- Both systems must have different computer names — I'll use WINSERVER and MAIN, but whatever names you like will work fine

- A network connection between the two

I would recommend not connecting their network to the Internet as the configuration that we're going to do won't allow them to properly route to the Internet.

Here's the most basic set of TCP/IP configuration tasks, and the first ones we'll tackle:

1. Set the IP address and subnet, default gateway, and DNS server.

2. Prepare the HOSTS file, if you're going to use one.

3. Test the connection with Ping.

Let's take a look at those steps, one by one.

Configuring TCP/IP with a Static IP Address

First, let's apply an IP address to the network interface card on WINSERVER. Do that by logging onto it as an administrator. Then get to its property page: click Start ➤ Settings ➤ Control Panel ➤ Network and Sharing Center and then, when your mouse is on Network Connections, *right*-click the mouse and choose Open. Windows will display the Network and Sharing Center window, which doesn't provide direct access to the network connections. Click "Manage network connections." You'll see something like Figure 10.9.

FIGURE 10.9
Network and Dial-Up Connections

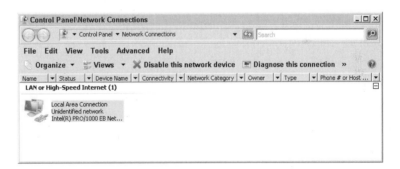

This window describes each NIC in your system and also lists every item in your Dial-Up directory — so if you've got your system set up to be able to dial an ISP or perhaps a distant Windows 2008 network, then you'll see a line for each of those DUN directory entries — as well as an icon that can start a wizard to add new Dial-Up entries. This computer hasn't got a modem and therefore has never dialed up anywhere.

Bring up the properties for the NIC by right-clicking the NIC (Local Area Connection is the name of the NIC in Figure 10.9) and choosing Properties. That will give you something like Figure 10.10.

Click Internet Protocol Version 4 (TCP/IPv4) and then the Properties button. You'll see a dialog box that looks like Figure 10.11, or anyway it will once we're through with it.

FIGURE 10.10
LAN Connection proper-
ties page

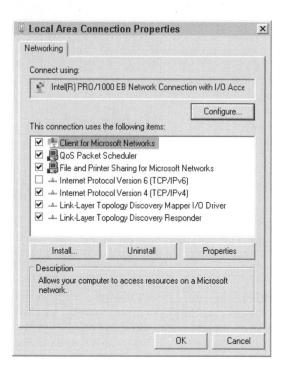

FIGURE 10.11
IP properties page after
modification

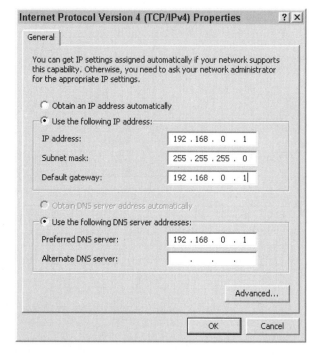

When you first see this dialog box, the "Obtain an IP address automatically" and "Obtain DNS server address automatically" radio buttons will be selected. You should click the "Use the following IP address" and "Use the following DNS server addresses" radio buttons. As mentioned earlier, you'll need to know four things to configure this screen: your IP address, the subnet mask, the IP address of your default gateway, and the IP addresses of one or more DNS server. In the case of the computer I'm configuring here, the IP address is 192.168.0.1, the subnet mask is 255.255.255.0, the default gateway is 192.168.0.1, and I've got a DNS server at 192.168.0.1. (We don't really need a default gateway or DNS server in this configuration, because this network is so simple — this is just an example.)

TIP

Do you recognize those IP addresses? They're in one of the RFC 1918 "nonroutable" ranges. It's safe to assume, then, that the router referred to at address 192.168.0.1 is a NAT router, even though in this particular case we've got two computers on a subnet that doesn't go anywhere — normally a 192.168 .0.x network goes *somewhere*; just not this one, and not today.

Click OK to clear the IP and LAN properties pages, and you'll have your IP address configured. But does it work? Read on.

Setting Up MAIN

Now that you've got WINSERVER set up with address 192.168.0.1, set up MAIN with IP address 192.168.0.2, subnet mask 255.255.255.0, and leave the default gateway and DNS fields empty.

Testing Your IP Configuration

There are two basic tools you'll use to verify that TCP/IP's working on your system: IPConfig and Ping.

IPCONFIG

First, check your IP configuration by opening a command prompt and typing **ipconfig /all**; if you run this from WINSERVER then you'll then see a screen like Figure 10.12.

FIGURE 10.12
Output of ipconfig
/all

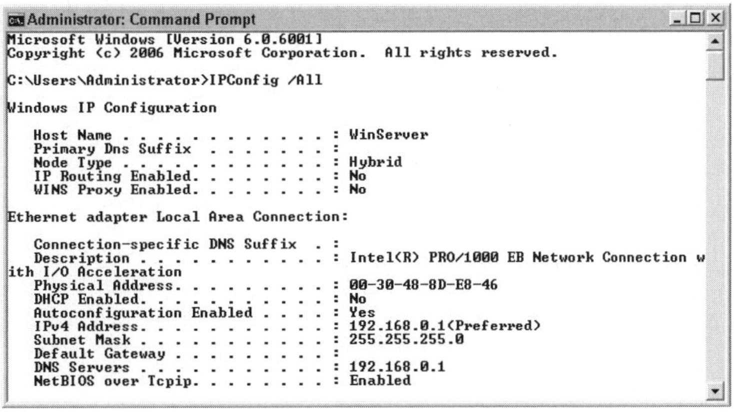

```
Administrator: Command Prompt                                              _ □ X
Microsoft Windows [Version 6.0.6001]
Copyright (c) 2006 Microsoft Corporation.  All rights reserved.

C:\Users\Administrator>IPConfig /All

Windows IP Configuration

    Host Name . . . . . . . . . . . . : WinServer
    Primary Dns Suffix  . . . . . . . :
    Node Type . . . . . . . . . . . . : Hybrid
    IP Routing Enabled. . . . . . . . : No
    WINS Proxy Enabled. . . . . . . . : No

Ethernet adapter Local Area Connection:

    Connection-specific DNS Suffix  . :
    Description . . . . . . . . . . . : Intel(R) PRO/1000 EB Network Connection w
ith I/O Acceleration
    Physical Address. . . . . . . . . : 00-30-48-8D-E8-46
    DHCP Enabled. . . . . . . . . . . : No
    Autoconfiguration Enabled . . . . : Yes
    IPv4 Address. . . . . . . . . . . : 192.168.0.1(Preferred)
    Subnet Mask . . . . . . . . . . . : 255.255.255.0
    Default Gateway . . . . . . . . . :
    DNS Servers . . . . . . . . . . . : 192.168.0.1
    NetBIOS over Tcpip. . . . . . . . : Enabled
```

ipconfig /all should be your first step when checking a TCP/IP installation or when troubleshooting one. This particular IPConfig output starts out with some general information about this machine and then displays specific information about the Ethernet adapter. It's laid out like this because, in some cases, you may have two or more NICs in a system, and each NIC will have an IP address. Additionally, you may have a modem on your system and may be connected to the Internet via a dial-up connection. In that case, you'd again have more than one IP address — your Ethernet card would have an IP address (the one you just assigned it if you were following along with the previous text), and your modem would have an IP address that your ISP gave it when you dialed up.

In the IPConfig output, WinServer is the machine's name.

WARNING

In general, you should avoid underscores in your computer names. Microsoft's old-style NetBIOS-based networking doesn't mind it, but the Internet document on legal Internet names, RFC 1123, doesn't permit underscores. According to RFC 1123 in its "assumptions" section, each piece of an Internet name can be no more than 24 characters long — that is, each piece between the periods — and the only legal characters are a–z, 0–9, and the hyphen/minus sign. In fact, the earliest 32-bit Microsoft TCP/IP software, the code that shipped with Windows for Workgroups 3.11, would simply refuse to work on a machine with an underscore in its name. That's not true anymore, and in fact, the Active Directory uses a fair number of underscored names, but that's acceptable, because AD communications will mainly just go on amongst computers running Microsoft software. But avoid underscores in workstation names as it may potentially cause trouble when trying to use resources on the Internet, which may be running on computers that aren't running Microsoft software.

Primary DNS Suffix is the end of the DNS name; if this computer had a full DNS name like ssdotnet.bigfirm.com, then the primary DNS suffix would be "bigfirm.com." (It *doesn't* have one because I've not told you how to configure one yet and, besides, we don't even have a DNS server running. We'll remedy that in Chapter 13.) Node Type answers the question, "How does the system convert an old-style NetBIOS name like \SNOOPY into an IP address?" That's a long and complicated story, and we'll take it up in the next chapter. IP Routing Enabled asks whether this computer is acting as an IP router. As you saw in the example in the beginning of the chapter with machines A through H, you've got to have two IP connections to do that. I will show you before the end of the chapter, how to make a Windows Server 2008 machine into an IP router. I'll explain WINS Proxy Enabled in Chapter 12.

Looking at the specific information under Ethernet Adapter Local Area Connection, the first entry is Connection-Specific DNS Suffix. This refers not to a Windows Server 2008 domain but to an Internet domain name, such as minasi.com, microsoft.com, or whitehouse.gov. Back in the NT 4 and earlier days, NT's TCP/IP software would only let you put a machine in just one Internet domain. That wasn't a big deal for most of us, but some people wanted their systems to be able to seem to be members of several domains, to have a sort of multiple citizenship in two or more domains. Such a machine might have a NIC in it that was connected to bigfirm.com's network, and it might have another NIC in it connected to minasi.com's network. If the machine's name were tadpole, then it might want to be able to be recognized both as tadpole.bigfirm.com and tadpole.minasi.com. Now, when configuring tadpole under NT 4, you would have had to choose whether tadpole was in bigfirm.com or minasi.com — you couldn't choose both as you had to choose domain membership for the whole machine. Under Windows Server 2008, however, you can say that one NIC is a member of bigfirm.com, and that the other is a member of minasi.com. In my particular case, I really have no need to do that, which is why Connection-Specific DNS Suffix is empty.

Next are an English-like description of the NIC's brand and type and the MAC address of the NIC. "DHCP Enabled" indicates whether I punched in the IP address directly or let DHCP set the IP address for me. As I set the IP address myself, the value is No. If it were Yes, then — as you'll see in the Chapter 14 — IPConfig would furnish more DHCP-specific information, like the IP address of the DHCP server who provided the IP address, and when the lease on that address runs out. "Autoconfiguration Enabled" says that if all else fails, APIPA is okay. IPConfig then reports the IP address, subnet mask, and default gateway. Finally, it displays the IP address of the DNS server that I configured.

PING

So all of the settings are correct — but can you reach out to the outside world? TCP/IP has a very handy little tool for finding out whether your TCP/IP software is up and running and whether you have a connection to another point: Ping. Before you can use Ping to check your connections, you must open the required feature in the firewall using the NetSH command as described in the following procedure.

1. Choose Start ➤ Programs ➤ Accessories.

2. Right click Command Prompt and choose Run as administrator from the context menu to open an Administrator command prompt.

3. Type **NetSH Firewall Set ICMPSetting 8 Enable** and press Enter. The utility will pause for a few minutes and then display a status message of OK.

Ping is a program that lets you send a short message to another TCP/IP node, asking, "Are you there?" If it is there, then it says "yes" to the ping, and Ping relays this information back to you. You can see an example of Ping in Figure 10.13; the first line of the screen shows you the syntax, ping *ipaddress*.

FIGURE 10.13
A sample Ping output

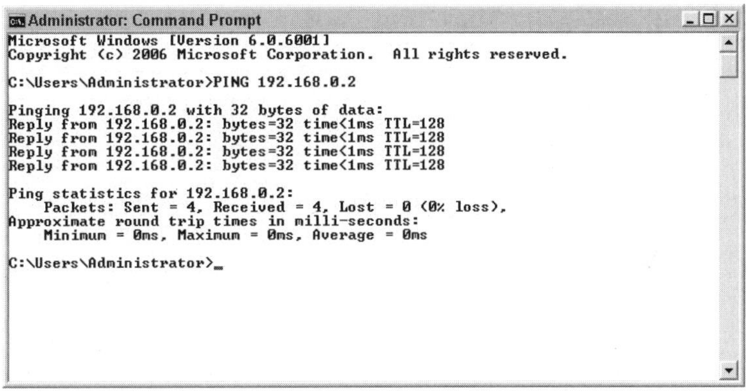

```
Administrator: Command Prompt                                          _ □ X
Microsoft Windows [Version 6.0.6001]
Copyright (c) 2006 Microsoft Corporation.  All rights reserved.

C:\Users\Administrator>PING 192.168.0.2

Pinging 192.168.0.2 with 32 bytes of data:
Reply from 192.168.0.2: bytes=32 time<1ms TTL=128
Reply from 192.168.0.2: bytes=32 time<1ms TTL=128
Reply from 192.168.0.2: bytes=32 time<1ms TTL=128
Reply from 192.168.0.2: bytes=32 time<1ms TTL=128

Ping statistics for 192.168.0.2:
    Packets: Sent = 4, Received = 4, Lost = 0 (0% loss),
Approximate round trip times in milli-seconds:
    Minimum = 0ms, Maximum = 0ms, Average = 0ms

C:\Users\Administrator>_
```

In the figure, I pinged the IP address of MAIN, the only other server on our little intranet.

> **TIP**
>
> If I were connected to *the* Internet, I'd try pinging 164.109.1.3, the IP address of a busy DNS server on the Internet. If pinging that address is successful, then it's a very telling test as the address is across the Internet from my system — the fact that I got a response from 164.109.1.3 means that not only is my TCP/IP software working across my segment and across my enterprise, but across the Internet as well. Another good one is 66.218.71.63, a Yahoo! DNS server.

Use the approach outlined in the sidebar "How Do I Make Sure That TCP/IP Is Set Up Properly?" to get the most out of Ping. You can also use the NetSH command to perform TPC/IP tasks at the command line. For example, to see your current IP configuration, type **Netsh Interface IP Show Config** and press Enter. The results are much like using Ping.

Unlike Ping, you can use NetSH to set the static IP address for an adapter, so you can use NetSH to correct configuration issues with your network. For example, to set MAIN to use a static address of 192.168.0.2 and rely on WinServer for DNS support, you would type **NetSH Interface IP Set Address "Local Area Connection" Static 192.168.0.2 255.255.255.0 192.168.0.1 1** and press Enter. In this case, you're setting the IP address of the Local Area Connection to a static address of 192.168.0.2. The address has a subnet mask for a class C address (one in which only the last quad contains a machine address, while the first three quads contain the subnet address). Because we want to use WinServer as a router, you set it as the default gateway using the next entry of 192.168.0.1 with a metric of 1. Don't worry too much about understanding the details of this command right now, Chapters 12 and 13 will provide more information on precisely what these settings mean.

Our static connection also requires a DNS and WINS server setup. The NetSH commands for performing these tasks are similar to setting the IP address. To set the DNS server address for WinServer, you would type **NetSH Interface IP Set DNSServer "Local Area Connection" Static 192.168.0.1** and press Enter. Likewise, to set the WINS server, you would type **NetSH Interface IP Set WINSServer "Local Area Connection" Static 192.168.0.1** and press Enter.

Configuration Continued: Setting Domain Suffixes

Thus far, my computer's name is just plain WinServer, which is a mite shorter than most Internet names; one might expect a name more like WinServer.bigfirm.com or the like, a name that looks like *specific machine name.organization name.root*, where *root* is a suffix like *com*, *gov*, or some country identifier.

I intend for my computer WinServer to be part of an Internet domain named bigfirm.com, so its complete Internet name will be WinServer.bigfirm.com. What that really means, in essence, is that if someone pings WinServer.bigfirm.com, I want the machine to respond. If I decide to run Web server software on it later, then I want people to be able to see whatever content is on it by pointing their Web browsers to http://WinServer.bigfirm.com rather than having to use http://192.168.0.1. (I know this probably seems obvious to many of you, but stay with me, there's a point coming.)

How Do I Make Sure That TCP/IP Is Set Up Properly?

With these ping tests, you're demonstrating two things: First, that your IP software can get a packet from your computer to the outside world (in other words, that your IP connectivity is functioning), and second, that your connection to a DNS server for name resolution is working.

First, test IP connectivity by pinging specific IP addresses.

In most cases, your connection will work the first time. Start out with an overall "does it work?" test by pinging some distant location on the Internet. Try pinging 164.109.1.3 or 66.218.71.63 — they're big DNS servers on the Internet. If that responds correctly, then you've demonstrated that your IP software can get out to the Internet and back.

If it doesn't work, then try pinging something not so far — your default gateway. (Actually, the next thing to do is to look around back and make sure the network cable is still in place. There's nothing more embarrassing than calling in outside network support only to find that your LAN cable fell out of the back of your computer.) If you can successfully ping the default gateway but not one of those big DNS servers, then either your firm's external Internet routers have failed or perhaps your default gateway is configured incorrectly. Another tool you might try is tracert, a souped-up Ping that shows you each of the hops that the IP packet had to use to get from your machine to the destination. It's a command-line command: Just type **tracert** followed by an IP address or DNS name. You can see a sample output in the following figure.

```
Administrator: Command Prompt                                        _ □ ×

C:\Users\Administrator>tracert 164.109.1.3

Tracing route to 164.109.1.3 over a maximum of 30 hops

  1    32 ms    31 ms    31 ms  dsl-lavalle2-129.lavalle.mwt.net [207.190.102.12
9]
  2    33 ms    33 ms    34 ms  207.190.94.199
  3    43 ms    38 ms    41 ms  camp-hill-eth-gw.direct.airstreamcomm.net [64.33
.130.139]
  4    49 ms    49 ms    48 ms  air-elk-7200-bdr-1-2.airstreamcomm.net [64.33.14
6.177]
  5    51 ms    50 ms    51 ms  12.116.253.61
  6    61 ms    60 ms    62 ms  tbr2.cgcil.ip.att.net [12.122.99.122]
  7    60 ms    60 ms    59 ms  ggr2.cgcil.ip.att.net [12.123.6.69]
  8    60 ms    60 ms    63 ms  0.so-1-1-0.BR6.CHI2.ALTER.NET [204.255.174.9]
  9    62 ms    62 ms    64 ms  0.so-0-0-0.XL1.CHI13.ALTER.NET [152.63.73.26]
 10    86 ms    83 ms    84 ms  0.so-5-0-0.XT1.DCA5.ALTER.NET [152.63.0.169]
 11    82 ms    82 ms    82 ms  0.so-2-0-0.HR1.DCA5.ALTER.NET [152.63.42.101]
 12    85 ms    85 ms    86 ms  POS9-0.UR2.BWI40.ALTER.NET [152.63.39.142]
 13    85 ms    86 ms    85 ms  pos2-0.dca2a-fdisa-dns-rtr1.netsrv.digex.net [16
4.109.3.62]
 14    80 ms    79 ms    79 ms  164.109.1.3

Trace complete.

C:\Users\Administrator>_
```

If you can't get to the default gateway, then try pinging another computer on your subnet. If you can get to another machine on your subnet but not the gateway, then perhaps you've got the wrong IP address for the gateway or perhaps the gateway is malfunctioning.

If you can't get to another system on your subnet — and I'm assuming that you've already walked over and checked that the other machine is up and running — then it may be that the IP software on your computer isn't running. Verify that by typing **ping 127.0.0.1**.

127.0.0.1 is the "loopback" address. IP software is designed to *always* report success on a ping to 127.0.0.1, if the IP software is functioning. Recheck that you've installed the TCP/IP software and rebooted after installing.

> Once you're certain that IP works, try out DNS. Try pinging a distant location, but this time, don't do it by IP address, do it by name — try pinging www.whitehouse.gov, www.internic.net, or www.minasi.com. If the ping works, great; if not, check that you've got the right address punched in for your DNS server and then check the DNS server.

I would have guessed that unless I found some way to tell WinServer that its full name was actually WinServer.bigfirm.com, it wouldn't know to respond when someone pinged it by its full name. But, as it turns out, that's wrong.

If you're sitting at your computer and you type **ping WinServer.bigfirm.com**, then your computer asks your local DNS server what WinServer.bigfirm.com's IP address is. *Then* your computer just pings that IP address, and WinServer.bigfirm.com never even knows *what* name your computer originally called it by. If one of the people running IBM's DNS servers were to decide on a whim to insert an entry into IBM's DNS database that said "iguana.ibm.com has IP address 206.246.253.1," then anyone anywhere pinging iguana.ibm.com would end up pinging my router at that address.

The point is, then, that in order to have my computer named WinServer recognized as WinServer.bigfirm.com, I've got to be concerned more with informing bigfirm.com's DNS server of WinServer's IP address than I should be concerned about telling WinServer that it's in bigfirm.com. So how do I ensure that bigfirm.com's DNS server finds out about WinServer? As it turns out, there are four ways to do this. (And even though handling DNS servers is a topic I won't get into until Chapter 13, it's worth covering this here.)

ADD A STATIC DNS ENTRY

The first way to make the DNS server for the Internet domain bigfirm.com know that there's a machine named WinServer.bigfirm.com whose IP address is 192.168.0.1 is for an administrator to simply sit down at the DNS server that holds the information about bigfirm.com and *tell* it that there's a host named "winserver" in that domain with IP address 192.168.0.1. Depending on what kind of machine the DNS server is running on, the admin will either edit a file or run some kind of management tool. (Again, you'll see how to do that with Windows Server 2008's DNS server in the Chapter 13.)

JOIN THE ACTIVE DIRECTORY DOMAIN OF THE SAME NAME

The second way to tell the DNS server for the Internet domain bigfirm.com to include ssdotnet.bigfirm.com in its list of known hosts is for WinServer to join the Active Directory domain *named* bigfirm.com, assuming that there is one. (I know I've not covered AD yet, but don't worry — this is all you need to know for the moment.) This is a positive side effect of Active Directory's unifying of AD domain names and Internet (DNS) domain names. If the server named WinServer joins an Active Directory domain named bigfirm.com, then by default the DNS server for the *Internet* domain named bigfirm.com adds a record in that Internet domain for WinServer .bigfirm.com. Don't worry too much about Active Directory for right now — we discuss it in the companion books of the *Mastering Windows Server 2008* series.

HACK THE REGISTRY TO TELL IT THE DNS SUFFIX

You can always tell a system what its primary DNS suffix is — or even override one that you got by joining an AD — by putting the value straight into the Registry:

1. Open Regedit.

2. Navigate to HKLM\SYSTEM\CurrentControlSet\Services\Tcpip\Parameters.

3. Look for a REG_SZ entry named "NV Domain." If there isn't one there, create it.

4. Set NV Domain to whatever primary DNS suffix you'd like it have.

5. Exit Regedit.

Alternatively, you can do this from the command line with REG, as in this example where I set the primary DNS suffix to "bigfirm.com:"

```
reg add HKLM\System\currentcontrolset\services\tcpip\parameters
/v "NV Domain" /d "bigfirm.com" /f
```

Handling Old Names: Configuring Your Workstation for WINS

Some older networks use a technology known as WINS. As mentioned in the "Internet Host Names" section of the chapter, WINS is a Windows-specific method of converting a network address into a human readable form and vice versa. Microsoft is slowly moving away from any use of WINS in order to provide a standardized method of name hosting. Even so, you may run into WINS at some point, so let's look at it. While in that advanced properties page for TCP/IP, click the WINS tab and you'll see something like Figure 10.14.

FIGURE 10.14
WINS client configuration tab

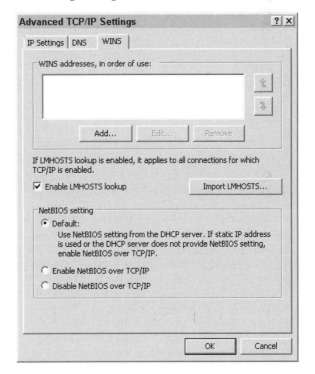

Now, if you're lucky, then you'll never have to look at this screen. If you have gotten rid of all of your older machines — those that contain anything older than Windows 2000, then you might never need to look at this dialog box. In fact, most companies are probably past the need to use this technology today.

WINS can become a complete topic and you may not even need it for many modern networks, but for now all you need to understand is that you have one or two Windows Server 2008 (or possibly NT) servers acting as name resolvers or WINS servers. This dialog box lets you fill in the names of a primary and secondary WINS server.

In brief, here's what WINS is all about. As you've read, most of the Internet in general as well as Windows Server 2008 uses something called DNS to convert network names to network addresses (or, in network lingo, to "resolve network names"), but now I'm saying that we'll *also* use something else, called WINS, to do what sounds like the same thing. What's going on? In truth, you shouldn't really have to set up WINS at all; NT and Microsoft enterprise networking in general should use DNS for all of its name resolution, but it didn't in Windows for Workgroups, Windows 9*x*, NT 3.*x*, and NT 4. It wasn't until Windows Server 2003 shipped that Microsoft networking started relying on Winsock and DNS.

The reason is that Microsoft wanted NT's networking modules to work like the already-existing LAN Manager system, and LAN Manager used a naming system based on its NetBIOS application program interface. A computer's NetBIOS name is the computer name that you gave it when you installed it. When you type **net view \\ajax**, something must resolve \\ajax into an IP address — a NetBIOS-to-IP resolution. WINS does that. In contrast, the rest of the Internet would see a machine called ajax as having a longer name, like ajax.bigfirm.com. If there were a Web server on ajax, then someone outside the company would have to point her Web browser to `http://ajax.bigfirm.com`, and some piece of software would have to resolve `ajax .bigfirm.com` into an IP address. That piece of software is the socket or Winsock interface, and in either case, it will rely upon not WINS but DNS to resolve the name. In a few words, then, programs written to employ NetBIOS will use WINS for name resolution, and programs written to employ Winsock use DNS for name resolution.

I can probably guess what you're thinking now, and, yes, DNS and WINS should be integrated, but they can't really ever be completely integrated, because, as you'll see in Chapter 13, DNS and WINS serve different masters — DNS serves standard Internet-type applications like Web browsers and newer Microsoft tools like Active Directory, and WINS serves older Microsoft-centric tools like network workgroups or NT 4 domains.

The bigger question at this point is *why am I even talking about this*? After all, it's Windows Server 2008. That bad old NetBIOS and NT 4 stuff is dead, right? Nope, not in most networks. You may have some Windows 98, Windows Me, and NT 4 systems still attached to your network. Hopefully, all of those Windows for Workgroups and Windows 95 systems are long gone. Back when Active Directory first appeared in Windows 2000, Microsoft kept promising us that WINS would no longer be necessary once 2000 Server — yes, that's 2000 Server, not Windows Server 2003 (and now Windows Server 2008) — had been out for a while, but there was some fine print, namely "so long as you throw away all of your old machines or put Windows 2000, XP, Vista, Windows Server 2003, or Windows Server 2008 on them." Some of us can't afford to do that, so we'll be living with WINS servers for the time being — which means that your Windows Server 2008 systems must know where those WINS servers are; hence this dialog box. (Remember that in our simple example we've not configured a WINS server yet, which is why that last figure had a blank "WINS addresses, in order of use" text box.)

I could tell this computer to use a WINS server at 192.168.71.10 by clicking Add, filling in the IP address, and clicking OK. You could only tell pre–2000 Server systems about two WINS servers, but for some reason 2000, XP, and Windows Server 2008 allow you to list as many WINS servers as you like in this dialog box.

Even at its best, WINS can't do the whole name resolution job. Some tough name resolution problems can only be solved with a HOSTS-like file called LMHOSTS. The "Enable LMHOSTS lookup" check box lets you use an LMHOSTS file if you've got one installed on your system. I'll explain LMHOSTS in detail in Chapter 12.

Below all that is a group of controls labeled "NetBIOS setting" offering three options:

◆ Default

◆ Enable NetBIOS over TCP/IP

◆ Disable NetBIOS over TCP/IP

If you're an old Windows 2000 hand, then you'll notice that these options changed a little bit — what is now Default used to be Use DHCP Setting.

The Enable NetBIOS over TCP/IP versus Disable NetBIOS over TCP/IP radio buttons embody a deceptively momentous choice, so it's odd that the choice is tucked away in this obscure properties page. Another way of phrasing the WINS-versus-DNS dichotomy is to say that all of the Microsoft operating systems prior to 2000 Server built all of their networking tools atop a programming interface called NetBIOS, and Windows 2000, XP, and Windows Server 2008 break with that tradition by instead using another programming interface called Winsock. An all–Windows-2000-or-later network would be perfectly happy running only network programs — Web servers, e-mail, file servers, even domain controllers for authentication — that used Winsock. But if those servers want to communicate with older Windows and NT systems, then they must use older networking programs that are compatible with these old systems, and those older networking programs are built atop NetBIOS.

That means that if your Windows Server 2008 system is acting as a file or print server for any older machines, it needs to keep NetBIOS around. If it's running any applications built for pre–2000 Server versions of NT, it'll probably need NetBIOS. Put simply, you can't shut off Net-BIOS until you're free of both old client machines and old network applications. But one day you'll be able to axe NetBIOS, and when you can, you should, because it'll reduce network chatter and free up server memory and CPU power.

Adding IP Addresses to a Single NIC

If you're still in the Advanced TCP/IP Settings page, click the IP Settings tab, and you'll see something like Figure 10.15.

This NIC already has the 192.168.0.1 IP address that I gave it earlier. But notice the Add button. This lets you attach different IP addresses to the NIC to assign more than one IP address to a single NIC.

TIP

You can also add addresses to the NIC using the NetSH utility at the command prompt. For example, say you want to add 192.168.0.122 as a second address — you'd type **NetSH Interface IP Add Address "Local Area Connection" 192.168.0.122** and press Enter. In this case, you're telling the NetSH utility to add a new IP address to the Local Area Connection of 192.168.0.122.

Why would you want to do that? Normally, you wouldn't. But there *is* one case where it would be very useful: when you're hosting multiple Web sites on a single Web server.

For example, suppose I've got two Internet domains, minasi.com and win2kexperts.com. I intend to put up a Web site for minasi.com (`www.minasi.com`) and another for win2kexperts.com (`www.win2kexperts.com`). But I want them to be very different Web sites; perhaps the minasi.com site is a personal site and the win2kexperts site is a business site. Even though `www.minasi.com` and `www.win2kexperts.com` are both hosted on a machine at 206.246.253.100, I don't ever want anyone visiting the business site to see pictures of my last vacation, and I don't think my friends care much about my professional résumé.

FIGURE 10.15
IP Settings advanced properties tab

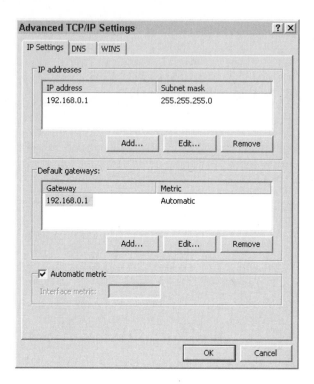

I separate the two by creating two *virtual sites*. There are two basic ways to give a single Web server "multiple personalities." If you ever need the slightly more expensive (and when I say *expensive* here, I mean that you'll have to use an IP address for each virtual site) method that works with *any* browser, then here's briefly how to do it — and it's a great example of why you'd put multiple IP addresses on a single NIC:

1. I assign an extra IP address to the Web server so that it now has two addresses — let's say they're 206.246.253.100 and 206.246.253.101.

2. I then set up DNS so that `www.minasi.com` points to the first address, 206.246.253.100, and `www.win2kexperts.com` points to the second address, 206.246.253.101.

3. I've already got the minasi.com Web site running, so I'll need a place to put the win2kexperts.com content. I just create a folder on the Web server called w2kx and put the HTML, images, and so on for win2kexperts.com there.

4. I next tell the Web server to create a "new site." It then basically needs to know two things: where to find the content (C:\w2kx) and which IP address to associate with the site. I've got to tell it to "start" the site, and I'm in business.

The important thing here is to understand that every one of these sites, each of these "personalities" of your Web server, burns up an IP address, and as you see, you use the IP Settings property tab to add those extra IP addresses to your Web server's NIC.

Whew! Getting IP running on that system was a bit of work. Good thing we can do most of our machines automatically with DHCP — but even that requires configuring, which is why we went through all of this detail. Now that we've got IP on a system, let's finish the chapter by making a 2008 box a "router lite" with ICS.

Lower-Cost LAN-to-WAN Routing with Internet Connection Sharing

I've already talked a bit about Internet Connection Service, ICS. Basically it acts as a NAT/PAT router, talking on one NIC to the Internet and talking on another NIC to your intranet.

Before we do this, I should offer a caveat. Once upon a time, knowing how to use a Windows box to share a single IP address was really useful, which is why I've put it in every edition of the book. In reality, though, there are now dedicated boxes called "Internet routers" from companies like Linksys, Dlink, Belkin, and others that are so cheap — usually under 50 bucks — that the only real reason to use a Windows server as a intranet/Internet router is just to get the practice. But it's still worth doing just to try it out, particularly if you want to go beyond what we're covering in this chapter and learn more about IP routing. (Which is the topic of Chapter 4 in the third book.)

As I've already said, the main aspects of this LAN/WAN connectivity are that:

◆ The only machine on the network with a "regulation," ICANN- or ISP-issued IP address is the gateway.

◆ The other machines have nonroutable addresses.

◆ All of the "heavy lifting," routing-wise, is being done by the gateway computer. In fact, the ISP has no idea whatsoever that all of those other computers are accessing the Internet via the gateway.

Recall from our earlier "routing the nonroutable" discussion that this functionality is generically called network address translation (NAT) routing and was until recently fairly expensive to implement, requiring special routers. But ever since Windows 98 Second Edition, Microsoft Windows OSes have included the ability to act as a NAT router. (Even XP, Vista, or 2000 Pro can do it.) Called Internet Connection Sharing, this will work on any kind of Internet connection, whether it's a modem, ISDN, cable modem, DSL, or whatever.

NOTE

Just to be on the safe side, check your "use agreement" with your ISP. Some ISPs specifically forbid any kind of sharing.

Basically, there are just four steps to make this work:

1. Attach all of your internal computers together in a network.

2. Connect one of the computers (the one running ICS) to the Internet either via a modem or another Ethernet card. And yes, that's *another* Ethernet card — you can't put the Internet

connection on the same segment as the connection to the internal, nonroutable machines. So if you wanted to share a cable modem or DSL connection with your Server system, then you'd have two Ethernet cards in your Server: one connected to your DSL/cable modem, and the other connected to your internal network.

3. You'll now have two connections on the ICS computer — one to the local Ethernet connecting the internal nonroutable machines, and one to the Internet. On the Internet connection, turn on ICS.

4. Tell all of the internal, nonroutable computers to automatically get their IP addresses (which they'll end up getting from the ICS machine), then reboot them.

Once you do all that, the internal systems will have nonroutable IP addresses in the range 192.168.0.2–192.168.0.254 — but they'll be able to access the Internet because of ICS's abilities.

> **WARNING**
>
> Before starting, ensure that Routing and Remote Access Services are *not* running on this computer. ICS will refuse to run on a system with RRAS enabled.

Step One: Connect the Internal Network — and Meet Automatic Private Internet Protocol Addressing (APIPA)

This is easy. Just put an Ethernet card in every computer in your home, small business, or whatever set of machines you need ICS for. (I'm kind of hoping you've already done this, or it's reasonable to wonder why you're reading this book!) When configuring the TCP/IP settings as you saw back in Figure 10.11, don't bother punching in any values; instead, just click the radio button labeled "Obtain an IP address automatically."

Now boot the systems and do an `ipconfig /all`. You'll find that they all have IP addresses in the range between 169.254.0.1 through 169.254.255.254. Where did *those* addresses come from? They're a feature of Microsoft networking since Windows 2000 called Automatic Private Internet Protocol Addressing (APIPA).

The idea in most IP-based networks, as you'll see in Chapter 13, is to set up a kind of server called a Dynamic Host Configuration Protocol (DHCP) server somewhere on the network. That DHCP server then automatically supplies IP addresses to all systems on the network, freeing you from having to walk around to every system and punch in a different IP address. But what happens if you have a system that (1) expects to find a DHCP server and therefore doesn't *have* a static IP address, but that (2) finds itself on a network without a DHCP server? Well, under NT 4, that system would basically just disable its TCP/IP software, and running IPConfig would just show your NIC with an IP address of 0.0.0.0. Under Windows 2000 and later OSes, however, it randomly assigns itself an address in the range of 169.254.0.1 through 169.254.255.254, checking to make sure that no one else has this address. Granted, it's not a terribly useful way to get IP addresses on important systems like Web servers, but for a small network that's not intending to talk to any other network, it's not a bad answer. But it's only a temporary answer, as we'll see, because ICS actually includes a basic, no-configuration-necessary DHCP server inside it, and so when we get ICS running, then its DHCP server will hand out more useful addresses to the machines on your internal network — your "intranet."

Step Two: Get Connected to Your ISP

The next step is just to get connected to your ISP. How you do that depends on whether you're dialing up or connecting via some high-speed connection like cable/DSL modem or directly via a corporate network. We'll look at how to get connected via dial-up first.

GET CONNECTED TO YOUR ISP (DIAL-UP)

> **NOTE**
>
> If you connect via DSL or cable modem, then skip this section and go to the next, "Get Connected to Your ISP (Cable Modem/DSL)."

As has been the case with Microsoft OSes since Windows 95, you tell your system to dial up to an ISP by creating a Dial-Up Connection object or, to use Microsoft's phrase, you will create a *connectoid*. (Where they come up with their "wordoids" is beyond me, although I *do* find the tech world's willingness to coin new phrases at a hatdrop — see, I can do it too — interesting.) The following steps tell you how to create the connection.

1. Click Start ➤ Settings ➤ Control Panel ➤ Network and Sharing Center. Click "Set up a connection" and you'll see the wizard shown in Figure 10.16.

FIGURE 10.16
Create a new connection for your machine.

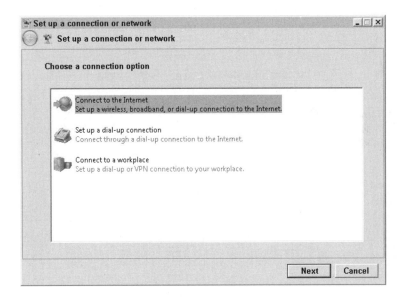

2. Choose "Set up a dial-up connection" and click Next. You'll see the "Set up a dial-up connection" dialog box shown in Figure 10.17 where you provide all of the information needed to create the connection.

FIGURE 10.17
Provide the connection information for the dial-up connection.

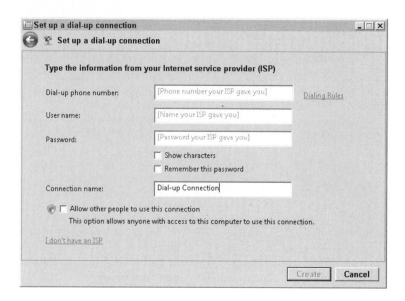

3. Type the "Dial-up phone number," your "User name" for the dial-up connection, and associated Password in the appropriate fields.

4. Check "Show characters" when you want to see the characters you're typing when you type the password. Normally, you don't want to see the characters — you want to see dots when you type the password to reduce the chance that someone will see your password.

5. Check "Remember this password" if you want Windows to supply the password automatically every time someone makes a connection. This option is helpful if you plan to share the connection. Otherwise, you have to give your password out to anyone else who uses the connection.

6. Type a name for the connection in the "Connection name" field. Choosing a descriptive name is important if you want to share the connection with other people.

7. Check "Allow other people to use this connection" if you want to share it with other people on the network using ICS. You still have to complete the ICS setup.

8. Click Create. Windows will create the new connection for you.

Click Start ➤ Settings ➤ Network Connections ➤ <Connection Name> to check your connectoid. Make sure that you can ping places on the Internet both by IP address and by name. Remember, *first* ping with IP addresses to ensure that routing is working. *Then* ping by DNS names, like www.minasi.com. If pinging by IP address works but pinging by DNS names does not, then the routing is working fine — the problem's with DNS. Then also check that you can ping inside your internal network, your intranet. Again, we're just worried about routing here, so just ping the internal systems by their IP addresses.

Hooked up and pinging okay? Great — then skip down to "Step Three: Turn ICS On."

GET CONNECTED TO YOUR ISP (CABLE MODEM/DSL)

If you connect to the Internet via DSL or cable modem, then you won't be creating one of those connectoids. Instead, as I said earlier in the chapter, you usually connect to a DSL/cable modem with a regular old Ethernet card. Typically, then, all you have to do is install an Ethernet card in your system — remember that it will be a separate Ethernet card from the one that connects to your other computers — and then run a standard Ethernet cable from your DSL/cable modem to the Ethernet card.

I said "usually" because you might choose instead to connect your DSL/cable modem to your PC with a USB connection. I recommend against this for reasons that I mentioned earlier. And once in a great while, you might have to load an extra bit of software on your computer to be able to communicate with your cable modem provider. I've never seen this myself but I'm told that some DSL modem companies make you install some extra piece of software that looks a bit like a modem dialer program so that you can log onto their cable modem network. (I'm *hoping* you don't have to use that kind of connection because honestly I can't advise you about how to share it, because there's no guarantee that such a nonstandard LAN/WAN connection would work with ICS.)

In most cases, though, it's simple: put the Ethernet card in your PC, connect it to the DSL/cable modem, and turn the computer on. A DHCP system at the DSL/cable provider will give your PC a routable IP address. Note that this will probably be an IP address that changes from time to time, so you may have to approach your provider about a static — that is, unchanging — address if you want to host Internet-visible services like Web or mail. Static addresses normally incur an additional cost.

Now try it before going any further. Make sure that the Windows Server 2008 machine attached to the DSL/cable modem connection can surf the Net without any trouble. And check that its other NIC also has a 169.254.x.x address, because there's no DHCP server on your intranet segment. An `ipconfig /all` should show one NIC with a routable address and another with a 169.254.x.x address. You should also be able to ping the computers inside your intranet.

At this point, you might be tempted to put a hub on that cable modem or DSL connection and then just hang your other internal PCs off that hub. *Don't*. At least, not if you want ICS to work.

Step Three: Turn ICS On

If you haven't already done it, go to Network Connections. (Click Start ➤ Settings ➤ Control Panel ➤ Network and Sharing Center and then, when your mouse is on Network Connections, *right*-click the mouse and choose Open. Windows will display the Network and Sharing Center window. Click "Manage network connections.") You'll see a dialog box like the one that you saw back in Figure 10.9, Network Connections. You'll see at least one Ethernet connection, probably labeled Local Area Connection, which represents the NIC attached to the internal network. You'll also see an object representing your connection to the Internet — if you dial up with a modem then it'll be a Dial-Up connectoid, or if you're using DSL or cable modem it'll be another Local Area Connection object.

Right-click that object and choose Properties, then in the resulting property page click Sharing. The Sharing page for a connectoid contains different information than the Sharing page of a connectoid for a network card, so you'll either see something like Figure 10.18 or Figure 10.19.

In those figures, check the box labeled "Allow other network users to connect through this computer's Internet connection," and click OK. When you click OK to clear the properties page, you may get a confirmation message saying something like this:

```
When Internet Connection Sharing is enabled, your LAN adapter will be set to
use IP address 192.168.0.1. Your computer may lose connectivity with other
computers on your network. If these other computers have static IP addresses,
you should set them to obtain their IP addresses automatically. Are you sure
you want to enable Internet Connection Sharing?
```

FIGURE 10.18
Advanced properties for
a dial-up connection

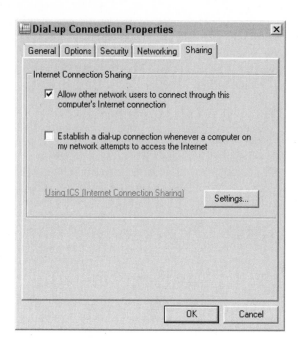

FIGURE 10.19
Advanced properties for
a network card

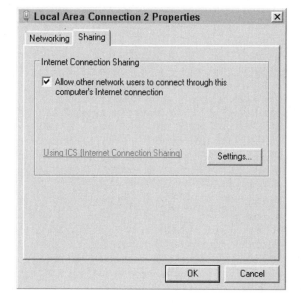

I say "may" because sometimes it pops up and sometimes it doesn't; I've not figured out what makes it appear or not.

Click OK and you'll return to Network Connections, where you'll see that your connectoid or NIC now have the status Shared in addition to Enabled, Connected, or the like. For example, the shared DSL connection produces a Network Connection window that looks like Figure 10.20.

FIGURE 10.20
Network Connections
with ICS enabled

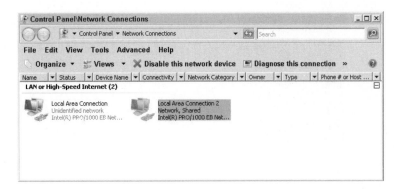

Step Four: Configure the Intranet Machines

You're now ready to share the wealth, Internet connection-wise. You have already configured your systems in your internal network, your intranet, to get their IP addresses automatically. "Automatically" means that they look for a DHCP server and if there is one then they get their IP addresses from that DHCP server. If there's no DHCP server — which has been the case until recently on your intranet — then they just give themselves APIPA addresses in the 169.254.x.x range.

Now that ICS is running, your network now has a DHCP server, because ICS includes a simple DHCP server. You need to go tell your systems on your intranet to try to find a DHCP server again and, while there are several ways to do that, the simplest is to just reboot. But before you do, check the machines — it appears that XP systems are smart enough to detect that there's now a DHCP server in residence, and so you'll probably find that they've *already* got an address. The client systems will all have addresses in the 192.168.0.x range.

What About the Firewall?

Windows Server 2008 comes equipped with a firewall. The firewall normally won't allow any access to your system at all. However, when you added file and folder sharing earlier, not only did Windows Server 2008 install the File Services role for you, but it also made the required changes to the firewall automatically. The same thing happens when you install ICS. The moment you install ICS, Windows Server 2008 is smart enough to add the required exception to the Windows Firewall. To see this for yourself, choose Start ➤ Settings ➤ Control Panel ➤ Windows Firewall to display the Windows Firewall window. Click "Change settings" to display the Windows Firewall Settings dialog box. Select the Exceptions tab and you'll see that it now contains an Internet Connection Sharing entry and that the entry is checked to allow the exception as shown in Figure 10.21.

FIGURE 10.21
Verify that Windows made the appropriate firewall exception for you.

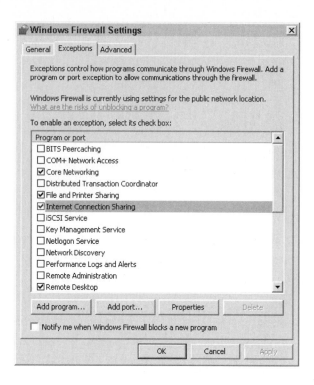

With our "phone numbers" — our IP addresses — in place, we need to add some people-friendly identifiers — a phone directory, you might say. We'll take that job on in the next three chapters, starting with an overview of name resolution in the next chapter.

Chapter 11

What's in a Name? Network Name Overview

Most things that we humans work with have names. Without a name, it's hard to identify an object or discuss it in any meaningful way. Effective names are ones that are easy to remember and understand. They also have context in that you associate the object with other objects. That's why names are so important to networks. If I were to say, "Come visit my Web site at 70.165.73.5," then I think it's safe to say that I wouldn't have to put in 20 servers to handle the overwhelming traffic, if you know what I mean — "`www.minasi.com`" is a bit easier to remember. Similarly, remembering that your intranet server "192.168.50.10" holds the bookkeeping data is a lot easier if you can name the server "Accounting."

Unfortunately, human names are inexact to a computer — examples are "Accounting," "the Accounting server," or "that stupid server that we really need to upgrade, but that those bozos in Accounting won't let us upgrade?" That's why the "true" address of a computer, its IP address, is numeric. But we humans *like* the idea of names, so we need some way to make both the silicon-based and carbon-based components of the network get along. The compromise that virtually all networks strike is the *network name*, a pairing of "human recognizable and remember-able" with "computer understandable."

To accommodate both humans and computers, vendors have had to develop a number of naming schemes over the years. These schemes help create a link between names and numbers. As with many things, as vendors and standards committees developed better ways to create naming schemes, the old naming schemes were abandoned, but not forgotten. In a Windows network, you will, for historical reasons, have to deal with two different naming systems.

When I've helped people solve problems on their networks over the years, I am not exaggerating when I say that at least half of the root causes of those problems are naming systems: people get them confused, they're not configured right, or there's some breakdown in the process whereby the computers on the network translate the sorta-human-friendly name to the computer-friendly IP address, a process called *name resolution*. That's why I felt that this topic was so important that we're devoting three chapters — this one and the next two — to name resolution, and you'll run into name resolution yet again in the companion book.

In this chapter, I want to set the scene by introducing the notion of name resolution and Windows' two name resolution systems.

What Is Naming All About: What a Name Server Does for You

As you've already read, name resolution is a "must" in networking. You'll find it in every operating system and there have probably been as many name resolution systems as there have *been* operating systems!

Of course, you need some way to store names permanently in a way that the software can access them. Even though names work fine for humans, they're ambiguous. Something's got to be able to answer the question, "what IP address corresponds to the name 'AccountingServer,'" and that something is generically called a *name server*. (Name servers can usually also perform the reverse task, of answering the question "what name does the system at 70.165.73.5 have," but that tends to be a less-used capability, as you'll see.)

At one time, all networks were small and you could use a single name to access a network object. You could call a server Accounting and have the name work perfectly well. Early networks relied on simple schemes because no one knew that we'd eventually end up with an Internet. Vendors also followed a number of routes to answer the need for naming. It was evident that networks required a naming scheme of some sort, but precisely how this naming scheme should work wasn't evident at all. But, like Nature, the IT business abhors a vacuum, and so many name resolution systems appeared.

As you'll see, getting rid of a name resolution system isn't easy. Both operating systems *and* applications are designed with particular name resolution systems in mind. That's why even though Microsoft has been trying to kill off its pre-year-2000 name resolution system (something called NetBIOS or WINS, depending on the context), many organizations find themselves unable to shut that old system off. You see, those organizations upgrade to the latest version of Windows on their desktops and servers, buy the latest version of Office ... but find that they can't part with some ten-year-old, home-grown application that was built in the pre-2000 days. Sometimes, though, there's a way around that, as you'll learn in the name resolution coverage in this book and the next.

Name Resolution in Perspective: Introduction to WINS, NetBIOS, DNS, and Winsock

Consider the following two commands, both issued to the same server:

```
ping server01.bigfirm.com
```

and

```
net use G: \\server01\
```

In the `ping` command, the server is referred to as `server01.bigfirm.com`. In the `net use` command, that same server is called \\server01. The difference is important for these reasons.

Ping relies upon a traditionally Internet-oriented programming interface called *Winsock*, and any program running Ping generally needs access to something called a *Domain Name System (DNS) server* in order to execute the `ping` command.

`net use` relies upon a traditionally Microsoft networking–oriented programming interface called *Network Basic Input/Output System (NetBIOS)*, and any program running `net use` generally needs access to something called a *WINS server* to execute the `net use` command.

Let's do a bit of background work in order to understand Winsock, DNS, NetBIOS, and WINS.

The Old: WINS, NetBIOS, and LMHOSTS

Back in the early '80s, IBM wanted to create a way to network PCs together. Like all successful technology companies, they wanted to own the whole idea from the ground up, and so they discarded the idea of using existing network hardware or software and set out to create their own. The hardware side was to be something called "token ring" that was sort of popular with some large organizations for a few years, but which was eventually supplanted by the cheaper and faster Ethernet. On the software side ... well, they were having success vis-à-vis operating systems with Microsoft, which was, believe it or not, little more than a startup at the time. So they asked Microsoft to build networking software for token ring, and Microsoft and IBM soon cooked up a network naming scheme whereby you could give a computer any name up to 16 characters. How to convert a name like PRINTSERVER into a network address? Simple: just broadcast. To figure out PRINTSERVER's network address, a client computer would just broadcast a "hey, which one of you guys is PRINTSERVER?" message, and every single computer on the network would stop what it was doing, listen to the message, and, if that computer was PRINTSERVER, would respond, "that's me." Inefficient? Yes. Likely to support big networks? Nope — can you imagine having to build a world-wide network that allowed broadcasts to travel the entire globe?

This name resolution system's name was "NetBIOS," which stands for "network basic input/output system" and no, that name doesn't seem to have much to do with name resolution — it's just one of those historical accidents — don't bother trying to pick apart its meaning. NetBIOS grew and changed over the years, as network name maximum lengths were shortened to 15 characters, and broadcasts became less important thanks to the introduction of a system of central servers who kept track of NetBIOS names called WINS — the Windows Internet Naming Service. As you'll learn in the next chapter, NetBIOS-aware systems could also use a sort of "helper file" to fill in the cracks in unusual cases, a file named "LMHOSTS." But even at its most modern, Net-BIOS never broke its habit of those messy broadcasts — when NetBIOS can't resolve a name with the newfangled software, it always returns to its mid-'80s roots.

By the late '90s, however, Microsoft — who by then had broken away from IBM and was fashioning its own empire — realized that while network naming hegemony would be nice, it wasn't gonna happen, because the rest of the world was moving to a different name resolution system. So, with the advent of Windows 2000 on 21 February 2000, Microsoft started the slow process of deemphasizing NetBIOS in their software — WINS, LMHOSTS, broadcasts and all. We're still in the post-NetBIOS transition phase, although brand-new networks running only the most up-to-date operating systems and applications can probably avoid WINS.

So if you're new to networking, do you need to know NetBIOS? When asked by people when they can turn off WINS and ignore NetBIOS altogether, I say, it seems this way to me:

◆ WINS, your days are numbered ...

◆ ... but unfortunately, that number seems pretty big.

Seriously, the answer is yes — I highly recommend that everyone in the networking business understand the NetBIOS-related technologies. token ring's gone, but you'll find its old naming buddy nearly everywhere, causing trouble.

The New: Domain Naming System (DNS)

At just about the same time that IBM and Microsoft were dreaming up NetBIOS, the ARPA guys were, you'll recall, dreaming up what would eventually become the Internet. When there were about 12 computers on the Internet, then name resolution was simple. Given that connecting systems across wide areas was part of the Internet's reason for existence, broadcasts were out from the beginning, and so instead every computer on the Internet — all 12 of them — had a text file on its hard disk called "HOSTS" which listed the names and IP addresses of every computer on the Internet — all 12 of them.

Realizing that this HOSTS thing wasn't going to work for an Internet bigger than, say, 20 machines, a fellow named Paul Mockapetris cooked up RFC 882 in November 1983. (I had the pleasure of spending a day with him at a conference in 2004. He's a very nice guy and modest to a fault. I could think of a few "big names" in our business who could do worse than to behave a bit more like Dr. Mockapetris — couldn't you?) Unassumingly titled "Domain names — concepts and facilities," this document laid out how to build a naming system that could grow and grow and grow through a hierarchical — that is, levels upon levels — system of names. When you see a name such as www.microsoft.com, what you're actually seeing is three levels of a hierarchy — the "com," "microsoft," and "www" pieces are all different levels. You'll learn about DNS in Chapter 13, followed by a more Active Directory- and 2008-centric discussion of DNS in the companion book in this series.

Two Different Lineages, Two Different Names

Let's return to the ping/net use command comparison and look a bit under the hood into what is technically "programmer territory," but that will make understanding why things work the way they do a bit easier. The ping command is clearly a TCP/IP/Internet kind of command. You can't run it unless you're running TCP/IP, and as a matter of fact, it's a valid command on a Unix, Virtual Memory System (VMS), Macintosh, or MVS (IBM mainframe) machine, so long as that machine is running a TCP/IP protocol stack.

In contrast, net use is a Microsoft networking command. You can do a net use on an NT or newer network (including Windows Server 2008) no matter what protocol you're running, but the command usually wouldn't be valid on a Unix, VMS, Macintosh, or whatever kind of machine. In general, Microsoft networking is pretty much built to work on PCs.

Application Program Interface = Modularity

The difference is in the network application programming interface (API) that the application is built atop. API? What's that?

Well, years ago, most PC software had no understanding of networks at all. But that's not true anymore; there are many "network-aware" programs around. For example, the software that lets a Windows Server 2008 system be a file server is network aware; what good would a file server be without a network? Other network-aware server software includes Web servers such as Internet Information Server (IIS) or e-mail servers such as Exchange.

Desktop machines — *clients* — use network-aware software as well. The program that lets you browse file servers with Network on Windows Server 2008 and Vista, My Network Places on Windows 2000 and later systems, and Network Neighborhood on Windows 9x and NT 4 systems is generically called a "client for Microsoft networking" and is network aware. The same holds true when you use command-line commands such as net view (which lets you view the servers in a workgroup or the shares on a server) or net use. So also is a Web browser (the client software for a Web server, like Internet Explorer) or an e-mail client.

But the programmers who build network-aware applications such as file server clients or Web browsers aren't generally the programmers who write the rest of the networking software — the NIC drivers, the protocols, and so on. Different pieces of network software are usually designed to fit together in a modular fashion. But the only way that the folks who write the Web browsers can remain compatible with the folks who write the TCP/IP code is if the application developers and the protocol developers agree on an interface, a kind of "software connector" between the two pieces of software. More and more, designers build software to be modular specifically so that the Web browser people don't have to coordinate closely with the TCP/IP protocol–writing people.

The interface between a protocol and the applications that rely on it is called the *application programming interface* (API). Think of an API as being something like the controls you use when driving a car. Your car's steering wheel, accelerator, and other controls form the interface that you see, and you learn to use them to operate the car. You might have no idea while you're driving what's under your car's hood — you just push down the accelerator and the car goes faster. If someone snuck into my garage tonight and replaced the internal combustion engine in my Honda with a magic engine that didn't use gas, I would have no idea, nor would I care until I eventually noticed that the gas gauge seemed to be broken. As a driver, I really don't have to know anything at all about engines — all I've got to know is that the pedal on the right makes the car go faster. So long as the magic engine makes the car go vroom-vroom when I push down the right pedal, I'm happy.

The "automobile API" consists of a few "primitive" commands: Brake the car, accelerate the car, shift the car's transmission, and so on. There is no command "back the car out of the driveway," and yet I can still back a car out of a driveway by just assembling several of the primitive commands into the actual action of backing a car out of a driveway. The best part about this generic automobile API is that once you learn how to drive one car, you can instantly use another. In other words, you are an "application designed for the car driver controls API."

In contrast, consider how private pilots learn to fly. They have two pedals on the floor of their plane, but the left pedal turns them left and the right pedal turns them right. Someone trained as a private pilot would be an "application designed for the private plane API." Taking someone who can fly a plane and plunking him down in a car without any other training wouldn't work too well. In the same way, if an application is built for *one* network API, then it won't work on another. But if you built a car whose controls acted like an airplane's, airplane pilots could drive the car without any trouble.

NetBIOS versus Winsock still not clear? Then consider one more analogy. Think of the APIs as communications devices. Telephones and the mail service are communications devices, also, so I'll use them in an analogy. Ping's job is to communicate with some other PC, and net use also wants to communicate with some PC. But Ping uses Winsock (the telephone) and net use uses NetBIOS (the mail). If you use the telephone to call a friend, then that friend's "name" as far as the phone is concerned may be something like (707) 555-2121. As far as the mail is concerned, however, the friend's "name" might be Charles Dwyer, 124 Main Street, Anytown, VA, 32102. Both are perfectly valid "names" for your friend Charles, but they're different because different communications systems need different name types. In the same way, server01.bigfirm.com and \\server01 are both perfectly valid but different names for the same server. (Refer to the "Sockets, Ports, and the Winsock Interface" section of Chapter 10 for additional information on Winsock.)

What's the bottom line here? Network programs are built atop APIs, and APIs are tied to name resolution systems. Thus, both operating systems and application programs are tied to name resolution systems, as I alluded to earlier. Keep that in mind when troubleshooting a network problem.

That's a quick look at name resolution; now we're ready to move on to Chapters 12 and 13. As you progress through the sections of those chapters, remember that the goal of a particular technology is to match a numeric identifier used by software with a text identifier used by humans — it really is that simple. The hard part comes in implementing a naming scheme in such a way that you can reliably identify machines and ensure those machines can connect to each other as needed. The name server provides this functionality using any of a number of standard protocols.

Chapter 12

Old Names: Understanding NetBIOS, WINS, and NetBIOS over TCP/IP

It's time to look at the "old" names in detail. So, let me pick up where the last chapter left off. I'm stretching a point a bit here, but I could say that cars and planes are just different ways of solving the same problem: transportation. In the same way, various network vendors over the years have tackled the same problem and come up with different solutions. In particular, Microsoft has, as you've already read, built its network applications atop a network API called the Network Basic Input-Output System (NetBIOS) that first appeared on a product from a company called Sytek and that was later promoted and expanded by IBM and Microsoft. The Internet world, on the other hand, has used a different network API called *sockets*. In the Microsoft world, we call our special version of sockets *Winsock*.

NetBIOS and Winsock

Recall that the value of an API is that it separates your network applications from your network vendor — you needn't buy your network operating system from the same people you bought your network fax software from. For example, if you buy a network fax application designed for a network API named NetBIOS, you should be able to run that network fax application on any network at all, so long as the network supports the NetBIOS API. Over time, we've seen a number of seemingly dissimilar networks that all sported NetBIOS as their API, including Lantastic, OS/2 LAN Server, LAN Manager, HP's LM/UX, Digital's PathWorks, Windows for Workgroups, Samba under Linux and Unix, NT and Windows Server family. Code written for one of these networks could run with little or no changes on any of the others.

Similarly, at one time there were several vendors selling a version of TCP/IP for Windows for Workgroups (WfW) back in 1992–1994, back before Microsoft released a TCP/IP stack for WfW. If the Winsock implementations of each of those TCP/IP versions were built right, then you should have been able to run the same copy of Eudora Light (a free Internet e-mail program) or Netscape Navigator on any of them.

Can your network live with just Winsock or NetBIOS programming interfaces and ignore DNS? I can't see how with today's networking demands. You want to run the NetBIOS-based programs because anything written for Microsoft networks prior to Windows 2000 was written to run on NetBIOS. And you want to run Winsock-based programs because so many Internet-type applications exist — the Web and e-mail stand out, but there are many more — and they're built to work with Winsock.

In fact, one of the major changes in NT wrought by Windows 2000 (and later OSes) was that almost all of Windows 2000's networking will work fine on Winsock and doesn't need NetBIOS at all. (Not everything; for example, some Exchange 2000 configurations need NetBIOS, and server clusters need NetBIOS, as does the ability to restrict users to only logging onto specific work-stations.) But any Windows 9*x*, Workgroups, or NT system needing to access data on Windows 2000/2003 or 2008 servers will do so via NetBIOS. Similarly, any pre–Windows 2000 applications running on a Windows 2000 system can run only atop NetBIOS, even if all of the systems in the network are Windows 2000 systems. The result is that virtually all Windows 2000 systems need a complete NetBIOS infrastructure.

Handling Legacy and NetBIOS Names: The Windows Internet Name Service

Anyway, for those of you hoping that WINS would bite the dust in Server 2008, I've got to report that, sorry, it looks like we've still got to support it on many networks, because many people still run applications that are tied to NetBIOS. (There is, however, something called a GlobalNames zone that's new to 2008 that may make even some of the old NetBIOS-addicted applications able to go cold turkey. We talk about the GlobalNames zone in the DNS chapter of the second book of the *Mastering Windows Server 2008* series.) So, let's see how to support this "legacy name resolving system." (*Legacy* is computer industry-ese for "crappy old stuff that we hate and that's why we upgraded in the first place, but we can't seem to get rid of all of it and so now we have to support both the new incomprehensible stuff *and* the crappy old stuff." But *legacy* sure makes it sound better, at least to me.)

NetBIOS atop TCP/IP (NBT)

The NetBIOS API is implemented on the NetBEUI, IPX/SPX, and TCP/IP protocols that Microsoft distributes. That makes Microsoft's TCP/IP a bit different from the TCP/IP you find on Unix (for example), because the Unix TCP/IP almost certainly won't have a NetBIOS API on it; it'll probably only have the TCP/IP sockets API on it. (Recall that as with all PC implementations of TCP/IP, Microsoft's TCP/IP form of sockets is called the Winsock API.)

NetBIOS on the Microsoft implementation of TCP/IP is essential, again to make older operating systems and applications happy. And NetBIOS over TCP (which is usually abbreviated NBT or NetBT) needs a name resolver.

Now, basic old NetBIOS converted names to network addresses by just broadcasting — "Hey, I'm looking for \\AJAX; if you're out there, \\AJAX, tell me your IP address!" — but clearly that's not going to be the answer in a routed environment; all of those "name resolution shouts" will stop dead at the routers. If \\AJAX is across a router from us, our software will never find \\AJAX.

NetBIOS name resolution over TCP/IP is, then, not a simple nut to crack. Many people realized this, and so there are two Internet RFCs (Requests for Comment) on this topic, RFC 1001 and 1002, published in 1986.

B NODES, P NODES, AND M NODES

The RFCs attacked the problem by offering options.

The first option was sort of simplistic: Just do broadcasts. A computer that used broadcasts to resolve NetBIOS names to IP addresses is referred to in the RFCs as a *B node*. To find out who server01 is, then, a PC running B node software would just shout out, "Hey! Anybody here named server01?"

Simple, yes, but fatally flawed: Remember what happens to broadcasts when they hit routers? As routers don't rebroadcast the messages to other subnets, this kind of name resolution would only be satisfactory on single-subnet networks.

The second option was to create a name server of some kind and to use that. Then, when a computer needed to resolve a name of another computer, all it needed to do was send a point-to-point message to the computer running the name server software. As point-to-point messages *do* get retransmitted over routers, this second approach would work fine even on networks with routers. A computer using a name server to resolve NetBIOS names into IP addresses using point-to-point messages is said to be a *P node*.

Again, a good idea, but it runs afoul of all of the problems that DNS had. *What* name server should be used? Will it be dynamic? The name server for NetBIOS name resolution is, by the way, referred to as a NetBIOS name server, or NBNS.

The most complex approach to NetBIOS name resolution over TCP/IP as described in the RFCs is the *M node*, or *mixed* node. It uses a combination of broadcasts and point-to-point communications to an NBNS.

MICROSOFT FOLLOWS THE RFCs, ALMOST

When Microsoft started out with TCP/IP, it implemented a kind of M node software. It was "point-to-point" in that you could look up addresses in the HOSTS file, or a file called LMHOSTS, and if you had a DNS server, then you could always reference that; other than those options, Microsoft TCP/IP was mainly B node-ish, which limited you to single-subnet networks. (Or required that you repeat broadcasts over the network, clogging up your network.) Clearly, some kind of NBNS was needed, and the simpler it was to work with, the better. As the RFCs were silent on the particulars of an NBNS, vendors had license to go out and invent something proprietary and so they did — several of them, in fact, with the result that you'd expect: None of them talk to each other.

That's where the Windows Internet Name Service, or WINS, comes in.

WINS is simply Microsoft's proprietary NBNS service. What makes it stand out from the rest of the pack is Microsoft's importance in the industry. They have the clout to create a proprietary system and make it accepted widely enough so that it becomes a de facto standard.

Microsoft's NetBIOS-over-TCP client software not only implements B, P, and M nodes, it also includes a fourth, non-RFC node type. Microsoft calls it an H, or Hybrid, node.

But wait a minute; isn't *M node* a hybrid? Yes. Both M nodes and H nodes use both B node and P node, but the implementation is different:

◆ In M node, name resolution would first broadcast (B node) and then, if that fails, communicate directly with the NBNS (P node).

◆ In H node, the NBNS is tried first. If it can't help you, then try a broadcast.

M NODE VERSUS H NODE

"Hmmm," you may be saying, "Why would anyone want to first broadcast, *then* look up the answer in the name server? Why clutter up the network cable with useless broadcasts when we could instead go right to the source and reduce network chatter?"

The answer is that it's a matter of economics. Recall that the RFCs on NetBIOS over TCP were written back in the mid-1980s, when a typical PC had perhaps an 8 MHz clock rate and a 5 MHz internal bus. A 10 megabit Ethernet full of mid-'80s PCs would have had a lot of trouble loading the network enough for anyone to even notice. The bottleneck in networks in those days was the CPU or disk speed of the network server. But if the network includes routers — and if it doesn't, then broadcasting is all you need — then consider what the routers are connected to: wide area network links, probably expensive 9600, 14,400, or 19,200bps leased lines. In a network like this, the LAN was a seemingly infinite resource, and wasting it with tons of broadcasts was of no consequence. In contrast, creating more traffic over the WAN by having every machine ask for NetBIOS names (presuming the NetBIOS Name Server was across the WAN link) could greatly reduce the effectiveness of that expensive WAN. Besides, the reasoning went, the vast majority of the time a PC only wanted to talk to another PC on the same LAN, so broadcasts would suffice for name resolution most of the time. The result? M nodes.

The economic picture in 1994, when Microsoft was inventing WINS, was another story entirely: LANs were clogged and WAN links were far cheaper — so H nodes made more sense.

The easiest way to configure the node type on a system is via DHCP, which we haven't yet covered (we'll get there in Chapter 14), but, in brief, DHCP is a way to centrally configure IP addresses and options for workstations and servers. One of those options lets you force any DHCP client to be a B, P, M, or H node. It shows up as a "WINS/NBNS Node Type." As you'll see in Chapter 14, you give DHCP a numeric value to set the client's NetBIOS name resolution technique. A value of 1 creates a B node, 2 is used for a P node, 4 for an M node, and 8 for an H node, the recommended node type.

UNDERSTANDING THE NBT NAMES ON YOUR SYSTEM

A major part of the NetBIOS architecture is its lavish use of names. A workstation attaches up to 16 names to itself. Names in NetBIOS are either group names, which can be shared — workgroups and domains are two examples — or normal names, which can't be shared, like a machine name.

NOTE

What's a workgroup? Every networked Windows system is said to be in a "workgroup" or a "domain." Recall that we introduced the idea of a domain in Chapter 3: A *domain* is a collection of Windows systems that trust a small number of servers to handle authentications for them. What, then, is the definition of a *workgroup*? It's a sort of negative definition: if you're a Windows box that does networking but you're not a member of a domain, then you're said to be in a workgroup. If you haven't joined your system to a domain, then by default Windows says that you are in a workgroup named "workgroup." You can, however, create a workgroup with any name that you like, although honestly with modern Windows systems there's very little reason to bother. You'll see me create one in a moment, but I only did it to clarify the point that workgroups don't *have* to be named "workgroup."

As you'll soon see that WINS keeps track of all of these names, you may be curious about what all of them *are* — so let's take a minute and look more closely into your system's NetBIOS names and how they're different in 2008.

You can see the names attached to your workstation by opening a command line from a Windows 9*x*, NT, Windows 2000/2003/2008, XP, or Vista machine and typing **nbtstat -n**. I created a server named s1.bigfirm.com, put it in a workgroup named "Markgroup," ran nbtstat -n, and got output like this:

```
C:\Users\Administrator>nbtstat -n

Local Area Connection:
```

```
Node IpAddress: [192.168.1.217] Scope Id: []

        NetBIOS Local Name Table

    Name              Type      Status
    ---------------------------------------------
    S1          <00>  UNIQUE    Registered
    MARKGROUP   <00>  GROUP     Registered
    S1          <20>  UNIQUE    Registered
```

Notice that S1 — NetBIOS doesn't know anything about DNS names, so the system's just "S1" rather than "s1.bigfirm.com" as far as nbtstat's concerned — registers only three names. Try running this command on a pre–Server 2008 system, and you'll see a lot more. In particular,

◆ The <00> record for S1 is unique, meaning that no other system should be allowed to register a record "S1<00>." This record registers the name of my system. (In this case, "register" means that my system broadcast a message saying, "is there anyone out there named 'S1?' 'Cause if not, then I'm taking this name!")

◆ The <00> record for "MARKGROUP" says that this system is signifying that it is a member of a workgroup named "MARKGROUP." That's why its type is "GROUP." More than one system can register that name for itself.

◆ The <20> record for S1, another unique one, advertises that this system is a file server.

I said that things changed under 2008 — how? By default, 2008 disables an ancient service called the "Computer Browser" or "browser" service, which sought to create a list of servers on each subnet. The browser service is pretty "chatty" and thus took up a fair amount of bandwidth on people's networks, and I'm guessing that's why Microsoft disabled it on 2008. I can re-enable it, however, by opening an elevated command prompt and typing this:

```
sc config browser start= auto
md c:\ftest
net share ftest=c:\ftest
sc start browser
```

If you want to try those commands, note that there must be a space between = and auto — that's a quirk of the sc command. I then included the last two commands to create a folder and share it (the browser service doesn't seem to want to run unless this system has at least one folder shared). Wait about five minutes — that's how long the browsing stuff needs to start working — and type **net view**. If you get a list of computers, even if it's only one, then browsing is working.

If I rerun the nbtstat -n command, I get this output:

```
C:\>nbtstat -n

Local Area Connection:
Node IpAddress: [192.168.1.217] Scope Id: []

            NetBIOS Local Name Table

     Name              Type       Status
    ---------------------------------------------
     S1           <00>  UNIQUE    Registered
     MARKGROUP    <00>  GROUP     Registered
     S1           <20>  UNIQUE    Registered
     MARKGROUP    <1E>  GROUP     Registered
     MARKGROUP    <1D>  UNIQUE    Registered
     .._MSBROWSE__.<01>  GROUP    Registered
```

Note the three new items — being a member of a group with the <1E> designation means "I'm willing to be a 'master browser,'" a computer that tries to build and maintain a list of other servers in the MARKGROUP workgroup and on the same subnet. Every system running the Computer Browser service announces that fact with the <1E> record. As it turns out, there *are* no other MARKGROUP servers on that subnet (or anywhere else in the universe, for that matter), so an election process gives S1 the title of "master browser for MARKGROUP on this subnet." S1 designates that he's the go-to guy if you need a list of local servers by registering the *unique* <1D> record for MARKGROUP. So, <1E>="I'm willing to be the master browser," and <1D>="I *am* the master browser." The one with the _MSBROWSE_ name makes it easy for other MARKGROUP master browsers on other segments to find S1. Again, you probably won't see those things on an nbtstat -n output from a 2008 system, but you can see it from any previous operating system, including Vista. You may also see records with <03> labels; those announce that this system is willing to accept messages from an old Windows service called the Messenger service. XP SP2 and 2003 SP1 disabled the service, and neither Vista nor 2008 has the service, but some older systems might, so you might sometimes see an <03> record on an nbtstat output.

TIP

Please note that I'm not suggesting that you leave the Computer Browser service enabled. I just wanted you to understand what you'll see on earlier systems. Restore the old state of affairs by typing **sc config browser start=disabled** and then **sc stop browser**.

Each NetBIOS name on the nbtstat -n output is, as I hope you can see by now, something that a system asserts about itself — this is my name, I'm a member of this workgroup or domain, I'm a server, and so on. For example, if some other user on the network wanted to connect to a share named STUFF on this computer, she could type **net use * \\s1\stuff**, and the redirector software (the client software for the file server service) on her computer would then do a NetBIOS name resolution on the name s1<00>, because the <00> suffix is used by the redirector.

You can see the list of registered names on any computer in your network by typing **nbtstat -a <ip address>**. Table 12.1 summarizes suffixes and the programs that use them.

No matter what kind of computer you have on a Microsoft enterprise network, it will have at least one name registered — the *<computer name>* [00] name. Most computers also register *<workgroup>* [00], which proclaims them as a member of a workgroup.

Adding file and/or printer sharing capabilities to a computer would add the *<computer name>* [20] name. Every system running the Computer Browser service (which is, again, disabled by default for Vista and 2008 but enabled for earlier versions of Windows) agrees to be candidates for browse master by default, so unless you configure a machine to *not* be a candidate for browse mastering, then the *<workgroup name>* [1E] name will appear on any machine offering file or printer sharing. If the machine happens to be the browse master, it'll have *<workgroup name>* [1D] as well. Workstations use the [1D] name to initially get a list of browse servers when they first start up: They broadcast a message looking to see if the [1D] machine exists, and if it does, then the [1D] machine presents the workstation with a list of potential browsers. Browse masters get the network name [01][02]__MSBROWSE__[02][01] as well — it's a group name, and only the *master* browsers are members. Master browsers use that name to discover that each other exists.

TABLE 12.1:   Examples of Machine Names

UNIQUE NAMES	WHERE USED
<computername>[oo h]	Workstation service. This is the "basic" name that every player in a Microsoft network would have, no matter how little power it has in the network.
<computername>[o3 h]	Deprecated for Vista and later OSes, but will appear for earlier OSes running the Messenger service. Used for administrative alerts or pop-up messages; NET SEND messages use this name.
<computername>[o6 h]	RAS Server service.
<computername>[1Fh]	NetDDE service; will only appear if NetDDE is active or if you're running a NetDDE application. (You can see this by starting up Network Hearts, for example.)
<computername>[2o h]	We used to call this the Server service, but now it is File Server; this name will only appear on machines with file/printer sharing enabled.
<computername>[21 h]	RAS Client service.
<computername>[BEh]	Deprecated on Vista and later OSes, but will appear for earlier OSes running the Network Monitor agent.
<computername>[BFh]	Deprecated on Vista and later OSes, but will appear for earlier OSes running the Network Monitor utility.
<domain name>[1Bh]	This system is the domain master browser which is the primary domain controller (or PDC emulator, if the domain is Active Directory). There is only one of these per domain.
<domain name>[1Ch]	This says that this machine is a domain controller on this domain. The PDC will register one and all DCs that are not the PDC will also register one. This is, therefore, not a unique name; more than one DC can exist, so more than one system can have this name.

TABLE 12.1: Examples of Machine Names *(CONTINUED)*

UNIQUE NAMES	WHERE USED
<domain name>[1Dh]	Master browser, which means "I create and maintain the browse list for members of this domain/workgroup *on this segment.*" Reports to the 1B system, the *domain* master browser. Thus, if your network has five segments, you will have four master browsers and one domain master browser, and the domain master browser will act as "browse master" on its segment. By default you won't see one of these on a 2008 system, as 2008 disables the computer browser service.
<domain name>[1Eh] or *<workgroup name>*[1Eh]	Used in browser elections, indicates that this computer would agree to be a browser. By default you won't see one of these on a 2008 system, as 2008 disables the browser service.
MSBrowse	Master browser for a subnet.

Name Resolution before WINS: LMHOSTS

Clients written prior to WINS, or clients without a specified WINS server, try to resolve a NetBIOS name to an IP address with several methods. The tools they'll use, if they exist, are:

◆ A HOSTS file, if present

◆ Broadcasts

◆ An LMHOSTS file, if present

◆ A DNS server, if present

You met HOSTS before — it's just a simple ASCII file in Chapter 11. Each line contains an IP address, at least one space, and a name. LMHOSTS works in a similar way to HOSTS. And yes, you'd do well to understand LMHOSTS, as it solves many name resolution problems with pre–Windows 2000 servers and perhaps even Windows 2003 Servers or Server 2008 machines in an enterprise with both Windows 2000– and NT 4–based domains.

Let me stress that: Don't skip this section. It's not a history lesson; it can sometimes be the only way to fix a networking problem even with Server 2008, believe it or not.

Introducing LMHOSTS

Recall that HOSTS is an ASCII file that lists IP addresses and Internet names, such as the following:

```
100.100.210.13 ducky.mallard.com
211.39.82.15 Exchange.minasi.com
```

Microsoft reasoned that if a simple ASCII file could supplement or replace DNS to resolve Winsock names, why not create an ASCII file to hold NetBIOS names? The result is the LMHOSTS file. LMHOSTS consists of pairs of IP addresses and names, like HOSTS, but the names are 15-character *NetBIOS* names that do not contain spaces or dots, not Internet-type names:

```
100.100.210.13 ducky
211.39.82.15 Exchange
```

I assumed in the previous example that the NetBIOS name is identical to the leftmost part of the Internet name, although that's not necessary, as you may recall from the earlier discussion in the previous chapter about setting up TCP/IP on a system.

REPRESENTING HEX SUFFIXES IN LMHOSTS

But how to handle the nonprinting characters in a NetBIOS name, the <1B> used by the primary domain controller, the <1C> used by all domain controllers? Recall that the hex suffixes are always the 16th character in a NetBIOS name, so write out a suffixed NetBIOS name like so:

◆ Enclose the name in quotes.

◆ Add enough spaces to the end of the name so that you've got 15 characters in the name.

◆ After the spaces, add \0x followed by the hex code.

For example, suppose I had a domain named CLOUDS and a domain controller named \\CUMULONIMBUS at address 210.10.20.3. I'm creating an LMHOSTS file that I can put on systems around the network so that they can find \\CUMULONIMBUS and recognize it as the primary domain controller for CLOUDS. The LMHOSTS file would look like this:

```
210.10.20.3 cumulonimbus
210.10.20.3 "clouds          \0x1Bx"
```

This indicates that the machine at IP address 210.10.20.3 has two names (or at *least* two names). As CLOUDS is a six-letter word, I added nine spaces to the end of it.

USING HEX SUFFIXES TO SOLVE AUTHENTICATION PROBLEMS

Suppose you have a system that absolutely cannot find a domain controller; no matter what you do, you get "no domain controller found." Or suppose you have two Active Directory domains that you are trying to build a trust relationship between, but the one domain seems unable to find the other domain.

In this case, you need desperate measures. You need LMHOSTS.

I'm going to show you a trick whereby you can take a particular system and "nail" it to a particular DC. Do this trick on a balky workstation and you do a couple of things. First, you force the workstation to use a particular DC when logging in — no ifs, ands, or buts. Second, you remove all of the workstation's normal methods of finding DCs...so the DC that you designate in LMHOSTS had better be up and running!

Systems connecting to Active Directories in mixed mode (again, apologies, we'll explain all of the ins and outs of domains in Chapter 15) query NetBIOS for a machine with a name equal to the domain's name, suffixed with a "1C." As you just learned, you can create an LMHOSTS entry that does this very thing by adding enough spaces so that there are 15 characters between the open double quote and where the \0x part starts. So let's suppose that I had a difficult system that seemed unable to see I had a DC named SATURNV in a domain named BOOSTERS. Let's also say that SATURNV is the PDC of that domain, and its IP address is 10.10.100.2. I'd create the following LMHOSTS entries:

```
10.10.100.2 saturnv
10.10.100.2 "boosters        \0x1C" #PRE
10.10.100.2 "boosters        \0x1B" #PRE
```

All three entries refer to the same computer. The first says that its name is saturnv, the second says that it is a domain controller of a domain named boosters, and the last says that it is not only *a* domain controller of boosters, it is *the* primary domain controller of that domain. I'll explain the #PRE in a few paragraphs.

A SPECIAL SUFFIX FOR DOMAIN CONTROLLERS: #DOM

In most cases, the only hex suffix you'll care about is <1C>, the suffix indicating a domain controller. You can create an entry for it as previously, with a \0x1C suffix, or you can use a special metacommand that Microsoft included in LMHOSTS: #DOM.

To indicate that a given entry is a domain controller, enter a normal LMHOSTS entry for it, but add to the end of the line #DOM: and the name of the domain controller. In the CUMULONIMBUS example, you could register CUMULONIMBUS's name and the fact that it is a domain controller for CLOUDS like so:

```
210.10.20.3 cumulonimbus #DOM:clouds
```

But \x01C and #DOM behave a bit differently, in my experience. If you enter a \x01C entry in an LMHOSTS, then NT will use it and only it, ignoring WINS or any other information — so if you're going to use an \0x1C entry, make sure it's right! Furthermore, if you try to tell NT about more than one domain controller in a given domain using the \0x1C suffix, it will only pay attention to the *last* one mentioned in the LMHOSTS file.

"LISTEN TO ME!": THE #PRE COMMAND

This is a bit out of order, as I haven't taken up WINS in detail yet, but as long as I'm discussing LMHOSTS, it kind of fits. As you'll learn later, a normal H node type of client will first send a name resolution question to a WINS server before consulting its local LMHOSTS file, if one exists. Only if the WINS server returns a failure, saying, "I'm sorry, I can't resolve that name," does the client look in its LMHOSTS file. But sometimes you want to tell a PC, "I have a particular entry here in LMHOSTS that is more important than anything that WINS tells you. If you need to look up this particular NetBIOS name, use the LMHOSTS entry rather than looking at WINS." For those entries, you can use the #PRE metacommand. In the case of CUMULONIMBUS, the previous line would look like:

```
cumulonimbus  #DOM:clouds #PRE
```

#PRE's job is this: If WINS and LMHOSTS offer conflicting answers to the question, "What's the IP address of CUMULONIMBUS?" then in general the client listens to WINS rather than LMHOSTS — in other words, by default WINS, uh, wins. But #PRE gives an LMHOSTS entry precedence over anything that WINS has to say.

CENTRALIZED LMHOSTS: #INCLUDE, #ALTERNATE

LMHOSTS is powerful but can require a fair amount of running around because for a user's PC to benefit from LMHOSTS, *the LMHOSTS file must be on the user's PC.* Yuck. That means you'd have to go out Amongst The Users, a happy time for some but a — ummm — mixed blessing for others. Every time you changed LMHOSTS, you'd have to walk around replacing the old LMHOSTS file with a new one on every single machine — ugh, double yuck. Is there a better way?

Sure. You can put a small LMHOSTS file on a user's machine with just one simple command: "Go to this server to read the 'main' LMHOSTS file." Even better, you can specify as many backups for this server as you like. You do it with the #INCLUDE and #ALTERNATE metacommands. Here's a sample LMHOSTS:

```
#BEGIN_ALTERNATE
#INCLUDE \\shadows\stuff\lmhosts
#INCLUDE \\vorlons\stuff\lmhosts
#INCLUDE \\centauri\stuff2\lmhosts
#END_ALTERNATE
```

You can use #INCLUDE without the #ALTERNATEs, but it seems to me that if you're going to go to all the trouble of having a central LMHOSTS, you might as well add some fault tolerance, right? And I would hope that it would go without saying that either \\SHADOWS, \\VORLONS, and \\CENTAURI would have to be on the same subnet as the client PC, or you should add a few lines above the #BEGIN ALTERNATE to tell the PC where to find those three servers.

```
#INCLUDE also takes local filenames:
#INCLUDE D:\MORENAME
```

LMHOSTS is a pretty powerful tool, and it still makes sense in today's NetBIOS-using networks because, as you'll see, WINS is not without its flaws.

WINS: A NetBIOS Name Service for Windows

You've seen that the world before WINS was a rather grim place, where everyone shouts and many questions (well, resolution requests) go unanswered. Now let's look at what happens with WINS.

WINS Needs NT or Later Server

To make WINS work, you must set up an NT 4 or later server to act as the WINS server. The WINS server then acts as the NBNS server, keeping track of who's on the network and handing out name resolution information as needed.

WINS Holds Name Registrations

Basically, when a WINS client (the shorthand term for "any PC running some kind of Microsoft enterprise TCP/IP network client software designed to use WINS for NBT name resolution") first boots up, it goes to the WINS server and introduces itself, or in WINS-speak, it does a name registration. (In fact, as you recall, most machines have several NetBIOS names, so clients register each of those names with WINS.) The client knows the IP address of the WINS server either because you hard-coded it right into the TCP/IP settings for the workstation or because the workstation got a WINS address from DHCP when it obtained an IP lease.

You may recall that the client could get *two* IP addresses, one for a "primary" and one for a "secondary" WINS server. The client tries to get the attention of the primary and register itself on that machine. But if the machine designated as a primary WINS server doesn't respond within a certain amount of time, the client next tries to register with the secondary WINS server. If the secondary will talk to the client and the primary won't, the client registers with the secondary. You can tell that this has happened by doing an `ipconfig /all` at the client. Among other things, this reports the address of the primary WINS server. If that address is the *secondary's* address, then you know that the primary was too busy to talk — and that turns out to be an important diagnostic clue, as you'll see later when I discuss how to design multiserver WINS systems.

In the process of registering its name with a WINS server, the workstation gets the benefit of ensuring that it has a unique name. If the WINS server sees that there's another computer out there with the same name, it will tell the workstation, "You can't use that name." The name registration request and the acknowledgment are both directed IP messages, so they'll cross routers. And when a workstation shuts down, it sends a "name release" request to the WINS server telling it that the workstation will no longer need the NetBIOS name, enabling the WINS server to register it for some other machine.

WINS Client Failure Modes

But what if something goes wrong? What if you try to register a name that some other workstation already has, or what if a workstation finds that the WINS server is unavailable?

Duplicate names are simple — instead of sending a "success" response to the workstation, the WINS server sends a "fail" message in response to the workstation's name request. In response, the workstation does not consider the name registered and doesn't include it in its NetBIOS name table; an `nbstat -n` will not show the name. I've usually found this to manifest itself by not being able to connect to servers outside of the client's own subnet. When I do an `nbtstat -n`, it shows the name missing and that's when I know to start looking for a duplicate name issue.

But if a workstation can't find the WINS server when it boots up, then the workstation simply stops acting as a hybrid NBT node and reverts to its old ways as a Microsoft modified B node, meaning that it depends largely on broadcasts but will also consult LMHOSTS (and perhaps HOSTS, if configured to do so) if they're present.

It's My Name, but for How Long?

Like DHCP, WINS only registers names for a fixed period of time called the *renewal interval*. By default, it's 6 days (144 hours), and there will probably never be a reason for you to change that.

In much the same way that DHCP clients attempt to renew their leases early, WINS clients send "name *refresh* requests" to the WINS server before their names expire — *long* before. According to Microsoft documentation, a WINS client attempts a name refresh very early after it gets its names registered — after one-eighth of the renewal interval. (My tests show that it's actually *three*-eighths, but that's not terribly important.) The WINS server will usually reset the length of time left before the name must be renewed again (this time is sometimes called the *time to live*, or TTL). Once the client has renewed its name *once*, however, it doesn't renew it again and again every one-eighth of its TTL; instead, it only renews its names every one-half of the TTL. (My tests agree with that.)

Installing WINS

Installing WINS is different from DHCP. With DHCP we added a Role; with WINS we add a feature.

When you're planning how many WINS servers you need and where to put them, bear in mind that you need not put a WINS server on each subnet (which is one of the great features of WINS). It *is* a good idea to have a second machine running as a secondary WINS server, however, just for fault tolerance's sake. Remember that if a workstation comes up and can't find a WINS server, it reverts to broadcasting, which will limit its name resolution capabilities to just its local subnet and will cause it to do a lot of shouting, which adds traffic to the subnet. Why would a WINS client not find a WINS server if there's a working WINS server?

Well, normally the client would find the server just fine, but in some small percentage of the cases, the WINS server might be too busy to respond to the client in a timely fashion, causing the client to just give up on the server. That will probably only happen rarely, unless you're over-loading the WINS server. Unfortunately, a very common way to overload a WINS server is to put the WINS server function on the same machine that's also acting as a domain controller. Think about it: When is a WINS server busiest? First thing in the morning, when everyone's booting up and registering names. When's a domain controller busiest? First thing in the morning, when everyone's logging in. That leads to a warning.

If possible, don't put the WINS server function on a domain controller. Or a system with more than one NIC.

That's where a secondary is useful. If you have a backup domain controller, then put a WINS server on that machine as well. The WINS software actually does not use a lot of CPU time, so it probably won't affect your server's performance unless you have thousands of users all hammering on one WINS server. If *that's* the case, I'd dedicate a computer solely to WINS-ing.

To get a WINS server set up, open Server Manager and highlight Features. Then click Add Features, as shown in Figure 12.1.

FIGURE 12.1
Adding a feature

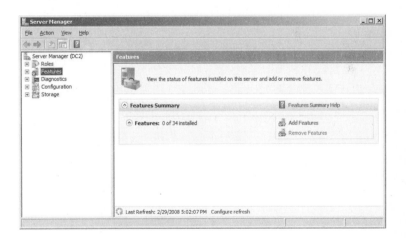

On the Selected Features page in the Features box, scroll down and put a check mark in the box next to WINS Server, as shown in Figure 12.2, and then click Next, Install, and Close.

FIGURE 12.2

Installing WINS

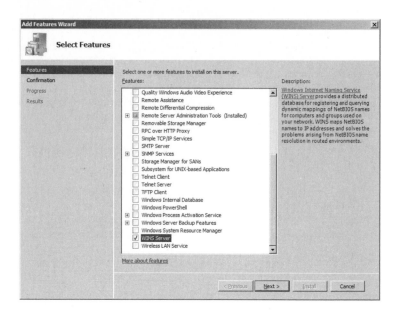

ADDING A FEATURE FROM THE COMMAND LINE

To add the WINS feature from a command line, type the following:

```
ServerManagerCmd -install wins-server
```

No reboots needed anymore — well, at least to add features. Removing a feature does require a reboot. You'll see in Start/Administrative Tools that you have a new snap-in to control WINS. Start it up, click the plus sign next to the server, and it will look like Figure 12.3.

FIGURE 12.3

The initial WINS manager screen

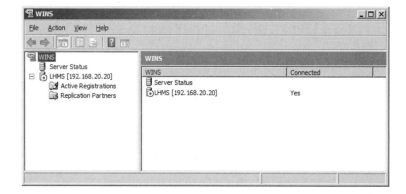

No need to authorize WINS servers, in case you're wondering. The first thing you should do on your WINS server is inform it of the machines on your subnet that are not WINS clients but use NetBIOS on TCP/IP. There won't be many of them, but they may exist; for example, you may have some old pre-1995 Microsoft Windows machines around. Machines with hard-coded IP addresses don't need to be entered, so long as they use WINS: If they know the address of a primary or secondary WINS server, they will register their names with that server. If you *do* have an old system requiring a static mapping, right-click Active Registrations and choose New Static Mapping. You then see a dialog box like the one shown in Figure 12.4.

FIGURE 12.4
New static mapping

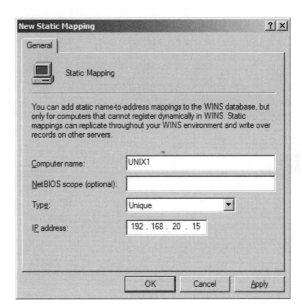

Alternatively, if you have an existing LMHOSTS file, you can click Active Registrations, click the Action menu, and then choose Import LMHOSTS File (or right-click Active Registrations). The program will take that information to build a static-mapping database.

ADDING A STATIC MAPPING FROM THE COMMAND PROMPT

To add a static mapping for a computer named Winsclient with an IP address of 192.168.20.99 from the command prompt, type this:

```
Netsh wins server add name name=winsclient ip={192.168.20.99}
```

Configuring a WINS Server

Right-click the server in the left pane of the WINS snap-in, and choose Properties. You'll see a properties page like the one in Figure 12.5.

FIGURE 12.5
WINS Server configuration properties page

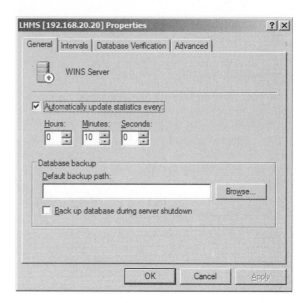

WINS will regularly back up its database — a good disaster recovery step — if you fill in a directory name in Default Backup Path. You can even use a UNC, such as \\ajax\central\wins or the like. A check box allows you to tell WINS to also do a backup specifically when the server is shut down.

Click the Intervals tab to see a page like Figure 12.6.

FIGURE 12.6
WINS Intervals tab

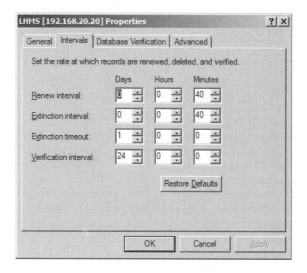

The "Renew interval" defines how often the client will renew its name with the WINS server. The default is every 40 minutes. The "Extinction interval" defines how much time will elapse between when a name is released and when it is marked as extinct. The default is also 40 minutes. After a name is marked as extinct, the "Extinction timeout" defines how long to wait before removing it from the WINS database. The default is 1 day. The "Verification interval" defines how often records received from a WINS partner (the owner of the records) are verified to be accurate.

SETTING INTERVALS FROM THE COMMAND PROMPT

To set the intervals from a command prompt, type the following:

```
set namerecord renew=4800 extinction=7200 extimeout=96400
                        verification=3073600
```

Click the Database Verification tab, and you'll see a page like Figure 12.7.

FIGURE 12.7
Configuring WINS
verification

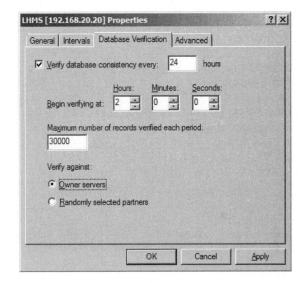

In the past, WINS was notorious for having corrupted WINS records that would get transmitted around the network, wreaking havoc and confusion on the databases. The corruption spreads, and before you know it, you're erasing your WINS databases and starting all over. The "Verify database consistency . . ." option at the top of the screen tells your WINS server to periodically check its records against those of any other server in your enterprise. It's a good idea. If you enable it, I'd let it check every 24 hours, as is the default, and to check against the *owner* rather than a random server (random server is the default). *Owner* in WINS terminology means "the WINS server that generated the original name record." Thus, it could be in a multi-WINS server world that I registered my PC's name with WINS Server 1, which then told WINS Server 2 about me. (This happens automatically, recall — you needn't do anything to get your system registered with WINS except to specify a WINS server in your TCP/IP settings.) WINS Server 2 might run into some kind of trouble and corrupt the record about my machine. But checking with WINS Server 1 would point out the problem, and WINS Server 2 would be set straight.

SETTING VERIFICATION OF THE DATABASE FROM THE COMMAND PROMPT

Setting verification of the database from the command prompt has more than one value that needs to be set. To set the verification of the database's consistency from the command prompt, type the following:

```
Netsh wins server set periodicdbchecking State=1 Maxrec=500
CheckAgainst=0 CheckEvery=3 Start=3600
```

In the previous command, the value of State=1 enables verification (0 disables it). Maxrec= sets the number of records to check during this verification process, which is 500 records this time. CheckAgainst=0 verifies the records from the WINS server that owns the records; 1 would be to verify against a randomly selected WINS server. CheckEvery=3 would set verification to run every three hours and start=3600 tells it to start the verification process in 3600 seconds or 1 hour.

Click the Advanced tab, and you'll see a page like the one in Figure 12.8.

FIGURE 12.8
Advanced WINS server configuration

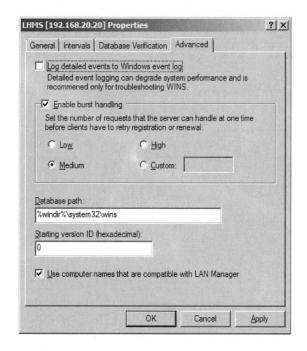

The first interesting thing here is logging. You can leave logging enabled, but think twice about logging detailed events. Basically, if you enable this, then WINS adds a lot of chatter to the Event Viewer, and WINS gets *really* slow. It's not a bad idea if you're trying to get some insight into what WINS does on a small network, but I've had it freeze a WINS server right up on me.

"Enable burst handling" is a workaround to handle an old WINS problem. WINS is busiest first thing in the morning, when everyone is logging on and trying to register their system names. Before registering a name, however, WINS must check its database to ensure that there's no duplication — that no one's trying to register a computer name that already exists. But that takes time, so WINS cheats.

The chances are good that early morning (the busy time) registrations are simply re-registrations, so WINS goes into burst mode, meaning it pretty much agrees to every registration request. It then says, "Come back and reregister in a few minutes," which gives it a chance to *really* check a registration when things are slower. It shifts into burst mode only when it has 500 outstanding registration requests in its queue by default (it's called a *Burst Queue*). But what happens when there are more or less? That's what the radio buttons are for — to set how soon WINS goes into burst mode based on the number of requests in its Burst Queue. Setting the burst mode to low allows a burst queue size of 300, medium is 500, and high is 1000. As you can see setting the burst handling to low would result in more accurate WINS registrations but a slower WINS server. There is also a Custom setting that allows you to input a number from 50 to 5000.

LOGGING FROM THE COMMAND PROMPT

Logging from the command prompt can be controlled by typing the following:

```
netsh wins server set logparam DBChange=1 Event=1
```

The DBChange parameter of 1 enables logging, 0 disables logging. Event=1 generates detailed events in the System event log, and 0 disables the generation of events.

BURST HANDLING FROM THE COMMAND PROMPT

Burst handling from the command prompt is done by typing the following:

```
netsh wins server set burstparam State=1 Value=5000
```

The State=1 enables burst handling, 0 disables it. The Value=5000 sets the burst queue size to hold 5000 outstanding registration/re-registration requests.

Designing a Multi-WINS Network

Thus far, I've discussed a situation where you have one WINS server and a bunch of clients. I've also mentioned the notion of a secondary WINS server, suggesting that at least one additional WINS server would be in order. How should you set up this second WINS server? And how about the third, fourth, and so on? And while we're at it, how many WINS servers should you have?

FROM MANY SERVERS, ONE DATABASE

The theory with multiple WINS servers is that you might have one in Europe, one in Africa, and one in North America. Europeans do their registrations with the European server, Africans with the African server, and Americans with the North American server. Then, on a regular basis, the three WINS servers get together and create a master worldwide list of WINS records, a kind of sort/merge amalgamating three different databases. But how to do it? We certainly don't want to have to transmit — *replicate* is the WINS term — the entire African name serving database over WAN links to Europe and America, particularly because the database probably hasn't changed all that much since yesterday.

As a result, WINS time-stamps and sequence-numbers name records so that it can take up less WAN bandwidth. That's great in theory, but in practice it means that WINS servers that are being asked to *do* all that sorting and merging will be pretty occupied CPU-wise, which will of course mean that they're falling down on the job as name resolvers. It also means that it might be a good idea to designate a relatively small number of servers — say, perhaps *one* — to essentially do nothing but the sort/merges.

Minimizing the Number of WINS Servers

People assume that as with domain controllers, it's a great idea to have a local WINS server, and lots of them. But it's not, and in fact you should strive to keep the WINS servers to an absolute minimum.

A local WINS server would be great because it could quickly perform NetBIOS name resolutions for nearby machines. And in fact it would be great if you could install a WINS server in every location that only did name resolutions — but remember that every WINS server does *two* things: name resolutions and name registrations. This, in my opinion, is the crux of why multiple WINS networks can be a pain. If you could simply say, "Go to local machine X for name resolutions, but for those infrequent occasions when you need to do a name *registration*, go across the WAN to the central WINS server named Y," then WINS would be more trouble free. Sure, a morning logon would get a bit slower, as the registration would happen over the WAN, but you'd not get the corrupted WINS databases that are sadly so common in big WINS installations.

Why this happens is easy to understand. Merging two WINS databases and "boiling them down" to one database is simple. Merging three is harder, and merging 100 could be, well, a lot of work, perhaps more than WINS's database engine is capable of. That's why for years, Microsoft has maintained that no enterprise on the entire planet needs more than 14 WINS servers. More than that, and database corruption becomes far more likely.

People want a local WINS server for name resolution, but actually they're not getting much for it. If your WINS server were across the WAN from you, how much time would a name resolution take? Well, an entire name resolution request and response is only 214 bytes. Let's see, at 56 Kbps that would be, hmmm, three-hundredths of a second. Here's a case where the wide area network will *not* be the bottleneck! WINS may have its drawbacks, but one thing that it was designed to do, and designed well, is to respond to name resolution requests quickly. Even a 66 MHz 486 running NT 4's WINS server can handle 750 resolution requests per minute — so when it comes to WINS servers, remember: Less is more.

Adding the Second WINS Server

Of course, having said that, a *second* WINS server isn't a bad idea.

When setting up a Microsoft TCP/IP client, you're prompted for both a primary and a secondary WINS server address. When your PC boots up, the PC goes to the primary WINS server and tries to register the PC's NetBIOS name with that WINS server. If it's successful, it never even tries to contact the secondary WINS server unless a subsequent name resolution attempt fails.

What that implies is important: Suppose you've been a good network administrator and created a backup WINS server, and then you've pointed all of your workstation's Secondary WINS Server fields to that backup. The primary goes down. Where are you?

Nowhere very interesting, actually. You see, that secondary WINS server doesn't know much, as no one has ever registered with it. If a WINS client successfully registers with its primary server, it does not try to register with the secondary server.

If the primary goes down and everyone starts asking the secondary to resolve names, the secondary will end up just saying, "Sorry, I can't answer that question." So you've got to convince the primary to replicate to the secondary. Fortunately, there's an easy way: *push/pull partners*.

Keeping the Second Server Up-to-Date

In general, you've got to configure two WINS servers to be push/pull partners, but it's possible to have them discover each other with a setting in the WINS snap-in. Right-click the Replication Partners folder, choose Properties, and click the Advanced tab. You'll see a screen like Figure 12.9.

FIGURE 12.9
Choosing automatic discovery of replication partners

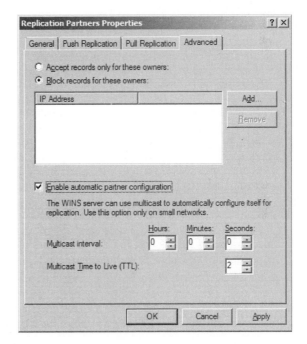

Here, I've checked the box "Enable automatic partner configuration," which will cause the WINS server to periodically broadcast (well, actually it will *multicast*) to find other WINS servers and from there automatically replicate. This will, however, work only for WINS servers on the same subnet, because most routers don't pass IP multicasts. On a big network, this is a bad idea, but for a small network (one that exists on just one segment, with no internal routers) it'll save the administrator a bit of time and trouble.

ENABLING AUTOMATIC PARTNER REPLICATION FROM THE COMMAND LINE

To enable automatic partner replication from the command line, type the following:

```
netsh wins server set autopartnerconfig State=1 Interval=3600 TTL=30
```

The State=1 enables automatic partner configuration (0 disables it). The Interval=3600 sets how often replication will occur, in this example — every 3600 seconds or 1 hour, and TTL=30 sets the multicast time to live to 30 (valid entries are 1–32).

Alternatively, you've got to introduce the replication partners. WINS database replications transfer data from a push partner to a pull partner. Those terms *push* and *pull* aren't *bad* terms description-wise, but they need a bit of illumination. Suppose for the purposes of the example that you have two machines named Primary and Secondary. Suppose also that Primary is the machine that gets the latest information, as it is the *primary* WINS server, and that all you really want to do with Secondary (the name of the machine that is the secondary WINS server) is have it act as a kind of backup to Primary's information. Thus, Secondary never really has any information to offer Primary. In that case, you'd have to set up Primary to *push* its database changes to Secondary.

You can tell a WINS server to create a push, pull, or push/pull relationship with another WINS server by right-clicking the folder labeled Replication Partners and choosing New Replication Partner. You're prompted for the IP address of the WINS server with which you want to establish a replication relationship.

In a push/pull relationship, data gets from Primary to Secondary in one of two ways. First, Secondary (the pull partner) can request that Primary (the push partner) update Secondary, telling Secondary only what has changed in the database. Alternatively, Primary can say to Secondary, "There's been a fair amount of changes since the last time I updated you. *You really should request an update*." I italicized the last sentence to emphasize that it's really the pull partner that does most of the work in initiating the database replication updates. All the push partner really "pushes" is a suggestion that the pull partner get to work and start requesting updates.

Having said that, could I just tell Secondary to be a pull partner with Primary, without telling Primary to be a push partner for Secondary? Wouldn't it be sufficient to just tell Secondary, "Initiate a replication conversation with Primary every eight hours"? It would seem so, as there wouldn't any longer be a need for Primary to do any pushing — but there's a catch. If Secondary starts pulling from Primary, Primary will refuse to respond to Secondary's pull request unless Primary has been configured as a push partner with Secondary, because WINS servers are configured by default to refuse replication requests from all machines but partners, remember?

WINS services are totally independent of Active Directory domain security. A WINS server can serve workstations throughout your network. In fact, if your network is connected to the Internet and doesn't have a firewall, you could actually publish your WINS server address, and other networks across the Internet could share browsing capabilities! I don't recommend exposing your WINS servers to the Internet because they contain sensitive information about your internal network.

CONTROLLING REPLICATION

So now you see that the right thing to do is to make Secondary a pull partner with Primary and make Primary a push partner with Secondary. What triggers the replication? What kicks off the process of WINS database replication? To see, right-click any server listed in the Replication

Partners folder, choose Properties, and click the Advanced tab. You'll see a screen like the one in Figure 12.10.

FIGURE 12.10
Configuring WINS
replication

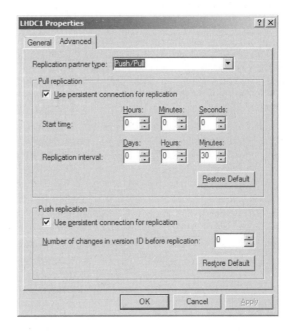

Well, recall that either the push partner or the pull partner can start the conversation. In the case of the former, you configure a push partner to tap its partner on the shoulder and suggest a replication session based on the number of database changes. You can tell Primary, "Notify Secondary whenever 50 changes have occurred to the WINS database on Primary," or whatever number you like to trigger replication. (You can alternatively trigger replication from the WINS snap-in.) The default, zero, essentially turns off push triggers.

A pull partner, in contrast, can't possibly know how many changes have occurred and so needs another way to know when to request updates. So pull partners request updates based on time — you configure a pull partner to contact its partner every so many minutes, hours, or days.

The bottom line, however, is that most of us will just set up our WINS replication relationships to the defaults, particularly if we set up our WINS enterprise as a hub-and-spoke design, as you're about to read. You *might* want to set your partners to replicate less often in a large enterprise. If you want to control your WINS replication traffic based on time, just inflate the push number to be something so great you would never hit that in the amount of time you specify for the pull parameter.

CONFIGURING WINS PULL PARAMETERS FROM THE COMMAND PROMPT

To configure WINS pull parameters from the command prompt, type the following:

```
netsh wins server set pullpartnerconfig state=1 server=192.168.20.20 start=3600
interval=10800
```

The previous command enables the pull parameter for the WINS server whose IP address is 192.168.20.20. Replication begins in 3600 seconds or 1 hour and will run every three hours.

The following command configures the push parameters to enable replication to server 192.168.20.10 whenever there are more than 500 updates from the command prompt:

```
Netsh wins server set pushpartnerconfig state=1 server=192.168.20.10 update=500
```

WINS REPLICATION DESIGN

Now that Microsoft has had years of experience supporting big clients using WINS, some Microsofties have recommended a push/pull partner architecture to me, something like a hub-and-spoke design. You see it pictured in Figure 12.11.

FIGURE 12.11
Suggested primary/secondary WINS server configuration

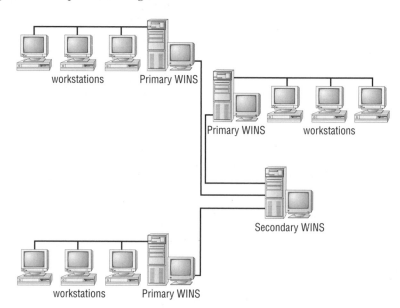

The goal of this design is to keep WINS servers responsive while still handling replication. In the picture, you see three different networks, each served by a WINS server labeled Primary WINS. In each network, each workstation points to the local WINS server as its primary server and the central machine labeled Secondary WINS as its secondary. In other words, then, every machine in the enterprise designates that one central machine as their secondary WINS server and a closer machine as their primary WINS server. This works because every WINS server hears about a particular machine from only one WINS server, instead of from several replication partners. Result? No confusion.

The main job of the central WINS server is to gather the three primary servers' databases, aggregate them into one enterprise-wide WINS database, and replicate that database out to the local primaries. Each primary WINS server, then, designates the central WINS server as its sole push/pull partner.

Many firms implement a mesh-type structure, where every WINS server designates every other WINS server as a push/pull partner. The result is a nightmare of corrupted WINS databases and lost records. To add another WINS server, just make sure that it has some kind of connectivity to the central WINS server and make it a push/pull partner of that machine. If you end up with too many WINS servers for one central machine, just put hubs and spokes on the ends of the hubs and spokes, building a hierarchy.

No matter what kind of WINS replication architecture you create, ensure that there are no loops in your replication. For example, if WINS server A replicated to B, which replicated to C, which replicated to A, then records can be replicated and re-replicated, causing WINS problems.

Avoiding WINS Problems

If you've ever had to track down WINS issues you know what an ordeal it can be. Here are a few tips to save you some time and help you avoid having to pay Microsoft more money to keep the product that you bought from them working.

WINS Servers Should Point to Themselves as a Primary WINS Server Only

When you're configuring the TCP/IP stack on a WINS server, do not fill in a value for a secondary WINS server, and in the Primary field, fill in the server's own value. This avoids a situation wherein the WINS server is busy but needs to reregister its own address. As it is busy, however, it cannot — believe it or not — respond quickly enough to *itself*. As a result, the WINS client software on the WINS server seeks out another WINS server, and so WINS server A's name registrations end up on WINS server B. The result is WINS instability, as the WINS server software is built assuming that each WINS server's name is registered on its own database.

Be Careful Replicating to "Test" WINS Servers

Don't set up a "test" WINS server, register a few names on it, have a "production" WINS server pull the names from the test server, and then shut off the test WINS server for good. WINS will refuse to delete names that it got from another server, no matter how old and expired they are, until it can do a final double-check with the WINS server that it got the names from originally; if you shut off the test and never turn it back on, those records will never go away without a bit of operator intervention!

To remove all of the records created by a defunct WINS server, go to one of its replication partners and start the WINS snap-in. Right-click the Active Registrations folder, then choose Delete Owner. Highlight the WINS server (you want to remove) in the list and choose "Delete from this server only," or if you want the deleted records to be removed from all WINS servers, choose "Replicate deletion to other servers," as shown in Figure 12.12. That allows WINS to finally purge the old owner's records.

Don't Make a Multihomed PC a WINS Server

A PC with more than one NIC can hear communications from several subnets. That's gotten WINS in trouble when a WINS server is multihomed, as WINS sometimes gets confused about where a name registration came in from. Several service packs have claimed to fix it, but each service pack brings more trouble reports. My suggestion: Don't make a multihomed machine a WINS server.

By the way, the same advice goes for PDCs. Multihomed PCs shouldn't be PDCs. The reason is that the PDC ends up being the master browser in a domain, and again, having workgroup announcements coming in from several different network segments causes problems for the browser software.

FIGURE 12.12
Deleting records from
WINS

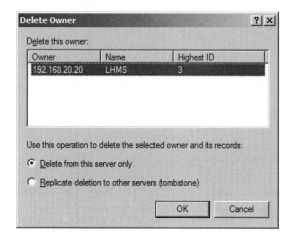

DON'T MAKE A DC A WINS SERVER

As explained earlier, both the domain controller and WINS functions are at their busiest at the same time. Mixing DC and WINS responsibilities on a single machine will make a mediocre DC and a mediocre WINS server. (Of course, on a small network this isn't the case; if you have 25 users, feel free to make one machine your domain controller, WINS, DHCP, DNS, and file server — but be sure you know how to do disaster recovery on it!)

Deleting, Tombstoning, and Purging WINS Records

You'll eventually look at your WINS name database and realize that there are a bunch of old, useless records that you'd like to get rid of. Some of those records may be, as mentioned earlier, garbage left over from an old, now-defunct WINS server. Those are easy to get rid of — just choose the Delete Owner function, as described earlier.

For other records, though, the approach is a bit different.

Consider how a record gets created and propagated around an enterprise. A machine named TRAY (what server doesn't have a tray?) registers itself with WINS Server 1. That generates a record in WINS Server 1's database. WINS Server 1 is said to be the "owner" of that record.

Now suppose WINS Server 1 replicates TRAY's name record (or more likely, records) to WINS Server 2. WINS Server 2 now contains copies of those records, but it also knows that WINS Server 1, not itself, originated — "owns" — those records. Even if WINS Server 2 were to replicate this record to yet another WINS server, then WINS Server 2 wouldn't "take credit for" this record; it would say to this new WINS Server, "Hey, just in case you don't know about this, here's a record for the TRAY computer — but I didn't discover TRAY, WINS Server 1 did. *It* owns TRAY's name record."

Now let's suppose we decommission the TRAY server. Working at WINS Server 2, you (an administrator) notice that the TRAY record is still in the WINS database, and so you delete the TRAY record. (In `Active Registrations`, right-click a record and choose Delete.) That causes the WINS snap-in to raise a dialog box asking whether you want to do one of two things:

◆ Delete the record only from this server, or

◆ Replicate deletion of the record to other servers (tombstone).

If you were to choose the first option, then TRAY would disappear from WINS Server 2's WINS snap-in . . . for a while. The next time that WINS Server 1 and WINS Server 2 replicated, then WINS Server 1 would say to WINS Server 2, "My goodness, why don't you have a TRAY record?" and quick as a wink, TRAY is *baaaaack*.

How, then, to stomp TRAY for good? With the alternative to deleting — tombstoning. When you tombstone a record, you don't remove it from the database; rather, it marks it as being in a *tombstone state.*

The purpose of the tombstone is this: WINS Server 2 has already written TRAY off, but it knows that the rest of the enterprise doesn't know that TRAY is history, because WINS Server 1 owns the TRAY record. So the next time WINS Server 1 replicates a TRAY record to WINS Server 2, WINS Server 2 may be tempted to insert a new record in its database for a machine named TRAY — but then it sees the tombstone record with TRAY's name and so can say, "Ah, I should just ignore that record; I have more up-to-date information than WINS Server 1 does." When WINS Server 2 next replicates to WINS Server 1, it'll tell WINS Server 1 that TRAY is tombstoned, and so WINS Server 1 will tombstone TRAY in its database as well. Eventually TRAY will be marked as tombstoned in the entire WINS enterprise.

By the way, tombstoned entries don't get purged from a WINS database until WINS runs a *scavenging operation.* That happens every three days by default, or you can initiate a scavenging operation from the WINS Manager by right-clicking a server, then choosing Scavenge Database.

If for some reason you stop the WINS service more often than every three days, your WINS database will never be scavenged. If that's the case, manually initiate scavenging from the WINS Manager.

Sometimes it may be necessary to manually clean up your WINS database but when do you choose delete or tombstone? When you delete a WINS record you get an option — delete or tombstone as you saw previously. You use tombstone if you want to delete a record on server X but you're working from server Y. You typically delete rather than tombstone if you're sitting right at the server that owns the record that you're about to delete. And if you find that you've been trying to get rid of a record but it keeps coming back, you tombstone it.

WINS Proxy Agents

Using an NBNS (NetBIOS naming server) such as WINS can greatly cut down on the broadcasts on your network, reducing traffic and improving throughput. But, as you've seen, this requires that the clients understand WINS; the older network client software just shouts away as a B node.

WINS can help those older non-WINS-aware clients with a *WINS proxy agent.* A WINS proxy agent is a regular old network workstation that listens for older B node systems helplessly broadcasting, trying to reach NetBIOS names that (unknown to the B node computers) are on another subnet.

To see how this would work, let's take a look at a simple two-subnet intranet, as shown in Figure 12.13.

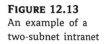

FIGURE 12.13
An example of a
two-subnet intranet

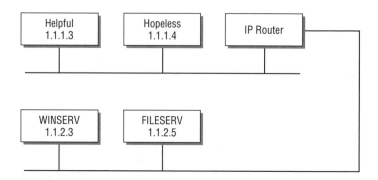

Here, you see two class C subnets, 1.1.1.0 and 1.1.2.0. There's a router between them that has two interfaces, one on the 1.1.1.0 subnet and the other interface on the 1.1.2.0 subnet. On 1.1.1.0, there are two workstations. One is a WINS-aware client named HELPFUL, which is also running a WINS proxy agent. The other is an old B node client named HOPELESS, which is not WINS-aware. On 1.1.2.0, there are a couple of servers, a machine acting as a WINS server and a regular old file server.

When HOPELESS first comes up, it'll do a broadcast of its names to ensure that no one else has them. The machine that it really should be talking to, of course, is WINSERV, but WINSERV can't hear it. HELPFUL, however, hears the B node broadcasts coming from HOPELESS and sends a directed message to WINSERV, telling it that there's a workstation named HOPELESS trying to register some names.

WINSERV looks up those names to ensure that they don't already exist. If they *do* exist, then WINSERV sends a message back to HELPFUL, saying, "Don't let that guy register those names!" HELPFUL then sends a message to HOPELESS, saying, "I'm sorry, but *I* already use the name HOPELESS." That keeps HOPELESS from registering a name that exists on another subnet.

Assuming that HOPELESS names do *not* currently exist in the WINSERV database, however, WINSERV does *not* register the names; putting a WINS proxy agent on 1.1.1.0 doesn't mean that the non-WINS clients will have their names registered with WINS. That means that it's okay to have the same NetBIOS name on two different computers, so long as they are both B node clients and are on different subnets.

Suppose then that HOPELESS does a `net use d: \\fileserv\files` — in that case, the name \\fileserv must be resolved. Assuming that HOPELESS does not have a HOSTS or LMHOSTS file, HOPELESS will start broadcasting, saying, "Is there anyone here named FILESERV? And if so, what's your IP address?" HELPFUL will intercede by sending a directed IP message to WINSERV, saying, "Is there a name registered as FILESERV, and what is its IP address?"

WINSERV will respond with the IP address of FILESERV, and HELPFUL will then send a directed message back to HOPELESS, saying, "Sure, I'm FILESERV, and you can find me at 1.1.2.5." Now HOPELESS can complete its request.

Make sure there is only one WINS proxy agent per subnet! Otherwise, two PCs will respond to HOPELESS, causing — how do the manuals put it? Ah yes — "unpredictable results."

Name Resolution in More Detail

Now that you know how to configure DHCP and WINS, you may be faced with a troubleshooting problem in reference to name resolution. Perhaps you try to FTP to a site inside your organization, but you can't hook up. Even though you know that `ftp.goodstuff.acme.com` is at one IP address, your FTP client keeps trying to attach somewhere else. You've checked your DNS server, of course, and its information is right. Where else to look?

Review: Winsock versus NBT

Remember first that there are two kinds of name resolution in Microsoft TCP/IP networking, Winsock name resolution and NetBIOS name resolution. A `net view \\`*somename* needs NetBIOS-over-TCP name resolution, or NBT name resolution. In contrast, because FTP is, like Ping, an Internet application, it uses Winsock name resolution. So, to troubleshoot a name resolution problem, you have to follow what your client software does, step by step.

DNS/Winsock Name Resolution

I type `ping lemon`, and get the response "unknown host lemon." But I suspect there's a lemon out there, and I'm not talking about a computer from a certain Texas computer company. How did Server 2008 decide that it couldn't find lemon? It certainly takes long enough to decide that it can't find lemon, after all — usually on the order of 20 to 30 seconds on a 400 MHz system. *Something* must be going on.

When faced with a question such as this, I turned to the Microsoft documentation for help, but there wasn't much detail. So I ran a network monitor and issued `ping` commands to computers that didn't exist, to see the sequence of actions that the network client software tried in order to resolve a name. The HOSTS and LMHOSTS files do not, of course, show up in a network trace, so I inserted information into those files that didn't exist on the DNS or WINS servers and then tried pinging again, to demonstrate where the HOSTS and LMHOSTS files sit in the name resolution hierarchy. (And if you think about it, LMHOSTS and WINS should have nothing at all to do with a Winsock resolution. Perhaps in a non-Microsoft world, but not in any version of Windows created after 1995.) Pinging for a nonexistent computer named apple, I found that the name resolution order proceeds, as shown in Figure 12.14.

Before I get into the details here, let me warn you that Microsoft has changed how their OSes resolve DNS names; in particular, Windows 2000 and later (XP, Vista, 2003, 2008) are a bit different, and I'll explain that as we go along. Step by step, it looks like this:

First, consult the HOSTS file, if it exists. If you find the name you're looking for, stop.

Next, look in the DNS cache. This only applies to Windows 2000 and later systems, and I'll cover this later, but basically all Win2K and later systems remember previously successful DNS name resolutions. So if I successfully looked up apple in DNS a moment or two ago, then my system would pull that successful resolution out of cache, and it'd be done. Note that this happens *after* the HOSTS lookup, contrary to some sources. You can, if you like, clear the DNS cache by typing **ipconfig /flushdns**. You can see the current contents of the DNS cache by typing **ipconfig /displaydns**.

Next, if there's a specified DNS server or servers, then query them. Most Microsoft OSes recognize that a name like apple clearly isn't a complete DNS name, as DNS names usually have parts to them like `apple.bigfirm.com` or the like. In a case like that, the system adds its DNS suffix to the query. For example, if I were sitting at a workstation named `mypc.bigfirm.com` and typed `ping apple`, then my workstation wouldn't query DNS for apple, it would query for "apple.bigfirm.com." You can, if you like, add even more DNS suffixes for your system to try when presented with a too-short DNS name; look in TCP/IP Advanced Properties, the DNS tab, and you'll see where you can add them. By the way, Windows 95 systems seem to not add the DNS suffix; a Win95 system would actually ask DNS to resolve apple in my theoretical case. If DNS finds the name, then stop.

FIGURE 12.14
The name resolution order

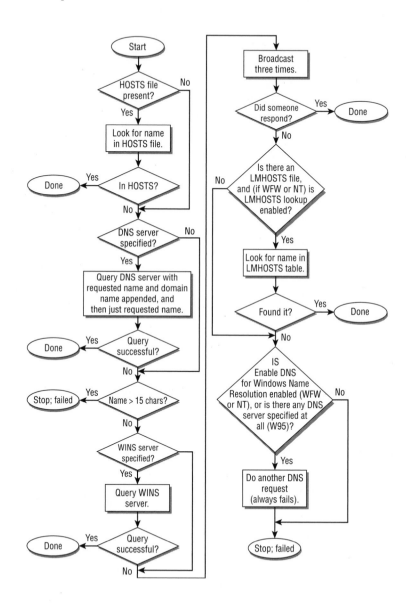

You would think that would be it for DNS name resolution, and indeed for most OSes it is — look in HOSTS, look in DNS and if there's no luck, then just stop looking. That's also how a Windows 2000 or later system works, if you have disabled NetBIOS over TCP/IP. (Almost no one does nowadays. But one day, when we're free of WINS . . .) Assuming that you're running NBT, though, Microsoft takes it further and involves its *NetBIOS* lookup engine as well. So if your system still hasn't gotten an answer to a name query . . .

If there's a specified WINS server or servers, then query the WINS server(s). The name WINS looks for is apple <00>, the name that *would* be registered by the Workstation service, if the apple machine existed.

If that fails, then do three broadcasts looking for a machine with NetBIOS name apple <00>, requesting that it identify itself and send back its IP address. Again, this would succeed with a workstation running some NetBIOS-over-TCP/IP client, even a relatively old one, as it would have registered the apple <00> name already, if only on its own name table. Unfortunately, this only works if the machine is on the same subnet.

If the name still hasn't been resolved, then the LMHOSTS file is read, unless configured to ignore LMHOSTS. Windows 2000 and later systems do *not* use LMHOSTS to assist in DNS/Winsock name resolution, whether configured to use LMHOSTS or not.

If the system still hasn't succeeded, then under some circumstances a pre-Win2K system will do yet another DNS lookup which will, of course, fail.

Summarizing, then, a Windows 2000 or later system first looks in its DNS cache, then its HOSTS file, then asks a DNS server, then a WINS server, and finally broadcasts. If you disable NetBIOS over TCP/IP then Win2K and later systems just look in the DNS cache, then HOSTS, and then ask the DNS server.

Why the broadcasts and the WINS lookup? I'm not sure, but I guess Microsoft just threw them in for good measure. The broadcasts are a pain because they waste network bandwidth, but they *would* be of benefit when you tried to execute a TCP/IP command on a computer in your network but wanted to use the shorter NetBIOS name rather than the longer DNS name, such as apple instead of `apple.bigfirm.com`.

Getting back to an earlier question, what happened on that workstation that could not access the FTP site? There was an old HOSTS file sitting in the Windows directory that pointed to a different IP address, an older IP address for the FTP server. Windows\System32\Drivers\etc directory is read before anything else, so the accurate information on the DNS or WINS servers never got a chance to be read. So be very careful about putting things in HOSTS if they could soon become out-of-date!

Controlling WINS versus DNS Order in Winsock

Now, what I just showed you is the order of events by default in NT, Windows 9*x*, or later clients. But if you feel like messing around with the way that Winsock resolves names, you can. As usual, let me take this moment to remind you that it's not a great idea to mess with the Registry unless you know what you're doing.

Look in the Registry under HKEY_LOCAL_MACHINE\System\CurrentControlSet\Services \Tcpip\ServiceProvider and you see HostsPriority, DnsPriority, and NetbtPriority value entries. They are followed by hexadecimal values. The lower the value, the earlier that HOSTS, DNS (and LMHOSTS), and WINS (and broadcasts) get done. For example, by default DNS's priority is 7D0 and WINS's (NetbtPriority) is 7D1, so DNS goes before WINS. But change DNS's priority to 7D2, and WINS does its lookup and broadcast *before* the client interrogates the DNS server.

Again, I'm not sure *why* you'd want to do this, but I include it for the sake of completeness and for the enjoyment of those who delight in undocumented features.

NetBIOS Name Resolution Sequence

Readers send me many questions about networking Microsoft OSes, but unfortunately I usually can't help much, usually because the problem boils down to either some hardware or software that I'm not familiar with, so all I can do is to make a few suggestions to help them try to smoke the problem out on their own. Of all of the troubleshooting suggestions that I make, however, here's the most common one.

Many problems sound like "I can't get X machine to connect to and communicate with Y machine," as in "I have a file server named ABEL that workstation BAKER can't access." Most people don't realize the very important fact that there are *two* problems to troubleshoot here:

1. First, you must have IP connectivity.

2. Second, you must have proper name resolution — and "proper" means DNS/HOSTS if the application is Winsock-based, or WINS/LMHOSTS if the application is NetBIOS-based.

I know I've touched on this elsewhere, but I really want to hit home with this point. First, make sure that the two systems can ping each other. Do a ping from each side to the other. Without the ability to transfer IP packets back and forth, your network can go no further — "don't mean a thing if you ain't got that ping," y'know.

Once you're sure that you have IP connectivity, check that your systems can resolve each other's names. Here's where I find that readers sometimes go wrong. Someone will tell me that workstation \\ABEL can't contact server \\BAKER, "even though I pinged BAKER from ABEL." In other words, the reader typed ping baker or something similar while sitting at ABEL. But Ping doesn't use NetBIOS to resolve the name "baker," of course — it uses DNS. That's no help, although it *does* demonstrate that there's IP connectivity. We need to test that ABEL can resolve the name \\BAKER via *NetBIOS*, not DNS. I'm not sure why, but Microsoft doesn't include a NetBIOS-based ping in any versions of NT and later OSes, and I wish it did. It'd make life a lot easier. About the closest thing that you can get to a NetBIOS-based ping is probably a `net view` command, as in `net view \\baker`. That command will list the shares on the BAKER server, but it's not a great test, as other irrelevant factors can cause it to fail.

To really chase down a NetBIOS name resolution problem, you've got to understand what's going on under the hood, exactly how the "WINS client" — the word for the piece of software that runs on your workstation and resolves NetBIOS names — operates.

I'll assume for this discussion that you haven't modified the way that the WINS client resolves NetBIOS names — that is, that you haven't told the client to disable the LMHOSTS file — and that you are using WINS. (Come to think of it, that's an important troubleshooting step: Make sure that all of the communicating parties are connected either to the same WINS server, or to WINS servers that replicate to each other.)

Summarized, the name resolution sequence appears in Figure 12.15.

FIGURE 12.15
Name resolution
sequence under NetBIOS

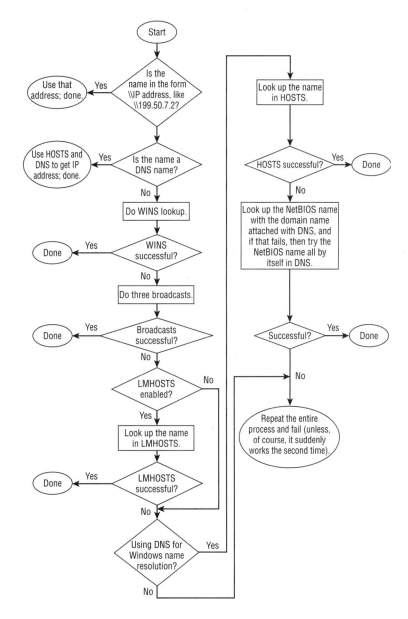

The NBT name resolver uses the following steps; if any succeed, then it stops looking:

◆ The resolver caches the result of NetBIOS-name-to-IP-address resolutions that have succeeded in the past 30 seconds, and looks first in that cache. You can see the current state of your NetBIOS name cache by typing **nbtstat -c**. You can clear and reload the cache by typing **nbtstat -R**.

◆ If the client is a Windows 98, Me, NT 4, Windows 2000, or later system, then the first thing to check is whether the name to the right of the \\ is either an IP address or a recognizable DNS name — that is, that it has a period in its name. If the name is just an IP address, as in a command like net use * \\199.33.29.15\Stuff, then forget the name resolution and just go to that IP address. If it's a DNS name, like net use * \\myserver.region8.acme.com\files, then resolve the name using the *DNS* client, not the WINS client (and you'll read about how DNS resolves names in the remainder of the chapter).

◆ If the name wasn't IP or DNS — or the client was too old to be able to respond to that — then the next part is the WINS client, if the client software is WINS aware.

◆ If WINS isn't being used, then the client does three broadcasts. For example, net view \\apple causes three broadcasts looking for a workstation with the name apple registered rather than apple.bigfirm.com or the like.

◆ Next, if LMHOSTS is enabled — and it appears that LMHOSTS is *always* enabled on Windows 95/98/Me/2000/XP/Vista/2003/2008 clients — then the client looks up the name in LMHOSTS. Surprised? When doing NBT name resolutions, LMHOSTS gets consulted *before* HOSTS, a reversal over Winsock name resolutions. Recall that LMHOSTS only contains 15-character NetBIOS names, not longer DNS-like names.

◆ If you've checked Enable DNS for Windows Name Resolution in a Workgroups, or if you have specified a DNS server in Windows 95/98/Me/2000/XP/Vista/2003/2008, then the workstation's client software will look at HOSTS, and if HOSTS can't help, it will interrogate the DNS server (or servers, as you can specify up to four DNS servers).

The NT/Workgroups clients and the 9*x* clients use DNS differently. The NT/Workgroups clients do a DNS query for the name with the domain name appended to it and then a DNS query of just the name. For example, if your domain is acme.com and you're doing a net view \\myserver, then an NT workstation will ask DNS first to resolve the name myserver.acme.com — it automatically adds the domain name for the first resolution. Then, if the DNS server can't resolve the name with the domain name attached, the client will request that the DNS server just resolve myserver.

In contrast, the Windows 9*x* client software only asks the DNS server to resolve the name with the domain name appended; in my example, a Windows 9*x* workstation would ask DNS to resolve myserver.acme.com but would not ask about myserver.

Then there's a final step in NetBIOS name resolution — it's an odd one. If the client software is the NT client (not the Workgroups or Win9*x* clients), and if it has been unsuccessful so far, then it goes back and does it all over again, I suppose in the hope that it'll work the second time.

Chapter 13

New Names: How DNS Works

As you've read in the past two chapters, being able to give names to networked servers, workstations, printers, and similar devices helps make networks more human-friendly. You've also read that the Internet has used a naming system first referred to by RFC 881 as the *domain name system*, or DNS, more than 25 years ago.

It seems to me that DNS is nothing short of amazing. Consider that if I were to type into my Web browser's address field **www.gov.au**, then my browser says to a local DNS server, "please find out what IP address goes with the name www.gov.au, and literally in seconds that DNS server searches the hundreds of thousands or possibly millions of DNS servers on the planet and returns the answer, even though the DNS server with that desired answer is half a planet away from me. Consider also that DNS is basically a database of names of computers on the Internet, a database consisting of untold billions of pieces of information, and that this worldwide database of names is designed in such a way that hundreds of thousands of people, people from every single country on the planet, can all manage their little parts of that database — and nothing falls apart, despite the fact that the entire planet seems unable to agree on virtually anything else. And finally, consider that this worldwide database of names is fairly inexpensive to participate in: as I write this, I've just discovered that I could register an Internet domain named worldofminasi.com for $6 a year. You've got to agree that DNS is a well-designed bit of work.

That's what impresses *me* about DNS — but why should *you* care about DNS? Because it's not only the database of computer names for the Internet, it is also the naming technology that Microsoft chose for Active Directory, and has been since Windows 2000. So before you can even think about setting up an AD, you've *got* to know DNS.

What DNS Does

As you've read earlier, a DNS server's main job is "name resolution," which means that you can ask a DNS server, "what IP address does the machine named www.minasi.com have?" That's important because computers don't care about names like www.minasi.com; they care about IP addresses like 70.165.73.5. The beauty of DNS, then, is that you can visit my Web site by firing up a copy of Internet Explorer and typing www.minasi.com into the address bar and then Internet Explorer asks a DNS server to resolve the name to an IP address. Once IE has got the IP address, it can take you to my Web site.

NOTE

By the way, my cable provider, Cox Communications, makes me pay considerably extra for a *static* — unchanging — IP address for my Web server, but they like to force me to change that IP address about every nine months (and if you're wondering exactly how that's "static," then don't ask me, I have no idea either), so if you try resolving www.minasi.com using the tools I'll show you later in this chapter, don't be surprised if your DNS server tells you a different IP address than 70.165.73.5. That's actually another neat thing about name resolution: it disconnects my Web site's name from its IP address. I've run a Web server with that name since about 1995, and over that time I've gotten my IP addresses from four different providers. None of my visitors were bothered by the changes, however, thanks to DNS. My business is associated with an online name, not an IP address, so I'm free to move my online presence to any ISP that I wish. Unlike Patrick McGoohan's character in the old TV series *The Prisoner*, I *am* a name — not a number! — and DNS makes that possible.

But simple name resolution isn't all that DNS does. DNS also does "reverse" name resolutions, wherein you ask a DNS server, "hey, what's the DNS name for the machine with IP address 70.165.73.5?" You might do that if your firewall logs showed that some jerk was trying to hack your network, but all the logs could tell you was that the jerk's IP address was 70.165.73.5. Thus, DNS servers can do forward lookups ("what IP address is associated with such-and-such machine?") and reverse lookups ("what DNS name is associated with such-and-such IP address?").

Because it's so widespread, well-understood, and efficient, people have given DNS other jobs as well. In modern networks you'll find that it's not just a database of names, it's also a database of functions. One of those functions involves one of the Internet's most important functions, e-mail. You see, whenever someone sends you an e-mail using your e-mail address, then their e-mail server must discover the name of your e-mail server. For example, if you send me an e-mail at help@minasi.com, then your e-mail server will extract the text to the right of the @, resulting in minasi.com, my e-mail address's *domain*, but merely knowing my DNS domain name doesn't tell your e-mail server the name of my domain's e-mail server. To find out my e-mail server's name, your e-mail server queries my DNS server for something called an *MX record*, as you'll see later. You'll run into another example of DNS's versatility when you're running an Active Directory, as the computers in your domain must be able to find your domain controllers. (Recall that DCs are the servers that provide authentication services for your AD.) How do your servers and workstations find DCs? By asking DNS. That's why I always tell my clients, "if you're not a DNS expert, then you're not an AD expert."

Anatomy of a DNS Name

Let's start understanding DNS by looking at a DNS name to know its parts and their significance. For example, one of my DNS servers is named netdoor.minasi.com. It appears, then, to have three parts — netdoor, minasi, and com. Specifically,

♦ Each of those parts (netdoor, minasi, and com) is called a *label* by RFC 882 and later DNS-related RFCs.

♦ DNS convention separates labels with a period.

♦ The maximum permissible length of a label is 63 characters (RFC 1035), and the maximum length for the entire DNS name is 254 characters (RFC 882).

♦ Labels can contain only letters, digits, and the hyphen (-) — no other punctuation is allowed by RFC 1035, and that includes the underscore!

DNS Labels 1: The Host Name

The leftmost label in the DNS name — `netdoor` in my example — is called the *host name* in Internet terms, and in the Windows world we'd call it the computer name or machine name. While the RFCs would be perfectly happy with a 63-character host name, that host name doubles as the NetBIOS name, which, as you know from the last chapter, can't exceed 15 characters. It's theoretically possible to make a computer name longer than 15 characters, but I recommend against it because there's so much Windows software out there that assumes a name of 15 or fewer characters that I think you're likely to run into a glitch or two with a longer name. Microsoft seems to agree, as the GUI interface for changing a system's host name automatically truncates any long names to 15 characters.

DNS Labels 2: DNS Domains or Zones

The remaining parts to the right of the first label are called the *DNS suffix* or *DNS domain* of the computer's name and so the DNS domain of the `netdoor.minasi.com` system is `minasi.com`. But don't think that DNS domain names always have just two labels, like `minasi.com`; they can, in fact, have one-label domain names, and domain names with more than two labels, like `westcoast.minasi.com` are perfectly valid. (We'll talk about three-plus label domain names later in this chapter.) Because a widely used kind of DNS server software called BIND refers to DNS domains as *zones*, the terms *DNS domain* and *zone* are considered synonymous, although that's technically not true. I often say *zone* instead of *domain* when speaking of DNS domains to try to minimize confusion about Active Directory domains versus DNS domains.

A system's complete name including its host name and DNS domain name, like `netdoor.minasi.com`, is sometimes called a *fully qualified domain name*, or FQDN.

DNS Domains Versus Active Directory Names

If you've been reading closely in the book to this point, then I may have confused you a bit in using the phrase *DNS domain*, as I've now used the word *domain* in two different ways, sometimes referring to Active Directory domains and other times to DNS domains. They are not the same thing, although they *are* related because every AD domain needs a DNS domain of the same name.

When the Internet folks laid down the early terminology for DNS in 1984, they decided to call the structure of their naming system the *domain* name system. They could just as easily have called them realms, organizations, or a number of other things, but *domain* is the name that stuck. Then, a few years later, Microsoft needed a phrase that they could use to characterize a group of systems that rely upon a common set of servers for authentication, and they decided to call that a *domain* — either out of a lack of creativity, or perhaps there weren't all that many words that would fit the job, after all.

Now, that didn't lead to all that much confusion initially, as NT prior to Windows 2000 had little use for DNS as its naming system, and so it was usually easy to figure out what someone meant when she said "domain" from the context. But with Windows 2000, Microsoft realigned their domain's name resolution system from NetBIOS to DNS, and that's where things got a bit ugly. Every Active Directory needs a name, and in particular a DNS name that matches the AD name. Thus, before I could create an Active Directory named `bigfirm.com`, I would first need a DNS domain named `bigfirm.com` in which to name resolution information about that `bigfirm.com` AD. We'll see more about that in this chapter, the next, and chapters in the companion book of the *Mastering Windows 2008* series because, as I've already said, AD is extremely dependent on DNS.

DNS from the Client Side

With those basics out of the way, let's start getting DNS working with a look at the part of DNS that you'll find on every system: the "DNS client." Every one of your systems, whether workstation or server, needs something that knows where to go to translate www.minasi.com to 70.165.73.5 or whatever my Web server's address happens to be at the time. Thus, every one of your systems is equipped with a piece of software that can answer the what-IP-address-goes-with-this-DNS-name question. *That* software is called a *DNS client*. In Windows, it's implemented as a service called, not surprisingly, the *DNS client service*.

Preferred and Alternate DNS Servers

The DNS client software on your computers works pretty hard for you and requires little in return, but it's not smart enough to go searching around the Internet finding DNS servers (remember, the *servers* can do that, not the clients) and so it *does* need one piece of information before the DNS client can be useful: the IP address of a DNS server to ask its questions of. Well, okay, it also likes one more piece of information: the IP address of a second DNS server to use if that first DNS server isn't available for some reason. (Windows calls them your system's *preferred* and *alternate* DNS servers, respectively, and in fact it's possible to feed a DNS client more than two DNS servers, as you'll soon see).

For example, suppose you've got a network all set up with two DNS servers, and their IP addresses are 10.2.2.2 and 10.50.7.2. You have configured both servers to be essentially identical, so it doesn't really matter which one you make the preferred and which the alternate, so you just arbitrarily decide to make the system at 10.2.2.2 the preferred DNS server for all of your workstations and servers and 10.50.7.2 the alternate DNS server for all of those systems. If you do that, then whenever one of your systems needs to resolve a DNS address into an IP address, then that system will ask 10.2.2.2, "are you available to answer a DNS question?" If 10.2.2.2 responds, "sure," then the client question will go to that computer. If 10.2.2.2 does not respond within a reasonable amount of time (I've never seen the number published, but it seems that Windows clients wait up to about eight seconds before giving up on a silent DNS server, depending on the circumstances), then the DNS client will ask 10.50.7.2 if *it* can resolve a DNS name. If neither respond, then of course the DNS client won't be able to resolve names for your computer.

Configuring Your DNS Client Software

You can tell the DNS client what IP address or addresses it should go to for DNS queries in one of three ways:

◆ If you get your IP address from DHCP, then DHCP can automatically provide your system with a preferred and alternate DNS server. (Recall that Chapter 10 explained that most systems get their IP addresses from a server called a *DHCP server*. You'll see how to set up a DHCP server in the next chapter, but for now all you need to know is that DHCP is the easiest, most automatic, and most common way to provide your systems with IP addresses, DNS server IP addresses, and other IP-related configuration items.)

◆ You can statically assign DNS servers to your system via the GUI in the Network and Sharing Center.

◆ You can statically assign DNS servers to your system via the command line and the netsh int ip set dns command.

You saw how to configure a preferred and alternate DNS server from the administrative GUI for your TCP/IP connections in Figure 10.11, but, as I've already said, you can go further and punch in more than just two DNS servers if you like. To do that, we'll need to go to the Advanced TCP/IP options on an adapter; here's how:

1. Open Control Panel.

2. Click Network Sharing Center.

3. To the left, click Manage Network Connections.

4. Locate the interface whose DNS servers you want to configure. Typically interfaces are, by default, named either Local Area Connection (the Ethernet connection) or Wireless Network Connection.

5. Double-click that interface. You'll see a dialog box named *ConnectionName* Status. Underneath it, you'll see a button labeled Properties; click that button.

6. The resulting dialog box is labeled *ConnectionName* Status. Locate the item in the box labeled Internet Protocol Version 4 (TCP/IP v4). Click that item, and then click Properties.

7. That will raise yet another dialog box that contains a button labeled Advanced; click that.

8. That raises a dialog box named Advanced TCP/IP Settings. Click the DNS tab in that dialog. It'll look like Figure 13.1.

FIGURE 13.1
Advanced TCP/IP
Settings DNS tab

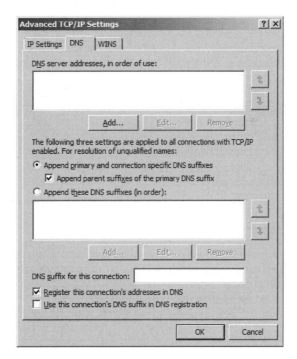

As you can see, clicking the Add... button under "DNS server addresses, in order of use:" lets you add DNS servers to your heart's content. Oh, by the way, if your DNS tab already has an address in there, don't worry about it, as your system needn't match mine in this figure.

Virtually all of your workstations will get the IP addresses for their preferred and alternate DNS servers via DHCP, but in contrast some of your servers will need static IP addresses, and with static addresses usually come statically assigned preferred/alternate DNS servers. You've already seen how to do that in the GUI, so now let's see how to do it from the command line. The command looks like this:

```
netsh int ip set dns adaptername static ipaddress
```

You can find the adapter's name in the Network and Sharing Center or from `ipconfig`. By default, Windows calls your Ethernet adapter Local Area Connection, and wireless adapters Wireless Connection. For example, look at an abbreviated version of an `ipconfig` command for the computer that I'm sitting at:

```
C:\>ipconfig

Windows IP Configuration


Wireless LAN adapter wireless:

   Media State . . . . . . . . . . . : Media disconnected
   Connection-specific DNS Suffix  . : apple-orchard.net

Ethernet adapter Local Area Connection:

   Connection-specific DNS Suffix  . : apple-orchard.net
   Link-local IPv6 Address . . . . . : fe80::217:a4ff:fed3:10ca%8
   IPv4 Address. . . . . . . . . . . : 10.50.50.110
   Subnet Mask . . . . . . . . . . . : 255.255.255.0
   Default Gateway . . . . . . . . . : 10.50.50.1
```

Your `ipconfig` will run longer than this because of a bunch of *tunnel adapters*, imaginary adapters created to make using IPv6 (a topic that you can safely ignore until the third book of the *Windows Server 2008* series, or, for many people, forever) easier to co-exist with IPv4, the version of IP that we've been talking about in this book and that the Internet mainly runs on. In my case, I ran this `ipconfig` on my laptop, which like most laptops has both an Ethernet and a wireless connection. As my wireless LAN adapter says "media disconnected," clearly it's not the adapter connecting me to the Internet.

Thus, I could tell my Ethernet adapter (the one named Local Area Connection) to use a DNS server IP of 164.109.1.3 by opening up an elevated command prompt and typing this:

```
netsh int ip set dns "local area connection" static 164.109.1.3
```

Notice that I surrounded `"local area connection"` with quotes; I needed to do that because there were spaces in its name. Once I wanted my laptop to return to getting its DNS from a DHCP server, I'd just type this:

```
netsh int ip set dns "local area connection" dhcp
```

How to add extra DNS servers? With a `netsh int ip add` command, rather than the `netsh int ip set` command we've used so far. It looks like this:

```
netsh int ip add dns adaptername ipaddress index=indexnumber
```

It looks like the `netsh int ip set` command, but now we've added an `index=` number and dropped `static`. For *indexnumber,* just use a number from 2 to whatever (1 is already in use holding the preferred DNS server); Windows then uses that to determine the order in which to try a DNS server. Thus, if I wanted to configure a system to use 10.10.1.2 as its preferred DNS server, 10.1.8.7 as its alternate, and 10.8.80.4 if both of those fail, I'd type three commands:

```
netsh int ip set dns "local area connection" static 10.10.1.2
netsh int ip add dns "local area connection" 10.1.8.7 index=2
netsh int ip add dns "local area connection" 10.8.80.4 index=3
```

As I noted before, I'm not quite certain of the maximum number of DNS servers that Windows Server 2008 will allow you to enter, but I've successfully input a list of 13 DNS servers and had Windows store and use those properly.

Configuring Your DNS Domain Membership

Back in Chapter 10, we briefly noted that you could give a system a "DNS suffix," which is another way of saying a "DNS domain." I said at the time that I intended for WINSERVER's full name to be `winserver.bigfirm.com`, and that I'd tell you how to configure it as such in this chapter. As with pointing the DNS client at a DNS server, we can set a machine's DNS suffix in one of three ways: by delivering it automatically via DHCP, by punching it into the GUI, or by doing it at the command line. Again, we're not handling DHCP until the next chapter, so we'll skip that for now and cover it in Chapter 14.

Suppose we wanted to give WINSERVER its long-awaited DNS suffix of `bigfirm.com`; here's how:

1. Logged onto WINSERVER as an administrator, click Start.

2. In the Start Search field, type **sysdm.cpl** and press Enter. That will open up Control Panel's System applet to the Computer Name tab. (Did you notice that we took a somewhat longer trip to get there back in Chapter 2? In Windows, there's *always* another way to skin a cat.)

3. Click the button labeled Change....

4. In the resulting dialog box Computer Name/Domain Changes, click the button labeled More... to see something like Figure 13.2.

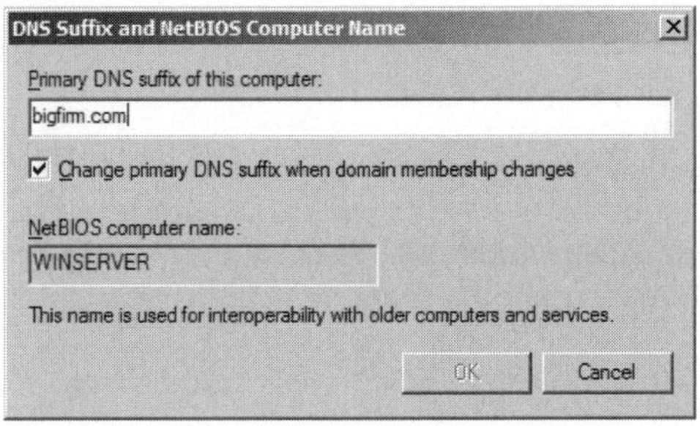

FIGURE 13.2
Entering the
bigfirm.com
DNS suffix

DNS Suffix and NetBIOS Computer Name

Primary DNS suffix of this computer:

bigfirm.com

☑ Change primary DNS suffix when domain membership changes

NetBIOS computer name:

WINSERVER

This name is used for interoperability with older computers and services.

OK   Cancel

Here, you can see that I've already entered **bigfirm.com**. Click OK to clear that dialog box and OK again to clear the previous one. You'll get an information message warning you that you've got to reboot to see your changes take effect (although why that requires a reboot has always been a mystery to me), OK to clear the information message box, and finally Close to clear the System properties dialog box. You can then choose either to reboot now or later — choose to reboot now.

You can alternatively change your DNS suffix from the command line and, as far as I can see, you needn't reboot. You see, there's no "official" command-line tool that I know of to change your DNS suffix, but I use this command to modify the Registry, which is where the DNS suffix is stored:

```
reg add HKLM\SYSTEM\CurrentControlSet\Services\Tcpip\Parameters
 /v "NV Domain" /d "bigfirm.com" /f
```

To see the effects of your efforts, open a command prompt, and type `ipconfig /all`. Next to Primary DNS Suffix, you'll see `bigfirm.com`.

Configuring the DNS Suffix Search List

If you work in an organization of any size, then many of the DNS names that you'll be typing into Windows won't include domain suffixes like `google.com`, `microsoft.com`, or `amazon.com` — they'll have your domain name as their suffix. If you worked at a place using the domain name `bigfirm.com`, then it would soon grow tiresome to have to tell your computer to go get something from names like `dc1.bigfirm.com` or `fileserver1.bigfirm.com` or `mailserver.bigfirm.com`; it'd be much easier to just refer to those systems as `dc1`, `fileserver1`, and `mailserver`.

In fact, you can do that, thankfully: if you type any one-label DNS name into Windows, then it automatically completes that name with whatever DNS domain your computer contains. Thus, if you're sitting at a system named `pc44.bigfirm.com` and you ask to ping something called server4, then your DNS client will assume that you mean `server4.bigfirm.com`, not server4, and chances are good that's what you meant. `Bigfirm.com` users are, then, set . . . whew! But wait . . . what if Bigfirm buys another firm?

Not every organization uses only one DNS domain name. Imagine, for example, that `bigfirm.com` bought `minasi.com` and decided not to change the domain suffixes on the `minasi.com` systems, leading to a network wherein some systems had a `bigfirm.com` DNS suffix, and some systems had a `minasi.com` suffix. In that case, then we'd lose the just-type-in-the-host-name-and-it-works benefit, as folks who worked at workstations whose DNS name ended in `minasi.com` could type just a host name for any system whose name ended in `minasi.com`, but not for the systems whose FQDNs ended in `bigfirm.com`. Arrgh.

The DNS client has an answer for that, though — a DNS domain suffix search order list. You can tell your DNS client, "if I give you a single label name, then first try `bigfirm.com` as a suffix and, if that doesn't work, try `minasi.com`." You can configure the DNS suffix search order list in one of two ways.

First, you can go to the DNS tab in Advanced TCP/IP Properties, the dialog that we met back in Figure 13.1. As the figure shows, you can punch in DNS suffixes; once you do that, your DNS client will try each of them when you offer it a single-label client. Windows stores this list as a simple text string with commas between the suffixes in the SearchList entry in the HKEY_LOCAL_MACHINE\SYSTEM\CurrentControlSet\Services\Tcpip\Parameters key.

Another approach involves Group Policy. In Computer Configuration/Administrative Templates/Network/DNS Client, there is a group policy setting called DNS Suffix Search List where you can type in a set of DNS suffixes to test. This isn't all that useful when you've got to type it in on a machine-by-machine basis but, as you'll learn in the companion book of the *Mastering Windows Server 2008* series, an Active Directory lets you put a set of group policies in a central location and then instructs all of the AD members to pull those policies from the central location and execute them, allowing you to put a DNS suffix search order list in just one place and seeing its effects all around the network.

Caching Query Results

While designing Active Directory, Microsoft considered that systems in a directory service like an AD domain talk to each other a lot; for example, if a workstation named pc44.bigfirm.com were being logged onto the domain by a domain controller named dc1.bigfirm.com, then pc44 would end up having to resolve the name dc1.bigfirm.com to whatever IP address dc1 had, and it would end up resolving it many, many times in the space of a few moments during the logon process. It would, Microsoft realized, be very dumb for pc44 to hammer its friendly neighborhood DNS server for something as silly as asking it the same question ("what's dc1.bigfirm.com's IP address?") over and over.

To reduce unnecessary DNS network traffic, the Windows DNS client software remembers recently asked queries and answers. The first time that pc44 asked its local DNS server for dc1.bigfirm.com's IP address, the DNS server would actually go out and find dc1's IP address and report that to pc44. The next time some software on pc44 needed to know dc1's address, however, the DNS client software on pc44 would instantly know the answer, at least for a while.

How long does the DNS client software remember an answer? It depends on which DNS domain the client has queried about. As you'll see later, the person who sets up a DNS domain on a DNS server must configure a *time to live* (TTL) for answers to DNS queries for that site. You can see your DNS client's current cache status by opening a command prompt and typing **ipconfig /displaydns**. For example, suppose you open up your Web browser and visit my home page at www.minasi.com. Under the hood, here's what happened:

◆ Your workstation's DNS client software queried your local DNS server — which may be your ISP's DNS server, if you're running from home, or your company's DNS server if you're at work — for the IP address of www.minasi.com.

◆ Your local DNS server found my DNS server and asked, "what's the IP address for www.minasi.com?"

◆ My DNS server replied, "it's 70.165.73.5, and you can remember that for 3600 seconds (one hour)."

◆ Your DNS server then reported that to your workstation.

At that point, running an ipconfig /displaydns might show, among other things, something like this:

```
www.minasi.com
----------------------------------------
Record Name . . . . . : www.minasi.com
Record Type . . . . . : 5
Time To Live  . . . . : 3502
Data Length . . . . . : 8
Section . . . . . . . : Answer
CNAME Record  . . . . : web2.minasi.com
```

Notice the `Time To Live` value, 3502 — yours will be different, but it'll be under 3600. That shows how many seconds that data will remain in your system's cache. It was originally 3600 when your DNS server delivered the information, but your DNS client watches the clock and reduces the TTL every second. Once my system counts down to zero, then it forgets that it knows what IP address `www.minasi.com` has, and if `www.minasi.com` has to be resolved after that point, then the DNS client on my system will have to go trouble a DNS server again to get `www.minasi.com`'s IP address.

Actually, what I just said isn't quite true; as it turns out, Windows won't cache something for more than a day. Windows stores that "maximum cache-able time" in the Registry in HKLM\SYSTEM\CurrentControlSet\Services\DNSCache\Parameters in a REG_DWORD entry called MaxCacheTTLLimit (you won't see the entry unless you create it), and its default value is 86400 (seconds).

Caching Negative Query Results

Your DNS client does more than just remember good news — it remembers bad news as well. As you've just learned, the result of a successful name resolution will stay in your DNS client's cache for however long that result's TTL specifies. But what happens after you ask to resolve a name that doesn't exist, such as when you try to ping a system named `weirdname.bigfirm.com`? There is no such host (and inasmuch as I own `bigfirm.com`, that will be true for the foreseeable future), and so any attempts at name resolution on that name fails. So what's there to cache? Failure, of course!

The Windows DNS cache remembers failed name resolutions for five minutes. The means that if you try to ping `weirdname.bigfirm.com`, then your system's local DNS server will search the Internet to find my DNS server, which holds the information for `bigfirm.com`, and my DNS server will say that there is no such host. Your DNS cache will remember that, so that if you try to ping `weirdname.com` again within five minutes, then your system will report failure . . . despite that it never even tried to requery its local DNS server to resolve `weirdname.bigfirm.com`. That behavior is called *negative caching*.

Sounds good, doesn't it? Normally, yes it is, but once in a while, you'll want the DNS client to *forget* what it's learned. For example, suppose you were building `bigfirm.com` from scratch, and one of the systems that you intended to create was named `reliableserver.bigfirm.com`, but you accidentally named the system `reliabulserver.bigfirm.com`. (We IT pros work late hours and after some point our "biological spelling modules" can fail, y'know?) You then sit down at some other machine and type **ping reliableserver.bigfirm.com**, and your system tells you that there's no machine by that name. You realize the error and go over to reliabulserver, rename it to reliableserver, and reboot it.

Now you go back over to your workstation and try another `ping reliableserver.bigfirm` `.com`, but it *still* tells you that there's no such system. Huh? You *fixed* the silly thing — *now* what's wrong? Negative caching, that's what; DNS isn't even going to try to resolve that name for another five minutes. Now, you *could* wait five minutes and try it again, but who the heck wants to do that? You can alternatively tell your system to forget all of its cached entries — negative and positive — with this command:

```
ipconfig /flushdns
```

So remember, when you're doing network troubleshooting, flush your DNS cache regularly so you don't get errors arising out of previously failed DNS resolutions that *shouldn't* fail anymore but that do anyway for some mysterious reason. Negative caching could be the cause of that mystery, so flush that cache after re-trying any failed command! And if you decide that five minutes is too long or too short a period to remember failed name resolutions, you can change that. Just look in the Registry in HKEY_LOCAL_MACHINE\SYSTEM\CurrentControlSet\Services\ Dnscache\Parameters to find the value entry named NegativeCacheTime. It's a value in seconds. 300 is the default, but you can set it to a larger or smaller value. Like the earlier entry, you won't see it in that key — you'll have to create the entry if you want to modify its value.

Setting Up a Simple DNS Server

We're done with the client, so it's time to set up a DNS server and a client of our very own. My plan here is to have you build a DNS server that can eventually host a DNS domain named bigfirm.com, but for now we're just going to get it set up and see that it can resolve names on the Internet. Now, I think I've figured out the simplest DNS server conceivable, *but* it needs something — an IP address that can get to the Internet.

Now, I know that some of you will just read along and not actually try this out, but let me counsel you *not* to do that. People often ask me how to learn a product — what books, seminars, videos, Web sites, or the like should they use? My answer is always the same: get a good basic text or other starting point, get a computer whose hard disk you don't mind wiping clean and rebuilding, and then just install the software and play with it. (I'm hoping that you've decided that you've got that "good basic text" in your hands, but use whatever works.)

As for machines, you've already got two — the ones you set up as WINSERVER and MAIN. Whether they're real systems or virtual machines, they don't need a tremendous amount of power. We'll only need WINSERVER for this next exercise.

Find Your IP Addresses

But what about those IP addresses? Well, again, I'm guessing that you have two machines to play with (you can actually get away with one for a lot of this) and they're on some small network like a home network with an Internet connection and some sort of device that allows you to share that connection, some sort of wired or wireless router, like the ones you can buy from Linksys, Dlink, Belkin, or the like.

So let's do a simple test:

1. We've had you build a couple of Windows Server 2008 systems so far. Start them up, and connect them to your network. (This is probably not a good idea if you're working on your *company's* network, by the way — at least check with the network folks before you do in that case.)

2. On each system, open up a command prompt, and use ipconfig to see whether you have any IP addresses on any of your network connections — remember, if you have an Ethernet connection, then it's likely to be called Local Area Connection, and if you have a wireless network card, then it's likely to be called Wireless Network Connection. And don't forget that IP addresses that start with 169.254 won't be any help, as they're local-only addresses. Ignore any adapters with "Tunnel" in their names.

3. Once you're satisfied that you've got what looks like a possibly good Internet connection, start up Internet Explorer and see whether you can get to any Web site on the Internet — Microsoft's, mine, Yahoo's, whomever.

If you can get to a Web site, great. If you can't, then it may be because my coauthors and I have sometimes asked you to configure systems with static IP addresses — telling your system to instead get its IP address from a local DHCP server might fix the trouble. Open an elevated command prompt and type **ipconfig /all**. If your wireless or Ethernet connection (you may not have both) says "DHCP Enabled . . . . . No," then tell it to use DHCP by modifying your network adapter's TCP/IP properties as you learned in Chapter 10; that may get you an address that can see the Internet. For example, if the system you're using to try to do this is connected with a wired (Ethernet) connection, then you can force it to get its IP address from DHCP by typing this:

```
netsh int ip set address "local area connection" dhcp
```

After running that command, give your computer a minute to talk with your local DHCP server (which, again, is probably housed in the Linksys/Belkin/Dlink device) and then try to connect with the Internet again. Don't forget to do an **ipconfig /flushdns** command first to defeat any negative caching!

Okay, now comes the big question: do you indeed have a working Internet connection on both systems, or at least one on WINSERVER (it's doing the DNS work, so it's the one that really needs it)? If so, then *write that address down* . . . we'll need it later.

> **NOTE**
>
> In general, real honest-to-God DNS servers that enterprises rely upon will have either static IP addresses, or unchanging IP addresses delivered via a DHCP reservation. Ultimately I'll have you set this machine to some IP address, but for now it doesn't matter because what we're doing is so simple. In these exercises, all you'll need is a system that can ping IP addresses to the public Internet.

Could you get to the Net? If so, then great, you'll be able to do this exercise. If not, then don't despair — you don't *have* to do this exercise, but if you don't, then please at least read along anyway, as we'll learn a few things in it and besides, we'll be disconnected from the Internet for most of this chapter's exercises.

We're going to do three things:

1. First, I'll show you how to install DNS server software on this system.

2. Then, once the DNS server software's installed, I'll have you configure your system so that it uses *itself* to resolve DNS names — in other words, you started out with a DNS client on your system (because *every* computer nowadays has a DNS client) and now you've got a DNS *server* on the system; now we'll hook 'em up.

3. With that in place, we'll try to surf the Internet. If the DNS server software is installed and functioning properly, then the system (which is configured to rely upon itself for DNS resolution) should be able to resolve DNS names, and you will have set up your first working DNS server.

Installing the DNS Server Software

I have to tell you, writing this section makes me *very* happy. You see, I love trying to make complicated computer things understandable (and I surely hope I'm succeeding with you), but I really hate having to describe in a click-by-click manner how to do something. Windows Server 2008, however, lets me avoid that altogether. In previous versions of Server, we'd be clicking around for about five minutes to find the place where we tell those earlier versions of Server to install a DNS server service. Here's how you do it in 2008:

1. First, open up an elevated command prompt.

2. Then, type this:

```
servermanagercmd -install dns
```

3. That's it. (Well, clearly don't forget to press Enter!) It will respond with this:

```
......................

Start Installation...
[Installation] Succeeded: [DNS Server].
<100/100>

Success: Installation succeeded.
```

4. Verify that it's running by typing **net start | findstr DNS**, and you should see "DNS Client" and "DNS Server."

Point the DNS Client to the DNS Server

Next, let's tell the DNS client software running on the server to direct its queries to the DNS *server* software that's running on the very same box. (You'd think they'd get acquainted all on their own, but they don't.) This is sometimes described as "telling the DNS server to point to itself." Do that by finding out your system's IP address — remember, ipconfig is the tool for that job — and then type into a command prompt:

```
netsh int ip set dns adaptername static ipaddress
```

What's that you say, you don't want to look up your IP address? Well, in that case, we can cheat a bit. Remember 127.0.0.1, the "loopback" address? When a computer asks to transmit information to 127.0.0.1, that information "loops back" to that computer. So, if the network adapter that's connecting you to the Internet is named Local Area Connection, then you could point your server's DNS client to itself by typing this:

```
netsh int ip set dns "local area connection" static 127.0.0.1
```

Remember also that your *adaptername* may not be "local area connection"; it might be "wireless connection" or something like that — recall that we've already seen in this chapter how to use ipconfig to find out your adapter's names.

Try Your DNS Server Out

With that open command prompt, try pinging my Web site by typing **ping www.minasi.com**. If that doesn't work, then maybe my ISP is making my life difficult again, and so try a few others, although the list of big-time Web servers that respond to pings is getting shorter. As I write this, www.google.com and www.yahoo.com still respond to pings. (Who *knows* what'll happen with the Yahoo! servers if Microsoft buys them?)

Did it work? If not, then do an **ipconfig /all** and double-check that the DNS server that ipconfig reports for your Internet-connected adapter is, indeed, either the same as the IP address reported for that adapter or 127.0.0.1.

Meet a Better DNS Tool: NSLOOKUP

Now, the whole idea of pinging my Web site was to exercise your newly constructed DNS server, but we've got a better tool for controlling DNS, a command-line tool named nslookup.

Open a command prompt (unless you've still got one open), type **nslookup**, and press Enter. You'll probably see something like this:

```
C:\>nslookup
DNS request timed out.
    timeout was 2 seconds.
Default Server: UnKnown
Address: 206.246.253.12
>
```

Your IP address will be different, but otherwise you'll probably see something like that. Don't worry about any timeout messages if they appear. Then, type

```
www.minasi.com
```

and again press Enter. You should see something like this:

```
> www.minasi.com
Server:   UnKnown
Address:  10.50.50.119

Non-authoritative answer:
Name:    web2.minasi.com
Address:  70.165.73.5
Aliases:  www.minasi.com

>
```

Again, the exact text may vary because your DNS server uses a different IP address than mine does, and I might well have reconfigured the IP address on my Web server by the time you try this out, and you may or may not get the "Non-authoritative answer" line. Here's the important thing: *it resolved a name on the Internet*. Not impressed, you say? Well, consider this: how much configuration did you do to the DNS server in order to "teach" it to resolve names on the public Internet? Answer: none.

That's *really* important. We're going to talk in the companion book of this series, *Mastering Windows Server 2008: Essential Technologies*, about something called *forwarders*. Many people somehow get an idea that they need to configure forwarders for DNS servers in order for the DNS servers to be able to resolve addresses on the Internet. It's not true; all a DNS server needs is a connection to the Internet and the list of 13 special servers called the *DNS root servers* — I'll be talking about them in a few pages. Again, the server's IP address needn't even be routable as long as it can surf the Internet through a NAT/PAT router. In other words, if you can read my home page or Microsoft's home page from your computer, then your computer has got sufficient juice to be a simple DNS server.

So when you set up a DNS server, make it a habit to do a simple little troubleshooting step as soon as you've got DNS on the system — point a system to that DNS server, start `nslookup`, and try to resolve a name out on the public Internet.

Troubleshooting the Simple DNS Server

What if your exercise *didn't* work? Check the following things:

- Double-check that the DNS service is actually running. From an elevated command prompt, type **net start** to see the list of running services; one should be named DNS Server. If it's not on the list, you might try typing **net start** "**dns server**" and pressing Enter.

- Check that the DNS server points to itself: do an `ipconfig /all` and ensure that the IP address and the address of the DNS server are the same (unless you used the all-purpose "myself" address, 127.0.0.1).

- Again, check that the server can route to the Internet. Try a ping to a few fairly reliable IP addresses like the ones that I mentioned a page or two back. If you can't ping to an IP address, then it's not a DNS problem; it's a router problem. (Or maybe a cable fell out of the back of a computer when you moved it, or perhaps — if you're using wireless networking — then maybe you've lost connectivity to the wireless access point.)

- Check that your network guys haven't installed some insanely paranoid firewall that's blocking your attempts to do DNS lookups. Type **nslookup**, press Enter, and then type **server 164.109.1.3** to point your system to that large ISP's DNS server. You should now be able to resolve www.ibm.com and the like. If not, then either you've got a really damaged copy of `nslookup` (something I've never seen) or your ability to communicate with the public Internet is being severely hampered by a firewall.

- Open the Event Viewer — click Start and, in the "Start search" field, type **eventvwr.msc** and press Enter. Once Event Viewer is open, open the Applications and Services Logs folder, and inside there you'll see a log named DNS Server. Sometimes the logs can offer valuable hints.

With hope, by now you've successfully set up a DNS server and gotten a bit hands-on with it.

We Just Built a "Caching-Only" DNS Server

So far, this DNS server isn't acting as *the* DNS server for any DNS domains — all it knows is how to take a query from a client and then search the Internet to find the particular DNS server that can answer its client's question. For example, the only DNS servers that can resolve www.google.com are the four DNS servers that Google runs, so before your newly built DNS server can find the IP address for www.google.com, it's got to find one of those four Google servers. And while accomplishing that is pretty neat, it means that no other DNS servers ever ask your new server to help them with questions.

> **NOTE**
>
> Okay, sure, any DNS server *can* resolve www.google.com — but they can't do it unless they can ultimately find and query Google's four DNS servers — those four hold the Google DNS information. In DNS terms, those four servers are said to be *authoritative* for the google.com DNS domain. Everyone else can resolve queries about google.com, but the answers that they provide are said to be non-authoritative. ("Non-authoritative" answers to queries makes them sound sort of illegitimate, but they're not — it's just a term.) Thus, to be authoritative for a domain, a DNS server must contain information about that domain, but that's not all — a server having information about a domain is not worth anything unless people know to ask that server about the domain. As we'll see later, that has to do with the "DNS hierarchy," which we're about to take up.

Such a server is called a *caching-only* DNS server. To understand that, imagine that you've been asked to run a network of 500 workstations, and so you've just installed the DNS server and configured all 500 systems to look to that server for DNS name resolution. The server still isn't authoritative for any DNS domains, but it does a fine job resolving queries for the 500 systems. But there's a bonus — remember caching? We said that the Windows DNS client caches answers to earlier-asked queries. Well, the DNS *server* does that as well, remembering the answers to queries. That's convenient because when Joe gets in early and visits some Web site with, one hopes, a big TTL, then that query stays in the DNS server's RAM for as long as its TTL allows, so when Susan arrives a few moments later and needs to visit that same Web site, then the DNS server can respond to her query instantaneously. Thus, any DNS server that's up and running, but not authoritative for any DNS domains is said to be a "caching-only" server.

DNS Concepts: "The Hierarchy"

Let's put WINSERVER away for a moment and look at how DNS servers relate to each other so that you'll be able to set them up properly and troubleshoot failures in DNS. Remember when I noted at the beginning of the chapter how fast DNS searches were, given the huge size of the Internet? Now I can explain how that's possible.

The key to DNS's speed and distributed nature is its structure. It's shaped in a tree structure or, rather, a "tree structure" in the sense that we techies mean when we say that, with a single "root" at the top of it with "branches" growing down from that root, then more "branches" spreading down off the higher branches and so on. (Roots in the air, branches below — only computer geeks would draw trees this way, you know?) Most people don't refer to "the DNS tree," however; instead, they say "the DNS hierarchy" or "the DNS namespace," which in all honesty mean the same thing.

Why care about how a DNS hierarchy or namespace works? You need to know this for a couple of reasons. First, you interact daily with the largest DNS hierarchy on the planet — the Internet's system of DNS servers. If you ever want to set up your own publicly visible DNS domain on the Internet, then it'll be good to know where you fit in the hierarchy. Second, you already know that you'll need *some* sort of DNS infrastructure before you can create an Active Directory, but you'll learn in the companion book, *Essential Technologies*, that I'll recommend that you keep your AD secure by creating its own DNS hierarchy separated from the Internet's DNS hierarchy — that way, it's harder for bad guys to find your network and try to attack it . . . and you can't build your own hierarchy without knowing how it's going to have to work. And, finally, I suppose that there is also a third reason to know this stuff — it's just plain interesting to understand how this essential part of the Internet works.

As I mentioned before, you'll see people use the term *namespace* and *hierarchy* when referring to DNS. I'll tend to use *hierarchy* here, but if you read something that refers to a *DNS namespace*, then just substitute *DNS hierarchy* and you'll be correct.

Introducing the Hierarchy: Back to Left-to-Right

You read DNS names left to right, whether they're names in the worldwide DNS hierarchy or in some private four-computer private intranet with its own DNS hierarchy. But what exactly *are* you reading? Let me explain this in some detail and use it as my vehicle to introduce how the DNS hierarchy works.

To return to a question I posed at the beginning of the chapter, "How on Earth could a database as large, widespread, and ever-changing as the DNS machine-name-to-IP-address database be managed and maintained and yet still offer reasonable query times?" Well, as you'll see later in this chapter, the *only* reason that it's possible is because no one person or organization must keep track of those names. Instead, the responsibility for keeping track of any given domain's name-to-IP-address relationship is maintained locally by administrators in that domain. For example, if you point your browser to www.minasi.com and your local DNS server then tries to figure out the IP address of www.minasi.com, then your local DNS server is eventually going to have to talk to *my* local DNS server to resolve that name. That means that it's *my* job to make sure that you can find the www machine in the minasi.com domain because minasi.com is my domain. If by contrast you go looking for www.acme.com and *Acme* drops the ball on keeping track of *their* domain, then it only affects the people trying to get to the Acme systems — you wouldn't be hampered at all in trying to find a computer in the minasi.com domain.

Let's consider a PC whose full name is mypc.test.minasi.com in order to start examining how the hierarchy works. What do the placements of the periods in the name — the parts of the name — tell us?

First, we know that its machine name is mypc. Second, we know that its DNS domain or zone is test.minasi.com.

But what *is* test.minasi.com? Well, reading left to right, you see that test is part of minasi.com, which is a DNS domain. What, then, is test? It's a DNS domain *inside* the minasi.com domain, and the RFCs refer to such a domain as a *child domain* or a *subdomain* — both terms get used in RFCs, so I don't think that either one is the "official" one. In the DNS hierarchy, child domains can be created only with the permission of whomever owns their parent domains, so whoever built test.minasi.com did it with the permission of whoever owns minasi.com.

Next, let's move to the right, and consider minasi.com. What is this domain? It is a child domain of a domain named, simply, com. (Yes, there is such a domain.) To create the minasi.com domain, someone (well, *me*, actually) needed to contact the people in charge of the com domain and get permission to create a subdomain of com named minasi or, in other words, minasi.com. That's what you do when you visit an Internet registrar like networksolutions.com, godaddy.com, register.com, or the like to try to register a new "dot-com" domain.

But where did the com domain come from? Is it a child of some other domain? Well, if it weren't for a very common bit of sloppiness, then it'd be more obvious. You see, mypc.test.minasi.com isn't, strictly speaking, a complete DNS name or, recall, an FQDN — instead, mypc.test.minasi.com. *is*. What's the difference? Look again — the correct one ends with a period. The com. domain is actually a child domain of a domain named just . that is, by the way, pronounced "dot" and is called the *root* of the DNS hierarchy.

Now you know why I've been calling the way that DNS stores names a "hierarchy" — DNS distributes responsibility. To create the com domain only required the permission — granted *once* — of whomever owned the root (.) domain. (Originally it was the U.S. government, but that responsibility has moved to a nonprofit group called the Internet Corporation for Assigned Names and Numbers, or ICANN; you may recall from Chapter 10 that they succeeded the IETF, the folks that were the central governing body for the Internet. The whole question of who ultimately "controls" the DNS hierarchy is and will probably forever be massively political, as you can imagine.) I got to register minasi.com because I provided some information and a credit card number to the people who run the com domain, Network Solutions. Now, if someone were to come to me and ask to create a domain named thisistheplace.minasi.com, she wouldn't have to talk to ICANN or Network Solutions — she'd only have to talk to me.

Let me underscore that. To create minasi.com, I only needed the permission of the people who run the .com domain. I didn't have to get permission from other .com companies, such as microsoft.com, ibm.com, or saralee.com — I just needed the OK from the .com parent domain, which is controlled by Network Solutions. Nor did Network Solutions have to ask the ICANN guys — once ICANN (the root people) delegated control of the com. directory to the Network Solutions folks, then ICANN doesn't care who Network Solutions delegates to. In the same way, if I wanted to create a subdomain of minasi.com, such as hq.minasi.com, then I not only needn't tell microsoft.com, ibm.com, or saralee.com, I also needn't tell Network Solutions.

Why Build the DNS Hierarchy This Way?

Let's back up for a bit and see what led to DNS looking as it does today. In the TCP/IP world, anything with an IP address is called a *host*. Back in the early '80s, when the Internet (which wasn't yet *called* the Internet — it was the ARPAnet then) consisted of only a few hundred computers, a server on MIT's campus held a file that listed the names and IP addresses of those few computers. That file was named HOSTS because it listed all of the hosts on the Internet. (Remember, "host" is Internet-ese for "something with an IP address.") When someone at some distant site added a computer to their local network and attached that computer to the ARPAnet, then he or she would just contact someone at MIT, who'd update the HOSTS file, and once a day everyone would attach to that MIT server and download the latest HOSTS file.

As you know, the HOSTS file still exists on every IP-using computer, although in a much less important role. But why not keep running things the old way, with one big central HOSTS file? Well, let's see: Assume 200 million computers on the Internet, and about 40 characters per HOSTS line; that'd be about 8 gigabytes. So every day you'd have to connect to some location and download 8 gigs — yuck. Even worse, every single time you put a computer on your network, adding pc0012 to acme.com, you'd have to tell someone at the one worldwide central repository of the HOSTS file and hope that they'd update the file in a timely fashion. And when you add a new system to your network, or perhaps assign a name to a different IP address — such as when you move www.acme.com from one machine to another, changing an IP address in the process — then you better hope that everyone out there in Internetland who you'd *like* to be able to find your Web server is working from the latest HOSTS file — ugh, double and triple yuck.

The Root, Top-Level, Second-Level, and Child Domains

Having explained how the hierarchy *doesn't* work, let's look at how it *does* work. Take a look at Figure 13.3.

TOP-LEVEL DOMAINS

Below the root are hundreds — yes, hundreds — of *top-level* domains. Most of the ones we tend to think of around the world are .com, .net, and .org, as they've become sort of the worldwide "catchall" domains. Then, each country has its own top-level domain — the United States has

.us, Canada .ca, the United Kingdom .uk, and so on. Some countries have decided to offer their top-level domain for registrations, as in the case of the Cocos Keeling Island, the owners of the .cc top-level domain that many are using as an alternative to .com, .org, or .net. The island has a total population of 596 (and you just have to wonder how many of them have Internet connectivity, don't you?). In another example, the somewhat-larger (population 12,000) island nation of Tuvalu ended up with the top-level domain with the salable name of .tv, and they make about 10% of their GNP from sales of .tv domains. Top-level domains .gov, .mil, and .edu tend to point to U.S. government, military, and educational institutions — remember what organization invented the Internet in the first place — although I guess in theory, groups of those types in other countries might register names under those top-level domains as well.

FIGURE 13.3
The public DNS hierarchy

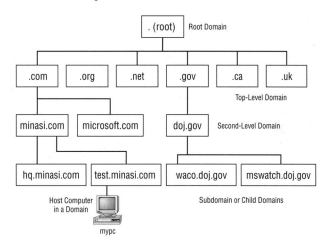

In November 2000, ICANN created several new top-level domains. I don't exactly get why they bothered with some of them, but they are presented in Table 13.1.

TABLE 13.1: Newer Top-Level Internet Domains

DOMAIN	PURPOSE	CONTROLLING ORGANIZATION
.aero	Aerospace-oriented firms, including airlines	Societe Internationale de Telecommunications Aeronautiques (Belgium)
.biz	Basically an "expansion area" for .com	JVTeam, LLC
.coop	Business cooperatives	National Cooperative Business Association
.info	Information sources	Afilias, LLC
.museum	Museums, clearly	Museum Domain Management Association
.name	People's names (see text)	Global Name Registry (the U.K.)
.pro	Various professional groups — doctors, lawyers, accountants, that sort of thing	RegistryPro (Ireland)

To tell you the truth, the effect of these "new" TLDs hasn't been great. The top-level domains `.biz` and `.info` are still, after eight years, both fairly wide-open domains that anyone can register names in. If you're Acme Termite Inspection service and you find that `acmetermite.com`, `acmetermite.net`, and `acmetermite.org` are taken, then you might still be able to get `acmetermite.biz` or `acmetermite.info`. The domain `.pro` is *not* wide open; there are people running various subdomains there. For example, you couldn't (as far as I can see) just register `engineer.pro`; rather, someone would administer `engineer.pro` and you'd get a name below that, like `janesconstruction.engineer.pro`. (As I write this, there's already a `cpa.pro`, `medical.pro`, and `legal.pro`.) The idea behind the `.name` domain is that someone would create an overall registry of people whose last name was Minasi and therefore control the `minasi.name` domain. I'd then get a subdomain under that called `mark.minasi.name`, although after eight years I have to say that `.pro` and `.name` don't seem to have gone very far — `.com` still seems to be *the* TLD to have.

Different organizations control different top-level domains. For example, clearly Ottawa designates who hands out registrations under `.ca`, and the `.tv` sellers couldn't be doing those sales without the permission of the Tuvalans. The top-level domains that are biggest by far, however, are of course `.com`, `.net`, and `.org`, all administered by Network Solutions, based in northern Virginia. Remember, though, that although Network Solutions controls the "waterfront property" in DNS-land, they don't control the rest of DNS — ICANN worries about *all* of the top-level domains.

ROLL-YOUR-OWN TOP-LEVEL DOMAINS: FOR INTERNAL USE ONLY!

Before I move to second-level domains, I want to toss in something that I'll be covering in detail later. Although the public Internet uses only a handful of top-level domains (TLDs in geek-speak), that doesn't mean you can't create others of your own sometimes. As you'll see, I strongly recommend that the DNS servers that support your Active Directory *not* be visible on the public Internet, if you can avoid it. You can, as you'll learn, create a DNS server that is perfectly capable of resolving names on the public Internet but that also hosts a domain that is "invisible" to the public Internet. (You'd do this for security's sake.) You can accomplish this in several ways, but one simple way is just to use a domain name with a nonstandard TLD. For example, suppose your company's publicly visible Internet domain name were `acme.com`; you might choose to create an Active Directory domain name of `acme.local`. Never heard of a domain called *something-dot-local*? No wonder — there's no such TLD on the Internet. But you can do anything you like on your *intra*net, creating domains with any TLD that you like. So I guess I *could* have an e-mail name of `mark@minasi` — but only people inside my company could use it! Again, we'll cover more on this later, but I wanted to plant that idea in your head now so I can expand on it later.

There was a proposed standard working its way through the RFC process that would have suggested a reserved internal-only top-level domain of `.pri` for "private" but it appears to have gone nowhere.

SECOND-LEVEL DOMAINS: SEARCHING THE HIERARCHY

Sadly, ICANN is not about to give me my own `.minasi` top-level domain, so I guess I won't be able to change my e-mail address to `mark@minasi` any time soon. So the second-level domains are the more interesting ones for most of us.

As you just read, you can create a second-level domain with the permission of the owner of the parent domain. To create your second-level domain, the parent domain only has to do one thing: "delegate" name responsibility for your second-level domain to some machine. That's an important concept, and I'll get to it in a minute. But first, let's see how DNS uses its hierarchical nature with an example.

Suppose you point your browser to www.minasi.com. Your browser needs to know the IP address of the www.minasi.com machine, so it asks the DNS client software on the same computer to resolve the name into an IP address. As you know, the local DNS client software passes the buck to a local DNS server. ("Tag — you're it!") Now where should your local DNS server go to ask the IP address of the www machine in the domain minasi.com? Simple — it should go to the DNS server for minasi.com.

Oh, sorry, what was I thinking? I guess I was in "outsourced technical support mode" for a moment, as I gave you an answer that was perfectly correct ... but not of much value. So let's see ... how is your DNS server supposed to find the DNS server for minasi.com? Well, in general, you can find the address of a domain's DNS server by asking the domain's *parent's* DNS server — in other words, the DNS servers in the com domain can tell you the addresses of the DNS servers in the minasi.com domain.

But we're still not done, because *now* the question is, "What is the IP address of the DNS server (or servers) for the com domain?" Well, as you just learned, you get a domain's DNS server addresses from the DNS servers in that domain's parent's DNS server, so you'd get com's DNS server address from the DNS servers for com's parent, ., which is the root.

Hmmm ... if you've been patient enough to follow this so far, then you've probably realized that we've run into a bit of a brick wall: to resolve www.minasi.com, we need the minasi.com DNS server, and to get the minasi.com server, we need the com DNS server, and to get the com server, we need the root DNS server. Where to find the root's DNS server? You find the DNS servers for minasi.com by asking the DNS servers for com, and you find the DNS servers for com by asking the root, but who do you ask to find out the DNS servers for the root, as the root has no parent? (Hey, that'd be a great computer trivia question: Which is the only "orphan" DNS domain?)

The answer is, "you cheat." Every piece of DNS server software that I've ever seen comes with a kind of a cheat sheet called the *root hints file*, which contains the name and, more important, IP addresses of the 13 root DNS servers. On a Microsoft OS-based DNS server, you'll find a file named cache.dns — an ASCII file that you can examine with Notepad — in \windows\system32\dns on any server that you've installed the DNS server service on. Anyway, once your DNS server has located a root DNS server's address in its root hints file, it asks that root DNS server for the addresses of the DNS servers for the com domain, then asks one of the com DNS servers for the address of the minasi.com DNS server, *then* asks the minasi.com DNS server for the address of the machine named www in the minasi.com domain and finally resolves the name for you. To summarize what happened when your local DNS server tried to resolve www.minasi.com:

1. First, your DNS server decided to find the minasi.com DNS server.

2. To find the minasi.com DNS server, your DNS server decided to look for the addresses of the com domain's DNS servers, as com is minasi.com's parent domain.

3. To find the com domain's DNS server, your DNS server decided to look for the root DNS servers.

4. It knew the IP addresses of the root DNS servers through its local root hints file.

5. Using the IP address of a root DNS server, it asked that root DNS server for the address of a DNS server for the com domain.

6. The root DNS server told your DNS server the addresses of the com domain's DNS servers.

7. Your DNS server then took one of those addresses and asked that com DNS server for the addresses of the minasi.com DNS servers.

8. That DNS server for the com domain told your DNS server the addresses of minasi.com's two DNS servers.

9. Your DNS server then asked one of minasi.com's DNS servers to resolve the name www.minasi.com.

10. The minasi.com DNS server resolved the address, returning the IP address of www.minasi.com to your DNS server.

Your DNS server cached that information just in case someone else in your organization needs to resolve www.minasi.com in the next hour, and passed www.minasi.com's IP address to you.

THIRD LEVEL, CHILD, OR SUBDOMAINS: MORE ON DELEGATION

Now suppose I choose to divide my domain into subdomains or child domains. Suppose I create a subdomain named hq.minasi.com. What's involved? Delegation.

DELEGATION INVOLVES SEPARATION

You saw from the previous example about resolving www.minasi.com that a DNS server resolves a name by working its way up the DNS hierarchy until it gets to the root, and then it works its way back down until it finally finds the DNS server that can answer its question. But, in some senses, *shouldn't* the root servers be able to resolve www.minasi.com? After all, www.minasi.com *is* in their domain, sort of. Or I could argue that the DNS servers for the com domain should be able to resolve www.minasi.com, as that address is inside the com domain, *sort* of "once removed," so to speak.

The answer is no, the root and com domains should *not* be able to resolve www in the minasi.com domain because they have *delegated* name resolution responsibility for minasi.com to a set of DNS servers, the minasi.com DNS servers.

When I say that "Network Solutions has delegated control of a minasi.com domain," I mean that something very specific has happened. minasi.com exists as a child domain of com because the Network Solutions folks put a bit of information into the com domain's DNS records that says, "there is a child of the com domain named minasi.com, and, to tell you the truth, we folks at Network Solutions have no idea what the heck's in there, but we *do* know that Mark's DNS server is named netdoor.minasi.com and can answer queries about any minasi.com hosts or subdomains."

DNS administrators insert this sort of information in their DNS zones by including a kind of record called an *NS record* — "NS" is short for "name server." The sequence of events that led to my getting a minasi.com domain, then, looks in more detail like this:

1. First, ICANN or, rather, its predecessor created the root domain. There are very few hosts in the root domain.

2. Very soon after, someone installed some NS records in the root saying, "we're creating a child domain of the root called com." We're not going to run it, Network Solutions is — and here are the names and addresses of the DNS servers that they're going to use for that domain. There is more than one NS record for com because DNS needs an NS record for each DNS server that the child domain's administrators want to set up.

3. Eventually, I set up a couple of DNS servers and gave Network Solutions some money, and they modified their COM domain DNS servers to contain two NS records naming their new child domain as minasi.com and pointing to my two DNS servers, the only two that can authoritatively answer questions about that domain.

Before I forget, let me note that word *authoritative*. We've seen it before, but now I'm ready to clarify what it means. For my `minasi.com` DNS servers to be authoritative for the `minasi.com` domain, they need two things. First, they've clearly got to contain an accurate list of names and IP addresses of systems in my domain, and, second, the rest of the Internet's got to be able to find those servers. From what we've seen in this discussion of the DNS hierarchy, I could host a thousand DNS servers, each of which contains an up-to-date copy of my DNS domain's information — but nobody's ever going to know about any of them except for the two in Network Solution's `com` domain. In this context, *authoritative* means "pointed to by the parent domain."

WHY CREATE SUBDOMAINS?

So why would I create a subdomain of `minasi.com`? Perhaps I've got the same kind of problem that Network Solutions does — that is to say, perhaps I want to enable a group to use DNS names within my domain, but I don't want to have to do the maintenance on the DNS records. Suppose, for example, that I buy a company in Singapore, 12 time zones away from me. Now suppose they put a new machine online and need a name resolution record for that machine installed in the `minasi.com` DNS database. They can't call me when they need that, as it's not only a long way away, but also because I'm usually asleep while they're working. That gets kind of annoying and after a while they say, "Can't you just give us control of the name resolution for our own machines?" Well, I'm not particularly keen about giving them control of the whole `minasi.com` domain, but I'd like to grant their request for local control of their machine names. So I create a subdomain and call it `test.minasi.com`. Making their subdomain a reality requires two things:

◆ First, they'll need to make one of their computers into a DNS server for the `test.minasi.com` subdomain. That machine will, of course, need to be on the Internet persistently with a static IP address.

◆ Second, I'll need to tell the rest of the world to look at their server when resolving names in the `test.minasi.com` domain. I do that by delegating name server responsibility, by placing an NS record in my `minasi.com` DNS database that says, "There's a subdomain named test in the `minasi.com` domain, and if you want to look up any names in that, then don't ask me, ask this other DNS server, the one in Singapore."

But that's not the only reason why I might want to create a child domain. Some people create child domains to highlight geographic realities, as might be useful if my PC were named, say, `pc39.dallas.bigfirm.com`. A look at the FQDN of that system would tell me where it's located, and that might be beneficial for network management. Alternatively, my machine might be named `pc39.consulting.bigfirm.com` to identify that it's being used (and perhaps owned) by a particular division of the company.

Yet another way to think about it is to follow the NS records. When someone wants to find, say, a machine named `pc21.test.minasi.com`, then their DNS server ends up doing this:

1. First asking the root domain's DNS servers for an NS record to locate the DNS servers in its `com` child domain.

2. Then asking the com domain's DNS servers for an NS record to locate the DNS servers in its `minasi.com` child domain.

3. Then asking the `minasi.com` domain's DNS servers for an NS record to locate the DNS servers in its `test.minasi.com` domain.

4. Finally, it asks the `test.minasi.com`'s DNS servers for a host name record for `pc21.test.minasi.com`.

You'll learn more about NS records a bit later, when I get more specific about building DNS zones, but in a nutshell that's all there is to delegation — it's a one-line command in a parent DNS server's database that says, "Hey, don't ask *me* — go talk to this other DNS server."

Building a More Complex DNS Server

Let's shift gears a bit now and start seeing how to get DNS zones onto a DNS server. Now, I want *everyone* to be able to follow along on this exercise, so we're no longer going to assume that your network can't necessarily attach to the Internet. We will, then, utilize our two Server 2008 systems, our old friends MAIN and WINSERVER. WINSERVER will be the one acting as the DNS server, and MAIN will mostly be acting as a client. (Yes, an XP or Vista box would make just as good a client ... but remember, Microsoft has got a free 180-day evaluation copy of Server 2008, *not* XP or Vista!) We'll set these systems up like so (I'll be taking you through the steps, don't try to do it just from this list):

WINSERVER will

◆ Have a machine name of "winserver" and a DNS suffix of "bigfirm.com."

◆ Have a static IP address of 192.168.1.1, a subnet mask 255.255.255.0, and no default gateway.

◆ Have the DNS server service installed.

◆ Point to itself (192.168.1.1) for DNS.

◆ Contain a zone named "bigfirm.com."

MAIN will

◆ Have a machine name of "main" and a DNS suffix of "bigfirm.com."

◆ Have a static IP address of 192.168.1.2, a subnet mask of 255.255.255.0, and no default gateway.

◆ Point to winserver (192.168.1.1) for DNS.

And it's not mandatory, but you'll probably find things a bit easier if you disable IPv6, as we're not ready to attack that just yet. The easiest way to disable IPv6 is probably with a Registry modification:

1. Open Regedit.

2. Navigate to HKLM ➢ SYSTEM ➢ CurrentControlSet ➢ Services ➢ Tcpip6 ➢ Parameters.

3. Add a REG_DWORD called "DisabledComponents."

4. Set its value to 0xFF hex (256 decimal).

5. Reboot your computer; do that for both WINSERVER and MAIN.

Connect and Name the Systems

First, hook up WINSERVER and MAIN onto the same switch or hub. Again, they needn't connect to the Internet, but they need to be able to connect to each other. Once the systems are up, check that they've got the right names by opening a command prompt and typing **hostname**. If you've forgotten how to rename a system, then refer to Chapter 2, where you've seen how to do it before, or use an elevated command prompt and type this:

```
netdom /renamecomputer %computername% /newname:winserver /force /reboot
```

(Clearly, that's the command for WINSERVER.) Check that the other system is named MAIN with a similar command.

Set Up the IP Addresses and Preferred DNS Servers

Assign MAIN the IP address of 192.168.1.2 with a subnet mask of 255.255.255.0 by opening up an elevated command prompt (you *are* still logged onto MAIN as an administrator, right?) and typing this:

```
netsh int ip set address "Local Area Connection" static 192.168.1.2 255.255.255.0
```

NOTE

In that example, I assumed that your network card had the name Local Area Connection. If you're not sure what your NIC's name is, just do an ipconfig command — that shows the names of your NICs, or look in the Network and Sharing Center in Control Panel, which also shows them.

Then do the same thing for WINSERVER, except use address 192.168.1.1. And by the way, it doesn't matter if you capitalize local area connection when you type the netsh command. Also, both systems' DNS clients should point to WINSERVER for their DNS needs, even if WINSERVER's not a DNS server just yet. On each system, just type this:

```
netsh int ip set dns "local area connection" static 192.168.1.1
```

Remember, type that same command at both systems because we want both systems to look to the same system for DNS — WINSERVER, at 192.168.1.1. After all, if MAIN asked itself to resolve DNS queries, it'd be up a creek, as MAIN is DNS-challenged.

Open the Firewalls to Allow Pings

At this point, I want to check connectivity by having the system at 192.168.1.1 ping the system at 192.168.1.2, and vice versa, but that probably won't work, as Server 2008 raises the firewall by default and blocks most traffic. (Don't get me started on the level of useless paranoia implicit in a firewall that doesn't even let you *ping*, for heaven's sake.) So let's make sure that the firewall's up — I mean, firewalls are a good idea, trust me — *and* then tell the firewall to relax a mite and let us ping.

On each system, type these two commands:

```
netsh firewall set opmode enable
netsh firewall set icmpsetting 8 enable
```

The first command turned on the firewall — again, yours was probably already on but it's a good idea to get used to having it on all the time — and the second told the firewall to enable ICMP — that's the protocol that Ping is built on — to request echoes, which is essential for Pings. The "8" refers to the fact that an echo request is "command type 8."

Test Connectivity

Now let's try those pings (remember, your network connection "don't mean a thing if it ain't got that ping")! From each system, ping the other system. But be sure to ping by IP address, *not* the machine name. For example, from WINSERVER you'd type this:

```
ping 192.168.1.2
```

And you would *not* type this:

```
ping main
```

That's an important point about network troubleshooting — start pinging from the IP address, not the name. If all's gone well so far for you, then you've got 192.168.1.2 pinging 192.168.1.1 without a hitch, but you'll see that pinging WINSERVER from MAIN, or vice versa, usually won't work without a working DNS server or two, because — as I've noted several times already — computers don't care about names, they care about IP addresses, and it's name resolution software that converts names into IP addresses, so we can't expect a DNS-less network to be able to do anything with just names . . . but in some cases it does, and that's why I said "usually." Some Microsoft software will, when faced with failing name resolution, just start *broadcasting* name requests, shouting "hey, is anyone on this line named 'winserver?'" and so sometimes you'll see name resolution happen even without DNS.

I should note that this test actually wasn't necessary at all, but I recommend it. Whenever I build a networked system, I take advantage of as many chances to test things as I can find — it makes troubleshooting later either easier or unnecessary.

Install DNS Suffixes

WINSERVER and MAIN need their `bigfirm.com` DNS suffixes, so please configure them with that suffix now as explained earlier. Use the GUI or hack the Registry directly, whichever suits you better. And now that they've got respectable multi-label names, we can start calling them `winserver.bigfirm.com` and `main.bigfirm.com` instead of all of that "WINSERVER" uppercase yelling!

At this point, an `ipconfig /all` on `winserver.bigfirm.com` will look something like this:

```
Windows IP Configuration

        Host Name . . . . . . . . . . . . : winserver
        Primary Dns Suffix  . . . . . . . : bigfirm.com
        Node Type . . . . . . . . . . . . : Hybrid
        IP Routing Enabled. . . . . . . . : No
        WINS Proxy Enabled. . . . . . . . : No
        DNS Suffix Search List. . . . . . : bigfirm.com
```

```
Ethernet adapter Local Area Connection:

    Connection-specific DNS Suffix  . :
    Description . . . . . . . . . . : Intel(R) PRO/1000 MT Network Connection
    Physical Address. . . . . . . . : 00-0C-29-00-15-3B
    DHCP Enabled. . . . . . . . . . : No
    Autoconfiguration Enabled . . . . : Yes
    IPv4 Address. . . . . . . . . . : 192.168.1.1(Preferred)
    Subnet Mask . . . . . . . . . . : 255.255.255.0
    Default Gateway . . . . . . . . :
    DNS Servers . . . . . . . . . . : 192.168.1.1
    NetBIOS over Tcpip. . . . . . . . : Enabled
```

An ipconfig /all for main.bigfirm.com will look like this:

```
Windows IP Configuration

        Host Name . . . . . . . . . . . : main
        Primary Dns Suffix  . . . . . . . : bigfirm.com
        Node Type . . . . . . . . . . . : Hybrid
        IP Routing Enabled. . . . . . . . : No
        WINS Proxy Enabled. . . . . . . . : No
        DNS Suffix Search List. . . . . . : bigfirm.com

Ethernet adapter Local Area Connection:

        Connection-specific DNS Suffix  . :
        Description . . . . . . . . . . : Intel(R) PRO/1000 MT Network Connection

        Physical Address. . . . . . . . : 00-0C-29-90-A7-D7
        DHCP Enabled. . . . . . . . . . : No
        Autoconfiguration Enabled . . . . : Yes
        IPv4 Address. . . . . . . . . . : 192.168.1.2 (Preferred)
        Subnet Mask . . . . . . . . . . : 255.255.255.0
        Default Gateway . . . . . . . . :
        DNS Servers . . . . . . . . . . : 192.168.1.1
```

Make Winserver a DNS Server

Next, we'll install the DNS server software on winserver.bigfirm.com. As before, open up an elevated command prompt and type **servermanagercmd -install dns** unless, of course, you've already installed the DNS server on this system in the earlier exercise. Alternatively, you can use Server Manager to install the DNS server like so:

1. Start Server Manager. (Click Start and you'll see it on the top of the menu on the left-hand side, or click Start, right-click Computer, and choose Manage. Or click Start, then All Programs, then Administrative Tools, and finally Server Manager. And heck, there are probably a few other ways to do it, but that's enough for now, right?)

2. Wait for Server Manager to start up, and then, in the left-hand-side pane of its window, notice that you can see Roles, Features, Diagnostics, Configuration, and Storage. Right-click Roles and choose Add Roles.

3. The Add Roles Wizard appears with a few bits of friendly advice that we can safely ignore at this point; click Next.

4. Next, you'll see a page named Select Server Roles, which offers about a dozen or so roles, each with check boxes next to them. Locate DNS Server and check the box next to it.

5. Click Next twice and then Install. Server Manager will work for a few minutes and report that DNS is now installed.

6. Click Close and then close Server Manager. DNS is now installed!

As I've already said (but can't resist resaying), I don't know about *you*, but I am *soooo* happy we've got `servermanagercmd`. It's hard to imagine *anyone* wanting to go through all that clicking when a simple `servermanagercmd -install dns` accomplishes the same thing!

TIP

If, however, you're paid by the hour, then I recommend the GUI approach. That's Windows Server 2008's great strength: it incorporates everyone's favorite GUIs ... all of them.

Creating bigfirm.com: The Birth of a Domain

Time to move from a simple caching-only DNS server to one ready to claim its birthright and be authoritative for something! Let us, then, create a `bigfirm.com` zone on `winserver.bigfirm.com`.

RUNNING THE NEW ZONE WIZARD

We can create DNS zones with either a GUI tool or from the command line, and the command line is the quicker way, but let's try our first DNS outing from the GUI. Click Start ➢ Administrative Tools ➢ DNS to open the DNS Manager, as you see in Figure 13.4. (If you like, then just follow along with the GUI, and when we're done clicking then I'll show you how to accomplish everything that all of the clicking accomplished in one command.)

FIGURE 13.4
The DNS Manager's opening screen

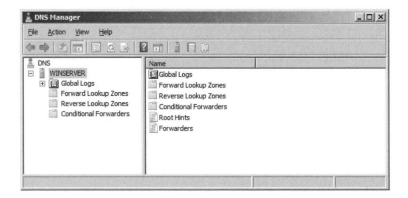

In the figure, I've opened up the WINSERVER icon to show the four objects in it. Global Logs is a view in the Event Viewer logs relevant to DNS, the log I mentioned earlier when offering a few suggestions about troubleshooting a DNS server. Forward Lookup Zones contains the places where DNS gets the information that it needs to answer forward queries ("what's the IP address for `www.minasi.com`?") and of course Reverse Lookup Zones contains the information for reverse queries ("what's the DNS name of the system with IP address 13.9.2.1?"). We won't have to worry about Conditional Forwarders for a while.

A `bigfirm.com` zone would be a forward lookup zone because, again, it lets DNS answer questions like "what IP address corresponds to the name `winserver.bigfirm.com`?" We can create one by right-clicking the Forward Lookup Zones folder and choosing New Zone. That opens a page labeled Welcome to the New Zone Wizard. Click Next to see the next page, as you see in Figure 13.5.

FIGURE 13.5

Choosing a zone type

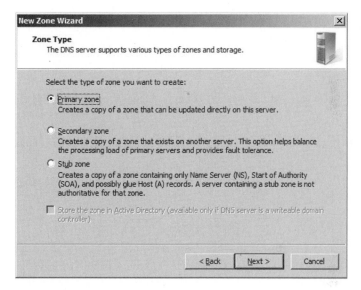

We'll cover more on these later, but in brief you create a "Primary zone" on a DNS server if you want to be able to modify and maintain your zone's (your DNS domain's, that is) information on this server. In contrast, you can create DNS servers that help share the load of answering queries by giving them *secondary* zones. Servers with secondary zones get the same information as servers with primary zones, but any administration of a zone's got to happen at a server with a primary zone. Thus, if you had one server with a primary zone for `bigfirm.com` and three servers with secondary zones for `bigfirm.com`, and you wanted to add or delete some information on the `bigfirm.com` domain, you'd have to make those changes on the server that contains the primary `bigfirm.com` zone. Don't worry about what stub zones do — they're not used as often and we'll take them up in the second book.

Choose "Primary zone" and click Next, and you'll see something like Figure 13.6.

Fill in **bigfirm.com**, and click Next to see the Zone File page, as you see in Figure 13.7.

Most varieties of DNS servers store their zone information in an ASCII text file, and by default Server 2008's DNS server is no exception. ("By default" because, as you'll see in the companion book, *Mastering Windows Server 2008: Essential Technologies*, you can choose to store the DNS information in Active Directory's database.) Unless you tell it otherwise, the DNS server creates a file named *zonename*.dns. The DNS server stores these files in \windows\system32\dns.

This is actually pretty convenient, as it makes disaster recovery on DNS a snap. If winserver croaked, then you could cook up a replacement in a twinkling, assuming that you've got a backup of `bigfirm.com.dns`. Just set up another 2000 or 2003 server as a DNS server, then take the `bigfirm.com.dns` file from the old server and copy it to `\windows\system32\dns` on the new server. Run the wizard as we're doing here, but at this page in the wizard choose "Use this existing file" and point the wizard at `bigfirm.com.dns`.

FIGURE 13.6
Specify the zone name.

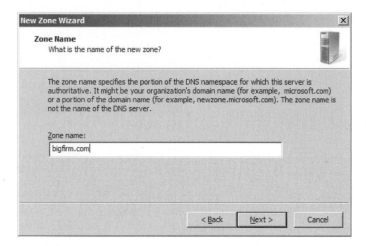

FIGURE 13.7
Where to store the zone?

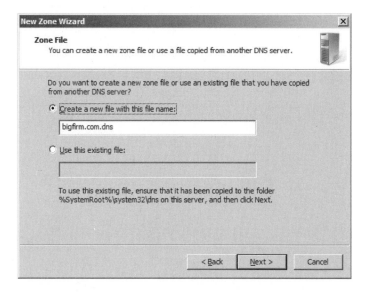

Click Next to accept the default filename and see the Dynamic Update page, as you do in Figure 13.8.

This is another topic we will take up later, but in brief, here's what it's all about. Until the latter part of the '90s, all DNS administration — adding records, deleting records — had to be done by an administrator. Add a new host, that host needs to be listed in the DNS zone, and so somebody had to type it in. Eventually an RFC came out describing how a host might be able to list *itself* in the DNS database, making life easier for the DNS administrators ... but it was not to be so. You see, most DNS administrators are among those paid by the hour, and so ... okay, I'm kidding, but most DNS administrators do not like dynamic DNS because they fear that if virtually anyone can modify the data in the DNS zone — a database, essentially — then they might pose security threats, so most places disable dynamic DNS. I like it quite a bit and we'll turn it on later, but leave it off for now — safety first and all that.

FIGURE 13.8
Allow dynamic updates?

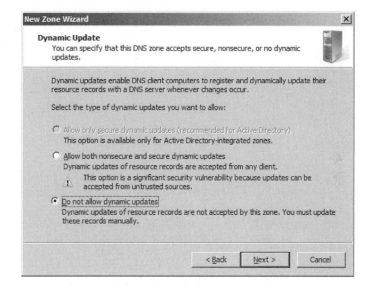

Click Next to get to the summary screen, Finish to dismiss it, and you've got your zone. Let's take a look at it, as you see in Figure 13.9.

FIGURE 13.9
bigfirm.com,
version 0.9

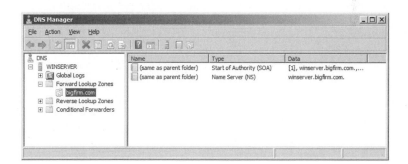

CREATING THE ZONE FROM THE COMMAND LINE

This zone is not yet useful, but it's a start. We'll get it to minimal completeness in a minute, but I've just got to point out that we could have accomplished everything that that wizard did with just this one line:

```
dnscmd /zoneadd bigfirm.com /primary
```

Configuring Your Zone with DNS Records

Now that you've built the zone, let's start making it useful by adding "resource records" and, in the process, we'll create another zone of a type called a *reverse lookup zone*.

Adding Hosts to a Zone: "A" Records

Look at Figure 13.9. Notice that it's got two pieces of information in it. Those pieces of information are called *resource records*. One is called an NS record — recall we've talked about those — and the other's called an SOA record. In brief, here's what they do:

◆ A "start of authority" or SOA record contains a few essential pieces of information that describes a zone — how long you can hold onto information from that zone before having to get more up-to-date information, the e-mail address of the person responsible for the domain, the name of the "primary" DNS server for the domain, a serial number that tells how many times the zone has been updated since its inception, and a few other bits of zone-specific trivia.

◆ NS records identify which servers are the DNS servers for the domain. ("NS" stands for "name server," which is the older name for a DNS server.)

Thus, the two records that you currently see in `bigfirm.com` describe the zone (SOA) and state that `winserver.bigfirm.com` is one of the servers that hold copies of the `bigfirm.com` zone. (There's only one now, but you can have as many as you like.) So far, so good . . . or is it? The SOA record says that the primary DNS server for this domain is named `winserver.bigfirm.com`, and the NS record says that `winserver.bigfirm.com` is one of the DNS servers for the `bigfirm.com` domain. (Of course, it' currently the *only* one for the domain, but that'll change in time.)

Now, that's great, but it's missing something *big* — a way to convert the name `winserver.bigfirm.com` into an IP address. We've got the name, but not the IP address, so how to get the IP address? Well, as I've said many times in this chapter, we need to resolve the name `winserver.bigfirm.com`, so we look in *what* zone? That's right — we look in the `bigfirm.com` zone.

And that's where the trouble arises. We're *looking* in the `bigfirm.com` zone, and there is no record that answers the question, "what IP address does `winserver.bigfirm.com` have?" Such a record is not an SOA or NS record; instead, it's called a "host" record and it has a record type of "A" rather than "SOA" or "NS."

We can see this problem if we try to use `nslookup` to get `winserver.bigfirm.com`'s IP address. Type **nslookup winserver.bigfirm.com**, and `nslookup` will respond with something like this:

```
DNS request timed out.
    timeout was 2 seconds.
Server:  UnKnown
Address:  192.168.1.1

*** UnKnown can't find winserver.bigfirm.com: Non-existent domain
```

So let's fix that by adding an "A" record to the `bigfirm.com` zone for winserver. Move back to `winserver.bigfirm.com` and open up the DNS manager and the `bigfirm.com` zone, if it's not already open. Right-click "bigfirm.com" under Forward Lookup Zones, and choose "New Host (A or AAAA) . . . , and you'll see a dialog box like Figure 13.10.

FIGURE 13.10
Adding an A record

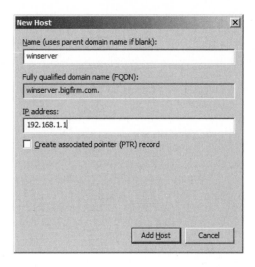

I've filled **winserver** into the Name field. I don't have to specify the FQDN with its incorporated domain suffix because I'm creating the record *inside* the bigfirm.com domain, and so DNS assumes that any record of any type inside the bigfirm.com zone automatically ends in .bigfirm.com. I've also typed in the IP address. The "Create associated pointer (PTR) record" would create the reverse-lookup version of an A record, a record that lets you query an IP address and get a host name back. (We'll build a reverse-lookup zone a bit later.) Click Add Host, and DNS will respond with a "The host record winserver.bigfirm.com was successfully created" information box — click it to make it go away — and the New Host dialog box will remain on-screen. Microsoft does that because they assume that there's a good chance that you'll want to punch in a bunch of A records, and so they're trying to save you clicks. Click Done, and the dialog box goes away, and you'll now see in the DNS manager a third record that looks like "winserver Host(A) 192.168.1.1." The bigfirm.com zone will now look like Figure 13.11.

FIGURE 13.11
bigfirm.com zone after adding host record for winserver

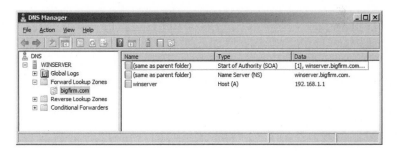

Now return to main.bigfirm.com and try that nslookup again, and you'll see something like this:

```
C:\>nslookup winserver.bigfirm.com
DNS request timed out.
    timeout was 2 seconds.
Server:  UnKnown
Address:  192.168.1.1
```

```
Name:    winserver.bigfirm.com
Address: 192.168.1.1
```

Which translates as "success." What would happen if `main.bigfirm.com` tries to resolve its own name? Clearly it will fail because there's no A record in `bigfirm.com` for main — so let's add one. Move back to `winserver.bigfirm.com`, and this time, type this at the command prompt:

```
C:\>dnscmd /recordadd bigfirm.com main A 192.168.1.2
```

And you'll see a result like this:

```
Add A Record for main.bigfirm.com at bigfirm.com
Command completed successfully.
```

That `dnscmd /recordadd` command is useful, so let's give it a closer look. Look in the GUI to see what you want the record to look like, as in "winserver A 192.168.1.1" — ignore the text in parentheses — and then construct the command like so:

```
dnscmd /recordadd zone-name desired-text-in-DNS-snap-in
```

As the zone that we're modifying is `bigfirm.com` and the text we're looking for is "main A 192.168.1.2" (and be sure to put at least one space between "main," "A," and "192.168.1.2), we end up with the command that I suggested earlier, `dnscmd /recordadd bigfirm.com main A 192.168.1.2`.

Well, congratulations; you've now set up a simple zone with a couple of systems in it. But we're not *nearly* done.

Setting Up Reverse Lookups

Thus far, I've described DNS's main task as converting host names such as `winserver.bigfirm.com` to IP addresses such as 192.168.1.1. But DNS can do the reverse as well; you can ask a DNS server, "What host name is associated with IP address 205.22.42.19?" As I've said before, this is called a *reverse name resolution*.

DNS maintains information about a given domain such as fruit.com in files called *zone files*. Bigfirm.com, then, has a zone file that DNS can use to look up `winserver.bigfirm.com`'s IP address. But where does DNS go to look up the host name associated with IP address 192.168.1.1? In the proper reverse lookup zone.

To create a reverse lookup zone, we need first to name it, and be warned that the *name* of the reverse lookup zone is odd-looking. To construct it, take the dotted quads that you're working with in your network — drop the ones that you control — and reverse them, then add `.in-addr.arpa` to the end of the name. Thus, suppose you've got a C network at 205.22.42.0; the corresponding reverse lookup zone would be called `42.22.205.in-addr.arpa`. A few other examples:

◆ 164.109.0.0/16, a class B network, would drop the two zeroed quads and reverse the remaining two to yield a reverse zone name of `109.164.in-addr.arpa`. Notice there were only two dotted numbers, as it's a B network and the owner controls the bottom two quads.

◆ 4.0.0.0/8, a class A network, would have reverse zone 4.in-addr.arpa. In the case of an A network, only the top quad is set, so there's only one number in the reverse zone.

◆ 200.120.50.0/24, a class C network, would drop the zeroed quad and reverse the numbers to get a reverse zone name of 50.120.200.in-addr.arpa.

CREATING A REVERSE LOOKUP ZONE

Armed with this information, let's create a reverse lookup zone for the 192.168.1.x IP address range that we've been working with so far. Here's the one-liner:

```
dnscmd /zoneadd 1.168.192.in-addr.arpa /primary
```

If you really want to use the GUI, then go back to the DNS GUI and, under bigfirm.com, you'll see a folder named Reverse Lookup Zones. Right-click it and you'll see that you can kick off a wizard that will create a reverse lookup zone for you.

CREATING REVERSE LOOKUP (PTR) ENTRIES

Just as forward lookup zones need an A record for each host in the zone, reverse lookup zones need something called a "PTR" record for each IP address used in their zone. PTR records look like A records reversed, like this:

```
2 PTR main.bigfirm.com.
```

Why "2"? For the same reason that we only specified "main" when creating main.bigfirm .com's A record. In main's case, its record was going in a domain named bigfirm.com, so DNS just assumes that we intend for the main record to be in the bigfirm.com zone. In the same way, any PTR record in the 1.168.192.in-addr.arpa zone doesn't have to specify the "192.168.1" part of its IP address of 192.168.1.2 — the "192.168.1" is just assumed. Think about the dnscmd /recordadd commands you've seen before — can you guess how to add a PTR record from the command line? I could insert that record into 1.168.192.in-addr.arpa with this command:

```
dnscmd /recordadd 1.168.192.in-addr.arpa 2 PTR main.bigfirm.com.
```

And what command would you expect would let you create a PTR record for 192.168.1.1, winserver.bigfirm.com? This, naturally:

```
dnscmd /recordadd 1.168.192.in-addr.arpa 1 PTR winserver.bigfirm.com.
```

If you take a look in the DNS GUI at this point, however, you'll see something like Figure 13.12.

FIGURE 13.12
Reverse lookup zone with two PTR records ... and an anomaly

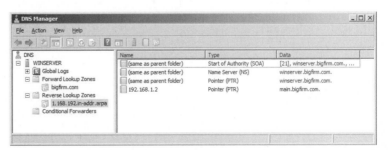

Notice that the record that looks like "192.168.1.2 Pointer (PTR) main.bigfirm.com" looks pretty much as we expected, but the entry above says not "192.168.1.1 Pointer (PTR) win-server.bigfirm.com," but instead "(same as parent folder) Pointer (PTR) winserver.bigfirm.com)." What's wrong with this line? It's a bug, I'm guessing, and we can see that by looking at the zone with nslookup instead of the GUI to verify that.

DOING REVERSE LOOKUPS

You can look up PTR records in nslookup just as you look up A records:

```
c:\>nslookup 192.168.1.2
Server:  winserver.bigfirm.com
Address:  192.168.1.1

Name:    main.bigfirm.com
Address:  192.168.1.2
```

And notice — those messages about DNS timing out are gone! We kept seeing messages that DNS wasn't responding quickly because nslookup likes to take your DNS server's IP address (which it knows because you gave your system the IP addresses of one or more DNS servers to use) and convert that to a DNS name by doing a reverse lookup. Our one DNS server didn't *have* any reverse lookup zones, however, but it went searching for one anyway, and that took time. Now that your DNS server can quickly reverse-resolve 192.168.1.2 or 192.168.1.1, there's no delay, and the opening output says "Server: winserver.bigfirm.com" rather than "Server: UnKnown." Try doing an nslookup 192.168.1.1 to see whether your PTR record for 192.168.1.1 worked, and you'll see that it did, despite that it doesn't show up properly in the DNS GUI.

Reading NS and SOA DNS Records

With our zones in place, let's see how to take a look at the contents of our zones using dnscmd rather than the DNS GUI. We can look at all of bigfirm.com's records by typing (at winserver) **dnscmd /zoneprint bigfirm.com** to see something like this:

```
;
;  Zone:    bigfirm.com
;  Server:  winserver.bigfirm.com
;  Time:    Mon Mar 17 13:00:26 2008 UTC
;
@ 3600 NS  winserver.bigfirm.com.
  3600 SOA winserver.bigfirm.com. hostmaster.bigfirm.com. 3 900 600 86400 3600
main 3600 A     192.168.1.2
winserver 3600 A       192.168.1.1


;
;  Finished zone: 3 nodes and 4 records in 0 seconds
;
```

The lines that start with semicolons (;) are comments, so you can ignore them. The remaining lines are all called *DNS resource records*, where the short all-caps item in the middle of the record — NS, SOA, and A in the records here — is the record type. The first line — @ 3600 NS winserver.bigfirm.com — is the NS record that declares, "winserver.bigfirm.com is a DNS server that holds zone information for bigfirm.com." The @ is shorthand for bigfirm.com when seen in DNS zone files, and so the record could just as correctly be written like this:

```
bigfirm.com. 3600 NS winserver.bigfirm.com
```

For the sake of brevity and because so many DNS records in a given domain's zone file start off with that domain's name, the developers of the earliest DNS server software, an application named BIND (short for Berkeley Internet Name Domain) decided to adopt the "@ equals the current domain's name" abbreviation, and most later DNS software — including Server 2008's DNS component — follows suit.

Notice the structure of this NS record, as DNS employs it for all of its records. bigfirm.com NS winserver.bigfirm.com (ignore the 3600 for a second) can be interpreted to mean "the thing on the left (bigfirm.com) has something described by the thing in the middle, the record type (a name server, in this case) that is the thing on the right (the system named winserver.bigfirm.com).

What's the 3600? It's the "time to live" for that record, a concept that we've discussed before in this chapter. Recall that a TTL means that anyone querying this DNS server for the answer to the question, "who are your name servers?" can cache the answer for no more than 3600 seconds, or one hour. Explicitly including the TTL on every record is optional because this zone has a default TTL of 3600, as you'll see soon.

The next record's a long one, and probably broke across a couple of lines on your page, although it's all one line. It looks like 3600 SOA winserver.bigfirm.com. hostmaster. bigfirm.com. 3 900 600 86400 3600. Here we actually see something of an idiosyncratic and annoying behavior of dnscmd /zoneprint: it left off the leading @, even though there *is* an @ in the actual record. (Technically this is correct, as BIND assumes that any record with nothing on its left corner carries the same value as the previous record that *did* have something on its left corner, but I find it somewhat obscure, and just another example of why programmers sometimes drive me crazy.) Anyway, this "Start Of Authority" or SOA record contains, in order:

◆ The invisible-to-dnscmd @, which means "this refers to the bigfirm.com zone."

◆ The 3600, which is the TTL for this SOA record.

◆ The SOA, which tells us that this is a Start Of Authority type of resource record. Note that while zones may have any number of NS or A records, to my knowledge you're only allowed one SOA record per zone.

◆ winserver.bigfirm.com, which says that of all of the DNS servers serving bigfirm.com that winserver hold the "primary" or "master" role. I've already hinted that most zones have more than one DNS server holding a copy of their zone information — so we want to avoid a situation wherein one of bigfirm.com's DNS servers holds (and disseminates) invalid zone information for bigfirm.com. Many DNS installations avoid this by anointing one of its DNS servers as the only one that an administrator makes changes on (the primary or master, depending on which RFCs you read), and all of the others get their zone information by just copying it from the master. This first parameter after "SOA" names that primary DNS server. We'll go into more detail on this soon, when we start setting up secondary DNS servers.

◆ hostmaster.bigfirm.com is Server 2008's guess about the e-mail address of whoever's in charge of the bigfirm.com zone. No, hostmaster.bigfirm.com isn't a valid e-mail address, but then recall that @ has a special meaning for DNS, and so since time immemorial (1984, that is), the e-mail address of the person responsible for any zone has his or her e-mail address written with a period instead of an @ in an SOA record. (I'll show you how to edit that value later.)

◆ 3 is the zone's *serial number*. DNS increments this value every time we change the zone in some way. The serial number is important for the zone's secondary DNS servers, as they can quickly find out if they've missed some changes by simply asking the primary for the SOA record and checking the serial number. If the serial number in the primary's SOA record is higher than the one stored at the secondary DNS server, then that secondary DNS server knows that it's time to ask the primary for any changes.

◆ 900 600 86400 are three time periods that tell secondary DNS servers how often to check for zone changes — I'll explain them later.

◆ Finally, 3600 declares the default TTL for records in this zone. It is because of this number that I commented earlier that the NS record didn't need to declare a TTL — this last number on the SOA record has already covered that.

Working with A Records and Understanding Glue Records

Following the SOA record, we've got two A records, `main 3600 A 192.168.1.2` and `winserver 3600 A 192.168.1.1`. Their meaning and structure should be obvious by now — they contain a host name; the 3600 second TTL; record type "A," which means "host name"; and the IP address associated with that host name. But there *is* one interesting nugget of information that I can talk about in these records — relative and absolute naming. Consider the first A record, without its TTL:

```
main  A 192.168.1.2
```

Notice that the record contains `main`, not `main.bigfirm.com`. The zone record needn't include the entire `main.bigfirm.com` name because any name you type on the left-hand-side of a resource record gets `bigfirm.com` tacked on the end of it automatically. If you absolutely wanted to go directly modify the DNS zone files (I'll show you how to later) to specify the whole FQDN on the left-hand side then you can, but only if you type it as an FQDN with a period on the end, as in

```
main.bigfirm.com. A 192.168.1.2
```

Once in while, DNS includes an A record with an FQDN on its left-hand side to speed up resolving A records from other domains. Consider, for example, a situation that we've not really discussed yet — what if one of `bigfirm.com`'s DNS servers wasn't a machine in `bigfirm.com`, but instead in `minasi.com`, a system called `dns1.minasi.com` with an IP address of 10.50.50.7?

Clearly it's easy enough to enter the new NS record to tell `bigfirm.com` that one of its DNS servers is named `dns1.minasi.com`:

```
dnscmd /recordadd bigfirm.com @ NS dns1.minasi.com.
```

Reviewing the `dnscmd` syntax, this says to create a name server record in `bigfirm.com` (the @, recall) and that the server's name is `dns1.minasi.com`. But suppose `winserver.bigfirm.com` needs to *find* that DNS server in `minasi.com` to notify it of available updates or the like? Well, in that case, then `winserver.bigfirm.com` will have to trek across the Internet to get `dns1.minasi.com`'s IP address, and *that's* not very efficient. So Server 2008's DNS software (and most other DNS software) lets you pre-install an A record right into the `bigfirm.com` zone for `dns1.minasi.com`, even though it's clearly not a member of the `bigfirm.com` zone. More precisely, creating an NS record that points to an out-of-zone DNS server in the GUI causes the GUI to insist on knowing not only the out-of-zone DNS server's name, but its IP address, and the GUI then creates an A record for the out-of-zone DNS server. The command line doesn't do that, and so if we wanted that faster, close-to-hand resolution that an A record for `dns1.minasi.com` would offer, we'd type an extra command:

```
dnscmd /recordadd bigfirm.com dns1.minasi.com. A 10.50.50.7
```

Notice the syntax here. It's an A record like others we've seen before, but as we've been discussing, there's that unusual situation wherein instead of a host name like winserver on the left-hand parameter, we've got the `dns1.minasi.com` FQDN, with a period on the end and all! Such an out-of-zone A record is called a glue record, as it glues the external DNS server to the zone that it's helping out. (We must have that period at the end of the name, or DNS would think that it referred to a system named `dns1.minasi.com.bigfirm.com`.)

But Server 2008's DNS does something kinda strange with glue records: it hides them. If we take a look in `bigfirm.com` in the DNS GUI, then the NS record for `dns1.minasi.com`'s there . . . but the A record for `dns1.minasi.com` isn't! Similarly, `dnscmd /zoneprint` has got something to hide as well, as you see in this run:

```
C:\>dnscmd /zoneprint bigfirm.com


;
;  Zone:     bigfirm.com
;  Server:   winserver.bigfirm.com
;  Time:     Mon Mar 17 20:30:27 2008 UTC
;
@ 3600 NS        winserver.bigfirm.com.
                 3600 NS         dns1.minasi.com.
                 3600 SOA        winserver.bigfirm.com. hostmaster.bigfirm.com.
15 900 600 86400 3600
main 3600 A     192.168.1.2
winserver 3600 A        192.168.1.1


;
;  Finished zone: 3 nodes and 5 records in 0 seconds
```

As I said, notice that there's a record for `dns1.minasi.com`'s DNS-ness, but no visible A record for `dns1.minasi.com`. But it's there, trust me! How do I know? Simple — try to delete that NS record from the GUI, and it'll ask if you want to delete the A record for `dns1.bigfirm.com`. Here's how:

1. On winserver, open the DNS snap-in, if it's not already open.

2. Locate and right-click the `bigfirm.com` zone.

3. Choose Properties.

4. In the resulting property page, click the Name Servers tab. It will look something like Figure 13.13.

FIGURE 13.13

Name Servers tab in
`bigfirm.com` properties

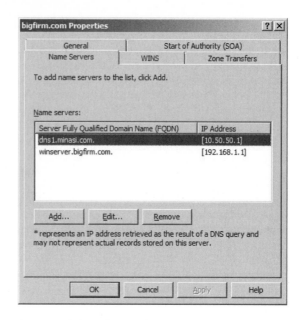

But if you click on `dns1.minasi.com` and then the Remove button and OK, you see the dialog in Figure 13.14.

FIGURE 13.14

The glue record is
revealed!

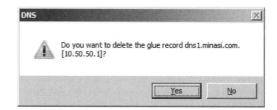

I dearly wish that 2008's DNS didn't engage in this sort of skullduggery, as the whole *point* of a GUI is to make things transparent, or at least I'm told.

Seeing All of the Records: The Zone Files Themselves

Thus far, we've seen that the DNS GUI and, to a smaller extent, `dnscmd /zoneprint` has offered us a few mysteries:

◆ We created PTR records for the 1 and 2 entries, but the 1 entry doesn't look at all like the 2 . . . so we've gotta wonder what DNS really thinks we meant there.

◆ Even though that SOA record is supposed to start with an @, `dnscmd /zoneprint` doesn't show it, and how can we sleep not knowing if that ''@'' is really there?

◆ Apparently DNS likes to create glue records, but the GUI *and* `dnscmd /zoneprint` refuse to show them to us, and it'd be nice to know where DNS hides those records.

I have to admit it, friends — I knew the answers to these mysteries almost immediately after they appeared, because I know a sneaky trick — I just bypass the DNS GUI and the `dnscmd` tool and go straight to the place on the server's hard disk where it keeps the DNS zone information itself. I also know *another* sneaky trick: DNS stores its data in simple text files that we can examine with nothing fancier than Notepad!

To make this a complete *"expose,"* let's restore the extra NS record and the glue record with these commands (type them into winserver, remember):

```
dnscmd /recordadd bigfirm.com @ NS dns1.minasi.com.
dnscmd /recordadd bigfirm.com dns1.minasi.com. A 10.50.50.7
```

READING AND WRITING ZONE FILES

Those two records we just typed (well, re-typed) are in the DNS server's memory, and it is acting on those commands, but it might not have had time to write that information out to the zone files, so let's force it to write that information out.

◆ From the GUI, right-click bigfirm.com and choose Update Server Data File.

◆ From the command line, type **dnscmd /zonewriteback bigfirm.com** and press Enter.

Once in a while you might need to do the reverse, and tell the DNS server to reload its data from the zone file in \windows\system32\dns. Here's how:

◆ From the GUI, right-click bigfirm.com and choose Reload.

◆ From the command line, type **dnscmd /zonereload bigfirm.com** and press Enter.

FINDING AND VIEWING ZONE FILES

Now, open up Explorer and navigate to C:\Windows\System32\DNS. In that folder, you'll see a number of files, but the two we're looking for are named bigfirm.com.dns (bigfirm's zone file) and 1.168.192.in-addr.arpa.dns (the reverse lookup zone's file).

> **TIP**
>
> Remember that if you haven't told Windows to show you file extensions, then you won't see the .dns extensions on those files.

Use Notepad to open up bigfirm.com.dns, and you'll see something like Figure 13.15.

Remember BIND, the granddaddy of all DNS server software? Well, BIND stores its information about zones in simple text files, and so by default Windows Server 2008 does the same thing, storing its zones in "BIND-compatible format." Take a look in that text file and you can see the @ in the front of the SOA record and the dns1.minasi.com. A 10.50.50.7 glue record. Similarly, if you open up 1.168.192.in-addr.arpa.dns in Notepad, you'll see that the PTR records named "1" and "2" are identical — why the GUI reports "same as parent zone" is clearly a bug.

Why'd I show you this? Because once in a while, DNS — like all software — gets stupid. Some bug appears and all of a sudden you're trying to figure out how to muscle the thing into doing something that it seems no longer capable of doing, or it does something puzzling (like leaving an @ out of a record) that makes you worry that there's something bad about to happen, and you want to check to see that things aren't as bad as they seem. We've seen the latter — peeking in the zone files — accomplished; how to do the former, and hand-modify the zone file?

FIGURE 13.15
`bigfirm.com`'s
zone file

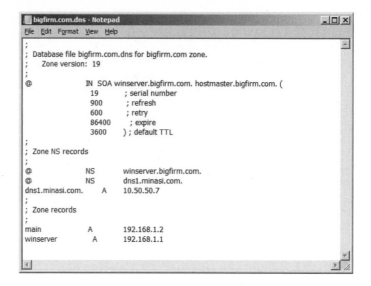

MODIFYING ZONE FILES

Let's create an A record for another system, `mailserver.bigfirm.com`, that has IP address 192.168.1.8, but let's do it by directly modifying bigfirm's zone file. To modify a zone file, it's best to follow this sequence:

◆ Stop the DNS server service.

◆ Modify the zone file.

◆ Restart the DNS server service.

The reason you have to start and stop the DNS service is that DNS re-writes the zone files on a regular basis, and you may find as a result that DNS simply refuses to read your updated zone file. Putting the DNS server to sleep before changing the file solves that problem.

You know by now that a basic A record for a system named "mailserver" with an IP address of 192.168.1.8 would look like this:

mailserver A 192.168.1.8

And that's what I'm going to have you type into the `bigfirm.com.dns` file. Here are the steps.

1. On winserver, stop the DNS service by typing **net stop dns**.

2. Open `c:\windows\system32\dns\bigfirm.com.dns` with Notepad.

3. Add a new line to the file and type **mailserver A 192.168.1.8**, ensuring to leave at least one space between `mailserver` and A, and at least one space between A and `192.168.1.8`. Also be sure to start `mailserver` on the *first* column of the line — don't leave any leading spaces.

4. Save `bigfirm.com.dns`.

5. Restart the DNS server service by typing **net start dns**.

6. Test to see whether DNS knows of mailserver by typing **nslookup mailserver.bigfirm .com**; it should report that there is indeed a system by that name at IP address 192.168.1.8.

Hey, look, I hope you never have to do it, but in case you ever need to do "zone surgery," at least you've seen it once!

BACKING UP AND RESTORING ZONE FILES: DNS DISASTER RECOVERY

Zone files are also useful to know about because they're useful for bringing a dead DNS server back to life. Suppose your main DNS server caught some awful virus and so first it stopped answering queries but instead pulled out a gun and threatened your employees and *then*, as you wondered what on Earth to do, the DNS server suddenly gasped, clutched its chest and fell over, *dead*. How to re-create `bigfirm.com`? Simple, actually — so long as you've been backing up your zone files.

The zone files are, as I've said, simple ASCII text files. They're never "locked open" like so many databases, so all you've got to do to back them up is to copy them somewhere off the server. Then, to restore your zones, just build a new DNS server with the same host name as the old one, copy the backed-up files to the c:\windows\system32\dns folder of the new server, and use a quick `dnscmd` command to tell DNS to recreate the zone using the file that you just restored:

```
dnscmd /zoneadd zonename /file restoredfilename /load
```

We can try this out with `bigfirm.com`'s zone. First, we'll copy the `bigfirm.com.dns` file to a file named `bigfirm.backup`. Then we'll delete the `bigfirm.com` zone, and finally we'll rebuild it by pointing DNS at the `bigfirm.backup` zone file. Sitting at winserver, try this out:

1. Back up the zone file by typing **copy c:\windows\system32\dns\bigfirm.com.dns c:\windows\system32\dns\bigfirm.backup**.

2. Delete the existing `bigfirm.com` zone by typing **dnscmd /zonedelete bigfirm.com /f** — most of that syntax should look as you expect except for the **/f**, which means "force." By default, `dnscmd` always asks you whether you're sure before deleting records or zones.

3. Now revivify `bigfirm.com` by typing a variation on the `dnscmd /zoneadd` command, **dnscmd /zoneadd bigfirm.com /primary /file bigfirm.backup /load**.

4. Using either the GUI, `dnscmd /zoneprint`, or `nslookup`, you should be able to verify that `bigfirm.com` is back.

Giving a Host Multiple Names with CNAMEs

Let's return to our look at DNS resource record types and consider system *aliases*, extra names. Many times, you'll need a host to respond to more than one name. Consider, for example, the way I set up my Web server. It's connected to the Internet on a NIC with the name web2.minasi.com. Thus, you could visit my Web server by using the URL http://web2.minasi.com.

USING CNAME/ALIAS RECORDS

Clearly, however, this isn't an optimal arrangement, as people assume that they'd access information on the minasi.com Web server by either surfing to http://minasi.com (which is inelegant in my opinion — you don't surf to domains; you surf to hosts, so giving your domain a host name has always seemed lame to me), or http://www.minasi.com. How to get my Web server to respond to the name www.minasi.com rather than just web2.minasi.com?

Well, I could surrender and just change web2.minasi.com's host (A) record to www.minasi.com. But now suppose this were *also* my ftp server that I wanted to name ftp.minasi.com?

Basically here I'm saying that in at least *this* case and, believe me, others, you'll sometimes want to give a system more than one name. You can do that with an alias resource record or, in DNS resource record-ese, a CNAME record. It's a record that lets me give a host extra names in addition to its host name.

> **NOTE**
>
> CNAME is short for "canonical name," which, I know, isn't the most enlightening phrase. (Why not use "alias"? It's got the same number of letters, if that was the issue.) My dictionary defines canonical as either "having to do with canon [church or secular] law, or of appearing in the Biblical canon, of or belonging to a cathedral chapter, music in the form of a canon," none of which are very helpful. But ah, here's a fourth definition: "conforming to orthodox rules, as of procedure." Ah, now that must be it. Naming a Web server has a sorta orthodox rule that you've got to give that system a name of "www."

Thus, a CNAME record says something like, "If someone asks for the machine that responds to www in this domain, then point to the machine at `web2.minasi.com`."

How do you add a CNAME to a zone? Well, I'm not going to let you mess with my Web server, so let's suppose we got Server 2008's Web server software running on `winserver.bigfirm.com` (we needn't) and wanted winserver to also respond to `www.bigfirm.com`. Here's how we'd add a www CNAME to the `winserver.bigfirm.com` host:

◆ From the GUI, right-click the zone file's folder (`bigfirm.com`'s, in this case) and choose New Alias (CNAME) and you'll get a dialog box named New Resource Record with two fields: "Alias name (parent domain if left blanks)," and "Fully qualified domain name (FQDN) for target host:." The alias name is "www" and the FQDN is "`web2.minasi.com`."

◆ From the command line, we'll use `dnscmd /recordadd`. Remember that it first needs the name of the domain to add the record to (`bigfirm.com`), and then the three parts that comprise most resource records: the label, the record type, and the object. Thus, we'd type **dnscmd /recordadd bigfirm.com www CNAME winserver.bigfirm.com**.

Once you've gotten that done, verify that it works with `nslookup` by typing **nslookup www.bigfirm.com** and you will see this:

```
C:\>nslookup www.bigfirm.com
Server:  winserver.bigfirm.com
Address:  192.168.1.1

Name:    winserver.bigfirm.com
Address:  192.168.1.1
Aliases:  www.bigfirm.com
```

Here, `nslookup` reports that there is indeed a `www.bigfirm.com`, but that it's a mere alias of `winserver.bigfirm.com`. (Again, you can try that out without having to actually install Microsoft's Web server software.) Typing **dnscmd /zoneprint bigfirm.com** again reveals the structure of a CNAME record:

```
www 3600 CNAME  winserver.bigfirm.com.
```

Notice that the left portion only says *www*, not www.bigfirm.com. This is another example of how DNS handles fully qualified or non-fully qualified names. If you create a CNAME within a given domain, the CNAME must be for a name that ends with the domain's name, hence www rather than www.bigfirm.com. In contrast, the machine that it's being equated to, winserver.bigfirm.com, need not be in the domain, and so its full name is entered in the DNS record.

ONLY ONE CNAME TO A NAME, PLEASE

For some reason, you're not allowed to have more than one of a given CNAME. For example, suppose I wanted to give the name www.bigfirm.com to both of our servers, that is, to both winserver.bigfirm.com and main.bigfirm.com. Can I create two CNAME www records in bigfirm.com?

You *can*, but it's not a good idea, or at least so I'm told. Supposedly RFC 1034 explains it, but I fear that I've never read it in enough detail to understand the problem, but several threads on the BIND support message boards suggest that a BIND server might not handle multiple www CNAMEs in the same zone. So, while you can force your 2008-based DNS server to accept multiple CNAMEs with the same name by directly editing the zone files, you could run into trouble if the person trying to visit your Web site was resolving your DNS names with a BIND-based DNS server. So to be safe, don't do multiple CNAMEs with the same name.

Just to make this very clear:

◆ You *cannot* use CNAMEs to give more than one IP address the name www.

◆ You *can* use CNAMEs to give more than one name to a given IP address — I could use a CNAME to give the www.bigfirm.com *and* the ftp.bigfirm.com names to winserver.bigfirm.com.

◆ There is no problem at all with multiple A records with the same name. You could have three different host records pointing to three different systems, and give them all the same name. Why might you do that? I'll answer that when we take up "round-robin DNS" later in this chapter.

YOU CAN'T *NET USE* TO A CNAME

Another quirk with CNAMEs arises when you try to connect to a file server using the NET USE command that we briefly introduced in Chapter 2. When you try, you'll get a misleading error message like "there is a duplicate server name" or something like that. If that's a problem, then you can get past it with a Registry modification. On the file server computer (the DNS server doesn't care), go to HKLM/System/CurrentControlSet/Services/Lanmanserver/parameters, create a REG_DWORD value named DisableStrictNameChecking, set it to 1, and reboot your computer (or restart the Server service). Microsoft explains this a bit further on their Web site at Knowledge Base article 281308.

Before we leave CNAMEs, here's a quick review. Suppose we were to set up main.bigfirm.com as an FTP server and wanted to give it the extra name of ftp.bigfirm.com. How would we do it? (Stop reading if you'd like to figure it out.)

Answer: we'd add a CNAME of "ftp" to the FQDN of main.bigfirm.com. I find it easiest to do this from the command lie:

```
dnscmd /recordadd bigfirm.com ftp cname main.bigfirm.com
```

Identify Your E-mail Servers with MX Records

If I send mail to bill@bigfirm.com, then I've told my e-mail program that I want the mail to go to someone named Bill and that Bill has an account on some server in the bigfirm.com domain.

What I *haven't* told my e-mail program is where exactly to send the e-mail for Bill, what his mail server's name is. If it's not immediately obvious why this is important, consider: If you know that my domain is named minasi.com, how do you know where to find my Web or FTP server? There's an *informal* convention in the world that I'd call my Web server www.minasi.com and my FTP server ftp.minasi.com, but nothing *requiring* that. You can't simply tell your Web server, "Go check out the minasi.com Web site." But you *can* tell an e-mail program, "Send this mail to minasi.com." That's because DNS includes something called a *mail exchange* or *MX* record, which answers the question, "Which machine is the mail server for minasi.com?" But DNS offers us the answer by providing a resource record that lets a domain say, "if you want to send e-mail to anyone in this domain, the mail server to send it to is such-and-such system." Here's how you'd find my e-mail server:

1. Open up an elevated command prompt.

2. Type **nslookup** and press Enter.

3. Type **set type=mx** and press Enter.

4. Type **minasi.com** and press Enter.

5. Then just type **exit** and Enter to get out of nslookup.

> **NOTE**
>
> Nslookup needs that new command, set type=mx whenever you're not searching for an A or PTR record. You could as easily use set type=ns or set type=soa to search for those records. There is even a set type=any to tell nslookup to get whatever it can. You can compress the whole thing into one line by adding a parameter -type=whatever between nslookup and the DNS address to look up. For example, we could have done the above query by typing **nslookup -type=mx bigfirm.com**.

Run that, and it'll look something like this:

```
> set type=mx
> minasi.com
Server:  nr1femantnc.mant.nc.charter.com
Address:  24.196.248.4

minasi.com      MX preference = 3, mail exchanger = minasi.com.s7b1.psmtp.com
minasi.com      MX preference = 4, mail exchanger = minasi.com.s7b2.psmtp.com
minasi.com      MX preference = 1, mail exchanger = minasi.com.s7a1.psmtp.com
minasi.com      MX preference = 2, mail exchanger = minasi.com.s7a2.psmtp.com
minasi.com.s7a2.psmtp.com       internet address = 64.18.6.13
```

Notice that there are four MX records here; that means that I've got four servers standing ready to receive e-mail. (That's how many reader e-mails I get a day — enough to require four servers! Okay, I'm lying — those are e-mail servers for a Google service that receives my mail, filters out the viruses and spam, and sends the rest to my company's e-mail server.) That advertises to the Internet at large that any e-mails to me should go through one of these servers.

A look at the MX records shows that they're a bit more complicated than A, NS, or CNAME records — they've got four parts to them, not three:

◆ The name of the domain that they serve (minasi.com)

◆ Their record type, "MX"

◆ Their "MX preference," the "=1...=2...=3...etc," which I'll explain in a moment

◆ The server that can accept the e-mail, systems with names like "minasi.com. s7b1.psmtp.com."

Thus, when you send an e-mail to someone@minasi.com, then your e-mail server would execute the equivalent of this nslookup command and get the names of these e-mail servers in return. Furthermore, your e-mail server would first try to send the mail to minasi.com.s7a1.psmtp.com, rather than the other three. Why? Read on.

MX AND MAIL FAULT TOLERANCE

Why wouldn't the distant mail server send mail to any one of the four e-mail servers, rather than minasi.com.s7a1.psmtp.com? Because of the "MX preference" value. Notice that minasi.com.s7a1.psmtp.com's MX preference value is 1, and its companions are 2, 3, or 4. E-mail servers know to examine the preferences on MX records that they receive and to always try to send the e-mail to those servers in the order of increasing preference. Thus, if you tried to send me an e-mail then your e-mail server would first try to send it to minasi.com.s7a1.psmtp.com, the "priority=1" system, but if that system were offline or too busy to respond then it would next try minasi.com.s7a2.psmtp.com, the "priority=2" system, and so on. By the way, the values needn't be consecutive; I could have reordered them from 1, 2, 3, 4 to 20, 27, 28, and 4000 with the same result.

The point of an MX preference value is to explain that while I run four e-mail servers or, rather, Google does, and for some reason Google prefers that I send incoming mail to minasi .com.s7a1.psmtp.com first rather than to the other three, probably because they're trying to balance the load of their zillions of customers across their e-mail servers.

But that's not the only possible use for an MX priority — some ISPs run "backup" e-mail servers for their small-company clients. So suppose bigfirm.com runs an e-mail server called mailserver.bigfirm.com, but Bigfirm's got unreliable Internet connectivity. In that case, Bigfirm might decide to pay their ISP a few bucks more every month to run a backup e-mail server called, say, email34.isp.com. Now, Bigfirm always wants their e-mail to come to mailserver.bigfirm.com, and to only go to email34.isp.com when mailserver.bigfirm.com doesn't respond. They can do this by putting two MX records in the bigfirm.com zone:

◆ First, an MX record naming mailserver.bigfirm.com and declaring an MX priority of 50, and

◆ Second, an MX record naming email34.isp.com and declaring an MX priority of 170.

The net effect would be that e-mail servers the Internet across will always try mailserver .bigfirm.com first, and only resort to email34.isp.com if mailserver.bigfirm.com doesn't respond. Again, I chose priorities of 50 and 170 arbitrarily, but 1 and 2 or 45 and 98 would have worked just as well. What happens if you advertise two MX records with the same priority? Then DNS will simply load-balance between the two.

Notice that you needn't actually create an MX record for each of your e-mail servers. For one thing, some very large organizations may handle so much e-mail that they may have servers that only *send* e-mail, and never receive it. As MX records are intended only to advertise whom to *send* e-mail to, there'd be no point in creating MX records for the sending-only servers. (That changes in an anti-spam technology called Sender Policy Framework or SPF, but that's a bit off-topic. If you'd like to read more about SPF, look at my site for my newsletters numbered 50 and 51.) Another reason that you might not want to skip creating an MX record for an e-mail server would be the same reason that I've omitted my internal e-mail server in my DNS zone — I want all external e-mail to first go through Google's servers.

In sum, then, MX priorities let us tell external servers in what order to address our e-mail servers, and lowest numbers come before higher numbers.

ADDING MX RECORDS

Let's set up `bigfirm.com` as if it actually did have an internal e-mail server named `mailserver.bigfirm.com` and a backup e-mail server named `email34.isp.com`, and give them MX priorities of 10 and 20, respectively. We'll create the first record with the GUI, and the second with the command line.

To create the `mailserver.bigfirm.com` MX record, right-click the `bigfirm.com` folder and choose New Mail Exchanger (MX) and you'll see a dialog box like Figure 13.16 — it should look familiar, as all DNS New Resource Record dialog boxes look similar.

FIGURE 13.16
Adding an MX record to
`bigfirm.com`

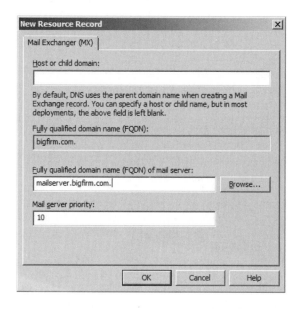

Notice that I didn't put anything in the "Host or child domain" field. As you've seen before, that's because for many DNS records, "blank" means "fill in the name of this domain automatically." As this will be an MX record for `bigfirm.com` and this is `bigfirm.com`'s zone file, just leave that field blank. In the "Fully qualified domain name (FQDN) of mail server" field, I fill in `mailserver.bigfirm.com`'s FQDN and, let me stress that this dialog needs an FQDN, not a host name, even if the e-mail server's in the that domain. The dialog box offers a priority of 10, which works just fine. Click OK to accept the new record.

Flush the zone to its zone file (right-click the zone and choose Update Server Data File, or go to the command line and type **dnscmd /zonewriteback bigfirm.com** or **dnscmd /zonewriteback bigfirm.com** and then look at Bigfirm's zone file (either `bigfirm.com.dns` or `bigfirm.backup`, depending on whether or not you did my short disaster recovery exercise) and see how DNS wrote out that MX record. Mine looked like

```
@    MX   10    mailserver.bigfirm.com.
```

That's not particularly surprising, but it's nice to see a record type once before taking a stab at creating one with `dnscmd /recordadd`. With this information, we can guess that adding `email34.isp.com` with an MX priority of 20 should be as simple as

```
dnscmd /recordadd bigfirm.com @ MX 20 email34.isp.com.
```

And a look at the DNS GUI confirms that that particular syntax worked fine, and Bigfirm now has two MX records.

Modifying Your Zone's SOA Record

We've looked at how to modify just about every "big" resource record type so far — but not SOA. So if you're skimming this chapter looking for advice on changing the SOA then I promise, I have it, but it's got to wait for a few pages, because the parameters on the SOA record don't make any sense unless you understand secondary DNS servers . . . which is our next topic. (And *then* we'll cover changing SOAs!)

Spreading the Work: Secondary DNS Servers

Now that we've got *one* DNS server running, let's next consider how to make this DNS database available under a large load, and able to survive the loss of our sole current DNS server. If a ton of people all decide at the same time to come surf `www.bigfirm.com`, then that means that a ton of DNS servers will all be trying at the same time to resolve the address `www.bigfirm.com`. But what if I configured `bigfirm.com` to have only one DNS server? That's asking for trouble. It'd be nice if I had more than one DNS server containing a copy of the `bigfirm.com` zone file; then those servers could share some of the burden of name resolution. (Of course, those extra DNS servers had better be listed as DNS servers for the `bigfirm.com` domain in the DNS servers for the com domain — if a DNS server isn't recognized as authoritative by being listed in its parent's DNS servers, then no one will ever know to even *try* to query the DNS server.)

But that might be a bit chaotic. Suppose I've got five DNS servers that all hold a copy of the `bigfirm.com` zone file. When I want to make a change to the zone file, perhaps to add or delete an A record, how do I do that? Must I make the identical change to each of the five copies of the zone file by hand? That doesn't sound like much fun.

Fortunately, I needn't do that. DNS has a built-in system for managing updates to copies of a zone's file sitting on multiple servers that keeps things consistent. Each domain has one and only one "primary" DNS server. That's the one that you make changes and updates to the zone file on. And when you set up a DNS server for a particular domain, you must tell the DNS server whether it is the primary DNS server for that domain. As I suggested a few pages back, you designate which DNS server is primary for a given zone by naming that DNS server in the SOA record for the zone. You can have only one primary DNS server for a given zone.

> **NOTE**
>
> A zone's primary DNS server is the only one that can accept additions, deletions, or changes to DNS records for that zone.

Secondary DNS Servers Hold Read-Only Zone Copies

You can have as many *secondary* DNS servers for a zone as you like, however. Secondary servers for a zone hold onto complete copies of the zone file for that zone and answer queries out of that file. Some people feel that the information in their zone files could help bad guys compromise their networks, and so most modern primary DNS servers won't just hand over a copy of a zone to anyone who asks, requiring instead some sort of security mechanism that lets you tell the primary DNS server, "only do zone transfers to the following systems" — we'll see how a bit later in this section.

> **NOTE**
>
> Note that any DNS server can act as the primary server for more than one zone. In fact, a DNS server can simultaneously act as the primary server for several zones while at the same time also acting as a secondary server for several zones. DNS servers can hold any number of zones. So strictly speaking, it's never meaningful to talk simply of a "primary DNS server" because heck, it might only be a primary DNS server from the point of view of one zone, like bigfirm.com, and it might also be a secondary DNS server from the point of some other zone, like minasi.com. To be more exact we should probably say things like "the DNS server holding the primary zone for bigfirm.com," but no one uses that sort of terminology — so please forgive me if I refer to "primary DNS servers" and "secondary DNS servers."

The main point to get out of this is that while a secondary DNS server for some zone can answer queries just as well as the primary can, each secondary DNS server treats *its* copy of the zone file as read-only, and will not allow an administrator to modify the secondary's zone file — admins must go to the primary DNS server to make zone changes.

How Primaries Keep Secondaries Up-to-Date

You've just read that secondary servers start out life asking primary servers for a copy of some zone, and that only the primary servers can accept changes to that zone, which clearly means that the secondary servers must get updated zone files from the primary periodically. How that update works depends partly on how you configure your primary, but basically zone replication works like this: every so often, the secondary says to the primary, "is anything new since last we spoke?" If nothing's new, then the secondary knows that it's already up to date. If something *is* new, then the secondary asks the primary for the new information.

ZONE SYNCHRONIZATION BASICS

More specifically, here's how a basic synchronization works:

1. The secondary keeps track of how long it's been since it's asked the primary for the latest information. That time period is called the "refresh period" and it's 900 seconds (15 minutes) by default on Windows DNS servers.

2. When a refresh period has elapsed, the secondary tries to contact the primary to ask it for the latest SOA record.

3. Assuming the primary responds (we'll get to what happens otherwise in a bit), the secondary now has the latest SOA record from the primary. The secondary then examines the *serial number* in the SOA record. Remember the serial number? It was one of the numbers in the SOA record, like this one:

```
@ SOA winserver.bigfirm.com. hostmaster.bigfirm.com. 3 900 600 86400 3600
```

The SOA record ends off with five numbers, only two of which I've defined so far. You may recall that the first number, the "3," is the serial number and it reveals how many times the zone has been modified. (By the way, the second number, the 900, defines the refresh interval that secondary servers should use in synchronizing their zones with the primary — that's the 15 minutes that I've just mentioned.) The secondary then compares the serial number in the SOA that it's just received to the serial number in its current copy of the zone file. If the new serial number is greater than the one in the current zone file, then the secondary asks the primary for the latest zone information.

4. The primary responds with the new information, and the secondary is now up to date.

Summarized, the secondary server starts a "retry interval" timer whenever it's got an up-to-date copy of the zone, setting the time to the second number in the SOA record. When the timer elapses, the secondary asks the primary for the latest SOA record and then examines the serial number in that SOA record (the first number in the SOA) to see if the zone has changed. If the zone has changed, the secondary asks for the changes, and restarts the retry interval time.

WHEN THE PRIMARY ISN'T PRESENT: RETRIES AND EXPIRY

That's how things work when the network is sunny, traffic is light, and every server's up, alert and able to respond to queries. Now let's consider the anomalies. The first is a lack of response on the primary server's part, whether because it's died, is being rebooted, is experiencing network problems, or whatever. The secondary last got an update 15 minutes ago (or whatever the refresh interval is), it asks the primary for an update . . . and nothing happens.

What to do? Wait another refresh interval? Nope; DNS also offers us a *retry interval*, which is the third value on the SOA record and is 600 seconds (10 minutes) by default on Windows DNS servers. If a secondary doesn't get a response from a primary, then it again asks the primary for the latest SOA record in 10 minutes and, if it still doesn't get a response, it tries again after 10 minutes, and so on, at least for a while.

Supposing that something really awful has happened and the primary's just not coming back, then at some point the secondary's got to give up the ghost and stop responding to requests on this beleaguered DNS domain, and the fourth number on the SOA record tells us when that point is. Set at 86400 seconds — one day — by default, the "expire" interval tells a secondary server, "if you've not been able to get a new SOA record from the primary in this many seconds, then stop acting as a secondary server for this zone."

Reviewing, then, the third and fourth numbers on the SOA record are known as the "retry" and "expire" interval and, in a trouble-free DNS setup, are never used. The retry interval says how often to retry a failed attempt to get the latest SOA record and the expire interval says when the secondary server should give up on the zone altogether.

MODIFYING A ZONE'S SOA RECORD

Now we've finally got enough background to see how to modify a zone's SOA record. There is, of course, the GUI way:

1. Open the DNS GUI.

2. Locate the folder for the zone whose SOA record you want to modify.

3. Right-click that folder and choose Properties.

4. In the resulting property page, click the Start of Authority (SOA) tab. (Alternatively, you can just open the zone and double-click the SOA record.)

5. You'll see a dialog box like the one in Figure 13.17.

FIGURE 13.17
Where to change SOA parameters

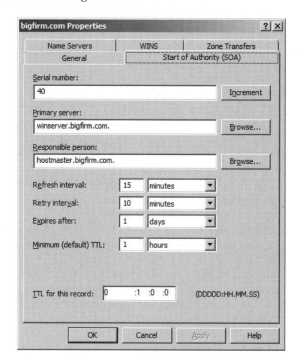

This dialog exposes all of the SOA record's parameters, letting you easily change any of them. But how to do it from the command line? The first time I set out to modify the SOA record from the command line, I supposed that I'd have to start out by deleting the existing SOA record, and `dnscmd` even told me that I'd succeeded ... but it lied. The answer seems to be to craft a `dnscmd /recordadd` statement that lays out the SOA record exactly as you'd like it. For example, to create an SOA record that set

♦ A primary DNS server of `winserver.bigfirm.com`

♦ A "responsible person" e-mail address of `mark@bigfirm.com`

♦ A serial number of 41 (this will be ignored if it is not greater than the current serial number; nevertheless, it's got to be there one way or another)

- A refresh interval of thirty minutes (1800 seconds)

- A retry interval of one minute (60 seconds)

- An expire interval of 30 days (2592000 seconds)

- A default TTL of two hours (7200 seconds)

you would type the following:

```
dnscmd /recordadd bigfirm.com @ SOA winserver.bigfirm.com
mark.bigfirm.com 41 1800 60 2592000 7200
```

I know, that's ugly, and it probably broke across two lines on the page, but you'd type it as just one line. Remember, we're covering this command-line stuff for a couple of reasons: first, you'll sometimes want to package up commands into one file, and you need command-line commands for that — mouse clicks don't go into a text file, and, second, Server 2008 offers the option of running "Server Core," a lightweight version of Server that runs faster and is more secure, but that doesn't have a GUI.

SECONDARIES HAVE DIFFERENT TTLs THAN EVERYONE ELSE

As long as we're re-examining the five numbers in an SOA record, let's take another look at the last one, the "default TTL," and point out that it's only the default — other records can have other values — and that it's the TTL for most of the Internet, but *not* the TTL for secondary DNS servers on that DNS domain.

Recall what happens when a DNS server that is *not* a secondary DNS server for a zone gets information from another DNS server. Suppose again that you visit my Web site. As you've already read, the DNS client on your computer asks your local DNS server for the IP address that corresponds to www.minasi.com, your DNS server searches for and finds my DNS server, and finally your DNS server gives your DNS client that IP address. But that's not all that happens — if you recall, your DNS server and your DNS client cache the IP address for www.minasi.com. How long do they cache it? As you've already read, they cache that information for the number of seconds specified in the TTL for that record.

That fifth number on the minasi.com zone's SOA record lays out a *default TTL* for all records in the minasi.com zone. It's 60 minutes by default, so any DNS server that does a name resolution on bigfirm.biz and then needs the same name resolved 59 minutes later need not re-query one of the bigfirm.biz DNS servers.

> **NOTE**
>
> Many references and in fact the Microsoft DNS server GUI refers to this default TTL as a "minimum (default)" TTL. I'm not sure where they got that "minimum" word from, as experimentation shows that it is *not* a minimum by any means — so when you see "minimum (default)," just read it as "default."

As its name suggests, a "default" TTL is just that — a default. The DNS GUI doesn't offer you a way to change a given record's TTL, but you can easily do it when creating a resource record from the GUI: just add the TTL *after* the item that goes in on the left-hand-side of the resource record, and *before* the record type. For example, to create an A record for "system4" with IP address 10.2.2.5, you'd normally type this:

```
dnscmd /recordadd bigfirm.com system4 A 10.2.2.5
```

To add a TTL for just this record of 20 minutes (1200 seconds), though, you'd type this:

```
dnscmd /recordadd bigfirm.com system4 1200 A 10.2.2.5
```

Similarly, to add a name server record for a system named "dns10" with IP address of 192.168.1.201 and a TTL of 86400, you'd type this:

```
dnscmd /recordadd bigfirm.com dns10 86400 A 192.168.1.201
```

Finally, let's consider the ugliest dnscmd line that I can imagine — an SOA record with a special TTL. Suppose we started from our SOA record of a page or two back, which declared an SOA of two hours, but we wanted just the SOA record to have a TTL of thirty minutes (1800), then we'd type this:

```
dnscmd /recordadd bigfirm.com @ 1800 SOA winserver.bigfirm.com
mark.bigfirm.com 41 1800 60 2592000 7200
```

Anyway, the point is that by default your DNS server caches my zone information for an hour, as an hour is my zone's TTL. But is that true for all DNS servers? Most of them, yes — any acting as caching DNS servers. But if you think about it, the SOA record's refresh, retry, and expire intervals constitute a sort of overriding TTL *for secondary servers*. If I set up my zone with the defaults, then any secondary DNS server on my zone will try to refresh every 15 minutes, but the one-day expire interval means that if all else fails, my secondaries won't forget my zone information for a whole day, rather than the one-hour TTL that any caching DNS server would see.

KEEPING THE BAD GUYS FROM OUR ZONE: CONTROLLING TRANSFERS

From what I've said so far, a secondary DNS server gets its zones by just asking the primary DNS server for a given zone for a copy of that zone. That troubles security folks, because the more a bad guy can find out about your network, the easier it is for him to start to probe and attack it.

> **NOTE**
>
> Reality check: most organizations have *internal* and *external* DNS zones that are completely different, as we'll discuss in Book 2. The bad guys in general can only get to the external zones, and a quick look at most external zones shows that they don't contain anything more than records for e-mail and Web servers — hardly top secrets. So I'm not all that paranoid about keeping "outsiders" from doing zone transfers, but a bit of low-cost security doesn't hurt anything — so it's worthwhile seeing how to control who can get your zones.

To control who a primary DNS server will synchronize with, right-click your zone and choose Properties, and then the Zone Transfers tab to see something like Figure 13.18.

FIGURE 13.18
Controlling zone
transfers

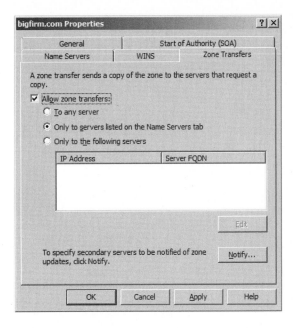

This dialog box offers us four options for controlling who's allowed to say, "I'm a secondary DNS server, please transfer a copy of the bigfirm.com zone to me":

◆ By un-checking "Allow zone transfers," you ensure that *nobody* is going to get your zones. Draconian, but I'm sure there's a place or two out there with high enough sphincter pressure to require this. You can also accomplish this by typing **dnscmd /zoneresetsecondaries bigfirm.com /noxfr**.

◆ By leaving the "Allow zone transfers" box checked and choosing the "To any server" radio button, you tell your server to share this zone with anyone who asks, the polar opposite of the last option. You can do that from the command line by typing **dnscmd /zoneresetsecondaries bigfirm.com /nonsecure**.

◆ The default stance, "Only to servers listed on the Name Servers tab," does what its label says — if you don't have an NS record, then you'll be denied any requests for a zone transfer. Command-line equivalent: **dnscmd /zoneresetsecondaries bigfirm.com /securens**.

◆ Finally, you can tell your DNS server exactly which IP addresses to send zone transfers to when requested by clicking the "Only to the following servers" radio button and then clicking the Edit button to add or remove IP addresses. From the command line, type **dnscmd /zoneresetsecondaries bigfirm.com /securelist ipaddr1 ipaddr2** ... and notice that you specify the list as a series of IP addresses with spaces between them. Note also that dnscmd will try valiantly to reverse-resolve those IP addresses, making your system crawl to a halt if it can't, so be careful about the IP addresses that you give it!

PRIMARY-INITIATED SYNCHS: NOTIFY

While in the Name Servers tab, you may have noticed the Notify button. Click that, and you'll see something like Figure 13.19.

FIGURE 13.19
Configuring
primary-to-secondary
notification

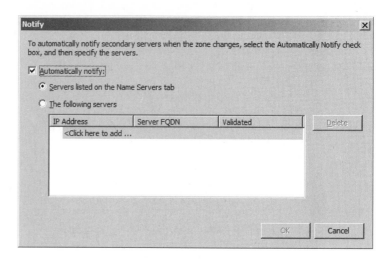

You've already learned that secondaries are the servers that initiate a primary-to-secondary zone synchronization, but in 1996, RFC 1996 appeared (how's *that* for synchronicity!) called "A Mechanism for Prompt Notification of Zone Changes (DNS NOTIFY)." RFC 1996 describes a standard mechanism whereby a primary DNS server can turn things around and initiate a zone synch. (I mention the RFC by name because I once wrote about DNS notification and got a tirade from a reader who claimed that DNS notification wasn't "real" DNS but instead a Microsoft plot.)

Anyway, this feature is enabled on Microsoft DNS servers by default, as you can see from Figure 13.18. If you needed to enable it from the command line, you'd do it by typing **dnscmd /zoneresetsecondaries bigfirm.com /notify**. You can disable notification (I can't imagine why you would) by either un-checking the "Automatically notify" box, or by typing **dnscmd /zoneresetsecondaries bigfirm.com /nonotify**. And if for some reason you only want to notify some small number of secondary DNS servers — a behavior that I would decry, as I have always loathed clique-ish behavior — then you can do it from the GUI as you see, or you can just type **dnscmd /zoneresetsecondaries bigfirm.com /notifylist** followed by a list of IP addresses for the "in crowd," in the same format as for controlling secondary updates in the last section.

CREATING A SECONDARY DNS SERVER ON Bigfirm.com

It's time to try something out, I think, so let's enlist main.bigfirm.com in our cadre of DNS servers. We'll make it a DNS server, give it an NS record in bigfirm.com, and then tell it to hold a secondary zone for bigfirm.com. Running the GUI would offer no surprises, as we've done that and done it again, so let's do it from the command line.

First, let's get bigfirm.com ready for main by adding an NS record in the bigfirm.com zone for main.bigfirm.com. By now I'll bet you can guess how to do that, so try it out if you like before reading any further, but here's the command, executed on winserver.bigfirm.com:

```
dnscmd /recordadd bigfirm.com @ NS main.bigfirm.com
```

And while we're at it, there's no sense in making winserver keep trying to connect to dns1 .bigfirm.com, as we've not created a system by that name. Let's remove *its* NS record:

```
dnscmd /recorddelete bigfirm.com @ NS dns1.bigfirm.com /f
```

Actually, I should mention briefly how you'd do that from the GUI, as Windows handles NS records strangely. You can't just right-click them and then delete them. Instead, you've got to go the zone's property page by right-clicking the zone, choosing Properties and then the Name Servers tab. You can then delete or modify name server records from there. (You'll notice how good I'm being about not mentioning how much easier the command line is in this context — but in the GUI's defense, recall that you might have to remember to delete a glue record if you use the command line *and* if the DNS server whose NS record you deleted is from another zone.)

Then it's time to prepare main.bigfirm.com to be bigfirm.com's secondary DNS server. We need to first install the DNS server service, and then create a secondary zone. On main, install the DNS server service as we have before:

```
servermanagercmd -install dns
```

And now we create the secondary bigfirm.com zone. Recall that we could create the primary zone on winserver by typing

```
dnscmd /zoneadd bigfirm.com /primary
```

So you *might* guess that on main we'd type **dnscmd /zoneadd bigfirm.com /secondary** ... and you'd be partially right. Secondary DNS servers need one more piece of information: who's the primary? (Yes, they could get that by just querying the Internet for the SOA record for bigfirm.com, but in really huge DNS installations people like to create levels upon levels of DNS servers, and so being able to "lie" to a DNS server about who's its primary can be useful.) As a result, dnscmd requires you to follow the parameter /secondary with the IP address of the master. At main then, we'd create that secondary zone by typing this:

```
dnscmd /zoneadd bigfirm.com /secondary 192.168.1.1
```

And in case it's not obvious, permit me to remind you that 192.168.1.1 is the IP address of winserver. Give main a minute or two to get replicated and then try a **dnscmd /enumzones** and **dnscmd /zoneprint bigfirm.com** and you'll see that you've got a real life secondary DNS server running on main!

How the Transfer Happens: Incremental Versus Complete

This is a sorta under-the-hood thing, but it's worth knowing. There are two ways that a secondary DNS server synchronizes with a primary DNS server. In fact, until the late '90s, DNS servers replicated data to their secondaries in a fairly primitive way.

The secondary servers in a domain periodically contacted the primary DNS server and copied its database to theirs. The *whole* database. So if a zone file contained 4000 lines of information and only one line changed, the secondary servers got the whole file when they requested an update.

RFC 1995 changed that, allowing for "incremental zone transfers." Put simply, RFC 1995–compliant DNS servers would know how to transfer just the few records that have changed, rather than resending the whole zone file. Server 2000, 2003, and 2008's DNS servers are RFC 1995–compliant, and will do incremental zone transfers whenever communicating between Windows DNS servers. If a Windows DNS server detects that it's talking to a DNS server running on something other than a Windows–based DNS server, however, then it will do complete zone transfers rather than incremental zone transfers.

You cannot to my knowledge configure Windows DNS servers to always do full zone transfers to other Windows DNS systems. But you can configure a Windows DNS server to do incremental zone transfers to non-Windows DNS servers.

1. Open the DNS snap-in (Start ➢ Administrative Tools/DNS).

2. Right-click the icon representing the server and click Properties.

3. Click the Advanced tab on the resulting properties page.

4. On the Advanced tab, uncheck the box labeled BIND Secondaries. Nonintuitive as this sounds, you must uncheck the box to have Windows' DNS do incremental zone transfers to non-Windows.

5. Click OK or Apply, and the server will do incremental zone transfers to all other DNS servers. Close the snap-in.

If you read about full transfers versus incremental transfers, you may stumble across an odd bit of terminology. When taking Microsoft's Windows 2000 certification exams, I ran across several DNS questions that referred to AXFR versus IXFR operations. I had no idea what they were talking about at first, but it quickly dawned on me that this idea of full versus incremental transfers was *another opportunity for an obscure acronym*! As you've probably guessed by now, AXFR just means "do a full zone transfer when updating a secondary," and IXFR means "do an incremental zone transfer when updating a secondary." The two phrases are apparently the internal commands that DNS servers use. In any case, don't blame Microsoft entirely for this — AXFR and IXFR are liberally used terms in DNS-related RFCs.

By the way, you can trigger a primary-to-secondary transfer on demand any time — you can even control whether it's an IXFR or AXFR. Go to any Windows secondary DNS server, start up the DNS administrative snap-in and open up the zone in question, then right-click that zone. You'll get a context menu that offers, among other things, Reload, Transfer from Master, and Reload from Master. Here's what they do:

◆ Reload looks like the "reload" command (**dnscmd /zonereload** *zonename* from the command line), except that it doesn't work at all unless you do something special. You see, for some reason, Microsoft secondary zones don't get written to \windows\system32\dns. As there is no zone file, choosing "reload" gets an error message. As far as I can see, the *only* way to get a secondary DNS server to keep a local zone file is to (1) create it from the command line and (2) add the **/file** *filename* option, as in **dnscmd /zoneadd bigfirm.com /secondary 192.168.1.1 /file bigfirmbackup.dns** or the like. (And even then, it's flaky.)

◆ "Transfer from Master" triggers an IXFR update. The corresponding CLI command is **dnscmd /zonerefresh** *zonename*.

◆ "Reload from Master" triggers an AXFR update. There's no corresponding CLI command that I know of, except to delete the secondary zone and then re-create it (which seems a bit harsh).

Delegating: Child Domains/Subdomains

As you learned when I explained how the DNS hierarchy works, the `minasi.com` and `bigfirm.com` zones are nothing more than child domains or subdomains of the "com" domain. But sometimes you'll want to create child domains of your own from *your* DNS domains, so let's look at how to accomplish that.

Revising Bigfirm

We've got `bigfirm.com` running well. But suppose we wanted to delegate control of a portion of the enterprise to another group, to give them the ability to control their DNS servers — how exactly would we do that? More specifically, suppose we wanted to create a `bigfirm.com` enterprise like the one in Figure 13.20?

FIGURE 13.20
Revised network

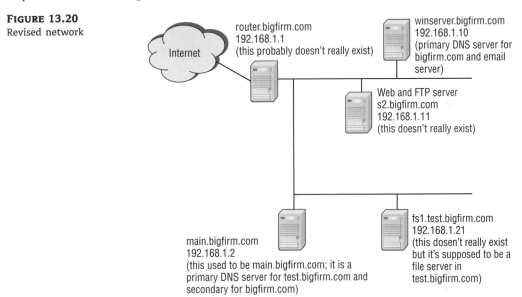

That figure probably looks sort of odd — why in the heck don't most of these systems exist? The answer is that on the one hand I'm trying to cook up an example of configuring DNS that isn't childishly simplistic and therefore of no instructional value, but on the other hand I want this to be a useful example that you can actually try out without having to go find more test systems than the two (main and winserver) that I've already asked you to find and install the 180-day evaluation copy of Server 2008 on. If you actually *do* have access to more systems or have enough RAM and a virtual machine manager to create a few more virtual machines, then that's great — but not necessary. Also, if you can put just one more machine together, then put together the "router.bigfirm.com" system with Internet Connection Sharing so your DNS servers can resolve names on the Internet.

NOTE

Okay, there's one wrinkle there — ICS hands out addresses in the 192.168.0.x range. But if you fiddle with its settings a bit, you can make it deliver addresses in the 192.168.1.x range.

Let me stress, however, that you don't need an Internet connection to do this. We will, however, have to reconfigure winserver and bigfirm a bit:

- Winserver needs a new IP address, 192.168.1.10, as routers should generally have the ".1" address and we're adding the imaginary system `router.bigfirm.com`, and we've got to free up the .1 address for it. Besides, real organizations reconfigure their networks now and then, so we might as well. Just make believe you've got this boss who arbitrarily decides to rearrange things now and then, and you'll be ready for a job in IT. (Okay, I'm kidding about that last point. Kind of.)

- We'll need to eliminate all of the records that we've created on the `bigfirm.com` DNS domain so far and get a fresh start.

- Then we'll need to create A records for our fictitious `router.bigfirm.com` and `s2.bigfirm.com` systems.

First, let's reconfigure winserver. Open an elevated command prompt and type these commands and `winserver.bigfirm.com` will be ready to go:

```
dnscmd /zonedelete bigfirm.com /f
dnscmd /zoneadd bigfirm.com /primary
dnscmd /recordadd bigfirm.com winserver A 192.168.1.10
dnscmd /recordadd bigfirm.com main A 192.168.1.2
dnscmd /recordadd bigfirm.com @ NS main.bigfirm.com
dnscmd /recordadd bigfirm.com @ MX 10 winserver.bigfirm.com
netsh int ip set address "local area connection" static 192.168.1.10 255.255.255.0
netsh int ip set dns "local area connection" static 192.168.1.10
```

Those eight commands delete the `bigfirm.com` zone ("/f" says "don't ask me if I'm sure, just delete it"), create a new `bigfirm.com` zone, install an A record for winserver, an A record for main, declare that main will be a DNS server for `bigfirm.com`, create an MX record declaring that winserver will receive e-mail for the `bigfirm.com` zone, changes winserver's IP address to 192.168.1.10, and instructs winserver's DNS client to query the DNS server at 192.168.1.10.

> **TIP**
>
> If you find yourself ever having to do this in the real world — doing a major network overhaul, that is — then here again is a place where the command line can be a big help. Very few of us can sit down and type a bunch of commands in the right order the first time, just as very few of us could sit down at the DNS GUI, start clicking, and remember everything that needed to get done. In this case, however, I sat down at `winserver.bigfirm.com` and got everything right, the first time. How? Simple — I had a test machine (a virtual machine running Server 2008, actually) configured like my actual `winserver.bigfirm.com` computer, and I tried out all of the commands on the test machine. If I got a command right, I just copied it from the command line to Notepad, building my list of commands slowly but surely. Then, once I'd figured out the commands just as I wanted them, I could either save those commands as a batch file and then run the batch file on the *real* `winserver.bigfirm.com`, or I could even have just copied them from Notepad and pasted them right into the command line. This also gave me yet *another* benefit: immediate documentation of what I did. Heck, if you're careful about keeping copies of all of the commands that you do on a zone, then you've got one big bunch of commands that can be re-executed, should you ever have to do a disaster recovery.

Do a **dnscmd /zoneprint bigfirm.com** at this point, and you'll get something like this:

```
;
; Zone:     bigfirm.com
; Server:   winserver.bigfirm.com
; Time:     Fri Mar 21 09:28:10 2008 UTC
;
@ 3600 NS          winserver.bigfirm.com.
                   3600 NS       main.bigfirm.com.
                   3600 SOA      winserver.bigfirm.com. hostmaster.bigfirm.com.
                                 5 900 600 86400 3600
                   3600 MX       10 winserver.bigfirm.com.
main 3600 A     192.168.1.2
winserver 3600 A      192.168.1.10


;
;   Finished zone: 3 nodes and 6 records in 0 seconds
;
```

NOTE

This may be obvious to some of you, but let me note that the DNS servers that you're setting up here can't be accessed from the public Internet. In order to set up a DNS server and zones that folks on the Internet can find, you've got to do two things: first, you've got to register a domain with some Internet registrar and, second, you need one or more unchanging ("static"), routable IP addresses to use for your DNS server or servers.

Next, go over to main.bigfirm.com and set it up with just a couple of commands, to delete and then rebuild its secondary zone for bigfirm.com and then to point it at the new IP address for winserver:

```
dnscmd /zonedelete bigfirm.com /f
dnscmd /zoneadd bigfirm.com /secondary 192.168.1.10
netsh int ip set dns "local area connection" static 192.168.1.10
```

With both systems reconfigured, we've still got two more bigfirm.com systems to set up:

◆ s2.bigfirm.com has an IP address of 192.168.1.11, and it acts as a Web server and so therefore should have an extra name of www.bigfirm.com and also acts as an FTP server and so therefore should have an extra name of ftp.bigfirm.com.

◆ router.minasi.com has an IP address of 192.168.1.1.

What DNS records do we need for those systems? If you've got winserver and main up and running, see if you can figure that out and give it a try before reading any further.

The answer is that we'll need four more resource records:

◆ An "A" record declaring that s2 has IP address 192.168.1.11

◆ A CNAME record giving s2 the alias "www"

◆ A CNAME record giving s2 the alias "ftp"

◆ An "A" record declaring that router has the IP address 192.168.1.1

A bit of clicking in the GUI will do it, or these commands will as well:

```
dnscmd /recordadd bigfirm.com s2 A 192.168.1.11
dnscmd /recordadd bigfirm.com www cname s2.bigfirm.com
dnscmd /recordadd bigfirm.com ftp cname s2.bigfirm.com
dnscmd /recordadd bigfirm.com router A 192.168.1.1
```

Once done, your zone should look (in the DNS GUI) like Figure 13.21.

FIGURE 13.21
Completely reconfigured
bigfirm.com

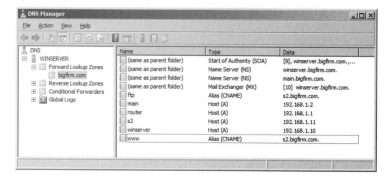

Time for a Subdomain: *test.bigfirm.com*

Now let's suppose that we've decided for some reason to create a subdomain of `bigfirm.com` called `test.bigfirm.com`. A subdomain is a domain, after all, and so it needs a DNS zone.

Recall, however, that every DNS zone has to fit into the DNS hierarchy, and so its parent domain needs to approve of its existence, just as I had to go to Network Solutions to get the okay to create `minasi.com` and `bigfirm.com`. The DNS phrase for "giving the okay" is actually "delegating control of a zone" or "delegating." That's mostly just a fancy name for creating an NS record for the child domain in the parent domain's zone. Here's what I mean by that. So far, we've created NS records that look like this one for main:

@ NS main.bigfirm.com.

Let's quickly review what that says. It's a DNS resource record and in particular an NS record, which just means that it names a DNS server. The DNS server's name is `main.bigfirm.com` ... but for what zone does `main.bigfirm.com` serve as a DNS server? The answer to that is "@," which means "this zone." Thus, the fact that I've got a record "@ NS `main.bigfirm.com`" *inside the* `bigfirm.com` *zone* means that `main.bigfirm.com` acts as a DNS server for `bigfirm.com`. But what if we created *this* record:

test NS main.bigfirm.com.

Let's see — @ means this domain, but putting a label at the beginning of a resource record means add this label to the domain's name, so `test` is just short for `test.bigfirm.com`. What would creating such a record do? Well, it's simple enough to find out by typing

```
dnscmd /recordadd bigfirm.com test NS main.bigfirm.com
```

If you then open up the DNS snap-in (or, if you've already got it open, press F5 to make it refresh the screen), then you'll see something like Figure 13.22.

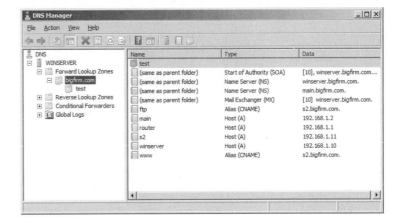

Rather than showing you the test NS main.bigfirm.com record — notice that there are two NS records, and this one isn't either of them — the GUI creates a ghostly gray folder named test. Right-clicking it and choosing Properties shows that main.bigfirm.com is the first and only DNS server for this not-yet-created zone. (In this case, dnscmd /zoneprint offers more straightforward information — test NS main.bigfirm.com.) We can then create the test.bigfirm.com zone, *but* recall that we haven't designated winserver as a DNS server for test.bigfirm.com, so we've got to move over to main.bigfirm.com to create the zone. We can then either use the GUI to create the test.bigfirm.com zone, or just type this:

```
dnscmd /zoneadd test.bigfirm.com /primary
```

At that point, go ahead and create the A record for fs1.test.bigfirm.com:

```
dnscmd /recordadd test.bigfirm.com fs1 A 192.168.1.21
```

Try an nslookup fs1.test.bigfirm.com, and you'll get a quick "Address: 192.168.1.21." Now that we've got that set up, let's review what we've seen in this section:

◆ Creating a subdomain or child domain (again, the two phrases mean exactly the same thing) involves doing just two things: first, create an NS record in the parent domain's zone that names the child domain and declares a DNS server for that child domain, and then go create the child domain on that DNS server.

◆ Creating that NS record that sort of announces the birth of a new domain is called *delegation.*

◆ main.bigfirm.com is not a member of the test.bigfirm.com domain, and yet it acts as the DNS server for test.bigfirm.com. That illustrates that a DNS server needn't be a member of a DNS domain, and in fact the majority of DNS domains on the Internet do *not* have DNS servers in their domain. In the case of Active Directory–related DNS servers, however, the opposite is true — most of the AD-related DNS domains you'll ever build will probably live on servers in those domains.

◆ As I mentioned earlier, the phrases "primary DNS server" or "secondary DNS server" are widely used but technically inaccurate. Look at `main.bigfirm.com`: is it a "primary DNS server" or a "secondary DNS server?" Well, it holds a secondary zone for `bigfirm.com`, but it also holds a primary zone for `test.bigfirm.com`.

Easier Record Maintenance: Dynamic DNS (DDNS)

By now, I'm hoping that you've got some feel for what's involved in running a DNS server and a zone or two, but now let's look more closely into what would be a part of your workload. We've seen how to add or modify SOA, A, NS, MX, PTR, and CNAME records, but consider: which sort will require the most attention? Well, there's only one SOA record, you won't have but a smattering of DNS and e-mail servers, so that takes care of the NS, MX, and CNAME records — there won't be too many of them. That leaves the A and PTR records, and on a goodly-sized network, there will be a *lot* of them — one for every workstation and server. Who wants to have to punch in all of those A and PTR records and, worse, keep track of how those records have to change as users move their computers from one subnet to another — ugh.

Fortunately, you needn't take on that drudgery, thanks to RFC 2136, "Dynamic Updates in the Domain Name System (DNS UPDATE)." It describes a way whereby PCs can contact their zone's primary DNS server and create their own A, PTR, and other records. Dynamic DNS (DDNS) is quite important for Active Directory, as you'll see in Book 2.

To make DDNS work, you need several pieces:

◆ You need a piece of DNS server software that knows how to accept DDNS updates. ("Updates" is the term that the RFC uses to describe the situation whereby a system goes to a DNS server and says, "please include this DNS record in your zone.")

◆ You've got to *enable* the DDNS feature on your server. Some people see DDNS as a horribly frightening security hole, and so every piece of DNS server software I've ever worked with has DDNS disabled by default.

◆ You need client systems that know how to initiate DDNS updates.

We have all of those pieces, as Windows 2000, XP, 2003, Vista, and 2008 all contain client software that knows how to do DDNS updates (oddly enough, it's in the DHCP client software rather than the DNS client software), and the DNS server software shipped with Windows 2000 Server, Windows Server 2003, and Windows Server 2008 can do DDNS.

Seeing DDNS Work

To see DDNS in action, let's make `main.bigfirm.com` a simple DNS client, rather than a server, so that we can use it to highlight how DDNS clients (like main) interact with a DDNS server (like winserver). To do that, we'll delete the secondary `bigfirm.com` zone on main, remove main's NS record on winserver, and remove main's static A and PTR records. Then we'll enable DDNS on the `bigfirm.com` and `1.168.192.in-addr.arpa` zones, and then ask `main.bigfirm.com` to dynamically register itself. First, delete main's NS, A, and PTR records from the `bigfirm.com` and `1.168.192.in-addr.arpa` zones and then erase all traces of `test.bigfirm.com` by going to `winserver.bigfirm.com` and either clicking on the records in the DNS GUI, or by typing these commands at winserver:

```
dnscmd /recorddelete bigfirm.com @ NS main.bigfirm.com /f
dnscmd /recorddelete bigfirm.com main A /f
```

```
dnscmd /recorddelete 1.168.192.in-addr.arpa 2 PTR /f
dnscmd /recorddelete bigfirm.com test ns /f
```

Notice that I didn't have to type the *entire* A and PTR records, just the left-hand-side label ("main" in the case of the A record, and "2" in the case of the PTR record) and the record type, and dnscmd does the rest. The /f says, again, "don't ask me if I really mean it, I *do* really mean it — just do it!"

Next, let's reconfigure the domains to accept dynamic updates. You can cause a zone to accept dynamic updates from the GUI by right-clicking the zone's folder in the DNS GUI, choosing Properties and then, at the General tab, choosing "Nonsecure and secure" in the "Dynamic updates:" single-selection drop-down. Or you can type these commands at winserver:

```
dnscmd /config 1.168.192.in-addr.arpa /allowupdate 1
dnscmd /config bigfirm.com /allowupdate 1
```

The /config option lets you reconfigure about 40 characteristics of a zone; /allowupdate turns DDNS on with a value of 1 or off with a value of 0. (On the off-chance that you're trying to do that on a Windows 2000 Server with the Windows 2000 version of dnscmd, you must type the option as /AllowUpdate with the capital A and W; later versions don't care about the case.)

Now that main's A and PTR records are gone and the forward and reverse lookup zones accept dynamic updates, move over to main.bigfirm.com and open an elevated command prompt. Then we'll delete the bigfirm.com secondary zone by typing (at main):

```
dnscmd /zonedelete bigfirm.com /f
dnscmd /zonedelete test.bigfirm.com /f
```

Once that's done, type **ipconfig /registerdns**. That's the command that causes main to ask winserver to register its A and PTR records. Wait a second or two — these updates take a little time — and return to winserver. Check either via an nslookup, a dnscmd /zoneprint, or in the GUI (don't forget to press F5 if you use the GUI), and you'll find that both the PTR and A records are back.

What DDNS Does, Under the Hood

Main did its DDNS update in eight steps:

1. First, main looked at its DNS suffix, bigfirm.com, to figure out what DNS domain to try to register with.

2. Then main asked winserver for the SOA record for bigfirm.com. It needed to do that to find the name of the primary DNS server for bigfirm.com. It needed to find that out because it wants to do an update to the bigfirm.com zone, if you recall, anyone modifying a zone must make those changes *on the server holding the primary zone file for that zone*. When winserver.bigfirm.com responded with the SOA record, it also said, "now that I'm telling you that winserver.bigfirm.com is the primary for this zone, I'm guessing that you'll next ask me to look up that IP address for that winserver.bigfirm.com system, so I'll save us both some time and include that answer in my response, even if you *haven't* asked me yet."

3. Armed with that information, main said to winserver (who main now knows holds the primary zone for bigfirm.com), "please register an A record for main.bigfirm.com."

4. Winserver responds that the update was successful.

5. Now it's time to register the PTR record. Once again, main asks for an SOA record, but this time it's the SOA record for `1.168.192.in-addr.arpa`.

6. As before, winserver gives main the SOA record as well as the IP address of the server identified as the primary server for the zone.

7. Main then sends its PTR update request to winserver.

8. Finally, winserver reports success, and we're done.

Why You Need a Dynamic Reverse Lookup Zone

Main's updates worked wonderfully, because we had both a dynamic forward lookup zone (`bigfirm.com`) and a dynamic reverse lookup zone (`1.168.192.in-addr.arpa`). But what if we'd only created a `bigfirm.com` zone, and skipped the reverse lookup zone? As it turns out, skipping the reverse lookup zone generates a fair amount of "junk traffic" on your network.

Consider what will happen when your systems query your local DNS server for the SOA record, but your DNS server doesn't have a reverse lookup zone. In that case, your DNS server says, "well, I don't have a `1.168.192.in-addr.arpa` zone, but maybe someone else does" — and so goes out on the Internet and asks one of the thirteen root servers if they can point it at the domain named `1.168.192.in-addr.arpa` zone. Of course, this should never happen, as the 192.168.x.x range is non-routable, and for private intranets only (remember RFC 1918). Now consider this question: how many systems on the planet are (1) running Windows 2000 or later and (2) have a non-routable address like 192.168.x.x or 10.x.x.x? I don't know the answer, but I'll bet it's a *lot* of systems, which means that those poor root servers probably get hammered every morning when all of those Windows clients start up and try to register their PTR records.

Actually, the ICANN guys know that, and so they've actually created a "black hole server" whose job it is to receive these PTR registration attempts. It smiles, nods politely at the system trying to register its nonroutable address, and says "thank you, your registration was successful," while actually ignoring the system. The server's name is `prisoner.iana.org`, and if we all told our non-routable systems not to try to register with it, then there'd be just a bit more bandwidth free on the Internet — precious bandwidth that could instead be used for downloading porn, stolen movies, music, and the like. (It's depressing sometimes to contemplate what a force for good the Internet was going to be in comparison with what it actually turned out to be.)

So be a good Netizen and set up a local dynamic reverse lookup zone, or tell your systems to *stop* trying to register their PTR records.

Keeping Your Systems from Registering PTRs

You can tell your clients and servers not to bother trying to register their PTR records with a Registry hack or a group policy setting. Open Regedit and navigate to HKLM\SYSTEM\CurrentControlSet\Services\Tcpip\Parameters. Then add a new REG_DWORD setting called DisableReverseAddressRegistrations and set it to 1.

Alternatively, you can tell your system to do that by looking in the Group Policy editor in Computer Configuration ➤ Administrative Templates ➤ Network ➤ DNS Client, where you'll see a setting named Register PTR Records. Set that to Disabled, and your system won't try to register its PTR records any more, but it *will* still register its A record.

What Triggers DDNS Registrations?

If you forgot to make the zones dynamic until after main booted, how can you force main to re-try registering? Well, clearly you could turn main on and off, but who wants to do that? You may recall that I had you type this at main:

```
ipconfig /registerdns
```

That command tells the DHCP client to re-register the A and PTR records. But that's not the only condition that triggers DDNS registrations. Remember that DDNS registrations are initiated by the client, not the server. The DNS server does not ask the client to register; instead, the client requests the registration of the server. Five events cause a client to register or, more likely, to *re*register:

◆ The computer has been rebooted and the TCP/IP software has just started.

◆ You've changed the IP address on a system with a static IP address. That also causes the system to ask DNS to delete the existing A and PTR records and replace them with its new ones.

◆ Your computer gets its IP address from DHCP and the computer has just renewed its DHCP lease.

◆ You type **ipconfig /registerdns**.

◆ 24 hours has passed since the last time the system registered with DDNS.

You can change that 24-hour period to another one with a Registry change to HKEY_LOCAL_MACHINE\SYSTEM\CurrentControlSet\Services\Tcpip\Parameters: add a new value entry DefaultRegistrationRefreshInterval of type REG_DWORD. You can then specify how often to reregister in seconds. The default is 86400, the number of seconds in a day.

While we're looking at the result of a successful dynamic registration, let's cover something that might surprise you. Go back to winserver and run **dnscmd /zoneprint bigfirm.com**. Main's A record will look interesting:

```
main [Aging:3569605] 1200 A   192.168.1.2
```

That number "3569605" tells Windows the time and date that this record was created. "Huh?," I hear you cry. Active Directory measures times and dates based on the number of hours since (as far as I can figure) roughly 1 January 1600. (Divide it by 24 (hours to days) and then by 365.25 (days to years) and you get roughly the number of years after 1600 that the record was created.) That date is important because Windows Server's DNS server can do "aging," wherein it deletes any records that haven't been updated in a while — but we'll get to that a bit later in this chapter. Notice also that this record has a TTL smaller than the zone's default of an hour; this one's set at 1200 seconds or 20 minutes. I guess Microsoft did that because workstations *might* change their IP addresses regularly, although I've never heard an "official" reason.

NOTE

You can change that 20-minute TTL value if you care to by creating a REG_DWORD value entry called DefaultRegistrationTTL in HKEY_LOCAL_MACHINE\SYSTEM\CurrentControlSet\Services\

Tcpip\Parameters. Fill the value entry with the length in seconds that you'd like the TTL set to. I can't think of a reason why you'd mess with it, but I include this for the curious. Please note that this is *not* how often your system reregisters with DDNS — there really isn't a Registry entry to affect that, as you'll see later in this chapter.

Stopping All DDNS Registrations

At some point, you may need to tell a Windows box not to do attempt any DDNS registration at all. As you've read, Windows systems automatically attempt to register their host names and IP addresses with the primary DNS server of the DNS domain that they belong to, as you've seen. But that can cause some problems in places that don't like DDNS for some reason.

I had a client that used Unix-based BIND servers and that hadn't made their DNS zone dynamic. (There wasn't any reason to, as they hadn't rolled out an AD yet.) The PC guys rolled out a few hundred Windows 2000 Professional systems.

The BIND guys — a different group — noticed.

All of a sudden, the DNS server logs were chock-full of warnings and errors about all of these computers trying to register with their static DNS zones. That worried the BIND guys, so they tracked it down to all of these then-new PCs. What to do? Well, the BIND folks could have just ignored the messages. But that *does* seem a bit inelegant. So rather than lowering the river, why not just raise the bridge? In other words, how could they get the Windows 2000, XP, Vista, 2003, and 2008 systems to stop bugging the DNS servers?

You can tell a Windows computer to forgo registering altogether either from the GUI or with a Registry hack. The Registry hack is in HKEY_LOCAL_MACHINE\SYSTEM\CurrentControlSet\ Services\Tcpip\Parameters. Add a new value entry, DisableDynamicUpdate — it's a REG_D-WORD entry — and set it to 1 and reboot the computer. That'll keep the computer from attempting a dynamic update whenever the computer has a static address or got it from DHCP. Or here's a (long) command line to do it:

```
reg add hklm\system\currentcontrolset\services\tcpip\parameters /v
DisableDynamicUpdate /t REG_DWORD /d 1 /f
```

That's all one line. You can even do it on a remote system by prefixing the Registry key's name with the system's name, so long as the remote system's firewall doesn't block you. For example, to reach across the network and make this change to Bigdog, you'd type (again, on one line)

```
reg add \\bigdog\hklm\system\currentcontrolset\services\tcpip\parameters /v
DisableDynamicUpdate /t REG_DWORD /d 1 /f
```

You can tell the computer not to try to update DNS in the GUI, as well; it's in the Advanced TCP/IP Settings property page, on the DNS tab. Uncheck the Register This Connection's Addresses in DNS box.

But what if you want to distribute this setting to bazillions of machines? Look to group policies for help here. Look in the Computer Configuration ➢ Administrative Templates ➢ Network ➢ DNS Client folder mentioned before, and you'll see a wealth of group policy options for reducing or eliminating DDNS registration attempts.

Troubleshooting Failed DDNS Registrations

Sometimes you'll be working with a network with a dynamic DNS infrastructure, or at least you're told that it's got DDNS running — but new systems don't seem to show up in DNS. Clearly something's keeping clients from successfully registering themselves in DNS — but what could it be? Here are the most likely causes:

♦ **There's a problem with connectivity to the primary — ping it to test**. If the cable's fallen out of the back of the system, then dynamic DNS is never gonna work.

♦ **Check that the client hasn't been instructed *not* to try to do a dynamic update**. Look in the same Registry key and group policy area that we discussed when showing how to stop PTR registrations, as there are settings that stop *all* attempts at dynamic registration (they'll be obvious).

♦ **DDNS isn't enabled**. On the primary DNS server, run a **dnscmd /zoneinfo** *dns-domain-name* and look for "update = 1" or look at the General tab of the zone's properties to ensure that you've made the zone accept dynamic updates.

♦ **The wrong SOA is being retrieved**. From the client, try running **nslookup -type=soa** *dns-domain-name* and check that there *is* an SOA record, and that what it calls the "primary name server" is indeed the DNS server that you expected it to be.

♦ **The SOA's being retrieved, but the A record for the primary DNS server is missing**. From the client, try running nslookup on the name of the primary DNS server to ensure that there's an A record for that system.

♦ **The preferred DNS server is offline**. The server may be online, but perhaps the DNS service isn't running at the moment for some reason. Go to the preferred DNS server, open an elevated command prompt, and type **sc query dns** and look for "STATE: 4 RUNNING."

♦ **You're running AD-integrated DDNS and the client is not part of the domain**. You'll learn later that you can skip the idea of primary and secondary DNS servers and instead do something called an Active Directory-integrated zone. One of the benefits of AD-I zones is that you can say to AD-I DNS servers, "only accept DDNS registrations from systems who have authenticated to the AD." Once you do that, then only domain members can do DDNS registrations.

Keeping Your Zones Clean with DNS Scavenging

When a system shuts down, it doesn't ask its zones' primary DNS server to remove its A and PTR records. As a result, DDNS zones are soon clogged with "junk" A and PTR records that don't apply to a working system any more. Windows Server's DNS system lets you keep a nice, clean zone through a process called *scavenging*. Scavenging keeps track of a record's age and, if it hasn't been re-created ("refreshed") recently, the DNS server removes the record. The idea is that if a machine named workstation391.bigfirm.com hasn't done a dynamic DNS update of its A record in a few weeks, then it's probably dead and thus that A record should be deleted.

Scavenging is not on by default, and it's a bit odd in the way that it works — you have to enable it first on the server, and then on the zone. You'd think that you could go to winserver.bigfirm.com and turn on scavenging and winserver would then start scavenging on all of its zones, but that's not how it works — you'd have to turn on scavenging first on winserver as a whole, and then on bigfirm.com.

CONTROLLING SCAVENGING: JUST THREE NUMBERS

To see how to set up scavenging, right-click the DNS server's icon in the DNS snap-in and choose Set Aging/Scavenging for All Zones and you'll get a dialog box like Figure 13.23.

FIGURE 13.23
Setting scavenging
parameters

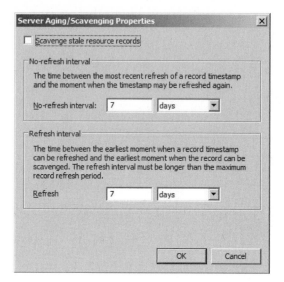

Check the box labeled "Scavenge stale resource records" and click OK twice (you'll see another dialog box asking about AD-integrated zones; again, just click OK to go with the defaults) to enable scavenging. But what about those two time values, the "No-refresh interval" and the "Refresh interval"? Well, there are three numbers relevant to how scavenging works; here, you see two of them — and I'll explain them in a minute, but if you're in a real rush, then here's the short version: turn scavenging on and just use the default time periods, they're fine.

But you're not done setting up scavenging. Right-click the server again, choose Properties, and click the Advanced tab. You'll see something like Figure 13.24. Check "Enable automatic scavenging of stale records" to kick off the scavenger on a regular basis.

The No-Refresh Interval

Now let's consider those three numbers.

Look back to Figure 13.23 and you'll see the first value, something called the No-refresh interval. It creates a period of time wherein your computer *cannot* reregister itself in DNS. So, for example, if the no-refresh interval were one day and your computer had reregistered at 9:00 A.M. on Tuesday morning, then any attempts to reregister itself before 9:00 A.M. Wednesday morning would simply be ignored by the DDNS server.

Why'd Microsoft bother with something like this? Mostly because you have the option, as I've mentioned (and will discuss in the companion book) to store your zones not in a traditional zone file, but instead in the Active Directory, a so-called "Active Directory–integrated zone." Any time that your system reregisters, that creates a change in the AD, and any change in the AD must be replicated to every other AD controller in the enterprise. Replication traffic can clog your WAN links and slow down the DCs, so I guess the idea with the no-refresh interval is to reduce the burden imposed on the AD by overzealously reregistering systems.

FIGURE 13.24
How often to scavenge?

If you're experimenting and want to force an immediate re-registration within the no-refresh interval, just open the zone in the DNS snap-in and use the GUI to delete the A record for the system that you want to register. Then go to the system that you want to reregister and type `ipconfig /registerdns` at a command line.

The Refresh and Scavenging Intervals

Figure 13.23 also includes a field called the "Refresh interval." But that's not a very descriptive name. A better name would be The Remainder of the Immunity from Scavenging Period. It's an interval that says to the scavenging routine, "If this record's age is less than the sum of its no-refresh and refresh intervals, then don't even *think* of scavenging it."

For example, suppose I've got a no-refresh interval of one day and a refresh interval of two days. And let's suppose that the scavenging routine runs every day. (You set the scavenging interval (period) shown in Figure 13.24.) Your system registers at 9:00 A.M. Tuesday morning. As you read before, that means that the DDNS server would be deaf to any attempts by your system to re-register. Let's say that the scavenging routine runs every evening. It sees that the no-refresh plus the refresh intervals equals three days. The scavenger then sees that your workstation's A record is less than a day old. That age is less than three days, so the scavenger leaves the record alone.

Let's suppose that you're on vacation for the week. So 9 A.M. Wednesday morning is when your DDNS server would accept a re-registration for your system, but your system's not on, so it doesn't try to re-register. Wednesday evening, the scavenger sees that your workstation's A record is about a day and a half old — still too young to scavenge. The same thing happens Thursday night, when the scavenger sees a two-and-a-half-day-old record. But on Friday night, your workstation's A record is three-and-a-half days old, so the scavenger munches it.

Simplified, think of it this way. Add the no-refresh and the refresh intervals together. That's how long you want a record to stay in a dynamic DNS zone.

Choosing a Good No-Refresh and Refresh Interval

There really isn't any relationship between the scavenging interval and the no-refresh/refresh intervals. But you should take a minute to ensure that you don't set the no-refresh/refresh intervals too small. The sum of those two should be larger than the frequency of re-registration.

Here's an exaggerated (and impossible) example of what I mean. Suppose that for some reason your system re-registers with DDNS only once every 30 days. But then suppose you set a no-refresh interval of six days and a refresh interval of seven days, and a scavenging interval of one day. Let's follow the process through from Jan. 1:

1. On Jan. 1, your system registers with DDNS.

2. The DDNS server will not accept another registration from your system until Jan. 7, but that's no problem — your system doesn't intend to re-register until Jan. 31.

3. Every day until Jan. 14, the scavenger runs and sees that your system's A record is less than 13 days (6 plus 7) old, and so leaves it alone.

4. Around Jan. 14, however, the scavenger runs, finds the record older than 13 days, and deletes it.

Remember that this is a client-driven registration system, so there's no method for the DDNS server to give the client a heads-up that it's time to re-register.

Clearly, then, you should set the sum of your no-refresh and refresh intervals so that they always exceed the maximum possible interval between subsequent re-registrations. But what's the maximum possible interval between re-registrations? Recall the things that trigger a re-registration: They happen every 24 hours (if the system stays up), upon a DHCP lease renewal, or when you turn your computer on. So the longest you'd probably ever go between re-registrations would be as long as you ever have your computer off — seven days, perhaps, unless you're in the habit of taking two-week vacations.

Setting Scavenging for One Zone

Figure 13.23 showed you how to set the scavenging values for all zones. To set a different set of refresh and no-refresh intervals for just one zone, then you'll need to right-click the zone and then choose Properties. Click the General tab and you'll see an Aging button; click it and you'll get a dialog box that looks like Figure 13.25.

Notice that it's identical to Figure 13.23. The defaults of seven days apiece are probably just fine. Notice the information field at the bottom of the dialog box — that says when scavenging could next occur. You may recall this bit of information from dnscmd /zoneprint:

```
main [Aging:3569605] 1200 A   192.168.1.2
```

Recall that I said that the 3569605 declares when the record was created in hours-past-1-January-1600 format.

In sum, then, to enable scavenging you must remember to:

◆ Set the no-refresh and refresh intervals for the server as a whole, as in Figure 13.23.

◆ Turn on scavenging, as in Figure 13.24.

◆ If you want to set different intervals for each zone, then adjust their specific refresh properties.

FIGURE 13.25
Scavenging settings for a particular zone

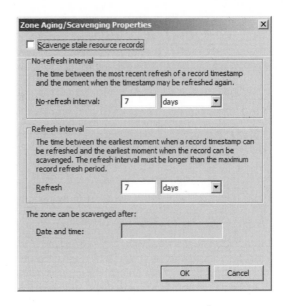

Viewing When a Record Will "Go Stale"

If you want, you can find out when a particular record will go stale, although not directly. Start up the DNS snap-in and choose View ➤ Advanced. Then right-click any record and choose Properties; you'll then see something like Figure 13.26.

FIGURE 13.26
Viewing a record's properties with View/Advanced enabled

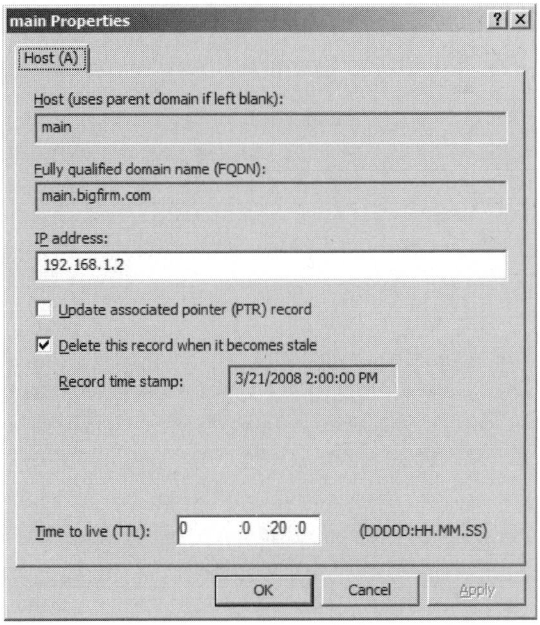

The date that you see of 3/21/2008 at 2 P.M. isn't telling me that this record goes stale at that time; instead, it's telling me that this record *was created* — registered — at that date. To find out when it'll go stale, I'd have to first add the no-refresh plus the refresh intervals. Suppose the no-refresh interval is two days, and the refresh interval is three days. That'd tell me that the earliest time that this record can go stale is five days later. But, of course, that's not the *only* information that I need. Recall that stale records only get deleted when the scavenging routine runs, so I'd need to know when the scavenging routine runs to determine exactly when this record will disappear.

Viewing Scavenging Logs

Windows 2000 Server and Server 2003–based DNS servers report what happened in every scavenging cycle in the Event Viewer in the System log. Just look for a DNS event with event ID 2501.

DDNS and Security

Sometimes you'll find yourself in an IT environment that *hates* the whole idea of dynamic DNS, and that enabling dynamic DNS is like turning off the firewalls and changing everyone's password to "password" or "secret." I agree that DDNS offers some security issues, but I'm not as paranoid as some — but here's the story.

One thing that troubles some people about vanilla, by-the-RFC DDNS servers is that they will accept a registration from anyone. So, for example, if `bigfirm.com`'s DNS server were "live" on the Internet, then anyone anywhere could just set their Windows computer's domain suffix to `bigfirm.com` and type `ipconfig /registerdns`. This would work even if that machine's local DNS server didn't do DDNS. Remember, all that your preferred DNS server must do is be able to retrieve the SOA record for `bigfirm.com` — and any DNS server can do that.

Should the `bigfirm.com` people care that people are registering on their domain? So what if the machine at 62.11.99.3 registers itself as `poindexter.bigfirm.biz`? A Microsoft person told me that it might matter. For example, he explained, consider the 128-bit downloadable versions of Internet Explorer. In the past, you weren't supposed to be able to download them if you weren't in the United States or Canada. Microsoft's Web site determined whether you were in the United States or Canada by looking at your domain. If `bigfirm.com`'s record in the Network Solutions database showed a U.S. address, then the download was okayed, so someone from outside the United States or Canada could sneak in that way.

Presumably, a hacker could first register with `bigfirm.com`, then try to hack some system. If the system administrator of the attacked system noticed that he was being hacked by someone at `bigfirm.com`, that might make for a bit of a hassle for the `bigfirm.com` administrator. Particularly if the hacker was trying to crack an NSA or CIA site.

Not every brand of DDNS server software is wide open. RFCs for secure DDNS have been around for over 10 years; RFC 3007 is the most recent that I know of. For some reason, though, Microsoft hasn't put RFC 3007 compliance into either their DNS client or server, so that's not an option for Windows users. You can, as I've suggested, secure a Microsoft DNS zone by making it AD-integrated; I'll cover that in Book 2.

Tweaking DNS Performance

Before we leave our look at the fundamentals of DNS, I should explain a couple of nice features of DNS that let you crank up your systems' performance a trifle — round robin and subnet mask ordering.

Cheap "Clusters": Building Fault Tolerance with Multiple A Records and Round-Robin DNS

If you've got a busy Web server (and don't we all hope to have that!) then you might need to build a second Web server to handle all of that load. But how to handle the load balancing? Well, Windows Server 2008 Enterprise Edition's got a nifty clustering tool to help there, but it's expensive. Alternatively, you might want to use a simple "load balancing" scheme built right into DNS.

How Round Robin Works

Suppose I've got a Web server at IP address 206.246.253.100. I've named it www.minasi.com because, well, that's what people expect the Web server at minasi.com to be named. But now let's suppose that several thousand people all decide at the same time to hit my Web site to find out how to hire me to speak at their next engagement. (Hey, it could happen.) At that point, my poor Web server's overloaded, lots of people get some kind of "server is too busy to respond to you" message, and I lose lots of potential business. That would be bad. Really bad.

Alternatively, I could set up three more machines with IIS on them, at IP addresses 206.246.253.101 through 206.246.253.103. *Then* — and here's the clever part — I just enter host name records, A records, for each of them and name *all* of them www.minasi.com.

Now that I've got all four machines, each named www.minasi.com, suppose someone points her browser to www.minasi.com. My DNS server is then asked by *her* DNS server to resolve the name www.minasi.com. So my DNS server looks at the four addresses that have www.minasi.com and responds with the four IP addresses, saying, "You can find www.minasi.com at 206.246.253.100, .101, .102, and .103." Then, seconds later, someone else's DNS server asks my DNS server what IP address goes with www.minasi.com. My DNS server then responds with the same information, but in a different order, offering first 206.246.253.101, then .102, .103, and finally .100. The DNS client will usually take the first address offered first, so the first visitor will tend to go to .100, and the second to .101. The third person to ask about www.minasi.com gets the four addresses in the order of .102/.103/.100/.101, the fourth as .103/.100/.101/.102, and then for the fifth, DNS cycles back to .100/.101/.102/.103.

This process, called *round-robin DNS*, spreads out the load on a machine. If I had these four Web servers set up, they each would get roughly one-fourth of the incoming Web requests. In that way, I could build a "scalable" Web site. Now, understand that this *isn't* a replacement for Enterprise Edition and multisystem clusters. DNS has no idea what's going on with the various Web servers, and if one of them goes down, DNS knows nothing of the problem and just keeps giving out the bad server's IP address to every fourth inquirer. But it's a free way of doing load balancing and worth a try before spending tens of thousands of dollars on cluster systems.

NOTE

Note that although I used an example of four consecutive IP addresses, you need not use consecutive addresses for your round-robin groups.

Configuring Round Robin

If you'd like, you can try it out with bigfirm.biz. First, check that the round-robin feature is enabled on your DNS server. It's enabled by default, but you can control it from your server's Advanced Properties page. To see that, right-click the server's icon (bigdog in our example) and choose Properties, then Advanced to see something like Figure 13.27.

FIGURE 13.27
A DNS server's
Advanced Properties
page

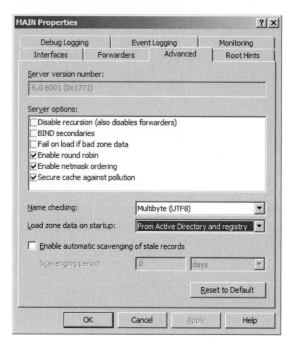

Note that one of the options is "Enable round robin," and it's checked. As far as I know, you can only configure round robin at the server level, not the zone level — a DNS server that contained a lot of zones could not do round robin on one zone and not another. Click Cancel to remove the dialog box.

To see this in action, we'll first delete the www CNAME record, as we can't have CNAMEs and A records conflicting. At `winserver.bigfirm.com`, type this:

```
dnscmd /recorddelete bigfirm.com www cname /f
```

(Notice that that I didn't type the entire record — `dnscmd /recorddelete` finds and deletes *all* records that start with "www cname" with this command.) Then create three A records all named "www" on IP addresses from 192.168.1.21 through 192.168.1.23, like so:

```
dnscmd /recordadd bigfirm.com www A 192.168.1.21
dnscmd /recordadd bigfirm.com www A 192.168.1.22
dnscmd /recordadd bigfirm.com www A 192.168.1.23
```

(I'm hoping by now that you've become comfortable with the "up" arrow on the command line interface!) Now we've got three A records declaring some host to have the host name of "www." Now try *this* out: type **nslookup www.bigfirm.com** and press Enter. Then run that command again, and again. You'll probably see something like this:

```
C:\>nslookup www.bigfirm.com
Server:  winserver.bigfirm.com
Address:  192.168.1.1
```

```
Name:      www.bigfirm.com
Addresses:  192.168.1.22
            192.168.1.21
            192.168.1.23


C:\>nslookup www.bigfirm.com
Server:  winserver.bigfirm.com
Address:  192.168.1.1

Name:      www.bigfirm.com
Addresses:  192.168.1.23
            192.168.1.22
            192.168.1.21


C:\>nslookup www.bigfirm.com
Server:  winserver.bigfirm.com
Address:  192.168.1.1

Name:      www.bigfirm.com
Addresses:  192.168.1.21
            192.168.1.23
            192.168.1.22
```

Neat, eh? Whenever some computer asks this DNS server for the IP address associated with www.bigfirm.com, the DNS server basically rolls the dice and hands the client all three names, in different order. As most clients just take the first address, the effect is that we end up with no-cost load balancing. Note that because Web servers are "stateless" — they don't remember you from page to page — then you can use this inexpensive approach to load balancing on Web servers. Most other sorts of servers — e-mail servers, file servers, FTP servers — aren't stateless (the opposite is "stateful," which sounds better than "state-ey," I suppose), and so round robin wouldn't work very well.

SIMPLE ROUTE OPTIMIZATION: SUBNET MASK ORDERING

If you've set up round-robin DNS, where you have several systems that have the same name but different IP addresses, then Windows DNS servers not only can do round robin for you, they can also ensure that clients get directed to the nearest server that matches their request.

Suppose I have 10 machines all named server1.minasi.com and 10 subnets on my network. Then suppose I have one of these machines on each subnet. Think about what happens when a computer on a particular subnet asks DNS to resolve server1.minasi.com. Simple round robin would just offer the 10 IP addresses in some random order. But clearly it'd make life easier on the routers if I could somehow tell DNS, "Listen — when someone asks for the IP address of server1.minasi.com, *and* if one of the server1.minasi.com systems is on the same subnet as that someone, then always offer the IP address of the *local* server1.minasi.com first." Windows DNS servers will do that — it's called *netmask ordering*. It is enabled by default. (You can turn it off in the Advanced tab of the DNS server's properties page that we saw while examining DNS round robin, as you'll see if you look back to Figure 13.27.)

If you feel like seeing this in action, go to bigfirm.com and delete the .21 and .22 entries for www.bigfirm.com. Then create a www.bigfirm.com entry in a different subnet, like 10.0.0.1. Then try the nslookup for www.bigfirm.com. You'll still get two answers in return, but the 192.168.0.23 entry will always be the first one, because it's on the same subnet as the computer that you're sitting at — it's subnet mask ordering that makes that happen.

dnscmd Cheat Sheet

This has been a long chapter, I know, and thank you for staying with me to its end. I cannot stress enough that knowing DNS is one of the most essential arts for any successful network administrator, and if you review and learn what we've covered here then you'll be well on the way to DNS proficiency. Before I go, however, I want to leave you with a small gift — my dnscmd cheat sheet. You've already heard me preach about the power and value of the command line, so I won't do that again, but I *will* agree that the CLI requires a bit more remembering than GUIs do, so I hope this table makes that remembering a bit easier. (And don't forget that there's still more to learn about DNS's AD-specific aspects — but we'll take those up in *Essential Technologies*!) This is by no means a complete explanation of everything that dnscmd does — just the stuff that I use regularly.

Function	*dnscmd* Option	Example	Comments
Do any dnscmd command on a remote system	dnscmd *remoteservername command*	dnscmd main.bigfirm.com /zoneprint bigfirm.com	
Create a primary zone	dnscmd /zoneadd *zonename* /primary	dnscmd /zoneadd bigfirm.com /primary	
Create a secondary zone	dnscmd /zoneadd *zonename* /secondary *master IP address*	dnscmd /zoneadd bigfirm.com /secondary 192.168.1.1	
Host a zone on a server based on an existing (perhaps restored) zone file	dnscmd /zoneadd*zonename* /primary /file*filename* /load	dnscmd /zoneadd bigfirm.com /primary /file bigfirm.com.dns /load	
Delete a zone from a server	dnscmd /zonedelete*zonename* [/f]	dnscmd /zonedelete bigfirm.com /f	(Without the /f, dnscmd asks you if you really want to delete the zone.)
Show all of the zones on a DNS server	dnscmd /enumzones	dnscmd /enumzones	
Dump (almost) all of the records in a zone	dnscmd /zoneprint *zonename*	dnscmd /zoneprint bigfirm.com	Doesn't show glue records.

Function	*dnscmd* Option	Example	Comments
Add an A record to a zone	dnscmd /recordadd *zonename hostname* A *ipaddress*	dnscmd /recordadd bigfirm.com mypc A 192.168.1.33	
Add an NS record to a zone	dnscmd /recordadd *zonename* @ NS *servername*	dnscmd /recordadd bigfirm.com @ A dns3.bigfirm.com	
Delegate a new child domain, naming its first DNS server	dnscmd /recordadd *zonename childname* NS*dnsservername*	dnscmd /recordadd bigfirm.com test NS main.bigfirm.com	This would create the test.bigfirm.com DNS child domain under the bigfirm.com DNS domain.
Add an MX record to a zone	dnscmd /recordadd *zonename* @ MX*priority servername*	dnscmd /recordadd bigfirm.com @ MX 10 mail.bigfirm.com	
Add a PTR record to a reverse lookup zone	dnscmd /recordadd *zonename lowIP* PTR *FQDN*	dnscmd /recordadd 1.168.192.in-addr .arpa 3 A pc1.bigfirm.com	This is the PTR record for a system with IP address 192.168.1.3.
Modify a zone's SOA record	dnscmd /recordadd *zonename* @ SOA *primaryDNSservername responsible-emailipaddress serialnumber refreshinterval retryinterval expireinterval defaultTTL*	dnscmd /recordadd bigfirm.com @ SOA winserver.bigfirm .com mark.bigfirm.com 41 1800 60 2592000 7200	Ignores the serial number if it's not greater than the current serial number.
Delete a resource record	dnscmd /recorddelete *zonename recordinfo* [/f]	dnscmd /recorddelete bigfirm.com @ NS main.bigfirm.com /f	Again, /f means "don't annoy me with a confirmation request, just do it."
Create a resource record and incorporate a nonstandard TTL	dnscmd /recordadd *zonename leftmostpartofrecord TTL restofrecord*	dnscmd /recordadd bigfirm.com pc34 3200 A 192.168.1.4	
Reload a zone from its zone file in \windows\ system32\dns	dnscmd /zonereload *zonename*	dnscmd /zonereload bigfirm.com	Really only useful on primary DNS servers.

Function	*dnscmd* Option	Example	Comments
Force DNS server to flush DNS data to zone file	dnscmd /zonewriteback*zonename*	dnscmd /zonewriteback bigfirm.com	
Tell a primary whom to allow zone transfers to	dnscmd /zoneresetsecondaries *zonename* /nonsecure|securens	dnscmd /zonereset-secondaries bigfirm.com /nonsecure	That example says to allow anyone who asks to get a zone transfer.
Enable/ disable DNS NOTIFY	dnscmd /zoneresetsecondaries *zonename* /notify|/nonotify	dnscmd /zonere-setsecondaries bigfirm.com /nonotify	Example disables DNS notification, which is contrary to the default settings.
Tell a secondary DNS server to request any updates from the primary	dnscmd /zonerefresh*zonename*	dnscmd /zonerefresh bigfirm.com	
Enable or disable dynamic DNS on a zone	dnscmd /config*zonename* /allowupdate 1|0	1 enables, 0 disables, 0 is default	
Stop the DNS service	Either net stop dns or sc stop dns		(No dnscmd command for this.)
Start the DNS service	Either net start dns or sc start dns		(No dnscmd command for this.)
Install the DNS service on a 2008 full install system	servermanagercmd -install dns		
Install the DNS service on a 2008 Server Core system	ocsetup DNS-Server-Core-Role		Case matters — ocsetup dns-server-core-role would fail.
Uninstall the DNS service on a 2008 Server full install system	servermanagercmd -remove dns		
Uninstall the DNS service on a 2008 Server Core system	ocsetup /uninstall DNS-Server-Core-Role		

Function	*dnscmd* Option	Example	Comments
Configure a client's preferred DNS server	`netsh int ip set dns`*connectionname* `static`*ipaddress*	`netsh int ip set dns ''local area connection'' static 192.168.1.7`	
Configure a client's alternate DNS server	`netsh int ip add dns`*ipaddress* `index=`*ordinal*	`netsh int ip add dns ''local area connection'' 192.168.1.200 index=2`	You may include as many extra DNS servers as you like; just change the index value.

Chapter 14

Automatic IP Setup: DHCP Essentials

Whether you're hooking up a two-computer intranet in your house to share an Internet connection or weaving a world-spanning Internet, you've got to solve two basic problems. First, every system on the network needs a unique IP address and requires configuration — it needs to know the address of its default router, what its domain name is, where the nearest DNS server is, and the like. Microsoft OS–based networks that are TCP/IP-based need the Dynamic Host Configuration Protocol (DHCP) to accomplish IP configuration.

This chapter will cover DHCP in an IPv4 environment. Server 2008 introduces some new DHCP topics that will be covered in the more advanced books in the *Mastering Windows Server 2008* series.

DHCP: Automatic TCP/IP Configuration

In Chapter 10, you learned how to set up IP on a Server 2008 system. Now ask yourself, "Do I really want to walk around to 3,000 workstations and do this by hand?" Auuugghhhh! Oops, sorry, what I really meant was, "Of course not." Who wants to have to remember which IP address you gave to *that* machine so you don't put the address on *this* machine? Or how'd you like to get a phone call every time some visiting dignitary needs an IP address for his laptop? No thanks. DHCP will greatly simplify the task, so let's see how to set it up.

By the way, this discussion assumes you've already read Chapter 10; don't think if you decided from the start to go with DHCP that you could jump in here without reading that chapter.

Simplifying TCP/IP Administration: BOOTP

"I have a little list / it never can be missed." Well, OK, that's not exactly what Pooh-Bah sings in *The Mikado*, but it fits here. You see, back when I first put TCP/IP on my company's computers, in 1993, I had to keep this list of PCs and IP addresses in a notebook. It was basically a kind of master directory of which IP addresses had been used so far.

Obviously, I had to consult it whenever I put TCP/IP on each new computer. Obvious, sure, but what's unfortunate is that I never seemed to have the notebook with me when I needed it. So I started keeping this list of computers and IP addresses on one of my servers, in a kind of common HOSTS file. It served two purposes: First, it told me what IP addresses were already used, and second, it gave me a HOSTS file to copy to the local computer's hard disk.

But, I recall thinking, this is silly. Keeping track of IP addresses and the machines using them is a rote, mechanical job — you know, the kind of job computers are good at.

Unknown to me, the Internet world apparently had a similar feeling and so invented a TCP/IP protocol called "the bootstrap protocol," usually abbreviated "BOOTP," which was first described in RFC 951. With BOOTP, a network administrator would first collect a list of MAC addresses for each LAN card. I've already mentioned the 48-bit identifiers on each network card, which are good examples of MAC addresses.

Next, the administrator would assign an IP address to each MAC address. A server on the company's intranet would then hold this table of MAC address/IP address pairs. Then, when a BOOTP-enabled workstation would start up for the day, it would broadcast a request for an IP address. The BOOTP server would recognize the MAC address from the broadcaster and would supply the IP address to the workstation. So BOOTP was (and is) a neat way to configure TCP/IP on a computer without having to travel to it.

But BOOTP doesn't stop there. Once a BOOTP server delivers an IP address to a computer, it also delivers a small startup operating system, a "bootstrap loader." (That's where the phrase "boot disk" comes from; in the old days, we'd have to hand-enter a small program into a computer to make the computer smart enough to be able to read its own disk drive or to start communicating on the network. That small program let a computer "lift itself by its own bootstraps," in the old phrase, and became known as a bootstrap loader and eventually just became "the boot loader," "boot disk" and similar phrases.) The idea with BOOTP was that you could have a computer that ran entirely off the network, with no local hard or floppy disks at all. As such a computer couldn't boot from its (nonexistent) floppy or hard disks, then it needed to get its startup programs from *somewhere*. A BOOTP server solved that by first handing the computer an IP address and then downloading a startup boot program.

This was a great improvement over the static IP addressing system that I've described so far. Administrators didn't have to physically travel to each workstation to give it its own IP address; they needed only to modify a file on the BOOTP server when a new machine arrived or if it was necessary to change IP addresses for a particular set of machines.

Another great benefit of BOOTP is that it provides protection from the "helpful user." Suppose you have user Tom, who sits next to user Dick. Dick's machine isn't accessing the network correctly, so helpful user Tom says, "Well, *I'm* getting on the Net fine, so let's just copy all of this confusing network stuff from my machine to yours." The result is that both machines end up with identical configurations — including identical IP addresses. So, Dick's machine will then encounter an IP Conflict error message, stating that this computer has the same IP address as another computer on the network. Tom's machine will continue to work fine, but Dick still cannot access the network! In contrast, if Tom's machine is only set up to go get its IP address from its local BOOTP server, then setting up Dick's machine identically will cause no harm, as it will just tell Dick's machine to get *its* address from the BOOTP server. Dick will get a different address (provided that the network administrator has typed in an IP address for Dick's MAC address), and all will be well.

DHCP: BOOTP Plus

BOOTP's ability to hand out IP addresses from a central location is terrific, but it's not dynamic, and in the PC world we typically don't care about getting bootstrap code from a central server; as you probably know, we tend to boot our computers from a local read-only memory chip called the BIOS and then from code on a local hard disk. Additionally, BOOTP requires the network administrator to find out beforehand all the MAC addresses of the Ethernet cards on the network. This isn't *impossible* information to obtain, but it's a bit of a pain (usually typing `ipconfig /all` from a command line yields the data). Furthermore, there's no provision for handing out temporary IP addresses, such as an IP address for a laptop used by a visiting executive. (I suppose you could keep a store of PCMCIA Ethernet cards whose MAC addresses had been preinstalled into the BOOTP database, but even so, it's getting to be some real work.) So someone came up with a somewhat simplified tool that is BOOTP-like but doesn't focus on delivering boot code: DHCP.

DHCP improves upon BOOTP in that you just give it a range of IP addresses that it's allowed to hand out, and it gives them out first come, first served to whatever computers request them. If, on the other hand, you want DHCP to maintain full BOOTP-like behavior, then you can; it's possible with DHCP to preassign IP addresses to particular MAC addresses (it's called *DHCP reservation*), as with BOOTP.

With DHCP, you only have to hardwire the IP addresses of a few machines, such as your BOOTP/DHCP server and your default gateway.

Both DHCP and BOOTP use UDP ports 67 and 68, so you won't be able to install both a BOOTP server and a DHCP server on the same computer. Now, Microsoft does not supply a BOOTP server; this note would mostly be relevant only if you tried to install a third-party BOOTP server. But Windows NT 4 Server and its newer siblings also allow you to make a computer a *BOOTP forwarding agent*. If you enable that software on a DHCP server, the server stops giving out IP addresses.

Let's see how to get a DHCP server up on your network so the IP addresses will start getting handed out, and then we'll take a look at how DHCP works.

Avoid Static IP: Use DHCP Everywhere!

In a minute, I'll get into the nitty-gritty of setting up DHCP servers and handing out IP addresses. But before I do, let's address a big, overall network configuration question: Which machines should have static IP addresses, and which machines should get their addresses from DHCP servers?

In general, the answer is that the only machines that should have static IP addresses should be your WINS servers, DNS servers, and DHCP servers. In actual fact, you'll probably put the WINS, DNS, and DHCP server functions on the same machines.

"But wait!" I hear you cry, "Are you suggesting that I let my domain controllers, mail servers, Web servers, and the like all have floating, random IP addresses assigned by DHCP willy-nilly?" No, not at all. Recall that you can assign a particular IP address to a particular MAC address using a DHCP reservation. My suggestion, then, is that you sit down and figure out which machines need fixed IP addresses, get the MAC addresses of the NICs in those machines, and then create reservations in DHCP for those machines. (You'll see how a bit later.)

Installing and Configuring DHCP Servers

DHCP servers are the machines that provide IP addresses to machines that request access to the LAN. DHCP works only if the TCP/IP software on the workstation is *built* to work with DHCP. That is, if the TCP/IP software includes a *DHCP client*. Nowadays, just about every network-aware OS includes DHCP clients — Macs, Linux, and every Microsoft desktop and server OS since 1994 have included them.

Installing the DHCP Service

To get ready for DHCP configuration:

◆ Have an IP address ready for your DHCP server — this is one computer on your network that *must* have a hardwired ("static") IP address.

◆ Know which IP addresses are free to assign. You use these available IP addresses to create a pool of IP addresses.

You install the software to make your server a DHCP server in the same way that you install most other network services — by adding a role. To add the DHCP Server role, open Server Manager from the Start menu (Start ➤ Server Manager), or click this button in the Quick Launch bar:

Highlight Roles, and click Add Roles, as shown in Figure 14.1.

FIGURE 14.1
Server Manager

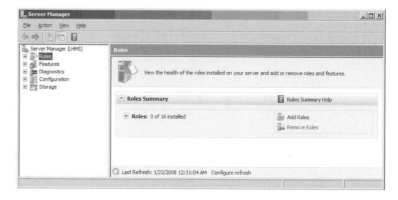

The Add Roles Wizard presents you with a Before You Begin page with suggestions on security settings such as ensure your administrator account has a strong password, set your IP address to static, and download the latest security updates. Click Next to get the Select Server Roles page. Place a check mark in the DHCP Server box, as shown in Figure 14.2, and click Next.

FIGURE 14.2
Select Server Roles page

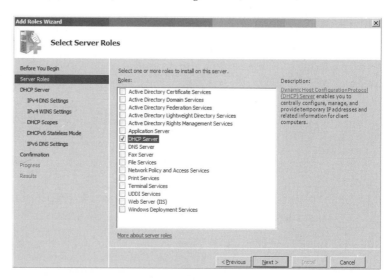

The DHCP Server page has some links for learning more about DHCP; click Next. Choose which network interface card (NIC) you want to bind DHCP to by selecting its IP address. Binding DHCP is telling DHCP which NIC it should listen on. If you have only one NIC, then of course you would want it bound to that NIC's IP address. If you have multiple network cards in your server, you could pick one, two, or all of them to listen for DHCP requests. Once you have configured your bindings, click Next. On the Specify IPv4 DNS Server Settings page, input your DNS server's IP address (this is a required field) in the Preferred DNS Server IPv4 Address box, and click the Validate button to ensure that you have indeed typed in the IP address of a server that is running DNS, as shown in Figure 14.3. Then click Next.

FIGURE 14.3
Specify IPv4 DNS Server Settings page

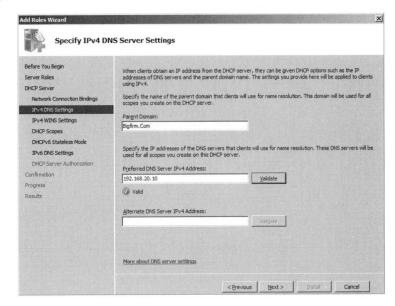

On the Specify IPv4 WINS Server Settings page, if your organization uses WINS input a preferred and alternate (if you have one) WINS server IP addresses, as shown in Figure 14.4, and click Next.

FIGURE 14.4
Specify IPv4 WINS Server Settings page

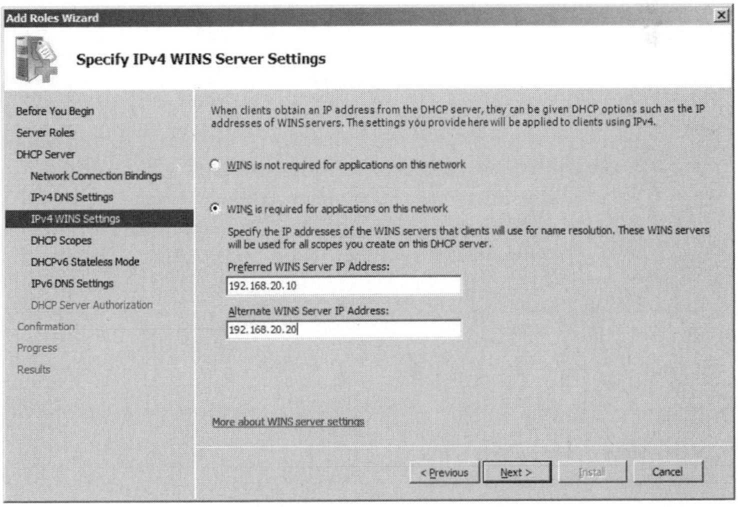

For DHCP to give out IP addresses, it must know the range of IP addresses that it can give out. Microsoft calls a range of IP addresses, and the descriptive information associated with them, a *scope*. To create a scope while installing DHCP, click the Add button on the Add or Edit DHCP Scopes page, as shown in Figure 14.5.

FIGURE 14.5
Add or Edit DHCP
Scopes page

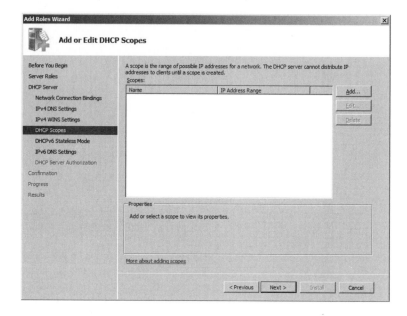

You will see the Add Scope dialog box. Give your scope a name (something descriptive), and then define the scope by inputting the starting and ending IP addresses along with a subnet mask and default gateway if you have one. The DHCP server in Figure 14.6 would hand out 192.168.20.50, 192.168.20.51, 192.168.20.52, and so on, until 192.168.20.100. Then the DHCP server would stop handing out IP addresses because it doesn't have any more in its scope. So, be sure you supply enough IP addresses for your environment. What happens if you or someone else set up a scope and you need to add to it? We'll get to that in a bit, as there are a couple of ways to handle that situation.

Notice the Subnet Type: the Wired option will have a lease duration of six days, and Wireless (click the down arrow to see Wireless) will have a default lease duration of eight days. The lease duration is how long a DHCP client will continue to use the IP address handed out by this DHCP server. What happens after six days (or eight days for Wireless)? The lease will have to be renewed by the client, but let's not get ahead of ourselves. I'll explain that later. The last thing you will need to do in this dialog box is decide whether you want to activate this scope. Activating a scope would tell the DHCP server to start handing out IP addresses as soon as you successfully complete this wizard. You could choose to set up a DHCP server by getting all your scopes created first and then activate the scope later. Click OK to take you to the Authorize DHCP Server page.

Now, before we go any further, I have to add a note here about DHCP and Active Directory because if you're running AD, then you won't be able to make your DHCP server work without a little adjustment — hence the note *now* rather than in the next chapter. If you're not running AD, then feel free to skip this section, but just remember that you saw this — or it'll come bite you *later*, when you've gotten your AD up and running.

FIGURE 14.6

Adding a scope

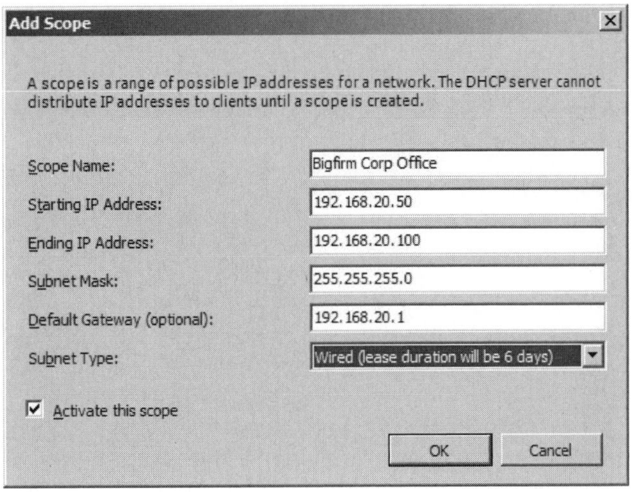

You see, under NT 4, 3.51, and 3.5, anyone with an NT Server installation CD could set up NT Server on a computer and make herself an administrator of that server. With administrative powers, she could then set up a DHCP server. Now, the job of a DHCP server, recall, is to hand out IP addresses to computers who want to be part of the network. The problem arises when the administrator of this new server decides just for fun to offer a bunch of meaningless IP addresses, a range of addresses that your firm doesn't actually own. The result? Well, the next time a machine in the company needs an IP address, it asks any server within earshot for an IP address. The server with the meaningless addresses responds, as do the valid servers — but the server with the bogus addresses is likely to respond more quickly than the valid servers (it doesn't have anything else to do) and so many client PCs will end up with IP addresses from the server with the bogus addresses. Those addresses won't route and so those people won't be able to get anything done on the network.

Why would someone set up a server with bogus addresses? Usually it's not for a malicious reason. Rather, it's more common that someone's just trying to learn DHCP and sets up a server to play around with, not realizing "test" DHCP servers are indistinguishable from "real" DHCP servers to the client machines. Such a DHCP server is called a *rogue* DHCP server.

Windows 2000 and later versions of Server solve the problem of rogue DHCP servers by disabling new DHCP servers until a member of AD's most powerful forest-wide group, the Enterprise Admins (you'll meet them in Chapter 15), "authorizes" them in the Active Directory. With those versions of Server, anyone can set up a DHCP server, but the server won't start handing out addresses until authorized. This isn't foolproof, as only machines that are members of Active Directory–based domains seek to be authorized. Someone who wanted to maliciously set up a rogue DHCP server could simply install a copy of Server 2003 and not join it to the domain, *then* set up a DHCP server — but, again, that's not the most common problem.

On the Authorize DHCP Server page shown in Figure 14.7, you'll have three options. If you're currently logged in as an Enterprise Admin, then you could select "Use current credentials." If you're not logged in as an Enterprise Admin, you could choose "Use alternate credentials" and then click the Specify button to type them in. The last option allows you to skip authorization altogether, but remember that before a DHCP server in an Active Directory domain can hand out IP addresses, it will have to be authorized. To authorize a DHCP server after the installation, please see the next section. After you have made your selection on this page click Next and on the

Confirm Installation Selections page review your choices as shown in Figure 14.8. If you would like to change anything just go back to that page and make your changes. You can go back by clicking the Previous button or on the left side of the screen where the pages of the wizard are listed simply click the page you want to go back to. If everything looks good on the Confirmation page click the Install button.

FIGURE 14.7
Authorizing the DHCP server

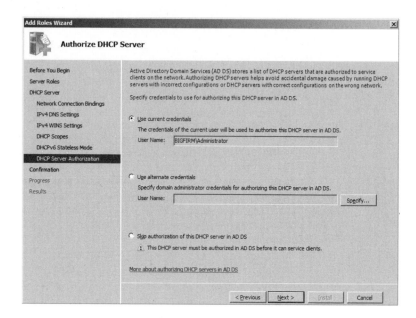

FIGURE 14.8
Confirmation screen

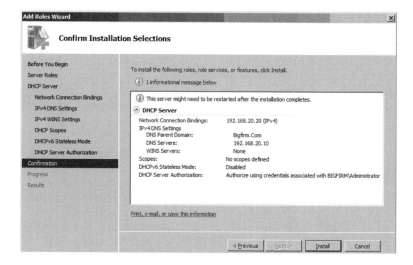

INSTALLING DHCP FROM THE COMMAND LINE

The tool you will use to install the DHCP Role is ServerManagerCmd.exe, and, no, it's not case sensitive. Type the following from a command prompt to install the DHCP role and store the log file containing any errors in an XML file called dhcpinstall.xml at the root of C:

```
servermanagercmd -install dhcp -resultpath dhcpinstall.xml
```

You'll like this; you needn't reboot afterward. You control DHCP with the DHCP snap-in, which you'll find in Administrative Tools: Start ➤ Administrative Tools ➤ DHCP. Start it up, and the opening screen looks like most MMC snap-ins, with the console pane on the left and the details pane on the right. This particular one lists your server, with a plus sign next to it. Click the plus sign and you'll see a screen like Figure 14.9.

FIGURE 14.9

DHCP manager opening screen

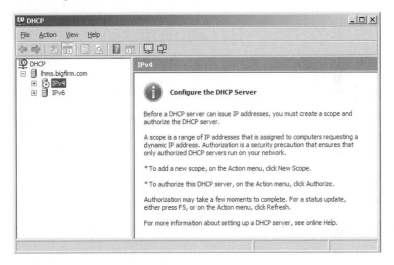

Notice that this snap-in lists the server in the console pane. That's because you can control as many DHCP servers as you like from this program. All you need do to add a DHCP server to the list of servers that you control is to highlight DHCP in the console pane and from the Action menu select Add Server.

AUTHORIZING DHCP SERVERS AFTER INSTALLATION (FOR ACTIVE DIRECTORY USERS)

If you didn't authorize your DHCP server during the installation, you'll need to before it will start handing out IP addresses. Click the plus sign next to the small icon that looks like a tower computer in Figure 14.9. You will see two nodes: IPv4 and IPv6. In this chapter we are covering only IP version 4 (IPv6 is a more advanced topic and is covered in *Mastering Windows Server 2008: Enterprise Technologies*, the third book in the *Mastering Windows Server 2008* series). Next to IPv4 there's a small circular blob. It's sort of small, so you may not be able to see it in the screen shot, but to the left of IPv4 is a small red arrow that points downward. That arrow represents a nice touch on Microsoft's part; it means the DHCP server is not yet authorized.

You authorize a server by starting up the DHCP snap-in while logged in as an Enterprise Admin. From the DHCP snap-in's Action menu, select "Manage authorized servers," and you'll see a dialog box like the one in Figure 14.10.

FIGURE 14.10
List of authorized DHCP servers

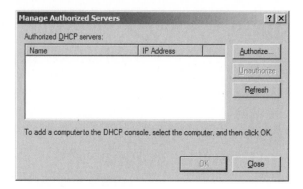

You can see that there are no servers authorized yet, so let's authorize this one. Click the Authorize button, and you'll see the dialog box in Figure 14.11.

FIGURE 14.11
Authorizing a DHCP server

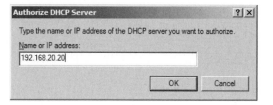

I've filled in the IP address of this server. Click OK, and you'll be asked to confirm that you do indeed want to authorize `1hms.bigfirm.com` with the IP address of 192.168.20.20. Click OK, and you'll return to the list of authorized servers. Click Close to close that dialog box and you'll see the DHCP snap-in looking as in Figure 14.9, save that the red down-pointing arrow is now a green up-pointing arrow.

You should be able to click the server and then press F5 to refresh the display to see the green arrow. In my experience, however, you usually have to close the DHCP manager and then reopen it to see the green arrow appear. (Once I not only had to close and reopen it, I also had to press F5. Clearly the DHCP manager isn't one of those chatty kinds of entities that constantly yammer on about their current condition — no, this app is downright reticent about its mood.)

Now you can offer IP addresses with this server.

If you *don't* have an Active Directory running, then you needn't authorize the server, as clearly there wouldn't be anything to authorize it *with*. But here's an interesting side effect of how 2000, 2003, or 2008 servers authorize DHCP servers. (Again, I know that some of you don't even *have* an Active Directory yet, but pay attention to this, or it'll bite you when you first set up your AD.)

If you are running a DHCP server on a network without an Active Directory, and all of a sudden bring up an AD, then the DHCP server will sense that, *even if it's not part of the AD domain*. It will then shut itself down. This *always* trips me up when I'm doing a class and I'm demonstrating Active Directory — first I get the DHCP and DNS servers up and running, then I create the AD, but then forget to authorize the already-running DHCP server that conveniently sniffs out the Active Directory and consequently disables itself. Anyway, just thought I'd mention it — now let's get back to the whys and wherefores of DHCP setup.

CREATING SCOPES AFTER INSTALLATION IS COMPLETE

To create a scope after DHCP has been installed, you'll go through the DHCP Management snap-in (Start ➤ Administrative Tools ➤ DHCP). Then expand your server's name, right-click IPv4, and choose New Scope. This launches the New Scope Wizard. Click Next from its opening screen, and you'll see a screen like the one in Figure 14.12.

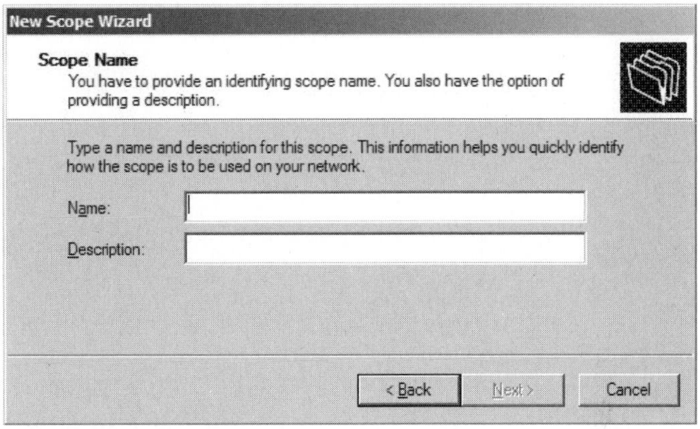

FIGURE 14.12

Naming the scope

In this screen, you simply identify the scope, giving it a name and a description. In my experience, I've never really figured out why there's a name *and* a description, as the name has no real use; it could well *be* a description, in effect. Fill in appropriate values for your network, and click Next to see a screen like Figure 14.13.

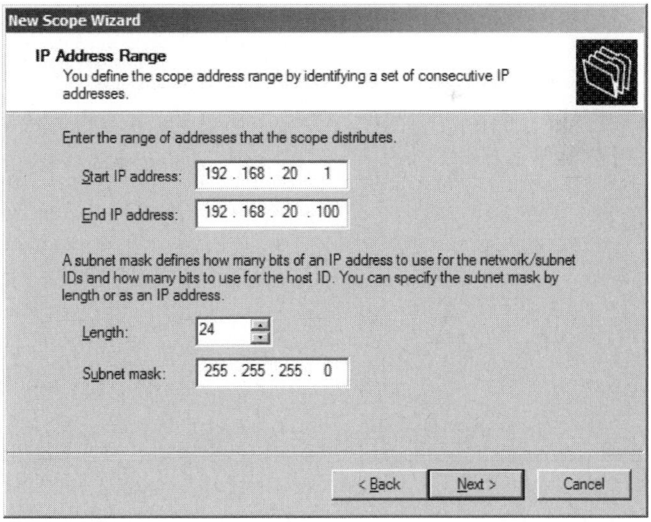

FIGURE 14.13

Defining the IP address range

SPECIFYING THE IP ADDRESS RANGE

As I've explained, a *scope* is simply a range of IP addresses — a pool from which they can be drawn. In the example in Figure 14.13, I've created a scope that ranges from 192.168.20.1 through

192.168.20.100 — in other words, I'm going to use DHCP to help me create and manage a class C intranet of nonroutable addresses.

I don't want to get too sidetracked on the issue of scopes just now (I'll cover multiscope considerations later), but let me mention why you'd have more than one scope on a DHCP server. You can assign a scope to each subnet serviced by your DHCP servers — and, yes, it is possible for one DHCP server to handle multiple subnets. In contrast, however, a DHCP server won't let you create more than one scope *in the same subnet*. I will, however, show you how to get more than one server to act as a DHCP server (for the sake of fault tolerance) in a minute.

I put DHCP in charge of giving out *all* of my Internet addresses, but clearly that makes no sense, as I must have at least *one* static IP address around — the one on my DHCP server. So I need to tell the DHCP server not to give *that* one away, but how to do it? Click Next to see the screen in Figure 14.14, where I'll tell the server what addresses to avoid.

FIGURE 14.14
Excluding address ranges

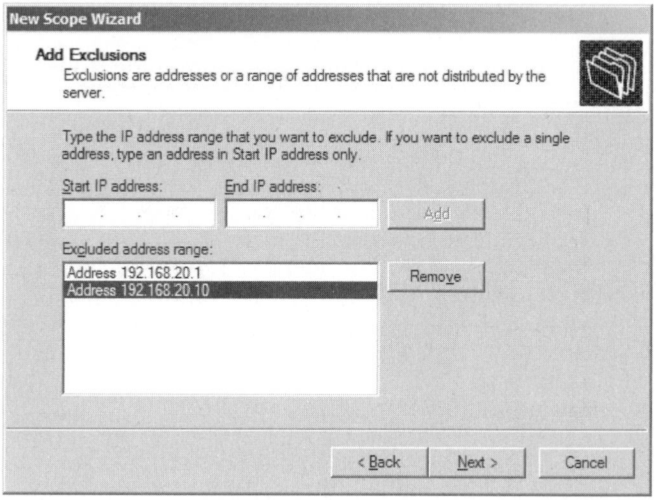

As you see, I've excluded several addresses: The .1 address is the default gateway, a NAT router, and the .10 address is this server itself. Notice that you can specify one address by itself; you don't *have* to specify starting and ending addresses in a one-address range.

SPECIFYING MORE RANGES: SUPERSCOPES

As you read in Chapter 3, in general there's a one-to-one relationship between physical network segments and subnets. IP was designed to let systems that could directly "shout" at each other do that, communicating directly rather than burdening routers.

Sometimes, however, you'll see two separate subnets on a single segment. That's often because a single network can't accommodate all of the segment's machines. For example, if you started your enterprise with 180 hosts and acquired a slash 24 network, you'd have enough addresses for 254 devices, presuming that you didn't subnet. But what about when your firm grows to need 300 machines? You might go out to your ISP and get another slash 24, another 254 addresses.

Now you've got two networks. You *could* break your network up into two segments and apply one set of network addresses to each segment. But you might not want to: Suppose your one segment can support all of your machines and you can't see the point in messing around with more routers — what then?

You create a *superscope*. The idea with a superscope is that it contains more than one range of IP addresses — more than one scope — but applies them to a single segment. You can do it simply — just define two separate scopes on a DHCP server, then right-click the server, choose New Superscope, and you'll have the superscope. You can then add scopes to the superscope as you like; don't forget that you might have to change the subnet mask to reflect the larger range of addresses.

But what about the mechanics of a superscope? When you put a new machine on this subnet and it broadcasts to find a DHCP server and get an IP address, will it get an IP address from the first scope or the second? The answer is that it doesn't matter. If you're just shoehorning two IP subnets onto the same physical segment simply because you're out of IP addresses on an existing subnet, then it doesn't matter whether a workstation gets an IP address from the first range of IP addresses or the second range of IP addresses, as all of the enterprise's routers know how to find either range.

Once in a while, however, you have two ranges of IP addresses on the same physical network for a reason — perhaps one range is composed of IANA- or ISP-assigned IP addresses and the other is composed of nonroutable addresses. You probably have good reasons, then, to put some computers on the routable addresses and some on the nonroutable addresses. But how to get DHCP to help there? After all, both the routable and nonroutable ranges are in the same shouting radius, so to speak. When a workstation asks DHCP for an address, how would DHCP know whether to give that workstation a routable or nonroutable address?

The answer is that DHCP can't — there's no magic here. There would have to be some kind of setting on the client that the client could use to give DHCP a clue about what network it wanted to be a member of, the routable or nonroutable. What you must do in a situation like that is decide which machines go in the routable network and which go in the nonroutable network and then enter their MAC addresses by hand into DHCP with *reservations* (which I'll cover later), much as network administrators must when using BOOTP instead of DHCP.

SETTING LEASE DURATION

Returning to the wizard, click Next, and you'll see a screen like Figure 14.15.

FIGURE 14.15
Setting lease duration

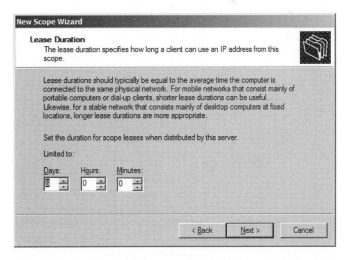

As you'll read in a few pages, when I explain the internals of DHCP, the DHCP server doesn't give the client PC an IP address to use forever. The client PC only gets the IP address for a specific period of time called a *lease*, and by the time the lease period's up, the client must either lease it or another address from a DHCP server, or the client must stop using IP altogether, immediately. But how long should that lease be? Although that was something of an issue when DHCP first appeared in NT 3.5, it doesn't matter all that much what you set it for now, so long as you set it for longer than a few days; the default of eight days is probably good.

Actually, what I just wrote is true unless, that is, you're creating a subnet that will serve computers connecting with wireless 802.1x network cards. Those connections tend to be more short-term, so in that case you might want to set the lease time shorter. What do you do if your subnet supports both wired and wireless connections? Then you have to make the call — short, long, or somewhere in between?

We'll talk more about lease durations when we discuss DHCP internals later. Click Next to move to Figure 14.16.

FIGURE 14.16
Configure DHCP Options screen

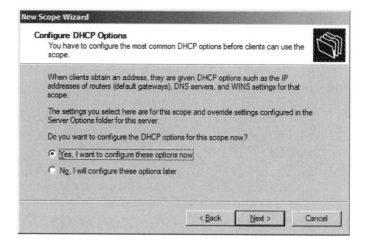

SETTING CLIENT OPTIONS

Remember all of those options in the Advanced tab for TCP/IP Properties when you configured static IP addresses in the preceding chapter? Well, you needn't travel around to the workstations and set them, as DHCP lets you configure those things right from the server. DHCP can provide default values for a whole host of TCP/IP parameters, including these basic items:

◆ Default gateway

◆ Domain name

◆ DNS server

◆ WINS server

Notice I said *default*. You can override any of these options at the workstation. For example, if you said that by default everyone's DNS server was 192.168.20.5 but wanted one particular PC to instead use the DNS server at 192.168.20.6, then you could just walk over to the PC and use the Advanced button in the TCP/IP properties page (see Chapter 10 if you don't recall how to find that) to enter a DNS name. Even though the DHCP server would offer a DNS server address of 192.168.20.5 to the PC, the PC's DHCP client software would see that the PC had been configured to use 192.168.20.6 instead and would use that address rather than 192.168.20.5. Any other DHCP-supplied options, however, wouldn't be ignored. The general rule is, then:

> *Any TCP/IP characteristic specifically configured on the client, such as a DNS server or WINS server, overrides any value that DHCP provides.*

Select "Yes, I want to configure these options now," and click Next to tell DHCP that you want to configure these options, and to see the first client option, shown in Figure 14.17.

FIGURE 14.17
Setting a default gateway

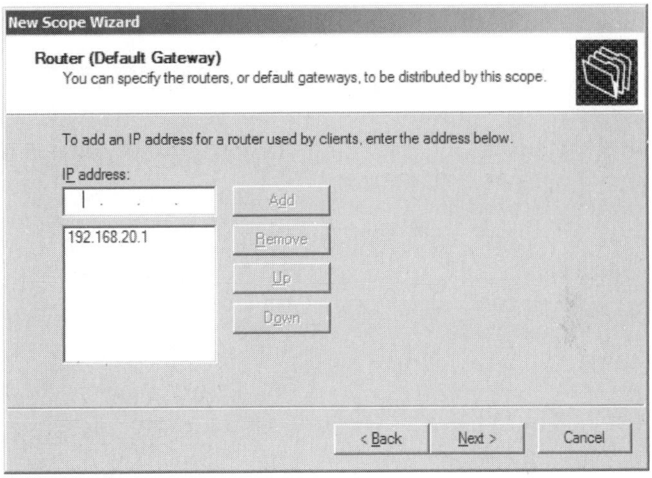

You may recall that in Chapter 10 I said that when configuring TCP/IP on a Windows system, there are four characteristics, so to speak: IP address, subnet mask, IP address of the default gateway, and address or addresses of local DNS server(s). By its nature, any DHCP lease gives the first two; this is the third.

Although you *can* enter any number of gateways, there's no point in entering more than one, as I've never found a situation wherein Microsoft's IP could use a second, third, or fourth possible gateway upon discovering that the first gateway is down. In fact, Microsoft specifically recommends that you only specify *one* default gateway on a system, even if it's got multiple NICs with independent Internet connections!

Following that advice, I've only specified one gateway, as you see in Figure 14.17. Click Next to see the next option screen, as in Figure 14.18.

In this Domain Name and DNS Servers screen, you tell the DHCP server that whenever it leases a client PC an IP address from this scope, it should also set that client PC's DNS domain name to — Bigfirm.Com, in this case — and to tell the client PC that it can find DNS servers at some address. I've chosen *not* to specify DNS servers, however, because *all* of the scopes in my enterprise share two DNS servers, and I don't want to have to reenter these DNS servers for every scope. As you'll see in a few pages, I can instead just tell this server, "Give this particular DNS server to *all* scopes." I have, however, specified a DNS suffix of Bigfirm.Com for all systems. That way, every system's DNS name ends with Bigfirm.Com and that means, as you'll see later in the DNS section, that the system registers itself with the DNS server for Bigfirm.Com. Click Next to see the WINS Servers screen, as seen in Figure 14.19.

Most of us will still have the necessary evil of WINS servers; here's where you tell the client where to find your enterprise's WINS servers.

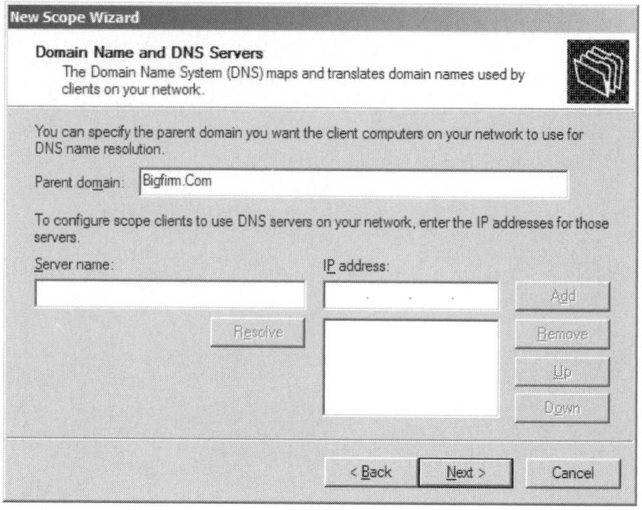

FIGURE 14.18
Setting the domain
name

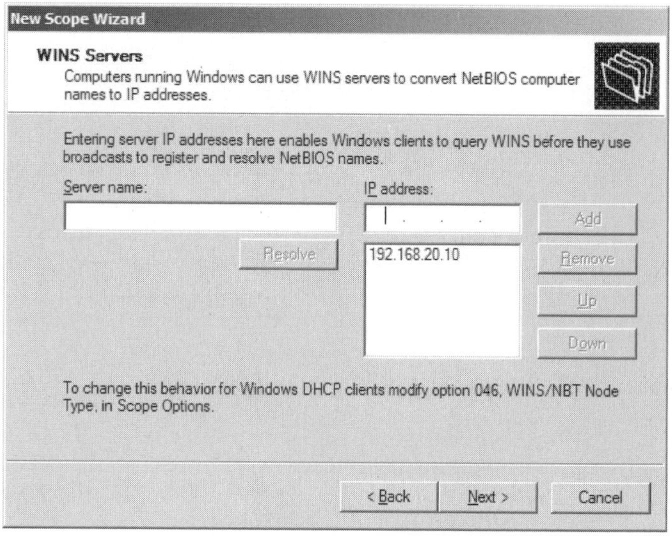

FIGURE 14.19
Setting the WINS
server(s)

ACTIVATING THE SCOPE

Click Next, and you can get the scope started, as you see in Figure 14.20.

That's all for the basic scope options, click Next and Finish to complete the wizard. The DHCP snap-in then looks like Figure 14.21.

Taking a minute and looking at the hierarchy in Figure 14.21 underscores a few things about how DHCP works. The snap-in enables you to control any number of DHCP servers from a central location, although you see only one in this example screen. Each server can have several subnets that it serves, with one range of IP addresses for each subnet. The ranges are called scopes, and again this example machine only shows one scope, but could host many — I've seen one large corporate DHCP server that hosts 1200 scopes! Within the scope there are several pieces of information: the range of addresses (Address Pool), the list of addresses that this server has given out

(Address Leases), addresses that we've preassigned to particular systems (Reservations, which I'll cover a bit later), and particular TCP/IP settings that the DHCP server should give to any clients (Scope Options). If you were to click Scope Options, then you'd notice that the options include something we didn't set — WINS/NBT Node Type. That's DHCP-ese for the fact that the client PC will be set up to use a WINS server — in other words — that the client will be set up as something called a *hybrid node*, which I'll cover later in this chapter in the WINS section.

FIGURE 14.20
Activating the scope

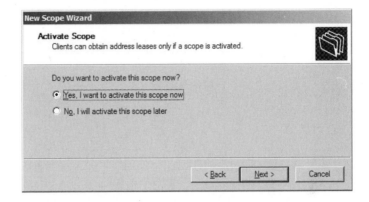

FIGURE 14.21
DHCP snap-in with activated scope

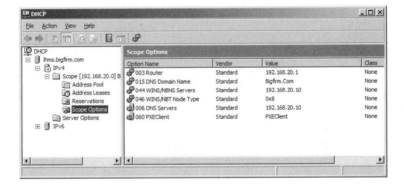

SETTING OPTIONS FOR ALL SCOPES

Notice the folder lower in the interface labeled Server Options in Figure 14.21. The server options are useful when you're putting more than one scope on a server. It could be that if you have three different subnets and a couple hundred machines, you've only got two DNS servers, and those machines serve your entire enterprise. When configuring those scopes, it would be a pain to have to retype in those DNS servers — the same two DNS servers — for all three scopes. Server Options solves that problem by allowing you to set options for *all* of a given server's scopes in one operation. Just right-click the Server Options folder and choose Configure Options to see a dialog box like the one in Figure 14.22.

Here I've selected the DNS servers box and you can see that it allows me to enter DNS server addresses, as the wizard did. A bit of scrolling down shows that there are a *lot* of potential DHCP options. But, despite the fact that there seem to be bushels of sadly unused parameters mutely begging to be used, *don't*. Even though they exist, the Microsoft DHCP *client* — the part of Windows,

DOS, Windows 9x, NT, Windows 2000, XP, 2003, and 2008 that knows how to get IP addresses from a DHCP server — does not know how to use any options save the ones I just mentioned. Microsoft included the other things just to remain compatible with BOOTP.

FIGURE 14.22
Server Options dialog box

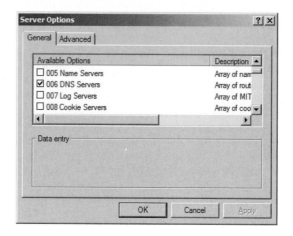

FORCING A PARTICULAR IP ADDRESS ON A CLIENT: DHCP RESERVATIONS

Sometimes, BOOTP doesn't seem like a bad idea. There are times that you'd like to be able to say, *this* computer gets *that* IP address. Fortunately, it's easy to accomplish that with DHCP reservations.

Look at the DHCP snap-in and you'll see a folder within your scope labeled Reservations. Right-click that folder and choose New Reservation. You'll see a dialog box like the one in Figure 14.23.

FIGURE 14.23
Reserving an IP address

Here, you see that I'm assigning the .25 address to a machine with a particular MAC address. So far, it sounds like DHCP pretty much hasn't changed since NT 4, and in large measure that's true. But it has added superscopes, support for dynamic DNS even on systems that don't understand dynamic DNS and now with Server 2008 IPv6 support. And there's one more interesting difference. Once you've created a reservation, open the Reservations folder and you'll see an object representing that reservation. Right-click it and you'll see Configure Options; click that and you'll see that you can set things like DNS server, domain name, WINS server, and the like for one specific reservation! Now, that's a pretty neat new feature.

ADVANCED OPTIONS: USING AND UNDERSTANDING USER AND VENDOR CLASSES

As you've seen, you can assign different DHCP options either to all scopes (the Server Options folder) or to a particular scope. You've even seen that you can assign DHCP options to a particular machine's reservation! But there's another way to assign options, through *user classes* and *vendor classes*. Here's how you use them.

You can make a machine a member of a user class by just telling the computer that it's a member of that class. You could have classes such as laptop or test computers.

Machines are also potentially members of vendor classes, some of which you can't control membership — it's hard-wired into their operating systems. For example, all Windows 2000 machines are automatically members of a vendor class called Microsoft and one called Microsoft Windows 2000; Windows 98 computers are automatically members of vendor classes Microsoft and Microsoft Windows 98. Vendor classes determine what options are available for you to give to your DHCP client.

You can use DHCP to apply a particular option to a particular system. The vendor class determines which options are available to the system — "default" includes the basic by-the-RFC stuff you've always seen, for example, Microsoft vendor options would offer nonstandard new options that would only be relevant to a system running a Microsoft operating system — and the user class determines whether to apply that option. Thus, you could use user and vendor options to say, "If this system is a member of the IBM-laptops class (a user class), then set the Router option (which is in the DHCP Standard Options vendor)."

You can see the user and vendor class controls like so:

1. Open the DHCP snap-in (Start ➤ Administrative Tools ➤ DHCP).

2. Open either a scope's options or the server options by right-clicking the Scope Options or Server Options folders and choosing Configure Options.

3. Click the Advanced tab. You'll see something like Figure 14.24.

FIGURE 14.24
Advanced tab showing "Vendor class" and "User class" drop-down lists

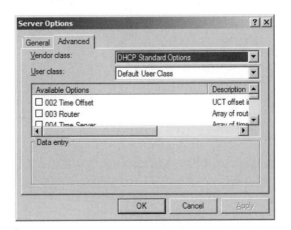

Prebuilt Vendor Classes

Click the "Vendor class" drop-down list, and you'll see four options: DHCP Standard Options, Microsoft Options, Microsoft Windows 2000 Options, and Microsoft Windows 98 Options. (Interesting that there are Win2K options, but no XP or 2003 options, hmmm?) While DHCP Standard Options is enabled, notice that you get all of the usual options — router, domain name, time server, name server, and so on. But click Microsoft Options, and you'll see a few non-RFC options that Microsoft added.

The Microsoft Disable Netbios Option tells the computer to shut down the NetBIOS-over-TCP (NetBT) interface. If you don't know what NetBT is, I covered it in Chapter 12, feel free to go back and read it if you skipped that chapter. But briefly, it's a piece of software that pretty much all NT-aware software built before Windows 2000 depends upon. If you've got an NT 4 workstation logging onto an Active Directory–based domain, then you need NetBT. Most modern networks still have enough pre-2000 stuff around that they still need NetBT, but in time I'd guess — most of us will be able to shut NetBT off. The result, once you can do it, is a noticeably faster network. To enable this — that is, to shut off NetBT — check the box next to Microsoft Disable NetBIOS Option, which will enable the Data Entry/Long field; enter **0x2**, as shown in Figure 14.25.

FIGURE 14.25
Disabling NetBIOS

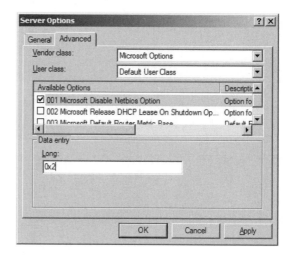

Check the Microsoft Release DHCP Lease on Shutdown Option and fill the Data Entry/Long field with **0x1** to enable. This tells a Windows 2000 system and later to release its DHCP lease upon shutdown, as the name indicates. Why is this useful? Consider this scenario: An employee works at her laptop in the office during the day, with her laptop connected to the company network via an Ethernet connection. The user shuts down the machine and takes it home. At home, she wants to check her mail, so connects her laptop to a phone line to dial in. She turns on the computer, which sees that it has an Ethernet card that has a DHCP lease. It tries to re-contact the DHCP server but fails, but that's no problem — it's got time on the lease and merrily sets up a TCP/IP stack atop an Ethernet card that's not attached to anything. The user dials up and now the computer has *two* IP stacks — one that actually goes somewhere, via the modem, and one that doesn't do anything. Some services bind to the useless Ethernet card and the user experiences either failures or slow service. One answer: Tell the user to disable the Ethernet card. Another answer: Tell the user to type **ipconfig /release** before shutting down the laptop at work. But the easier answer is to enable this feature — shutdowns lead to DHCP lease releases. (This would also bedevil users with Ethernet connections at home, so it's a good practice in that case also.)

The third option lets you modify the default metric of DHCP-supplied gateways. I'm honestly not sure where this would be useful.

Click Microsoft Windows 2000 Options, and you'll get the same three options. Click Microsoft Windows 98 Options, and you won't see any options — apparently Microsoft has hard-coded the vendor class into 98 but didn't do much with it.

Prebuilt User Classes

Next, click the "User class" drop-down list, and you'll see four prebuilt user classes: Default BOOTP Class, Default Network Access Protection Class, Default Routing and Remote Access Class, and Default User Class. Here's where you'll see each of the classes:

Default BOOTP Class   All of your Windows 2000, XP, and 2003 systems will be members of this class.

Default Network Access Protection Class   Server 2008 now offers a new user class as a component for using Network Access Protection or NAP. NAP allows you to configure specifications for every machine that is plugged into your network. If the specifications are not met the machine is assigned an IP address that quarantines it. Or rather, puts it in a subnet that cannot harm your production environment. Some of those specifications can mandate service pack or patch levels or ensuring their anti-virus scanning signatures are up to date. NAP is a very complex technology and way outside the scope of this chapter. For more detailed information on NAP, please see the third book in this series: *Mastering Windows Server 2008: Enterprise Technologies*.

Default User Class   The class that a system reports if it lacks class (finds belching in public funny, blue screens just for the heck of it, that kind of thing) or, more likely, has a DHCP client that simply doesn't understand what a user class is in the first place — DHCP user classes weren't even a fully accepted RFC standard when Microsoft released the original version in Windows 2000. An NT 4 system, then, would end up with Default User Class.

Default Routing and Remote Access Class   If you're connected via RRAS, then you're in this class. This is potentially a pretty useful class; for example, the DHCP Help for Windows 2008 shows you how to set the lease times for remote/dial-in users — members of the Default Routing and Remote Access Class — to smaller values than for other users; that way, folks who typically only visit a site for a day end up with a day-long rather than a week-long lease.

You can see which user classes a system belongs to (there is no way to view the vendor classes for a system) by typing **ipconfig /showclassid ***; a sample run might look like the following:

```
C:\>ipconfig /showclassid *

Windows IP Configuration

DHCP Class ID for Adapter "Local Area Connection":
      DHCP ClassID Name . . . . . . . . : Default
         Routing and Remote Access Class
      DHCP ClassID Description  . . . . : User
        class for remote access Clients
      DHCP ClassID Name . . . . . . . . : Default BOOTP Class
      DHCP ClassID Description  . . . . : User class for BOOTP Clients
      DHCP ClassID Name . . . . . . . . : Laptop
         DHCP  ClassID  Description   . . . . :  Identifies  laptops
```

Here, this computer is a member of three user classes — Default BOOTP Class (it's a Windows 2000 computer), Default Routing and Remote Access Class, and a class called Laptop (which I created). *Note*, however, that you may get different results from an `ipconfig /showclassid *` if you try it on different OSes; for some reason I sometimes get different class IDs when running this on 2000 machines than I do on XP, 2003, or 2008 machines.

User-Defined User and Vendor Classes

How did I define my own user class? In two steps. First, I told the DHCP server about the new user class and, second, I told some of my workstations that they were members of the class.

You create a new user class in the DHCP snap-in. Right-click the IPv4 node and choose Define User Classes, and you'll get a dialog box like the one in Figure 14.26.

FIGURE 14.26
DHCP user classes

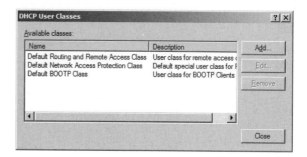

This dialog box doesn't show the Default User Class; however, your DHCP server — *every* 2000-based and later DHCP server, in fact — has it. Let's create a new user class and use it. Suppose I want all of the people in the headquarters office building to use different DNS servers than the other buildings on campus. To create the new user class, I click Add from Figure 14.26. Then in "Display name" I fill in **Headquarters**, and in Description I fill in **Headquarters DNS Servers**, as you see in Figure 14.27.

FIGURE 14.27
New user class for
Headquarters building

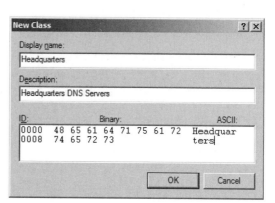

The only non-straightforward part of filling out the dialog box was the ID part; it's not obvious, but you've got to click the mouse in the empty area below the word *ASCII* to be able to type in the class identifier. You can't have blanks in the identifier. Click OK and Close to return to the DHCP snap-in. Now right-click Server Options again and choose Configure Options, click Advanced, and notice that under User Class, there is now a class called Headquarters. (Case doesn't matter anymore — so "Headquarters" or "headquarters" will work the same.) Choose Headquarters under User Class. Now you want to assign the DNS servers 192.168.20.5 and 192.168.20.6 to the Headquarters users class, and that's in the default options, so for Vendor Class just choose DHCP Standard Options. Look for the line 006 DNS Servers, choose it, and in the Date Entry/IP Address field, enter the IP addresses of the DNS servers clicking the Add button after each to see a figure similar to Figure 14.28. Then click OK. You're ready on the server side. Don't worry about the hex on the left side; it's just an alternative way of entering the data.

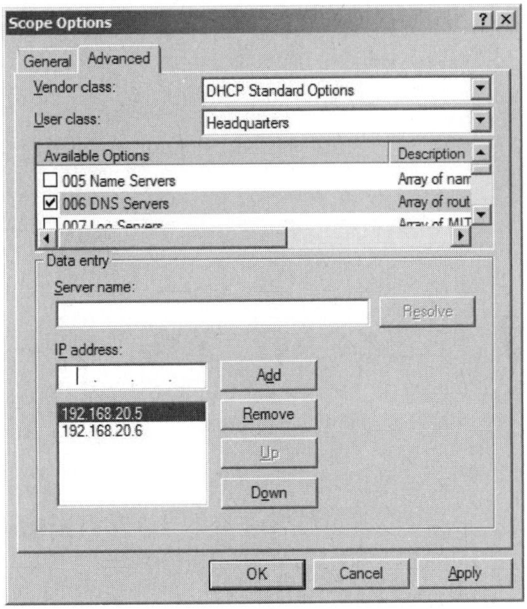

FIGURE 14.28
Configuring DNS servers for Headquarters user class

Next, find a machine in the Headquarters building and make it a member of the Headquarters user class. To do this you'll need to open a command line and type this:

```
ipconfig /setclassid "Local Area Connection" Headquarters
```

Then type **ipconfig /renew** and **ipconfig /all**. You should get an output something like this:

```
Windows IP Configuration

        Host Name . . . . . . . . . . . . : lhms
        Primary Dns Suffix  . . . . . . . : Bigfirm.Com
        Node Type . . . . . . . . . . . . : Hybrid
        IP Routing Enabled. . . . . . . . : No
        WINS Proxy Enabled. . . . . . . . : No
        DNS Suffix Search List. . . . . . : Bigfirm.Com

Ethernet adapter Local Area Connection:

        Connection-specific DNS Suffix  . :
```

```
Description . . . . . . . . . . . . : Intel(R) PRO/1000 MT Network Connection
Physical Address. . . . . . . . . : 00-0C-29-A3-82-AE
DHCP Enabled. . . . . . . . . . . : Yes
Autoconfiguration Enabled . . . . : Yes
IPv4 Address. . . . . . . . . . . : 192.168.20.40(Preferred)
Subnet Mask . . . . . . . . . . . : 255.255.255.0
Default Gateway . . . . . . . . . : 192.168.20.1
DHCP Class ID . . . . . . . . . . : headquarters
DNS Servers . . . . . . . . . . . : 192.168.20.5
DNS Servers . . . . . . . . . . . : 192.168.20.6
NetBIOS over Tcpip. . . . . . . . : Enabled
```

Two notes on this:

First, notice in the `ipconfig /setclassid` line where I have `"Local Area Connection"` in quotes. That is the *name* of your network adapter. Didn't know that it *had* a name? To see it, click the Start button and right-click Network and choose Properties. In the Network and Sharing Center under the domain name your network cards will be listed along with their name. The default name is *Local Area Connection,* but you can rename it. If you have more than one NIC, then you'll have a different name.

If this doesn't work the first time that you do it, don't be surprised — this often behaves a bit flakily the first time you use it — I have no idea why. Try an `ipconfig /release` after you do the `/setclassid` command before the `ipconfig /renew`.

The DHCP user class will survive reboots; to clear the user class info, type this:

```
ipconfig /setclassid "Local Area Connection"
```

And if your NIC has a different name than Local Area Connection, then substitute that, of course.

If you script your installs, then you can also set an adapter's class ID by adding this parameter to its [MS_TCPIP parameters] section:

```
DHCPClassId = name
```

The steps for creating a vendor class are identical to a user class except for two things. First, when you right-click IPv4, choose Define Vendor Classes. Second, the settings you can configure are a little more complicated. Hardware vendors have specifications for their hardware. These specifications can be set in a DHCP vendor class so that when a Dell machine boots, these Dell specs tell the DHCP server that it is a Dell computer. The specifications are set differently for each vendor. If you need to create a vendor class, you'll have to get those specs from the specific computer company. To fully understand vendor classes, you can refer to RFCs 1700, 2131, and 2132, which document them in great detail.

ADVANCED SERVER CONFIGURATION

Before leaving configuration, let's take a look at some overall server configuration items — in particular, logging and DNS client registration. In the DHCP snap-in, right-click the IPv4 node and choose Properties. You'll see a page with four tabs. The first is named General, as you see in Figure 14.29.

FIGURE 14.29
General server
configuration page

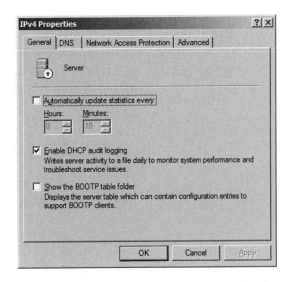

The main thing to notice here is the logging option. It's a default option, so don't worry about having to check it. But where is the log kept? Well, for one thing, there are seven logs, one for each day of the week — that makes finding a record for an action on a particular day easier. The logs are in simple ASCII format, so you can examine them with Notepad, although it would be nicer if the DHCP snap-in would go get them *for* you. They're in C:\Windows\system32\dhcp in files whose names include the day of the week like DhcpSrvLog-Mon, DhcpSrvLog-Tue, and so on. Part of one log looks like the following:

```
00,01/12/08,11:13:51,Started,,,,,0,6,,,
55,01/12/08,11:13:51,Authorized(servicing),,Bigfirm.Com,,,0,6,,,
24,01/12/08,11:13:52,Database Cleanup Begin,,,,,0,6,,,
25,01/12/08,11:13:52,0 leases expired and 0 leases deleted,,,,,0,6,,,
63,01/12/08,00:12:00,Restarting rogue detection,,,
51,01/12/08,00:12:30,Authorization succeeded,,Bigfirm.com,
11,01/12/08,00:12:45,Renew,192.168.20.56,
PC400.Bigfirm.com,00105A27D97A
10,01/12/08,00:48:00,Assign,192.168.100,
PC405.Bigfirm.com,5241532000105A27D97A000000000000
```

Rogue detection is a process whereby the DHCP server seeks to find unauthorized DHCP servers. To entrap these dastards, the DHCP server craftily pretends it is just a PC looking for an IP address. It gets offers from other DHCP servers, and the DHCP server then checks their IP addresses against the list of authorized DHCP servers in the Active Directory. If it finds a scoundrel, then it reports that in the Event Viewer.

On the seventh line, you see that the machine at 192.168.20.56 has "renewed" its IP address — that is to say, it has said to the DHCP server, "You once gave me this IP address and the lease is running out. May I extend the lease?" Line nine assigns 192.168.20.100 to computer PC405.

The properties page has another interesting tab, the DNS tab. Click it, and you'll see a screen like the one in Figure 14.30.

FIGURE 14.30
Configuring the dynamic
DNS client from DHCP

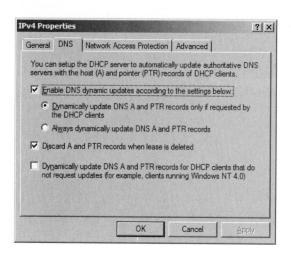

Although DNS is a topic for later in the book let me jump ahead a bit and explain briefly how it works. DNS is a database of machines and names: My local DNS server is the machine that knows there's a machine named dc1.bigfirm.com with an IP address of 192.168.20.11. But how does it *know* that? With DNS under NT 4, I'd have to start a program called the DNS Manager and hand-enter the information. But with the DNS client built into Windows 2000 and later OSes, dc1.bigfirm.com is smart enough to talk to its local DNS server and say, "Listen, I don't know if you knew this, but I'm a machine on the network, my name's dc1.bigfirm.com, and my IP address is 192.168.20.11." Additionally, the DNS server — which is running Server 2008, although any DNS server on Windows 2000 Server or later will work — is smart enough to *hear* this information; older DNS servers wouldn't be expecting machines to register themselves with their local DNS server, and the local DNS server wouldn't have a clue about what to do with the information anyway. But post-1998 DNS servers have a feature called *dynamic* DNS, which enables them to accept this name/address (*name registration*) information from other machines rather than having to have a human type the information in.

There are two important points to notice in the preceding paragraph. First, the DNS server's got to be smart enough to listen to and act upon the name registrations when they come from the clients. Second, the clients have to be smart enough to *issue* name registration information! If my workstation's running NT 4 rather than Windows 2000 or later, then it hasn't been programmed to offer name/address information to its DNS server because the whole dynamic DNS technology didn't even exist in 1996 when Microsoft wrote NT 4! From the point of view of the state-of-the-art DNS server running on the Windows 2000 or Server 2003, then, the old Windows 9*x*, Windows for Workgroups, and NT clients are just plain dumb. Or, more exactly, from the point of view of the DNS server, those clients *don't even exist*. There's no way that the DNS server could figure out they are there.

That's what the dialog box in Figure 14.30 accomplishes. This DHCP server will notice when it's handing out an IP address to a machine that doesn't know about dynamic DNS; although the DHCP server cannot modify the code running on the older client, it can fill in for the older client's lack of knowledge, and register the client's name/address with DNS for it. Notice the option labeled "Dynamically update DNS A and PTR records for DHCP clients that do not request updates"; that's the feature I've been discussing here. Make sure that box is checked, and DHCP will handle the DNS registrations for the older systems.

The Network Access Protection tab is covered in Chapter 6 in the third book, *Mastering Windows Server 2008: Enterprise Technologies.* Click the Advanced tab to see the conflict detection settings, audit log file path (your logs), DHCP server bindings, and the DNS dynamic updates registration credentials, as shown in Figure 14.31.

FIGURE 14.31
Advanced settings

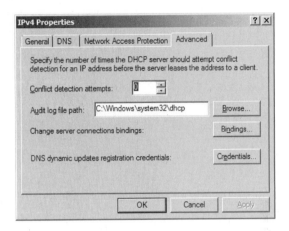

Conflict detection can be performed as a fail safe to ensure that the IP address the DHCP server is about to hand out is not currently in use. The way conflict detection works is before a DHCP server hands out an IP address, it will ping it *x* number of times. If the DHCP server receives a PING response, then it knows that the address is currently in use and will try another one. So, once again, it will begin by pinging the address it is going to give out.... Okay, first, the number of times that a ping is performed is based on the number you change the 0 to. If you change the 0 to 1, then the DHCP server will ping an IP address only one time. If you set this to 2, then two pings will be sent to each IP address before that IP address can be distributed. Enabling conflict detection can impose some additional overhead on a server and setting the conflict detections attempts higher than 2 is not recommended because it puts an unnecessary load on the server.

You can change which network card listens for DHCP requests by clicking the Bindings button and selecting the NIC's IP address.

The DNS dynamic updates registration credentials can be set from the Credentials button. Simply input the username and password of an account that will own the DNS records when the DHCP server dynamically registers on the client's behalf. Ownership of DNS records? Yes, in the past there were issues with who the owner of a DNS record was and which other servers could then modify the record. Here was the problem: Client1 would get an IP address from DHCPSrv1, who would then register Client1's name and IP address with a DNS server (often they are the same machine so there was no additional network traffic generated). So, DHCPSrv1 would be the owner of Client1's DNS record and no other computers could modify the record (not even Client1). This doesn't sound like much of a problem until Client1 attempts to modify its own record in DNS *or* DHCPSrv1 dies and you bring up a new DHCP server named DHCPSrv2 who cannot modify any DNS registrations made by DHCPSrv1. The answer in the past was to put all DHCP servers in an Active Directory group named DnsUpdateProxy. Whenever a DNS registration is performed by a member of the DnsUpdateProxy group, the group owned the record. So, in the previous scenario, all that had to happen when DHCPSrv1 dies and you bring DHCPSrv2 online is to put the computer account for DHCPSrv2 in the DnsUpdateProxy group. With Server 2008 you can specify a user to be the owner of the DNS records registered by a DHCP server.

Monitoring DHCP

Once you've got a DHCP server set up and running, you may want to find out how many leases remain, who's got those leases, and the like. Open the Address Leases folder and you'll see something like Figure 14.32.

FIGURE 14.32
Assigned leases

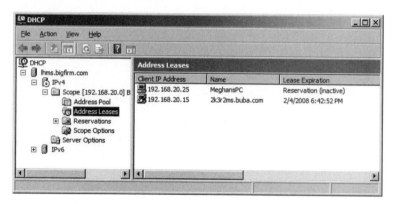

This folder displays all of the leases that DHCP has currently outstanding, which machine (by name) has them, as well as the machine's MAC address.

But how many addresses are left? Right-click any scope and choose Display Statistics, and you'll see a message box like Figure 14.33.

FIGURE 14.33
Lease statistics

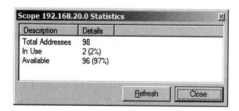

With just a few clicks, you can bring up this message box and find out whether your network's hunger for IP addresses is being met.

Rebuilding a Damaged DHCP Server

Once in a while, something goes wrong and you lose a DHCP server. The scopes, reservations, classes . . . all go poof! and you're in for an hour or two of configuration, assuming that you kept good documentation. If you didn't, well, then it'll take longer . . .

You can avoid that with just one command. Server 2003 lets you get your DHCP server just so, just as you like it, and then lets you back up the DHCP server's configuration with just one command:

```
netsh dhcp server dump
```

Or, if you're not sitting at the server, use this:

```
netsh dhcp server ipaddress dump
```

That spews line after line of configuration information to your screen. Save it by redirecting it to an ASCII file:

```
netsh dhcp server dump > dhcpbackup.txt
```

Then, if the DHCP server falls apart, all you have to do is make sure you have a copy of the dhcpbackup.txt file (you could have named it anything), and use netsh exec, like so:

```
netsh exec dhcpbackup.txt
```

With Server 2003 you could put the DHCP server service on some other machine, copy over your backup file, and perform the same netsh exec command. But I am writing this based on RC1, and I can't get the file to run properly on another server. So, I am hoping by the time Server 2008 is released to market (RTM'd) that should be fixed.

You won't get back the lease information, but you'll get everything else — classes, options, scopes, reservations, and so on.

DHCP on the Client Side

Now that you've set up DHCP on a server, how do you tell clients to use that DHCP? Simple. Any Microsoft operating system from Windows for Workgroups to Windows 9*x* to NT to XP, to Vista, to Windows 2000 up through 2008 all have DHCP configuration as an installation option, although some of those clients refer to it as "automatic" configuration rather than DHCP configuration. (By the way, the Microsoft Client software for DOS and Windows supports DHCP as well.)

Once a system has gotten an IP address, you can find out what that address is by going to that system, opening a command line, and typing **ipconfig /all**. On a Windows 95 workstation, click Start ➤ Run, and then type **winipcfg** and press Enter. Windows 98 supports both IP-Config *and* WINIPCFG. Windows NT only supports IPConfig. IPConfig's useful for other DHCP client–fiddling, as well. You can force a DHCP client to abandon its DHCP-supplied IP address and look for a different one by typing first **ipconfig /release** and then **ipconfig /renew**.

Windows XP, Vista, Server 2003, and later Windows versions (including Server 2008) support an all-in-one command to rebuild an IP connection:

```
netsh int ip reset filename
```

where *filename* is a file that reports the command's progress. I highly recommend learning this command if you've got XP / 2003 or later (and if you didn't have 2008 then I'm not sure why you'd be reading this book); it's more reliable than the pair of ipconfigs.

DHCP in Detail: How DHCP Works

That's setting up DHCP. But how does it work, and unfortunately, how does it sometimes *not* work?

DHCP supplies IP addresses based on the idea of *client leases*. When a machine (a DHCP client) needs an IP address, it asks a DHCP server for that address. (*How* it does that is important, and I'll get to it in a minute.) A DHCP server then gives an IP address to the client, *but only for a temporary period of time* — hence the term *IP lease*. You might have noticed you can set the term of an IP lease from DHCP; just right-click any scope and choose Properties, and it's one of the settings in the resultant window.

The client then knows how long it's got the lease. Even if you reboot or reset your computer, it'll remember what lease is active for it and how much longer it's got to go on the lease.

FINDING THE CLIENT LEASE INFORMATION

On a Windows 3.*x* machine, lease information is kept in DHCP.BIN in the Windows directory. On a Windows 95 machine, it's in HKEY_LOCAL_MACHINE\System\CurrentControlSet\Services \VxD\DHCP\Dhcp-infoxx, where xx is two digits. And if you want to enable or disable the error messages from the DHCP client on a Windows 95 machine, it's the value PopupFlag in the key HKEY_LOCAL_MACHINE\System\CurrentControlSet\Services\VxD\DHCP; use "00 00 00 00" for false, or "01 00 00 00" for true. Alternatively, opening a command line and typing **ipconfig /release** will erase this information. To find the place in the Registry holding DHCP lease information on an NT machine, run REGEDIT and search for DHCPIPAddress in HKEY _LOCAL_MACHINE\System\CurrentControlSet. The key or keys that turn up are the location of the DHCP lease info. On a Windows 2000 system, it's probably HKEY_LOCAL_MACHINE\SYSTEM \CurrentControlSet\Services\TCPIP\parameters\Interfaces; within there you'll find GUIDs (Global Unique IDs, the things that look like CE52A8 C0-B126-11D2-A5D2-BFFEA72FC) for each adapter and potential RAS connection. There's a DHCPIPAddress value in each adapter that gets its addresses from DHCP. On Windows XP systems, it's just HKEY_LOCAL_MACHINE\SYSTEM \CurrentControlSet\Services, and you'll notice those keys with GUID names right up top; each of those keys has a Parameters\TCPIP key within it. Delete the GUID's key and you eliminate any settings for that adapter. As to figuring out which GUID goes with which adapter, ummm, well, that's a matter of trial and error.

So, if your PC had a four-day lease on some address and you rebooted two days into its lease, then the PC wouldn't just blindly ask for an IP address; instead, it would go back to the DHCP server that it got its IP address from and request the particular IP address that it had before. If the DHCP server were still up, then it would acknowledge the request, letting the workstation use the IP address. If, on the other hand, the DHCP server has had its lease information wiped out through some disaster, then either it will give the IP address to the machine (if no one else is using the address), or it will send a *negative acknowledgment* (NACK) to the machine, and the DHCP server will make a note of that NACK in the Event Log. Your workstation should then be smart enough to start searching around for a new DHCP server. In my experience, sometimes it isn't.

Like BOOTP, DHCP remembers which IP addresses go with what machine by matching up an IP address with a MAC (Media Access Control — that is, Ethernet) address.

Normally a DHCP server can send new lease information to a client only at lease renewal intervals. But DHCP clients also "check in" at reboot, so rebooting a workstation will allow DHCP to reset any lease changes such as subnet masks and DNS services.

GETTING AN IP ADDRESS FROM DHCP: THE NUTS AND BOLTS

A DHCP client gets an IP address from a DHCP server in four steps:

1. A *DHCPDISCOVER* broadcasts a request to all DHCP servers in earshot, requesting an IP address.

2. The servers respond with *DHCPOFFER* of IP addresses and lease times.

3. The client chooses the first offer it receives and broadcasts back a *DHCPREQUEST* to confirm the IP address.

4. The server handing out the IP address finishes the procedure by returning with a *DHC-PACK*, an acknowledgment of the request.

Initial DHCP Request: DHCPDISCOVER

First, a DHCP client sends out a message called a DHCPDISCOVER saying, in effect, "Are there any DHCP servers out there? If so, I want an IP address." Figure 14.34 shows this message.

FIGURE 14.34
DHCP step 1:
DHCPDISCOVER

**DHCP
client**

**DHCP
server**

Enet addr: 00CC00000000
IP addr: 0.0.0.0

"Is there a DHCP server around?"

IP address used: 255.255.255.255 (broadcast)
Ethernet address used: FFFFFFFFFFFF (broadcast)
Transaction ID: 14321

Enet addr: 00BB00000000
IP addr: 210.22.31.100

You might ask, "How can a machine communicate if it doesn't have an address?" Through a different protocol than TCP — UDP, or the *User Datagram Protocol*. It's not a NetBIOS or NetBEUI creature; it's all TCP/IP-suite stuff.

Now, to follow all of these DHCP messages, there are a couple of things to watch. First of all, I'm showing you both the MAC addresses (the 48-bit unique Ethernet addresses) and the IP addresses because, as you'll see, they tell somewhat different stories. Also, there is a *transaction ID* attached to each DHCP packet that's quite useful. The transaction ID makes it possible for a client to know when it receives a response from a server exactly *what* the response is responding to.

In this case, notice that the IP address the message is sent to is 255.255.255.255. That's the generic address for "anybody on this subnet." Now, 210.22.31.255 would also work, assuming that this is a class C network that hasn't been subnetted, but 255.255.255.255 pretty much always means "anyone who can hear me." If you set up your routers to forward broadcasts, then 255.255.255.255 will be propagated all over the network; 210.22.31.255 would not. Notice also the destination Ethernet address, FFFFFFFFFFFF. That's the Ethernet way of saying, "Everybody — a broadcast."

DHCP Offers Addresses from Near and Far

Any DHCP servers within earshot — that is, any that receive the UDP datagram — respond to the client with an offer, a proposed IP address, like the one shown in Figure 14.35. Again, this is an offer, not the final IP address.

This offering part of the DHCP process is essential because, as I just hinted, it's possible for more than one DHCP server to hear the original client request. If every DHCP server just thrust an IP address at the hapless client, then it would end up with multiple IP addresses, addresses wasted in the sense that the DHCP servers would consider them all taken, and so they couldn't give those addresses out to other machines.

FIGURE 14.35
DHCP step 2:
DHCPOFFER

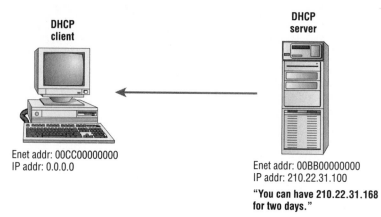

Enet addr: 00CC00000000
IP addr: 0.0.0.0

Enet addr: 00BB00000000
IP addr: 210.22.31.100

**"You can have 210.22.31.168
for two days."**

IP address used: 255.255.255.255 (broadcast)
Ethernet address used: 00CC00000000 (directed)
Transaction ID: 14321

Side Note: Leapfrogging Routers

Before going further, let's consider a side issue that may be nagging at the back of your mind. As a DHCP client uses *broadcasts* to find a DHCP server, where do routers fit into this? The original UDP message, "Are there any DHCP servers out there?" is a broadcast, recall. Most routers, as you know, do not forward broadcasts — which reduces network traffic congestion and is a positive side effect of routers. But if DHCP requests don't go over routers, then that would imply that you have to have a DHCP server on every subnet — a rather expensive proposition.

The BOOTP standard got around this by defining an RFC 1542, a specification whereby routers following RFC 1542 would recognize BOOTP broadcasts and would forward them to other subnets. The feature must be implemented in your routers' software, and it's commonly known as *BOOTP forwarding*. Even if you live in a one-subnet world, by the way, that's worth remembering, as it's invariably a question on the Microsoft certification exams: "What do you need for client A to communicate with DHCP server B on a different subnet?" Answer: The router between A and B must either "be RFC 1542–compliant" or "support BOOTP forwarding."

Okay, so where do you *get* an RFC 1542–compliant router? Well, most of the IP router manufacturers, such as Compatible Systems, Cisco, and Bay Networks, support 1542. You would be hard pressed in this day and age to purchase a router that doesn't support 1542; older routers may require a software upgrade. Another approach is to use a Windows 2000 or later system as a router (you could do the same with NT, but it is no longer supported by Microsoft), as Windows 2000 and later OSes includes 1542 compliance. But what if you've got dumb routers, or router administrators who refuse to turn on BOOTP forwarding? Then you can designate an NT, Windows 2000/2003/2008 machine as a *DHCP relay agent*.

A DHCP relay agent is just a computer that spends a bit of its CPU power listening for DHCP client broadcasts. The DHCP relay agent knows there's no DHCP server on the subnet (because you told it), but the relay agent knows where there *is* a DHCP server on another subnet (because you told it). The DHCP relay agent then takes the DHCP client broadcast and converts it into a directed, point-to-point communication straight to the DHCP server. Directed IP communications can cross routers, of course, and so the message gets to the DHCP server.

What do you need to make a DHCP relay agent? Well, with NT 4, you could use any NT machine — workstation or server. For some annoying reason, Windows 2000/2003/2008 only include software to make a DHCP relay agent with Server.

Under no circumstances should you make a DHCP server into a DHCP relay agent. The net effect will be for the DHCP server to essentially "forget" that it's a DHCP server and instead just forward every request that it hears to some other DHCP server. This prompts me to wonder why the silly DHCP relay agent function isn't grayed out altogether on a DHCP server — certainly the Obtain an IP Address from a DHCP Server option is.

To make a Windows 2000/2003 and 2008 Servers system — remember, Server only — into a DHCP relay agent, you've got to use Routing and Remote Access Service (RRAS). Basically any RRAS configuration will do; you needn't enable WAN routing or dial-in. Look to Chapter 4 in the *Mastering Windows Server 2008: Enterprise Technologies*, the third book in this series, to see how to configure an RRAS system — again, click Start ➤ Administrative Tools ➤ Routing and Remote Access, then right-click the server's name and choose Configure and Enable Routing and Remote Access to start the wizard, then choose Custom Configuration, click Next, check the box next to LAN Routing, and finish the wizard. If asked to start the Routing and Remote Access service click the "Start service" button. You'll see a screen like the one in Figure 14.36.

FIGURE 14.36
RRAS main screen

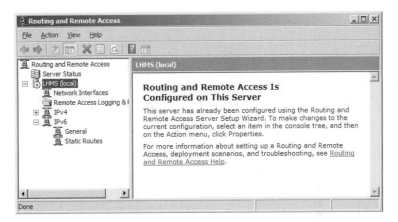

Open the IPv4 node (click the plus sign) and one of the objects you'll see inside it will be a folder labeled General. Right-click the General folder and choose New Routing Protocol to see another dialog box. One of the options offered will be DHCP Relay Agent; choose it and click OK. Back in the RRAS snap-in, you'll now have an object under IPv4/General named DHCP Relay Agent, as you see in Figure 14.37.

Right-click the DHCP Relay Agent object and choose Properties and you'll see a dialog box like the one in Figure 14.38.

You configure the agent by telling it where to find DHCP servers. Enter the IP address of the DHCP server and click Add to add a server to the list. Finally, you've got to enable the agent to listen on the local network for DHCP requests to forward. Right-click DHCP Relay Agent and choose New Interface. Choose Local Area Connection and the agent will then be active on the network.

Discussion of relay agents and 1542-compliant routers leads me to yet another question. What if a DHCP server from another subnet gave an IP address to our client? Wouldn't that put the client in the wrong subnet? If a DHCP server serves a bunch of different subnets, how does it know which subnet an incoming request came from? DHCP solves that problem with BOOTP forwarding.

FIGURE 14.37
RRAS console with
DHCP Relay Agent
highlighted

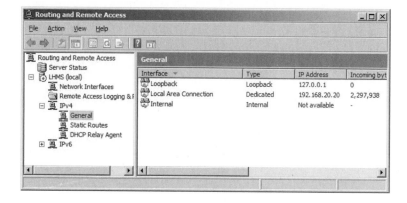

FIGURE 14.38
Relay agent
configuration screen

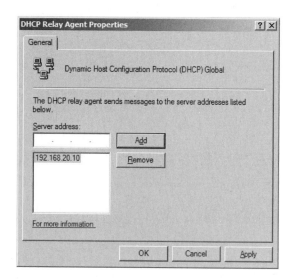

Assuming that your routers implement BOOTP forwarding, then a client's original DHCP request gets out to all of them. But how do you keep a DHCP server in an imaginary subnet 200.1.2.z from giving an address in 200.1.2.z to a PC sitting in another imaginary subnet, 200.1.1.z? Simple. When the router forwards the BOOTP request, it attaches a little note to it that says, "This came from 200.1.1.z." The DHCP server then sees that information, and so it only responds if it has a scope within 200.1.1.z.

Notice that although to the higher-layer protocol (UDP) this is a broadcast, the lower-layer Ethernet protocol behaves as though it is not, and the Ethernet address embedded in the message is the address of the client, not the FFFFFFFFFFFF broadcast address. Notice also that the transaction ID on the response matches the transaction ID on the original request. End of side trip, let's return to watching that client get its address from DHCP.

Picking from the Offers

The DHCP client then looks through the offers it has and picks the one that's "best" for it, or so the Microsoft documentation says. In my experience — and I've done a bunch of experiments — "best" means "first." It seems that the first server that responds is the one whose offer it accepts. Then it sends another UDP datagram, another broadcast, shown in Figure 14.39.

FIGURE 14.39
DHCP step 3:
DHCPREQUEST

DHCP client

DHCP server

Enet addr: 00CC00000000
IP addr: 0.0.0.0

Enet addr: 00BB00000000
IP addr: 210.22.31.100

"Can I have the 210.22.31.168 IP address, and thanks for the other offers, but no thanks."

IP address used: 255.255.255.255 (broadcast)
Ethernet address used: FFFFFFFFFFFF (broadcast)
Transaction ID: 18923

It's a broadcast because this message serves two purposes. First, the broadcast *will* get back to the original offering server if the first broadcast got to that server, which it obviously did. Second, this broadcast is a way of saying to any *other* DHCP servers who made offers, "Sorry, folks, but I'm taking this other offer."

Notice that both the Ethernet and the IP addresses are broadcasts, and there is a new transaction ID.

The Lease Is Signed

Finally, the DHCP server responds with the shiny brand-new IP address, which will look something like Figure 14.40.

It also tells the client its new subnet mask, lease period, and whatever else you specified (gateway, WINS server, DNS server, and the like). Again, notice it's a UDP broadcast, but the Ethernet address is directed, and the transaction ID matches the previous request's ID.

You can find out what your IP configuration looks like after DHCP by typing **ipconfig /all**. It may run off the screen, so just scroll back to the top. You can see a sample run of ipconfig /all below. Windows 95 machines have a graphical version of IPConfig called WINIPCFG.

```
Windows IP Configuration

        Host Name . . . . . . . . . . . . : 1hms
        Primary Dns Suffix  . . . . . . . : Bigfirm.Com
        Node Type . . . . . . . . . . . . : Hybrid
        IP Routing Enabled. . . . . . . . : No
        WINS Proxy Enabled. . . . . . . . : No
```

```
        DNS Suffix Search List. . . . . . : Bigfirm.Com

    Ethernet adapter Local Area Connection:

        Connection-specific DNS Suffix  . :
        Description . . . . . . . . . . . : Intel(R) PRO/1000 MT Network Connection
        Physical Address. . . . . . . . . : 00-0C-29-A3-82-AE
        DHCP Enabled. . . . . . . . . . . : Yes
        Autoconfiguration Enabled . . . . : Yes
        IPv4 Address. . . . . . . . . . . : 192.168.20.73(Preferred)
        Subnet Mask . . . . . . . . . . . : 255.255.255.0
        Default Gateway . . . . . . . . . :
        DHCP Server . . . . . . . . . . . : 192.168.20.10
    DNS Servers . . . . . . . . . . . : 192.168.20.10
        NetBIOS over Tcpip. . . . . . . . : Enabled
```

FIGURE 14.40
DHCP step 4: DHCPACK

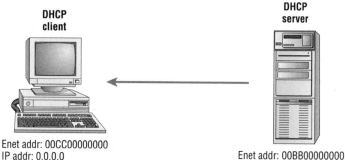

IP address used: 255.255.255.255 (broadcast)
Ethernet address used: 00CC00000000 (directed)
Transaction ID: 18923

Lost Our Lease! Must Sell!

What happens when the lease runs out? Well, when that happens, you're supposed to stop using the IP address. But you're not likely to lose that lease — Windows DHCP client software is pretty vigilant about keeping its DHCP leases as long-lived as is possible.

When the lease is half over, the DHCP client begins renegotiating the IP lease by sending a DHCP request to the server that originally gave it its IP address. The IP and Ethernet addresses are both specific to the server.

The DHCP server then responds with a DHCPACK. The benefit of this is that the DHCPACK contains all of the information that the original DHCPACK had — domain name, DNS server, and so on. That means you can change the DNS server, WINS server, subnet mask, and the like, and the new information will be updated at the clients periodically, but no more than 50 percent of the lease time.

Now, if the DHCPACK doesn't appear, then the DHCP client keeps resending the DHCP request out every two minutes until the IP lease is 87.5 percent expired. (Don't you wonder where they get these numbers from?) At that point, the client just goes back to the drawing board, broadcasting DHCPDISCOVER messages until someone responds. If the lease expires without a new one, the client will stop using the IP address, effectively disabling the TCP/IP protocol on that workstation.

But if you've messed with the DHCP servers, then the renewal process seems to get bogged down a bit. It's a good idea in that case to force a workstation to restart the whole DHCP process by typing `ipconfig /renew` or, better, `ipconfig /release` followed by `ipconfig /renew`; that will often clear up a DHCP problem.

Even with an infinite lease, however, a DHCP client checks back with its server whenever it boots. Therefore, you can often change from infinite to fixed leases by just changing the lease value at the server. Then stop and restart the DHCP service.

Designing Multi-DHCP Networks

Clearly the function of the DHCP server is one that shouldn't rest solely on the shoulders of one server (well, okay, servers don't have shoulders, but you know what I mean). So, how can you put two or more DHCP servers online to accomplish some fault tolerance? If you had two different DHCP servers on the same subnet, and they both thought that they could give out addresses 202.11.39.10 through 202.11.39.40, then there would be nothing keeping the first server from giving address 202.11.39.29 to one machine while simultaneously the other server was giving out that same 202.11.39.29 address to another machine.

In the past Microsoft has recommended an 80/20 rule. What I mean by that is you have two DHCP servers on different subnets. DHCP1 is on subnet 1 with a 192.168.20.0 scope and DHCP is on subnet 2 with a 10.10.10.0 scope. So if DHCP2 died how could clients from the 10.10.10.0 subnet receive or renew IP Addresses? Only 80% of the 10.10.10.0 scope should be on DHCP2, the other 20% of the scope should live on DHCP1 and be active. When clients on the 10.10.10.0 subnet no longer receive IP addresses locally the router between the two will forward (if BOOTP enabled) the DHCPREQUEST to DHCP1 who has a small scope for that subnet.

I guess I should note for the sake of completeness that you can provide fault tolerance for DHCP servers by putting your DHCP server on a cluster of two or more machines. A perfectly valid answer, but not a very cheap one.

Chapter 15

Things to Come: A Peek at Active Directory

If you've made it this far, then let me thank you again. Of all the sorts of books that I like writing, my favorite are books that introduce people to an area of the world.

But what, exactly, have we introduced you to? Well, in a sense, we've introduced you to some of the firmament of networks, the infrastructure that every network needs, no matter whether it's built on technology from Microsoft, Sun, Linux, or whatever. And I hope you don't mind that despite the fact this is a "beginner" book, we've gotten pretty nitty-gritty about things like the chapters about Windows storage, DNS, and DHCP.

In another sense, though, this book has laid the foundation for the most integral, fundamental technology in a Microsoft network — Active Directory. We'll take that up in earnest in the second book of the series, *Mastering Windows Server 2008: Essential Technologies* (and please forgive me if it's not yet on the shelves once you finish this volume — please understand that I'm working very hard to make sure that it's worth your time, and that *takes* time!), but it just wouldn't feel right to end the book without at least a short discussion about what AD is, and what it'll do for you.

Active Directory is Microsoft's offering in the field of network software called *directory services*. We discussed the value of directory services a bit back in Chapter 3, but it's worth repeating and extending some of that.

Put simply, directory services mainly exist for one reason: your organization's data and server resources are in some senses nothing more than one big cookie jar, and if you don't put a lock on that jar, then dirtbags assume that you have no problem with them absconding with your cookies. Make no mistake, directory services do more than secure your network, but when all's said and done, most of what a directory service does is to make securing your network easier: directory services are all about security, plain and simple.

When you stop and think about it, isn't the idea that *security* is the central organizing theme for network software bizarre? I mean, if I were to explain to you what an automobile does, can you imagine me starting out by saying, "this thing has these neat locks that you can lock and unlock remotely, and if you unlock and get into it, it also takes you places?" Viewed in that light, I guess it's kinda sad, but the fact is that in the modern world security *is* the story. As a result, we are all unfortunately forced to run our networks like gulags; ah well.

That's the negative side, but there is a strongly positive side: easier management. Security was the initial reason to bind together systems in a domain, but as the years have gone by, Microsoft and third-party independent software vendors have exploited the centralization exacted by security needs and transmuted it into a set of tools that make it possible for a small cadre of IT pros to keep a network up and running. In this short chapter, I want to introduce you to some of AD's tools and benefits.

Centralized User Accounts and Authorization

Now that we've established that security is a major concern for network operating systems, let's see what sorts of problems it creates, and how a directory service like Active Directory can help.

Recall that in Chapter 2 we talked about the fact that Windows, like virtually every modern operating system, has a local list of known users and passwords, an encrypted file named SAM. We also talked at the time about the management nightmare of having to keep track of thousands of SAMs and thousands of accounts in each one. In other words, it's nice to have a local security system, but it's just not practical for every system to maintain its own list of known users in a network of any size.

Just as we centralize file storage space, printers, and databases on small numbers of file, print, and database servers, centralizing authentication services seems a good idea, and from that we get a class of servers that I think of as "authentication servers." In a network consisting of a few thousand workstations and a couple hundred servers, the job of worrying about the bulk of the work of authentication can be handed over to a mere dozen or so servers dedicated to the task. Those "authentication servers" are actually called *domain controllers*, or DCs, in Microsoft networking terminology. That creates two classes of servers, the domain controllers and the *member servers*, the term for any server that's not acting as a DC. The workstations and member servers that trust the DCs to authenticate for them, as well as the DCs themselves, comprise an *Active Directory domain*.

ADs save you from having to have an account on every workstation and server in the domain, which makes password-changing-day a lot easier to live through. (You'll find that most workplaces have password requirements that are considerably more stringent than the ones required by your online banking or ecommerce sites, and it's not unusual for companies to require you to change your network password every six weeks or so — and so making password changes less burdensome is a very good thing indeed!) Having one account that gives you access to many servers is referred to as *single sign-on*, or SSO, and it's sort of a Holy Grail of network computing. Systems aren't "SSO" versus "not SSO" — it's a matter of degree. For example, in my domain I use just one password to log onto my Windows domain controllers, file servers, database server, print server, and terminal server . . . nice. But my e-mail server is a third-party product that doesn't really do a good job of integrating with AD domains, so it maintains a separate account and password for my e-mail. Similarly, my Linux server isn't terribly adept at accepting AD credentials, meaning that I've achieved only something like 75 percent SSO-ness.

Now, I *could* crank up my "SSO quotient" (SSOQ?) a trifle by getting rid of my existing e-mail server and replacing it with Microsoft Exchange Server, Microsoft's enterprise-level e-mail server. Exchange used to maintain a separate list of users and passwords like my current e-mail server, but when AD debuted in the year 2000, then Microsoft implemented SSO between Exchange and AD accounts.

AD is not the only directory service product out there, nor is it the oldest, but it *is* the most widely used. That probably means that as time goes on, more and more server products will integrate with AD. We even see a bit of this in Server 2008, as one of Windows Server's biggest features, Terminal Services, didn't really do SSO with AD. Yes, Terminal Services exploited the same list of user names and passwords as did AD, but you had to explicitly log onto a terminal server to use its services, *even if you were already logged onto the domain*. In retrospect, that's kinda goofy, sort of like if you logged onto your Windows XP or Vista desktop, tried to open Notepad and were presented with a dialog box requiring you to log onto Notepad!

Group Policy Centralizes Management, Security, and Configuration

Keeping track of one computer is easy — keeping its patches updated, configuring it, backing it up. Adding a second computer doubles the workload, the third triples it, and so on. PC software is so complex nowadays that trying to keep more than a handful of systems properly updated by actually sitting down at those systems to manage them has become horribly expensive — one analysis that I saw figured that companies that didn't use centralized management tools ended up spending on average about $1200 per PC per year. That's almost the cost of buying a new PC — the hardware, at least — every year!

And that's just managing the computers; users need management also and can run costs up even more. Anything that lets us centralize user and computer management is clearly well worth examining. You've already met the Group Policy editor, an MMC snap-in that lets you control the thousands of possible group policy settings on any given computer. But when you add AD to group policy, you get domain-based group policies. That's exciting because this means that once you've built your AD and joined dozens, hundreds, or thousands of machines to the domain, then you can create policies that sit centrally on the domain, and can configure those machines.

Group policies sit on domain controllers, and domain member systems ask the DCs now and then for the latest policies, and the members then execute those policies. Think of it this way — ever worked at a place with a coffee room? There's usually a corkboard on the wall in those rooms, and management likes to post notices about new policies there. Thus, when a manager posts a policy, she knows that it won't be followed immediately, but that in time, everyone will eventually see (and, she hopes, comply with) the policy.

What can you control with group policies? By my rough estimation, about 70 percent of what you can do from the command line or the GUI. Password policies, many settings on server and client tools, and the very useful logon, logoff, startup, and shutdown scripts that let you control very closely what a workstation can and can't do.

Nevertheless, "70 percent" is sort of a problem — but 2008 offers a solution. Domain-based Group Policy objects (GPOs) are great in that they're easy to document and they apply uniformly to an entire domain or a designated part of a domain ... but what about the things that there aren't yet policies for? A new-to-2008 tool called Group Policy Preferences lets you roll your own GP settings. Pretty neat, and we'll discuss them if you join us for Book 2, *Essential Technologies*.

AD Provides a Central List of Resources

So suppose you've got a network with thousands of workstations and a hundred or so servers ... how the heck do you find things? Which server has the annual report data? Where's the online human resources manual? In most networks, you get the answers to those questions by asking someone "in the know." But that's silly; computers are *designed* to keep track of things.

Despite that truth, many directory services haven't been very good about that. AD, in contrast, has a nice system for letting you tell people about what's on the servers on your network. In AD-ese it's called "publishing" and sadly most people to this day have not made use of AD's publishing abilities ... but they should. You can create a file share and advertise that it contains such-and-such data, or publish a print share so it's easy to locate based on its physical location.

Most AD admins do not use this feature, but you'll learn how in Book 2, *Essential Technologies* — and I hope you take the time to do so.

Your Data Follows You Around, and It's Easier to Secure

I've been using computers since 1973, and maybe that's why I don't trust them. Hard drives fail, keys get gummed up ("okay, maybe I *did* spill a soda on the keyboard, but it wasn't my fault"), and, well, I'm pretty sure that whoever designed the first computer was an acolyte of the Church of Murphy, which would explain why it seems true that with computers, everything that can go wrong does, and with a startling amount of reliability. (Don't believe me? Buy an HP inkjet printer. They're great, work fine, and are inexpensive . . . until 24 hours after the warranty runs out. Uncanny!)

The computers that run server software aren't really all that different from those that run workstation software and often are not different at all. The difference usually boils down to one simple thing: the data on servers gets backed up regularly and automatically. I like that idea — no, scratch that, I *love* it — but I work on several systems at different times, and some of them aren't reliably connected to my network. How can file servers help me? In an AD domain, they can help in many ways.

- ◆ You can take the items in your Documents folder and your Desktop and store them not on your computer, but instead on a folder on a file server. That data is then backed up daily or thereabouts, using a feature called "roaming profiles." Furthermore, once you authenticate as you, the domain knows to deliver the contents of the Documents and Desktop folders to whatever computer you're working at. Thus, if you store your stuff entirely in the Documents folder, you need never worry about losing things.

- ◆ When you're offline, there's a very nice "offline files folder" feature that's been around since 2000 and that, sadly, again many people haven't figured out. When you're not online, you can still get to your oft-used files that you keep on a server, because your Windows system caches those things, and it goes so far as to essentially lie to you and tell you that sure, you're online, and here are the files. Of course, when you get back to the mother ship, then there's the "how do I reconcile the differences?" issue, but Offline Files gives you some useful options there.

- ◆ Roaming profiles are nice, but if you've got a lot of data in your profile then they can be slow. Windows offers a faster but more bandwidth-dependent feature called *folder redirection* that may be a better trade-off. With folder redirection, you keep the Documents folder and the Desktop's files on the file server. If you've got the network speed and your users don't travel a lot, then this is a decent answer.

These are pretty useful options, but none of them work in the Windows world without AD. The bottom line is that in this short AD introduction I've hardly scratched the surface. I'll be honest — AD can be complex, but it *can* be mastered with a bit of work, and I hope you'll join us in Book 2 to learn how to do that work.

Whether you do indeed join us in *Essential Technologies* or not, thank you for letting me show you a few things in Windows networking, and don't forget to come visit our friendly online forum at www.minasi.com/forum, browse my free technical newsletters at www.minasi.com /nwstoc.htm, or perhaps join me for an in-person seminar. Thanks and best of luck!

Index

Note to the Reader: Throughout this index **boldfaced** page numbers indicate primary discussions of a topic. *Italicized* page numbers indicate illustrations.

A

A records
    adding hosts to zones, **384–386**, *385*
    fault tolerance, **427–430**, *428*
    working with, **390–392**, *392*
Access Control Entries (ACEs), 48, 111–112
access control lists (ACLs), **46–48**, *47*
accessing resources, **33–35**, *34–35*
accounts
    central, **44–45**, **474**
    user, **27–30**, *27–30*
ACEs (Access Control Entries), 48, 111–112
ACLs (access control lists), **46–48**, *47*
Action menu, 96
Actions menu, 184
Actions pane
    Disk Management, 184
    MMC, 94
activation, scope, **450–451**, *451*
Active Directory, **473**
    central list of resources, **475**
    centralized user accounts and authorization, **474**
    encryption keys, 240
    Group Policy, 161, **181–182**, **475**
    joining domains, **300**
    names, **355**
    security, **476**
Active Directory Certificate Service, 72
Active Directory Domain Services, 72
Active Directory Federation Services, 72
Active Directory-integrated zones, 422
Active Directory Lightweight Directory Services, 72
Active Directory Rights Management Services (AD RMS), 73
active partitions, **192–193**
Active Scope page, 451, *451*

AD RMS (Active Directory Rights Management Services), 73
Add Exclusions page, 446, *446*
Add Features Wizard, 86–87, *87*
Add Mirror dialog box, 205–206, *206*
Add New Quota Entry dialog box, 227, *228*
Add or Edit DHCP Scopes page, 440, *440*
Add or Remove Snap-ins dialog box, 94–95, 101–103, *102*
Add/Remove Templates dialog box, 172, *172*
Add Roles Wizard, 82–84, *83–84*
    DHCP, 438–442, *438–440*, *442*
    DNS, 380
Add Scope dialog box, 440–441, *441*
Address Resolution Protocol (ARP), 266
addresses
    IP. *See* IP addresses
    MAC
        BOOTP, 436
        Ethernet boards, **260–261**
        vs. IP addresses, 262
    socket, 280
ADM templates, **172–174**, *172–173*
administrator-friendly folder options, **92–93**
Administrator screen, 21
administrators, LGPOs, **166–167**, *166*
ADMX files, **174**
ADMX Migrator tool, 173
Advanced dialog box for snap-ins, 103
Advanced Attributes dialog box, 235–236, *236*
Advanced page
    command prompt, 119–120, *120*, 123
    DHCP
        classes, 453, *453*
        clients, 448
        servers, 410, 461, *461*
    MMC, 101

path information, 123
replication partners, 339, *339*, 341, *341*
round robin DNS, 427, *428*
WINS, 336, *336*
zone scavenging, 422–423, *423*
Advanced Research Projects Agency (ARPA),
   255
Advanced Security Settings for SecureFolder
   dialog box, 51–53, *51–52*
Advanced Sharing dialog box, 32, *32*
Advanced TCP/IP Settings dialog box
   DNS, *357–358*, *357*, 360, 420
   NIC, 303–305, *304*
   WINS, 301, *301*
adware, 38
.aero domain, 371
Alias records, *395–397*
#ALTERNATE command, *329*
alternate DNS servers, *356*
APIPA (automatic private IP address)
   benefits, *263–264*
   ICS, *306*
   nonroutable addresses, 270
APIs (application programming interfaces),
   316–317
Appearance page, 185, *185*
applets, 27
application programming interfaces (APIs),
   316–317
application quirks with Registry, *149–150*
application servers
   description, *73*
   purpose, 5
arguments, command line, *125–127*, *126*
ARP (Address Resolution Protocol), 266
ARPA (Advanced Research Projects Agency),
   255
ARPANET, *255–257*, *255–256*
Assign Drive Letter or Path page, 222, *223*
asterisks (*)
   command line arguments, 125
   file searches, 130–131
at signs (@)
   batch files, 134
   NS records, 389
authentication
   vs. authorization, *40–42*

hex suffixes for, *327–328*
   process, *42–46*
Author mode in MMC, 96
authoritative servers, 368, 375
authorization, *46*
   Active Directory, *474*
   vs. authentication, *40–42*
   DHCP servers, *440–444*, *442*, *444*
   files and folders, *50–54*, *51–54*
   legacy support, *50*
   permissions and ACLs, *46–48*, *47*
   tokens, *48–50*, *49*
Authorize DHCP Server dialog box, 444,
   444
Authorize DHCP Server page, 440–441, *442*
automatic private IP address (APIPA)
   benefits, *263–264*
   ICS, *306*
   nonroutable addresses, 270
automatic resource access, *34–35*, *35*
Automatically fix file system errors option, 246
Automatically select the certificate store based
   on the certificate option, 243
AXFR operations, 410

B
B node in NBT, *320–321*
backbones, 257, 266
Background Intelligent Transfer Service (BITS)
   server extensions, 76
backing up
   encrypted files, 237
   Registry, *151–152*, *159–160*
   zone files, *395*
Ballmer, Steve, 12
Base64 Encoded X.509 format, 242
basic disks, *189–190*
   active partitions, *192–193*
   converting dynamic to, *198*
   converting to dynamic, *196–197*, *197*
   deleting partitions, *195*
   extending partitions, *193*, *194*
   primary partitions, *190–192*, *190–192*
   shrinking partitions, *194–195*, *194*
batch files, 107, 110, *131–134*, *132*, *134*
BIND-based DNS servers, 397

BIND-compatible format, 393
biometrics, 43
BitLocker drive encryption, 76
$bitmap file, 244–245
BITS (Background Intelligent Transfer Service)
    server extensions, 76
.biz domain, 371–372
Bolt, Beranek, and Newman contractors, 256
Boot drive letters, 216
BOOT.INI file, 141
Boot partition, 190
BootMGR file, 190
BOOTP, *435–437*, 466, 468
bootstrap loader, 436
breaking mirrored volumes, *208*
broadcasts
    DHCP, 466
    reserved addresses, *271*
Browse for a Group Policy Object dialog box,
    166–168, *166*
Buffer Size setting, 115
burst handling, 336–337
Burst Queues, 337

C
cable, *7–8*
cable modems
    connections, *308–309*
    overview, *291*
cached mode for smart cards, 240
caching-only DNS servers, *367–368*
caching query results, *361–363*
canonical names, 396
case sensitivity
    command line, 126
    file searches, 131
CD command, 111, 132
central list of resources, *475*
centralized accounts, *44–45*, *474*
centralized management, *475*
Cerf, Vinton, 256
Certificate Export Wizard, 241–242
certificates
    certificate authorities, 72
    encryption, 235, 240–243, *242*
Certificates dialog box, 242, *242*
Change an Account window, 29–30, *29*

Change Drive Letters and Paths dialog box,
    216, 216–217
Change Settings window, 67, *67*
checksum headers, 277
child domains, 369, *374–376*, *411–416*, *411*,
    414–415
CHKDSK tool, *244*
    from command prompt, *246–248*
    from Explorer, *245–246*, *246*
    operation, *2445*
ChkNTFS command, 132, 247
CIDR (Classless Inter-Domain Routing),
    275–277
CIPHER utility, *237*, 243
classes
    DHCP, *453–458*, *453–454*, *456–457*
    network, *267–269*, *268*
Classic Start menu, 91, *92*
Classless Inter-Domain Routing (CIDR),
    275–277
clean installations, 63
cleaning zones, *421–426*, *422–423*, *425*
client programs, 279
    DHCP, *463*
        lease information, *464*
        server options, *448–449*, *449–450*
    DNS
        pointing to servers, *365*
        software, *356–363*, *357*, *359*
    FTP, 279
    mail, 289
    network-aware, 316
    networks, *2–4*
    protocols, *10–12*
    Telnet, 80
    WINS failure modes, *330*
Client Side Extensions (CSEs), *176–180*, *176*
clusters, 216
CMAK (Connection Manager Administration
    Kit), 76
CMD program, *121–123*, *122*
CNAMEs, *395–397*
color
    Command Prompt window, *117*, *118*
    primary partitions, 191, *192*
Colors page, *117*, *118*
.com domain, 371

Command History settings, 115
command line, *107–108*
    batch files, *131–134*, *132*, *134*
    benefits, *108–110*
    CHKDSK, *246–248*
    descriptions, *127*
    DHCP installation, 443
    Disk Defragmenter, *249–250*, *250*
    disk quotas, *229*
    DiskPart, *185–186*, *186*
    elements, *112–113*
    encryption, *237*
    formatting disks, *220–221*
    help, *124*, *125*
    internal vs. external commands, *121–124*,
        122–123
    limitations, *110–111*
    locating files, *130–131*, *130*
    parameter lists, *127*
    Registry, *143*, *145*, *151*
    rights, *113–114*, *113*
    special usage information, *127–128*
    switches and arguments, *125–127*, *126*
    syntax, *124–127*, *126*
    system status, *128–129*, *129*
    task management, *129–130*, *130*
    VSS, *234*
    WINS
        automatic partner replication, 340
        burst handling, 337
        features, 332
        interval settings, 335
        logging, 337
        pull parameters, 341–342
    zone creation, 383
Command Prompt window, *114*, *114*
    Colors page, *117*, *118*
    Font page, *116*, *116*
    Layout page, *116–117*, *117*
    Options page, *115–116*
    personalization, *118–121*, *119–121*
comments in resource records, 388
committing transactions, 244
compatibility, protocols for, 254
complete zone transfers, *409–410*
COMPMGMT.MSC tool, 97
Computer icon, 90, 92

computer information in installation, *65–66*
Computer Management console, *97–99*, *97–98*
Computer Name/Domain Changes dialog box,
    25–26, *26*, 359, *359*
computer names
    changing, *24–26*, *25–26*
    DNS, 355, 369
    examples, *324–326*
    legal characters in, 296
computer node for LGPOs, *168–170*, *168*
Configuration Installation Selections page, 85
Configure DHCP Options screen, 448, *448*
Confirm Installation Selections page, 442, *442*
Connection Manager Administration Kit
    (CMAK), 76
connections
    DNS server systems, *376–378*
    Internet, *289–292*, *292*
    ISP, *307–309*, *307–308*
    network hardware, *6*
connectors, *7*, *7*
Console pane, 184
consoles, MMC, *95–99*, *96–98*
containers, snap-ins, 95
content
    encryption keys, 241, *241*
    locating files based on, *130–131*, *130*
Content page, 241, *241*
Control Panel
    LGPOs, *164*, *164*
    Registry as, *136–137*
    user accounts, 27, *27*
CONVERT command-prompt utility, 221–222
Convert to Dynamic Disk dialog box, 197, *197*
converting
    basic disks to dynamic, *196–197*, *197*
    dynamic disks to basic, *198*
    FAT format to NTFS, *221–222*
.coop domain, 371
copying encrypted files, 237
core MSC files, *99–101*
countries in top-level domains, 370–371
Create associated pointer (PTR) record option,
    385
Create New Account window, 28, *28*
Create Password window, 29

Cryptographic Message Syntax Standard
   certificate type, 242
cryptographic service provider (CSP), 235
CSEs (Client Side Extensions), *176–180, 176*
CurrentControlSet key, 141, 158
Cursor Size option, 115
custom installations, 63
customizing servers, *69–70, 69–70*

D

DACLs (discretionary ACLs), 47
DAD (Duplicate Address Detection), 264
daisy chaining, 8
data types, Registry, *145–146*
Database Management System (DBMS), 72
Database Verification page, 335–336, *335*
databases
   securing, *44*
   WINS, *335–338, 335*
Datacenter edition, *56*
Datacenter Server, 13
Date and Time dialog box, 65
DBMS (Database Management System), 72
DCs (domain controllers), 45, 474
DDNS. *See* Dynamic DNS (DDNS)
decrypting files, *240*
Default BOOTP class, 455
default gateways, 265, 448–449, *449*
Default Network Access Protection class, 455
default route addresses, 271
default router addresses, 266, 271–272
Default Routing and Remote Access class,
   455–456
default TTLs, 405
Default User class, 455
defrag command, *250–251*
defragmenting disks, *248–251, 249–250*
delegation, DNS, *374–375, 411–416, 411,
   414–415*
Delete Owner dialog box, 343, *344*
deleting
   partitions, *195*
   Registry entries, *150–151*
   volumes, *204*
      mirrored, *208–209, 209*
      RAID-5, *213*
   WINS records, *344–345*

Deny disk space to users exceeding quota limit
   option, 225
DER (Distinguished Encoding Rules) format,
   242
descriptions
   command line, *127*
   scopes, 445
Desktop, *89–90*
Desktop Experience feature, 76
Desktop Icon Settings dialog box, 90, *91*
Desktop icons, restoring, *90–92, 91–92*
Desktop Properties dialog box, 90
details pane in MMC, 97
Device Manager, 98
DHCP. *See* Dynamic Host Configuration
   Protocol (DHCP)
DHCP.BIN file, 464
DHCP-provided addresses, *263*
DHCP User Classes dialog box, 456, *456*
DHCPACK messages, 464, *470–471*
DHCPDISCOVER messages, *464–465, 465*, 471
DHCPOFFER messages, *464–465, 466*
DHCPREQUEST messages, 464, *469, 469*
Dial-up Connection Properties dialog box,
   309–311, *310*
dial-up connections, *307–308, 307–308*
Digital Rights Management (DRM), 73
Dir command, 122, 132
disaster recovery in DNS, *395*
Discard Old Duplicates option, 115
discretionary ACLs (DACLs), 47
Disk Defragmenter, *248–251, 249–250*
disk duplexing, *207*
disk geometry, *216*
disk management and Disk Management
   utility, 104, *104, 183*
      basic disks. *See* basic disks
      CHKDSK, *244–248, 246*
      defragmentation, *248–251, 249–250*
      drive letters, *216, 216–217*
      dynamic disks. *See* dynamic disks
      encryption. *See* encryption
      formats, *217–220, 218*
      formatting, *220–224, 221, 223*
      maintenance tools, *244*
      mounted drives, *222–224*

overview, *183–185*, *184–185*
physical/logical disks, *186–189*, *187–188*
quotas, *224–229*, *225–228*
RAID, 189, *204–205*
 mirrored volumes, *205–209*, *206*, *209*
 RAID-5 volumes, *210–213*, *211–212*
 striped volumes, 201
Remote Storage feature, *251–252*
VSS, *230–234*, *232–233*
Disk Operating System (DOS), 107
DiskPart utility, 183, *185–186*, *186*
 active partitions, 193
 converting basic disks to dynamic, 197
 deleting partitions, 195
 deleting volumes, *204*
 extending partitions, 193
 mirrored volumes, *207–209*
 missing disks, 214–215
 mounting drives, *224*
 primary partitions, 192
 recovering failed RAID-5 volumes, *212–213*, *212*
 shrinking partitions, 194
 simple volumes, 199
 striped volumes, *202–204*, *203*
Display Options settings, 115
Distinguished Encoding Rules (DER) format, 242
DNS. *See* Domain Name System (DNS); Domain Name System (DNS) servers
DNS Manager dialog box, 380–381, *380*, 385, *385*, 415, *415*
DNS page, *357–358*, *357*, 360, 420, 460, *460*
dnscmd, command summary, *430–433*
dnscmd /AllowUpdate command, 417
dnscmd /config command, 417
dnscmd /enumzones command, 409
dnscmd /recordadd command, 386, 396–397, 404, 406, 408, 412, 414, 428
dnscmd /recordall command, 387, 390–391, 393
dnscmd /recorddelete command, 409, 416–417, 428
dnscmd /zoneadd command, 383, 395, 409, 412–413, 415
dnscmd /zoneall command, 387
dnscmd /zonedelete command, 395, 412–413, 417

dnscmd /zoneinfo command, 421
dnscmd /zoneprint command, 388, 391–392, 396, 409, 413, 419, 424
dnscmd /zonerefresh command, 410
dnscmd /zonereload command, 393, 410
dnscmd /zoneresetsecondaries command, 407–408
dnscmd /zonewriteback command, 393
documentation of Registry entries, 146
#DOM command, *328*
domain controllers (DCs), 45, 474
Domain Name and DNS Servers page, 449, *450*
Domain Name System (DNS), 24, 73, 286, *315–316*, 353
 caching query results, *361–363*
 clients
  pointing to servers, *365*
  software, *356–363*, *357*, *359*
 CNAMEs, *395–397*
 DDNS. *See* Dynamic DNS (DDNS)
 disaster recovery, *395*
 dnscmd summary, *430–433*
 domains, 355, *369–370*
  creating, *380–383*, *380–383*
  delegation, *374–375*, *411–416*, *411*, *414–415*
  historical development, *370*
  membership, *359–360*, *359*
  second-level, *372–374*
  subdomains, *375–376*
  third-level, *374*
  top-level, *370–372*, *371*
 fault tolerance, *427–430*, *428*
 functions, *353–354*
 hierarchy, *368–376*
 name anatomy, *354–355*
 name resolution, *347–349*, *348*
 overview, *287–288*
 performance, *426–430*, *428*
 records, *384*
  A, *384–386*, *385*, *390–392*, *392*
  MX, *398–401*, *400*
  NS and SOA, *388–390*, 401
  reverse lookups, *386–388*, *387*
  viewing, *392–395*, *394*
 route optimization, *429–430*

servers. *See* Domain Name System (DNS)
   servers
suffixes, 355
   installing, *378–379*
   Registry for, *300–301*
   search list, *360–361*
Winsock order, *349–350*
Domain Name System (DNS) servers, 11, 73,
   287–288
   complex, *376*
      connecting and naming systems,
         376–377
      connectivity testing, *378*
      creating, *380–383*, *380–383*
      IP addresses, *377*
      opening firewalls, *377–378*
      suffixes, *378–379*
      winservers, *379–380*
   preferred and alternate, *356*, *377*
   root, 366
   secondary, *401*
      creating, *408–409*
      primary-initiated synchs, *407–408*, *408*
      read-only zone copies, *402*
      retries and expiry, *403*
      SOA records modification, *404–405*, *404*
      transfers, *406–407*, *407*, *409–410*
      TTLs, *405–406*
      updating, *402–403*
   setup, *363*
      caching-only, *367–368*
      finding IP addresses, *363–364*
      nslookup command, *366–367*
      pointing clients to, *365*
      software installation, *364–365*
      troubleshooting, *367*
      trying out, *365–366*
   static entries, *300*
domains, 3, 286
   Active Directory, 474
   DNS, *355*, *369–370*
      creating, *380–383*, *380–383*
      delegation, *374–375*, *411–416*, *411*,
         414–415
      historical development, *370*
      membership, *359–360*, *359*
      second-level, *372–374*

subdomains, *375–376*
third-level, *374*
top-level, *370–372*, *371*
joining, *300*
in security, *44–45*
suffixes, *298–301*
vs. workgroups, 322
DOS (Disk Operating System), 107
dotted quad notation, *261–262*, *262*
downloading Windows Server 2008, *16–17*
drive letters
   changing, *216*, *216–217*
   partitions, 191
   spanned volumes, *200*
drives. *See* disk management and Disk
   Management utility
DRM (Digital Rights Management), 73
DSL connections, *291*, *308–309*
dumb terminal connections, *290*
duplexing, disk, *207*
Duplicate Address Detection (DAD), 264
DVD installation method, *59–65*, *59–64*
dynamic disks, 189, *195–196*
   converting basic to, *196–197*, *197*
   converting to basic, *198*
   moving, *214–215*
   volumes, *198–204*, *199–203*
Dynamic DNS (DDNS), *416*, 460
   operation, *416–417*
   registrations
      failed, *421*
      PTR, *418*
      stopping, *420*
      triggers, *419–420*
   reverse lookup zones, *418*
   security, *426*
   zone scavenging, *421–426*, *422–423*, *425*
Dynamic Host Configuration
   Protocol (DHCP), 11, *435*
      authorizing, *443–444*, *444*
      benefits, *435–437*
      client options, *448–449*, *449–450*
      configuration, *458–461*, *459–461*
      description, *73*
      installing, *437–443*, *438–443*
      IP address ranges, *445–447*, *446*

IP addresses from, 262–263, 306, *464–471*, *465–470*
leases, 463
    duration, *447–448*, *447–448*
    expiration, *470–471*
    information, *464*
    signing, *469–470*, *470*
monitoring, *462*, *462*
multi-DHCP networks, *471*
operation, *463–464*
rebuilding, *462–463*
relay agents, 466–467
reservations, 437, *452–453*, *452*
scopes, 263
    activation, *450–451*, *451*
    adding, *440–441*, *441*
    creating, *445–446*, *445–446*
    options, *451–452*, *452*
    superscopes, *446–447*
user and vendor classes, *453–458*, *453–454*, *456–457*
Dynamic Update page, 382–383, *383*
Dynamically update DNS A and PTR records for DHCP clients that do not request updates option, 460

E
e-commerce online stores, 6
e-mail
    names, *288–289*, *288*
    servers, 5, *398–401*, *400*
Edit Options settings, 115–116
Edit System Variable dialog box, 123
editing Registry, *137–138*, *143–145*
editions, selecting, *55–57*
.edu domain, 371
effective permissions, 52
EFI (extensible firmware interface), 188
EFSINFO utility, 239
8.3 filenames, 218
Enable automatic partner configuration option, 339
Enable automatic scavenging of stale records option, 422
Enable burst handling option, 336
Enable LMHOSTS lookup option, 302

Enable round robin option, 428
Enable Windows Automatic Updating and Feedback dialog box, 66
Encoded Binary X format, 242
Encrypt contents to secure data option, 235
encryption, *235*
    from command line, *237*
    decrypting files, *240*
    document creator information, *238–239*, *238–239*
    file recovery, *243–244*
    vs. hashing, 44
    key protection, *240–243*, *241–242*
    logons, 46
    new features, *240*
    passwords, 43
    process, *235–237*, *236*
Encryption Warning dialog box, 236, *236*
End Of File markers, 244
Enterprise edition, *56*
entries, Registry, 142
    creating and deleting, *150–151*
    editing, *143–145*
    types, *145–146*
    values, *148–150*, *148*
Environment Variables dialog box, 121, *121*, 123
error detection and correction
    IP, *277–278*
    MMC, 95
    TCP, *279*
    TCP/IP, 258
Ethernet addresses, *260–261*
Ethernet segments, 259
Event Viewer, 95–96, 104
    for failed volumes, 207
    logs, 98, 223, 381
Exceptions page, 311, *312*
excluding IP address ranges, 446, *446*
expiration
    leases, *470–471*
    secondary DNS servers, *403*
Explorer, CHKDSK tool from, *245–246*
Extend Volume Wizard, 193, *194*, 200
extended partitions, 189, *193*, *194*
extensible firmware interface (EFI), 188

extensions
  BITS, 76
  CSEs, *176–180*, *176*
  MMC, 95, 103
Extensions for Computer Management dialog box, 104, *105*
external commands vs. internal, *121–124*, *122–123*
external DNS zones, 406
Extinction interval setting, 334
Extinction timeout setting, 334

F

failed DDNS registrations, *421*
failover clustering, *77*
failure recovery, TCP/IP design for, 258
FAT (file allocation table) and FAT32 format, *217*, *219*
  basic disks, 191
  CHKDSK with, 248
  converting to NTFS, *221–222*
  on system partition, *220*
fault tolerance
  A records, *427–430*, *428*
  mail, *399–400*
  RAID, 189, *204–205*
    mirrored volumes, *205–209*, *206*, *209*
    RAID-5 volumes, *210–213*, *211–212*
    striped volumes, 201
  Registry, *157–158*
Favorites menu in MMC, 97
FAX servers, 73
fdisk utility, 185
features
  installing, *86–87*, *86*
  need for, *71–81*
  vs. roles, *70–71*
  server, 6
File Server Resource Manager (FSRM), 224
File Transfer Protocol (FTP), 279
files
  batch, 107, 110, *131–134*, *132*, *134*
  encrypting. *See* encryption
  finding, *130–131*, *130*
  long filenames, *218–219*, *218*
  security, *50–54*, *51–54*
  servers, 5

services, 74
  zone. *See* zone files
Find dialog box, Registry, 147, *147*
finding
  files, *130–131*, *130*
  IP addresses, *363–364*
  zone files, *393*, *394*
FindStr utility, 130–132, *130*
fingerprint readers, 43
firewalls
  configuring, 70, *70*
  opening, *377–378*
  TCP/IP, *311–312*, *312*
flags for security descriptors, 48
floppies, file formats on, 218–219
flow control, TCP for, 279
folders
  administrator-friendly, *92–93*
  encrypting. *See* encryption
  for mounted drives, 222
  security, *50–54*, *51–54*
  shared, 98
Font page, *116*, *116*
format command, 220–221
Format New Volume dialog box, 220–221, *221*
formats, disks, *217–220*, *218*
formatting disks, *220–224*, *221*, *223*
Forward Lookup Zones folder, 381
forwarding, BOOTP, 466, 468
FQDNs (fully qualified domain names), 355, 390, 400
fragmented disks, *248–251*, *249–250*
FSRM (File Server Resource Manager), 224
Fsutil command, 229
FTP (File Transfer Protocol), 279
Full Installation option, 19
full version installation, *57–58*
  choices, *58–59*
  DVD method, *59–65*, *59–64*
fully qualified domain names (FQDNs), 355, 390, 400

G

gateways, default, 265, 448–449, *449*
General page
  DDNS, 417, 421, 424
  DHCP servers, 458–459, *459*

encryption, 235, 240
folders, 93
geometry, disk, *216*
GetMAC command, 133, 261
Global Logs view, 381
Globally Unique Identifiers (GUIDs), 133, 464
GlobalNames zone, 320
glue records, *390–392*, *392*
.gov domain, 371
GPOs (Group Policy Objects), 161
GPT (GUID Partition Table) partition style, *187–188*
   basic disks, 190
   mirrored volumes, 207
grace writes, 229
Graphical User Interfaces (GUIs), 107
Group Policy, 77, 161
   Active Directory, 161, *181–182*, *475*
   centralized management, *475*
   importance, *161–163*, *162–163*
   LGPOs. *See* Local Group Policy Objects (LGPOs)
   Registry settings, 137
   scripts in, *180–181*, *180*
   tattooing, *169–170*
Group Policy Object editor, 165
Group Policy Objects (GPOs), 161
group scheduling servers, 5
GUID Partition Table (GPT) partition style, *187–188*
   basic disks, 190
   mirrored volumes, 207
GUIDs (Globally Unique Identifiers), 133, 464
GUIs (Graphical User Interfaces), 107

H

H node in NBT, *321–322*
hard quotas, 225, *226*
hardware for networks, *6–10*, *7*, *10*
hardware RAID systems, 205
hashed passwords, 43
hashing vs. encryption, 44
Healthy status, 214
help, command line, *124*, *125*
Help and Support dialog box, 60
hex suffixes for LMHOSTS file, *327–328*
Hidden option in Disk Management utility, 185

Hide File Extensions for Known File Types option, 93
Hide Protected Operating System Files (Recommended) option, 93
hierarchy, DNS, *368–369*
   domains, *368–370*
      historical development, *370*
      second-level, *372–374*
      subdomains, *375–376*
      third-level, *374*
      top-level, *370–372*, *371*
   overview, *369–370*
hives, Registry, *156–158*
HKEY_CURRENT_USER key, *141–142*, *142*
HKEY_LOCAL_MACHINE key, *141*, 169
HKEY_Users key, 169
hosts and host names, *285–286*
   CNAMEs, *395–397*
   DNS, *287–288*, *355*, 370
   e-mail names, *288–289*, *288*
   HOSTS file, *286–287*, 315–316, 370
   independence, 258
   WINS configuration for, *301–303*, *301*
   for zones, *384–386*, *385*
HOSTS file, *286–287*, 315–316, 370
HTTP (HyperText Transfer Protocol), 4
hubs, *8*
hybrid node in DHCP, 451
HyperText Transfer Protocol (HTTP), 4
hyphens (-) in command line, 125–126

I

IANA (Internet Assigned Numbers Authority), 267
ICANN (Internet Corporation for Assigned Names and Numbers), 267–268, 287, 370
ICS (Internet Connection Sharing), *305–306*, 411
   connections, *306–309*, *307–308*
   machine configuration, *311*
   overview, *282–284*
   turning on, *309–311*, *310–311*
IGRP (Internet Group Management Protocol), 266–267
Import Certificate Wizard, 242–243
#INCLUDE command, *329*

incremental zone transfers, *409–410*
independence, TCP/IP design for, 258
.info domain, 371–372
.ini files, 135
Initial Configuration Tasks window, *65–70*, *65–70*
Initialize Disk Wizard, 187, *187*
Insert Mode option, 116
Install Windows dialog box, 18–21, *18–21*, *59–65*, *59–64*
installation, *18–21*, *18–21*, *55*
    edition choices, *55–57*
    full version, *57–65*, *59–64*
    Initial Configuration Tasks window, *65–70*, *65–70*
    roles and features, *70–71*
        need for, *71–81*
        process, *81–87*, *82–87*
interactive logins, 44, 139–140
internal commands vs. external, *121–124*, *122–123*
internal DNS zones, 406
internal top-level domains, *372*
Internet, 257
    connections, *289–292*, *292*
    host names. *See* hosts and host names
Internet Assigned Numbers Authority (IANA), 267
Internet Connection Sharing (ICS), *305–306*, 411
    connections, *306–309*, *307–308*
    machine configuration, *311*
    overview, *282–284*
    turning on, *309–311*, *310–311*
Internet Corporation for Assigned Names and Numbers (ICANN), 267–268, 287, 370
Internet Group Management Protocol (IGRP), 266–267
Internet Options dialog box, 241, *241*
Internet Packet Exchange/Sequenced Packet Exchange (IPX/SPX), 11
Internet Printing Client, 77
Internet Protocol. *See* IP (Internet Protocol)
Internet Protocol Configuration. *See* ipconfig command
Internet Protocol Version 4 (TCP/IPv4) Properties dialog box, 293, *294*

Internet service providers (ISPs)
    connections, *307–309*, *307–308*
    IP addresses for, 267–268
Internet Storage Name Server (iSNS), 77
internets, 257
Intervals page, 334–335, *334*
intranets, 257–258
    domains, 372
    machine configuration, *311*
IP (Internet Protocol), *253*, 259
    error checking, *277–278*
    Ethernet/MAC addresses, *260–261*
    ipconfig for, *273–275*
    leases, 463
    port numbers, *280–281*
    routers, *259–260*, 265
    routing, 265–267
    subnets, *259–260*
    testing configuration, *295–300*, *295*, *297*, *299*
    versions, 2
IP Address Range page, 445, *445*
IP addresses
    APIPA and IPv4 link-local addresses, *263–264*
    CIDR, *275–277*
    DHCP-provided, *263*, *464–471*, *465–470*
    DNS servers, *377*, *445–447*, *446*
    finding, *363–364*
    forcing, *452–453*, *452*
    network classes, *267–269*, *268*
    quad format, *261–262*, *262*
    routable and nonroutable, *269–270*
    for single NICs, *303–304*
    source, *262–264*
    special, *270–271*
    static, *264*, *292–295*, *293–294*
    subnet masks, *272–273*
    terminal connections, *291–292*, *292*
IP Settings page, 303–305, *304*
ipconfig command
    description, 133
    DNS, 358
ipconfig /all command
    DHCP, 457, 463, 469
    DNS server setup, 364, 366, 378–379
    network information, *273–275*
    TCP/IP testing, *295–297*, *295*

ipconfig /displaydns command, 348, 361

ipconfig /flushdns command, 348, 362, 364

ipconfig /registerdns command, 417, 419, 423, 426

ipconfig /release command, 454, 458, 463–464, 471

ipconfig /renew command, 457–458, 463, 471

ipconfig /setclassid command, 457–458

ipconfig /showclassid command, 455

IPv4 link-local addresses, *263–264*

IPv4 Properties dialog box, 458–461, *459–461*

IPX/SPX (Internet Packet Exchange/Sequenced Packet Exchange), 11

Irfanview viewer, 150

iSNS (Internet Storage Name Server), 77

ISPs (Internet service providers)
connections, *307–309*, *307–308*
IP addresses for, 267–268

Itanium Processor edition, 57

IXFR operations, 410

J

joining Active Directory domains, *300*

junction points, 222

K

Kahn, Robert, 256

Kerberos authorization, 50

keys
encryption, 235, *240–243*, *241–242*
Registry, *139*
backing up and restoring, *151–152*
HKEY_CURRENT_USER, *141–142*, *142*
HKEY_LOCAL_MACHINE, *141*
permissions, *152–154*, *153–154*
profiles, *139–141*, *140*

L

labels for DNS names, *354–355*

LAN Connection properties page, 293, *294*

LAN Manager, *12–13*, 302

languages, 17, 19, 60

LANs (local area networks), 2
architectures, 259
connections, 291

LAN-to-WAN routing, *305–311*, *307–308*, *310–311*

Layout page, *116–117*, *117*

leapfrogging routers, *466–468*, *467–468*

Lease Duration page, 447–448, *447*

leases, DHCP, 463
duration, *447–448*, *447–448*
expiration, *470–471*
information, *464*
signing, *469–470*, *470*

leaves in snap-ins, 95

legacy names, *320*

legacy security support, *50*

LGPOs. *See* Local Group Policy Objects (LGPOs)

licenses, 19–20, 62

link-local addresses, *263–264*

links, networks, *6*

LMHOSTS file, 302, *326*
centralized, *329*
hex suffixes, *327–328*
name resolution, *314–315*, 352
overview, *326–327*

local accounts, 44

Local Area Connection Properties dialog box, 293, *294*

local area networks (LANs), 2
architectures, 259
connections, 291
LAN-to-WAN routing, *305–311*, *307–308*, *310–311*

Local Group Policy, *165–166*, *165*

Local Group Policy Editor dialog box, 172, *172*

Local Group Policy Objects (LGPOs), 161–163, *162–163*
Active Directory, *182*
ADM templates, *172–174*, *172–173*
administrators and non-administrators, *166–167*, *166*
ADMX files, *174*
computer node vs. user node, *168–170*, *168*
CSEs, *176–180*, *176*
Local Group Policy, *165–166*, *165*
non Registry-based, *174–175*, *175*

organization and structure, *168–175*, *169–170*, *172–173*, *175*
Registry values, *169–171*, *170*
user specific, *167–168*, *168*
working with, *163–165*, *164*
local logons, 44
local users and groups management, 98
Locally Unique Identifiers (LUIDs), 48
locating
    files, *130–131*, *130*
    IP addresses, *363–364*
    zone files, *393*, *394*
$Logfile file, 244
logical disks, *186–189*, *187–188*, 191
Logoff scripts, 181
logons
    interactive, 44, 139–140
    local, 44
    across networks, *45–46*
    scripts, 181
logs
    Event Viewer, 98, 223, 381
    Registry, 157–158
    scavenging, 426
    transaction, 244
long filenames, *218–219*, *218*
loopback addresses, 271
lost allocation units, 248
LPR Port Monitor, 77
Lucida Console font, 116
LUIDs (Locally Unique Identifiers), 48

M

M node in NBT, *320–322*
MAC (Media Access Control) addresses
    BOOTP, 436
    Ethernet boards, *260–261*
    vs. IP addresses, 262
machine names
    changing, *24–26*, *25–26*
    DNS, 355, 369
    examples, *324–326*
    legal characters in, 296
machine profiles, 139
mail clients, 289
mail fault tolerance, *399–400*

mail routers, 289
Manage Accounts window, 28–29, *28*
Manage Authorized Servers dialog box, 444, *444*
Manually Configure Settings window, 66–67, *66*
Map Network Drive dialog box, 34–35, *35*
masks, subnet, *272–273*
master boot records (MBRs)
    basic disks, 190
    dynamic disks, 196
    mirrored volumes, 207
    partition style, *187–188*
master browsers, 324
master file table ($MFT) files, 244
Media Access Control (MAC) addresses
    BOOTP, 436
    Ethernet boards, *260–261*
    vs. IP addresses, 262
member servers, 474
Message Queuing, 77
metadata, 245
$MFT (master file table) files, 244–245
Microsoft Disable Netbios Option, 454
Microsoft Management Console (MMC), *89–90*
    administrator-friendly folder options, *92–93*
    benefits, *94*
    building tools, *101–106*, *101–106*
    Computer Management console, *97–99*, *97–98*
    core MSC files, *99–101*
    Desktop icons and Start menu, *90–92*
    limitations, *95*
    new features, *94–95*
    terms, *95–97*, *96*
Microsoft Release DHCP Lease on Shutdown Option, 454
Microsoft Saved Consoles (MSCs) files, 95–96
    building, *101–104*, *101–105*
    core, *99–101*
Microsoft Windows NT Server, 13
.mil domain, 371
mirrored volumes, *205–209*, *206*, *209*
missing disks, 214–215

MMC. *See* Microsoft Management Console (MMC)
Mockapetris, Paul, 316
modifying
    Registry, *137–138*, *143–145*
    SOA records, *401*, *404–405*, *404*
    zone files, *394–395*
modularity, API for, *316–317*
monitoring DHCP, *462*, *462*
mounted drives, *222–224*
moving
    dynamic disks, *214–215*
    encrypted files, 237
MS-NET tool, 12
MSC (Microsoft saved console) files, 95–96
    building, *101–104*, *101–105*
    core, *99–101*
multi-DHCP networks, *471*
multi-WINS network, *337–339*
multicasts, 269, 339
multihomed computers, 265, *343–344*
Multipath I/O feature, 78
.museum domain, 371
MX records, 354
    adding, *400–401*, *400*
    e-mail servers, *398–401*, *400*
    mail fault tolerance, *399–400*
My Shared Folder Properties dialog box, 31, 33

N

NACK (negative acknowledgments), 464
.name domain, 371–372
name registrars, 287
name resolution, *313–314*
    DNS. *See* Domain Name System (DNS); Domain Name System (DNS) servers
    LMHOSTS, *314–315*, *326–329*, 352
    NetBIOS, *314–315*, *350–352*, *351*
    WINS, *314–315*
    Winsock, *347–349*, *348*
name server (NS) records, 374–375, 384, *388–390*
name servers, 287, *313–314*, 391, *392*
Name Servers page, 391, *392*
names

Active Directory, *355*
filenames, *218–219*, *218*
machine
    changing, *24–26*, *25–26*
    DNS, 355, 369
    examples, *324–326*
    legal characters in, 296
    NetBIOS, 302–303
    network, *26–27*
    scopes, 445
    WINS registrations, *329–330*
    zones, 382, *382*
naming domains, 287
NAT (network address translation)
    characteristics, *270*
    vs. PAT, *284–285*
National Research and Education Network (NREN), 257
National Science Foundation, 257
NBT (NetBIOS atop TCP/IP), *320*
    names, *322–326*
    nodes, *320–322*
    RFCs, *321*
    vs. Winsock, 347
nbtstat -c command, 352
nbtstat -n command, *322–324*
nbtstat -R command, 352
NCP (Network Control Protocol), 256
negative acknowledgments (NACK), 464
negative query results caching, *362–363*
Net command, 133
.net domain, 371
.NET Framework 3.0 features, 76
Net Share command, 108–109, *109*
net start command, 365, 367
net use command, 314, 324
    CNAME, 397
    vs. ping, *316*
net view command, 316, 323
NetBEUI (Network Basic Input/Output System Extended User Interface), 11
NetBIOS (Network Basic Input/Output System) API, 314, *319–320*
    name resolution, *314–315*, *350–352*, *351*
    names, 302–303
    WINS. *See* Windows Internet Name Server (WINS)

NetBIOS atop TCP/IP (NBT), 320
    names, *322–326*
    nodes, *320–322*
    RFCs, *321*
    vs. Winsock, 347
netdom command, 377
netmask ordering, *429–430*
netsh dhcp server dump command, 462–463
netsh exec command, 463
netsh firewall set command, 377
netsh int ip add command, 303, 359
netsh int ip rest command, 463
netsh int ip set address command, 364, 377, 412
netsh int ip set dns command, 356, 358–359, 365, 377, 412
netsh wins server command, 336–337, 340–342
netstat command, 133, 281
Network Access Protection page, 461
network address translation (NAT)
    characteristics, *270*
    vs. PAT, *284–285*
Network and Sharing Center window, 22, 23, 293
network-aware clients, 316
Network Basic Input/Output System (NetBIOS) API, 314, *319–320*
    name resolution, *314–315*, *350–352*, *351*
    names, 302–303
    WINS. *See* Windows Internet Name Server (WINS)
Network Basic Input/Output System Extended User Interface (NetBEUI), 11
Network Connections window, 65
Network Control Protocol (NCP), 256
Network Discovery, 22
Network icon, 90, 92
network interface cards (NICs)
    characteristics, *7*
    IP addresses for, *303–304*
Network Load Balancing (NLB), 78
Network Policy and Access Services, 74
network-ready devices, *8–9*
Network Solutions company, 370
Network window, 22, 22
networks, *1*
    building, *15*
        180-day version, *17–18*

    machine names, *24–26*, *25–26*
    network names, *26–27*
    resource access, *33–35*, *34–35*
    resource sharing, *30–33*, *31–33*
    setup, *22–24*, *22–24*
    user accounts, *27–30*, *27–30*
    Windows Server 2008 download, *16–17*
    Windows Server 2008 installation, *18–21*, *18–21*
classes, *267–269*, *268*
client and server software, *3–4*
hardware, *6–10*, *7*, *10*
IP. *See* IP (Internet Protocol)
links, *6*
logons across, *45–46*
names, *26–27*
numbers, *271*
purpose, *1–3*
server types, *5–6*
TCP/IP. *See* TCP/IP (Transmission Control Protocol/Internet Protocol)
transport protocol, *10–12*
types, *3*
New Class dialog box, 456, *456*
New Host dialog box, 384–385, *385*
New Mirrored Volume Wizard, 207
New RAID-5 Volume dialog box, 210–211, *211*
New Reservation dialog box, 452–453, *452*
New Resource Record dialog box, 396, 400, *400*
New Routing Protocol option, 467
New Scope Wizard, 445–451, *445–451*
New Simple Volume Wizard, 190–191, *191*, 198
New Spanned Volume Wizard, 199, *199*
New Static Mapping dialog box, 333, *333*
New Striped Volume Wizard, 201, *201*
New Superscope option, 447
New User Variables dialog box, 121
New Zone Wizard, *380–383*, *380–383*
NICs (network interface cards)
    characteristics, *7*
    IP addresses for, *303–304*
NLB (Network Load Balancing), 78
No-refresh interval setting, *422–424*
nodes
    CMC, *97–99*
    LGPO, *168–170*, *168*

NBT, *320–322*

snap-ins, 95–96

non-administrators, LGPOs, *166–167*, *166*

non-cached mode for smart cards, 240

nonroutable IP addresses, *269–270*

nonroutable machines, *283–284*

Notepad application

command-line switches, 110

Registry settings, 143

Notify dialog box, 407–408, *408*

Novell NetWare, 12–13

NREN (National Research and Education Network), 257

NS (name server) records, 374–375, 384, *388–390*

NSFNet network, 257

nslookup command, *366–367*

CNAMES, 396

e-mail servers, *398–401*, *400*

reverse lookups, 388

zone hosts, 384–385

NT Advanced Server, 13

NT Workstation, 14

NTDS.DIT file, 45

NTFS format, *217*

basic disks, 191

converting FAT or FAT32 to, *221–222*

vs. FAT, *219*

NTUSER.DAT file, 140

Number of Buffers setting, 115

O

Obtain an IP address automatically option, 295

Obtain DNS server address automatically option, 295

180-day version, *17–18*

Open Shortest Path First (OSPF) protocol, 266

opening firewalls, *377–378*

Options page, *115–116*

.org domain, 371

OS/2 operating system, 12

OSPF (Open Shortest Path First) protocol, 266

owners in WINS, 335

P

P node in NBT, *320–321*

packet switching, 290

parameter lists, *127*

parity, 210

partitions, 187

active, *192–193*

deleting, *195*

extending, *193*, *194*

primary, *189–192*, *190–192*

shrinking, *194–195*, *194*

styles, *187–188*

passive opens, 281

passwords

dial-up connections, 308

encrypted files, 243

installation, 21

requirements, 41

setup, 29, *30*

storing, *43*

PAT (port address translation), 270

vs. NAT, *284–285*

overview, *284*

Path environment variable, 123–124

paths

command line, 123–124

drive letters, *216*, *216–217*

Peer Name Resolution Protocol (PNRP), 78

per-user encryption, 240

performance

DNS, *426–430*, *428*

logs and alerts, 98

permissions, 39

authorization, *46–48*, *47*

command line, *113–114*, *113*

effective, 52, *53*

Registry subkeys, *152–154*, *153–154*

resource sharing, 32–33, *32*

security, 53, *53*

Permissions for My Shared Folder dialog box, 32–33, *32*

Permissions for SecureFolder dialog box, 53, *53*

Personalization window, 90

physical disks, *186–189*, *187–188*

physical security, 44

PIDs (Program Identifiers), 129–130, *130*

ping command, 133, 378
    DDNS registrations, 421
    DNS servers for, 314
    IP configuration, *297–299*, *297*
    vs. net use, *316*
    opening firewalls for, *377–378*
pipe symbol (|) in command line, 127
platters, 216
plenum cable, 8
plug-ins, 95
PNRP (Peer Name Resolution Protocol), 78
Point-to-Point Protocol (PPP), *289–290*
policies vs. preferences, *171*
Policy Templates dialog box, 172
POP (Post Office Protocol), 288
port address translation (PAT), 270
        vs. NAT, *284–285*
        overview, *284*
port numbers, *280–281*
ports
        TCP/IP, *280–282*
        well-known, 280
Post Office Protocol (POP), 288
PowerCfg command, 133
PPP (Point-to-Point Protocol), *289–290*
#PRE command, *328*
prebuilt classes
        user, *455–456*
        vendor, *454–455*, *454*
preferences vs. policies, *171*
preferred DNS servers, *356*, *377*
Previous Versions page, 232–233, *233*
primary DNS servers, *402–403*
Primary DNS Suffix setting, 296
primary-initiated synchs, *407–408*, *408*
primary partitions, *189–192*, *190–192*
primary WINS servers, 340, *343*
primary zones, 381
print servers, 5
Print Services, 74
private encryption keys, 235
privileges. *See* permissions
.pro domain, 371–372
product keys, 19, 60–61
profiles for Registry keys, *139–141*, *140*
Program Identifiers (PIDs), 129–130,
    130

prompt, command line, *114*, *114*
    Colors page, *117*, *118*
    Font page, *116*, *116*
    Layout page, *116–117*, *117*
    Options page, *115–116*
    personalization, *118–121*, *119–121*
Prompt environment variable, 119–121, *119*
protocols, *10–12*, 253–254, *254*
proxy agents, *345–346*, *346*
PTR records, 392–393
    creating, *387–388*
    DDNS, *418*
public encryption keys, 235
purging WINS records, *344–345*
push/pull partners, *339–343*, *339*, *341–342*

Q
quad format, *261–262*, *262*
Quality Windows Audio Video Experience
    (Qwave), 78
query results caching, *361–363*
question marks (?)
    command line arguments, 125–126
    command line help, 124
    file searches, 130
QuickEdit Mode, 115
Quota page, 225, *225*
quotas, *224*
    managing, *228–229*
    user, *224–228*, *225–228*
Qwave (Quality Windows Audio Video
    Experience), 78

R
RAID (Redundant Arrays of Independent
    Drives), 189, *204–205*
    mirrored volumes, *205–209*, *206*, *209*
    RAID-5 volumes, *210–213*, *211–212*
    striped volumes, 201
ranges, IP address, *445–447*, *446*
Raster Fonts option, 116
RDC (Remote Differential Compression)
    feature, 78
read-only zone copies, *402*
reading zone files, *393*
rebooting for Registry changes, *144*

rebuilding DHCP servers, *462–463*
Reconnect at logon option, 35
records
  DNS, *384*
    A, *384–386*, 385, *390–392*, 392
    MX, *398–401*, 400
    NS and SOA, *388–390*, 401
    reverse lookups, *386–388*, 387
    viewing, *392–395*, 394
  WINS, *344–345*
recovery
  DNS, *395*
  encrypted files, *243–244*
  mirrored volumes, *207–208*
  RAID-5 volumes, *212–213*, 212
  TCP/IP design for, 258
Recovery Agents, 239
Recovery Console, 220
Recycle Bin and quotas, 229
Redundant Arrays of Independent Drives
  (RAID), 189, *204–205*
  mirrored volumes, *205–209*, 206, 209
  RAID-5 volumes, *210–213*, 211–212
  striped volumes, 201
refresh
  secondary DNS servers, 402–403
  WINS, 330
  zone scavenging, *422–424*
Refresh interval setting, *422–424*
reg add command, 360, 420
REG_BINARY type, 145
REG_DWORD type, 145–146
reg.exe command, 143
REG_EXPAND_SZ type, 145
REG_MULTI_SZ type, 145
REG_SZ type, 145–146
Regedit tool, 138, *138*, *143–145*
Regional Internet Registries (RIRs), 267
registrations
  DDNS
    failed, *421*
    PTR, *418*
    stopping, *420*
    triggers, *419–420*
  Windows Server 2008, 17
Registry, *135*
  application quirks, *149–150*
  backing up and restoring, *151–152*, *159–160*

command line for, *143*, *145*, *151*
computer configuration, *135–136*
contents, *138–139*, 138
as Control Panel, *136–137*
data types, *145–146*
DNS suffix, *300–301*
editing, *137–138*, *143–145*
entry creation and deletion, *150–151*
fault tolerance, *157–158*
hives, *156–158*
keys, *139*
  backing up and restoring, *151–152*
  HKEY_CURRENT_USER, *141–142*, 142
  HKEY_LOCAL_MACHINE, *141*
  permissions, *152–154*, 153–154
  profiles, *139–141*, 140
LGPOs, *169–171*, 170
rebooting for, *144*
remote modification, *158–159*
researching, *146–150*, 147–148
security, *152–156*, 153–154
switch settings, *149*
Registry Editor, 115
Rekeying Wizard, 240, 244
relay agents, 466–467
reliable services, 278
Remote Assistance feature, 78
Remote Desktop connections, 70
Remote Differential Compression (RDC)
  feature, 78
remote operations
  computer management, 97
  Registry modification, *158–159*
Remote Server Administration Tools, 79
Remote Storage feature, *251–252*
Removable Storage Manager (RSM), 79, 98,
  104–106, 105–106
Removal Progress page, 86
Removal Results dialog box, 86
Remove Features Wizard, 86
Remove Mirror dialog box, 209, 209
Remove Roles Wizard, 85, 85
removing
  mirrored volumes, *208–209*, 209
  roles, *85–86*, 85
renewal intervals for WINS, *330*, 334
Repair your computer option, 60
replication, WINS, *339–343*, 339, 341–342

Replication Partners Properties dialog box, 339, *339*
Rescan option, 187
reservations, DHCP, *452–453*, *452*
reserved addresses, 269, *271*
resource records
    NS, 374–375, 384, *388–390*
    SOA, 384, *388–390*, 392
resources
    accessing, *33–35*, *34–35*
    sharing
        command line for, 108–109, *109*
        ICS, *309–311*, *310–311*
        process, *30–33*, *31–33*
restoring
    Desktop icons and Start menu, *90–92*, *91–92*
    Registry, *151–152*, *159–160*
    zone files, *395*
Resuming Configuration dialog box, 86
retries, secondary DNS servers, *403*, 405
Reverse Lookup Zones folder, 381
reverse lookups, 354
    dynamic zones, *418*
    setting up, *386–388*, *387*
RFC 1918, *269–270*
rights and permissions, 39
    authorization, *46–48*, *47*
    command line, *113–114*, *113*
    effective, 52, *53*
    Registry subkeys, *152–154*, *153–154*
    resource sharing, 32–33, *32*
    security, 53, *53*
RIP (Routing Information Protocol), 266
RIRs (Regional Internet Registries), 267
rogue detection, 459
rogue DHCP servers, 441
roles
    adding, *82–84*, *82–84*
    DHCP, 438–442, *438–440*, *442*
    vs. features, *70–71*
    installing, *81–86*, *82–86*
    need for, *71–81*
    removing, *85–86*, *85*
    server, 6
root DNS servers, 366
root hints file, 373
round robin DNS, *427–429*, *428*

routable addresses, *269–270*, *283–284*
route optimization, *429–430*
Router (Default Gateway) page, 449, *449*
routers, *8*
    default, 266
    IP, *259–260*, *265*
    leapfrogging, *466–468*, *467–468*
    mail, 289
routing
    IP, *265–267*
    LAN-to-WAN, *305–311*, *307–308*, *310–311*
Routing and Remote Access Service (RRAS), *467–468*, *467–468*
Routing Information Protocol (RIP), 266
RPC over HTTP Proxy feature, *79*
RSM (Removable Storage Manager), 79, 98, *104–106*, *105–106*
Run dialog box, 90
Run link, 90
Russinovich, Mark, 137

S
SACLs, 51, *52*
SAM (Security Account Manager), 43–45
SANs (Storage Area Networks), 80
Save As dialog box
    batch files, 131, *132*
    for tools, 106
Scaling page, 185
Scan for and attempt recovery of bad sectors option, 246
scavenging
    logs, 426
    WINS, 345
    zones, *421–426*, *422–423*, *425*
schedules
    CHKDSK, 246
    tasks, 98
Scope Options dialog box, 457, *457*
scopes, DHCP, 263
    activation, *450–451*, *451*
    adding, 440–441, *441*
    classes, 457, *457*
    creating, *445–446*, *445–446*
    options, *451–452*, *452*
    superscopes, *446–447*
Screen Buffer Size setting, 117
screen savers, 136–137

ScreenSaveActive entry, 142
ScreenSaveIsSecure entry, 142
scripts in Group Policy, *180–181*, *180*
second-level domains, *372–374*
secondary servers
    DNS, *401*
        creating, *408–409*
        primary-initiated synchs, *407–408*, *408*
        read-only zone copies, *402*
        retries and expiry, *403*
        SOA records modification, *404–405*, *404*
        transfers, *406–407*, *407*, *409–410*
        TTLs, *405–406*
        updating, *402–403*
    WINS, 340
secondary zones, 381
sectors, 196, 216
SecureFolder Properties dialog box, 50, *51*, 53–54
security, 3, *37*
    Active Directory, 473, *476*
    authentication
        vs. authorization, *40–42*
        hex suffixes for, *327–328*
        process, *42–46*
    authorization. *See* authorization
    DDNS, *426*
    encryption. *See* encryption
    methods, *38–40*
    need for, *37–38*
    Registry, *152–156*, *153–154*
Security Account Manager (SAM), 43–45
security descriptors, 47–48, *47*
Security Identifiers (SIDs), 48, 224
Select Computer dialog box, 106
Select Disks page, 201, *201*
Select Group Policy Object dialog box, 165, *165*, 167–168
Select Server Roles page, 83, *83*, 380, 438, *438*
Select User or Group dialog box, 52, *53*
Select Users dialog box, 227, *227–228*, 239
Select Users or Groups dialog box, 33, *33*
Selected Color Values option, 117
Selected Features page, 331–332, *332*
semicolons (;) in resource records, 388
sendmail program, 288
separation, DNS, *374–375*

sequencing, TCP for, 279
Serial Line Interface Protocol (SLIP), 290
serial numbers
    in SOA records, 403
    zones, 390
Server Aging/Scavenging Properties dialog box, 422, *422*
Server Core version, 57–58, 110, 136–137
Server Manager, 183
    DHCP, 438, *438*
    winservers, *379–380*
Server Options dialog box, 451–453, *452–453*
servermanagercmd -install dhcp command, 443
servermanagercmd -install dns command, 365, 379–380, 409
servermanagercmd -install wins-server command, 332
servers
    customizing, *69–70*, *69–70*
    DHCP. *See* Dynamic Host Configuration Protocol (DHCP)
    DNS. *See* Domain Name System (DNS) servers
    e-mail, 5, *398–401*, *400*
    FTP, 279
    name, 287, *313–314*, *391*, *392*
    networks, *2–4*
    protocols for, *10–12*
    types, *5–6*
    updating, *66–68*, *66–68*
    WINS. *See* Windows Internet Name Server (WINS)
Services and Applications node, 97, *99*
Set up a dial-up connection dialog box, 307–308, *308*
Settings dialog box, 185, *185*
Shadow Copies property page, 231, *232*
Share utility, 111
shared folders, 98
SharePoint servers, 5–6
Sharing page, *309–311*, *310–311*
sharing resources
    command line for, 108–109, *109*
    ICS, *309–311*, *310–311*
    process, *30–33*, *31–33*
shortcuts, command line, 111
Show Hidden Files and Folders option, 93

Shrink Volume Wizard, 194
shrinking partitions, **194–195**, *194*
Shutdown scripts, 181
SIDs (Security Identifiers), 48, 224
Simple Mail Transfer Protocol (SMTP), 79, 288–289
Simple Network Management Protocol (SNMP) services, 79
Simple TCP/IP Services, 79
simple volumes, **198–199**
single large expensive drives (SLEDs), 196
Single Sign-On (SSO), 240, 474
64-bit version, *17*
size
    screen buffer, 117
    sectors, 196
    volume, 191, *191*, 250
    window, 117
slashes (/) on command line, 125–127
SLEDs (single large expensive drives), 196
SLIP (Serial Line Interface Protocol), 290
smart cards, 42, 240
SMTP (Simple Mail Transfer Protocol), 79, 288–289
snap-ins, **94–96**
SNMP (Simple Network Management Protocol) services, 79
SOA (start of authority) records, 384, **388–390**, 392
    DDNS, 417–418
    modifying, **401, 404–405**, *404*
    serial numbers in, 403
socket addresses, 280
sockets
    TCP/IP, **280–282**
    Winsock, **285**
soft quotas, 225
software-based RAID systems, 205
software compatibility, protocols for, 254
SOFTWARE key, 141
spanned volumes, **199–201**, *199–200*
special usage information, command line, **127–128**
Specify IPv4 DNS Server Settings page, 439, *439*
Specify IPv4 WINS Server Settings page, 439, *439*
Specify Volume Size page, 191, *191*

square brackets ([]) on command line, 126–127
SSO (Single Sign-On), 240, 474
Standard edition, **56**
Start menu, restoring, **90–92**, *91–92*
Start Menu page, 91, *92*
Start Menu Properties applet, 92
Start of Authority (SOA) page, 404, *404*
start of authority (SOA) records, 384, **388–390**, 392
    DDNS, 417–418
    modifying, **401, 404–405**, *404*
    serial numbers in, 403
Startup scripts, 181
static DNS entries, **300**
static IP addresses, **264, 292–295**, *293–294*, **437**
status of system, **128–129**, *129*
Storage Area Networks (SANs), 80
storage concepts, 183
    disk management. *See* disk management and Disk Management utility
    evolution, **252**
Storage Manager, 80
Storage node, **97–99**
striped volumes, **201–204**, *201–203*
SUA (Subsystem for UNIX-based Applications) feature, 80
subdomains, 369, **374–376, 411–416**, *411, 414–415*
SubInACL utility, 111–112
subnet masks
    ordering, **429–430**
    overview, **272–273**
Subnet Type: the Wired option, 440
subnets, **259–260**, 268
Subsystem for UNIX-based Applications (SUA) feature, 80
suffixes
    DNS, 355
        installing, **378–379**
        Registry for, **300–301**
        search list, **360–361**
    domain, **298–301**
    LMHOSTS file, **327–328**
superscopes, **446–447**
switches, **8**
    CHKDSK, **247**

command line, *125–127*, *126*
defrag, *250–251*
Notepad, 110
Registry, *149*
synchronization
secondary DNS servers, *407–408*, *408*
zones, *402–403*
syntax, command line, *124–127*, *126*
system data, transaction logging, 244
System drive letters, 216
SYSTEM hive, 141, 158
System partition, 190, *220*
System Properties dialog box, 92
command prompt, 119–120, *120*
computer names, 24–25, *25*, 66
path information, 123
Remote Desktop, 69, *69*
System Recovery Options dialog box, 60
system status, *128–129*, *129*
System Tools node, *97–98*
System Volume Information folder, 231
SystemInfo utility, 128–129, *129*

T

Tab key for command line, 111
tape storage, *251–252*
Task Scheduler, 98
TaskKill utility, 129
TaskList command, 122, 126, *126*
tasks
scheduling, 98
viewing and managing, *129–130*, *130*
tattooing, *169–170*
TCP (Transmission Control Protocol),
278–279
TCP/IP (Transmission Control
Protocol/Internet Protocol), 2, 11, *253–254*
design goals, *257–258*
DHCP. *See* Dynamic Host Configuration
Protocol (DHCP)
domain suffixes, *298–301*
firewalls, *311–312*, *312*
history, *254–255*
host names, *285–289*, *288*
ICS, 282
Internet connections, *289–292*, *292*

IP. *See* IP (Internet Protocol)
LAN-to-WAN routing, *305–311*, *307–308*,
310–311
origins, *255–257*, *255–256*
ports, *280–282*
sockets, *280–282*
static IP addresses, *292–295*, *293–294*
TCP, *278–279*
Windows for Workgroups, 319
Winsock sockets, *285*
TCP/IP suite, 258
Telnet protocol, 80
templates, ADM, *172–174*, *172–173*
temporary resource access, *34*, *34*
terminal connections, *290–292*, *292*
terminal servers, 5
Terminal Services, 74
testing
DNS server connectivity, *378*
IP configuration, *295–300*, *295*, *297*, *299*
WINS servers, *343*, *344*
text colors on command prompt, *117*
TFTP (Trivial File Transfer Protocol), 80
third level domains, 374
time to live (TTL)
DDNS, 419
DNS, 361–362
secondary DNS servers, *405–406*
SOA records, 389
WINS, 330
tokens, *48–50*, *49*
tombstone state, 345
tombstoning WINS records, *344–345*
tools
building, *101–106*, *101–106*
CHKDSK, 245–246, *246*
MMC, 95
Tools page, 245–246, *246*
top-level domains, *370–372*, *371*
TPM (Trusted Platform Module) chips, 76
tracert tool, 299, *299*
transaction logs, 244
transfers with secondary DNS servers, *406–407*,
407, *409–410*
Transmission Control Protocol (TCP), *278–279*

Transmission Control Protocol/Internet Protocol. *See* TCP/IP (Transmission Control Protocol/Internet Protocol)
transport protocols, *10–12*
triggers, registration, *419–420*
Trivial File Transfer Protocol (TFTP), 80
troubleshooting
    DDNS registrations, *421*
    DNS servers, *367*
    mirrored volumes, *207–208*
Trusted Platform Module (TPM) chips, 76
TTL (time to live)
    DDNS, 419
    DNS, 361–362
    secondary DNS servers, *405–406*
    SOA records, 389
    WINS, 330
tunnel adapters, 358

U
UAC (User Account Control) feature, 49, 113, 241
UDP (User Datagram Protocol), 465
Universal Description, Discovery, and Integration (UDDI) service, 75
Unix operating system, 257
updating
    secondary DNS servers, *402–403*
    server, *66–68*, *66–68*
Updating and Feedback dialog box, 66
upgrade installations, 63
Use alternate credentials option, 441
Use current credentials option, 441
Use the following DNS server addresses setting, 295
Use the following IP address setting, 295
Use Windows Classic Folders option, 93
User Account Control (UAC) feature, 49, 113, 241
user accounts, *27–30*, *27–30*
    Active Directory, *474*
    database security, *44*
user classes in DHCP, *453–458*, *453–454*, *456–457*
User Datagram Protocol (UDP), 465
user-defined DHCP classes, *456–458*, *456–457*

user mode in MMC, 96
user node in LGPOs, *168–170*, *168*
user-specific hive files, 156
user-specific LGPOs, *167–168*, *168*
users
    profiles, 139–140
    quotas, *224–228*, *225–228*
    storing, *43*

V
vendor classes, *453–458*, *453–454*, *456–457*
Verification interval setting, 335
viewing
    tasks, *129–130*, *130*
    zone files, *393*, *394*
virtual private networks (VPNs), 2
virtual sites, 304
viruses, 38
Volume Shadow Copy Service (VSS), *230*
    applications, *230–231*
    command line, *234*
    enabling, *231*, 232
    operation, *232–234*, *233*
    previous versions, *231*
Volume size setting, 250
volumes, 187
    deleting, *204*
    mirrored, *205–209*, *206*, *209*
    simple, *198–199*
    spanned, *199–201*, *199–200*
    striped, *201–204*, *201–203*
VPNs (virtual private networks), 2
VSS. *See* Volume Shadow Copy Service (VSS)
VSS Coordination Service, 230
VSS Provider, 230
VSS Requester, 230
VSS Writer, 230–231
VSSadmin utility, *234*

W
WAN (wide area network) connections, 2, 291
WAPs (wireless access points), *9–10*, *10*, 259
Web browsers, 2, 4
Web edition, *56–57*
Web servers, *4*, 75

Welcome to the New RAID-5 Volume Wizard, 210

Welcome to the New Zone Wizard, 381

well-known ports, 280

What to know before installing Windows option, 60

WhoAmI command, 134

wide area network (WAN) connections, 2, 291

wildcard characters
command line, *125–127*, *126*
file searches, 130–131

Window Position setting, 117

Window Size setting, 117

Windows, history, *12–14*

Windows 2000 operating system, 14

Windows Active Directory domain, 45

Windows can't check this disk while it's in use message, 246

Windows Deployment Services, 75

Windows Error Reporting Configuration dialog box, 67, *68*

Windows Firewall Settings dialog box, 70, *70*, 311–312, *312*

Windows for Workgroups (WfW), 319

Windows installation method, *58–59*

Windows Internal Database feature, 80

Windows Internet Name Server (WINS), 11, 81, 287, *320*
client failure modes, *330*
installing, *331–333*, *331–333*
issues, *343–344*, *344*
multi-WINS network, *337–339*
name registrations, *329–330*
name resolution, *314–315*
proxy agents, *345–346*, *346*
records, *344–345*
renewal intervals, *330*, 334
replication, *339–343*, *339*, *341–342*
server configuration, *333–337*, *334–336*
Winsock order, *349–350*
workstation configuration for, *301–303*, *301*

Windows Live ID, 17

Windows PowerShell command line, 80

Windows Process Activation Service feature, 81

Windows Recovery Disc, 81

Windows Server Backups feature, 81

Windows SharePoint Services, 75

Windows System Resource Manager (WSRM) feature, 81

winipcfg command, 463, 469

WinLoad.exe file, 190

WINS. *See* Windows Internet Name Server (WINS)

WINS page, 301, *301*

WINS Servers page, 449, *450*

winservers, *379–380*

Winsock API, 303, 319
name resolution, *347–349*, *348*
sockets, *285*
WINS vs. DNS order, *349–350*

Winsock name resolution vs. NBT, 347

wireless access points (WAPs), *9–10*, *10*, 259

Wireless Local Area Network (WLAN) service, 81

workgroups, 3, 45, 322

workstations, *301–303*, *301*

World Wide Web (WWW), 4, 256

writing zone files, *393*

WSRM (Windows System Resource Manager) feature, 81

WWW (World Wide Web), 4, 256

Z

Zone Aging/Scavenging Properties dialog box, 424, *425*

Zone File page, 381, *382*

zone files, 386, *392–393*
backing up and restoring, *395*
finding and viewing, *393*, *394*
modifying, *394–395*
reading and writing, *393*

Zone Name page, 381, *382*

Zone Type page, 381, *381*

zones
A records, *390–392*, *392*
creating, *380–383*, *380–383*
hosts for, *384–386*, *385*
NS and SOA records, *388–390*
read-only copies, *402*
reverse lookups, *386–388*, *387*
scavenging, *421–426*, *422–423*, *425*
synchronization, *402–403*

Targeting what you need for Windows Server® 2008

Leading Windows authority and author of the bestselling book *Mastering Windows Server 2003*, Mark Minasi, has set his sights on Windows Server 2008. Look for his three new, targeted books on Windows Server 2008, each addressing the specific needs of Windows Server administrators.

978-0-470-24984-0

978-0-470-24991-8

978-0-470-24992-5

Designed for new network administrators, this book presents Mark Minasi's in-depth knowledge of networking concepts as well as basic instruction on Windows Server 2008 installation and management.

Covers the critical tasks that are crucial to the day-to-day administration of Windows Server 2008 and offers plenty of workarounds, undocumented features, and much more. This is the in-depth book that all Windows Server administrators will want to keep within reach.

This unique book goes beyond the day-to-day tasks of Windows Server 2008 administration with coverage of topics and issues that will help IT professionals gain maximum control of their complex enterprise networks.

Get more information about all of the Windows Servers 2008 books from Sybex at www.sybex.com/go/ws2008

An Imprint of ⊛WILEY
Now you know.